Challenging Cases in Clinical Research Ethics

Clinical research ethics consultation has emerged in the last 15 years as a service to those involved in the conduct of clinical research who face challenging issues for which more than one course of action may be justified. To respond to a growing field and need for opportunities to share knowledge and experience, the Clinical Research Ethics Consultation Collaborative, established in 2014, holds monthly webinars for its 90 members to present their most challenging cases to each other and engage in substantive discussion. Every year, the group selects the four most interesting cases with accompanying commentaries for publication in the *American Journal of Bioethics*.

This timely book brings together these cases and commentaries under a range of common themes for the first time, creating a permanent collection in book format that encourages and supports readers to gain a better understanding of the ethical challenges that they may face, and providing them with a convenient and reflective resource to reference in their own deliberations.

Key Features:

- Comprehensive collection of cases and commentaries, chosen to reflect the range of issues faced by clinical researchers and oversight committees and illustrate the diversity of analysis that can arise
- Supplemented by short introductions to each section
- Focus on ethical rather than regulatory issues
- Essential reading for graduate students in bioethics and postdoctoral bioethics fellows, and useful for all participants in training grants that are funded by either the NIH or NSF

Presenting challenging cases to stimulate reflection, the book provides invaluable guidance to clinicians in training and in practice and to investigators, bioethics consultants, regulators, and oversight bodies.

Benjamin S. Wilfond is an Investigator in the Treuman Katz Center for Pediatric Bioethics and Palliative Care at the Seattle Children's Research Institute, and Professor in the Division of Bioethics and Palliative Care at the Department of Pediatrics, University of Washington School of Medicine, Seattle, WA, USA.

Devan M. Duenas is a Clinical Research Coordinator and the Coordinator for the Research Ethics Consultation Service at the Treuman Katz Center for Pediatric Bioethics and Palliative Care at the Seattle Children's Research Institute, Seattle, Washington, USA.

Liza-Marie Johnson is an Investigator and Associate Member (Professor) in the Department of Oncology at the St. Jude Children's Research Hospital, Memphis, Tennessee, USA.

Holly A. Taylor is a Research Bioethicist in the Department of Bioethics, Clinical Center at the National Institutes of Health, Bethesda, Maryland, USA.

Challenging Cases in Clinical Research Ethics

Edited by
Benjamin S. Wilfond, Devan M. Duenas, Liza-Marie Johnson,
and Holly A. Taylor

CRC Press
Taylor & Francis Group
Boca Raton London New York

CRC Press is an imprint of the
Taylor & Francis Group, an **informa** business

Contents

Foreword

Attention to the ethics of conducting clinical research has been intense since the end of World War II, when concern about dangerous research without the consent of participants was brought to light. Yet efforts by ethics consultants to offer advice to improve the ethical conduct of clinical research is a rather recent development that has lagged behind ethics consultation in the healthcare setting.

This book marks a particularly valuable development in clinical research ethics consultation. It reflects the initiation of clinical research ethics consultation services at universities and research centers around the United States that was largely prompted by the National Institutes of Health (NIH) Clinical and Translational Science Awards (CTSA) Program—a funding program that supports a national network of medical research institutions that work together to improve the translational process of designing and disseminating medical treatments. Because of a funding requirement of the CTSA Program that institutions have some kind of ethics support services, nearly 60 institutions created ethics consultation services (see "History—CRECC," iths.org). Together they formed the Clinical Research Ethics Consultation Collaborative (CRECC) in 2014.

The book before you reflects the novel and exciting way in which research ethics consultation has grown as a collective effort in a virtual space. The ethics consultations featured in this book were first requested by investigators at research institutions throughout North America, and were then presented and discussed by research ethicists in virtual meetings of the CRECC. From start to finish, each consultation presented in this book involved numerous individuals who participated in some step of the process: receiving a consultation request, offering consultative advice, presenting to the CRECC, writing up a case for publication, or preparing a commentary. In sum, each section of the book involved approximately 30 to 50 ethics consultants. It is hard to imagine that such a successful collaborative effort among scholars who are so geographically dispersed would have been possible before the advent of videoconferencing platforms. Those of us who are interested in preserving such thriving collaborative intellectual work will need to seriously consider how to sustain thriving human endeavors like this as machine learning and natural language processing tools driven by artificial intelligence technology gain an expanding role in our intellectual efforts.

This book represents a maturation in ways of thinking about research ethics; it is published over a decade after the first casebook of research ethics consultation cases was published by research ethics consultants in the intramural program of the NIH (Danis et al. 2012). That earlier publication demonstrated that research ethics consultation could be useful over the entire duration of a research project—ranging from the time of initial study design all the way to study completion. The editors of this new casebook offer the reader the opportunity to think about ethics consultation along various dimensions: according to topics of interest, including population, study type, research feature, or oversight, as well as ethical principles and values. Accordingly, the book can provide a very flexible source of teaching material.

Given the collaborative human scholarship that this book represents, let's hope that it has a wide audience of readers who access it in print and/or online and appreciate the carefully articulated and diverse perspectives it contains.

Marion Danis, MD
Head, Section on Ethics and Health Policy
Chief, Bioethics Consultation Service
National Institutes of Health
Bethesda, Maryland, USA

REFERENCE

Danis, M., E. Largent, C. Grady, D. Wendler, S. C. Hull, S. Shah, J. Millum, and B. Berkman. 2012. *Research ethics consultation: A casebook*, New York: Oxford University Press.

Contributors

Brooklyn Aaron
Georgia State University
Atlanta, Georgia

Cheryl Abbate
University of Colorado
Boulder, Colorado

Melissa E. Abraham
Massachusetts General Hospital
and
Harvard Medical School
Boston, Massachusetts

Sanjeev Akkina
Loyola University Chicago Stritch School of
    Medicine
Chicago, Illinois

Megan A. Allyse
Mayo Clinic
Rochester, Minnesota

Emily E. Anderson
Loyola University Chicago Stritch School of
    Medicine
Chicago, Illinois

Armand H. Matheny Antommaria
Cincinnati Children's Hospital
    Medical Center
University of Cincinnati
Cincinnati, Ohio

W. Patricia Bandettini
National Heart, Lung, and Blood Institute
Bethesda, Maryland

Amrutha Baskaran
University of California-San Diego
San Diego, California

Lee Beers
Children's National Health System
Washington D.C.

Daniel J. Benedetti
Vanderbilt University Medical Center
Nashville, Tennessee

Benjamin E. Berkman
National Institutes of Health
Bethesda, Maryland

Laura M. Beskow
School of Medicine
Duke University
Durham, North Carlina

Jessica Blanchard
University of Oklahoma
Norman, Oklahoma

Shannon Blee
Winship Cancer Institute
Emory University School of Medicine
Atlanta, Georgia

John Bond
Roche Pharmaceuticals
Schweiz, Switzerland

Jeffrey R. Botkin
University of Utah
Salt Lake City, Utah

Andrew D. Boyd
University of Illinois
Chicago, Illinois

Andrea Branch
Icahn School of Medicine
Mount Sinai, New York

Derek W. Braverman
Johns Hopkins University School of Medicine
Baltimore, Maryland
and
National Institutes of Health
Bethesda, Maryland

Stephen D. Brown
Harvard Medical School
Boston, Massachusetts

Amy E. Caruso Brown
SUNY Upstate Medical University
Syracuse, New York

Nancy J. Burke
University of California-Merced
Merced, California

Kristin Canavera
St. Jude Children's Research Hospital
Memphis, Tennessee

Alexander Capron
University of Southern California
Los Angeles, California

Yvonne Carroll
St. Jude Children's Research Hospital
Memphis, Tennessee

Bora Chang
Children's National Health System
Washington D.C.

Stephanie C. Chen
National Institutes of Health
Bethesda, Maryland

Mildred K. Cho
Stanford University
Stanford, California

Cynthia Chuang
Penn State College of Medicine
Hershey, Pennsylvania

Reginald Claypool
National Institutes of Health
Bethesda, Maryland

Elaine Collier
National Center for Advancing
    Translational Sciences
Bethesda, Maryland

Kate E. Creevy
College of Veterinary Medicine
    & Biomedical Sciences
Texas A&M University
College Station, Texas

Joshua S. Crites
Cleveland Clinic
Cleveland, Ohio

Richard Culbertson
LSU School of Public Health
New Orleans, Louisiana

Reid Cushman
Miller School of Medicine
University of Miami
Miami, Florida

Marion Danis
Clinical Center
National Institutes of Health
Bethesda, Maryland

Michael Danziger
SUNY Downstate Medical Center
College of Medicine
New York City, New York

Christopher R. DeCou
University of Washington School
   of Medicine
Washington D.C.

Arthur R. Derse
Medical College of Wisconsin
Milwaukee, Wisconsin

Neal W. Dickert
Emory University
Atlanta, Georgia

Anne Dimmock
Penn State College of Medicine
Hershey, Pennsylvania

Margie Dixon
Winship Cancer Institute
Emory University School of Medicine
Atlanta, Georgia

Sam Doernberg
Clinical Center
National Institutes of Health
Bethesda, Maryland

Adélaïde Doussau
McGill University
Montreal, Quebec, Canada

Leah R. Eisenberg
University of Arkansas for
   Medical Sciences
Little Rock, Arkansas

Emily Evans
Georgetown University
Washington, D.C.

Rachel Fabi
Berman Institute of Bioethics
Bloomberg School of Public Health
Johns Hopkins University
Baltimore, Maryland

Jeffrey S. Farroni
University of Texas Medical Branch
Galveston, Texas

Stuart G. Finder
Cedars-Sinai Medical Center
Los Angeles, California

Robin N. Fiore
Miller School of Medicine
University of Miami
Miami, Florida

Jill A. Fisher
University of North Carolina
Chapel Hill, North Carolina

Kathy Forte
Nell Hodgson Woodruff School of Nursing
Emory University
Atlanta, Georgia

Nanibaa' A. Garrison
Stanford University
Stanford, California

Luke Gelinas
Harvard Law School
Cambridge, Massachusetts

Cynthia M. A. Geppert
U.S. Department of Veterans Affairs
Washington, D.C.

Philip Ghobrial
Stritch School of Medicine
Loyola University of Chicago
Chicago, Illinois

Jessica C. Ginsberg
Wellstar Health System
Marietta, Georgia

Hannah Giunta
Michigan State University
East Lansing, Michigan

Cory E. Goldstein
Western University
London, Canada

Christine Grady
National Institutes of Health
Bethesda, Maryland

Mary Greiner
Cincinnati Children's Hospital Medical Center
University of Cincinnati
Cincinnati, Ohio

Clark B. Hanmer
Retired family physician

Catherine Haywood
Louisiana Community Health Outreach Network
Baton Rouge, Louisiana

Elizabeth Heitman
Vanderbilt University Medical Center
Nashville, Tennessee

Vanessa Hiratsuka
University of Alaska Anchorage
Anchorage, Alaska

Stacy Hodgkinson
Children's National Health System
Washington D.C.

Elizabeth Hohmann
Massachusetts General Hospital
and
Harvard Medical School
Boston, Massachusetts

Steven M. Holland
National Institutes of Health
Bethesda, Maryland

Amy P. Hsu
National Institutes of Health
Bethesda, Maryland

Caroline J. Huang
Clinical Center
National Institutes of Health
Bethesda, Maryland

Sara Chandros Hull
National Institutes of Health
Bethesda, Maryland

Nora Hutchinson
McGill University
Montreal, Canada

Wenke Hwang
Penn State College of Medicine
Hershey, Pennsylvania

Kent P. Hymel
Penn State College of Medicine
Hershey, Pennsylvania

Brian Michael Jackson
Childrens Hospital
Aurora, Colorado

Bobbie Johannes
Penn State College of Medicine
Hershey, Pennsylvania

Arthur Johnson
Lower Ninth Ward Center for
    Sustainable Engagement
    and Development
New Orleans, Louisiana

Sandra Juul
University of Washington School
    of Medicine
Seattle, Washington

Matt Kaeberlein
School of Medicine
University of Washington
Seattle, Washington

Ruquyyah Abdul Karim
National Institutes of Health
Bethesda, Maryland

Scott Y. H. Kim
National Institutes of Health
Bethesda, Maryland

Bryan H. King
University of Washington
and
Seattle Children's Hospital
Seattle, Washington

Esther Elise Knapp
University of Louisville
Louisville, Kentucky

Alex Kolevzon
Icahn School of Medicine
Mount Sinai, New York

Stanley Korenman
UCLA Medical Center
Los Angeles, California

Stephanie A. Kraft
Treuman Katz Center for Pediatric Bioethics
    and Palliative Care
Seattle Children's Research Institute
and
University of Washington School
    of Medicine
Seattle, Washington

Ellen Kuwana
Treuman Katz Center for
    Pediatric Bioethics
Seattle Children's Research Institute
Seattle, Washington

Emily A. Largent
Perelman School of Medicine
University of Pennsylvania
Philadelphia, Pennsylvania

Susannah W. Lee
Wellstar Health System
Marietta, Georgia

Jason Lesandrini
Wellstar Health System
Marietta, Georgia

Amy Lewin
Children's National Health System
Washington, D.C.

Emily Y. Liu
Stanford University
Stanford, California

Holly Fernandez Lynch
Perelman School of Medicine
University of Pennsylvania
Philadelphia, Pennsylvania

Marsha Mailick
Madison and Morgridge Institute
    for Research
University of Wisconsin
Madison, Wisconsin

Jeff Matsler
Wellstar Healthcare System
Marietta, Georgia

Jennifer B. McCormick
Penn State College of Medicine
Hershey, Pennsylvania

Ross E. McKinney
Duke University School of Medicine
Durham, North Caroline

Ann J. Melvin
University of Washington
Seattle, Washington

Matthew Memoli
National Institute of Allergy and
    Infectious Diseases
Bethesda, Maryland

Diana Meyers
St. Anna Episcopal Church
and
Anna's Place NOLA
New Orleans, Louisiana

D. Gibbes Miller
National Institutes of Health
Bethesda, Maryland

Joseph Millum
National Institutes of Health
Bethesda, Maryland

Lauren C. Milner
Stanford University
Stanford, California

Douglas B. Mogul
Johns Hopkins University School
    of Medicine
Baltimore, Maryland

Kathleen M. Mohan
University of Washington
Seattle, Washington

Christian Morales
Berman Institute of Bioethics
Bloomberg School of Public Health
Johns Hopkins University
Baltimore, Maryland
Megan Morash
Partners HealthCare
Massachusetts General Hospital
Boston, Massachusetts

Ryan R. Nash
Ohio State University
Columbus, Ohio

Lindsay D. Nelson
Medical College of Wisconsin
Milwaukee, Wisconsin

Robert M. Nelson
Johnson & Johnson
New Brunswick, New Jersey

Alan Nyitray
Medical College of Wisconsin
Milwaukee, Wisconsin

Pilar Ossorio
University of Wisconsin
Madison, Wisconsin

Lawrence A. Palinkas
Suzanne Dworak-Peck School of Social Work
University of Southern California
Los Angeles, California

Erin Talati Paquette
Ann & Robert H. Lurie Children's Hospital of
   Chicago
and
Northwestern University
Chicago, Illinois

Anuradha Paranjape
Lewis Katz School of Medicine
Temple University
Philadelphia, Pennsylvania

Kendra Parris
St. Jude Children's Research Hospital
Memphis, Tennessee

Rebecca D. Pentz
Winship Cancer Institute
Emory University School of Medicine
Atlanta, Georgia

Ponni Perumalswami
Icahn School of Medicine
Mount Sinai, New York

John Phillips
National Institutes of Health
Clinical Center
Bethesda, Maryland

Kathryn M. Porter
Seattle Children's Research Institute
Seattle, Washington

Daniel Promislow
University of Washington School of Medicine
Seattle, Washington

Naresh M. Punjabi
Johns Hopkins University School of Medicine
Baltimore, Maryland

Lynne M. Quittell
College of Physicians and Surgeons
Columbia University
New York City, New York

Rosamond Rhodes
Icahn School of Medicine
Mount Sinai, New York

John M. Ringman
UCLA Medical Center
Los Angeles, California

Lainie Friedman Ross
MacLean Center for Clinical Medical Ethics
University of Chicago
Chicago, Illinois

Mark A. Rothstein
University of Louisville School of Medicine
Louisville, Kentucky

Henry Sacks
Icahn School of Medicine
Mount Sinai, New York

Robert M. Sade
Medical University of South Carolina
Charleston, South Carolina

Lauren A. Sanchez
National Institutes of Health
Bethesda, Maryland

Daniel Sarpong
Xavier University of Louisiana
New Orleans, Louisiana

Adam I. Schiffenbauer
National Institute of Environmental Health
    Sciences
National Institutes of Health
Bethesda, Maryland

Toby Schonfeld
U.S. Department of Veterans Affairs
Washington, D.C.

Anita Shah
University of Washington School
    of Medicine
Seattle, Washington

J. Jina Shah
Roche Pharmaceuticals
Basel, Switzerland

Seema K. Shah
Ann & Robert H. Lurie Children's Hospital of
    Chicago
and
Northwestern University
Chicago, Illinois

Akshay Sharma
St. Jude Children's Research Hospital
Memphis, Tennessee

Richard R. Sharp
Mayo Clinic
Rochester, Minnesota

Hannah Claire Sibold
Winship Cancer Institute
Emory University School of Medicine
Atlanta, Georgia

Tomas J. Silber
Children's National Health System
Washington, D.C.

Anne R. Simpson
University of New Mexico
Mexico City, Mexico

Ryan Spellecy
Medical College of Wisconsin
Milwaukee, Wisconsin

Michael A. Spinner
National Institutes of Health
Bethesda, Maryland

Benjamin F. Springgate
LSU School of Medicine
New Orleans, Louisiana

Robert Steel
National Institutes of Health
Bethesda, Maryland

Mark A. Stein
University of Washington
and
Seattle Children's Hospital
Seattle, Washington

Anne Stevens
Seattle Children's Hospital and Research
    Institute
and
University of Washington School
    of Medicine
Seattle, Washington
and
Janssen Research and Development
Titusville, New Jersey

Olivia Sugarman
LSUHSC Center for Healthcare Value
    and Equity
New Orleans, Louisiana

Haley K. Sullivan
National Institutes of Health
Bethesda, Maryland

Eric S. Swirsky
University of Illinois
Chicago, Illinois

Emma Tumilty
University of Texas Medical Branch
Galveston, Texas

Jessica M. Turnbull
Vanderbilt University Medical Center
Nashville, Tennessee

Yoram Unguru
The Herman and Walter Samuelson Children's
    Hospital at Sinai
and
Berman Institute of Bioethics
Johns Hopkins University
Baltimore, Maryland

Anna Wald
University of Washington
Seattle, Washington

Rebecca L. Walker
University of North Carolina
Chapel Hill, North Carolina

Charles Weijer
University of Western Ontario
London, Canada

Kenneth B. Wells
Los Angeles Semel Neuropsychiatric Institute
University of California-Los Angeles
Los Angeles, California

David Wendler
Johns Hopkins University School of Medicine
Baltimore, Maryland
and
National Institutes of Health
Bethesda, Maryland

Ashley Wennerstrom
LSUHSC Center for Healthcare Value
    and Equity
New Orleans, Louisiana

Cynthia Wetmore
Aflac Cancer & Blood Disorders Center
Children's Healthcare of Atlanta
and
School of Medicine
Emory University
Atlanta, Georgia

Danielle Whicher
Patient-Centered Outcomes
    Research Institute
Washington D.C.

Albert W. Wu
School of Public Health
Johns Hopkins University
Baltimore, Maryland

Joel T. Wu
University of Minnesota
Minneapolis, Minnesota

Mark Yarborough
University of California-Davis
Davis, California

Jamila M. Young
Wellstar Distribution Center
Marietta, Georgia

Joon-Ho Yu
Seattle Children's Hospital and
    Research Institute
and
University of Washington
Seattle, Washington

Jennifer Zabrowski
St. Jude Children's Research Hospital
Memphis, Tennessee

Acknowledgments

The cases included in the collection were presented to the Clinical Research Ethics Consultation Collaborative and published in the *American Journal of Bioethics* Challenging Cases in Research Ethics Series. The case presentations were revised by the editors of this collection, with contributions by prior managing editors of this series, including Ellen Kuwana, Christian Morales, and Jennifer Zabrowski, as well as the original case presenters. The collaborative is supported by the National Center for Advancing Translational Sciences of the National Institutes of Health (NIH) under Award no. UL1 TR002319. Dr. Taylor is funded by the Intramural Program of the NIH Clinical Center. This content is solely the responsibility of the authors and does not reflect the view of the National Institutes of Health, the Department of Health and Human Services, or the U.S. government.

Introduction

BENJAMIN S. WILFOND, LIZA-MARIE JOHNSON, DEVAN M. DUENAS, AND HOLLY A. TAYLOR

The cases and commentaries in this collection were identified by research ethics consultants who are members of the Clinical Research Ethics Consultation Collaborative. The Collaborative currently has more than 70 members across North America who are affiliated with research ethics consultation services. The Collaborative is a network that shares consultation practices and discusses challenging cases at monthly virtual meetings. The Collaborative was established in 2014 by members of the Clinical and Translational Science Award Consortium Clinical Research Ethics Consultation Working Group with support from the Institute of Translational Health Sciences (https://www.iths.org/crecc/). The primary mission of the Collaborative is to improve the quality of clinical research ethics consultation services and recommendations.

One strategy to achieve this mission is sharing practices and experiences related to clinical research ethics consultation services. Members of the Collaborative (and the prior working group) have published several manuscripts that address a range of research ethics consultation practice issues. They initially explored the relationships between consultation services and institutional review boards (IRBs) (Beskow et al. 2009) and, more recently, established strategies for developing new research ethics consultation services (Taylor et al. 2021). They proposed specific data to be collected and documented about consultations (Cho et al. 2015) and published the collective experience of 10 consultation services with data from over 350 consultations (Porter et al. 2018a). They have explored professional practice challenges commonly faced by consultation services (Sharp et al. 2015) and identified emerging practice issues that will require further consideration (Porter et al. 2018b). They conducted a survey of research ethics practices and experiences in 2013 (McCormick et al. 2013) and published a follow-up survey in 2022 that illustrates the growth of such services (Taylor et al. 2022).

The second strategy to support its mission is for collaborative members to present their most challenging cases to the group. Since 2013, up to four of these cases have been selected each year to be published in the *American Journal of Bioethics* (AJOB) Challenging Cases in Research Ethics Series. Each case in the series is accompanied by two to four commentaries. For some cases, the commentators reach the same conclusions but for different reasons. Yet in other cases, the conclusions are different. The value of this collection is both in the range of cases and in reading about the different approaches and conclusions that scholars articulate.

The purpose of this collection is to be a resource for those who want to think more about challenging cases in research ethics and/or are interested in the practice of clinical research ethics consultation. These can be useful for research ethics consultants, graduate students and fellows in bioethics, clinical

DOI: 10.1201/9781003335306-1

researchers, and members of IRBs, Human Subjects Protection Programs, and related programs in other countries.

A FRAMEWORK FOR RESEARCH ETHICS

The editors of this collection are current and past editors of the AJOB series and leaders within the Collaborative. The editors have organized the book into five thematic sections that reflect principles (requirements) for research ethics that were initially articulated in a seminal paper by Emanuel, Wendler, and Grady (2000); further expanded in a follow-up article (Emanuel et al. 2004); and summarized in a book chapter (Emanuel, Wendler, and Grady 2008). Many research ethics consultants in the Collaborative use these principles to systematically analyze a particular ethical question. Many of the cases in this collection involve more than one principle, which at times can conflict and must be juggled. Thus, the identification of the principles at stake does not itself resolve the ethical question in a particular case, as much as provide a structure for the analysis.

The editors appreciated that these cases could have been organized differently, so we created a framework of topics, values, and principles to which each case is assigned. We reviewed the cases in this collection and identified 18 topics related to research studies or specific ethical questions. We also identified three core values that relate to many of the cases. For each case, we list the principles, topics, and values in the case introduction. An astute reader will notice that there are five sections but eight principles. We included legal/regulatory oversight as a *topic* to replace the principle of independent review. We also included social value as a *value*, rather than a principle. We did not categorize the cases according to the principle of scientific validity.

To facilitate the reader rapidly identifying cases that may be of interest, Appendix A lists the cases grouped by the five principles, including the cases that were identified as secondarily related to the principle (p. 303). Appendix B organizes the cases by topics (p. 307). Appendix C organizes the cases by values (p. 312).

PRINCIPLES OF RESEARCH ETHICS

Four of the eight principles focus on key aspects related to the research question and study design: social value, scientific validity, favorable risk–benefit ratio, and fair subject selection.

Social value describes the importance of the research question. For some studies, answering the research question may have a significant impact on health, healthcare, or future research. However, some studies, even if successful, may have limited impact on society. Of course, the determination of social value is subjective, and there can be differing views between researchers themselves, as well as between researchers and communities in which the research is taking place. Social value is important, as it can be a pivotal principle to balance with other principles and making decisions about study design.

Scientific validity refers to the capability of a particular study design to answer a research question. For example, placebo-controlled trials rely on an ethical justification of scientific validity. Scientific validity refers to importance of rigorous science to answer the question at hand. While a randomized trial can be more definitive than observational studies, observational studies can still address more limited questions. Scientific validity is necessary but not sufficient for a design to be ethically justified. There may need to be tradeoffs between principles to decide which study design is optimal.

Favorable risk–benefit ratio requires that the study design balances the benefits of knowledge and the direct benefit to participants with risks of study participation. It requires that risks be minimized and that benefits be enhanced. The application of this principle can be complex because benefits can accrue to one group and risks may be experienced by other groups.

Fair participant selection regards the study design decisions around whom to include in or exclude from research participation. When a particular study is viewed as having a favorable risk–benefit ratio, there will more attention to ensure that inclusion is fair. But when the risk–benefit ratio to the individual participants appears to be less favorable, the concern will be to ensure that groups are not being targeted unfairly.

The other four principles are not specific to the research question and study design, per se, but are related to the research process more generally: informed consent, independent review, respect for participants, and collaborative partnership.

Informed consent is neither necessary nor sufficient for research to be ethical, yet it is a critical principle. Ideally, participants should be aware of research and understand enough that they can make a voluntary decision around participation. However, questions about what details are important and what actions may unduly influence a decision can be challenging. Considerations of informed consent must also be balanced with the other principles in this framework.

Independent review is the principle that determinations about the other principles above should be done by those who are independent of the research. This is the ethical rationale for oversight programs, including IRBs and data and safety monitoring committees. Many studies will also create ad hoc advisory committees, as well, to provide additional input to promote quality science and get advice about ethical challenges.

Respect for participants, while articulated as early as the *Belmont Report*, may be the most difficult to define. Respect is a rationale for many of the decisions and approaches in clinical research, such as protecting privacy, allowing participants to withdraw, compensating participants for their time, and communicating research results. The definition of respect is ultimately determined by the participants themselves.

Collaborative partnership refers to the critical importance of researchers partnering with the community with whom they are engaging. This principle was not included in the initial framework but was later added as an eighth principle to address concerns that the seven principles were not sufficient to address concerns about the conduct of research in developing countries. The argument is that collaborative partnerships are necessary to evaluate each of the other principles from the community's perspective. Questions about social value, favorable risk–benefit ratios, fair participant selection, informed consent, and respect for participants may be considered differently by communities than by researchers or regulators. This principle is the justification for community engagement practices that have become commonplace over the last 20 years for all research, not just research in developing countries.

TOPICS IN RESEARCH ETHICS

The topics are intended to highlight the subject matter of each case. These topics were initially developed using a previous categorization system for the AJOB series, which assigned each case to one of 10 categories. The initial topical categories were revised by two of the editors (DD and HT) and reconceived so each case could be included in multiple topics. The topics were then reviewed and finalized by all the editors to ensure clarity and consistency of application. The goal was to create topics related to thematic areas of interest and promote accessibility to readers.

The topics span four major categories. The first category (populations) involves groups that were historically designated as "special populations," including children, adolescents, and young adults; people who are or can become pregnant; and those with a disability or who represent neurodiversity. The second category (study type) includes specific types of trials such as phase I trials or pragmatic trials or approaches such as genetics or health record review. The third category (research features) relates to specific features in a research study that raise ethical challenges, such as disclosing research results, clinician and researcher obligations, and research impact on family members. The final category is legal and regulatory oversight. Below is a list of the topics and descriptions for those topics (other than the topics within the population category).

Table: Topics in research ethics

Population	
Pediatrics	
Adolescents and Young Adults	
Pregnancy	
Disability and Neurodiversity	
Animal Research	
Study type	
Drugs and Devices	Cases involving research on the development or testing of medications or devices
Phase I Trials	Cases involving a trial to test a drug or intervention in a small group of participants with the purpose of evaluating safety and dosage
Pragmatic Trials	Cases involving a trial comparing two standard treatments currently offered to patients
Electronic Health Record	Cases involving research using data from electronic health records
Genetics	Cases involving research on the collection or use of genetic information
Research features	
Results Disclosure	Cases involving disclosing a clinical or research result to a participant or to all participants
Payment	Cases involving payment to research participants, including compensation and incentives
Off-Label Drug Availability or Use	Cases involving access to or use of a drug other than for its FDA-approved indication
Privacy	Cases involving the protection of data and information
Family Impact	Cases involving research that has collateral effects on a research participant's family members
Social Media	Cases involving the use of internet-based technologies developed to facilitate the sharing of information through virtual networks and communities
Clinician and Researcher Obligations	Cases involving the duties and responsibilities of a clinician and/or researcher when engaging in research with human participants
Legal and Regulatory Oversight	Cases involving laws or regulations regarding research, as well as the approaches to oversight

VALUES OF RESEARCH ETHICS

Research is a social activity. It engages an array of stakeholders to advance science and knowledge. People who volunteer to participate in research deserve protection and respect as essential tenets of the research enterprise. The values below are meant to be universal in the sense that all are key to the ethical conduct of research. That is, every case involves each of the values below. But for the purpose of this collection, we have assigned one or more of these values to cases where one or more is key to the analysis of the case.

Social value

As noted above, whether a research project has social or scientific value is essential to the evaluation of any research endeavor. We categorized those cases that present a dilemma in which the social value of a project is in tension with other ethical principles. For example, a project with high social value may not provide any direct personal benefit. While the social value can be considered in the ethical evaluation of the case, it may not be high enough to outweigh the level of risk to which participants would need to be exposed to answer the research question.

Equity

Traditionally, the term justice is used in research ethics discourse to bring attention to the distribution of the benefits and burdens of research. We chose the term equity to go beyond distribution. We categorized cases under equity when not only the distribution of benefits and burdens is a concern but also how those benefits and burdens are distributed, and care should be taken to avoid further disadvantaging any disadvantaged group (Ballantyne 2019).

Trustworthiness

As opposed to focusing on trust and mistrust, which are attributes that describe the relationship between an individual and another individual or institution, trustworthiness emphasizes how actions by an institution can be considered worthy of the trust of individuals and/or groups of individuals (Sheehan et al. 2020). The values of transparency and accountability are related to trustworthiness, as a commitment to either or both conveys a commitment to being worthy of trust. We categorized cases under trustworthiness where earning or maintaining trust from the community is especially relevant.

SUMMARY

The cases in this collection were generated over a decade. These cases, and listed topics, are not exhaustive or necessarily representative of all research ethics cases. Furthermore, the commentaries are intended to illustrate scholarly approaches to addressing the cases but should not be considered definitive. Often the commentators disagree. However, one of the key learnings from the Collaborative is that sharing research cases and exploring solutions and reasons will ensure, over time, that we can improve the quality of our collective analyses of challenging cases in research ethics.

REFERENCES

Ballantyne, A. 2019. Adjusting the focus: A public health ethics approach to data research. *Bioethics* 33(3):357–66.

Beskow, L. M., C. Grady, A. S. Iltis, et al. 2009. Points to consider: The research ethics consultation service and the IRB. *IRB* 31(6): 1–9.

Cho, M. K., H. Taylor, J. B. McCormick, et al. 2015. Building a Central repository for research ethics consultation data: A proposal for a standard data collection tool. *Clinical and Translational Science* 8(4): 376–87.

Emanuel, E. J., D. Wendler, and C. Grady. 2000. What makes clinical research ethical? *The Journal of the American Medical Association* 283(20):2701–11.

Emanuel, E. J., D. Wendler, and C. Grady. 2008. Chapter 11 - An ethical framework for biomedical research. In: *The Oxford textbook of clinical research.* Edited by E. J. Emanuel, C. Grady, R. A. Crouch, R. K. Lie, et al. Oxford University Press: New York, pp. 123–35.

Emanuel, E. J., D. Wendler, J. Killen, and C. Grady. 2004. What makes clinical research in developing countries ethical? The benchmarks of ethical research. *The Journal of Infectious Diseases* 189(5):930–37.

McCormick, J. B., R. Sharp, A. L. Ottenberg, and C. R. Reider, et al. 2013. The establishment of research ethics consultation services (RECS): An emerging research resource. *Clinical and Translational Science* 6(1):40–44.

Porter, K. M., M. Danis, H. A. Taylor, M. K. Cho, and B. S. Wilfond. 2018a. Clinical research ethics consultation collaborative repository group. The emergence of clinical research ethics consultation: Insights from a national collaborative. *The American Journal of Bioethics* 18(1):39–45.

Porter, K. M., M. Danis, H. A. Taylor, M. K. Cho, and B. S. Wilfond. 2018b. Defining the scope and improving the quality of clinical research ethics consultation: Response to open Peer commentaries about the national collaborative. *The American Journal of Bioethics* 18(2):W13–15.

Sharp, R. R., H. A. Taylor, M. A. Brinich, M. M. Boyle, et al. 2015. Research ethics consultation: Ethical and professional practice challenges and recommendations. *Academic Medicine* 90(5):615–20.

Sheehan, M., P. Friesen, A. Balmer, C. Cheeks, et al. 2020. Trust, trustworthiness and sharing patient data for research. *Journal of Medical Ethics* 18:medethics-2019-106048.

Taylor, H. A., K. M. Porter, E. T. Paquette, J. B. McCormick, et al. 2021. Creating a research ethics consultation service: Issues to consider. *Ethics and Human Research* 43(5):18–25.

Taylor, H. A., K. M. Porter, C. Sullivan, and J. B. McCormick. 2022. Current landscape of research ethics consultation services: National survey results. *Journal of Clinical and Translational Science* 6(1):e148.

Section 1

Collaborative partnership

BENJAMIN S. WILFOND

As noted in the introduction, collaborative partnership was added to the initial seven principles in the framework to explicitly consider the challenges when research is conducted in resource-limited settings and the risk of exploitation of the participants and the communities can be heightened. However, the value of a collaborative partnership to mitigate healthcare and health inequities is relevant to domestic contexts as well. A collaborative partnership refers to the importance of engaging communities and other stakeholders in development of research questions, study design, analysis, and implementation.

The initial contribution in this section is not a specific case but comprises four narrative reflections on different contexts in the United States where collaborative partnerships with communities are explored. The first of the five subsequent cases in this section regards a study of a vaccine to prevent dementia in participants from a Mexican community; this complex case is also categorized under respect for participants, fair participant selection, favorable risk–benefit ratio, and informed consent. The other four cases are also categorized with at least one of these principles. Three of the cases involve explicit considerations of the social context of the research, including health inequities due to racism, economic injustice, and a non-ideal healthcare system. For each of these, collaborative partnerships with communities are key considerations in addressing the question. The final case is sui generis; it considers the ethics of a clinical trial in dogs trained as companion animals and is an illustration of a community for whom protection from exploitation is paramount.

CASE 1.1: SUPPORTING COMMUNITY–ACADEMIC RESEARCH PARTNERSHIPS: REFLECTIONS FROM THE GROUND (OCTOBER 2021)

Principles: Respect for Participants

Topics: Genetics

Values: Social Value, Trustworthiness, Equity

The first commentary (Springgate et al., this volume, p. 15) is a description of a community-based partnership in southeast Louisiana created with the framework of "community partnered participatory research." This partnership began as a coalition between healthcare, public health, social services, and community-based organizations (CBOs) to address the impact of climate change and related disasters on the community. The commentary describes the conceptual origins of

---

DOI: 10.1201/9781003335306-2

the approach, the leadership structure, and evolving approaches to community engagement that develop, implement, and evaluate interventions to benefit the community. Because this partnership was established in the late 2000s, it was well positioned in 2020 to be a focal point in addressing the impact of the COVID-19 pandemic, as well as the impacts of structural racism on minority communities. This narrative underscores the potential of long-term impact by a geographically based community partnership.

The second commentary (Yu, this volume, p. 18) is the reflection of an Asian American leader describing his journey from a leader in a community-based healthcare organization to an academic researcher partnering with other organizations. He also describes an innovative approach, creating a "learning community-based organization" in which each project, including its successes and failures, becomes the inspiration for ongoing innovations.

The third commentary (Carroll, this volume, p. 20) is written by a sickle cell disease advocate who describes her perspective from 20 years of experience working with CBOs and academic researchers. She emphasizes the importance of community-based participatory research, including the effort to engage people with sickle cell disease as partners in the design and implementation of research projects. She notes that researchers need to acknowledge the mistrust of the African American community and the effort needed to become trustworthy.

The final commentary (Blanchard and Hiratsuka, this volume, p. 23) describes the partnership between American Indian communities and academic researchers in the context of genomic research. The authors describe the approaches to the partnership and highlight the importance of tribal sovereignty and the management of data. A key focus of this narrative is suggestions to ensure that data collected are used to benefit the community. The authors discuss the concept of "being in good community," which describes the value of academic researchers advocating for communities to allow those communities to flourish.

Each of these four narratives emphasizes the long-term nature of the partnerships and deep commitments required of both researchers and community partners.

CASE 1.2: PROTECTING RESEARCH SUBJECT WELFARE IN PREVENTATIVE TRIALS FOR AUTOSOMAL DOMINANT ALZHEIMER'S DISEASE (2015)

Principles: Respect for Participants, Fair Participant Selection, Favorable Risk–Benefit Ratio, Informed Consent

Topics: Drugs and Devices, Phase I Trials, Genetics, Results Disclosure

Values: Equity, Trustworthiness

This case involves a placebo-controlled trial of a vaccine to prevent a monogenetic form of Alzheimer's disease. The target population are members of an extended family in rural Mexico who have been enrolled in an observational cohort study. Some of the family has migrated to Mexico City, and others to the United States. The cohort study involves imaging and neuropsychological testing. Participants also can have clinical genetic testing done. The vaccine study would be a first-in-human trial, stratified by research genetic testing. Those who enroll who carry a pathogenic variant would be randomized to a vaccine or placebo, while those who do not carry a pathogenic variant would only get the placebo vaccine. The participants in the cohort study have a range of English proficiency, literacy, and medical sophistication.

The first commentary (Yarborough, this volume, p. 28) focuses on the impact of targeting a select population. This includes the requirement for a genetic test that would predict their development of Alzheimer's disease. Participants have the option to opt for or against receiving the results of the test. But there is a chance that their genetic status may be inferred if they experience side effects from the vaccine. This could cause distress and, if disclosed to others, stigmatization. While cohort members do not have to join the trial, the commentator raises the second concern that potential participants may feel pressure to join a study that could benefit others in their community. The commentator does not offer solutions to these concerns, but suggests robust community partnership, with attention to language, culture, and familial issues, as a path forward.

The second commentary (Korenman, Finder, and Ringman, this volume, p. 30) considers the case through a lens of vulnerability. They are specifically concerned about the potential for "therapeutic misconception." To promote clear understanding about the goals, risks, and benefits of the study, they advocate for community outreach prior to the beginning of enrollment, to both educate the community and tailor the consent process.

The third commentary (Simpson, this volume, p. 32) also focuses on the challenge of informed consent and reviews recent literature to suggest specific steps the researchers can take. One key suggestion for this study is utilizing bilingual research coordinators from the community and emphasizing their role to ensure that participants understand the information disclosed and are making a voluntary choice. They also endorse involving community members as research coordinators to build community partnerships.

This case is included in community partnerships because the solutions to the questions raised by this case can be best addressed by a robust partnership with the specific community who would be involved in this research to ensure trustworthiness and equity.

CASE 1.3: STUDYING THE ROLE OF FINANCIAL INCENTIVES TO PROMOTE HEPATITIS B VACCINATION IN A COMMUNITY CLINIC (2016)

Principles: Respect for Participants, Favorable Risk–Benefit Ratio, Informed Consent

Topics: Drugs and Devices, Clinician and Researcher Obligations, Payment

Values: Trustworthiness, Social Value

This case asks whether it is appropriate to test the role of differential incentives among participants eligible to receive the hepatitis B virus (HBV) vaccine. The study site is a U.S. health clinic that primarily serves African-born immigrants. The HBV vaccine is considered safe and effective and is a routine infant vaccine in the United States. Among clinic patients, 25% of the population is at risk for HBV, as 75% were previously infected. However, only 10% of those who may benefit from vaccination have followed through on the three-vaccine series over three months, even when offered free of charge, at this clinic. Community focus groups did not offer clear insight regarding the barriers. The clinic staff proposes to conduct a study that randomizes clinic attendees to an education control group versus $10 versus $20.

The first commentary (Giunta, this volume, p. 36) is very skeptical of this study. Her central concern is that the goal of increasing vaccine uptake by clinicians offering payment for recommended care is misguided. First, she is concerned that clinicians offering to pay patients for routine medical care is a fundamental departure from the classic physician–patient relationship, and one that can undermine the overall effectiveness of that relationship. Her second concern is that even though the focus groups have not identified a clear reason, it is necessary to understand and address the underlying concerns. More attention to engaging the community about the vague concerns is what is needed.

The second commentary (Doussau and Grady, this volume, p. 38) has concerns about the study design. One concern is about the education control group, which may limit the opportunity to observe the impact of the financial incentive, if the education control also is effective. The commentators are also concerned that for the study to be successful, it may be necessary to not disclose to participants what the other groups are getting, as that knowledge could impact each group's behavior. They do not suggest that such a deception is unethical as much as state that the decision to do this would require community involvement in the decision.

The third commentary (Perumalswami, Branch, and Rhodes, this volume, p. 40) addresses potential concerns that paying patients is ethically problematic and suggests that the consequences of improving health could justify it ethically. Furthermore, they raise the framework of behavioral economics to suggest that such strategies for encouraging behavior that is in the patients' interests not only may be effective but also are used routinely in other contexts. These considerations would be helpful to community groups who are considering these questions.

The three commentaries approach this question from different perspectives and came to different conclusions. A robust community partnership could consider these perspectives as part of the decision-making process.

CASE 1.4: A CLUSTER RANDOMIZED TRIAL TO SCREEN FOR ABUSIVE HEAD TRAUMA IN THE PEDIATRIC INTENSIVE CARE UNIT: HOW TO MANAGE SITE-SPECIFIC EVIDENCE OF RACIAL/ETHNIC DISPARITY (2019)

Principles: Respect for Participants, Favorable Risk–Benefit Ratio

Topics: Pragmatic Trials, Pediatrics, Results Disclosure

Values: Social Value, Equity

This case is about a cluster randomized trial at eight institutions comparing usual care to a recently validated screening tool to identify which children admitted to a pediatric intensive care unit with a head injury should be evaluated for child abuse. The rationale for developing the tool was to avoid implicit bias about race and ethnicity by clinicians who may over- or under-identify families to be evaluated for abuse. The investigator conducted an interim analysis after year 1 and determined that one of four sites using the screening tool evaluated only 53% of their 15 high-risk patients. The other three sites evaluated 86–100% of high-risk children. The four control sites did not have any disparities in evaluations between sites. The interim analysis was conducted in response to a finding, upon secondary analysis of the initial validation study, that two of 18 sites were much more likely to report Black or Hispanic families as families to evaluate for potential abuse. One of these sites was the same site in the intervention arm that underreported abuse, and the other site was in the control group for the current study. The investigator questioned whether the two sites in the implementation study should be told about their data from the initial study and whether that would jeopardize the integrity of the implementation study. His second question is whether the study should be stopped or modified as families were being subjected to the very implicit biases that the tool was intended to address.

The first commentary (Tumilty and Farroni, this volume, p. 45) notes that, ideally, the data monitoring committee would have established stopping rules before the implementation study began, but also notes that these are rarely done in cluster trials. The commentators recommend that all eight sites offer an educational program to reduce bias in abuse evaluations, rather than just the two sites. They note that the results can be analyzed to compare pre/post education to address scientific concerns about the influence of the educational program.

The second commentary (Jackson, this volume, p. 47) does not recommend stopping or modifying the study. First, he points out that the clinical trial is not the cause of bias. Second, the finding of racial disparity in evaluating abuse has been previously reported and is well known. Third, completion of the trial may help decrease implicit bias if the study results demonstrate this tool is useful. For these reasons, he does not think the two sites should be informed of their behavior until the current study is completed.

The third commentary (McCormick and Hymel, this volume, p. 50) also does not recommend stopping or modifying the study. They point to the importance of the trial to address the serious underlying problem of implicit bias. They do not recommend notifying the two sites from the prior study but encourage all sites to consider the potential for bias. In addition, they suggest that the aggregate interim data for the trial be provided to all the sites as well.

This case is not explicitly grounded in community partnerships. Instead, the focus of the commentators is to balance the importance of the study to change behavior even while the study is documenting that biased evaluations for abuse are occurring. Because the issues addressed in this study would be important to communities, it becomes evident that the equity and social value questions raised by this case could be addressed in part with robust community partnership in place.

CASE 1.5: WHEN A CLINICAL TRIAL IS THE ONLY OPTION (2016)

Principles: Fair Participant Selection, Informed Consent, Respect for Participants

Topics: Clinician and Researcher Obligations

Values: Trustworthiness, Equity

This case involves a patient with myelofibrosis, a gradually progressive blood disorder. The patient is a 55-year-old from Central America who speaks Spanish, is undocumented, and is not eligible for government financial assistance programs. He has been in the hospital for three weeks, getting daily platelet transfusions and other treatments for symptom control. The palliative care service has arranged for him to be sent home, receiving hospice care provided by a local charity. Just before discharge, another clinician identified a clinical trial for a bone marrow transplant (BMT) at a center 900 miles away. The clinical trial would cover the associated costs of the transplant. The five-year survival with a transplant is 30%. The costs of posttransplant care are also very expensive. He has one sibling in Texas and two siblings in Central America. If one of the siblings in Central America is a match, the sibling would need to apply for a medical visa, which could take weeks to months. There is disagreement between team members whether to tell the patient about the clinical trial option. The main concern is that the logistical and financial complexities will remain, and enrollment in a trial may be misunderstood as medical treatment.

The first commentary (Fabi, this volume, p. 53) considers it a moral imperative to tell the patient about the trial. She initially raises the concern that some of the hesitation may be an implicit bias related to his immigration status. She suggests that talking about the study conveys respect and treats him as we would treat any other patient. She argues clinicians have an obligation to disclose the options so the patient can decide what is the right decision for him and his family.

The second commentary (Heitman, this volume, p. 55) offers a more qualified recommendation to disclose. She first suggests detailed discussion about the goals of care, and to be clear about the limited chance of even clinical success of the BMT. She then describes in vivid detail the range of costs and complexities that might occur, even with the coverage of the transplant. She suggests that these issues need to be discussed in detail with the family to better position themselves to make a decision they will not regret.

The third commentary (Burke, this volume, p. 57) concludes the study should not be offered. She counters what she frames as a "logic of choice" with a "logic of care." By this, she means that we are not obligated to offer all choices. She argues that the contextual situation and the clinical situation portend a poor outcome for the patient and family. However, once offered, it may be too difficult to achieve the nuance about the expected outcomes proposed by the second commentator. Rather, she suggests that a "logic of care" would direct the team to continue with the current plan.

Like the prior case, these commentators do not explicitly discuss community partnerships. Rather, this case speaks to potential for implicit bias, the reality of inequitable care, and its relevance to research. This case begins in the clinical context and can be understood as a dilemma for the overlap of clinical and research obligations. This is also a topic that can benefit from community engagement.

CASE 1.6: A RANDOMIZED TRIAL OF RAPAMYCIN TO INCREASE LONGEVITY AND HEALTH SPAN IN COMPANION ANIMALS: NAVIGATING THE BOUNDARY BETWEEN PROTECTIONS FOR ANIMAL RESEARCH AND HUMAN SUBJECTS RESEARCH (2018)

Principles: Respect for Participants, Fair Participant Selection, Favorable Risk–Benefit Ratio, Informed Consent

Topics: Drugs and Devices, Animal Research, Pediatrics

Values: Social Value

The study team has proposed a randomized clinical trial in middle-aged companion dogs to assess the impact of rapamycin on longevity and health span. Rapamycin is a transplant immunosuppressive drug that has also been shown in small laboratory animals to increase lifespan. The placebo-controlled trial will include one year of treatment and two years of follow-up. The dose proposed will be low, but it is not known what the side effect profile will be in dogs. The commentators explore the relationship between animal and human research regulations, and the unique questions about the obligations researchers may have to the dog owners.

The first commentary (Abbate, this volume, p. 61) explores the contours of disclosure during informed consent with owners, with recommendations for key points to include. She considers that the model of human research regulations, with a focus on social value and risk–benefit ratio, is important for companion animal research. She then points out that laboratory animals are even more vulnerable than companion dogs, yet the animal welfare regulations still permit life-and-death decisions that we would never accept in companion dogs.

The second commentary (Walker and Fisher, this volume, p. 63) also draws attention to how concerns for companion animal research can direct attention further to laboratory animal research. The commentators then turn to the potential for "therapeutic misconception" of dog owners in the rapamycin trial and the need for thoughtful informed consent materials.

The third commentary (Wilfond et al., this volume, p. 65) focuses explicitly on the pediatric framework in the federal regulations, and suggests that this can guide approval considerations in companion animal research and that institutional review boards (IRBs) should be involved, as some data will be collected from the owners. The commentators also consider how a data and safety monitoring committee can also play a role in oversight of this sort of research.

All three commentaries note the chasm between traditional animal regulations and human subjects' regulations: both how ethical analysis of companion animal research benefits from each approach but also how this research illustrates the limitations of the animal research regulations. Getting input from dog owners can be part of the resolution for how to approach the rapamycin study, but perhaps the greatest potential ethics legacy of this study is to further the community dialogue about laboratory animal research.

CASE 1.1: SUPPORTING COMMUNITY–ACADEMIC RESEARCH PARTNERSHIPS: REFLECTIONS FROM THE GROUND

INTRODUCTION

Currently, there is consensus that community engagement and partnerships are essential to inclusive patient-centered clinical research. Yet there is variation about what it means to do this well, and there are diverse implementation strategies.

The role of the communities in decision making about research and policy was elevated in the 1980s by AIDS activists who demanded a place at the table when research policy decisions affecting their health and welfare were at stake. They formed national advocacy organizations to make sure their communities' voices were heard: taking their demands to the Food and Drug Administration (FDA) and National Institutes of Health (NIH), protesting the slow pace of drug approval, and demanding the expansion of clinical trials to include more women and people of color. In the subsequent 40 years, community partnerships have developed in a variety of contexts. Several contemporary NIH research programs illustrate the legacy of these community activists in their approach to trial design, conduct, and oversight in partnership with communities. For example, the All of Us Research Program (NIH 2021), which seeks to develop a diverse biorepository of samples for future health research, and the Rapid Acceleration of Diagnostics—Underserved Populations projects (RADx-UP 2021), which aim to improve COVID-19 testing and health support for affected individuals from underserved and/or vulnerable populations, have deliberate approaches to community engagement and partnerships.

Communities can be defined by a variety of contexts—disease, geography, race, Indigenous sovereignty, as well as combinations of the above—which complicates a single paradigm of "community partnerships." The four commentators in this series all have experience with community partnerships and offer insights based on their experience on the ground. The authors reflect on their experiences with community partnerships in distinct contexts and offer insights for researchers, communities, and others who may be involved in creating new partnerships.

Yvonne Carroll, from St. Jude Children's Research Hospital, reflects on the experience of the predominately Black communities with sickle cell anemia. She discusses the importance of community partnerships in the context of systemic racism to advance research that is meaningful to the community.

Jessica Blanchard, from the University of Oklahoma, and Vanessa Hiratsuka, from the University of Alaska Anchorage, reflect on community partnerships with American Indian and Alaska Native communities. They emphasize the importance of appreciating the impact of Indigenous sovereignty in establishing partnerships and highlight the efforts of a research center to acknowledge the importance and impact of Indigenous sovereignty.

Joon-Ho Yu, from the University of Washington, has the unique perspective of working both at an academic institution and in an official capacity for the Korean Community Service Center (KCSC) in Seattle. He describes both his personal journey and how he has supported a community group in establishing the terms of the partnerships to embed research as part of the group's mission.

Benjamin Springgate and colleagues from the Louisiana State University (LSU) Health Sciences Center–New Orleans together with collaborators from the Community Resilience Learning Collaborative and Research Network (C-LEARN) community–academic partnership describe a unique academic–community partnership in southeastern Louisiana that is grounded in the concept of community-partnered participatory research (CPPR). This approach was adopted to allow a collaboration between a variety of community groups in partnership with academic institutions to develop public health strategies to enhance community resilience in the context of climate change and related natural disasters.

Collectively, these four commentaries share approaches and rationales that can inspire researchers to prioritize community partnerships in the development of new research to ensure that research that is conducted has the greatest opportunity to benefit the communities the research is designed to serve.

REFERENCES

NIH (National Institutes of Health). 2021. All of us research program. Accessed July 6, 2021. https://allofus.nih.gov/.

RADx-UP. 2021. Rapid Acceleration of Diagnostics-Underserved Populations (RADx-UP). Accessed July 6, 2021. https://radx-up.org/.

COMMENTARY 1.1.1: COMMUNITY-PARTNERED PARTICIPATORY RESEARCH IN SOUTHEASTERN LOUISIANA COMMUNITIES THREATENED BY CLIMATE CHANGE: THE C-LEARN EXPERIENCE

BENJAMIN F. SPRINGGATE, OLIVIA SUGARMAN, KENNETH B. WELLS, LAWRENCE A. PALINKAS, DIANA MEYERS, ASHLEY WENNERSTROM, ARTHUR JOHNSON, CATHERINE HAYWOOD, DANIEL SARPONG, AND RICHARD CULBERTSON

Community-partnered participatory research (CPPR) is grounded in the ethical principle of respect for persons participating in the research enterprise. The critical importance of respect for persons on an individual level was recognized in the *Belmont Report*, and is a foundation of consent in clinical ethics (Jonsen, Siegler, and Winslade 2015). However, as population-driven research shifts focus from individuals to communities, a new view of the role of the community in assessing collective benefit and harm is essential (Erikainen et al. 2021). The community is no longer an amalgam of participants but an active partner over the course of investigation. The case example of the C-LEARN network will illustrate this ethical imperative in action.

The Community Resilience Learning Collaborative and Research Network (C-LEARN; https://www.c-learn.org/) began in 2017 as a community–academic partnered study in southeastern Louisiana seeking to enhance community and individual resilience in communities threatened by climate change and related disasters through a collaboration of partners in healthcare, public health, and CBOs, including faith-based groups, neighborhood associations, and social services (Springgate et al. 2018). Based on a 13-year history of collaboration and funded by the National Academies of Sciences Gulf Research Program (NAS-GRP), multiple community organizations and three academic institutions developed this community–academic partnered program in three temporal phases:

1. Partners co-developed qualitative processes to assess community perceptions of resilience and to inform subsequent interventional study phases (Pollock et al. 2019).
2. Partners initiated a community-partnered, two-level randomized controlled trial to test interventions and assess impacts on community and individual resilience (particularly depression, mental health–related quality of life, and social determinants of health).
3. When the COVID-19 pandemic interrupted the trial, partners recognized the shifting landscape and impacts on the study and communities. They modified the study using a rapid assessment methodology to learn how the pandemic was affecting southern Louisiana communities and their ongoing preparedness efforts for future climate-related disasters.

Loretta Jones defined CPPR as "a variant of CBPR (community-based participatory research) emphasizing partnership in all aspects of research and capacity building, developed specifically for health research to include clinician investigators and community partners representing under-resourced communities" (Jones 2018). C-LEARN represented the newest iteration of CPPR among community and academic partners across New Orleans, Louisiana, and Los Angeles, California. The CPPR model was developed by Loretta Jones of Healthy African American Families ii (https://www.haafii.org/) and colleagues, adapted for behavioral health with Kenneth Wells of UCLA's Center for Health Services and Society (Wells and Jones 2009). CPPR emphasizes authentic partnerships between community and academic stakeholders, including for implementation of evidence-based practices. Such partnerships meaningfully engage community members in all phases of work, holding scientific perspectives of academic partners and lived experience of community members as "PhDs of the sidewalk" in equally high regard, to ensure that research goals, processes, and outcomes are credible, equitable, and meaningful to communities affected by conditions studied. Applications of CPPR to behavioral health originated with the Witness for Wellness study of depression in South Los Angeles, which informed engagement of community leadership in subsequent partnered projects with a focus on depression (Bluthenthal et al. 2006). The New Orleans and Los Angeles projects, as well as community and scientific contributions applying CPPR over more than 20 years, are well documented (Wells et al. 2013). Applying CPPR-initiated innovations reflects the involvement of diverse partners in all phases of research from conceptualization to community engagement, design of interventions and data collection tools, analysis, development of products, and dissemination of results. The principles of partnership emphasize explicit attention to power and resource sharing to address systemic inequities (e.g., racism), commitment to the scientific process, and sharing benefits of results among participants.

In addition to adopting an underlying conceptual model for partnership, C-LEARN drew from experiences and lessons of historical applications of CPPR, including developing structures and processes reflective of community and academic co-leadership, applying community expertise to enhance study design and implementation, and relying on community strengths to overcome unexpected challenges.

For instance, a Leadership Council consisting of academic scholars and community leaders from local nonprofit organizations met regularly to oversee decision making related to the project. The Leadership Council wrote, revised, and subscribed to a set of principles formalized in a Collaboration Agreement, which was designed to ensure agreed-upon mutual goals, opportunities for contribution, and measures of accountability. Study plans and progress were reviewed and modified based on regular input with the Leadership Council.

Study processes benefited from expertise of community partners, including critical review and refinement of study methods, as well as insightful contributions to data analyses. While some critics may point to the slower initial pace of study progress as partners engage across cultures, demands on academic and community partners to work with one another and come to consensus in decision making, and the dilution of authority involved in community–academic partnered research processes as drawbacks or limitations, in our opinion the additional time and effort to gather diverse perspectives among stakeholders and to realize associated improvements in processes and outcomes are both warranted and worthwhile. For example, in C-LEARN, partnered research processes led to successful co-development of interview guides, surveys, intervention tools, and community engagement processes benefiting from extensive community and academic input.

Community forums were held to engage and inform other community partners at the study's onset as well as periodically. Disseminations of findings and products in academic and community settings, including peer-reviewed papers, were co-led and coauthored by academic and community partners—a critical process to ensure equitable credit for contributions and opportunities for shared benefit among participating stakeholders. Additionally, plans for interventions to promote resilience, while based on evidence-based toolkits, were iteratively tailored to communities and the local context of disaster preparedness and social determinants of health, through reviewing community input in interviews and adapting programs and training plans with stakeholder consensus.

When the pandemic interrupted trial recruitment, the strength of partnership was evident. Even as community and academic co-leads struggled with impacts of the pandemic in their personal and work lives, they came together to identify paths forward for the study and apply CPPR principles to enhance knowledge and inform southeastern Louisiana communities. Recognizing that the new pandemic might affect how community members and organizations sought to address ongoing threats of climate-related disasters such as hurricanes and severe weather events, the Leadership Council worked to adapt the study design. This led to a novel application of Rapid Assessment Procedure-Informed Community Ethnography (RAPICE) to inform understanding of what help might be needed to address ongoing disaster preparedness during a pandemic (Palinkas et al. 2021). Furthermore, the increased concern about racial/ethnic discrimination events like the murder of George Floyd prompted community discussions of how to incorporate a concern with individual and structural racism into the assessment. Given the collaborative, participatory nature of CPPR and the tradition of responding in partnership to events, these discussions were open conversations about implications for resources, training, and partnerships (e.g., collaborations among health, social services, and faith-based organizations).

In conclusion, the CPPR model, structures, and processes supporting community and academic partners as co-equal were critical to both the initial goals and design of C-LEARN, and to reframing and identifying an approach to examine environmental disaster and pandemic resilience as original goals for the study were disrupted by the pandemic. Nevertheless, partnership in reframing led to expanded lessons learned and broader community dialogue and support, reinforcing the value of ethical principles of trust, respect, power sharing, and two-way cultural exchange in knowledge, attitudes, and behaviors for supporting together resilient individuals and communities.

References

Bluthenthal, R. N., L. Jones, N. Fackler-Lowrie, M. Ellison, T. Booker, F. Jones, S. McDaniel, M. Moini, K. R. Williams, R. Klap, et al. 2006. Witness for wellness: Preliminary findings from a community-academic participatory research mental health initiative. *Ethnicity & Disease* 16(1 Suppl 1): S18–S34.

Erikainen, S., P. Friesen, L. Rand, K. Jongsma, M. Dunn, A. Sorbie, M. McCoy, J. Bell, M. Burgess, H. Chen, et al. 2021. Public involvement in the governance of population-level biomedical research: Unresolved questions and future directions. *Journal of Medical Ethics* 47:522–525.

Jones, L. 2018. Commentary: 25 years of community partnered participatory research. *Ethnicity & Disease* 28(Suppl 2):291–4.

Jonsen, A., M. Siegler, W. Winslade. 2015. *Clinical ethics*, 8th ed. New York, NY: McGraw-Hill.

Palinkas, L. A., B. F. Springgate, O. K. Sugarman, J. Hancock, A. Wennerstrom, C. Haywood, D. Meyers, A. Johnson, M. Polk, C. L. Pesson, et al. 2021. A rapid assessment of disaster preparedness needs and resources during the COVID-19 pandemic. *International Journal of Environmental Research and Public Health* 18(2):425.

Pollock, M. J., A. Wennerstrom, G. True, A. Everett, O. Sugarman, C. Haywood, A. Johnson, D. Meyers, J. Sato, K. B. Wells, et al. 2019. Preparedness and community resilience in disaster-prone areas: Cross-sectoral collaborations in South Louisiana, 2018. *American Journal of Public Health* 109(S4):S309–15.

Springgate, B., A. Arevian, A. Wennerstrom, A. Johnson, D. Eisenman, O. Sugarman, C. Haywood, E. Trapido, C. Sherbourne, A. Everett, et al. 2018. Community Resilience Learning Collaborative and Research Network (C-LEARN): Study protocol with participatory planning for a randomized, comparative effectiveness trial. *International Journal of Environmental Research and Public Health* 15(8):1683.

Wells, K., and L. Jones. 2009. "Research" in community-partnered, participatory research. *JAMA* 302(3):320–1.

Wells, K. B., B. F. Springgate, E. Lizaola, F. Jones, and A. Plough. 2013. Community engagement in disaster preparedness and recovery: A tale of two cities-Los Angeles and New Orleans. *The Psychiatric Clinics of North America* 36(3):451–66.

COMMENTARY 1.1.2: LEVERAGING ACADEMIC INSTITUTIONAL STRUCTURES TO SUPPORT ASIAN AMERICAN COMMUNITY ORGANIZATIONS' ENGAGEMENT IN RESEARCH: THE KOREAN COMMUNITY SERVICE CENTER

JOON-HO YU

My research partnership with the Korean Community Service Center (KCSC) of Seattle is the deepest research relationship I have had since transitioning from working with a national "minority health" organization, the Asian & Pacific Islander American Health Forum (APIAHF), to academic research. As director of the APIAHF Chronic Disease Programs, I served local community-based organizations (CBOs) like KCSC. My subsequent academic scholarship has focused on community engagement and community-based research but from a perspective primarily situated outside of the community. My relationship with KCSC, an organization founded by locally defined Korean American stakeholders to serve the Korean American community, began in 2018 on a small limited project (the Korean American Youth Survey) and over time has blossomed into my current role as part-time deputy director and director of assessment, research and evaluation. Through this ongoing journey, I have learned much about community–academic collaborations; thus, I offer my reflections on the KCSC "partnership" because of its unique qualities and my deep involvement.

Partnership vision and strategies

The overall vision of research partnership is to develop and promote a model in which the KCSC is a learning CBO akin to learning healthcare organizations (Greene, Reid, and Larson 2012). This approach is a significant shift for an organization founded 37 years ago for mutual aid and service. For example, the parent/caregiver education implementation project sponsored by Best Starts for Kids (BSK) (King County-DCHS 2021) has been our most important investment of time and energy because it provided access to key capacity-building resources (e.g., staffing and organizational development, data platform development, and data visualization trainings).

To realize this vision, four strategies have been vital to success. (1) As a learning CBO, we adopted an implementation science approach that serves as a framework for iterative learning and action. (2) Although we partner with University of Washington (UW) researchers to contribute generalizable knowledge, additional assessment, research, and evaluation activities are supported through philanthropic funds to inform flexible program and community initiative development (i.e., in contrast to generalizable knowledge). (3) As part of our BSK project planning, we established culturally informed principles of partnership that we revisit while engaging in the work. (4) We ground our work in living logic models (i.e., evolving explanatory models of cause and effect that inform our program planning and evaluation) informed by both our community's lived experiences and the available literature. These models encapsulate the "why" behind our efforts. They bring staff, advisors, funders, and community members together in common understanding, and force us to better center our strategies and identify intermediary outcomes and measures of change. Taking BSK as an example, we've adopted a trauma-informed intergenerational approach where we connect our elders' traumas (e.g., Japanese occupation and the Korean War) to waves of subsequent U.S. immigration and the cultural conflicts that exist between first- and second-generation worldviews. We applied this to the development of culturally relevant parenting education that raises community awareness in the short term and encourages family communication as an intermediary outcome, ultimately toward measurable change in parenting behaviors and children's mental health.

Six intensive practices have been critical for our program development and research efforts. (1) Months of weekly conversations with leadership about the organization, community, and research led to a shared vision for how to move forward: both with the initial Korean American Youth Survey and more broadly in our working relationship. (2) We check in with community members (staff and volunteers) at initial stages of every project's development before formal community engagement to ensure that we are on the right track. (3) In parallel, we convene advisory committees of subject matter experts from the Korean American community for both program and research activities. (4) We routinely conduct formative qualitative research with community members for new projects and to inform iterations of program implementation in varied contexts (Cho et al. unpublished). (5) We invest in staff training conducted by experienced researchers so that KCSC staff are empowered to conduct research activities. (6) Finally, we actively "return results" by convening forums to share our findings, engage community stakeholders and decision makers, and disseminate through ethnic print, radio, online media, and social media platforms.

Key accomplishments

The most significant accomplishment has been conducting research that matters to the community and informs allocation of public and private resources for community-based prevention and intervention programs and services. For the organization, coupling research and organizational capacity building has been a decisive advantage in demonstrating our relatively sophisticated model and vision of becoming a learning CBO. By taking the initiative to seek out and develop research partnerships where KCSC leads and UW researchers serve as consultants and collaborators (e.g., BSK projects), we have flipped the model to yield direct community benefits while still contributing to generalizable research. From a capacity-building perspective, we have been able to make space for subject matter experts, many of whom were former academics in Korea, to contribute their skills to community-based projects. Perhaps the best marker of our success has been the increasing interest from government agencies and foundations for KCSC to conduct robust, research-informed development of services and programs.

Challenges

New models of research present challenges. To this day, we still advocate for disaggregating data from population-based studies because "Asian" or "AANHPI" (Asian Americans, Native Hawaiians, and Pacific Islanders) promotes the myth that we are a *model* minority and fails to represent ethnic and community-specific inequities and priorities. Yet, with the advent of "big data," the potential for disaggregating existing data to answer questions of community priority may be possible, though to do so will require a new cadre of community-oriented bioinformatics researchers (Grayson, Doerr, and Yu 2020). Such innovations will likely resurge issues of community engagement, governance, and what constitutes trustworthy practices. For instance, community engagement has been instrumental for establishing community consent, culturally appropriate recruitment approaches, and acceptable data collection procedures. In the context of preexisting aggregated datasets, stakeholders will need to look at community engagement in the context of explicit third-party data use and the potential risk of harms derived from data harmonization and aggregation. Furthermore, as big data become more widely available to individuals untethered from the primary research institution, self-governance may become the principal approach to protecting communities from derived harms.

A professional challenge is making transparent the potential conflicts I feel as both a research faculty member and a member of the KCSC leadership. For example, while I am responsible for research collaborations between KCSC and other academic and governmental researchers, any research activities involving my own academic work is decided by the agency's executive director and managers.

Lessons learned for researchers and funders creating new partnerships

(1) Get out there and be part of "the community"; otherwise, your relationships will always be utilitarian such that conflicts of purpose, benefits, and risks may impede success. (2) By prioritizing and rewarding collaboration in funding initiatives, local funders encouraged many of the structural and process-oriented practices we have adopted. Take advantage of these opportunities to try out and explore new configurations for collaborative research. (3) The implicit value of working with diverse communities, such as AANHPIs, as a microcosm of the larger diversity of these United States of America needs to be more explicit. Yet, to do so, we must move from cultural to community competence (Robinson 2005), from understanding a community bound by static notions of culture to recognizing the need for deeper community competence as a generalizable approach to partnership. (4) CBOs can be hubs for community-based research independent of academic research institutions. In part, this reflects the broader shift toward patient-led research and citizen science, and the community's needs to control data, samples, and research agendas most clearly demonstrated in Indigenous communities' efforts. In an AANHPI context, it also demonstrates a need for establishing independent routes for research and funding for Native Hawaiian and Pacific Islander communities.

Conclusion

The diversity of AANHPI and, more generally, BIPOC (Black, Indigenous, People of Color) communities and experiences requires a commitment to recognizing our communities' unique intersectional perspectives, especially when attempting to connect the production of generalizable knowledge to real-world practices. This commitment holds promise as a unifying approach to research partnerships.

References

Cho, Y., R. Lee, J. H. Park, J. H. Yu, and E. Kim. (unpublished). Comparison of perceptions on traditional parental virtues between Korean- and English-speaking Korean immigrants.

Grayson, S., M. Doerr, and J. H. Yu. 2020. Developing pathways for community-led research with big data: A content analysis of stakeholder interviews. *Health Research Policy and Systems* 18(1):76.

Greene, S. M., R. J. Reid, and E. B. Larson. 2012. Implementing the learning health system: From concept to action. *Annals of Internal Medicine* 157(3):207–10.

King County-DCHS. 2021. Best Starts for Kids. Accessed April 20, 2021. https://kingcounty.gov/depts/community-human-services/initiatives/best-starts-for-kids.aspx

Robinson, R. G. 2005. Community development model for public health applications: Overview of a model to eliminate population disparities. *Health Promotion Practice* 6(3):338–46.

COMMENTARY 1.1.3: ENGAGING THE SICKLE CELL COMMUNITY IN PARTICIPATORY RESEARCH

YVONNE CARROLL

Community-based participatory research (CBPR) is an effective tool in engaging underrepresented minorities in research (Brewer et al. 2019). To be successful, CBPR must be culturally sensitive, respectful, and engage stakeholders in a collaborative and equitable manner (Ward et al. 2018); this is especially true when engaging stakeholders with sickle cell disease (SCD). People with SCD are often disenfranchised by the healthcare system. SCD is a blood disease that causes life-threatening complications and affects approximately 100,000 people in the United States, mostly of African ancestry.

Excruciating pain is a hallmark of the disease (Yawn et al. 2014). People with SCD are stigmatized and experience a plethora of health disparities (Bulgin, Tanabe, and Jenerette 2018). According to the Centers for Disease Control and Prevention (CDC), people with SCD have a life expectancy 30 years shorter than those without the disease, the rate of stroke in adults (35–64 years old) is three times higher, and they wait longer to receive pain medication and see a physician in the emergency room (CDC Foundation n.d.). Additionally, SCD receives less research funding compared to other orphan diseases; e.g., SCD affects more than twice as many people in the United States as cystic fibrosis (CF), which mostly affects Whites, but receives 3.5 times less government funding and 400 times less from foundations (Cystic Fibrosis Foundation n.d.; Lee et al. 2019). Also, SCD lags far behind other diseases in the number of drugs available for treatment, e.g., four for SCD versus 15 for CF (Power-Hays and McGann 2020). Researchers can help improve these statistics by involving SCD stakeholders in the research process. Developing a successful CBPR program can be challenging, but successful collaboration can be mutually beneficial and can be achieved by employing two basic principles: (1) building a solid foundation and (2) listening to the SCD community.

There are many local and regional SCD CBOs and two national organizations that are at the fore-front of representing the patient voice for people with SCD. The Sickle Cell Community Consortium is a group of sickle cell CBOs whose mission is to "harness and amplify the power of the patient voice," and the Sickle Cell Disease Association of America is a coalition of 48 member CBOs whose goal is "to advocate for people affected by the sickle cell condition." There are multiple ways to engage SCD stakeholders: through CBOs, advisory committees, social media, surveys, focus groups, partnerships, and collaborative conversations.

As a nurse, lawyer, sickle cell advocate, and board member and past president of the International Association of Sickle Cell Nurses and Professional Associates (IASCNAPA), I have worked with the SCD community and CBOs for more than 20 years. My introduction to SCD was through interaction with parents of infants newly diagnosed with SCD. I saw firsthand the impact the disease had on families. Also, as an African American, I recognized the systemic racism and stigma associated with SCD. I made a conscious decision to become a SCD advocate and to engage in CBPR. After partnering with the SCD community for many years, several joint CBPR projects have proven impactful and mutually beneficial. Many of the ideas generated by SCD stakeholders have resulted in significant research awards. Some of the projects include the development of a SCD peer-mentoring program, numerous SCD educational projects, and a SCD community awareness program. CBPR is a valuable research tool and can be used effectively if researchers are willing to take the time to build a solid foundation and listen to the SCD community.

Building a solid foundation

Justifiably, minorities have a long history of mistrust of the medical community; this mistrust was spurred by the Tuskegee experiments, but has been reinforced by structural racism and implicit bias in the healthcare community (Jaiswal 2019; Stevens et al. 2016). Cultural competency, mutual respect, honesty, and collaboration are core values of CBPR (Brown Speights et al. 2017; Jagosh et al. 2015). Researchers must establish a relationship with the SCD community before asking them to participate in research. To do this, researchers must first face their own implicit biases. Researchers acknowledge that implicit bias exists and affects the delivery of care to people with SCD (Burnes et al. 2008; Jaiswal 2019), but often fail to recognize their own biases. There are a multitude of implicit bias materials available to researchers. Taking an implicit bias test is a good start: The Implicit Association Test (IAT) developed by Harvard University is a test that measures attitudes and beliefs (Harvard 2021). Taking the IAT can help researchers identify and address their biases before engaging in a CBPR project.

Secondly, researchers must be willing to make a sustained commitment to the community. Anecdotally, people with SCD feel as if they are used as guinea pigs for the purpose of advancing research and are not regarded with respect as individuals with unique needs and lived experiences. They feel powerless in an unjust system without recourse or redress and are suspicious of the motives of SCD researchers. These perceptions are not easily overcome. CBPR is a time-consuming and labor-intensive process, and researchers are busy, but they must be willing and able to dedicate time and effort to build a successful CBPR partnership.

Listening to the SCD community

The core of CBPR is involving the community in the development of research projects. SCD community members have a unique perspective of the disease. They understand barriers to clinical trial participation, the impact of stigma, the environment, depression, and complications of SCD. They understand how SCD affects them, their loved ones, the medical community, and the community at large. To take advantage of their expertise, researchers must engage the SCD community. Some of the ways to connect with SCD stakeholders are through referrals, CBOs, SCD influencers, caregivers, SCD advocates, interviews, webinars, podcasts, emails, websites, and newsletters.

Whatever methods researchers use to engage the SCD community, it must be sincere and involve a committed, sustained partnership. Goals must be developed in conjunction with the SCD community, and researchers cannot lead the conversation. One of my current projects, SCDGENE (CERA Working Groups n.d.), is an example of a collaboration between academia, SCD patients, and family stakeholders. The goal of the project is to identify best practices to develop educational material for gene therapy for SCD. The SCD community, academia, clinicians, community advocates, and ethicists are equal partners in the project. People with SCD are engaged via deliberate stakeholder consultation and are instrumental in guiding the direction of the project.

As demonstrated, there are many ways to engage SCD stakeholders in CBPR. When done correctly, CBPR is a proven method to engage the SCD community and can be a powerful tool for researchers.

References

Bulgin, D., P. Tanabe, and C. Jenerette. 2018. Stigma of sickle cell disease: A systematic review. *Issues in Mental Health Nursing* 39(8):675–86.

Brewer, L. C., S. N. Hayes, A. R. Caron, D. A. Derby, N. S. Breutzman, A. Wicks, J. Raman, C. M. Smith, K. S. Schaepe, R. E. Sheets, et al. 2019. Promoting cardiovascular health and wellness among African-Americans: Community participatory approach to design an innovative Mobile-health intervention. *PLoS ONE* 14(8):e0218724.

Brown Speights, J. S., A. Nowakowski, J. De Leon, M. M. Mitchell, and I. Simpson. 2017. Engaging African American women in research: An approach to eliminate health disparities in the African American community. *Family Practice* 34(3):322–9.

Burnes, D. P., B. J. Antle, C. C. Williams, and L. Cook. 2008. Mothers raising children with sickle cell disease at the intersection of race, gender, and illness stigma. *Health & Social Work* 33(3):211–20.

CDC Foundation. n.d. Sickle cell disease health disparities. Accessed June 15, 2021. https://www.cdcfoundation.org/sites/default/files/files/SickleCellDisease-HealthDisparities-FactSheet021618.pdf

CERA Working Groups. n.d. Accessed June 30, 2021. https://elsihub.org/about/cera-working-groups

Cystic Fibrosis Foundation. n.d. About cystic fibrosis. Accessed June 23, 2021. https://www.cff.org/What-is-CF/About-Cystic-Fibrosis/

Harvard. 2021. Project implicit. Accessed June 23, 2021. https://implicit.harvard.edu/implicit/takeatest.html

Jagosh, J., P. L. Bush, J. Salsberg, A. C. Macaulay, T. Greenhalgh, G. Wong, M. Cargo, L. W. Green, C. P. Herbert, and P. Pluye. 2015. A realist evaluation of community-based participatory research: Partnership synergy, trust building and related ripple effects. *BMC Public Health* 15:725.

Jaiswal, J. 2019. Whose responsibility is it to dismantle medical mistrust? Future directions for researchers and health care providers. *Behavioral Medicine* 45(2):188–96.

Lee, L., K. Smith-Whitley, S. Banks, and G. Puckrein. 2019. Reducing health care disparities in sickle cell disease: A review. *Public Health Reports* 134(6):599–607.

Power-Hays, A., and P. T. McGann. 2020. When actions speak louder than words—Racism and sickle cell disease. *The New England Journal of Medicine* 383(20):1902–3.

Stevens, E. M., C. A. Patterson, Y. B. Li, K. Smith-Whitley, and L. P. Barakat. 2016. Mistrust of pediatric sickle cell disease clinical trials research. *American Journal of Preventive Medicine* 51(1):S78–S86.

Ward, M., A. J. Schulz, B. A. Israel, K. Rice, S. E. Martenies, and E. Markarian. 2018. A conceptual framework for evaluating health equity promotion within community-based participatory research partnerships. *Evaluation and Program Planning* 70:25–34.

Yawn, B. P., G. R. Buchanan, A. N. Afenyi-Annan, S. K. Ballas, K. L. Hassell, A. H. James, L. Jordan, S. M. Lanzkron, R. Lottenberg, W. J. Savage, et al. 2014. Management of sickle cell disease: Summary of the 2014 evidence-based report by expert panel members. *JAMA* 312(10): 1033–48. Erratum in: *JAMA* 2014;312(18):1932. Erratum in: *JAMA*. 2015;313(7):729.

COMMENTARY 1.1.4: BEING IN GOOD COMMUNITY: ENGAGEMENT IN SUPPORT OF INDIGENOUS SOVEREIGNTY

JESSICA BLANCHARD AND VANESSA HIRATSUKA

Authentic community engagement in Indigenous communities insists on the exercise of tribal sovereignty over research. American Indian and Alaska Native (AI/AN) tribes are sovereign nations with unique governing structures, data needs, and community expectations for research, and these are all local considerations that should form the basis of community engagement activities in tribal contexts. As sovereign nations, tribes have the authority to govern research that occurs within their tribal jurisdictions, and best practices for the conduct of responsible research with tribes establishes that researchers must engage appropriate tribal governance structures (Claw et al. 2018). Tribal sovereignty, however, continues to be disregarded as a guiding principle of ethical research by some, especially in fields like genomics (Claw et al. 2018; Jooma et al. 2019; West, Blacksher, and Burke 2017).

The Center for the Ethics of Indigenous Genomic Research (CEIGR), a National Human Genome Research Institute–funded Center of Excellence in Ethical, Legal and Social Implications (ELSI) Research, is a multidisciplinary research consortium focused on systematic inquiry into tribal concerns about genomic research (https://ou.edu/cas/anthropology/ceigr). CEIGR began as a partnership between traditional academic researchers at the University of Oklahoma and three Indigenous-led research groups based in AI/AN communities, but has continued to grow with the addition of new partner sites. A central focus of CEIGR's work is promoting more meaningful dialogue with AI/AN community members about the role of genomics research in their communities (Hiratsuka, Beans, Reedy et al. 2020a). This center grew out of the collaborative efforts of community-based and academic partnerships, and these collaborations are premised on an approach to research that is inclusive of community-based investigators and prioritizes community-driven initiatives (Blanchard et al. 2020; Hiratsuka, Beans, Reedy et al. 2020a; Reedy et al. 2020). As researchers with CEIGR, we advocate for the assertion of tribal sovereignty as a guiding principle for more ethical, community-engaged research with tribes.

CEIGR takes seriously the importance of finding balance between the collective goals of the consortium and the local priorities at each partner site. The key to achieving this balance is trust building, growing interpersonal relationships among the partners within the consortium itself, and investigators who are willing to and abide by community values and direction for the research agenda and processes. A core tenet of CEIGR has been cultivation of cultural competence as a center and within each of the investigators (Cross et al. 1989). CEIGR researchers across all partner sites expect trust and relationship building to be central tenets of the community engagement process, especially given the persistence of mistrust as a result of generations of unethical research practices in many of the Indigenous communities with whom we work (Claw et al. 2018). The center emerged as an amalgam of individual researchers and research groups, each with established working relationships with different tribal communities. The work of building trust and interpersonal relationships within the center itself, among the consortium of researchers and ahead of any actual research activities in community settings, was a bit more unexpected for us. We needed to learn how to combine our efforts in ways that worked toward collective goals as a research consortium, while also honoring the established obligations between researchers and the tribal communities they serve. Creating opportunities to build trust and be "in good community" with each other—through regular interpersonal communication, conflict resolution, and a shared leadership structure—prepared a foundation for CEIGR to work toward shared research goals across distinct tribal contexts.

One of these shared research initiatives was the development and implementation of community-based deliberations at each of the three tribal partner sites. We proceeded with the understanding that each CEIGR partner site would have its own goals for public deliberation (Blacksher et al. 2021; Blanchard et al. 2020). We have now completed deliberations at each of the existing partner sites and expect that additional deliberations will occur as CEIGR expands to new partner sites (Blacksher et al. 2021; Blanchard et al. 2020; Hiratsuka, Beans, Blanchard et al. 2020b; Reedy et al. 2020).

Driving our collective approach to deliberation planning with all CEIGR partners was the commitment to uphold the exercise of tribal sovereignty over the entire research process. In practice, this means that the design, review, and conduct of research activities are regulated by the governance structures and oversight mechanisms at each tribal site. It also means that data management plans, including any decisions to have tribal data reside with the tribe and not the researcher, are negotiated with each tribal partner site prior to collection. Data practices present innumerable opportunities for the exercise of tribal sovereignty over research.

These deliberations were unique in that they were conducted in exclusively tribal contexts with AI/AN participants, but also because our cross-site approach affirmed the possibility of designing research that is both applicable across sites with varied geographies, cultures, histories, and research capacities and also directly responsive to the goals and needs of local communities (Blacksher et al. 2021; Blanchard et al. 2020).

Recognizing a tribe's sovereign right to govern their own data creates an imperative for researchers to reimagine the goals of community engagement and partnerships with tribes. Indigenous data sovereignty (IDS) is an inherent right of "Indigenous peoples and tribes to govern the collection, ownership, and application of their own data," including data collected by tribal or nontribal entities (Carroll, Rodriguez-Lonebear, and Martinez 2019). It is incumbent on all researchers working with tribal communities and tribal data to actively disrupt data practices that simply promote the extraction of samples and knowledge from communities without any return of benefit and discontinue paternalistic models of data ownership that challenge tribes' sovereign authority to govern their own data (Tsosie et al. 2020). It is best to engage tribal communities specifically about how to best center Indigenous data needs as the primary drivers of research.

Global calls to address the management of all kinds of research data in responsible and equitable ways is part of a growing movement known as the "data revolution." The moment to improve the quality of data for decision making, accountability, and sustainable problem solving is upon us (United

Nations, Independent Expert Advisory Group on a Data Revolution for Sustainable Development 2014), and it is imperative that calls to improve data needs extend to Indigenous communities. It is due time that researchers support an Indigenous data revolution, already underway with the growing efforts of Indigenous peoples to reclaim sovereignty over their data in ways that are meaningful and responsive to the needs of the community. Desi Rodriguez-Lonebear (2016) identifies intertribal partnerships—tribes helping tribes—as a key component of the data sovereignty revolution underway across AI/AN communities right now. As a research consortium composed of community and academic partners, CEIGR understands that the work we do must strive to be "in good community" with our tribal partners and in service of this data sovereignty revolution. CEIGR researchers have used their access to federal staff, academic institutions, and scientific venues to hold space for tribal partners and hold conversations on IDS.

The work described here compelled the center to examine our collective willingness to be "in good community" with each other as colleagues and as people, ahead of our research goals; centering relationships in this way contributed to our ability to then conduct more authentic and engaged research in the communities. We hope these considerations speak to the need for a more serious role for community engagement in the research enterprise. The work of "being in good community" is rarely the kind of work acknowledged in grant proposals, project evaluations, and academic promotions, but it absolutely should be. It should be the case that researchers growing research relationships be granted the time needed to establish trustful and collaborative relationships. It should be the case that academic tenure and promotion of researchers be grounded in community-aligned values, such as returning results and ensuring community benefit from research, alongside more conventional academic standards like peer-reviewed publishing. It is also the case that standards for identifying research priorities and evaluating measures of program success also need to be aligned with community expectations and data sovereignty goals, and not individual researcher priorities. It is the case that the pressure to show success in tribal programs often outweighs recognition of what may have led to previous failures—the lack of sufficient time to build trust, effective communication between all participants, and inclusive working relationships (Chino and DeBruyn 2006, 597).

As CEIGR moves forward and grows into the next iteration of what it will be, we know that the work ahead is not just with new community partners but with ourselves.

References

Blacksher, E., V. Y. Hiratsuka, J. W. Blanchard, J. Lund, J. Reedy, J. A. Beans, B. Saunkeah, M. Peercy, C. Byars, J. Yracheta, et al. 2021. Deliberations with American Indian and Alaska native people about the ethics of genomics: An adapted model of deliberation used with three tribal communities in the United States. *AJOB Empirical Bioethics* 12(3):164–78.

Blanchard, J., V. Hiratsuka, J. A. Beans, J. Lund, B. Saunkeah, J. Yracheta, R. B. Woodbury, et al. 2020. Power sharing, capacity building, and evolving roles in ELSI: The Center for the Ethics of indigenous genomic research. *Collaborations: A Journal of Community-Based Research and Practice* 3(1):18.

Carroll, S. R., D. Rodriguez-Lonebear, and A. Martinez. 2019. Indigenous data governance: Strategies from United States native nations. *Data Science Journal* 18(1):31.

Chino, M., and L. DeBruyn. 2006. Building true capacity: Indigenous models for indigenous communities. *American Journal of Public Health* 96(4):596–9.

Claw, K. G., M. Z. Anderson, R. L. Begay, K. S. Tsosie, K. Fox, N. A. Garrison, and Summer internship for INdigenous peoples in Genomics (SING) Consortium. 2018. A framework for enhancing ethical genomic research with Indigenous communities. *Nature Communications* 9(1):2957.

Cross, T., B. Bazron, K. Dennis, and M. Isaacs. 1989. *Towards a culturally competent system of care*. Vol. 1. Washington, DC: Georgetown University Child Development Center, CASSP Technical Assistance Center.

Hiratsuka, V. Y., J. A. Beans, J. Reedy, J. M. Yracheta, M. T. Peercy, B. Saunkeah, R. B. Woodbury, M. O'Leary, and P. G. Spicer. 2020a. Fostering ethical, legal, and social implications research in tribal communities: The Center for the Ethics of indigenous genomic research. *Journal of Empirical Research on Human Research Ethics* 15(4):271–8.

Hiratsuka, V. Y., J. A. Beans, J. W. Blanchard, J. Reedy, E. Blacksher, J. R. Lund, and P. G. Spicer. 2020b. An Alaska Native community's views on genetic research, testing, and return of results: Results from a public deliberation. *PLoS ONE* 15(3):e0229540.

Jooma, S., M. J. Hahn, L. A. Hindorff, and V. L. Bonham. 2019. Defining and achieving health equity in genomic medicine. *Ethnicity and Disease* 29(Suppl 1):173–8.

Reedy, J., J. W. Blanchard, J. Lund, P. G. Spicer, C. Byars, M. Peercy, B. Saunkeah, and E. Blacksher. 2020. Deliberations about genomic research and biobanks with citizens of the Chickasaw nation. *Frontiers in Genetics* 11: 466.

Rodriguez-Lonebear, D. 2016. Building a data revolution in Indian country. *Indigenous Data Sovereignty: Toward an Agenda* 14:253–72.

Tsosie, K. S., R. L. Begay, K. Fox, and N. A. Garrison. 2020. Generations of genomes: Advances in paleogenomics technology and engagement for Indigenous people of the Americas. *Current Opinion in Genetics & Development* 62:91–6.

United Nations, Independent Expert Advisory Group on a Data Revolution for Sustainable Development. 2014. *A world that counts: Mobilising the data revolution for sustainable development.* Independent Advisory Group Secretariat. https://www.undatarevolution.org/wp-content/uploads/2014/11/A-World-That-Counts.pdf

West, K. M., E. Blacksher, and W. Burke. 2017. Genomics, health disparities, and missed opportunities for the Nation's Research Agenda. *JAMA* 317(18):1831–2.

CASE 1.2: PROTECTING RESEARCH SUBJECT WELFARE IN PREVENTIVE TRIALS FOR AUTOSOMAL DOMINANT ALZHEIMER'S DISEASE

INTRODUCTION

With advances in medical science come new challenges in protecting the welfare of human subjects. Our ability to identify individuals at risk of catastrophic illness may lead us to new understandings of subject vulnerability. How ought we identify and recruit genetically unique research subject populations from whom much can be learned but for whom direct benefits are absent? What level of understanding ought we require of these subjects, and how must we assess their understanding? The case we present here and three accompanying commentaries address these issues in the context of early-phase preventive trials for Alzheimer's disease.

Accompanying the case summary is a commentary by Mark Yarborough, PhD, University of California, Davis, who discusses how highly targeted recruitment from a narrowly defined population places a "high price of admission" in terms of the burden on potential research subjects. Stanley Korenman, MD, John M. Ringman, MD, both of UCLA Medical Center, and Stuart Finder, PhD, of Cedars-Sinai Medical Center focus on the ways in which the eligible patient population may be vulnerable and recommend measures to best protect their welfare. Then Anne Simpson, MD, CMD, from the University of New Mexico Health Science Center Institute for Ethics, explores barriers and facilitators to potential subjects' understanding of research.

CASE SUMMARY

Investigators requested an ethics consultation about a proposed study for a vaccine to prevent a monogenetic version of Alzheimer's disease. Ongoing research with two large family cohorts identified an autosomal dominant, fully penetrant gene. Symptom onset is between 35 and 50 years of age. Many family members live in a rural area of Mexico, while others have migrated to Mexico City and the United States. Members of these families are aware, to varying degrees, of their susceptibility to early-onset dementia. The educational level, degree of acculturation, English language proficiency, medical sophistication, and attitudes toward research participation vary greatly among family members.

Subjects enrolled in the cohort studies travel to the United States to undergo imaging, as well as neuropsychological, behavioral, and biochemical testing. Genetic testing results are not returned as part of the research protocol per se, but if subjects want to know their genetic status, the investigators facilitate their meeting with a genetic counselor and subjects can undergo testing outside the study, at no cost to them.

The study team's proposed plan is to conduct a randomized, placebo-controlled trial of an experimental Alzheimer's prevention agent (a β-amyloid antibody). The goal of the trial is to prevent or delay cognitive decline. All eligible asymptomatic family members will be recruited to participate in the trial. All subjects enrolled in the intervention study would undergo genetic testing on a research basis. Subjects found to carry the mutated gene would be randomized such that two-thirds would receive active treatment and one-third would receive placebo for the duration of the study. Subjects found to not carry the mutated gene undergo all study procedures but receive placebo. Although subjects will not be explicitly told their mutation status, persons having—or believed to be having—side effects from the intervention might infer (rightly or wrongly) that they carry the mutated genes. Similarly, the genetic status of all study subjects might be inferred by others in the communities.

This is an investigational vaccine that has not been used in humans before. The study team expects some subjects to experience serious adverse events, although the exact nature and likelihood are impossible to predict. Subjects who do not have the mutated gene undergo the risks of participation (including study interventions and the inference of genetic status) without any prospect of personal benefit.

The investigators were seeking advice about how to provide appropriate protections to a cohort with varied levels of education, acculturation, medical sophistication, knowledge, and attitudes toward research participation. This study raises questions about risks, results disclosure, and consent. How would you recommend that these and other ethical issues be addressed for this study?

COMMENTARY 1.2.1: WHEN THERE ARE ONLY TWO WHO CAN TANGO: ETHICAL CONCERNS AT THE JUNCTURE OF HIGHLY NOVEL INTERVENTIONS AND PRECISELY TARGETED RESEARCH POPULATIONS

MARK YARBOROUGH

Among the many instructive features of the case study about the preventive trial for autosomal dominant Alzheimer's disease is how it illustrates the impact of new technologies on research. Advances in fields such as genomics, genetics, and stem cell research are leading to the development of precisely targeted and often truly novel interventions that, if successful, will represent true game changers in the treatment of serious diseases such as Alzheimer's disease. But there is much to learn along the arduous path to enhanced benefit, with critical ethical issues at each juncture. As this study illustrates, one of these junctures arises from the fact that because the intervention is so precisely targeted, it requires recruitment from a small subset of the population affected by a disease. In this brief commentary, I focus on two commingled ethical issues that can accompany such targeted recruitment. One is the relatively high "price of admission" that can be required for entry into a trial, and the other is the extent to which consent for participation may be a "foregone conclusion" for many of these individuals.

As experimental interventions become more targeted, the research community becomes increasingly dependent on access to narrowly defined populations, populations who in turn must disproportionately bear the demands imposed by early research protocols studying novel developments. How high can we reasonably set the price of admission for these prospective research subjects in order to facilitate the precisely targeted research? The price of admission may go far beyond being subjected to the risks of a new intervention. Invasive monitoring procedures, such as a lumbar puncture, or surgical procedures may also be part of the protocol. For example, a recent Phase I study of a stem cell intervention to study amyotrophic lateral sclerosis (ALS) required subjects to undergo a laminectomy (Riley et al. 2014).

These burdens of participation can push the limits of what we normally are inclined to tolerate for early trials, but the new technologies can require imposing such risks at the very outset in order to be able to test new approaches. This is especially challenging given that the likelihood of personal medical benefit for trial subjects is remote. For example, there is no escaping the high failure rate of vaccine and other pharmaceutical trials. Indeed, 85 to 90% of all investigational trials fail to lead to Food and Drug Administration (FDA)-approved interventions (Davis et al. 2011; DiMasi, Hansen, and Grabowski 2003). We always hope that novel developments, such as being able to so precisely target a treatment, will increase the odds of success—but that hope, we must recognize, is speculative, while the burdens imposed by the protocols are genuine and possibly quite serious.

With respect to this vaccine trial, we must consider the consequences of requiring a predictive genetic test so that researchers can be assured that they can study the targeted population. While subjects can request shielding themselves from the results of the predictive test, the fact of the matter is that a price of admission to the trial is the discovery of predictive knowledge that the subject might desire under different circumstances never be known, by anyone. Thus, someone from the affected community who wants to see the research go forward must submit to what is otherwise an undesired procedure. This could lead to a range of undesirable consequences.

Due to their involvement in the vaccine trial, subjects may focus more than they otherwise would on their risk for Alzheimer's disease and they may have a tendency as a result to overattribute a range of health symptoms to Alzheimer's, likely increasing their pondering about whether to undergo predictive testing. Knowing that there is someone who already knows their test results might create additional pressure for people to learn what they otherwise would prefer not to know. In other words, a preferred state of ignorance may be easier to maintain when specific test results are merely a possibility rather than a reality. In this instance, it becomes a matter of you learning what someone else already knows about you. What was once a mystery to all and in the hands of fate is now simply hidden from you; this may push people to obtain predictive information that they would never otherwise pursue if not for their trial participation.

To fully consider the required forfeiture of ignorance imposed by this trial, we need to be mindful of how novelty aggravates the concern. This feature of the trial may be of less concern, perhaps, in a different population. For example, we might be a little less concerned if the targeted research population were the Huntington's disease (HD) community, because that group now has decades of experience dealing with the availability of predictive testing. People affected by HD are now able to give prolonged consideration to whether, or under what circumstances, they would consider permitting a predictive test that may affect them. They can discuss with others whether or not this is information worth knowing, as well as observe others grappling with the same issues over time. The targeted population for the predictive vaccine trial in this case lacks this important history, and this fact may increase the psychological burdens posed by knowing that definitive predictive information is now known by someone and thus is fairly easily available to obtain for themselves. The only way to avoid this burden is to choose not to enroll in the trial.

While nonparticipation is certainly an option, it may be a less likely and more difficult choice for some to make than we might suppose. This brings us to the commingled second ethical issue, the implications that targeting very specific, and thus likely small, groups of people can have for the informed consent process. Specifically, the more that a rare disease, or rare variant of one, is concentrated in families, the more there is a legacy of the disease. Longing for the time when the family is rid of the scourge of the disease or having a commitment to fight the disease in any and all ways available might easily be a part of the narrative arc in the lives of people in the affected community. Thus, consenting to trial participation may be an entirely characteristic decision for them to make, such that they will not be very motivated to learn much about matters such as risks and benefits. They may be more motivated instead to do what they can to contribute to a cure. This could in effect make trial participation a "foregone conclusion." This should by no means disqualify them from participating, but the research community must take note of this feature of affected communities and explore what extra steps might be required in the consent process.

These are just two concerns raised in settings like the preventive vaccine trial. Such trials highlight the extent to which researchers can be entirely dependent upon the participation of small populations in order to carry out their research. At the same time, there likely will be substantial social and familial inertia for trial participation among the members of these populations, despite the risks and other burdens such participation may entail.

References

Davis, M. M., A. T. Butchart, J. R. Wheeler, M. S. Coleman, D. C. Singer, and G. L. Freed. 2011. Failure-to-success ratios, transition probabilities and phase lengths for prophylactic vaccines versus other pharmaceuticals in the development pipeline. *Vaccine* 29:9414–16.

DiMasi, J. A., R. W. Hansen, and H. G. Grabowski. 2003. The price of innovation: New estimates of drug development costs. *Journal of Health Economics* 22:151–85.

Riley, J., J. Glass, E. L. Feldman, et al. 2014. Intraspinal stem cell transplantation in amyotrophic lateral sclerosis: A phase I trial, cervical microinjection, and final surgical safety outcomes. *Neurosurgery* 74:77–87.

COMMENTARY 1.2.2: CONCEPTUALIZATION AND ASSESSMENT OF VULNERABILITY IN A COMPLEX INTERNATIONAL ALZHEIMER'S RESEARCH STUDY

STANLEY KORENMAN, STUART G. FINDER, AND JOHN M. RINGMAN

With an aim toward preventing cognitive loss, the extension study described in the case summary entails administering an experimental Alzheimer's disease prevention agent to persons inheriting fully penetrant autosomal dominant mutations prior to the loss of cognitive function. Conducting this study with this population thus raises concern about vulnerability. When considering the potential vulnerability of potential subjects and the associated obligations to ensure protection, however, we believe it beneficial to think about vulnerability not in terms of the bureaucratically shaped notion reflected in the Code of Federal Regulations (U.S. Department of Health and Human Services 2009, 45 CFR 46 Sections A, B, C, and D), but in terms of a more expansive conception of vulnerability. One such expanded conception is the one put forth by the Council for International Organizations of Medical Sciences (CIOMS), which defines vulnerable persons as "those who are relatively (or absolutely) incapable of protecting their own interests" such that, more formally, they are seen as potentially lacking "sufficient power, intelligence, education, resources, strength, or other needed attributes" (CIOMS 2002). Coleman's three-part conception of vulnerability—which not only addresses ability to comprehend research and its implications but also takes into consideration the ability to understand and assess risk as well as implications of belonging to a group that can be coerced or enticed to participate in research—further amplifies the need for such an expanded conception (Coleman 2009).

Interestingly, two decades ago in the *American Journal of Bioethics*, Levine and colleagues raised a similar point about the need to expand how vulnerability is understood in the research context; their focus was on the importance of the particular features of individual research projects (Levine et al. 2004). Their aim was to reinvigorate a sense of responsibility toward subjects among researchers. In an associated commentary, it was suggested that as part of fulfilling such responsibility, researchers need to directly attend to the experience of being a research subject, especially the attendant ambiguities and uncertainties (Finder 2004). With all of these more expanded notions at hand, there are thus several concerns meriting attention related to vulnerability pertinent to the proposed study.

The first is that the individuals who might qualify as potential subjects have already been identified as carriers of the relevant mutation associated with Alzheimer's. A subset of these individuals may have opted to speak with a genetic counselor and are therefore aware of their carrier status; the possibility of facing their own cognitive decline due to Alzheimer's may, by itself, be overwhelming (Anderson et al. 2009; Nelson 2005). In addition, many will come from local communities or from families in which having Alzheimer's creates a significant stigma—for themselves as potential sufferers as well as for their families as carriers (Blay and Toledo Piza Peluso 2010; Piver et al. 2013; Werner et al. 2012). Add into the mix that this is a complicated study, and now the issue of possible hurdles to understanding the details of this study becomes prominent. In short, to qualify for participation, potential subjects need, at the very least, to understand that:

1. This is a research study, and not everyone with the genetic defect will be treated (subjects will be randomized to treatment or placebo).
2. The primary goal of the study is to determine scientifically whether the medication has the proposed effect, and hence the aim is not to provide therapeutic treatment to research subjects.
3. Treatments for Alzheimer's disease thus far have had only slight efficacy, and there has been no preventive therapy proved to be effective.
4. Serious adverse events are possible.
5. There are, in addition to the preceding, other medical, psychological, and social implications of having the mutations causing autosomal dominant early-onset Alzheimer's disease.

Internalization of these kinds of facts typically is difficult for many people and frequently leads to therapeutic misconceptions (as has been well established for decades). Having to do so in the face of the self-recognition that one may be standing on the precipice of falling into a slow cognitive decline, as well as having to respond to the potential stigma associated with such decline, only complicates matters.

Perhaps more importantly, a portion of these individuals will very likely lack the educational and scientific background to understand the study itself. This is a common problem in much clinical research, but one heightened here by the fact that the communities from which potential subjects will be drawn explicitly includes parts of rural Mexico, where general educational levels, let alone science educational levels, are relatively low (Organization for Economic Cooperation and Development [OECD] 2013). Thus, it is reasonable to begin not only with a recognition that at least some of the potential trial participants will be vulnerable to misunderstanding and, accordingly, in need of additional protections, but with a concurrent recognition that there may be great need to help create a more educated populace. A step toward this goal is to reach out to the community far in advance of the study itself coming online and interact with the community from which individuals may qualify as potential subjects.

As part of such an "advance outreach" effort to limit vulnerability, one key initiative should be to identify what potential participants do or do not already understand, in general, about their potential to serve as research subjects. Such work with communities in advance of pursuing recruitment of potential research subjects, indeed, has been done, the results of which are indicated in Figure 1.2.1, (Hooper et al. 2013).

What stands out to us in this work is that the percentage of individuals consenting to a hypothetical trial fell with the intensity and invasiveness of the trial, from around 90% to around 40%. The proposed use of a placebo reduced the likelihood of participation in the most benign study, while it increased participation in the others. Having this kind of advance knowledge about the

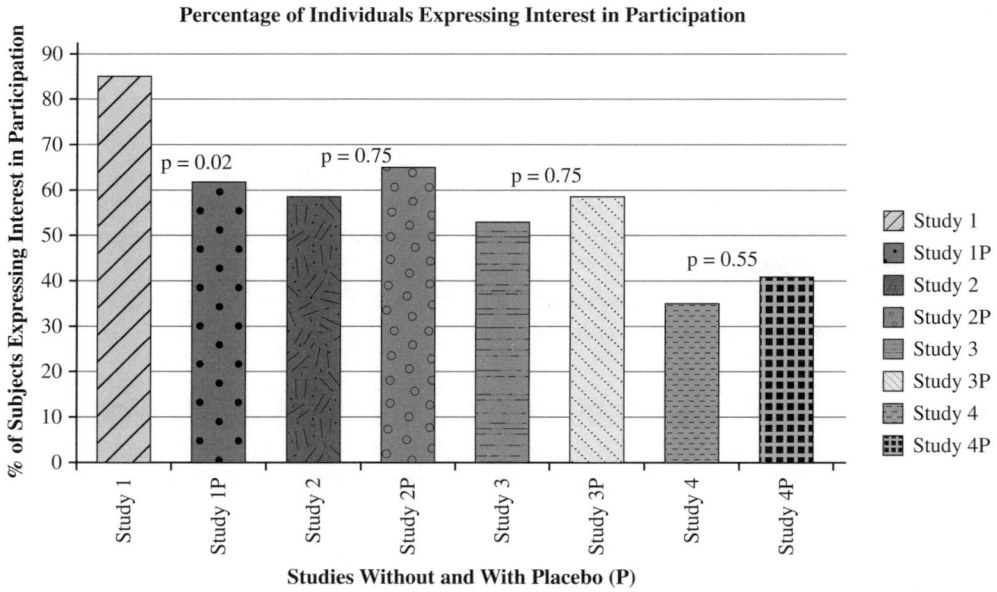

Figure 1.2.1 Percentage of subjects expressing an interest in undergoing revealing genetic testing in order to participate in clinical trials to prevent familial Alzheimer's disease (FAD) of increasing invasiveness, without or with (P) a 50% chance of receiving placebo. (Reprinted with permission of Elsevier. © 2013 Elsevier.)

community allows researchers to better understand their potential research subjects and, in turn, to develop informed consent procedures and processes that will be better attuned to the vulnerabilities associated with being a subject in the proposed study. In so doing, the researchers more fully respond to the lack of "sufficient power, intelligence, education, resources, strength, or other needed attributes" of the potential subjects, and hence fulfill the responsibility the researchers owe to vulnerable subjects.

References

Anderson, L. A., K. L. Day, R. L. Beard, P. S. Reed, and B. Wu. 2009. The public's perceptions about cognitive health and Alzheimer's disease among the U.S. population: A national review. *Gerontologist* 49(suppl 1):S3–S11.

Blay, S. L., and E. Toledo Piza Peluso. 2010. Public stigma: The community's tolerance of Alzheimer disease. *American Journal of Geriatric Psychiatry* 18(2):163–71.

Coleman, C. H. 2009. Vulnerability as a regulatory category in human subject research. *Journal of Law Medicine and Ethics* 37(1):12–18.

Council for International Organizations of Medical Sciences (CIOMS). International Ethical Guidelines for Biomedical Research Involving Human Subjects. 2002.

Finder, S. 2004. Vulnerability in human subject research: Existential state, not category designation. *American Journal of Bioethics* 4(3):68–70.

Hooper, M., J. D. Grill, and Y. Rodriguez-Agudelo, et al. 2013. The impact of the availability of prevention studies on the desire to undergo predictive testing in persons at risk for autosomal dominant Alzheimer's disease. *Contemporary Clinical Trials* 36(1): 256262.

Levine, C., R. Faden, C. Grady, D. Hammerschmidt, L. Eckenwiler, and J. Sugarman. 2004. The limitation of "vulnerability" as a protection for human research subjects. *American Journal of Bioethics* 4(3):44–49.

Nelson, T. D. 2005. Ageism: Prejudice against our feared future self. *Journal of Social Issues* 61(2):207–21.

Organization for Economic Cooperation and Development. 2013. Available at: http://skills.oecd.org/informationbycountry/mexico.html.

Piver, L. C., P. Nubukpo, A. Faure, N. Dumoitier, P. Couratier, and J. P. Clement. 2013. Describing perceived stigma against Alzheimer's disease in a general population in France: The STIGMA survey. *International Journal of Geriatric Psychiatry* 28(9):933–938.

U.S. Department of Health and Human Services. 2009. Final rule 45 CFR 46 Sections A,B,C, and D. Protection of human subjects. Revised January 15. Available at: http://www.hhs.gov/ohrp/humansubjects/guidance/45cfr46.html (accessed January7, 2015).

Werner, P., M. S. Mittelman, D. Goldstein, and J. Heinik. 2012. Family stigma and caregiver burden in Alzheimer's disease. *Gerontologist* 52(1):89–97.

COMMENTARY 1.2.3: BARRIERS AND FACILITATORS TO THE CONSENT PROCESS IN A STUDY OF COMPLEX GENETIC FACTORS

ANNE R. SIMPSON

Alzheimer's disease and other dementias have an enormous impact on patient, family, and the community. Studying and developing curative interventions will be of benefit to society as a whole. The proposed study in this case is focused on a specific variant of Alzheimer's disease that is of significant relevance to the research subject cohort.

Many principles, such as those presented in the World Medical Association's (WMA) Declaration of Helsinki (WMA 2013), guide the ethical practice of research and the process of informing potential research subjects. In consideration of the diverse makeup of the cohort to be studied, ensuring that each member of the cohort is informed is essential but might prove challenging, given the complexity of issues inherent in the study. The burden of ensuring the subject's capacity for understanding and delivering a noncoerced agreement rests on the investigator.

The focus of this commentary is on the key concepts those eligible for enrollment will need to understand, as well as some barriers and facilitators to understanding. The subjects approached to consider enrollment in the study described a need to understand that they are being asked to enroll in a research study and not being offered medical treatment. According to the study protocol, "Subjects found to carry the mutated gene would be randomized such that two-thirds would receive active treatment and one-third would receive placebo for the duration of the study." If the "active treatment" referenced is the drug under study, then it needs to be clearly articulated during the process of informed decision making to avoid therapeutic misconception. In addition, the drug under study has been approved only for use in research; it has never before been used in humans, and therefore side effects for humans are not known. Potential subjects should be told of side effects that were observed in animal studies. They also need to understand that the study drug is not an approved treatment, that the drug may be of no benefit to them, and that some of the subjects will not receive the study drug.

Research has shown that a person's level of education plays a role in how well a potential subject can answer questions about the study they are considering participating in (Shafiq and Malhotra 2011). Those with lower education levels are less able to answer questions correctly. For all subjects, there are key research concepts such as randomization and placebo that are hard to understand (Ndebele et al. 2014). While some suggest approaches to simplifying the language used in consent forms and attending to the format in which the information is presented, others suggest that the best way to help subjects understand is to provide potential research subjects the opportunity to discuss their decision to enroll with someone other than the principal investigator (Naanyu, Some, and Siika 2014). A study team member other than the principal investigator may be better able to convey complex concepts in ways the average subject can best understand. It has also been shown that low-income and minority women overwhelming prefer (97%) the opportunity to discuss the consent form with a member of the study team when compared to reading the form on their own (Jallo et al. 2013). And, relatedly, it has been recommended that those tasked with reviewing the consent form with the potential subject be adequately trained, and preferably be a member of that cultural community (Ndebele et al. 2014). One way to assure that potential subjects understand the information conveyed is to administer a quiz of understanding (Shafiq and Malhotra 2011).

This summary of recent findings has implications. Explaining concepts such as randomization, double-blind study design, and placebo to a group with diverse education, culture, and literacy will require time and one-on-one engagement to ensure understanding, but participant comprehension and competency are required. For true informed decision making, all has to be divulged to the participants using language and terminology they understand. Members of the research team who are bilingual and have a detailed understanding of the study should engage in an ongoing dialogue between participants and investigator to attend to the participant's knowledge and understanding throughout. Understanding the cultural values of the cohort members is important. For example, the eligible population or subpopulation of the group may subscribe to a notion of community consent. If so, it will be important to make sure that each individual understands what the group may or may not be consenting for and that as an individual the person continues to have a right to not participate even if the majority chooses to participate. How do participants understand the disease under study and how it relates to them as family and each as an individual? This may help to ascertain their understanding of the genetic relevance of the study; in addition, it offers an opportunity to gain insight into cultural beliefs that might be associated with the disease and ways to tread with respect.

To ensure subject understanding, the investigator can use the Informed Consent Comprehension Questionnaire, have bilingual/bicultural team members hold group and individual meetings with subjects, and reiterate the subjects' right to voluntary participation in the study.

References

Jallo, N., D. E. Lyon, P. A. Kinser, D. L. Kelly, V. Menzies, and C. Jackson-Cook. 2013. Recruiting for epigenetic research: Facilitating the informed consent process. *Nursing Research and Practice* 2013:935740.

Naanyu, V., F. F. Some, and A. M. Siika. 2014. "I understood … but some parts were confusing and hard to grasp": Patients' perception of informed consent forms and clinical trials in Eldoret, Kenya. *Perspectives in Clinical Research* 5(1):20–24.

Ndebele, P., D. Wassenaar, F. Masiye, and E. Munalula-Nkandu. 2014. Trial participants' understanding of randomization, double-blinding, and placebo use in low literacy populations: Findings from a study conducted within a microbicide trial in Malawi. *Journal of Empirical Research on Human Research Ethics* 9(3):2–10.

Shafiq, N., and S. Malhotra. 2011. Ethics in clinical research: Need for assessing comprehension of informed consent form. *Contemporary Clinical Trials* 32(2):169–72.

World Medical Association (WMA). 2013. WMA Declaration of Helsinki—Ethical principles for medical research involving human subjects; 64th General Assembly, Fortaleza, Brazil, October 2013. *Journal of the American Medical Association* 310(20):2191–94.

CASE 1.3: STUDYING THE ROLE OF FINANCIAL INCENTIVES TO PROMOTE HEPATITIS B VACCINATION IN A COMMUNITY CLINIC

INTRODUCTION

Hepatitis B virus (HBV) is a bloodborne virus that is transmitted most commonly from mother to child (perinatal) and by sexual contact. About one-quarter of those infected with HBV develop chronic hepatitis B. While relatively uncommon in the United States, chronic HBV affects more than 250 million people worldwide (Centers for Disease Control and Prevention [CDC] 2016). Those with chronic HBV are at high risk of developing cirrhosis and liver cancer, both of which can be fatal. The current HBV vaccine is very safe and highly efficacious, and since 1991 it is routinely given to newborns in the United States. It is synthetic and cannot initiate an HBV infection. Severe allergic reactions are believed to occur less than once in a million doses. The case described in the following focuses on the question of the ethical appropriateness of conducting a clinical trial to assess the impact of financial incentives on the uptake of HBV vaccination among a community-based population of adult immigrants to the United States. This question straddles public health, clinical care, and human subject research, and can be considered from all three vantage points.

From the clinical care angle, the question can be framed balancing patients' well-being and the boundaries of acceptable approaches to influencing healthcare decisions. As our commentators note, while financial incentives have been used to promote health behaviors, doing so is not without some ethical concerns. From a public health perspective, this case shines light on public health benefits of vaccines. As a case involving a community health clinic that serves immigrant populations, questions about the acceptability of this approach to the community and population must be considered. Finally, from a research perspective, the case raises questions about study design and the ethical appropriateness of testing the utility of financial incentives. None of the three commentators raises serious objections to the underlying concept of financial incentives for participation in research, and at a fundamental level, this could be considered one of the areas of consensus in research ethics. But the question of the suitability of adopting financial incentives to encourage the uptake of standard interventions remains.

The first commentary, written by Hannah Giunta from Michigan State University, looks at this case from a community perspective and raises questions about how such research, and any subsequent clinical interventions, would be received by the community and whether such approaches would undermine the relationships between providers and the community. The second commentary, written by Adelaide Doussau and Christine Grady from the National Institutes of Health (NIH) Clinical Center, considers this case from the research perspective, explores how well this study design is likely to answer the research question, and also points to the importance of the availability of such an incentive outside of the study to justify the research. Doussau and Grady also consider the ethical challenges in communicating a study design that compares different incentives and whether a deception is justified. The final commentary, written by Ponni Perumalswami, Andrea Branch, and Rosamond Rhodes from the Icahn School of Medicine at Mount Sinai, concludes that the study's clinical approach can be ethical and supports such research to learn more about its impact.

CASE SUMMARY

Up to 75% of African-born men and women living in the United States have evidence of past infection with HBV or an ongoing chronic infection. At least 25% remain at risk for HBV infection. As part of ongoing screening efforts, in one community with a large population of African-born men and women, at-risk adults are advised to undergo vaccination. Only 10% of these at-risk adults completed the three-dose regimen when it was offered to them free of charge.

Focus-group discussions were conducted to assess the causes underlying the low acceptance rate. Participants expressed no particular objection to the vaccination itself. Their responses were vague, and it was hard to tell whether denial, fear of the U.S. medical establishment, lack of understanding, or inertia contributed to the low acceptance of vaccination.

The investigators propose to study two different interventions in an identified cohort of African-born men and women to increase the number of people who receive HBV vaccinations. The study aims at determining whether education on the benefits of vaccination or a financial incentive will be more effective in having people accept vaccination for HBV and following through with the vaccine's three doses over six months. Some groups of participants will receive $10, others $20, and those in the education group will receive no financial incentive. This study cannot be accomplished using historical controls because that would not provide information about the specific subgroup of patients in the community. Furthermore, the factors leading to acceptance of vaccination might vary between groups. A contemporaneously enrolled comparison group is required for the scientific validity of this study.

The investigators requested a research ethics consultation to consider whether it is ethically acceptable to offer financial incentives for accepting HBV vaccination in this randomized trial. Should investigators initiate a study involving physicians offering an inducement for receiving healthcare?

REFERENCE

Centers for Disease Control and Prevention (CDC). 2016. Hepatitis B FAQs for health professionals. Available at: http://www.cdc.gov/hepatitis/hbv/hbvfaq.htm#overview (accessed June 29, 2016).

COMMENTARY 1.3.1: TREATMENT INCENTIVES AND THE NATURE OF THE DOCTOR–PATIENT RELATIONSHIP

HANNAH GIUNTA

In the present case study, researchers wish to assess the impact of offering modest financial incentives on adherence with the recommended three-dose hepatitis B vaccine series among at-risk African-born adults in a community clinic. When those at risk were initially offered the vaccine series free of charge, only 10% completed the series in full. Subsequently, researchers conducted focus groups to determine what barriers exist to vaccination and received vague responses. Possible hypothesized barriers garnered from focus-group interviews included denial, fear of the medical establishment, lack of understanding, and inertia. In response, researchers now wish to study the impact of modest financial incentives on patient adherence by enrolling participants in one of three research arms where they will receive $10, $20, or education about the vaccine only.

Based on previous studies, it is likely that financial incentives would increase vaccine coverage in the at-risk population. Among individuals who inject drugs, recent studies have shown an increase in hepatitis B vaccine series completion when incentives are offered. A UK study demonstrated significant increases in vaccination rates when participants were offered £30 worth of vouchers during series completion (Weaver et al. 2014), and an Australian study revealed that small financial incentives (A$30) significantly increased rates of vaccination among inner-city patients who injected drugs (Topp et al. 2013). A 2003 U.S. study went so far as to suggest that modest financial incentives could be used to improve future compliance with HIV vaccination strategies (Seal et al. 2003). However, I suggest that financial incentives are unlikely to be the best solution to the current quagmire.

There are three important points to consider in this case. First, the situation is complicated because participants are in fact being compensated for receiving standard medical care, raising questions about appropriate inducements, consent, and autonomy. It is one thing to compensate patients when they enroll in a clinical trial that may bring additional inconveniences, though there are legitimate ethical qualms about where to draw the line between appropriate compensation and undue inducement. It is another thing to compensate patients for merely acquiescing to standard care. While insurance companies and employers have begun relying on financial incentives to shape behaviors (i.e., premium rebates for certain outcomes or lifestyle changes), medical professionals still rely on a more covenantal rather than contractual relationship. The success of the doctor–patient relationship does not merely depend on patient compliance but on the reasons for that compliance. The relationship ought to be patient centered. Physicians have a responsibility to empower and educate patients as partners in clinical decisions, rather than merely inducing a certain behavior. This is the true difference between the physician–patient relationship and other merely contractual relationships. The insurance company does not particularly care why a person complies, but physicians should because they want patients to participate in their own healthcare rather than simply acquiescing to recommendations. Healing is a joint enterprise. Of course, physicians routinely attempt to persuade patients to take certain courses of action, but this persuasion usually renders the intervention more understandable or desirable to the patient. The monetary incentive in this case does not serve to remedy barriers or change beliefs about the vaccine. It is a simple inducement.

Second, in this case, financial incentives actually do little to address the researchers' own hypothesized barriers to vaccination and instead may continue the historical pattern of professionals deciding what is best for disadvantaged patients. Researchers did assess possible reasons for vaccine nonadherence in the present case, but now they appear to have decided that those reasons do not merit additional consideration. A financial incentive is a potentially efficient solution that does not take the hypothesized barriers into account. Researchers apparently asked but do not intend to rely on participant answers. Thus, if skepticism about the medical profession or the business of medicine is the underlying barrier, then payment in order to induce patients might very well make the situation worse. Additionally, denial, inertia, and poor understanding are not remedied by financial incentives. The U.S. medical community does in fact have a long history of imposing what it thinks is best for patients through overly paternalistic intervention, especially when those patients are disadvantaged, uneducated, or overly skeptical. Because vaccine refusal is such a complicated issue, multicomponent interventions that emphasize dialogue and communication between patient and provider are more likely to positively impact patients as they make future health decisions and actually address some of the root issues in this case (Jarrett et al. 2015). Merely offering an inducement may mean not taking participants' reasons for refusal seriously because they do not comport with what we consider to be acceptable reasons for reluctance.

Finally, researchers may very well miss an opportunity to better understand their patients and empower them by relying primarily on financial incentives to induce compliance. This approach may impact patients' future behavior when receiving healthcare. It is simply impractical for practitioners to routinely compensate patients for seeking preventative care or complying with disease management or treatment, and doing so would change the doctor–patient relationship for the worse. Unless providers plan to begin paying patients for multiple standard procedures, they are unlikely to make much difference overall. The better approach is to explore the real barriers to vaccine adherence, even if it takes longer and requires more steps. Eliminating barriers allows patients to seek future care unencumbered.

Incentives are commonly and sometimes legitimately offered to patients who participate in clinical trials. But compensating patients for receiving routine care, especially when identified barriers have not been conclusively identified or mitigated, is not a good practice. Most importantly, we must remember that offering an inducement may say as much about our own inability to appreciate patients' perspectives as it does about patients' true motivations. Respect should involve working to overcome obstacles, rather than simply trying to move forward in some predetermined direction.

References

Jarrett, C., R. Wilson, M. O'Leary, E. Eckersberger, and H. J. Larson; SAGE Working Group on Vaccine Hesitancy. 2015. Strategies for addressing vaccine hesitancy—A systematic review. *Vaccine* 33(34):4180–90.

Seal, K. H., A. H. Kral, J. Lorvick, A. McNees, L. Gee, and B. R. Edlin. 2003. A randomized controlled trial of monetary incentives vs. outreach to enhance adherence to the hepatitis B vaccine series among injection drug users. *Drug and Alcohol Dependence* 71(2):127–31.

Topp, L., C. A. Day, H. Wand, et al.; Hepatitis Acceptability and Vaccine Incentives Trial (HAVIT) Study Group. 2013. A randomised controlled trial of financial incentives to increase hepatitis B vaccination completion among people who inject drugs in Australia. *Preventive Medicine* 57(4):297–303.

Weaver, T., N. Metrebian, J. Hellier, et al. 2014. Use of contingency management incentives to improve completion of hepatitis B vaccination in people undergoing treatment for heroin dependence: A cluster randomised trial. *Lancet* 384(9938):153–63.

COMMENTARY 1.3.2: THE ETHICS OF STUDYING FINANCIAL INCENTIVES IN PUBLIC HEALTH IMPLEMENTATION: STUDY DESIGN CHALLENGES

ADELAIDE DOUSSAU AND CHRISTINE GRADY

This study aims to compare the effectiveness of education about vaccine benefits to financial incentives in increasing hepatitis B vaccine uptake and completion of three vaccine doses among African-born men and women. The study will compare the effects of two different levels of financial incentive to education alone. Determining the ethics of studying financial incentives for accepting HBV vaccination in this randomized trial depends on two considerations: (1) the social value and validity of the study design, and (2) the acceptability of offering financial incentives to research participants.

Social value and validity of the study design

Clinical research is considered ethical when its results will add scientific knowledge that brings social value (Emanuel, Wendler, and Grady 2000). Necessary conditions for research to promote social value are (1) a good research question and (2) a valid methodology. This proposal is designed with three arms: (1) a $10 incentive, (2) a $20 incentive, and (3) education. The primary aim is to determine whether financial incentives affect vaccine uptake more than education does; a secondary aim might be whether the amount of money makes a difference.

Evaluating the social value of a research protocol includes consideration of what will be done if the results are positive. Social value includes planning for adopting the intervention if the study finds that financial incentives increase vaccination uptake more than education in this subpopulation. Indeed, social value entails anticipation of questions such as: Who should have access to the financially incentivized vaccination program if it is effective? This local community? All the African-born in a larger community? A wider population?

A negative outcome in this trial could mean either that financial incentives do not increase vaccination uptake as compared to education, or that the amount of financial incentives was insufficient to have an impact. The education control group may confound the ability to detect the impact of financial incentives. A factorial trial design could address this: vaccination free of charge (control) versus financial incentives (A) versus education (B) versus financial incentive + education (A + B). This would generate data on the effect of each intervention and their potential synergy.

In this case, clarifying what scientific knowledge is necessary to proceed to wider implementation is important, particularly given existing literature about the positive effects of financial incentives on hepatitis B vaccination uptake in drug users (Rafia et al. 2016; Weaver et al. 2014). The impact of financial sanctions on childhood vaccination has also been studied (Kerpelman, Connell, and Gunn 2000). Indeed, if monetary incentives have been shown efficacious in increasing vaccination uptake and there is already evidence to support this practice, then pragmatic approaches might be warranted to show effectiveness in real-life settings such as this one. A pragmatic approach, such as a stepped wedge design, could have been considered in which the monetary incentives would be rolled out over time to several outreach care units; this design is increasingly used in implementation science (Prost et al. 2015), when data support that the intervention is likely to produce more benefit than harm. The classical stepped wedge design might not be applicable to the setting of a study in a single clinic, as the stepped wedge design usually involves random sequential rollout of the intervention to clusters over several time periods. A variation of the stepped wedge design might still be considered in a single-clinic setting. Indeed, a study of implementation of preventive tuberculosis treatment in HIV+ workers used a design where the subjects were randomly staggered over time to receive an invitation letter to join the intervention, thus providing an example of an individually randomized stepped wedge design (Grant et al. 2005). Stepped wedge studies, however, require careful consideration of additional scientific and ethical challenges (Hemming et al. 2015; de Hoop et al. 2015).

Financial incentives and deception

A second consideration is the ethics of offering financial incentives to patients to accept an intervention that is considered standard of care. Although financial incentives for participants are often used in the research setting, some worry about the possibility that a financial incentive will have an undue influence on their behavior. Scholars have clarified that financial payment could result in undue influence if it distorts the potential participant's judgment about research risks and benefits (Largent et al. 2013). Reviewing the risks and benefits in this case, hepatitis B vaccine is safe with almost no risk and is accepted standard practice in the general population, including in infants. Some participants screened for this study might learn that they are already infected. Despite some risk of social stigma with hepatitis B infection, a diagnosis might trigger medical care, treatment, and prevention of transmission. Hepatitis B infection screening is currently recommended in the United States for those at risk of infection. Thus, the low risk and possible benefits of being screened or enrolled in this trial avert concerns about undue influence from small amounts of money.

If there is agreement that it is ethically appropriate to offer monetary incentives to these potential participants, we ought to consider whether there are any ethical concerns about giving monetary incentives to only two-thirds of those enrolled. Specifically, we need to consider whether this project as designed requires deception. If participants are informed about the three arms before being randomized, this could pose challenges for study validity. Indeed, as this immigrant population is socioeconomically disadvantaged, possibly a main reason to enroll in the study is the hope of receiving money in addition to being vaccinated. Participants who are randomized to $10 or education might regret not being in the $20 arm. If so, they may be less likely to return to the clinic to receive their second and third vaccinations. Their failure to return could lead to a disproportionate loss to follow-up in the $10 and education arms, could reduce vaccination uptake in the $10 and education arms, or could inflate the vaccination uptake of participants who are randomized to $20 as well. Furthermore, to the extent that increased vaccine uptake in the group receiving $20 is a result of their knowledge that they are receiving more money than the other groups, this effect may not be sustained when implemented without a comparison arm. Altering the traditional consent process by withholding information or by deception (giving false information) is controversial but sometimes justified to enhance the validity and social value of public health research (McCambridge et al. 2013). In this case, not telling participants what the three interventions are, or the aim of the trial, might have more advantages than drawbacks. Such deception is ethically more acceptable when the community is engaged or informed about the study design, or the design can be communicated to participants after the fact.

Conclusion

In conclusion, there is negligible ethical concern in financially incentivizing a subset of participants of the trial. However, some aspects of the study design should be clarified. The optimal design is that which will maximize the expected social value, while respecting participants. Further consideration ought to be given to a plan for adoption of the intervention if the trial is successful. Furthermore, given that some but not all participants will be incentivized, withholding some features of the study design from participants might be ethically justified in order to optimize the social value of the study.

References

Emanuel, E. J., D. Wendler, and C. Grady. 2000. What makes clinical research ethical? *Journal of the American Medical Association* 283(20):2701–11.

Grant, A. D., S. Charalambous, K. L. Fielding, et al. 2005. Effect of routine isoniazid preventive therapy on tuberculosis incidence among HIV-infected men in South Africa: A novel randomized incremental recruitment study. *Journal of the American Medical Association* 293(22):2719–25.

Hemming, K., T. Haines, P. Chilton, A. Girling, and R. Lilford. 2015. The stepped wedge cluster randomised trial: Rationale, design, analysis, and reporting. *British Medical Journal* 350:h391.

de Hoop, E., I. van der Tweel, R. van der Graaf, et al. 2015. The need to balance merits and limitations from different disciplines when considering the stepped wedge cluster randomized trial design. *BMC Medical Research Methodology* 15:93.

Kerpelman, L. C., D. B. Connell, and W. J. Gunn. 2000. Effect of a monetary sanction on immunization rates of recipients of aid to families with dependent children. *Journal of the American Medical Association* 284(1):53–59.

Largent, E., C. Grady, F. G. Miller, and A. Wertheimer. 2013. Misconceptions about coercion and undue influence: Reflections on the views of IRB members. *Bioethics* 27(9):500–7.

McCambridge, J., K. Kypri, P. Bendtsen, and J. Porter. 2013. The use of deception in public health behavioral intervention trials: A case study of three online alcohol trials. *American Journal of Bioethics* 13(11):39–47.

Prost, A., A. Binik, I. Abubakar, et al. 2015. Logistic, ethical, and political dimensions of stepped wedge trials: Critical review and case studies. *Trials* 16(1):351.

Rafia, R., P. J. Dodd, and A. Brennan, et al. 2016. An economic evaluation of contingency management for completion of hepatitis B vaccination in those on treatment for opiate dependence. *Addiction.* doi:10.1111/add.13385.

Weaver, T., N. Metrebian, J. Hellier, et al. 2014. Use of contingency management incentives to improve completion of hepatitis B vaccination in people undergoing treatment for heroin dependence: A cluster randomised trial. *Lancet* 384(9938):153–63.

COMMENTARY 1.3.3: YOU CAN LEAD A HORSE TO WATER, BUT CAN YOU PAY TO MAKE HIM DRINK? AN ETHICAL ANALYSIS OF RESEARCH ON USING INCENTIVES TO PROMOTE PATIENT HEALTH

PONNI PERUMALSWAMI, ANDREA BRANCH, AND ROSAMOND RHODES

In the mid-1980s, advances in vaccine technology led to the development of a safe and highly effective vaccine for the prevention of HBV infection (Andre 1989; Szmuness et al. 1980; Zajac et al. 1986). There is no question that more extensive use of this vaccine in high-risk populations would save lives, but, as illustrated by this case, questions remain about the pros and cons of direct payment to potential study participants and about the larger issue of direct payment to patients and members of the general public. Behaviorism has taught us that as long as sufficient incentives are provided, the desired behavior is promoted.

The question in this case is whether incentives have a place in the practice of medicine. If there are persuasive reasons for prohibiting them, payments for accepting medical care should not be allowed. But if there are none, and if incentives promise significant benefits to individual patients and society, they should be allowed. Although we believe that payments are acceptable as a means of encouraging health-promoting choices (including the decision to become vaccinated), in what follows, we consider objections that others might raise.

Pay-for-performance initiatives encourage desired behavior in a variety of domains. Within healthcare, employers use them to encourage employees to exercise and receive annual checkups. Hospitals use them to encourage the physicians they employ to practice efficiently and uphold the standard of care. Most recently, medical insurers are considering the use of payments to encourage people to accept medical screening interventions that they would otherwise eschew, such as stool sampling or mammography. These examples do not involve physicians providing incentives to patients and therefore do not involve the physician–patient relationship. Yet it's not at all clear that incentives should be prohibited within the sphere of physician–patient interaction. After all, incentives paid to patients could prevent illness, mitigate the impact of disease, save lives, conserve medical resources, and save money.

Behavioral economics (BE) provides a framework for understanding the possible need for incentives. BE is the study of psychology related to the economic decision-making processes of individuals and institutions (Posner 1997). Most traditional theoretic models conceptualize behavior as driven by deliberative thought processes (Lowenstein and O'Donoghue 2015). BE has established that even when people have all of the relevant information, good intentions, and knowledge of what they should do, they often fail to do what reason would dictate, even when it involves health. BE theory posits that the well-timed and delivered use of incentives, as well as "nudges," can overcome barriers, influence decisions, and promote intentional follow-through. BE interventions incorporate strategies to overcome or utilize biases and make use of low- or no-cost strategies to influence behavior.

Some might imagine that the offer of money to patients would amount to coercion. Would the offer of $10 or $20 coerce patients to accept a vaccine that they previously refused? Coercion involves an unjust threat of harm, but no significant risks are associated with HBV vaccination. The live attenuated vaccine offered before 1985 exposed patients to a risk of HBV. Today's vaccine is so safe that it is recommended for newborns, and children are required to be vaccinated before starting school (Andre 1989). The vaccine itself comes with the benefit of preventing HBV infection. Hepatitis B is a sexually transmitted disease that increases the incidence of liver cancer, and acute hepatitis B can be fatal. Because the voluntary acceptance of payment and health-promoting medical interventions are benefits, and not harms, the offer of money should not be considered a source of undue influence on a patient's decision to be vaccinated.

A related concern might be that using money to motivate action undermines autonomy. It is hard to imagine that an offer of $10 or $20 could be such a powerful incentive as to disable people's ability to make their own decisions. Actually, money promotes liberty by giving people the freedom to do what they like with what they have or what they can do. Voluntary exchanges of money promote autonomy by allowing people to make choices that express their values and priorities. And even if payment would encourage poor people to accept interventions that they otherwise might refuse, the pressure comes from the participants' own values and priorities and therein expresses their autonomy. In that way, cash can promote well-being by allowing people to determine for themselves what will make them better off. Related concerns over the possibility of "undue inducement" would also be misplaced. Worries about undue inducement are concerns about encouraging risk taking, whereas incentives for beneficial medical care aim at reducing health risks. These considerations explain why the proposed study does not run afoul of either respect for autonomy or undue inducement.

Some might find this study of payment for accepting healthcare objectionable because it targets poor people. Even if incentives encouraged a disproportionate number of poor people to accept health-promoting interventions, it's hard to see that as unjust. Injustice involves some people getting either more or less than what is due them. When the poor get improved health, they are not left with less than they deserve, and providing the poor with a little extra money could not be giving them more than their due. Thus, even if this study targets a population of people who are poor, it is not unjust or objectionable on those grounds.

Another concern might be raised about how payment for healthcare could alter the doctor–patient relationship. Introducing incentives into healthcare would certainly involve doing things differently, but, in itself, change is neither bad nor immoral. And perhaps cash payments are not all that different from the treats that have been provided by pediatricians and dentists at the end of a visit. A more general worry would be that introducing payment for accepting treatment could also diminish patient willingness to accept unpaid treatment in the future. Ultimately, this would be a cost-effectiveness issue, an empirical question that would have to be studied, not a matter of ethics. To provide a net benefit, payments could be selective and targeted at interventions that would provide a net financial advantage to the health system. For example, cash payments could be offered for disease screening and to high-risk populations for receiving the HBV vaccine and, thus, provide a net benefit in efficiency.

We appreciate the investigators' concern for their at-risk patients, their frustration with the patients who did not accept the vaccination that would protect them from a serious disease, and their efforts to help those reluctant patients to accept the treatment that they clearly needed. Based on the factors we have considered, instead of seeing the introduction of incentives as an ethical problem, we regard it as a creative and courageous approach that serves the interests of patients. Unless there is some remaining issue that we have overlooked, we find no ethical impediments to proceeding with the proposed study. Despite the anticipated benefits of incentives, however, whenever a physician or healthcare institution is in a position to profit from the incentivized procedure, a potential conflict of interest exists that needs to be thoughtfully and transparently managed.

References

Andre, F. E. 1989. Summary of safety and efficacy data on a yeast-derived hepatitis B vaccine. *American Journal of Medicine* 87:14S–20S.

Lowenstein, G., and T. O'Donoghue. 2015. Animal spirits: Affective and deliberative processes in economic behavior. Available at: http://ssrn.com/abstract=539843 (accessed May 31, 2016).

Posner, R. A. 1997. Rational choice, behavioral economics, and the law. *Stanford Law Review* 5(5):1551–75.

Szmuness, W., C. E. Stevens, E. J. Harley, et al. 1980. Hepatitis B vaccine: Demonstration of efficacy in a controlled clinical trial in a high-risk population in the United States. *New England Journal of Medicine* 303:833–41.

Zajac, B. A., D. J. West, W. J. McAleer, and E. M. Scolnick. 1986. Overview of clinical studies with hepatitis b vaccine made by recombinant DNA. *Journal of Infection* 13(Suppl A):39–45.

CASE 1.4: A CLUSTER RANDOMIZED TRIAL TO SCREEN FOR ABUSIVE HEAD TRAUMA IN THE PEDIATRIC INTENSIVE CARE UNIT—HOW TO MANAGE SITE-SPECIFIC EVIDENCE OF RACIAL/ETHNIC DISPARITY

INTRODUCTION

Abusive head trauma is the leading cause of traumatic death and disability during infancy and early childhood. Typically, physicians elect to evaluate and report suspected abuse in young, acutely head-injured patients based on their individualized assessment that the injury was possibly due to nonaccidental trauma. With no standardized set of criteria, these decisions are subject to individual variability and provider bias.

Under- or overreacting to potential abuse can have serious implications for the child and caregivers. A flawed decision to forgo an abuse evaluation allows substantial risk of additional injury for the abused, head-injured child returned to his or her abusive caregivers (Jenny et al. 1999). A flawed decision to launch an abuse evaluation when the injury is not the result of nonaccidental trauma can also have negative consequences, including exacerbation of parental stress, strain on the clinician–parent relationship, and exposure of the child to additional risks (e.g., sedation and radiation), and it may increase overall healthcare costs.

In the case outlined here, a research team has developed a screening tool based on observational data to remove individual variability and improve the accuracy of these clinical decisions. The team has initiated a multisite implementation study to assess the tool's effectiveness, but because of an interim analysis, the principal investigator is now concerned that in spite of the tool, implicit biases may still be influencing decisions about abuse evaluations at some sites. The investigator faced a dilemma of how to respond to this new information, given that the study was ongoing.

In the first commentary, Emma Tumilty and Jeff Farroni of the University of Texas Medical Branch at Galveston argue for the importance of having initial pretrial discussions before opening a cluster randomized trial, where the study team clearly outlines (1) safety monitoring and/or stopping rules and (2) a mechanism to document the implementation process and provider efficacy around using or incorporating the practice being studied. Unlike the second commentary, which argues for nonintervention, the authors in this first commentary suggest a broad educational intervention across all sites that aims to teach providers about implicit bias while reinforcing the correct use of the screening tool. In the second commentary, Brian Jackson of the University of Colorado argues for nonintervention and letting the validation trial of the screening tool continue as originally planned because the trial itself is not the cause of bias. Disparities in clinician judgment occur independently from the trial, and therefore "the implementation trial may result in a more effective strategy to reduce the effect of implicit biases" compared to the current standard of care (i.e., clinician discretion). In the final commentary, Jennifer McCormick and Kent Hymel of Pennsylvania State University also argue for continuation of the trial, but suggest that results of the interim analysis and concern for ongoing provider biases in reporting be presented to study sites in aggregate for the purpose of raising awareness about implicit bias. This can allow providers at the study sites to reflect on how these biases may be influencing their decision making around reporting suspicions of nonaccidental trauma.

CASE SUMMARY

The sequential, observational, prospective study of 500 acutely head-injured children (<3 years old) conducted from 2010 and 2013 at 18 pediatric intensive care unit (PICU) sites has resulted in the development of a validated screening tool for pediatric abusive head trauma. The screening tool has a positive predictive value of 0.55 and a negative predictive value of 0.93. The screening tool recommends that patients who present with one or more of its for-predictor variables be considered "higher risk" and "thoroughly evaluated for abuse" (Hymel et al. 2013, 2014).

Subsequently, an implementation study was initiated at eight sites using a cluster randomized design. The primary aim of this trial is to assess the tool's clinical impact when applied in PICU settings and used in clinical decision making. At four of the intervention sites, research teams are deploying active implementation strategies designed to encourage PICU physicians to apply the screening tool and to follow its recommendations. At the other four matched control sites, physicians are practicing "abuse screening as usual." At all eight participating sites, investigators are collecting the same historical, clinical, and radiological data captured in the initial observational studies. At the four intervention sites, investigators are collecting additional data regarding physicians' decisions to follow or ignore the screening tool recommendations.

During year 1 of the implementation trial, the investigators published a secondary analysis of the data from the initial observational studies (Hymel et al. 2018). This analysis revealed significant race/ethnicity-based disparities in abuse evaluation and reporting practices at two of the 18 sites (not identified), where ethnic and racial minorities were 8–16 times more likely to be evaluated and reported for suspected abuse than White/non-Hispanic patients. Analysis of confounders did not explain the observed disparities, suggesting they may represent local physicians' implicit bias.

These two initial sites are involved in the current implementation trial—one in the intervention arm (Site X), and the other in the control arm (Site Y).

Alerted to the potential for racial or ethnic bias at Sites X and Y, the investigator analyzed current abuse evaluation trends at Sites X and Y more closely, and found the following: Through year 1 of the implementation trial, physicians at Site X evaluated 53% of their 15 higher-risk patients thoroughly for abuse, while physicians at the three remaining intervention sites evaluated 88% of 16, 100% of 14, and 6 (86%) of 7 of their higher-risk patients thoroughly for abuse. Equivalent analyses failed to reveal similar discrepancies between Site Y and the three remaining control sites during year 1. The trial's data and safety monitoring committee endorsed the investigator's plan to request a research ethics consultation to determine whether the two sites should be informed of the racial/ethnic disparities at their sites.

Cognizant of the physical and psychosocial risks of potentially underreporting certain racial groups while overreporting others, the principal investigator requested a research ethics consultation to explore the following specific question: Do these potential risks justify informing the two sites that their physicians are likely practicing with racial/ethnic disparity and bias—at the cost of compromising the integrity of the implementation trial? Lacking definitive evidence that any patient(s) at Site X have been harmed, is the potential for harm enough to warrant trial termination or modification?

REFERENCES

Hymel, K. P., V. Armijo-Garcia, R. Foster, et al. 2014. Validation of a clinical prediction rule for pediatric abusive head trauma. *Pediatrics* 134(6):e1537–44.

Hymel, K. P., A. L. Laskey, K. R. Crowell, et al. 2018. For the pediatric brain injury research network (PediBIRN) investigators. Racial/ethnic disparities and bias in the evaluation and reporting of abusive head trauma. *The Journal of Pediatrics* 198:137–43.e1.

Hymel, K. P., D. F. Willson, S. C. Boos, et al. 2013. Derivation of a clinical prediction rule for pediatric abusive head trauma. *Pediatric Critical Care Medicine* 14(2):210–20.

Jenny, C., K. P. Hymel, A. Ritzen, S. E. Reinert, and T. C. Hay. 1999. Analysis of missed cases of abusive head trauma. *Journal of American Medical Association* 281(7):621–6.

COMMENTARY 1.4.1: ISSUES OF JUSTICE AND RISK: SETTING STOPPING CRITERIA IN CLUSTER RANDOMIZED TRIALS

EMMA TUMILTY AND JEFFREY S. FARRONI

Justice issues are typically about the fair distribution of benefit or risk within relevant populations and their subgroups. In this case, there is a potential unfair risk burden: Provider racial/ethnic bias represents a safety risk to participants related to the consequences of over- and underscreening (Johnson, Zabrowski, and Wilfond 2019). In an ideal situation, stopping criteria around over- or underscreening would be established at the beginning of the trial. A data monitoring committee can ensure trial data validity while periodically monitoring trial data to assess the efficacy, futility, and safety of a trial intervention so that they can make recommendations about whether a study should continue, be modified, or be terminated. Generally, data and safety monitoring plans will describe when and how interim analyses will occur, as well as stopping criteria. Stopping criteria assess futility, efficacy, and safety of the intervention related to measurable risks and benefits that are predetermined. In this case, prior to initiating the study, the team would determine threshold rates at which they believe either under- or overscreening constitutes a harm that would stop the study (i.e., X percent over a specified rate or X percent under a specified rate). They would determine these thresholds using a combination of current standard screening rates combined with the new tool's specificity and sensitivity information from their previous research. They can also use these criteria for racial bias analyses. That is, if the total cohorts from each site do not meet stopping criteria but racial/ethnic subgroups do, then you have an issue of racial bias in the tool's use, which may warrant intervention or termination of the study on further examination.

The investigators could have used their previous work on prevalence and screening to accomplish this (Hymel et al. 2018; Jenny et al. 1999). If this was not included in the data safety monitoring plan, then the team must complete specific analyses of both over- and underscreening by each site compared against previous data and include a race/ethnicity analysis. What will be limiting in this case are the small numbers—often an issue at interim analyses. Given these small numbers, a site-specific analysis using case note review of potential abuse would be the most robust way of establishing screening validity within the site.

The current case as described raises an issue rarely dealt with in the ethics of cluster randomized controlled trials specifically, but also in clinical trials and data–safety monitoring more generally: justice considerations (harm distribution) in safety stopping criteria. In discussing the ethics of cluster randomized controlled trials, Weijer et al. (2011) made no mention of data safety monitoring and stopping guidelines. The authors' discussion of justice only referred to the general aspects of fair representation and the distribution of benefits and burdens in regard to trial enrollment and participation (Weijer et al. 2011). The CONSORT (Consolidated Standards of Reporting Trials) guidelines acknowledge the absence of stopping criteria for many cluster randomized trials and the difficulties in determining appropriate interim analyses time frames, but make no specific recommendations to investigators for trial monitoring (Campbell et al. 2012). Similarly, the Council for International Organizations of Medical Sciences (CIOMS 2016) included a section on cluster randomized trials, but this section also fails to address the complexities of data–safety monitoring in cluster randomized trials. While the current CIOMS *Guidelines* discuss risk extensively and the need for instituting stopping criteria, these do not refer specifically to the complexities of monitoring cluster randomized controlled trials (CIOMS 2016).

It appears that Site X has a lower screening rate for its high-risk abusive head trauma cases than the other sites. This could be because the tool has greater negative predictive value than positive predictive value (which would be an indication that the other sites were overscreening, rather than

Site X was underscreening, but this is unlikely). It also appears that Site Y's current screening practices are in line with the other control sites despite its history of racial bias found in the retrospective data review. The current case provides no description of the racial and ethnic makeup of the interim analysis data.

For implementation of cluster–cluster randomized control trials, an important first step in understanding differences in clinical outcomes between sites is determining whether providers have changed their practice or whether implementation of the tool has failed or is less than ideal. The team can do this by interrogating screening rates. It is unclear whether the investigators, when analyzing confounding factors and eliminating them, included the implementation of the tool itself and whether it was effective at intervention Site X.

The options available to the team are:

- *Option 1—Termination of Site X*: If the data analyses establish underscreening at Site X, then given that underscreening carries the greatest risk, the team should terminate this site and they should inform the institution and the providers immediately of why this was necessary so that they can provide an intervention (education/training).
- *Option 2—Termination of Sites X and Y*: Given that historical data show biases at these sites, despite equivocal data currently reported, the research team should terminate these sites and inform the institution and the providers immediately of why this was necessary so that they can provide an intervention.
- *Option 3—Modification of Site X*: If intervention Site X has failed in implementing the tool, understanding why is an important part of an implementation project. It is possible to try further intervention to implement the tool at Site X and to continue to monitor data. The team would have to describe clearly this secondary intervention, and ongoing monitoring would be required to ensure that this addressed the issue of the lower screening rates.
- *Option 4—Modification of All Sites*: If the implementation of the tool was working, and the team believed the mis-screening was due to provider bias, then the research team could provide further education tailored to identifying and removing racial/ethnic bias from all sites (both intervention and control). Again, this would divide data between pre- and post-education for reporting purposes, and monitoring would be required to ensure that this addressed bias at Site X and did not cause unintended consequences at the remaining sites.

Without knowing more data and information, we endorse Option 4, that is, an intervention to reduce racial bias in screening at all sites with ongoing monitoring. Modifications are justifiable in situations where data are equivocal. The research team has a duty to inform the institutions immediately that there may be racial/ethnic bias in their organizations, regardless of which of these options they chose.

This case highlights that it is very important, even in cluster randomized control trials, to engage in the same initial discussions about data safety monitoring and stopping criteria that traditional clinical triallists do. These criteria should be determined using relevant available clinical data and research evidence. It is crucial when conducting implementation projects that intervene on providers to document the implementation itself and monitor its effectiveness on providers, not just the effect on clinical outcomes. Lastly and most importantly, issues of justice are often issues of harm, whether by action or by omission, and these can be quantified and measured and should always be acted upon.

References

Campbell, M. K., G. Piaggio, D. R. Elbourne, and D. G. Altman. 2012. Consort 2010 statement: Extension to cluster randomized trials. *BMJ* 345: e5661.

Council for International Organizations of Medical Sciences (CIOMS). 2016. 2016 International Ethical Guidelines for Health-related Research Involving Humans. Fourth Edition. Geneva. https://cioms.ch/shop/product/international-ethical-guidelines-for-health-related-research-involving-humans/ (accessed May 29, 2019).

Hymel, K. P., A. L. Laskey, K. R. Crowell, et al. 2018. Racial/ethnic disparities and bias in the evaluation and reporting of abusive head trauma. *The Journal of Pediatrics* 198: 137–43.e1. Available at (accessed January 25, 2019).

Jenny, C., K. P. Hymel, A. Ritzen, S. E. Reinert, and T. C. Hay. 1999. Analysis of missed cases of abusive head trauma. *JAMA* 281(7):621–6.

Johnson, L., J. Zabrowski, and B. Wilfond. 2019. A cluster randomized trial to screen for abusive head trauma in the pediatric intensive care unit—How to manage site-specific evidence of racial/ethnic disparity. *American Journal of Bioethics* 19(4):108–9.

Weijer, C., J. M. Grimshaw, M. Taljaard, et al. 2011. Ethical issues posed by cluster randomized trials in health research. *Trials* 12(1): 100.

COMMENTARY 1.4.2: CLINICAL TRIALS NOT CAUSING HARM WITH POTENTIAL FOR REALIZING BENEFIT SHOULD CONTINUE

BRIAN MICHAEL JACKSON

This secondary analysis of observational research and the subsequent interim analysis of an interventional trial using a decision aid to identify possible abusive head trauma raise concerns (though not definitive proof) of implicit ethnic and racial bias at two research sites (Johnson, Zabrowski, and Wilfond 2019). Revealing these concerns to these sites could invalidate the implementation trial. I argue that unmasking of individual sites should not be done because the research did not cause the disparity, this disparity is not novel, and completing the validation of the implementation trial may result in a more effective strategy to reduce the effect of implicit biases on patients and families.

The clinical trial is not the cause of bias

Removing Sites X and Y from the ongoing implementation study would likely require premature closure of the trial or would at least significantly limit the results of the study. Removing two sites that are thought to be different in some way (in this case, because of racially disparate rates of reporting child maltreatment) would undermine the randomization strategy that was created a priori. Generally, early termination of clinical trials is justified when new information is uncovered that raises concerns about the relative risks and benefits of the ongoing study. This information usually relates to one of four features of the research: participant safety, futility/feasibility, efficacy, or economic considerations (Malmqvist et al. 2011). Each of the reasons relates to a flaw in the study itself: Either the study is designed such that it cannot be completed successfully, or the study is causing potential harm to participants. The study itself must be the agent that is responsible for the harm for premature closure of a clinical trial to be justified. To close a study early for other reasons is to have put previously enrolled participants at risk without benefit (i.e., they were exposed to the risk of the study), as no clear conclusion can be made from the trial.

In the present study, the research itself is not causing known harm, nor is continuation of the trial infeasible or futile. The observational portion of the research simply describes current features of the clinical landscape at the sites in question, and neither the investigators nor the research procedures can reasonably be held responsible for the preexisting environment. The interim analysis of the interventional portion of the research suggests continuing differences for Site X, but not for Site Y. It is not clear from the reported information whether the differences in evaluation of potential abuse victims at

Site X correlate with racial or ethnic categories of participants. Furthermore, no evidence is reported that the study intervention (use of a structured screening tool) is the cause of any difference in workup rates by race. Given this, the harms of stopping the study to reveal the sites with evidence of possible racial or ethnic bias are not justified by the potential benefits and may in fact result in unnecessary harm to participants who have already completed the study.

The apparent racial disparity has been previously reported

Disparities in rates of reporting potential child abuse have been observed for nearly four decades (Hampton and Newberger 1985). More recent studies have demonstrated that these disparities have not decreased over time, but differ as to whether those differences are due to bias or social determinants of health that increase the risk for child abuse and neglect (Drake et al. 2011; Drake, Lee, and Jonson-Reid 2009). There is debate in the literature about whether the racial disparities can be explained solely by other factors (such as poverty) or whether race plays a more direct role. However, the studies are clear that people are more likely to make reports regarding Black and Latino children than White children. Some recent studies suggest that there is geographic variability to the disproportionality of child abuse reporting (Ards et al. 2003; Krase 2013; Maguire-Jack et al. 2015). These data show that racial disparities in child abuse reporting vary between states, as well as between counties within states. A national county-by-county analysis showed more disparity in very rural and very urban areas and less racial disparity in areas of moderate population density (Maguire-Jack et al. 2015).

Given these data, the results of the secondary analysis of observational data are precisely what one would have predicted. The secondary analysis shows that some (but not all) sites had disproportionate reporting related to race/ethnicity, but was not able to determine whether these differences were due to underlying risk factors or implicit bias (though the examination of confounding variables suggested the latter). Either way, these results are consistent with well-known features of assessment of possible child abuse that result in disproportionate attribution of nonaccidental trauma to nonwhite parents. These features are known, or should be known, to the research sites. Because early stopping of a trial should be based on newly discovered information, stopping the trial early when expected results are uncovered is not justified.

Completion of the study may help decrease implicit bias

Implicit bias is widely recognized within the healthcare system at a variety of levels. Multiple studies have demonstrated disproportionately bad outcomes for nonwhite patients (Zestcott, Blair, and Stone 2016). There are also reports that suggest descriptions of biases often do not help practitioners who believe their implicit biases do not affect patient care (Gonzalez, Kim, and Marantz 2014). These data suggest that the present researchers' informing Sites X and Y of their racially disproportionate assessment of possible child abuse and neglect is unlikely to create lasting change in practice patterns at the sites, even if these differences are the result of implicit bias.

On the other hand, completion of the study and validation of an objective screening tool to determine which patients and families require additional evaluation may help to reduce the effect of implicit biases. Some guidance for reducing the impact of implicit bias suggests that moving from subjective determinations to objective decision aids may help to reduce the impact of implicit biases on decision making (Casey et al. 2013). Other work has suggested that under complex workloads (such as in an intensive care unit), healthcare professionals tend to show increased evidence of implicit bias (Dovidio and Fiske 2012). It is therefore possible that reducing the cognitive workload by outsourcing the decision making about further child abuse workup to an objective decision tool may reduce the effect of bias on patients and families. This study has the potential to reduce the effect of implicit biases in the target population.

Conclusion

The study is not the cause of the racially disproportionate decision making revealed by the observational study. In fact, these differences were well described long before this study was conceived. Furthermore, revealing the disproportionate results to the sites is not likely to have a significant long-term effect on their practice behavior. Finally, this study has the potential to validate a new, objective tool that may help to reduce the effect of implicit biases on patients and families. Sites should not be informed of site-specific results, and the implementation trial should continue unchanged. At the conclusion of the implementation trial, all sites can be informed of their site-specific results and how they compare to the pooled results. This approach maximizes the potential benefit of the study without exposing participants to unnecessary risk.

References

Ards, S., S. Myers, A. Malkis, E. Sugrue, and L. Zhou. 2003. Racial disproportionality in reported and substantiated child abuse and neglect: An examination of systematic bias. *Children and Youth Services Review* 25(5–6):375–92.

Casey, P. M., R. K. Warren, F. L. Cheesman, and J. K. Elek. 2013. Addressing implicit bias in the courts. *Court Review* 49:64.

Dovidio, J. F., and S. T. Fiske. 2012. Under the radar: How unexamined biases in decision-making processes in clinical interactions can contribute to health care disparities. *American Journal of Public Health* 102(5):945–52.

Drake, B., J. M. Jolley, P. Lanier, J. Fluke, R. P. Barth, and M. Jonson-Reid. 2011. Racial bias in child protection? A comparison of competing explanations using national data. *Pediatrics* 127(3):471.

Drake, B., S. M. Lee, and M. Jonson-Reid. 2009. Race and child maltreatment reporting: Are blacks overrepresented? *Children and Youth Services Review* 31(3):309–16.

Gonzalez, C. M., M. Y. Kim, and P. R. Marantz. 2014. Implicit bias and its relation to health disparities: A teaching program and survey of medical students. *Teaching and Learning in Medicine* 26(1):64–71.

Hampton, R. L., and E. H. Newberger. 1985. Child abuse incidence and reporting by hospitals: Significance of severity, class, and race. *American Journal of Public Health* 75(1):56–60.

Johnson, L.-M., J. Zabrowski, and B. S. Wilfond. 2019. A cluster randomized trial to screen for abusive head trauma in the pediatric intensive care unit—How to manage site-specific evidence of racial/ethnic disparity. *American Journal of Bioethics* 19(4):108–9.

Krase, K. S. 2013. Differences in racially disproportionate reporting of child maltreatment across report sources. *Journal of Public Child Welfare* 7(4):351–69.

Maguire-Jack, K., P. Lanier, M. Johnson-Motoyama, H. Welch, and M. Dineen. 2015. Geographic variation in racial disparities in child maltreatment: The influence of county poverty and population density. *Child Abuse & Neglect* 47:1–13.

Malmqvist, E., N. Juth, N. Lynöe, and G. Helgesson. 2011. Early stopping of clinical trials: Charting the ethical terrain. *Kennedy Institute of Ethics Journal* 21(1):51–78.

Zestcott, C. A., I. V. Blair, and J. Stone. 2016. Examining the presence, consequences, and reduction of implicit bias in health care: A narrative review. *Group Processes & Intergroup Relations* 19(4):528–42.

COMMENTARY 1.4.3: RESPONDING TO IMPLICIT BIAS IN ABUSIVE HEAD TRAUMA EVALUATIONS AND REPORTING IN THE PICU: ETHICAL CONSIDERATIONS DURING A CLINICAL TRIAL

JENNIFER B. McCORMICK AND KENT P. HYMEL

When considering the ethical nature of a research study, we find it helpful to specify the potential social relevance or importance of the research study's goals (Emanuel et al. 2000). Abusive head trauma is the leading cause of traumatic death and disability during infancy and early childhood. During 1999–2014, abusive head trauma resulted in nearly 2,250 deaths among children in the United States aged younger than 5 years (Spies and Klevens 2016). Morbidity ranges from mild learning disabilities to severe cognitive or physical abnormalities. Recent evaluations of reported cases show that between 2009 and 2014, abusive head trauma continued to be a major cause of pediatric morbidity and mortality (Barr et al. 2018; Joyce and Huecker 2019; Lind et al. 2016; Tilak and Pollock 2013). However, clinicians have limited evidence-based approaches at their disposal when assessing whether a pediatric head trauma case is the result of abuse (Hymel et al. 2013, 2014).

The study in question (Johnson, Zabrowski, and Wilfond 2019) is testing the implementation of an evidence-based screening tool they previously developed (Hymel et al. 2013), since the tool will only provide benefit if physicians find the tool acceptable and are willing to use and integrate it into their practice. Having an evidence-based tool that physicians will embrace and integrate into their practice has the potential for significant impact by reducing harms and costs at both the individual and societal levels.

This case raises questions about the role of implicit bias in the context of the clinical decision-making tool. Increasingly, health organizations are becoming more aware of the impact implicit bias has on the care of patients and the interactions among employees. Implicit, or unconscious or hidden, bias can encompass both favorable and unfavorable assessments and is activated involuntarily. That is, an individual is unaware of when their implicit biases are influencing decisions, attitudes, and actions. Moreover, implicit biases are learned behaviors, derived over a long period of time from an individual's social and cultural environment. As such, alerting or eliminating one's implicit biases requires that person to recognize that biases exist and to make a cognizant effort to eliminate them in his or her interactions, decisions, and attitudes. Many medical centers have begun administering the Implicit Association Test (IAT; https://implicit.harvard.edu/implicit/aboutus.html), which is designed to assess conscious and unconscious preferences across a range of different topics, including ethnicity and race. Medical centers that used this test for assessing the level of implicit bias have found notable pro-White biases among their staff members, including physicians (Joint Commission 2016). While the clinical decision tool under investigation in this trial is aimed at removing biases from the equation of whether to report head trauma as potentially nonaccidental, it is unknown whether the tool actually eliminates implicit bias from a physician's decision making, given how these biases are embedded in an individual's subconscious. For instance, even when and how the physician applies the tool can be influenced by that individual's unconscious biases.

The study interim data indicate that one of the intervention sites is applying the clinical decision-making tool recommendations at a much lower rate than the other intervention sites. What are unknown are the reasons why the recommendations of the tool are being ignored. It is not clear that it can fairly be stated that the reasons are grounded in biases. Furthermore, it is not clear what telling or accusing physicians at a specific site that their racial and ethnic biases are influencing their practice will accomplish with respect to evaluations of higher-risk head trauma cases. Changing learned attitudes like implicit bias means that individuals must accept these biases and be willing to make concerted efforts to change their hidden partialities. All the sites in the study are aware of the results from the observational study involving 18 sites that identified two sites where implicit racial bias appears to be influencing physicians' decisions about which acutely head-injured patients to evaluate for child abuse (Hymel et al. 2018). While they don't know which sites these two specific sites are, the existence of this finding ought to give each site pause and reason to engage in internal evaluation. Finally, we should consider whether any individual has been harmed because of the use or lack of use of the tool. The case description fails to present evidence that solid harm has come to any patients at any of the eight sites in the trial.

With all of this in mind, we make the following recommendations. We recommend that the study not be stopped, based on the current preliminary analysis. Additionally, we encourage the investigator to continue to track the abuse evaluation trends at each site, and to continue to report the aggregate data to each site as it compares to the other sites. Finally, since this study is part of a larger network of centers where research on pediatric brain injury is conducted, we strongly encourage the investigators to urge the network member sites to consider the findings from Hymel et al. (2018) as an impetus to engage in internal reflection on their own practices and the possible role that biases have in clinical decision making, in particular with those decisions regarding whether head trauma cases are thoroughly evaluated for abuse.

References

Barr, R. G., M. F. Barr, C. Rajabali, et al. 2018. Eight-year outcome of implementation of abusive head trauma prevention. *Child Abuse & Neglect* 84:106–14.

Emanuel, E. J., D. Wendler, and C. Grady. 2000. What makes clinical research ethical? *Journal of the American Medical Association* 283(20):2701–11.

Hymel, K. P., D. F. Willson, S. C. Boos, et al. 2013. Derivation of a clinical prediction rule for pediatric abusive head trauma. *Pediatric Critical Care Medicine* 14(2):210–20.

Hymel, K. P., V. Armijo-Garcia, R. Foster, et al. 2014. Validation of a clinical prediction rule for pediatric abusive head trauma. *Pediatrics* 134(6):e1537–44.

Hymel, K. P., A. L. K. R. Laskey, and M. Crowell, et al. 2018. Pediatric brain injury research network (PediBIRN) investigators. Racial/ethnic disparities and bias in the evaluation and reporting of abusive head trauma. *Journal of Pediatrics* 198: 137–43.e1.

Johnson, L., J. Zabrowski, and B. Wilfond. 2019. A pragmatic trial of suicide risk assessment and ambulance transport decision making among emergency medical services providers. *American Journal of Bioethics* 19(4):108–9.

Joint Commission, Division of Health Care Improvement. Implicit Bias in Health Care. *Quick Safety*, Issue 23, April. 2016. https://www.jointcommission.org/assets/1/23/Quick_Safety_Issue_23_Apr_2016.pdf (accessed May 10, 2019).

Joyce, T., and M. R. Huecker. Pediatric Abusive Head Trauma (Shaken Baby Syndrome) [Updated February 11, 2019]. *StatPearls [internet]*. Treasure Island (FL): StatPearls Publishing. https://www.ncbi.nlm.nih.gov/books/NBK499836/ (accessed February 11, 2019)

Lind, K., H. Toure, D. Brugel, P. Meyer, A. Laurent-Vannier, and M. Chevignard. 2016. Extended follow-up of neurological, cognitive, behavioral and academic outcomes after severe abusive head trauma. *Child Abuse & Neglect* 51:358–67.

Spies, E. L., and J. Klevens. 2016. Fatal abusive head trauma among children aged <5 years — United States,1999–2014. *Morbity and Mortality Weekly Report* 65:505–9.

Tilak, G. S., and A. N. Pollock. 2013. Missed opportunities in fatal child abuse. *Pediatric Emergency Care* 29(5):685–7.

CASE 1.5: WHEN A CLINICAL TRIAL IS THE ONLY OPTION

INTRODUCTION

The case presented here, along with three commentaries, focuses on whether the option of enrollment in a clinical trial involving a bone marrow transplant (BMT) ought to be presented to a medically eligible cancer patient who has exhausted all available standard treatment options. The answer to this question is complicated by the fact that the patient is an undocumented immigrant with limited financial resources. Whether the trial option ought to be offered turns on an assessment of how best to respect the autonomy of the patient and what is in the best interest of the patient and his family as they all deal with a life-threatening diagnosis. The three commentaries weigh these considerations and come to different conclusions. Rachel Fabi from the Johns Hopkins Berman Institute of Bioethics and Bloomberg School of Public Health argues that the patient's undocumented status is not a morally relevant consideration with regard to his eligibility for enrollment in clinical research. Based on a set of key considerations relevant to whether the patient is capable of making an autonomous choice, she concludes that the patient's care team has an obligation to disclose the option of enrollment in a potentially lifesaving trial. Elizabeth Heitman from Vanderbilt University School of Medicine assumes that a therapeutic BMT was not previously offered to the patient due to his likely inability to afford the cost of treatment. She notes that while enrollment in a clinical trial may be an alternative point of access to a BMT, it is far from an inexpensive option, and that if the team agrees to present the option to the patient and his family, all of the potential costs and benefits of enrollment must be considered. Nancy J. Burke from the University of California, Merced, applies Annmarie Mol's critique of patient-centered care to the case of the undocumented patient in need of medical care, a "situation of choice." Reviewing the case through the lens of a "logic of care," she concludes that this patient should not be considered a candidate for enrollment in the trial.

CASE SUMMARY

A member of the palliative care service contacted the research ethics consultant for help in defining the goals of care for a 55-year-old Central American man with a recent diagnosis of myelofibrosis. Myelofibrosis is a rare cancer that results in the proliferation of abnormal blood cells and extensive scarring of the bone marrow. There is no cure for the disorder. If a matched donor is available, allogenic BMT offers the possibility of remission. The patient had been admitted to the hematology service through the emergency department (ED) three weeks earlier. Since his admission, he has received almost-daily platelet transfusions, prophylactic antibiotics, and steroids for symptom control. The patient is weak but alert and readily cooperates with all treatment. He and his wife are able to communicate clearly with caregivers through the hospital's Spanish-language interpreters.

The patient works for a landscaping company that does not provide health insurance. He is an undocumented immigrant, and therefore ineligible for federal- or state-funded financial assistance programs. He is stable enough to receive palliative treatment in the outpatient clinic or at home, but neither the hospital nor other local healthcare groups will provide such services without an identified source of payment. Earlier in the week, the head of the hospital's transition management office contacted the patient's medical team to encourage them to make a discharge plan. The palliative care team has arranged for the patient to be discharged to his home, where a local charity group has agreed to provide hospice care.

In the interim, a fellow on the hematology service has discovered a clinical trial for BMT at an academic medical center 900 miles away, for which the patient is medically eligible. The five-year survival rate for myelofibrosis after BMT is approximately 30%. However, the BMT process itself involves prolonged hospitalization and close supportive care for months after discharge. A successful BMT can also result in debilitating graft-versus-host disease (GVHD). The posttransplant drug regimen, essential to promoting new bone marrow and to suppressing both the original myelofibrosis and GVHD, may cost more than $100,000/year, even for well-insured patients.

The study will enroll participants without regard to immigration status or ability to pay. In order to be evaluated for the study, patients must have an identified human leukocyte antigen (HLA)-matched related donor; the patient has two siblings in Central America and one in Texas willing to be tested. The fellow has also found a private philanthropic organization to cover the costs of HLA testing (including shipping). If one of the siblings living in Central America is a match, he or she will need to apply for a medical visa for entry into the United States, a process that typically takes weeks to months. The hospital has also agreed to cover the costs of the patient's transfusions and drugs as an outpatient for a few weeks as he waits to learn whether one of his siblings might be a suitable donor.

The palliative care team is seeking guidance from the ethics consultant because its members disagree with the hematology team's plan to notify the patient about the study. The patient can explain that he has "blood cancer," but it is not clear whether he fully understands that no curative treatment is available or how clinical research differs from established treatment. Should the patient be told about the clinical trial? If so, what should he be told about the nature of the medical intervention and the complex logistical and financial hurdles he would face? What responsibilities would the patient's current caregivers have to facilitate his enrollment into the study?

COMMENTARY 1.5.1: "RESPECT FOR PERSONS," NOT "RESPECT FOR CITIZENS"

RACHEL FABI

Imagine for a moment that this case was about a medically and socioeconomically identical American citizen. He has limited English proficiency and requires an interpreter. He has siblings in the United States and abroad. He is uninsured, perhaps because he falls into the coverage gap created when his state chose not to expand Medicaid. Would this citizen's care team inform him of a potentially life-extending clinical trial? If the answer to this question in the analogous case is yes, then the correct course of action for the original patient should be obvious. Respect for patient autonomy requires that the team inform him about all of his treatment options, including the clinical trial. I argue that respect for patient autonomy is not a duty owed solely to compatriots, but rather to all humans, regardless of their immigration status. Although the case does not explicitly state that the palliative care team's primary concern is the patient's immigration status, consideration of the case with that variable removed could yield clear guidance. Immigration status is morally irrelevant, and the medical team should consider only the morally relevant facts in deciding whether or not to inform the patient about the clinical trial.

Duty to respect autonomy transcends immigration status

The principle of respect for autonomy can be derived from the Kantian categorical imperative that we treat each person as an end in himself and never merely as a means (Beauchamp and Childress 2009). It calls on us to recognize the unconditional worth of individual persons, and to respect their capacity to decide for themselves those ends that they find most valuable and worthy of pursuit. Kant does not restrict the application of the categorical imperative only to those persons with whom we share a nationality. Indeed, Kant does not even restrict the categorical imperative to humans, but claims that it applies to all rational beings (Kant, Gregor, and Timmermann 2012).

Non-Kantians might base a duty to respect autonomy on John Stuart Mill's harm principle, which requires that society "should permit individuals to develop according to their own convictions, as long as they do not interfere with a like expression of freedom by others or unjustifiably harm others" (Beauchamp and Childress 2009). Like Kant, Mill makes no distinction between citizens and noncitizens in his theory; noninterference in the pursuit of projects is owed to all.

We need not focus only on the theoretical roots of respect for autonomy in determining to whom it is owed. Modern ethical guidelines for physicians similarly reject any differential duties on the basis of citizenship or immigration status. The 1964 update to the Hippocratic Oath contains the promise, "I will remember that I remain a member of society, with special obligations to all my fellow human beings, those sound of mind and body as well as the infirm" (Lasagna 1964). When new physicians swear this oath, they acknowledge that their obligations extend to all their fellow human beings; citizenship is not a precondition for the fulfillment of their duties.

Physician duty to disclose

Having established that the duty to respect patient autonomy is not dependent on citizenship or legal status, we can dive into the details of this case to determine whether its morally relevant characteristics entail a duty to disclose the option of the clinical trial. For the purposes of this analysis, we examine the morally (rather than legally) relevant considerations from the consent literature that might override the requirement that patients be fully informed of all potential treatment options. These include diminished capacity to consent, the futility of the treatment option, and medical contraindication of disclosure (Beauchamp and Childress 2009). I examine each of these in the context of this case, and evaluate whether any are legitimate reasons for the care team to withhold treatment information from the patient.

First, the patient's capacity to understand and consent should be considered. From the case description, it is clear that the patient retains full capacity. He is alert and compliant with treatment, and is able to communicate through interpreters. Although he is unable to describe his condition beyond recognition that he has "blood cancer," it seems unlikely that even many fluent English speakers could describe myelofibrosis with more detail or medically relevant information than that it is a cancer of the blood. Capacity to consent is therefore not at issue in this case.

The second consideration that might allow the medical team to withhold information about a treatment option would be the futility of the option. Although determinations of medical futility can be subjective and can vary from patient to patient, a physician is not morally required to provide treatment that is "highly unlikely to be efficacious," and "may not even be required to discuss the treatment" (Beauchamp and Childress 2013). While the BMT trial in this case is experimental, the facts of the case do not indicate that enrolling in this trial would be prima facie futile. Indeed, there seems to be a good chance that BMT could be a viable option for this patient; siblings typically experience a one-in-four chance of being a HLA match, and with three siblings, our undocumented patient has a decent chance of finding a match among his siblings (Be the Match 2016). If a sibling match could be identified, a 30% five-year survival rate after BMT could yield a strong positive benefit for the patient. Thus, while the benefits of enrolling in the trial are uncertain, it cannot be argued that it would be futile for this patient.

Finally, it might, under very specific circumstances, be ethical for a medical team to withhold information about a treatment option if informing the patient about it is medically contraindicated. This idea, known as the therapeutic privilege, applies when the disclosure itself could cause harm to the patient's health (Beauchamp and Childress 2009). Although this patient may find it distressing to hear of the potentially expensive long-term costs associated with the BMT procedure, the disclosure itself would likely not cause any deterioration of the patient's condition, especially given his stable status. The emotional and psychological burden this choice could place on an uninsured and vulnerable patient may be heavy, but the existence of such a trade-off should not outweigh the duty to allow him to make his own choices.

Conclusion

Immigration status is not morally relevant to this decision, and the criteria that are morally relevant suggest that the medical team has an obligation to inform their patient of the potentially life-extending clinical trial for which he is eligible. They must review, through the interpreter, all of the risks, benefits, and costs associated with each option, including the trial and the palliative care at home, and do their utmost to ensure that he comprehends them. A patient's noncitizenship does not absolve the medical team of their duty to respect autonomy. If anything, the patient's status as a member of a vulnerable population only strengthens the obligations of the medical team to ensure that he is able to choose the best option for his own life. Furthermore, as the physicians with whom he has an established relationship, they have a duty to facilitate his exercise of that choice, or to transfer his care to someone else who will.

References

Be the Match. 2016. HLA matching. Available at: https://bethematch.org/for-patients-and-families/finding-a-donor/hla-matching/(accessed on May 9, 2016).

Beauchamp, T. L., and J. F. Childress. 2009. *Principles of biomedical ethics*, 6th ed. New York, NY: Oxford University Press.

Beauchamp, T. L., and J. F. Childress. 2013. *Principles of biomedical ethics*, 7th ed. New York, NY: Oxford University Press.

Kant, I., M. J. Gregor, and J. Timmermann. 2012. *Groundwork of the metaphysics of morals*, Cambridge, UK: Cambridge University Press.

Lasagna, L. 1964. Hippocratic oath, modern version. Available at: http://www.aapsonline.org/ethics/oaths.htm

COMMENTARY 1.5.2: THE POTENTIALLY HIGH COST OF A FREE CLINICAL TRIAL

ELIZABETH HEITMAN

Despite the rarity of the disease in question and the patient's status as an undocumented immigrant, the primary ethical challenges in this case reflect complex phenomena that affect most medical care and clinical research in the United States. For the research ethics consultant, the most pressing of these issues are the financial and social barriers that limit access to medical care, divergent perspectives among members of the multidisciplinary care team, and the subtle power of the therapeutic misconception.

The appropriate use of BMT for many hematologic cancers, including myelofibrosis, remains a source of ethical debate because of its extraordinary financial cost, its intense and often protracted physical burden, and its relatively low survival rate (Experts in Chronic Myeloid Leukemia 2013; Himmelstein et al. 2009). Nonetheless, the hematology–oncology team likely would have offered BMT soon after diagnosis if the patient had had comprehensive insurance or the personal wealth to fund the procedures and the lifelong posttransplant drug regimen. If a related donor were not readily available, his physicians probably would have sought a nonrelated donor through the National Marrow Donor Program (https://bethematch.org). However, it appears that the team has not even mentioned BMT to the patient in the three weeks since admission, most probably because they understood the intervention to be financially inaccessible to him. Instead, the palliative care service has been consulted for a shift to comfort measures and home hospice care.

There is general consensus that physicians have no ethical obligations to offer treatments of limited effectiveness, including available clinical trials, especially when such intervention also imposes high physical burden, likelihood of suffering, and financial costs (American Thoracic Society Ad Hoc

Committee on Futile and Potentially Inappropriate Care 2015). However, following a life-threatening diagnosis, it is also best practice for physicians to talk with the patient and family about goals of care and recommended options, including why some interventions are not recommended or are not truly options (Bernacki and Block 2014). While the team's initial decision not to discuss BMT may have seemed like a compassionate response to the patient's insurmountable financial barriers to treatment, the discovery of the clinical trial and possible "free" treatment highlights the paternalism of that unilateral decision. Moreover, raising the possibility of a clinical trial with BMT at this late date would likely introduce the therapeutic misconception into the patient's assessment of BMT's benefits and burdens: *Why would the team offer the possibility of BMT now if they did not recommend it before? Surely, entering the trial must be in my best interests.*

A central task for the research ethics consultant is to help the multidisciplinary members of the care team identify their common goals of care for this patient and how the clinical trial fits or does not fit within them. Up to this point, the financial inaccessibility of BMT has apparently helped to bridge the divergent professional perspectives of the multidisciplinary care team on the goals of care. Now, however, before raising the possibility of the study with the patient and his family, the multidisciplinary caregivers need to come to a common understanding of what is truly involved in the trial and whether it changes their previous assessment.

Over the past two decades, ethicists and regulators have increasingly emphasized the need for clinical investigators to disclose the full financial costs of participating in a clinical trial as part of the study's informed consent process (U.S. Department of Health and Human Services 1998; Wong et al. 2016). Not only will such consideration be essential to the ethics of this study's enrollment process, but also the current care team needs to appreciate the significant expenses and logistical demands that the patient and his family will encounter in order just to be evaluated for eligibility. While the hematology fellow appears to have resolved concerns about the costs of HLA testing through a private charity, many other expenses will need to be met before the patient can qualify for the trial. The research ethics consultant should encourage the team, especially the fellow advocating for the clinical trial, to identify these other likely financial and logistical hurdles, together with any possible sources of support or means to overcome them. Only then can a comprehensive calculation of benefits and burdens begin. For example, the team will need to consider and seek answers to the following set of questions:

- What costs would the patient, together with a required family caregiver and potential sibling donor, incur in traveling to the study site, as well as for housing, meals, and ground transportation during the study?
- Although the patient appears stable enough to be discharged for palliative care at home, will the 900-mile journey require expensive medical transport?
- If the patient should become significantly sicker while at the study hospital, what might it cost for other family members already in the United States to be with him in his final days?
- If he should die during the study, what will it cost to transport his body for burial, either back to his U.S. home or to his native country?
- If one of the siblings in Central America is the best match, does he or she have a passport? If not, how long will it take to get one, and at what cost?
- How long will it take to get a medical visa for travel to the United States, and what costs will be incurred in that process, including application fees and travel to their country's U.S. embassy for an interview?
- Can the sibling leave work and family for the time it may take to be evaluated for the study and, if suitable, donate marrow? If so, how much will he or she lose in unpaid wages?

Moreover, as undocumented immigrants who speak no English, the patient and his wife—and his potential donor sibling in Texas—are at higher risk for detection, detention, and even deportation if they travel long distances into an unfamiliar environment. Hospitals have no legal duty to report unauthorized immigrants, but the need to present identification in commercial and even private travel may result in the patient's interception outside the hospital. Not only would detention eliminate the possibility of the patient taking part in the study, but it would also likely interrupt even his basic palliative care. An investigation by immigration officials would also likely reveal any other members of the patient's family not authorized to be in the United States. The cost of legal representation, if available, could be staggering.

Once the medical team has clarified its recommendations about the trial and can present them in practical terms of benefits, costs, and burdens, the patient and his family need to be brought into the discussion. Not only does shared decision making respect the patient's individual autonomy, but also the patient's and family's own knowledge of their personal resources, limitations, and values is an essential element in the larger assessment of available treatment options. And even if ultimately the medical team is unwilling to recommend the BMT trial, both they and the patient and his family may find comfort in knowing they have evaluated and rejected that option, and go home reassured that their plan for hospice care is the best choice from among everything available (American Thoracic Society Ad Hoc Committee on Futile and Potentially Inappropriate Care 2015; Bernacki and Block 2014).

References

American Thoracic Society Ad Hoc Committee on Futile and Potentially Inappropriate Care. 2015. Responding to requests for potentially inappropriate treatments in intensive care units. *American Journal of Respiratory and Critical Care Medicine* 191(11):1318–30.

Bernacki, R. E., and S. D. Block, for the American College of Physicians High Value Care Task Force. 2014. Communication about serious illness care goals: A review and synthesis of best practices. *JAMA Internal Medicine* 174(12):1994–2003.

Experts in Chronic Myeloid Leukemia. 2013. The price of drugs for chronic myeloid leukemia (CML) is a reflection of the unsustainable prices of cancer drugs: From the perspective of a large group of CML experts. *Blood* 121(22):4439–42.

Himmelstein, D. U., D. Thorne, E. Warren, and S. Woolhandler. 2009. Medical bankruptcy in the United States, 2007: Results of a national study. *American Journal of Medicine* 122(8):741–46.

U.S. Department of Health and Human Services, Office for Human Research Protections. 1998. Informed consent checklist. Available at: http://www.hhs.gov/ohrp/regulations-and-policy/guidance/checklists/index.html

Wong, Y.-N., M. D. Schluchter, and T. L. Albrecht, et al. 2016. Financial concerns about participation in clinical trials among patients with cancer. *Journal of Clinical Oncology* 34(5):2463–78.

COMMENTARY 1.5.3: CONTEXTUALIZING "CHOICE" FOR UNDOCUMENTED IMMIGRANTS IN U.S. CLINICAL TRIALS RESEARCH

NANCY J. BURKE

This consultation about the ethics of offering a clinical trial to an undocumented and uninsured immigrant with a diagnosis of myelofibrosis raises two primary questions. One is posed by the case presentation: Should the patient and his wife be informed of the trial? And the second is a larger question of how we understand and mobilize "choice" in oncology, and how patients' life history and social context are incorporated into care.

In her 2008 book, philosopher Annemarie Mol took on the troubling issue of patient-centered medicine. Through a close reading of the daily interactions, challenges, and clinical practices involved in diabetes care, she distinguished between the "logic of choice" and the "logic of care." In the following, I draw upon this work to delineate different aspects of the patient–care matrix evoked in this case. Specifically, I unravel concerns related to the patient as consumer of medical care and the patient as living subject and part of a collective.

According to Mol, the "logic of choice" builds upon the value of information and the delivery of value-free information. It holds individuals as autonomous subjects able to weigh risks and benefits, to hear information presented by providers, and to make appropriate decisions. But, Mol asked, in any situation in which dire outcomes and the loss of health are the likely results of a choice, is any information really value-free? And in this case, is it appropriate to ignore the social reality of the patient—an undocumented Central American migrant with no health insurance, low English proficiency, little experience with the U.S. healthcare system, and a family support system that spans national borders and therefore is subject to immigration delays? Each of these aspects of the patient's life presents challenges to receiving and understanding the gravity of his diagnosis of myelofibrosis and the lack of cure for the disease, let alone understanding differences between standard care and experimental treatment.

The "situations of choice" present in this case counter clear action. While informed choice may be a great ideal, it is only so in situations where people are actually able to make their own choices. When they are patients, people often lack this ability (Mol 2006, 7). For the hematology fellow, locating a clinical trial that will accept this patient is a coup both for the patient and for his medical center, as recruitment of minority and medically underserved patients into clinical research has been a priority of the U.S. National Cancer Institute for the last 20-plus years (Epstein 2008). It also fulfills the noted oncological imperative to sustain hope as long as possible for the patient and his family (Del Vecchio Good et al. 1994). The patient is medically eligible and therefore, according to the logic of choice, should be informed of this option. Then he and his wife, as responsible consumers of medical care (though without the resources to choose what to consume), can make the choice of the best course of action for themselves. The information, according to this logic, is value-free. It is their (patient's and wife's) responsibility to consider their own values when digesting the information. The situations of choice include the scientific imperative as one context, and the reality of poverty, lack of legal status, and no follow-up care as the other. The values, perspectives, and priorities of each lead one to a very different choice, and result in the destabilization of what should be an opportunity to provide care to a suffering patient and family.

Mol highlighted situations of choice in order to identify the parameters of a logic of care. A logic of care attends less to information and more to practice, to actions that become a part of the patient's daily living and that fit within that life. The logic of care posits patients as part of a collective. The collective here is the patient's wife and potential donor matches, who would have to apply for visas, cover travel costs, and cover living expenses and any additional healthcare expenses incurred as a result of the procedure. If informed of the possibility, one can assume that they would likely agree to do this for their family member in the hope that the procedure would extend his life. In this case, the life extension is very short and the potential impact on other lives is great. Once they know, once the collective has been given the value-free information that they could extend their family member's life, it becomes their responsibility. If they refuse, his death also becomes their responsibility (Kaufman 2015).

Within the logic of care, the clinical trial in this case does not represent a choice. Rather, offering participation in the trial would further complicate an already fraught situation in which low English proficiency, lack of experience with the U.S. healthcare system, and low health literacy likely undermine effective communication. Especially important in clinical trials communications is the relationship between therapeutic misconception—the conflation of treatment with the experimental aims of research—and health literacy, the latter defined as "the cognitive and social skills which determine the motivation and ability of individuals to gain access to, understand, and use information in ways which promote and maintain good health" (World Health Organization [WHO] 1998). Only 12% of the U.S. population is estimated to have adequate health literacy (U.S. Department of Health and Human Services 2016). Those with low health literacy are particularly at risk for misunderstanding a cancer diagnosis, its treatment, and what clinical trials have to offer (e.g., therapeutic misconception). Furthermore, the uninsured and undocumented status of this patient undercuts equitable engagement; if one is on the receiving end of charity care, one is less likely to question the options presented.

The question posed by the consultation focuses on the discrete choice of whether or not to provide a financially, linguistically, and socially disadvantaged terminal cancer patient the choice to participate in a clinical trial. This consideration is linked to the larger question of the trial design and how it might fit into a logic of care, despite its experimental aims. The 1993 National Institutes of Health (NIH) Inclusion Act mandated equitable inclusion of women and ethnic minorities in clinical research in the United States. Millions of dollars since have been devoted to understanding the best ways to recruit patients into trials, but the majority of this research has focused on patient attitudes, fears, and misconceptions (Epstein 2008). What has not been addressed is the need for changes in clinical trial design that accommodate the different life contexts of medically underserved and ethnic minority patients. These include accommodations for those "outside" the healthcare system, without adequate health insurance or financial resources to support trial participation at a distance; ensuring cultural and linguistic competence of trial coordinators (translating 18-page consent forms is not enough); and providing resources for caregivers who form the patient's collective, among other considerations.

Offering participation in a clinical trial to this family undermines a logic of care by offering them a constrained moment of hope within the knowledge (of those doing the offering) of ultimate failure. Unless travel and living expenses related to trial participation and follow-up supportive care are covered by the trial sponsor, this patient should not be considered a candidate.

References

Del Vecchio Good, M. J., T. Munakata, Y. Kobayashi, C. Mattingly, and B. J. Good. 1994. Oncology and narrative time. *Social Science and Medicine* 38:855–62.

Epstein, S. 2008. The rise of 'recruitmentology' clinical research, racial knowledge, and the politics of inclusion and difference. *Social Studies of Science* 38:801–32.

Kaufman, S. 2015. *Ordinary medicine: Extraordinary treatments, longer lives, and where to draw the line*, Durham, NC: Duke University Press.

Mol, A. M. 2006. *The logic of care: Health and the problem of patient choice*, New York, NY: Routledge.

U.S. Department of Health and Human Services. 2016. Health literacy fact sheet. Available at: http://health.gov/communication/literacy/quickguide/factsbasic.htm (accessed April 24, 2016).

World Health Organization (WHO). 1998. *Division of health promotion, education and communications health education and health promotion unit. health promotion glossary*. Geneva, Switzerland: World Health Organization. Available at: http://www.who.int/healthpromotion/about/HPR%20Glossary%201998.pdf

CASE 1.6: A RANDOMIZED TRIAL OF RAPAMYCIN TO INCREASE LONGEVITY AND HEALTH SPAN IN COMPANION ANIMALS: NAVIGATING THE BOUNDARY BETWEEN PROTECTIONS FOR ANIMAL RESEARCH AND HUMAN SUBJECTS RESEARCH

INTRODUCTION

Rapamycin is FDA approved as an immune-suppressive and anticancer drug and is routinely used as an anti-rejection drug in transplants (Li, Kim, and Blenis 2014). Rapamycin has also been extensively studied in rodents, where there is evidence that it extends lifespan and prolongs length of optimal health, including the delay of age-related declines in kidney, heart, muscle, immune, and cognitive function as well as reducing cancers and bone loss (An et al. 2017; Johnson et al. 2015). There is similar evidence that rapamycin can improve heart function in middle-aged dogs, and several clinical trials are underway to determine whether rapamycin can increase survival in dogs diagnosed with cancer (Larson et al. 2016; Urfer et al. 2017).

A study team has developed a research agenda to understand the biological and environmental causes of aging by studying middle-aged companion dogs. The scientific premise is that the anticipated findings can advance the understanding of the aging process in humans. As mentioned above, one study in dogs suggests that rapamycin can delay age-related cardiac dysfunction during aging (Urfer et al. 2017), as one potential mechanism for increased longevity. Since rapamycin is commercially available, some dog owners have expressed interest and even sought it out for their dogs outside the context of clinical research.

Accompanying the case summary are three commentaries. Cheryl Abbate from the University of Colorado concludes that it is ethically justifiable, under certain conditions, to expose companion dogs to risk, and she proposes a set of key information that canine guardians must have in order to make an informed decision about enrollment. Rebecca L. Walker and Jill A. Fisher from the University of North Carolina at Chapel Hill use this case to identify and consider three ethical concerns given the limitations of applying the standard approach to the review and oversight of laboratory animal research to research with companion animals and their guardians. Benjamin Wilfond and Kathryn Porter from Seattle Children's Hospital, along with Kate E. Creevy from Texas A&M University and Matt Kaeberlein and Daniel Promislow from the University of Washington, consider whether the regulatory framework for pediatric research is a useful starting place for both researchers and those charged with oversight for companion animal research.

CASE SUMMARY

One component of the proposed research agenda is an intervention trial of approximately 600 dogs to assess the impact of rapamycin on canine longevity and health span. For the intervention trial, the team would recruit approximately 600 healthy, middle-aged dogs (after an assessment based on laboratory and echocardiography screening that they are free of detectable diseases) for a three-year randomized, placebo-controlled trial. As there is no information available about potential side effects from rapamycin in dogs in advance of the study, the investigators will be concerned primarily about those they would expect to see in humans, including the potential for increased risk of infection and side effects such as mouth sores, gastrointestinal distress, increased blood glucose and lipids, and impaired wound healing. One potential ethical concern regards the goals of research around extending longevity and health span (in dogs and, by extension, in people) and whether this is an important enough research question to justify funding and support.

A second concern regards the appropriateness of the intervention trial and how to assess if the dog's participation is ethically appropriate. Is our standard approach to animal welfare for laboratory-based animal research sufficient, or does our approach to human subject research offer additional guidance for review and oversight? How should we consider our obligations to the dog owners? How should we consider the potential for direct benefit and harm to the dogs?

REFERENCES

An, J. Y., E. K. Quarles, S. Mekvanich, et al. 2017. Rapamycin treatment attenuates age-associated periodontitis in mice. *GeroScience* 39(4):457–63.

Johnson, S. C., M. Sangesland, M. Kaeberlein, and P. S. Rabinovitch. 2015. Modulating mTOR in aging and health. Interdisciplinary Topics in Gerontology 40:107–27.

Larson, J. C., S. D. Allstadt, and T. M. Fan, et al. 2016. Pharmacokinetics of orally administered low-dose rapamycin in healthy dogs. *American Journal of Veterinary Research* 77(1):65–71.

Li, J., S. G. Kim, and J. Blenis. 2014. Rapamycin: One drug, many effects. *Cell Metabolism* 19(3):373–9.

Urfer, S. R., T. L. Kaeberlein, and S. Mailheau, et al. 2017. A randomized controlled trial to establish effects of short-term rapamycin treatment in 24 middle-aged companion dogs. *Geroscience* 39(1):43–127.

COMMENTARY 1.6.1: RAPAMYCIN: RISKING HARM FOR CANINE LONGEVITY

CHERYL ABBATE

Because the average life expectancy of a dog (10–13 years) is so much shorter than the average human lifespan, most canine guardians desire that their dogs live longer (healthy) lives. Scientists are therefore looking into ways to extend canine lives. The proposed study in this case concerns the testing of the drug rapamycin in dogs, which researchers suspect may promote not only canine longevity but also canine *health span*. It should be emphasized that the goal of the study is not to extend low-quality older years—it's aimed at extending the healthy period of canine lives. For instance, it's suspected that rapamycin may delay the onset of age-related cardiac dysfunction, which means that dogs who are given rapamycin could live longer lives and remain optimally healthy while doing so.

The proposed rapamycin research differs significantly from standard animal research, which often subjects animals to excruciating pain and suffering, confines animals to small and artificial research facilities for the duration of their lives, and ends with the death of animal subjects when they are no longer useful to researchers (Garrett 2012). The dogs used in the rapamycin study presumably will not be confined to research labs, as the "recruited" canine participants will already have both "owners" and homes, and the dogs will not be killed when the study is complete.

Based on the expected rapamycin side effects in humans, the researchers suspect that canine participants may experience the following mild side effects: "mouth sores, gastrointestinal distress, increased blood glucose and lipids, and impaired wound healing." The case study also points out that rapamycin has been extensively studied in rodents and that there is evidence that it prolongs the length of optimal rodent health. Yet information gained from research on rodents and humans cannot be reliably extrapolated to dogs. And the information gained from research on dogs cannot be reliably extrapolated to humans, as some medications that are deemed safe for one species often have harmful effects in others (Greek and Greek 2000). Thus, if one goal of this research is to extend longevity and health span in humans, as the case study suggests, the researchers ought to consider different research methods to achieve this goal.

Setting aside questions about the transferability of information gained to humans, because the rapamycin study will force a potentially harmful drug into the body of a healthy animal, those who "own" dogs might, on ethical grounds, hesitate to enroll their dogs in this study. Yet acts that put canines at risk aren't always impermissible. After all, when it comes to making decisions about the well-being of companion animals, animal guardians must make trade-offs quite frequently. Those who live with cats often confine them to the indoors, at least in the evenings, in order to protect them from larger predators. Essentially, cat guardians cause the harm of confinement in order to extend feline lives. When our companion animals become sick, they are often given lifesaving (and thus life-extending) medications that carry the risk of uncomfortable side effects. Exposing our companion animals to risk of harm in an attempt to extend their lives is, under certain conditions, justifiable.

Efforts to advance veterinarian medicine are often made to save (and thus extend) the lives of companion animals when they become sick or injured. If it's important to develop and use medications and technologies to treat illnesses in our nonhuman companions after they've occurred, it's hard to see why researching medication that will prevent illness from occurring in the first place is not important enough to justify funding and support, even if the research is challenging, expensive, and time-consuming. With the development of both treatment medication and preventative drugs, the end is the same: the extension of lives.

In the United States alone, 89.7 million dogs live in households (American Pet Products Association 2018). Because 89.7 million dogs and their human companions stand to benefit significantly from rapamycin research, the goal of the proposed study is certainly worthwhile. But even so, this does not mean that any *method* used to achieve the goal is thereby justified. In this case, researchers should consider investigating the potential side effects of rapamycin in dogs through the use of microdosing technology, in silico technology, or tests on dog tissues in vitro, which may provide important information about how rapamycin will be absorbed and metabolized by dogs, before the proposed rapamycin study is conducted (Engel 2012). Only after such tests have been conducted should the rapamycin study begin.

Because dogs cannot consent to participate in this research, canine guardians must give informed consent on their behalf. For their consent to be informed, they should, at the very least, receive the following information:

1. *Information about the possibility of benefits*: Participants should be given an accurate projection of the likelihood that their dog will personally benefit from the trial.
2. *Information about the possibility of no benefits*: As the case study reports, some canine guardians have expressed interest in rapamycin and actively sought it out for their dogs. Presumably, they desire that their canines participate in the study because they want their dogs to receive rapamycin; thus, it ought to be emphasized that not every dog in the trial will receive rapamycin and that their dog may receive placebo pills.
3. *Information about side effects*: Participants should be told (1) how likely it is that their dogs will experience negative side effects, and (2) how long the side effects are likely to last.
4. *Information about the dosing and duration of rapamycin and how this informs the risk assessment*: Participants should know the exact dose of rapamycin that will be given to the dogs and how frequently it needs to be administered. If the dose and frequency of rapamycin administration carry increased risks, this should be made clear.
5. *Clarification about prior studies*: Some people may attempt to enroll their canines in the study because they're aware of the Dog Aging Project's first rapamycin study, which reported no clinical side effects of rapamycin in dogs (Urfer et al. 2017). However, this study was only 10 weeks long and there were only 24 canine participants. Researchers ought to emphasize that the side effects observed in this small, short-term study are not strong indicators of the possible side effects dogs might experience in a three-year rapamycin study.
6. *Information about the danger of extrapolation in research*: Although low doses of rapamycin seem to have only rare, mild adverse reactions in mice and humans, researchers ought to explain that medications that are safe for humans or mice might have very harmful consequences for dogs.

7. *Information about the monitoring procedures*: The participants should be informed of the monitoring procedures that are part of the protocol and how often the dogs must undergo "checkups." They should be made aware of the harms that the dogs might endure when researchers periodically assess them throughout the study.

One final question that is asked in the case study is this: Could the approach to research on human subjects offer better guidance than the standard approach to animal welfare for laboratory-based animal research? From an ethical perspective, one wonders why this question arises only in discussions about research on companion animals, and not in discourse about research on other sentient creatures, like rats and mice, who are just as capable of suffering as are dogs. These researchers ought to use the approach used in research on humans, not because dogs deserve special protection, but because they are sentient, and researchers ought to give equal weight to the interests of all sentient animals used in research.

References

American Pet Products Association. 2018. Pet Industry Market Size & Ownership Statistics. Available at: http://www.americanpetproducts.org/press_industrytrends.asp (accessed May 5, 2018).

Engel, M. 2012. The Commonsense Case Against Animal Research. *The ethics of animal research*. Edited by J. Garrett. Cambridge, MA: MIT Press, pp. 215–36.

Garrett, J. ed. 2012. *The ethics of animal research*, Cambridge, MA: MIT Press.

Greek, C., and J. Greek. 2000. *Sacred cows and golden geese: The human cost of experimenting on animals*, New York: Continuum.

Urfer, S., T. Kaeberlein, and S. Mailheau, et al. 2017. A randomized controlled trial to establish effects of short-term rapamycin treatment in 24 middle-aged companion dogs. *Geroscience* 39(2):117–27.

COMMENTARY 1.6.2: COMPANION ANIMAL STUDIES: SLIPPING THROUGH A RESEARCH OVERSIGHT GAP

REBECCA L. WALKER AND JILL A. FISHER

In human subject research ethics, we appeal to principles of respect for persons, beneficence, and justice. In laboratory animal studies, the three Rs (reduce, refine, and replace) are key touchstones, along with an overarching principle of promoting animal welfare—when consistent with the needs of science and within the constraints introduced by the institutional setting. Underlying these different approaches to research oversight are moral status assumptions regarding human and nonhuman animals. Independently of whether appeals to moral status are a specious mechanism to differentiate the two research contexts, there are important structural differences in how the research is typically conducted: in an animal "confinement" facility where conditions are controlled and consent need not be sought, versus with human participants in society whose consent and active compliance are critical.

The featured companion animal longevity study (CALS) falls in a liminal space between these human and nonhuman animal practices and highlights the ethical tensions produced by compartmentalizing these two domains of research oversight. As nonhuman animals in research, dogs are typically regulated by laboratory animal oversight. However, the study's structural features to test the efficacy of rapamycin in increasing dogs' longevity and "health span" more closely reflect those of human clinical trials. While some institutions require additional ethical oversight of companion animal studies (Hampshire 2003), this is a relatively ad hoc solution to the oversight problem. We identify here several particular ethical concerns with CALS that raise important questions about companion animal studies more generally.

In the United States, oversight of animal research is typically conducted by institutional animal care and use committees (IACUCs), which are mandated both by the Animal Welfare Act and by the Public Health Service. Yet, this oversight structure generally contains features that may limit the protections that animals receive (Walker 2006). Most relevant for CALS, IACUC review, unlike in human subject research, does not require a risk–benefit analysis of individual animal research protocols (Carbone 2014). While federal funding mechanisms require assessment of the science value of the research, this is not the same as balancing potential (or actual) harms to animals with proposed benefit to animals and humans. Furthermore, for studies that are funded by private sources—as studies like CALS are likely to be—even an impartial science value assessment may be missing. Similarly, the FDA's Center for Veterinary Medicine (CVM) requires evidence of a "rational basis" to undertake companion animal clinical trials (Hampshire 2003, 193) and subsequent reporting of any adverse experiences, but this also does not amount to a risk–benefit analysis. Furthermore, it is unclear from the case description whether CALS falls under CVM oversight, which is applicable when drug sponsors seek approval for a new animal drug application.

An important ethical question for CALS, then, is whether an impartial analysis would determine that the risks to the study dogs are justified by the potential for benefit to these animals, other animals, and/or society generally. Leaving aside larger social questions of the value of longevity research, we may focus on the concrete harms and benefits at issue in this study. Because the dogs proposed for inclusion are healthy, the analogue risk assessment in human trials would set a higher bar for acceptable risks. It would also warrant independent data and safety monitoring to ensure that participants are protected from unnecessary harm and that objective criteria determine rules for the study's discontinuation should harms prove unacceptable. While the CALS case presentation states that there is "no information" available about potential adverse effects of rapamycin in dogs, it is more correct to say that such information is limited. Studies have shown severe adverse effects in dogs, including death, with high dosage (aimed at immune suppression), but rapamycin has been well tolerated at low doses for up to 10 weeks (Larson et al. 2016; Urfer et al. 2017). As CALS is a three-year intervention, it is all the more crucial within a risk–benefit analysis to consider how and when to withdraw dogs or to stop the entire trial should safety concerns emerge (or, for that matter, clear evidence of drug benefit). Human trials are a much better guide than is laboratory animal practice for setting "humane endpoints" to companion animal studies, since laboratory practices typically dictate euthanasia as the appropriate endpoint.

On the benefits side of the calculus, CALS's aim of increased health span in particular, while raising the specter of enhancement, potentially offers individual direct benefit (avoiding disability in dogs' older years) alongside a hope of meaningful benefit to other companion animals and, eventually, humans. The animals' guardians (legally "owners"), too, might benefit by facing fewer veterinary costs for and/or gaining more time with their dogs. Yet it is important to recall that although rapamycin is an approved immune-suppressive and anticancer drug in human medicine, it has not been FDA approved either for veterinary use or for the off-label use of increasing longevity and health span in either humans or companion animals.

Although laboratory animal research in the United States could offer risk (or harm)–benefit analysis as a regular part of its oversight (as occurs in the European Union), this would not close the gap in regard to companion animal research. Specifically, there is little room in the framework of conventional animal research oversight to account for other ethical considerations that make companion animal research structurally more like human clinical trials. For example, because biomedical research institutions "own" their laboratory animals, no outside consent to research participation is sought. In any companion animal study, however, there should be a robust consent process involving the guardians of the animals.

As part of a consent process in a study like CALS, many of the ethical complexities typical to human subject research will arise. The potentials for both therapeutic misconception and undue inducement are significant, particularly if investigators emphasize that rapamycin is already FDA approved for human use. While the notion of a therapeutic misconception is perhaps odd for healthy dogs, the animals' guardians, despite the lack of evidence, may expect a longevity benefit. Moreover, such a perception may result from the (perhaps unwitting) enthusiasm of the investigators. The potential for undue inducement arises because of the high cost of commercially available rapamycin combined with insufficient attention to the likely risk of harms. Relatedly, borrowing from a human subject framework, CALS might also be said to require a plan for posttrial provision of the study drug. At the conclusion of the three-year period, if enrolled dogs have benefited from rapamycin, provision of this expensive drug is important to consider, particularly for those dogs randomized to the placebo group.

Important ethical considerations raised in CALS reveal the inadequacy of the system of laboratory animal research oversight to protect companion animals and their guardians. These are significant concerns, particularly when coupled with the science value question of whether CALS's enhancement orientation and health span gains should even be perceived as potential medical benefits. Leaving contentious social issues of enhancement aside, CALS illuminates a gap between the oversight of laboratory animal and human subject research. What is the rationale, we might wonder, of two separate oversight systems based on unstated moral status assumptions, rather than a unified system that attends to structural factors in the science and offers respect for all subjects?

References

Carbone, L. 2014. Justification for the Use of Animals. *The IACUC handbook*. Edited by J. M. A. Silverman, S. Suckow, and Murthy. Boca Raton, FL: CRC Press, pp. 211.

Hampshire, V. A. 2003. Regulatory issues surrounding the use of companion animals in clinical investigations, trials, and studies. *ILAR Journal* 44(3):191–6.

Larson, J. C., S. D. Allstadt, T. M. Fan, et al. 2016. Pharmacokinetics of orally administered low-dose rapamycin in healthy dogs. *American Journal of Veterinary Research* 77(1):65–71.

Urfer, S. R., T. L. Kaeberlein, S. Mailheau, et al. 2017. A randomized controlled trial to establish effects of short-term rapamycin treatment in 24 middle-aged companion dogs. *Geroscience* 39(2):117–27.

Walker, R. L. 2006. Human and animal subjects of research: The moral significance of respect versus welfare. *Theoretical Medicine and Bioethics* 27(4):305–31.

COMMENTARY 1.6.3: RESEARCH TO PROMOTE LONGEVITY AND HEALTH SPAN IN COMPANION DOGS: A PEDIATRIC PERSPECTIVE

BENJAMIN S. WILFOND, KATHRYN M. PORTER, KATE E. CREEVY, MATT KAEBERLEIN, AND DANIEL PROMISLOW

This proposed rapamycin trial in companion dogs raises the question of the social value of research designed to increase healthy lifespan (or "health span") in animals. Concerns have been raised about the appropriateness of promoting "longevity" as a goal of the research. This broad question is enduring and is related to the distinction between health and disease and the goals of medicine. It evokes a recurrent theme in literature from Wilde (*The Picture of Dorian Gray*) to Thomas ("Do not go gentle into that good night") about our acceptance of aging. While it is beyond the scope of this commentary to explore this concern in detail, we think that efforts to extend the duration of healthy life of humans and companion animals through the prevention and treatment of conditions of aging, including cardiovascular disease, cancer, and immune decline, are suitable goals for medicine. Of course, another complementary goal of medicine is also to assist patients and families making deliberative choices toward the end of life, and appreciating that death, while often tragic and sad, is part of what makes us human (or canine, as the case may be).

The case also raises the question about the appropriateness of the dogs' participation. While the inclusion of animals in research is typically viewed in the context of laboratory-based animal research, the companion dogs in this study are being enrolled as "study participants," making the situation bear striking similarities to pediatric research in which parents enroll their children. The medical care of companion animals and children shares another common feature: Much is done without evidence from randomized controlled trials. Just as there has been an increase in pediatric clinical research over the past decade, there has also been an increase in the availability of clinical trials for companion animals. Most notably this has occurred in oncology, and, as with pediatric medicine, such research is typically done in the context of providing medical care for companion animals. In fact, it is precisely the ongoing use of clinical interventions without evidence that provides the strongest ethical justification for conducting clinical research in both populations. And just as it is important to think deliberately about how best to engage and respect parents when they are asked permission to enroll their young children in clinical research, it is necessary to think deliberately about how best to engage and respect the "owners" when they are asked to give permission to enroll their companion animals in research.

The pediatric research ethics framework

Thus, the framework that has been developed for pediatric research under the federal regulations (Department of Health and Human Services 2005) can be a useful starting place in guiding both researchers and those charged with oversight for companion animal research. A key component of this framework is the concept of parental permission, which is distinct from consent, as it is a decision made by a surrogate on behalf of a participant who cannot make a decision for him- or herself (Katz et al. 2016). A related aspect of this framework is the importance of independent assessments of benefits and risks, before parents are even given an opportunity to give permission (Freedman, Fuks, and Weijer 1993). A third aspect of this framework is the useful distinction between research activities that offer a prospect of direct benefit, and those that are justified on the basis of the advancement of scientific knowledge (Roth-Cline and Nelson 2015).

The proposed rapamycin trial offers a prospect of direct benefit to extend lifespan based on previous animal studies. Within the context of the pediatric regulations, such a study would also have a balance of benefits and risks such that the risks are justified by the anticipated benefits, and such that the balance is as favorable as that provided by available alternative approaches. It is beyond the scope of this commentary to assess the risks and benefits of this trial, other than to suggest that it is plausible for such a trial to meet these criteria.

One challenge for the rapamycin study will be to develop a sound recruitment and permission process. This is especially important given the likely motivation of owners to extend the healthy lifespan of their own companion animal, rather than being motivated to ask their dog to sacrifice for the pursuit of generalizable knowledge. Furthermore, given the natural lifespan of dogs, we can anticipate that a proportion of the enrolled animals will die during the study. This reinforces the importance of developing materials and communication approaches to set realistic expectations. It may also be valuable to empirically evaluate owners' motivations and experiences to inform future recruitment approaches.

Approaches to oversight

Another opportunity to borrow from the world of human subjects' protection is to consider what approaches for independent oversight of clinical trials for companion animals should be used. While the IACUC is an important starting place for oversight for the use of animals in research, IRBs would be involved in this study since data are collected from the owners, making them research subjects themselves. In pediatric research, IRBs also consider not only the interests of children, but also the rights and welfare of the parents as decision makers for their children. However, an IRB would not typically be involved in overseeing how veterinary researchers interact with owners as the surrogate decision makers for their dogs. In this case, since the IRB is already involved because of the data collection from owners, the IRBs could also consider how the researchers interact with the owners as the responsible party for the companion animals.

Having IRBs expand their focus to consider the owners as *in loco parentis* may be useful for those studies designed to offer a prospect of direct benefit and especially when the prospect of direct benefit either is more tenuous or is not the primary goal, as would be the case for Phase I oncology studies or studies like the rapamycin study. The IRB could review recruitment and promotional materials to ensure that the owners have appropriate expectations for the trial.

A data monitoring committee is another important oversight mechanism of clinical research that may play a valuable role here, even though there are not typically external requirements for such an oversight process in companion animal research. Committee members could be selected to have the relevant expertise to assess study design, clinical risks and benefits, statistics, and ethics. Furthermore, the committee would have access to interim data to ensure the appropriate and timely evaluation of adverse events, as well as determining stopping rules for such a trial.

Conclusion

The overarching relevance of the pediatric framework for studies to improve health span in companion animals, as in the rapamycin study, is to consider the impact on the dogs, as well as the indirect impact on owners serving as surrogate decision makers. Researchers should aim to treat both with respect and dignity, and to value their contribution to scientific discovery. Empirical social science research about owners' experiences in this study can advance the evidence base, so that future research can be conducted appropriately.

References

Department of Health and Human Services. 2005. Protection of Human Subjects (The Common Rule): Additional Protections for Children Involved as Subjects in Research. 45 CFR 46.401-409. Available at: https://www.hhs.gov/ohrp/regulations-and-policy/regulations/45-cfr-46/index.html#subpartd (accessed June 6, 2018).

Freedman, B., A. Fuks, and C. Weijer. 1993. In loco parentis. Minimal risk as an ethical threshold for research upon children. *Hastings Center Report* 23(2):13–9.

Katz, A. L., S. A. Webb, and Committee on Bioethics. 2016. Informed consent in decision-making in pediatric practice. *Pediatrics* 138(2):e20161485.

Roth-Cline, M., and R. M. Nelson. 2015. Ethical considerations in conducting pediatric and neonatal research in clinical pharmacology. *Current Pharmaceutical Design* 21(39):5619–35.

Section 2

Respect for participants

HOLLY A. TAYLOR

The principle of respect for participants is a reminder to investigators that their obligations to participants begin prior to enrollment and may not end once the study has completed. The key components of respect for participants noted by Emanuel, Wendler, and Grady (2000) are promoting the well-being of participants, keeping promises to participants about how they will keep private data confidential, voluntariness and respecting a participant's request to withdraw, sharing the aggregate results of research with participants, and assuring that those participants in need of ongoing access to healthcare are referred to an appropriate source of care.

The seven cases in this section, categorized under the principle of respect for participants, are also secondarily categorized under the principles of favorable risk–benefit ratio and/or informed consent. In addition, each of the cases is categorized by the topic of disclosure of research results, and the majority by the topic of clinician and researcher obligations. This is perhaps not surprising, as the obligation to respect participants overlaps with the investigator's commitment to minimizing risks and communicating with participants. Some of the cases deal with the disclosure of research-related information beyond individual results.

CASE 2.1: ETHICAL CONSIDERATIONS FOR UNBLINDING A PARTICIPANT'S ASSIGNMENT TO INTERPRET A RESOLVED ADVERSE EVENT (2018)

Principles: Respect for Participants, Favorable Risk–Benefit Ratio

Topics: Results Disclosure, Clinician and Researcher Obligations, Drugs and Devices, Phase I Trials, Legal and Regulatory Oversight

Values: Trustworthiness, Social Value

In this case, the participant has enrolled in a trial and is seeking information about the treatment to which she was assigned. She experienced a medical complication and wants to understand whether the treatment is in any way responsible for the complication. While not a question about

DOI: 10.1201/9781003335306-3

the disclosure of results in the traditional sense, she wants access to information related to her enrollment that is otherwise not available until the trial is completed. She was aware of the blinding component of the study design upon enrollment. The investigator, also blinded, does not know whether the complication is related to the study treatment. On the other hand, the particular complication was not one the investigators had anticipated, and the complication was treated and resolved. The investigator asked the Data Monitoring Committee (DMC) for permission to unblind the participant's assignment. In other words, the investigator, wearing his clinician "hat," erred on the side of pursuing information that may be in the best interest of their patient. The principle of respect for participants has to be considered and balanced with the potential benefit that may accrue to the participant and whether disclosure may diminish the social value of the overall study.

The first commentary (Shah and Bond, this volume, p. 78) evaluates the case according to U.S. Food and Drug Administration (FDA) guidelines regarding investigational drugs and devices to consider whether unblinding and disclosure are advisable in this case. They review the obligation of the investigator and DMC to assess whether the adverse event was related to the study treatment. They conclude that, given the information shared in the case, unblinding and disclosure are not likely prudent in this case. They also conclude that the informed consent process could be revised to note this potential complication to make future participants aware of the issue. The commentators prioritize the social value of the research as well as promote the trustworthiness of the regulatory process of drug development.

The second commentary (Steel and Danis, this volume, p. 80) sets regulatory concerns aside and focuses on the communication and management of research risk. They describe the obligation of the DMC to manage the knowledge they have about the trial and the participant through a variety of assumptions about the likelihood of the adverse event being related to the study drug as well as the seriousness of the adverse event. They note that the potential relationship of the risk to the study drug as well as how that risk has been minimized also need to be weighed against the scientific value of the study itself. In the end, they conclude similarly to the first commentary that, while the consent form could be revised to alert future participants about this particular risk, the question of disclosure to the participant must be weighed against any negative consequences the disclosure may have to the value of the study.

The third commentary (Quittell, this volume, p. 82) first describes the importance of blinding to control bias but that traditionally a blind may be broken when doing so is in the best interest of the participant. She covers some of the points made in the first commentary about the process by which adverse events ought to be investigated in compliance with FDA guidance and notes that, while the investigator may want to disclose to satisfy the participant's desire, it is the DMC that is the arbiter of whether unblinding is warranted. While she concludes that, given the case as described, disclosure is not warranted, she notes that not disclosing can have negative consequences for how others perceive the trustworthiness of the research enterprise if the participant publicizes her frustration if the information is not shared with her.

There is a clear consensus among the commentators that, while the participant deserves respect, there is a trade-off between the desires of the participant (and, in this case, the investigator on behalf of the participant) and the integrity of the scientific enterprise and preserving the social value of this particular trial.

CASE 2.2: SHOULD RESEARCH PARTICIPANTS BE NOTIFIED ABOUT RESULTS OF CURRENTLY UNKNOWN BUT POTENTIAL SIGNIFICANCE? (2019)

Principles: Respect for Participants, Favorable Risk–Benefit Ratio, Informed Consent

Topics: Results Disclosure, Clinician and Researcher Obligations, Drugs and Devices

Values: Trustworthiness, Social Value

The investigator is conducting a study of the deposition of a common contrast agent used during magnetic resonance imaging (MRI). The study population is healthy volunteers who have been exposed to the agent multiple times while enrolled in previous research protocols. The study is in response to an FDA Communication noting the lack of safety information beyond the nephrotoxic effects among those with kidney failure. The goal of the study is to systematically assess whether increased exposure to the agent predicts an increased risk of adverse clinical effects. The question in this case is whether research results indicating the levels of contrast deposition among participants who join the study should be communicated to them.

The first commentary (Brown, this volume, p. 86) argues that research participants should be asked whether they want to receive information about contrast deposition as it may, at least, inform future decisions they make about joining trials using the same contrast agent. It is respectful to the participant to allow them to decide about future exposure whether or not this study (or a future study) concludes that contrast deposition is clinically harmful.

The second commentary (Huang, Bandettini, and Danis, this volume, p. 88) agrees that respect for participants favors giving participants the option of receiving information about their personal level of contrast deposition as disclosure, as the information may influence future decisions (i.e., they can opt out if they would prefer). They conclude that special attention to the informed consent process is warranted given the current, uncertain clinical significance of contrast deposition. Research participants should be informed that there is no evidence of adverse clinical effects at this time.

The final commentary (Hutchinson, Capron, and Doussau, this volume, p. 90) concurs with the two previous commentaries and adds that the investigators should share aggregate results with the participants once the study is completed.

There is a clear consensus among the commentators that results of tests with uncertain significance should be shared with participants.

CASE 2.3: THE ETHICS OF CONTACTING FAMILY MEMBERS OF A SUBJECT IN A GENETIC RESEARCH STUDY TO RETURN RESULTS FOR AN AUTOSOMAL DOMINANT SYNDROME (2013)

Principles: Respect for Participants, Favorable Risk–Benefit Ratio

Topics: Results Disclosure, Clinician and Researcher Obligations, Genetics, Family Impact, Privacy, Legal and Regulatory Oversight

Values: None

In this case, the investigator's objective was to identify genetic mutations responsible for a unique syndrome. Having successfully done so, the investigators sought help in navigating what they owe those related to the original cohort, some of whom are currently at risk of developing a preventable, treatable disease and/or may also be considering reproductive options. As with the cases above, this case places the investigator in the position of both investigator and clinician. The dilemma is how to balance respect for participants (some of whom are deceased), as planned and documented in the informed consent process (in which disclosure to family members was not mentioned), with consideration of the risks and benefits of tracking down family members and offering them access to potentially life-altering information.

The first commentary (Shah et al., this volume, p. 94) notes there is general agreement that clinicians have an obligation to provide genetic results to relatives when the results are clinically actionable, and this obligation has to be balanced with the duty to respect the confidentiality of information they have about their patients. They agree that this pair of obligations are also relevant in the context of research. They conclude that, even if they had an indication that a now-deceased participant had strong feelings about keeping their genetic information private, the potential benefits of disclosure for their relatives outweigh the participant's right to privacy. As it relates to original cohort members who are still alive, the commentators note that the disclosure ought to be done with the participant's permission and handled respectfully, but also note that a duty to warn may override the participant's desire to keep their genetic information private.

The second commentary (Rothstein, this volume, p. 96) brings a legal lens to the case. Dealing first with what to do in cases where the research participant has died, according to the HIPAA Privacy Rule, the investigator must first find the "personal representative" of the participant to propose disclosure to genetic relatives of the participant. From this point, the commentator agrees with the first set of commentators that the potential benefit to genetic relatives may outweigh the desire of the former research participant or their personal representative to protect the privacy of the genetic information.

The final commentary (Milner, Liu, and Garrison, this volume, p. 98) analyzes the case from a different perspective. While they agree that the disclosure of results to genetic relatives may result in some benefit, the strength of the investigator's obligation to facilitate the disclosure depends on the strength of the relationship between the investigator and the original research participant. They conclude that if the relationship between the investigator and research participant is based only on the participant's enrollment in the trial, the investigator has no obligation to disclose the results to genetic relatives. They argue that the investigator's obligation is to the research enterprise and to maximize benefit for the participants in their research, not their genetic relatives. If, on the other hand, the investigator was also the participant's clinician, a duty to warn similar to what the first set of commentators proposed would make disclosure mandatory. But they add that in cases such as this, when the potential harm of withholding the information from genetic relatives is high and the harm that will accrue to alive or deceased participants upon disclosure is low, the balance tips in favor of disclosure.

All three commentaries come to similar conclusions (disclosure to genetic relatives should occur) but use slightly different arguments and justifications.

CASE 2.4: ETHICS OF CONTINUING TO PROVIDE A DRUG ON AN OPEN-LABEL EXTENSION STUDY FOR AN "UNAPPROVED INDICATION" (2014)

Principles: Respect for Participants, Favorable Risk–Benefit Ratio

Topics: Results Disclosure, Clinician and Researcher Obligations, Drugs and Devices

Values: Trustworthiness

A key question in respecting research participants regards what investigators and sponsors owe participants in terms of posttrial access to an intervention found to be beneficial. This is most commonly a question in the context of a trial where the novel treatment has been found to be better than the standard treatment (or placebo) for the majority of participants who received the novel treatment and will eventually be approved for use. The question in this case is a variation on this theme. After the trial was completed and during an open-label extension of the trial (during which participants received intervention at no cost), the intervention was found to be beneficial for a particular subgroup of participants and approved for use in this subgroup. Based on the knowledge gained by the study, the participants not in the subgroup (n = 19) are not likely to benefit and may even be harmed by continued use. The sponsor has proposed that the off-label extension be discontinued. If discontinued, the patients' clinicians could prescribe the intervention off-label, but the intervention is expensive and insurance coverage for off-label use is uncertain. This case puts respect for participants in conflict with finding a fair risk–benefit ratio. And, as with the cases above, the commentaries focus on what investigators owe to participants in terms of sharing information gained during the study and the differences between the obligations of the clinician and those of the investigator.

The first commentary (Crites, this volume, p. 101) reviews two rationales for conducting an extension: (1) to contribute to generalizable knowledge (i.e., social value) and (2) to benefit participants. He notes that, given these rationales, an open-label extension can represent a convergence of investigational and therapeutic objectives. To aid investigators in navigating this convergence, he emphasizes that it is the investigators' responsibility to inform the participant at the time they are offered enrollment in the extension that the purpose is to gather additional data (a continuation of research objectives) and that additional risks may be identified, and to share the range of potential outcomes, including the circumstances of a case like this one—with the collection and analysis of additional data, it may be in their best interest to stop taking the intervention. Providing this information will allow the investigator to better navigate their commitments to the research and to the benefit of the participant. The commentator concludes that, if some participants stand to benefit, then continued access to the intervention should be facilitated; if no participants stand to benefit, the open-label extension should be closed.

The second commentary (Nash, this volume, p. 103) opens his narrative with a reminder that research ethics is built on an ethic of permission. He begins his analysis of the case with two questions: (1) Is there enough information to determine that the intervention is harmful? And (2) can valuable information be gained by continuing the open-label extension? If there is uncertainty about the answer to either question, the commentator concludes that continuing the extension may make economic sense for the sponsor if additional information might lead to evidence of effectiveness. If there is harm and no additional information can be gained, the commentary comes to the same conclusion as the first: The information known should be shared with the participants, and the extension should be closed.

The third commentary (Cho, this volume, p. 105) opens with two questions as well: (1) Should the sponsor close the extension and inform the investigators and participants of the unpromising results? And (2) if a participant, in consultation with their physician, decides to continue on the intervention despite the unpromising results, should the sponsor cover the cost? As noted by the first commentary, the purpose of the extension—research or treatment—is key to the analysis of the case. She also adds that the purpose of the extension and the possible outcomes should have been reviewed with participants at the time they enrolled. The third commentator agrees with the first two commentators that, if there is a currently enrolled participant clinically benefiting from the intervention, they should be given the option, upon consultation with their physician, to continue the intervention at no cost.

The three commentators come to the same conclusions from slightly different directions.

CASE 2.5: SUPPORTING INVESTIGATORS IN CHALLENGING CASES: UNEASE IN THE FACE OF AN ETHICALLY APPROPRIATE ACTION (2021)

Principles: Respect for Participants, Favorable Risk–Benefit Ratio

Topics: Results Disclosure, Clinician and Researcher Obligations

Values: Social Value

The goal of the research in this case is to discover whether a biomarker (i.e., a measure of methylation) will be useful in assessing risk of developing cancer. The methylation results will be compared to the outcome of the standard diagnostic test. The latter results will be disclosed to participants. As the measure of methylation is not yet known to be predictive of risk of cancer, these results are not disclosed to the participants. The investigator observes a very high level of methylation in one participant. The participant is well known to the investigator, and the investigator wants to share this information with the participant. An initial ethics consultation recommends not disclosing the result, as intended by the study originally, and the key issue in this case is how to help an investigator navigate their roles as clinician and investigator and to address their distress with that approach.

The first commentary (Schonfeld and Geppert, this volume, p. 108) focuses on the moral distress of the investigator. They posit that if the investigator is also the participant's clinician, they are caught in a moral dilemma. They have two strongly held values—respect for the individual participant and their obligation to the integrity of the science underway—that are in conflict. The commentators conclude that in a case like this, the consultant can help the investigator name and explore this conflict of values.

The second commentary (Blee et al., this volume, p. 110) provides a three-step process to address the investigator's moral distress (they use the term "angst"). The first step is in harmony with the first commentary's approach: Help the investigator explore their apparent moral dilemma caused by competing values. If, after the exploration, the investigator remains in a state of moral distress, the commentators suggest looking at the circumstances that lead to the distress. In this case, a key question is why the lab staff chose to reach out to the investigator with identifiable results. Adopting an institutional policy to return only clinically actionable results to participants and to otherwise avoid providing research results with personal identifiers to investigators may reduce, if not eliminate, this source of moral distress. They suggest a second institutional-level policy that respects the participants but balances the risks and benefits more favorably: posting a lay summary of the aggregate results. Research participants receive the information about whether there is a possible link between the methylation and their risk of cancer, and consider the implications with their clinicians.

The third commentary (Spellecy and Nyitray, this volume, p. 112) discusses the investigator's knowledge of the participant and his belief that the participant would want to know the results, even though the methylation results are not (yet) a valid measure of cancer risk. The commentators acknowledge that the investigator may feel conflicted because it is not always the case that the risk–benefit balance in a situation such as this favors withholding of research results. The investigator may both respect the participant and believe that having these nonclinically actionable research results may result in a net benefit to the participant. But, as they assume that the participant was told as a part of the consent process that research results would not be disclosed, these results must not be disclosed. The commentary comes full circle in the end and agrees with the previous commentaries that the best approach is to help the investigator explore the values placing them in a moral dilemma.

Ultimately, all three sets of commentators conclude that a conversation with the investigator probing his concerns and underlying values is the best approach to resolve his moral distress.

CASE 2.6: RECONTACT AND RECRUITMENT OF YOUNG ADULTS PREVIOUSLY ENROLLED IN NEONATAL HERPES SIMPLEX VIRUS RESEARCH (2015)

Principles: Respect for Participants, Informed Consent

Topics: Results Disclosure, Adolescents and Young Adults, Family Impact, Privacy

Values: Trustworthiness, Social Value

In contrast to the first five cases, the last two cases involve the principles of informed consent along with respect for participants. The investigators want to contact the potential participants to directly document their health and determine if they continue to shed the virus responsible for their newborn infection. Doing so would disclose health information previously unknown to them: that their mother had transmitted a sexually acquired infection. The investigators' initial recruitment plan, focused on contacting the parents or guardians to locate the potential participants, was unsuccessful. Parents and guardians were reluctant to provide the contact information. Their new proposal is to directly contact those over 18 who were exposed as newborns. The investigators are seeking advice if it is acceptable to contact the adults directly, when the parents have declined to pass along the information.

The first commentary (Melvin et al., this volume, p. 116) quickly sets up this case as a set of competing interests: the social value of the research, respect for the original participants, and the interests of the potential participants. The principle of respect for participants conflicts with the value of the science proposed and pushes the limits of informed consent. The commentators make the case that the research has social value for all exposed to herpes in utero and may even benefit the potential participants. They add that the concerns about the consequences of disclosure demand that the original participants are respected. They point to the precedent in genetics, where priority is placed on the desires of the original participants (parents). Finally, they posit that the potential participants (the children) have a right to their health history and contemporary implications. They compare the circumstances to newborn HIV infection, where failure to disclose newborn infection has clear negative consequences. The commentary concludes that one path to resolution would be to respectfully engage with the parents, emphasizing the social value of the research proposed. They do not endorse going directly to the potential participants.

The second commentary (McKinney, this volume, p. 118) adds an additional stakeholder to the analysis: the sexual partners of the potential participants. The first commentators mentioned this group but noted that the risk of transmission from those infected at birth to sexual partners is unknown. The commentary considers the role of the investigators as advocates for advancing knowledge and, as such, advocates for exposed newborns including the potential participants. The commentary considers that the potential participants (given the assumed lack of knowledge about their newborn exposure and its implications) have priority in the ethical analysis, noting that the utility of the knowledge withheld is marginal but the right to know is substantive. The commentary also notes that the argument in favor of directly recruiting the possible participants must be balanced with the family impact of ignoring the stated preferences of the parents. The commentary concludes that the value of the information to the potential participants is not sufficient to override the parents' preferences but is generally in favor of encouraging the parents to have frank discussions with their children, whether or not this leads to their enrollment. They do not endorse going directly to the potential participants.

The third commentary (Paquette and Ross, this volume, p. 120) posits that the key to this case is what the original participants agreed to surrounding future contact with children as part of their informed consent process. If not agreed to or disclosed in the consent, direct contact with the potential participants would be unacceptable. The commentary makes a similar recommendation to previous commentators in eliciting more information from the parents or guardians (inviting them to participate in a study to do so) or offering the parents or guardians a reasonable incentive to contact their children.

The commentators all come to the same conclusions, each prioritizing slightly different ethical principles in the process.

CASE 2.7: GENOTYPE-DRIVEN RECRUITMENT IN POPULATION-BASED BIOMEDICAL RESEARCH (2017)

Principles: Respect for Participants, Informed Consent

Topics: Genetics, Results Disclosure

Values: Trustworthiness, Social Value

This case is about how best to respect a research participant when it comes to the disclosure of research-related results of uncertain clinical value. The population of interest in this case are women who previously provided biospecimens to a research repository and who have a particular genotype (fragile X carriers) that may place them at elevated risk for poor outcomes and/or place their offspring at risk for poor outcomes. The investigators in this case want to recruit women who are fragile X carriers as well as a group of women without the genotype to better understand the fragile X phenotype. The repository consent form notified women that no research results would be disclosed. A list of women, without genotype status, will be provided to the study team to facilitate recruitment (i.e., investigators are blinded). The question in this case is whether it is ethical to offer enrollment to eligible women without disclosing the underlying research question and design: a case control study of phenotypic characteristics among carriers. This is a case where disclosing the genotypic information would violate the previous informed consent (no return of biobank results) but requires a type of deception to recruit the women needed to complete the study.

The first commentary (Ossorio and Mailick, this volume, p. 124) focuses on the meaning of deception. They lead with an assumption that the social value of completing this research is high. They argue that parsing a technical definition of deception can lead to a way in which withholding genotypic results from an individual potential participant does not disrespect them or put them at risk of harm. A key assumption in their analysis is that not enough is known about the genotype for the women approached to enroll to have any preconceived notions about the meaning of the results or to feel that something of value is being withheld if they do not receive the results. They add that clinically actionable information will be provided to all women enrolled in the study. They provide an example of information that could be provided during the informed consent process that both respects the participants and provides them with adequate information about the purpose and design to allow for an informed decision to enroll.

The second commentary (Doernberg and Hull, this volume, p. 127) takes a different tack than the first. The commentary concludes that the study as designed is deceptive, as key information about the purpose and design of the study is being withheld to avoid disclosing genotypic results to potential participants. While the commentators note that the use of deception is not always unethical, it is in this case, as the specifics fail to meet the regulatory standard of when withholding some or all of the required elements of informed consent can be justified. Their conclusions are supported by their arguments that the study as designed (no disclosure of genotypic results to individuals) could result in three harms. The first two harms are consequences of withholding health information that may be of relevance to their own health status and to fertility or reproductive decision making. The third potential harm created by the study design is an incomplete clinician referral if clinically actionable information (related or unrelated to the genotype) is given to a participant; it is incomplete given that the genotypic information is not provided to the participant or their clinician. This particular harm could be avoided by debriefing the participants, although part of the design is that investigators don't have this information.

The last commentary (Beskow, this volume, p. 129) zeros in on the key tension in the case of genotype-driven recruitment, how to avoid harm (withholding information) and avoid deception. The commentary advocates for an evidence-based approach to recruitment, a clear description of the purpose and eligibility, as well as giving the potential participants the option to not know their individual genotype results. She adds that the consent form, containing similar information, should offer disclosure and provide the potential risks and benefits of the results. Acknowledging that there are a variety of considerations in disclosing genotypic information and that providing genotypic results after participation in a trial is possible, the commentator states that this case is not in that category. Respect for participants during the recruitment process demands the offer of disclosure to those approached to enroll.

All three commentaries focus on the harms of withholding genotype information and whether deception is acceptable. They come to different conclusions as to whether the proposed study design is ethical.

CASE 2.1: ETHICAL CONSIDERATIONS FOR UNBLINDING A PARTICIPANT'S ASSIGNMENT TO INTERPRET A RESOLVED ADVERSE EVENT

INTRODUCTION

A participant's request to be unblinded during an ongoing clinical trial places two important ethical benchmarks in clinical research in conflict: the scientific validity of the study and respect for participants. Typically, the decision about unblinding is managed by a DMC, and participants are informed that they will not know which arm they were assigned to until the completion of the trial. While there are specific criteria for unblinding a participant during the trial, such as the protection of a participant's well-being, the case below presents a subtler rationale for the request involving the participant's personal assessment of the value of information to her. It is possible that knowing her treatment assignment will help her better understand if a medical complication she experienced was because her disease is worsening, or, less consequentially, might just be a complication of trial participation. Her request is not solely based on protecting her health, but also includes a request for the demonstration of respect and caring.

Accompanying the case summary is a commentary by J. Jina Shah and John Bond from Roche Pharmaceuticals, who describe the regulatory framework utilized by drug sponsors and overseen by the FDA to guide DMCs when making decisions about unblinding. This is followed by a commentary by Robert Steel and Marion Danis from the National Institutes of Health (NIH), who articulate the ethical considerations that DMC members need to grapple with when making their decision. The final commentary is by Lynne Quittell from Columbia University, who is the associate chair of the Cystic Fibrosis Data Monitoring Program. She offers the perspective of a sponsor that maintains a close relationship with the community and points to the special challenges to DMCs' considerations that are raised by the use of social media by trial participants.

CASE SUMMARY

A patient with systemic lupus erythematosus had enrolled in and completed participation in a Phase 1B (safety and efficacy) research study. The study was a randomized, controlled, and blinded trial of a drug that was already FDA approved for rheumatoid arthritis— another autoimmune condition—but was being tested for efficacy in managing lupus. After finishing the intervention phase of the study, she continued to be followed. The study was still enrolling patients and had a DMC.

During her first follow-up visit, the investigator determined that the participant had pancytopenia with a dangerously low platelet count that put her at risk for bleeding. The research team successfully treated this problem but did not know whether it was a result of the study drug since they were blinded and did not know which arm of the study she had been in.

It is possible that the low blood count was caused solely by the regular course of the patient's lupus. But it is also possible that it could have been caused by her earlier receipt of the study drug and its subsequent withdrawal: The study drug's mechanism of action is such that the cessation of its administration could, at least theoretically, have caused such an event—for example, such as through a mechanism of an exuberant reconstitution of the immune system. However, this possibility had not been anticipated by the investigators when the study began, thus participants were not aware of this risk. Furthermore, the investigators did not know whether the patient had ever received the study drug at all, and so it was correspondingly unknown to investigators whether the adverse event could indicate a potential safety risk for the study drug.

The investigator requested that the DMC allow the investigator and the participant to be unblinded, such that the investigator could better determine the possibility that the adverse event was related to the study drug or a natural progression of her disease. If it turned out she had only ever been on the placebo treatment, then the patient would know that this was from her lupus, and there would be less concern that other participants would be at risk. An ethics consultation was requested by the DMC to consider whether the participant's assignment in the original research study ought to be disclosed, and the impact of that on the study. The ethics consultant also was asked to address whether this adverse event necessitated breaking the blind altogether and stopping the study, and, if not, how this possibly study-related event should be communicated to current and future research participants in the study, given that it indicated an uncertain but possibly significant research-related risk.

COMMENTARY 2.1.1: CONSIDERATIONS FOR UNBLINDING IN BIOPHARMACEUTICAL INDUSTRY–SPONSORED TRIALS

J. JINA SHAH AND JOHN BOND

The case scenario as described is from the perspective of an investigator who has asked the DMC to unblind the treatment assignment of a patient who experienced a resolved adverse event of pancytopenia. The DMC then asked for a research ethics consultation. Supposing the scenario came from an industry-sponsored trial, the DMC would then have to make recommendations to the sponsor. This commentary is written from the perspective of an industry sponsor for a multisite, multinational study.

Industry sponsors are bound by regulations such as 21 CFR 312.32 in the United States and 2001/20/EC in the European Union, and guidances such as ICH E2 and E6 that mandate protection of individual patient safety, timely reporting of adverse events, and maintenance of study integrity by unblinding only specific people in specific circumstances.

When should a patient's treatment assignment be unblinded to the investigator?

The investigator must be unblinded to the patient's study treatment assignment when knowledge of the study treatment is required to treat an adverse event. Then, there is a clear need for the individual subject's welfare to take precedence over concerns about study integrity. However, in this case, pancytopenia was effectively treated without knowledge of the study treatment assignment.

In this scenario, the investigator considers breaking the blind to determine whether the pancytopenia may represent a new safety risk, but treatment assignment (active versus placebo) is just one factor in ascertaining adverse event causality. Biological plausibility and the occurrence of pancytopenia upon treating and withdrawing the study drug again would be other factors to assess adverse event causality. Whether the adverse event also occurs in some patients as part of the natural history of a disease is also relevant. Even if the pancytopenia were due only to lupus, it could still occur in the active treatment arm by chance. Certain adverse events have no known background incidence in the disease population, so a single occurrence of an adverse event suggests a possible drug-related risk. But for those events that may also be signs or symptoms of the underlying disease (e.g., pancytopenia in patients with lupus), unblinded aggregate data (as opposed to a single case) have to be analyzed to assess causality.

FDA drug safety guidances (U.S. Food and Drug Administration 2012, 2015) suggest that a DMC or independent sponsor safety team could conduct such aggregate analyses to avoid unblinding the investigator and others responsible for study conduct, analysis, and interpretation of results.

Unblinding in the case of a suspected, unexpected, serious adverse reaction (SUSAR)

Any adverse event occurring in a clinical trial that is considered to be a suspected, unexpected, serious adverse reaction (SUSAR) requires expedited reporting from the investigator to the sponsor and from the sponsor to regulatory agencies, institutional review boards (IRBs), and investigators on the study. Companies have to report SUSARs to the FDA within 15 days.

The investigator's suggestion that pancytopenia may represent a new risk suggests that it might be "unexpected" per the trial's reference safety information (RSI). "Unexpected" is a regulatory term meaning that the particular adverse event has not been previously reported in the clinical experience with the particular investigational medicine. The regulatory term "unexpected" may not correlate with whether an adverse event is "medically expected." For example, pancytopenia is known to occur in patients with lupus, but if it has not previously been reported as an adverse event (and therefore listed in the RSI) for this investigational medicine, it is termed "unexpected." The RSI is usually the investigator's brochure, summarizing safety and efficacy across investigational studies, or a local label with the safety and efficacy of marketed products such as the U.S. package insert.

There are a number of criteria to define seriousness, including events that result in outcomes such as death or disability, require hospitalization, and are life-threatening. Another category of serious events is those that are medically significant, defined as an important medical event that may jeopardize the patient and may require medical or surgical intervention to prevent one of the ultimate outcomes listed in the previous sentence.

In this case, the investigator suspects a possible causal relationship between the pancytopenia and the withdrawal of the study drug; therefore, this is considered a "suspected adverse reaction." A sponsor may disagree with an investigator's causality assessment but may not change it, in which case both opinions are included in the expedited report to regulatory authorities. Most regulatory authorities require expedited reporting of serious unexpected adverse events assessed as related to the study drug by either the investigator or the sponsor. The U.S. FDA only requires expedited reporting when the sponsor assesses the adverse event as related to the drug, in which case it is called an investigational new drug (IND) safety report.

Once the investigator reports a SUSAR to the sponsor, specific personnel within the company who are not involved in running the study unblind the study treatment and, if the patient received the study drug, report it to regulatory authorities. Regulatory agencies receive unblinded SUSAR reports. While DMCs may also receive unblinded SUSAR reports, investigators and IRBs may get either blinded or unblinded reports depending on local regulatory requirements and the sponsor's policy. The Council for International Organizations of Medical Sciences (CIOMS) Working Group 6 raised the question of whether it is advisable or appropriate to keep cases blinded for investigators when unblinded reports are sent to regulators, data and safety monitoring boards (DSMBs), and trial ethics committees, but concluded that guidance on this issue was beyond its scope (Council for International Organizations of Medical Sciences 2005).

How are potential safety risks such as pancytopenia evaluated?

The investigator, sponsor, DMC, IRB, and regulatory authorities all have responsibilities to determine whether a drug's risks outweigh the potential benefit for patients.

The DMC has an unblinded view of the whole study. According to a safety monitoring plan that would have been established at the beginning of the study, it reviews cumulative safety data periodically, and on an ad hoc basis for rare, severe events. After reviewing the data, the DMC will consider recommending continuing the study without change, holding enrollment for further data review, or stopping or modifying the study. Independent DMCs can communicate their findings and recommendations to sponsors, to IRBs, and directly to regulatory agencies.

Although the DMC may review only unblinded information from the concerned study, the sponsor is able to review the total frequency of similar adverse events from all studies and from postmarketing experience across all indications for the drug. Sponsors can determine whether the adverse event represents a new safety concern and can take appropriate action.

Regulatory authorities can evaluate SUSARs in the context of safety data from multiple drugs with similar mechanisms of action and any other relevant data. They can mandate changes to informed consent, restrictions in the study population, and changes to the study conduct, and can suspend or even terminate a trial if they believe it is in the best interests of patients.

Should information about the adverse event of pancytopenia be added to the informed consent form?

With a single case of pancytopenia that could be associated with the underlying disease, there is too little information to understand whether current or future study participants are at increased risk. A change in the informed consent form can be considered after a thorough evaluation of the event by the DMC, sponsor, and regulatory agencies, which does not require unblinding of the investigator.

References

Council for International Organizations of Medical Sciences. 2005. *Management of safety information from clinical trials: Report of CIOMS working group VI*, Geneva: Council for International Organizations of Medical Sciences.

U.S. Food and Drug Administration. 2012. *Safety reporting requirements for INDs and BA/BE studies. Guidance for industry and investigators*, Rockville, MD: U.S. Department of Health and Human Services.

U.S. Food and Drug Administration. 2015. *Safety assessment for IND safety reporting. Guidance for industry and investigators*, Rockville, MD: U.S. Department of Health and Human Services.

COMMENTARY 2.1.2: BLINDS AND RESEARCH RISKS

ROBERT STEEL AND MARION DANIS

This case raises several ethical issues related to the communication and management of research risk. The ethical resolution of many of those issues will depend on matters of expert clinical judgment. We bracket regulatory issues, assuming that reporting requirements are fulfilled and that the DMC, investigators, and relevant bodies comply with their various mandates. Our focus is on the general ethical considerations they confront as they do so.

The case report describes the sudden appearance, and management, of an unanticipated adverse event. The first and most dramatic question posed is whether this ethically demands stopping the study altogether. If so, many other questions about the trial are rendered moot. To be clear, our understanding is that the affected patient was successfully treated and at no ongoing risk, so the relevant risks are just those to participants going forward. Do those risks require stopping the trial?

Begin with the most unfavorable assumption: Assume the patient who experienced the adverse event was known by the DMC to have been previously enrolled in the active arm of the drug trial. Thus, the DMC knows that the study drug may have caused the adverse event, a theory supported by reasonable hypotheses about the drug's mechanism of action—that is, that it might lead to exuberant reconstitution of the immune system upon cessation.

But even if the patient is assumed to be on the study drug, that fact alone would not guarantee that the study drug was actually the cause of the event. Thus, the DMC would still have to go on to make its best assessment as to the likelihood of that relationship. In making a judgment here, the DMC would need to draw on its understanding of the underlying disease course, the pharmacological properties of the study drug, and the full weight of its data about other subjects' outcomes.

In addition to assessing its likelihood, the DMC would also need to assess the seriousness of the risk. This would involve attention to the monitoring and treatments plans of the study in terms of how well they can catch and mitigate future events of the same character.

Depending on how both the likelihood and seriousness judgments are filled in, they could result in a wide range of ultimate risk assessments. Once such a risk assessment is made, how might the DMC proceed? In general, bodies regulating research risk must consider absolute risk thresholds, risk–benefit ratios, and the overall minimization of risk, and we discuss these in order.

Within research ethics, many believe that once the risks to participants exceed a certain absolute threshold they render a trial impermissible, although there is a lack of consensus on what precisely that threshold is or what justifies it; points of comparison in establishing such a threshold have included socially tolerated but risky altruistic activities like organ donation or volunteer firefighting (London 2006; Miller and Joffe 2009). If the DMC came to believe on the basis of this new information that the trial exceeds a threshold of this kind, it could not be allowed to proceed. But we suspect, and will assume for the sake of further analysis, that a sufficiently close monitoring plan could bring the absolute risks of participation within reasonable limits. We similarly assume that the trial's social value is sufficient to produce an adequate risk–benefit ratio.

This brings us to the question of risk minimization. For research to be ethical, it must minimize the risk to enrolled subjects. But this injunction is not absolute. Research will often involve additional risks that one would not face in clinical care; this is part of what differentiates the two enterprises. Rather, researchers must minimize risk insofar as is consistent with the scientific value of the research, and this may involve difficult trade-offs.

In this case, it is fortunate that the clinical care necessary for addressing this adverse event was independent of whether the participant had been on the active or control arms. It was not the case, for instance, that there was any potential interaction between the clinical care and the study drug, nor did the participant require a specific antidote. This substantially reduces the tension between the scientific value of maintaining the blind and the imperative to minimize risks to enrolled subjects.

We can underline this point by considering a poignant story of an unblinding event in Spain (Eduardo and MacKillop 2001). A doctor, in a panic upon finding the participant he's treating entering a hypotensive crisis, calls the sponsor to demand that it break the blind. The sponsor initially resists, but, upon repeated demands, eventually relents and supplies the unblinding code. The patient is successfully treated. But the treatment did not depend on the patient's study enrollment arm—it was completely standard treatment for hypotension, which resolved in a completely standard way. And in this particular case, not only were the participant's own data compromised, but worse yet the study was arranged in blocks such that the unblinding of one participant de facto unblinded several others.

Insofar as risks can be acceptably mitigated by close monitoring and a readiness to provide treatment that doesn't depend on whether participants are in the active or control arms, this allows researchers an attractive way to protect both the blind and the participants. Still, even when such a proposal is a feasible way of managing newly discovered risks, it is imperative that the consent process be updated to include any salient new information. Informed consent must always reflect the researchers' best current understanding. In any case, these are the sorts of ethical issues that investigators and regulators will have to confront.

All of the preceding discussion has proceeded under the assumption that the DMC knows that the patient who experienced the adverse event had been previously enrolled in the active arm. Suppose, finally, that this is not so. In one respect, this greatly simplifies the case. If the patient was not in the active arm, then the patient's experience cannot indicate the possibility of a formerly unknown risk with the drug. Nonetheless, the DMC must still make a decision about disclosure. If for no other reason than peace of mind, the patient and investigator are likely both concerned to know whether the adverse event could be drug related. But even this benign disclosure, that the patient never received the study drug and so could not have been harmed by it, will itself have to take place in consideration of the impact that disclosure has on the data and the value of the research as a whole.

References

Eduardo, A., and N. MacKillop. 2001. Educating investigators to understand when to break the blind. *Applied Clinical Trials* 8(11). http://www.appliedclinicaltrialsonline.com/educating-investigators-understand-when-break-blind

London, A. J. 2006. Reasonable risks in clinical research: A critique and proposal for the integrative approach. *Statistics in Medicine* 25(17):2869–85.

Miller, F. G., and S. Joffe. 2009. Limits to research risks. *Journal of Medical Ethics* 35(7):445–9.

COMMENTARY 2.1.3: THE SCIENTIFIC AND SOCIAL IMPLICATIONS OF UNBLINDING A STUDY SUBJECT

LYNNE M. QUITTELL

Bias can occur at multiple levels throughout a clinical trial and has the potential to undermine the validity and accuracy of a study. Bias is best described as the "difference between the true value and that actually obtained due to all causes other than sampling variability" (Mausner and Bahn 1974). As a result, it is standard practice that clinical trials be double blinded, where neither the investigators nor the study subjects are aware of the study drug or intervention assignment. Blinding aims to preclude bias due to differences in clinical management, interpretation of test results, and preconceived notions about the efficacy and safety of the study drug or intervention.

Should a patient be unblinded at his or her request?

The case presented describes a situation in which both a patient and investigator request that the DMC allow them to be unblinded to better understand if a serious adverse event was related to the study drug. The study drug is a previously FDA-approved medication under study for a new indication. The study subject had already completed active study participation when she developed pancytopenia, a possible complication of her underlying lupus.

This case underscores the importance of having a comprehensive charter that not only addresses study monitoring but also includes stopping rules and guidelines for unblinding. The dilemma and challenge of this case might have been avoided with anticipatory planning in place before the start of the study. An outline for unblinding and transmission of information to those who need to know but maintaining the blind for those doing the analysis would minimize the risk of bias in assessing the study outcomes.

There are circumstances where unblinding the assignment of individual patients may be needed to dictate care, but these are rare and usually clear-cut. It is accepted practice that unblinding be done when it is clinically in the best interest of the patient. However, as illustrated in this case presentation, determining what "best interest" means is not well defined and may have different interpretations. For example, unblinding might be necessary if a patient needs to be taken off the active study drug and the medication requires tapering. Unblinding might also be warranted when there is concern about safety for future patients, although this is rarely the case when there is an isolated incident. Since this is an FDA-approved drug and not part of an investigational new drug (IND) application, one can assume that there is a previously well-defined safety profile.

What are the potential ramifications of unblinding?

This case raises several questions: (1) When does unblinding impact the scientific validity of a study? (2) Would unblinding of one patient impact this study and future phases of the study? (3) Should a patient know his or her study arm assignment, and when should this be done? (4) What is the public perception of a study subject's right to know about study assignment and adverse events during a clinical trial?

Unblinding has the potential to bias a study. Since the natural tendency is to be optimistic that a new treatment is effective, unblinded investigators and study subjects may be more likely to report benefits if they are on a study drug, and unblinded investigators may be more likely to attribute adverse events to a study drug. Previous work has shown that poorly blinded studies tend to show a larger treatment effect (Schulz et al. 1995).

In this case, where the study drug is an already FDA-approved drug, it is unlikely that there are significant side effects that have not yet been described. In addition, the study has been monitored by a DMC with access to unblinded data. A strong safety signal for hematologic events should have been identified in previous studies, making it less likely that this is an issue with the study drug. The investigator's and patient's concern that this knowledge would be important to protect other study participants is out of their purview and rests with the DMC, which is charged with protecting the welfare of study subjects. Furthermore, the patient has completed the active phase of the study and has returned to baseline clinically. The development of pancytopenia should trigger a hematologic evaluation, and alterations to her treatment regimen at this point would not be expected by unblinding. Most likely, time will tell whether this is part of her disease process, but there should be a commitment on the part of the study team to ensure that she has access to the study code at the completion of the study, which would allow her and the care team to make informed decisions about her healthcare and potential use of the study drug moving forward if the risk–benefit ratio is favorable.

If the investigators are concerned that the subject's development of pancytopenia is related to the study drug, this would be classified as a SUSAR and would require reporting to the FDA. For INDs, FDA regulation requires unblinded reporting to ensure that patients receive proper care and safety for other participants in a clinical trial. The FDA clearly states that the unblinding of a single or small number of patients does not have implications for the integrity of the study. It also addresses the need for a plan that limits the number of people that need to be unblinded. In the case presented, the patient and local investigator cite concern for her future heath and the protection of future study subjects, but there is no discussion on how to limit the number of people who are unblinded. Either way, it is important to maintain the blind for those individuals charged with completing the study analysis (U.S. Food and Drug Administration 2018).

An issue often not addressed is the impact of social media within the realm of clinical trials. For years, patients have used various forms of peer-to-peer communication to share their experiences and learn from each other. These networks have become more mainstream, sophisticated, and elaborate with social media. More recently, social media are increasingly being utilized for education and recruitment for clinical trials. As social platforms become mainstreamed into the clinical trial sphere, we should anticipate the potential impact. If this patient attributes her pancytopenia to the study drug and this is confirmed through unblinding, she might use social media to discourage other patients from enrolling in clinical trials. If unblinding is not done, the patient might choose to spread her frustration on social network platforms among disease groups, which could impact the ability of the sponsor to recruit patients for this and future studies.

Summary

The case represents the disconnect between patient expectations and what researchers perceive clinical trial participants understand about safety monitoring during clinical trials (Flynn et al. 2013). It highlights the need to anticipate and address patient expectations before study enrollment. This can be accomplished by ensuring that consent forms are written simply and clearly and that expectations for the clinical trial process are understood before enrollment. In addition, study charters should have well-thought-out and documented parameters for issues such as unblinding.

References

Flynn, K. E., J. M. Kramer, C. B. Dombeck, et al. 2013. Participants' perspectives on safety monitoring in clinical trials. *Clinical Trials (London, England)* 10(4):552–9.

Mausner, J. S., and A. K. Bahn. 1974. *Epidemiology: An introductory text*, Philadelphia: W.B. Saunders.

Schulz, K. F., I. Chalmers, R. Hayes, et al. 1995. Empirical evidence of bias: Dimensions of methodological quality associated with estimates of treatment effects in controlled trials. *JAMA* 273(5):408–12.

U.S. Food and Drug Administration. 2018. Guidance (Drugs). Available at: http://www.fda.gov/Drugs/GuidanceComplianceRegulatoryInformation/Guidances/default.htm (accessed on June 13, 2018).

CASE 2.2: SHOULD RESEARCH PARTICIPANTS BE NOTIFIED ABOUT RESULTS OF CURRENTLY UNKNOWN BUT POTENTIAL SIGNIFICANCE?

INTRODUCTION

In the past 20 years, there has been increasing recognition that clinical research results be communicated to study participants after completion of the research study. At a minimum, research results are presented in aggregate format; however, an evolving standard is the return of individual research results. Individual research results may provide greater personal utility by allowing the study participant to more accurately determine whether the research findings may have implications for their future health. One area of controversy in the return of individual research results is "what" to return to participants, particularly when the information is incidental to the original study or of uncertain significance (Botkin et al. 2018).

Discussions around the return of individual research results have largely occurred in the context of genomic sequencing, where research studies can generate tremendous amounts of data revealing incidental genetic information or discovery of variants of uncertain significance or actionability. In the context of genomic research, some researchers have elected to return everything (i.e., the ceiling), nothing (i.e., the floor), or something in between to interested study participants (Jarvik et al. 2014). The wide variability in practice provides little guidance to IRBs and researchers seeking guidance on "what" individual results to return during the conduct of clinical research.

In the case described here, researchers have developed a protocol incorporating MRI in a study of healthy individuals previously exposed to gadolinium-based contrast agents (GBCAs) to examine the extent and consequences of gadolinium exposure. Like genomic results where the implications of many variants are unclear, the consequences of gadolinium deposition from GBCAs in tissues are of uncertain significance and may or may not have implications for an individual's future health. This case highlights the challenge for researchers and IRBs in determining what individual results should be returned to participants, particularly when questions surround the significance of the research result to be returned.

Three commentaries accompany this case. Stephen Brown from Boston Children's Hospital argues that gadolinium deposition is not incidental, and results should be disclosed to participants. Extending his rationale beyond this case, he makes a wider appeal that, due to potential public health concerns, transparency is broadly needed during informed consent and other study-related conversations as the safety of GBCAs is investigated in clinical research. Caroline Huang and Marion Danis of the NIH Clinical Center and Patricia Bandettini of the National Heart, Lung, and Blood Institute call upon the genomic return of results literature to argue for return of individual MRI results about gadolinium deposition in tissues. The three argue that, while this information is not medically actionable in the traditional sense, it may become potentially actionable in the future and knowledge about one's personal result may inform future decision making. These authors also ask whether failure to return results in this present study may impact willingness to enroll in future studies on the safety of GBCAs, potentially slowing the progress of research in this important area. Nora Hutchinson and Adélaïde Doussau of McGill University and Alexander Capron of the University of Southern California argue for disclosure of individual results of unknown but potential significance to interested participants and encourage investigators to provide participants with this option during the informed consent conversation.

CASE SUMMARY

An investigator is planning a study that will examine the extent and consequences of accumulation of GBCAs in individuals who have undergone repeated MRI studies. GBCAs are the most commonly used contrast agents for MRIs. Recent reports indicate that small amounts of gadolinium may be left behind in the brain, bone, and skin. While GBCAs may increase the risk of nephrogenic systemic fibrosis in people with severe kidney failure, the FDA issued a December 2017 Drug Safety Communication stating that "gadolinium retention has not been directly linked to adverse health effects in patients with normal kidney function." However, the FDA has directed GBCA manufacturers to carry out additional safety research and approved new patient Medication Guides for all GBCAs in May 2018. The study investigator plans to use blood tests and MRI to study healthy volunteers who have been repeatedly exposed to gadolinium, typically from past participation in research using GBCAs. The protocol states that the investigator will report "significant" incidental MRI findings to participants. The IRB to which the investigator has submitted the research protocol has requested that the investigator speak with the Bioethics Consultation Service to discuss the advisability of notifying research participants about their personal study results, particularly any gadolinium deposition in the brain and other tissues. The IRB is aware that there are no currently identified adverse effects of gadolinium in healthy participants and no actionable results, but is concerned that this situation may change in the future.

REFERENCES

Botkin, J. R., M. Mancher, E. R. Busta, and A. S. Downey. 2018. *Returning individual research results to participants: Guidance for a new research paradigm*, Washington, DC: National Academic Press.

Jarvik, G. P., L. M. Amendola, J. S. Berg, et al. 2014. Return of genomic results to research participants: The floor, the ceiling, and the choices in between. *The American Journal of Human Genetics* 94(6): 818–26.

COMMENTARY 2.2.1: THE NEED FOR NATIONAL GUIDANCE AROUND INFORMED CONSENT ABOUT GBCA SAFETY

STEPHEN D. BROWN

Since GBCAs were approved in 1988, they have become an indispensable adjunct to MRI (McDonald et al. 2018; Rozenfeld and Podberesky 2018). GBCAs have been widely considered safe for patients with normal renal function, but recent concerns have arisen regarding gadolinium accumulation in brains, bones, livers, and other organs of exposed individuals (McDonald et al. 2018; Rozenfeld and Podberesky 2018). A conspicuous knowledge gap now exists about its safety. Symptoms, dose thresholds, at-risk populations, and latency periods for gadolinium deposition are undefined. Tests to detect it may be insensitive (McDonald et al. 2018). To address this gap, the NIH, in collaboration with the American College of Radiology (ACR), the Radiological Society of North America (RSNA), and an assortment of industry and academic experts, issued a comprehensive "Research Roadmap" for the rigorous approach necessary to determine the effects of gadolinium retention (McDonald et al. 2018).

At issue in the present case is whether the offered guidance suffices to manage attendant informed consent issues (Johnson, Zabrowski, and Wilfond 2019). The research protocol under discussion highlights where the NIH Roadmap around GBCAs falls short. The protocol proposes to perform blood tests and MRIs in "healthy volunteers who have been repeatedly exposed to gadolinium, typically from past participation in research using GBCAs." It calls for informing participants of "significant" incidental MRI findings. At the direction of the IRB, the investigator seeks guidance on whether participants should be informed about gadolinium deposition demonstrated in their brains or other tissues.

Guidance from recommendations about genetic research

The IRB should first clarify that gadolinium deposition is not incidental in this study. The deposition and its consequences are the primary investigative targets; the participants are specifically at risk.

Potential guidance about when to inform participants about their gadolinium deposition is found in NIH consensus recommendations about genetic research results, which, like gadolinium deposition, may be of uncertain but potential significance (Fabsitz et al. 2010). These recommendations are that findings should be disclosed if they carry established health implications, if clinically actionable interventions exist, if the tests are valid, and if participants opt in to disclosure. Gadolinium deposition would not meet this threshold because its health implications are unknown and the tests may not be valid.

Whether gadolinium retention would be actionable is arguable. Therapeutic interventions do not exist and may never be necessary. However, unlike genetic mutations, gadolinium deposition results from external exposure. Moreover, the exposure may be ongoing. Previously exposed individuals may confront decisions regarding additional exposures from present or future clinical care. Even if individuals understand that the significance of deposition is unknown, and that current tests may be insensitive to measure retention or effects, they might still reasonably decide to minimize or avoid further exposure until more is known. It is empirically groundless to establish that IRBs or individual investigators should retain decisional discretion over the balance of harms and benefits for individual participants. Discretion should be left to individual participants following informed consent.

Precarious conditions for informed consent

More problematically, prospective participation recruits were exposed to GBCAs specifically because they volunteered (often repeatedly) to receive the agent in prior research. Many were likely told the agent was entirely safe. Compared to genetic information, this presents a more precarious set of conditions for informed consent. The recruitment may create harms even in advance of informed consent conversations. Unless the investigators seek (inappropriately) to conceal the protocol's purpose, merely approaching these individuals to participate will necessitate informing them that previous exposures may not have been as safe as was previously indicated. The nagging anxiety created simply by recruitment may be compounded if participants are informed that tests available to study the problem may be insensitive. Thus, once recruits are informed of the possibility of retention, potential psychological harm already exists. No empirical claim can be made that participants would be more harmed to know that deposits had been identified than to know the possibility exists but they will not be informed. It would add insult to potential injury not to empower these individuals with the decision.

The informed consent process may also elicit anger and distrust from some who bristle at being told they were exposed through volunteer research but cannot now decide for themselves how to handle the matter. These conditions present distinctly delicate communication challenges. Prohibiting opt-in to receive results seems disrespectful not only to participants but also to individual investigators faced with recruitment and informed consent responsibilities.

Wider public health concerns

This protocol raises narrow informed consent questions that belie deeper public health concerns: Namely, should we inform the hundreds of millions of children and adults exposed to GBCAs over the past three decades, and the many millions more who face exposure while safety is reevaluated? Certainly, retaining a formal research paradigm seems essential to establishing requisite systematic rigor. Broad public awareness prior to firm evidence may create widespread, unnecessary anxiety. Still, studies will ultimately require the participation of individuals exposed to GBCAs previously as patients, who vastly outnumber those exposed through research. If genuine risks exist, individuals exposed during childhood, the elderly, and those exposed multiply are likely particularly vulnerable. Without including these populations within research protocols, the safety studies may never identify small high-risk cohorts, such as children with certain conditions of the brain, bone, liver, and so on. Thus, even as a research matter, recruitment will require outreach to sizable populations, which may itself raise public awareness and anxiety. Previously exposed individuals who are not informed may later legitimately cry foul, particularly given that GBCAs understood as most closely associated with gadolinium retention have already been removed from markets in Europe but not the United States (McDonald et al. 2018; Rozenfeld and Podberesky 2018). If safety concerns are eventually validated, those who were previously exposed, or who were exposed as patients while research was ongoing, may have compelling grievances about not having been informed earlier. Researchers, institutions, manufacturers, and the government may face substantial liability risk. The ACR, which has recommended against actions that Europe has taken, risks a loss in public credibility, as does the NIH, which has not addressed the informed consent issues substantively (Malayeri et al. 2016; McDonald et al. 2018; Rozenfeld and Podberesky 2018).

Conclusion

These wider implications have direct relevance to the investigator and IRB involved in the submitted protocol, because responsibility for addressing informed consent currently falls individually to them and their institutions. The NIH Roadmap represents an admirable effort to create a systematic approach to investigating GBCA safety, but it leaves investigators and IRBs on their own to devise ad hoc solutions for thorny issues of informed consent that are matters of larger public interest. If gadolinium deposition proves to cause adverse effects, hundreds of millions will have been previously exposed; costs will be in the billions. Ironically, gadolinium deposition could be a boon to the very institutions and manufacturers responsible for mass GBCA exposure, because MRI will be a principal investigative and clinical tool. This could confound conflicts of interest already weighing against public disclosure (and removal from U.S. markets). For these reasons, stakeholders represented in the NIH Roadmap should regroup together with those representing broader public interests to establish national, central guidance around informed consent for GBCA exposure in patients and research participants. The investigator and IRB in this case should not go it alone.

References

Fabsitz, R. R., A. McGuire, and R. R. Sharp, et al. 2010. Ethical and practical guidelines for reporting genetic research results to study participants: Updated guidelines from a National Heart, Lung, and Blood Institute working group. *Circulation Cardiovascular Genetics* 3(6):574–80.

Johnson, L. M., J. Zabrowski, and B. S. Wilfond. 2019. Should research participants be notified about results of currently unknown but potential significance? *American Journal of Bioethics* 19(4):73–74.

Malayeri, A. A., K. M. Brooks, L. H. Bryant, et al. 2016. National Institutes of Health perspective on reports of gadolinium deposition in the brain. *Journal of the American College of Radiology* 13(3): 237–241.

McDonald, R. J., D. Levine, J. Weinreb, et al. 2018. Gadolinium retention: A research roadmap from the 2018 NIH/ACR/RSNA workshop on gadolinium chelates. *Radiology* 289(2):517–34.

Rozenfeld, M. N., and D. J. Podberesky. 2018. Gadolinium-based contrast agents in children. *Pediatric Radiology* 48(9):1188–96.

COMMENTARY 2.2.2: RETURNING INDIVIDUAL RESEARCH RESULTS REGARDING GADOLINIUM DEPOSITION IN THE BRAIN IS THE PREFERABLE CHOICE

CAROLINE J. HUANG, W. PATRICIA BANDETTINI, AND MARION DANIS

Per the Secretary's Advisory Committee on Human Research Protections, there is a "rebuttable presumption in favor of returning individual results" to participants based on the principles of respect for persons and beneficence (Office for Human Research Protections 2016). To determine whether that presumption should be rebutted in this gadolinium study (Johnson, Zabrowski, and Wilfond 2019), some relevant factors to consider include (1) the actionability of a result, (2) the potential for a result to cause harm, and (3) the impact of receiving one's individual research result.

The American Society for Human Genetics discusses several ways in which genetic tests may reveal secondary findings that are "medically actionable, meaning they prompt clinical action by the patient's medical provider" (The American Society of Human Genetics n.d.). Common examples include pathogenic mutations in genes associated with familial breast and ovarian cancer, familial hypertrophic cardiomyopathy, and Marfan syndrome (Kalia et al. 2017). Other potentially actionable findings include pharmacogenomics results, which might impact a person's response to certain drugs, and carrier status results, which might influence a person's reproductive and lifestyle decisions.

There are clear parallels between secondary findings in genetic testing and potential findings in this gadolinium study. Because there are no identified adverse effects of gadolinium deposition in the brain and no available treatments for removing gadolinium deposits (Levine, McDonald, and Kressel 2018), evidence of gadolinium deposition in the brain does not trigger immediate clinical action. However, it is reasonable to think that this result would fall under the second kind of potentially actionable findings that may modify future decision making. Awareness of the presence or absence of gadolinium deposition in the brain may inform a participant's decision to undergo future imaging involving a GBCA, request a nephrology consultation to check kidney function, or seek to enroll in future studies on the health effects of or treatment for gadolinium deposition.

Related to the lack of available treatments, finding out that there is evidence suggestive of gadolinium deposition in the brain may be distressing to some participants. This concern may be mitigated by the clearly stated purpose of the study, which aims to assess gadolinium deposition in the brain in people with prior exposure to GBCAs, and language in the participant information sheet explaining that there are no known adverse clinical effects of gadolinium deposition in the brain at this time. To further address this concern, the researchers could consider providing participants the opportunity to opt in or out of learning their result, though the result would likely be determinable if researchers asked participants to return for subsequent imaging or invited them to participate in future studies about gadolinium deposition. Not receiving a result from participation in the present study might also make participants less likely to enroll in future studies investigating the health effects of GBCAs, which could slow the progress of research on GBCAs and thus delay or prevent participants from benefiting from any eventual outcomes of this research.

In this case, returning the results of MRI scans for gadolinium deposition is the preferable choice for several reasons:

1. *Respect for persons*: Participants may want to know their individual results, particularly since they would be enrolled in a study that aims to assess whether they have deposits.
2. *Reassurance*: Participants who have concerns about gadolinium deposition may be reassured if they find out there is no evidence of gadolinium deposition.
3. *Consistency*: If the research team wants to invite people with gadolinium deposition to participate in future studies, the participants will have to be informed of their results.
4. *Actionability*: These results are actionable in that they can inform choices about nonclinical scans involving GBCAs, facilitate potential participation in future trials about the effects of gadolinium, and possibly lead to care if an agent is identified to remove gadolinium.

Implementing this recommendation in practice will require careful discussion of the return of results in the participation information sheet and consent form. In general, it would be prudent to focus on the specific findings (e.g., evidence or no evidence of gadolinium deposition) and the uncertain significance of deposition, and to avoid any mention of an "abnormal" brain. Additional guidance may also be forthcoming from organizations including the NIH, ACR, and RSNA, which cosponsored a workshop on gadolinium retention in February 2018 and subsequently released a research roadmap in September 2018 (McDonald et al. 2018).

References

Johnson, L. M., J. Zabrowski, and B. S. Wilfond. 2019. Should research participants be notified about results of currently unknown but potential significance? *American Journal of Bioethics* 19(4):73–4.

Kalia, S. S., K. Adelman, S. J. Bale, et al. 2017. Recommendations for reporting of secondary findings in clinical exome and genome sequencing, 2016 update (ACMG SF v2.0): A policy statement of the American College of Medical Genetics and Genomics. *Genetics in Medicine* 19(2): 249–55.

Levine, D., R. J. McDonald, and H. Y. Kressel. 2018. Gadolinium retention after contrast-enhanced MRI. *Journal of the American Medical Association* 320(18):1853–4.

McDonald, R. J., D. Levine, J. Weinreb, et al. 2018. Gadolinium retention: A research roadmap from the 2018 NIH/ACR/RSNA workshop on gadolinium chelates. *Radiology* 289(2):517–34.

Office for Human Research Protections. 2016. "Attachment B: Return of Individual Research Results." Text. HHS.Gov. July 21, 2016. Available at: https://www.hhs.gov/ohrp/sachrp-committee/recommendations/attachment-b-return-individual-research-results/index.html (accessed November 20, 2018).

The American Society of Human Genetics. n.d. Medically actionable secondary or incidental results. *Clinical Sequencing Exploratory Research Toolkit* (Blog). Available at: https://www.ashg.org/education/csertoolkit/medicallyactionable.html (accessed November 20, 2018).

COMMENTARY 2.2.3: RESEARCH PARTICIPANTS SHOULD HAVE THE OPTION TO BE NOTIFIED OF RESULTS OF UNKNOWN BUT POTENTIAL SIGNIFICANCE

NORA HUTCHINSON, ALEXANDER CAPRON, AND ADÉLAÏDE DOUSSAU

The FDA recently identified the need for further safety studies of GBCAs due to uncertainty regarding the effects of gadolinium retention in individuals with normal renal function (U.S. Food and Drug Administration 2017). Research to specify and quantify the consequences of gadolinium accumulation in order to establish what constitutes a "significant" deposition, based on correlating the health and well-being of individuals with their different levels of case involves studying healthy volunteers who have undergone multiple MRI scans with GBCAs (Johnson et al. 2019). The IRB wants the investigator to consider whether these participants should be notified of their personal study results, including gadolinium deposition in the brain, given that such results would not be actionable at this time but adverse effects may be established in the foreseeable future.

What duty do investigators have toward participants regarding the disclosure of study results of unknown but potential significance? The answer to this ethical issue was once regarded as straightforward: At least when dealing with healthy volunteers, investigators' obligation was not to create harm or to worsen participants' health; hence, there was no obligation to provide personalized research findings. This view rested on three propositions. First, a person who enrolls in research does not have a patient–physician relationship with the investigator, absent an explicit agreement. It was thought that the contrary view would unduly burden investigators—and the sponsors of research—and also potentially create an undue inducement for people to enroll in research as a means of getting medical care. This connects to the second reason: It was thought that when investigators behave like care providers, they aggravate the "therapeutic misconception," namely, the tendency of people to agree to participate in research under the misimpression that investigators aim to advance patients' individual interests when in fact their principal objective is advancing scientific knowledge. Third, the return of results was opposed because of their potential unreliability (often involving measurements that have not been validated to the level of accuracy and reliability required for clinical use) and lack of utility (causing alarm to the recipient unduly, precisely because the appropriate medical response to a particular finding is not yet established).

In recent years, the traditional view has come under challenge, propelled by new thinking about so-called "incidental findings" (Presidential Commission for the Study of Bioethics Issues 2013). Expanding on this line of argument, we conclude first that the participants in the current study should be informed of the presence of significant gadolinium deposition, second that the information in question should be regarded as actionable, and third that participants should be able to opt out of disclosure. Furthermore, in line with established ethical codes, the overall results of the completed study should be provided to research participants. The consensus emerging in the literature on investigators' ethical obligations to provide participants with findings uncovered during research MRI scans, and similarly in genome sequencing, is informative for this research ethics consultation, even though any finding of gadolinium deposition would be a primary, rather than an incidental, finding in this study.

The movement toward communicating potentially serious incidental findings to research participants rests both on the principle of justice and on participants' assessment of their own interests. While the creation of a duty to warn imposes a burden on investigators, withholding information about serious risks seems unfair in light of participants' contributions to the research. Furthermore, participants apparently do not buy into the nonmaleficence claim that conveying potentially upsetting findings, which they did not anticipate receiving when they enrolled in the research, creates an unjustified harm. For example, more than 90% of those surveyed in a study about their participation in neuroimaging research wished to be informed of the results of their MRI scans, irrespective of the severity of the findings (Kirschen, Jaworska, and Illes 2006). Similarly, Phillips and colleagues found that greater than 80% of participants wished to know whether their MRI scans were deemed normal or whether either a treatable or an untreatable condition was identified (Phillips et al. 2015). For participants, access to their study results was thus of preeminent importance, irrespective of the clinical significance and actionability of findings. Assuming the methods used in this study to measure gadolinium deposition are scientifically valid, research participants should be informed if significant gadolinium accumulation is found, notwithstanding the uncertainty regarding the pathogenicity and clinical significance of such deposition.

Although clinical guidelines for either reversing gadolinium accumulation or treating its effects do not yet exist, a finding of gadolinium deposition is nevertheless actionable, namely, by potentially refraining from participating in future studies that involve GBCAs. Thus, healthy participants in this study who wish to adhere to the precautionary principle could benefit by responding to their study results and reducing a potential future health risk. Although this unknowable future risk is certainly in a lesser category than a life-threatening but treatable brain tumor uncovered by chance in a research MRI study, preserving patient choice and the opportunity to avoid amassing potential risk is compelling.

Furthermore, out of respect for patient autonomy, participants should be given the chance to opt out of being informed of significant gadolinium deposition. This position aligns with arguments made regarding disclosure of incidental discoveries in cerebral MRI research scans in which the ability to opt out of being informed of findings (Illes et al. 2006), particularly findings that are deemed less serious in nature (Royal and Peterson 2008), is endorsed. Similarly, the American College of Medical Genetics and Genomics (ACMG Board of Directors 2015) recently changed its recommendations from full disclosure (Green et al. 2013) to allowing individuals to choose not to have analyses performed for 56 sequence variations that are known, or expected, to cause disorders (ACMG Board of Directors 2015). In the current study, where the potential implications of the results are much less certain and, based on present knowledge, much less severe, the case for allowing an opt-out is even stronger. (Admittedly, in the ACMG context, the choice allowed is not to test for the variations, whereas in this study, the option would be not to receive the results, since gadolinium analysis is inherent in the research.) Therefore, when a participant is being recruited, the informed consent process should clearly detail the possibility and likelihood of identifying gadolinium deposition, the option to receive individual results or not, and the potential actionability of this information. Additionally, unless they indicate that they do not want the information, research participants should be informed of the overall outcomes of the research study, as outlined in the World Medical Association (WMA) Declaration of Helsinki (World Medical Association 2013). It is also desirable that participants be informed of any additional newly discovered risks of gadolinium deposition, out of respect for their welfare (Emanuel, Wendler, and Grady 2000).

In sum, we believe that investigators should provide research participants not only with the overall study results but also with their own individual gadolinium findings, which have potential, albeit still uncertain, health significance. Furthermore, we believe that individuals should have the choice to opt out of this disclosure, even though some participants will treat the information as actionable by avoiding further studies with GBCAs. Our conclusions are based on the central importance of respecting participants' ability to act as informed decision makers, able to individually assess the trade-off between knowing and not knowing research information of uncertain significance.

References

ACMG Board of Directors. 2015. ACMG policy statement: Updated recommendations regarding analysis and reporting of secondary findings in clinical genome-scale sequencing. *Genetics in Medicine* 17(1):68–9.

Emanuel, E. J., D. Wendler, and C. Grady. 2000. What makes clinical research ethical? *The Journal of the American Medical Association* 283(20):2701–11.

Green, R. C., J. S. Berg, W. W. Grody, Genetics American College of Medical, and Genomics, et al. 2013. ACMG recommendations for reporting of incidental findings in clinical exome and genome sequencing. *Genetics in Medicine* 15(7): 565–74.

Illes, J., M. P. Kirschen, E. Edwards; Research Working Group on Incidental Findings in Brain Imaging, et al. 2006. Ethics. Incidental findings in brain imaging research. *Science* 311(5762): 783–4.

Johnson, L. M., J. Zabrowski, and B. S. Wilfond. 2019. Should research participants be notified about results of currently unknown but potential significance? *American Journal of Bioethics* 19(4):73–4.

Kirschen, M. P., A. Jaworska, and J. Illes. 2006. Subjects' expectations in neuroimaging research. *Journal of Magnetic Resonance Imaging* 23(2):205–9.

Phillips, J. P., C. Cole, J. P. Gluck, J. M. Shoemaker, L. Petree, D. Helitzer, R. Schrader, and M. Holdsworth. 2015. Stakeholder opinions and ethical perspectives support complete disclosure of incidental findings in MRI research. *Ethics and Behavior* 25(4):332–50. doi: 10.1080/10508422.2014.938338.

Presidential Commission for the Study of Bioethics Issues. 2013. Anticipate and Communicate: Ethical Management of Incidental and Secondary Findings in the Clinical, Research, and Direct-to-Consumer Contexts (accessed 9 December 2018).

Royal, J. M., and B. S. Peterson. 2008. The risks and benefits of searching for incidental findings in MRI research scans. *The Journal of Law, Medicine & Ethics* 36(2):305–314, 212.

U.S. Food and Drug Administration. 2017. FDA warns that gadolinium-based contrast agents (GBCAs) are retained in the body; requires new class warnings. Available at: https://www.fda.gov/downloads/Drugs/DrugSafety/UCM589442.pdf (accessed 27 October 2018).

World Medical Association. 2013. World medical association declaration of Helsinki: Ethical principles for medical research involving human subjects. *Journal of the American Medical Association* 310(20):2191–2194. doi: 10.1001/jama.2013.281053.

CASE 2.3: THE ETHICS OF CONTACTING FAMILY MEMBERS OF A SUBJECT IN A GENETIC RESEARCH STUDY TO RETURN RESULTS FOR AN AUTOSOMAL DOMINANT SYNDROME

INTRODUCTION

This case explores the ethical landscape around recontacting a subject's relatives to return genetic research results when the informed consent form signed by the original cohort of subjects is silent on whether investigators may share new information with the research subject's family. As a result of rapid advances in genetic technology, methods to identify genetic markers can mature during the life course of a study. In this case, the investigators identified the genetic mutation responsible for the disorder after a number of their original subjects had died. The researchers now have the ability to inform relatives of the subject about their risk of developing the same disease. Seema Shah, JD, and colleagues at the NIH and University of California, Los Angeles (UCLA), discuss whether and how requirements of the duty to warn are applicable in this case. Mark Rothstein, JD, from the University of Louisville School of Medicine, provides an overview of the medical/scientific, legal, and ethical issues underlying this case. Lauren Milner, PhD, and colleagues at Stanford University explore how the relationship between researcher and subject affects this debate.

In the early 1990s, a research team identified a small cohort of subjects suffering from a unique syndrome. As the research progressed, the team learned that the syndrome affected multiple generations of the index subjects' families. Those with the syndrome were found to be susceptible to life-threatening infections and blood cancers. The syndrome was fatal in nearly 50% of cases. Over time, the team found that certain interventions, including bone marrow transplant, could help to prevent or even cure diseases that occur with this syndrome. Importantly, if a bone marrow transplant from a related donor is a possibility, it is critical to the success of the transplant that the related donor does not also have the syndrome.

In 2011, the team identified the genetic mutation responsible for the syndrome. The disorder is autosomal dominant, which means that affected individuals have a 50% chance of passing the mutation on to their children. The principal investigator's laboratory is Clinical Laboratory Improvement Amendments (CLIA) certified to test for the mutation. Three other independent groups have identified mutations in this gene as the cause of various other clinical syndromes.

The team has maintained contact with many, but not all, former research subjects. It has identified a number of at-risk children who are descendants of the original study population. For more than half of these children, the parent who was in the study is deceased. Some of the descendants are now at reproductive age and may be making decisions to have children of their own.

Because this syndrome is heritable and can be very severe, and because potential interventions may help to prevent or even cure disease, the research team felt an obligation to reestablish contact with the original cohort of surviving subjects in order to offer genetic testing, counseling, and education to the subjects' relatives.

The consent form does not address the contact of family members of deceased subjects. The team requested an ethics consultation to address the following questions: (1) Do the investigators have an ethical obligation to disclose the risk of a novel mutation to the descendants of former research subjects? (2) If so, how should these at-risk individuals be identified and informed?

COMMENTARY 2.3.1: WHAT DOES THE DUTY TO WARN REQUIRE?

SEEMA K. SHAH, SARA CHANDROS HULL, MICHAEL A. SPINNER, BENJAMIN E. BERKMAN, LAUREN A. SANCHEZ, RUQUYYAH ABDUL-KARIM, AMY P. HSU, REGINALD CLAYPOOL, AND STEVEN M. HOLLAND

We all have a duty to warn others when we can easily provide information to protect them from significant harm. In the medical context, a duty to warn patients and research subjects who are at risk of a disease is widely recognized. More recently, a similar duty to warn relatives of patients or research subjects has been discussed in the literature (Offit et al. 2004).

Several prominent organizations have provided guidance on the disclosure of genetic information to family members in the clinical context (American Society of Clinical Oncology 2003; American Society of Human Genetics [ASHG] 1998; Green et al. 2013; Institute of Medicine Committee on Assessing Genetic Risks 1994; President's Commission for the Study of Ethical Problems in Medicine and Biomedical and Behavioral Research 1998). These groups agree that healthcare professionals have an obligation to inform patients about the potential for genetic risks to relatives (ASHG 1998). McGuire and colleagues have proposed that this duty expands to include individuals participating in research when the relevant information or tests have been validated (McGuire, Caulfield, and Cho 2008). Most commentators and organizations argue that this duty has to be balanced against the obligation to maintain the confidentiality of genetic information and to respect the desires of those who wish not to know certain information.

In the case presented, there is a strong ethical justification to inform subjects' relatives about the mutation and the availability of genetic testing and counseling. The research team is in the unique position of having information that is clinically actionable and could prevent serious harm in some people with the genetic mutations. There are several interventions, including treatment with preventive antibiotics, vaccination, and bone marrow transplant, that could prevent or possibly cure disease. Without knowledge of this syndrome, therapeutic interventions may be delayed, overlooked, or mismanaged. For example, prior to discovery of the mutation in question, a patient could receive a bone marrow transplant from a sibling who unknowingly carried the same mutation. This could contribute to a patient's subsequent relapse and death after transplant. For this reason, it is critically important to screen related donors for the relevant mutations. Additionally, this genetic information can be relevant when making reproductive decisions. In many respects, therefore, failure to disclose this information could lead to significant harm.

Although there is a strong justification for disclosing this information, how the information should be disclosed is not straightforward. First, it is important to consider the value of respecting the confidentiality of subjects who may not want their health information disclosed to family members. Some of the subjects who were involved in the study are now deceased. With respect to deceased subjects, in the absence of a prospective conversation about disclosure after death, the researchers would not know whether the deceased subjects had preferences to keep their information confidential that would be violated by contacting their relatives. Even if deceased subjects had previously expressed a desire to maintain confidentiality, however, it is difficult to see how they would be harmed by disclosure after their death, and these desires likely would be outweighed by the potential to prevent serious harm to their relatives (Chan et al. 2012).

With regard to living subjects, family-mediated contact may be the best approach. Ideally, the subject would share information with the research team about family members who may be at risk and would facilitate contact with those family members. Family members may sometimes neglect to, or choose not to, disclose health information within their family (Gaff et al. 2007), however, which raises the question of what the research team should do if some living subjects do not wish to reveal their health information.

In some cases, parents may decide that they would not like to have their children tested for the genetic mutation. Acknowledging that parents are given considerable discretion over medical decision making for their children and that the syndrome may not affect some individuals until they are adults, the wishes of a parent with regard to genetic testing generally should be respected if the child is a minor. Nevertheless, given that there are medical interventions that can help prevent or cure disease, it would be reasonable for researchers to urge reluctant parents to have their children tested for the mutation. For parents who continue to decline testing for their children, it will be important to try to foster an ongoing conversation with the point of contact so that even if the information is not shared with an at-risk individual immediately, there is still some possibility of sharing the information at a later date.

When a subject does not want the team to contact relatives who are adults, however, the team should weigh the ethical duty to warn against the duty to maintain confidentiality in each case, and there will likely be cases in which the duty to warn trumps confidentiality.

The American Society of Human Genetics permits unauthorized disclosure when:

attempts to encourage disclosure on the part of the patient have failed;

the harm is highly likely to occur and is serious, imminent, and foreseeable;

the at-risk relative(s) is identifiable; and

the disease is preventable, the disease is treatable, or medically accepted standards indicate that early monitoring will reduce the genetic risk.

(ASHG 1998, 474)

These conditions appear to be met in this case, given the potential for serious harm, the options for treatment and prevention, and the fact that early monitoring and intervention could reduce the risks of serious complications in the future. Thus, unauthorized disclosure may be permissible if attempts to encourage disclosure fail, but it should be considered an option of last resort.

Finally, the approach to disclosure should not merely be a way to increase recruitment for the research, and would ideally include genetic counseling to convey the information appropriately. For this reason, it is important to explain to individuals how they can obtain testing and treatment even if they decline study participation, and to provide genetic counseling to all individuals about the test and their results.

References

American Society of Clinical Oncology. 2003. Policy statement of the American Society of Clinical Oncology Update: Genetic testing for cancer susceptibility. *Journal of Clinical Oncology* 21:2397–406.

American Society of Human Genetics [ASHG]. 1998. ASHG statement. Professional disclosure of familial genetic information. The American Society of Human Genetics Social Issues Subcommittee on Familial Disclosure. *American Journal of Human Genetics* 62:474–83.

Chan, B., F. M. Facio, H. Eidem, S. C. Hull, L. G. Biesecker, and B. E. Berkman. 2012. Genomic inheritances: Disclosing individual research results from whole-exome sequencing to deceased participants' relatives. *American Journal of Bioethics* 12(10):1–8.

Gaff, C. L., A. J. Clarke, P. Atkinson, et al. 2007. Process and outcome in communication of genetic information within families: A systematic review. *European Journal of Human Genetics* 15:999–1011.

Green, R. C., J. S. Berg, W. W. Grody, et al. 2013. ACMG recommendations for reporting of incidental findings in clinical exome and genome sequencing, American College of Medical Genetics
and Genomics. Available at: http://www.acmg.net/docs/ACMG_Releases_Highly-Anticipated_
Recommendations_on_Incidental_Findings_in_Clinical_Exome_and_Genome_Sequencing.pdf
(accessed March 25, 2013).

Institute of Medicine Committee on Assessing Genetic Risks. 1994. *Assessing genetic risks:
Implications for health and social policy*, Washington, DC: National Academies Press.

McGuire, A., T. Caulfield, and M. K. Cho. 2008. Research ethics and the challenge of whole-
genome sequencing. *Nature Reviews Genetics* 9:152–6.

Offit, K., E. Groeger, S. Turner, E. A. Wadsworth, and M. A. Weiser. 2004. The "duty to warn"
a patient's family members about hereditary disease risks. *Journal of the American Medical
Association* 292(12):1469–73.

President's Commission for the Study of Ethical Problems in Medicine and Biomedical and
Behavioral Research. 1998. *Screening and counseling for genetic conditions: The ethical, social,
and legal implications of genetics screening, counseling, and education programs*, Washington,
DC: U.S. Government Printing Office.

COMMENTARY 2.3.2: SHOULD RESEARCHERS DISCLOSE RESULTS TO DESCENDANTS?

MARK A. ROTHSTEIN

One of the possible benefits of new genetic research is that genetic information discovered about a research subject may have important implications for the health of a research subject's family members. When research subjects are available at the time of the discovery, assuming they have not indi-cated they do not want to be recontacted, it is relatively easy to contact them and advise them of the familial significance of research findings. Then the research subjects can decide whether to inform their relatives, authorize the researcher to do so, or decline to inform family members. In cases where the research subjects have died and the original informed consent document does not address disclo-sure of results to family members after the death of the research subject, researchers face a dilemma. Disclosure seems to be a way to avert harm to the relatives, but it is not clear whether disclosure is legally permissible, is ethically desirable, or could potentially be the cause of unintended consequences.

There are three types of issues to consider. First are scientific and medical issues, such as the strength of the association, severity of the condition, degree of penetrance, variability of expression, length of latency, and degree to which early intervention is valuable. Because these issues have been widely dis-cussed in various other reviews of genetic risk (Berg, Khoury, and Evans 2011), I do not address them in this short commentary. Second are legal issues, especially those arising under the Health Insurance Portability and Accountability Act (HIPAA) Privacy Rule. Third are ethical issues, including the most appropriate way of offering information to at-risk relatives.

At the outset, it is important to note that a researcher's legal and ethical obligations to a research subject are not the same as the obligations owed by a physician to a patient. The physician–patient relationship—but not the researcher–research subject relationship—is what the law terms a fiduciary relationship, where one person (the physician) has a duty to act primarily for the benefit of another (the patient) with regard to a specific undertaking (medical care) (Hafemeister and Spinos 2009). Consequently, a physician's duties to a patient are more extensive than the narrow duties owed by a researcher to a research subject. Although researchers have fewer duties than clinicians do, they still have legal and ethical duties that could extend beyond the research protocol, possibly including offer-ing unexpected research findings to research subjects or even to the family members of a deceased research subject.

Disclosure of a deceased research subject's genetic information to a family member raises important issues under the HIPAA Privacy Rule. Because an academic medical center is classified as a healthcare provider and therefore is considered a covered entity under HIPAA (45 C.F.R. § 160.102(a)(3)), a researcher at such an institution would be subject to the HIPAA Privacy Rule. The provisions of the HIPAA Privacy Rule expressly apply to the protected health information (PHI) of a deceased individual (45 C.F.R. §164.502(f)). The HIPAA Privacy Rule defers to state law on who is an executor, administrator, or other person authorized to act on behalf of a deceased individual or the individual's estate. Under the HIPAA Privacy Rule, this individual is considered a "personal representative" and has the same rights that the deceased individual had to access PHI or authorize the disclosure of PHI to other individuals or entities (45 C.F.R. §164.502(g)(4)).

The U.S. Department of Health and Human Services Office for Civil Rights, which enforces the HIPAA Privacy Rule, has indicated it is permissible for a covered entity to disclose a decedent's PHI to a healthcare provider for treatment of a relative of the decedent (U.S. Department of Health and Human Services 2013). This clarification would seem to apply only if a healthcare provider treating the relative of the decedent contacted the researchers in search of genetic results. It would not permit the unsolicited, direct disclosure of PHI to a decedent's relative without the prior authorization of the decedent. Therefore, if there has been no prior authorization for disclosure signed by the decedent, a researcher seeking to offer information to at-risk relatives would need to contact the decedent's personal representative, who could contact the relatives or sign an authorization for the researcher to do so.

Establishing the lawful method for contacting at-risk relatives does not resolve the issue of when it is ethically appropriate to do so. Although offering to disclose or actually disclosing potentially important and medically actionable information might seem to represent a clear case of beneficence, receiving the information may have negative consequences for the relatives. By definition, the finding has come in a research study and therefore the results may be ambiguous or indeterminate for any particular individual. The information may lead to an expensive, time-consuming, stressful, and unsuccessful diagnostic odyssey. It also could lead several family members from multiple generations to become committed to a lifetime of medical surveillance with little clinical utility. Furthermore, the family members could suffer from psychological, social, or economic harms.

Prospectively, researchers can avoid the quandary of whether to notify descendants by ensuring that consent forms and discussions with research subjects make explicit mention of when, if at all, researchers are authorized to inform at-risk family members of research findings, both during the lifetime of the research subject and after the research subject's death. For legacy studies, such as the case under consideration, the HIPAA Privacy Rule mandates that surviving relatives may be contacted only through the decedent's personal representative. Ethically, an interesting question is whether, if the personal representative refuses to authorize notification of family members, it is justifiable to override this decision and contact the relatives directly. Because of the life-and-death nature of the condition in this case, it is reasonable to expect that the personal representative will grant permission to contact descendants.

References

Berg, J. S., M. J. Khoury, and J. P. Evans. 2011. Deploying whole genome sequencing in clinical practice and public health: Meeting the challenge one bin at a time. *Genetics in Medicine* 13(6):499–504.

Hafemeister, T. L., and S. Spinos. 2009. Lean on me: A physician's fiduciary duty to disclose an emergent medical risk to the patient. *Washington University Law Review* 86(2):1167–210.

U.S. Department of Health and Human Services. 2013. Frequently asked questions about the HIPAA Privacy Rule: How can family members of a deceased individual obtain the deceased individual's protected health information that is relevant to their own health care? Available at: http://www.hhs.gov/ocr/privacy/hipaa/faq/smaller_providers_and_businesses/222.html (accessed May 8, 2013).

COMMENTARY 2.3.3: RELATIONSHIPS MATTER: ETHICAL CONSIDERATIONS FOR RETURNING RESULTS TO FAMILY MEMBERS OF DECEASED SUBJECTS

LAUREN C. MILNER, EMILY Y. LIU, AND NANIBAA' A. GARRISON

The obligation to return genetic results to the biological relatives of research subjects is an emerging issue in research ethics. The lack of consensus regarding this type of third-party disclosure is apparent in both bioethics literature and human subjects research guidelines (Tassé 2011). Here, we argue that the ethical obligation to return genetic results to a subject's relatives depends as much on the relationship between the researcher and the subject as on the results obtained. Specifically, the researcher's ethical obligation to disclose genetic results depends on whether his or her relationship with the subject exists exclusively within the research context or whether the researcher also serves as the subject's physician.

If the relationship between researcher and subject exists only within the context of the study, the researcher has no obligation to return results to the subject's relatives. This position is based on arguments asserting that a researcher's primary duty is to produce reliable research that advances general knowledge, rather than to provide benefits to individual research subjects, and that actively disclosing individual results to any subject would place undue burden on the research enterprise (Clayton and McGuire 2012). There is a growing consensus, however, that the return of analytically valid and clinically actionable genetic results falls within the scope of researcher duties to provide subjects with information that may be particularly beneficial to their physical or psychological health (Fabsitz et al. 2010, 575; Ravitsky and Wilfond 2006, 9). This beneficence-based argument for disclosure rests on two assumptions: first, that the researcher's duty extends only to the research subject (and not to the subject's relatives); and, second, that the subject could directly benefit from the results to be returned, either by allowing the subject to seek clinical care for a condition or by informing important life choices (such as reproductive decisions).

In the case considered here, we assume that the research team's goal in disclosing results is to benefit subjects' families rather than the subjects themselves, as noted by their intent to "offer genetic testing, counseling, and education to [subjects'] relatives." We also assume that the direct benefit to subjects in this case is negligible, because the subjects are already aware of their condition and treatment options and are beyond reproductive age. Because there is presumably no direct benefit to subjects themselves, the researchers have no ethical obligation to disclose results to subjects' relatives.

The ethical obligation to report analytically valid, clinically actionable genetic results to a subject's relatives may change if the researcher is also the subject's physician. In this scenario, the physician-researcher *may* have an ethical obligation to disclose to subjects' relatives based on a physician's "duty to warn" patients' relatives of their risk for a hereditary condition (Laberge and Burke 2009; Offit et al. 2004). Physicians' obligation to disclose genetic results to patients' relatives has been raised in both case law and genetic testing guidelines, although a general consensus about this issue has not been reached. In U.S. case law, a precedent has been set for obligatory disclosure of genetic results to relatives: In *Pate v. Threlkel* (1995), the state court ruled that physicians have the duty to disclose genetic risks to a patient's children, although they also noted this duty is met by warning the patient of their children's risk for developing the condition. In *Safer v. Estate of Pack* (1996), the court extended the physician's duty to include taking "reasonable steps" to directly inform a patient's immediate relatives of their genetic risk for a severe and clinically actionable condition.

Unlike case law, national and international guidelines for disclosure of clinical genetic results vary considerably. While many guidelines cite a physician's duty to respect patient confidentiality as the principle consideration for disclosure, others assert that beneficence toward patients' relatives supersedes patient confidentiality in specific circumstances, such as in cases where genetic information relates to a life-threatening illness for which an effective intervention exists (Black and McClellan 2011, 608).

The genetic information presented in this case fits these specific circumstances, and the harm to relatives resulting from nondisclosure far outweighs the potential harm to living or deceased subjects resulting from a confidentiality breach. Furthermore, in the absence of explicit wishes from deceased subjects, many favor the disclosure of genetic results on the presumption that the deceased subject would consent to providing medical information relevant to the health of his or her relatives (Wertz, Fletcher, and Berg 2003, 85). Taken together, we believe that the circumstances arising in this research study suggest that a physician-researcher should take additional steps to ensure that they disclose results to the immediate biological relatives of their subject-patients, either by encouraging living subjects to share the results with their families or by directly informing the relatives of deceased subjects.

Regardless of the relationship, the return of genetic results in this case is ethically permissible if disclosed responsibly. The case description notes that the researchers feel it is appropriate to disclose results and are in a position to do so (i.e., the tests are being performed in a CLIA-certified laboratory). A number of key issues must be addressed, however, before establishing contact with relatives. Researchers must first decide upon a reporting plan that addresses how to contact relatives, how to disclose results, and what types of support and education services will be provided. Unless the researcher is a physician with an existing relationship with the family and extensive experience in returning genetic results, the disclosure process must involve genetic counselors. Additional questions to be addressed include who will disclose results (researchers, outside physicians, or genetic counselors) and to what extent the living subjects themselves will be involved in the disclosure process to their relatives. Once a plan has been established, researchers must ensure that the necessary resources are in place before contacting relatives. These practical considerations are critical to the ethical permissibility of returning genetic results—because the ethical basis for disclosure to subjects' relatives is beneficence. Therefore, failure to offer adequate follow-up support and services would undermine the ethical justification for return of results by potentially generating significant harms for individuals, such as heightened anxiety over their risk for developing the condition or detrimental behavioral changes based on misinterpretation of genetic results. However, if a comprehensive plan addressing these issues is established prior to initiating contact, then we strongly recommend the team return genetic results to biological relatives of the research subjects in this study.

References

Black, L., and K. A. McClellan. 2011. Familial communication of research results: A need to know? *Journal of Law, Medicine & Ethics* 39(4):605–13.

Clayton, E. W., and A. L. McGuire. 2012. The legal risks of returning results of genomics research. *Genetics in Medicine* 14(4):473–7.

Fabsitz, R. R., A. McGuire, R. R. Sharp, et al. 2010. Ethical and practical guidelines for reporting genetic research results to study participants: Updated guidelines from a National Heart, Lung, and Blood Institute working group. *Circulation Cardiovascular Genetics* 3(6):574–80.

Laberge, A. M., and W. Burke. 2009. Duty to warn at-risk family members of genetic disease. *Virtual Mentor* 11(9):656–60.

Offit, K., E. Groeger, S. Turner, E. A. Wadsworth, and M. A. Weiser. 2004. The "duty to warn" a patient's family members about hereditary disease risks. *Journal of the American Medical Association* 292(12):1469–73.

Pate v. Threlkel. 1995. 661 So.2d 278 (Fla. 1995).

Ravitsky, V., and B. S. Wilfond. 2006. Disclosing individual genetic results to research participants. *American Journal of Bioethics* 6(6):8–17.

Safer v. Estate of Pack. 1996. 291 N.J. Super 619, 667 A.2d 1188 (N.J.Super.App.Div. 1996).

Tassé, A. M.. 2011. The return of results of deceased research participants. *Journal of Law, Medicine & Ethics* 39(4):621–30.

Wertz, D. C., J. C. Fletcher, and K. Berg. 2003. *Review of ethical issues in medical genetics*, Geneva: World Health Organization.

CASE 2.4: ETHICS OF CONTINUING TO PROVIDE A DRUG ON AN OPEN-LABEL EXTENSION STUDY FOR AN "UNAPPROVED INDICATION"

INTRODUCTION

This case explores the ethical obligations regarding open-label extension trials in groups of patients in whom the drug did not demonstrate sufficient efficacy to garner regulatory approval. This case involves adults with primary pulmonary hypertension for which current treatments have limited effectiveness and are costly. All three commentators come to similar conclusions, but for different reasons. All think that the open-label extension trials should be allowed, provided participants are informed about (1) what they received during the study and (2) the study results. None argued there is a clear obligation to offer the open-label extension to this population.

Joshua S. Crites, PhD, from Penn State College of Medicine, raises the question of whether researchers' obligations are different from a clinical or research perspective, and suggests that these perspectives converge and do not support an obligation to offer the open-label extension because of lack of efficacy. Ryan R. Nash, MD, MA, from the Ohio State University Center for Bioethics and Medical Humanities, considers this from the perspective of uncertainty (clinical, economic, and ethical) and suggests that these uncertainties mitigate the researchers having any such obligations. Mildred Cho, PhD, from Stanford University, focuses on the goals of this type of research, and suggests that an open-label extension, while not obligatory, should be designed to maximize the goals of generalizable knowledge and potential for individual benefit.

CASE SUMMARY

Subjects were enrolled in a randomized clinical trial of an investigational drug for pulmonary hypertension that was followed by an open-label extension. The analysis for the primary endpoints showed that the drug benefited only one clinical subgroup (with *primary* pulmonary arterial hypertension) and the drug was approved for use in this population. The requestor's primary question was whether there are any ethical concerns with researchers mandating that subjects in these other clinical subgroups stop receiving the drug, or should the researchers merely inform participating clinicians and subjects about the risks suggested by recent findings?

Pulmonary hypertension is a lethal disease with a median survival time of 2.5 years if untreated. Current approved treatments have limited long-term effectiveness and are quite expensive. The approved drugs are most effective in individuals with *primary* pulmonary hypertension; the benefit is less clear to patients in other subgroups who have secondary pulmonary hypertension, such as those whose pulmonary hypertension is secondary to lung disease.

The 24-week multisite/multicenter study enrolled patients with both primary and secondary pulmonary hypertension. The subjects were able to discontinue the drug at their or the investigator's discretion. At the end of 24 weeks, the subjects were rolled over into a long-term extension trial. The ongoing extension trial has 19 subjects with lung disease enrolled in the United States, Canada, and Australia. Patients in the extension trial are permitted to take more than one drug for pulmonary hypertension.

The six-minute walking distance was the primary endpoint. This patient-oriented outcome has a subjective component. Subjects with lung disease showed no improvement in walking distance, although there was an improvement of some of the secondary endpoints related to cardiac function. Other studies using this and other drugs in patients with lung disease show conflicting evidence of worsening and improving lung function in this population.

Based on the results from the study, and with the potential harm to subjects with lung disease noted in some other studies, the sponsor is considering discontinuing the open-label extension for these individuals. If the extension is discontinued for these patients, clinicians can continue to prescribe the drug off-label. However, the drug is extremely expensive and difficult to reimburse for off-label use. Given the potential risks and benefits, does the sponsor have an obligation to subjects to allow interested subjects to remain in the trial to receive the drug at no cost?

COMMENTARY 2.4.1: WHEN SHOULD OPEN-LABEL EXTENSION STUDIES BE STOPPED?

JOSHUA S. CRITES

There are two rationales for conducting open-label extension studies (OLEs). The investigational objective most often cited for an OLE focuses on "gathering information about safety and tolerability of the new drug in long term, day to day use" (Taylor and Wainwright 2005). A second objective, therapeutic in nature, relates to "ongoing access to an effective but otherwise unobtainable medicine by the volunteers who participated in the Phase III … trials" (Day and Williams 2007).

There is doubt whether, due to limitations in study design, OLEs can answer questions about longer-term tolerability. In this case, this concern may be mitigated because the patient population with this disease is relatively small, and subsequently, even small numbers of OLE subjects may sufficiently power statistical analysis or allow investigators to draw other scientific conclusions. Concerns about the second objective often are stated more strongly and relate to the view that an individual's ability to provide adequate informed consent to participate in an OLE is severely limited for two reasons. (1) As Wainwright concludes, "The one piece of information the participant will not be given—must not be given, if one accepts the arguments of the investigators—is whether she has been taking active medication during the first part of the trial or whether she has been taking placebo" (Wainwright 2002). (2) This information is necessary, according to Taylor and Wainwright, because without it subjects are making enrollment decisions based on "their experience during the trial and their perception of the efficacy of the treatment they have received," not on actual outcomes that would be part of the as-yet-unanalyzed aggregate data from the parent study—data that may reveal the study drug to be better (or worse) than the standard of treatment (Taylor and Wainwright 2005).

These objectives and their corresponding criticisms set up a contrast that follows the contours of a debate pervasive throughout clinical research ethics: whether and to what extent research and therapy overlap. One way to determine the guiding ethical principles involved in OLEs might be to determine whether OLEs are purely (or at least primarily) research or therapy, declare allegiance to the "similarity position" or the "difference position" (Miller and Brody 2003), then assign corresponding researcher responsibilities. However, OLEs seem to fall outside the traditional research–therapy dichotomy, instead garnering legitimacy largely from satisfying objectives from both domains. Thus, the most productive way to understand OLEs may be as a convergence of investigational and therapeutic objectives. This approach reveals that investigator responsibilities borrow from the ethics of research and of clinical care.

Ideally, the researcher should inform individuals who consent to participate in an OLE that they are enrolling in an activity with inherent (and sometimes unknown) risks, and that at the time of enrollment there can be no definitive conclusions drawn from the parent study about efficacy. Despite the fact that all subjects will be receiving the study drug, investigators should inform subjects that the OLE might be stopped should new information arise about significant adverse effects. This reiterates that one aim of the OLE is to gather data to answer a research question—but it is an important contextual element of the investigator–subject relationship. Subjects should understand that one objective of the OLE is to "contribute to the likelihood that the subjects in the parent trial will benefit from the knowledge to be gained" (Casarett et al. 2001). This obligates researchers to make decisions based on subjects' best medical interests, similar to the ethical principles undergirding a physician–patient relationship. Though these commitments seem to conflict and pull the researcher in opposing directions, they can be navigated by recognizing that "investigators' professional integrity requires them to assess each intervention with a patient-subject in order to discern whether it is aimed at patient care or at research" (Miller and Rosenstein 2003). Making this judgment allows a researcher to determine whether a decision is guided by a duty to the subject or by a commitment to acquiring knowledge to benefit future patients.

Turning to the specific questions raised in the case, with the OLE underway, what obligations do researchers and/or the study sponsor have to subjects in light of final data from the parent study and evidence from other studies that there may be increased risk of a worsening condition when taking the study drug?

Even without case specifics, three possible scenarios can guide our thinking about ethical obligations. In all scenarios, it is important to recall that an OLE is justified (either at the outset or at any time during the study) only if it contributes to generalizable knowledge through sufficiently powered statistical analysis or other legitimate inferential interpretation and it is clinically benefiting at least some subjects. Stated alternatively, if no subjects are benefiting (even if it can contribute to generalizable knowledge) or if investigators lose the ability to draw conclusions based on data gathered during the OLE, the study loses ethical justification and should be closed.

- *Scenario 1*: The case summary indicates, "subjects with lung disease showed no improvement in walking distance," although it is not clear whether this is true for all subjects in that subgroup or only true in the aggregate. Inferring that this evidence indicates only that there was no aggregate improvement (i.e., there were at least a few individuals in the subgroup who demonstrated clinical improvement of the primary endpoint) creates one possible scenario. Some individuals likely enrolled in the OLE thinking it was the only way to receive potential benefit from the study drug outside of the parent study. Because newly discovered information about efficacy and risk clearly is relevant to making this kind of treatment decision, investigators should disclose this information to subjects and participating clinicians. Disclosure respects individual autonomy, facilitates informed decision making regarding continued participation (thereby respecting the inherent therapeutic intent of OLEs), and recognizes that OLEs may yield valuable scientific knowledge. In this scenario, the study should remain open because it meets both of its convergent objectives.
- *Scenario 2*: Another possible scenario is that some subjects in the OLE benefit from the study drug, but, as is likely to be the case upon disclosure of parent study findings, some subjects choose to withdraw. Investigators would be obligated to determine whether they could draw scientifically meaningful conclusions without data from those who withdraw. Should the researchers determine they could not, the study will not be justified and should be closed. Investigators should advocate for an off-label, compassionate-use mechanism for continued access to the drug for those who benefited.
- *Scenario 3*: Another scenario is that no subjects demonstrate benefit along the primary endpoint of the parent study and that improvement in some of the secondary endpoints does not outweigh risks. It is clear that the study does not meet its therapeutic objective, therefore losing ethical justification. Investigators should close the OLE, disclosing findings from the parent study as explanation. They would have no obligation to provide the study drug off-label because none of the subjects has demonstrated clinical improvement.

Researcher obligations in the context of an OLE stem from the convergence of investigational and therapeutic objectives such that neither may be prioritized over the other: They must be considered as being on equal moral footing. Of note, there is nothing that justifies maintaining the status quo. Not disclosing efficacy analysis from the parent study and new data about potential harms from other studies while continuing this OLE essentially would be equivalent to subject exploitation.

References

Casarett, D., J. Karlawish, P. Sankar, K. B. Hirschman, and D. A. Asch. 2001. Open label extension studies and the ethical design of clinical trials. *IRB: Ethics and Human Research* 23(4):1–5.

Day, R. O., and K. M. Williams. 2007. Open-label extension studies: Do they provide meaningful information on the safety of new drugs? *Drug Safety* 30(2):93–105.

Miller, F. G., and H. Brody. 2003. A critique of clinical equipoise: Therapeutic misconception in the ethics of clinical trials. *Hastings Center Report* 33(3):19–28.

Miller, F. G., and D. L. Rosenstein. 2003. The therapeutic orientation to clinical trials. *New England Journal of Medicine* 348(14):1383–6.

Taylor, G. J., and P. Wainwright. 2005. Open label extension studies: Research or marketing? *British Medical Journal (Clinical Research Edition)* 331(7516): 572–4. doi:10.1136/bmj.331.7516.572.

Wainwright, P. 2002. Consent to open label extension studies: Some ethical issues. *Journal of Medical Ethics* 28(6):373–6.

COMMENTARY 2.4.2: THE ROLE OF CLINICAL EQUIPOISE AND PRACTICAL CONSIDERATIONS IN DECIDING WHETHER TO CONTINUE TO PROVIDE A DRUG ON AN OPEN-LABEL EXTENSION STUDY FOR AN "UNAPPROVED INDICATION"

RYAN R. NASH

"Doing" bioethics in our pluralistic society presents great challenge. As we do not agree on where we come from and where we are going and what the good, the valuable, and the right are or what the proper authority is—we do not agree on a content-rich, consensus bioethics. For this reason, research ethics is done predominately at law and public policy. Research ethics, at least the *modus vivendi* (the way of living with a compromise that allows disputing sides to move forward) that has been established at law and public policy, is usually determined in the realm of regulation and compliance. The thin foundation on which research ethics is based is an ethic of permission. This ethic of permission comes from the English common law or Lockean tradition of forbearance rights (Engelhardt 1996). Though there has been a movement to develop a more content-rich ethic based on a particular cosmopolitan, European view of human rights (Trotter 2009), this has not yet become the standard at law and public policy and therefore is not the realm in which research ethics is encountered in the United States (Cherry 2009). Beyond the ethic of permission, it is difficult to claim an ethical obligation in clinical research (basic values such as truth-telling, authorship, and freedom from fraud can fall into this ethic of permission based on forbearance rights). Though one can make a deep ethical argument in this case from a particular moral narrative, such a narrative will not be convincing to all and likely should not be grounds to compel others to follow a directive based on nonshared values and judgments.

With this preamble and the limitations of finding a consensus bioethical position, I argue that the present case largely is asking a clinical and practical question. It deals more with the questions of "Is this effective?" or even "Is this worth the money?" and less about the more clearly ethical "Should we do such a thing?"

The first question often is cast as ethical, but is more a clinical judgment (Anderson 2010): Are there enough data to consider treatment in the secondary pulmonary hypertension group to be harmful? In other words, is there clinical equipoise (Freedman 1987; Shaw and Chalmers 1970)? If there is not clinical equipoise—in other words, if sufficient data exist to suggest that continued treatment in this group is harmful—then the study should be stopped in this group.

The second significant question ultimately may be economic: Does sufficient question remain as to whether the drug is effective in the treatment of secondary pulmonary hypertension? If sufficient uncertainty persists, then continuing the study in the secondary pulmonary hypertension group, or expanding meaningful measures, and even following the cohort until death may be reasonable. How is this an economic determination? Some would be concerned that using an expensive medication without sufficient effect could cost some persons, companies, or even society unduly at the expense of other potentially more effective interventions. The more pressing economic concern, however, may be from the perspective of the pharmaceutical company. Were the study to stop now and the working rule in medicine become not to use the medication for secondary pulmonary hypertension, the company could lose a large population and thus lose revenue in sales. Were the study to continue, and if it ended up showing some benefit, then utilization of the drug might grow. Thus, it could be argued that continuing the treatment in the secondary pulmonary hypertension cohort may be a good business decision.

To close this brief consideration of the case, the following observations and opinions are offered:

1. Clinicians can prescribe medicines off-label if, in their clinical judgment, such medicines are potentially effective. This utilization, whether in a trial or not, will have costs that may seem not worth the cost by many (particularly those who are not the patient seeking treatment). This consideration does not prohibit the prescribing, but also does not oblige the provision of a medication by a company or other entity, such as the state.
2. The basic ethic of permission, at least the particular version that has governed ethics in the United States, demands that the needed information for an opportunity for refusal and participation be shared with the research subject (Engelhardt 1996; Faden and Beauchamp 1986).
3. As to whether the drug company or sponsor of the study has an ethical obligation to continue treating the secondary pulmonary hypertension cohort—in the absence of clear consensus (and there is no consensus in this case)—there is no obligation. But if studying this group offers relative safety for the subjects; if it asks a reasonable, unresolved scientific question with clinical significance; and if subjects are willing to continue in the trial, then continuing seems like a prudent idea.

References

Anderson, J. A. 2010. Clinical research in context: Reexamining the distinction between research and practice. *Journal of Medicine and Philosophy* 35(1):46–63.

Cherry, M. J. 2009. UNESCO, 'universal bioethics,' and state regulation of health risks: A philosophical critique. *Journal of Medicine and Philosophy* 34(3):274–95.

Engelhardt, H. T. 1996. *The foundations of bioethics*, 2nd ed. New York, NY: Oxford University Press.

Faden, R. R., and T. L. Beauchamp. 1986. *A history and theory of informed consent*. New York, NY: Oxford University Press.

Freedman, B. 1987. Equipoise and the ethics of clinical research. *The New England Journal of Medicine* 317(3):141–5.

Shaw, L. W., and T. C. Chalmers. 1970. Ethics in cooperative clinical trials. *Annals of the New York Academy of Sciences* 169:487–95. doi: 10.1111/j.1749-6632.1970.tb54759.x.

Trotter, G. 2009. The UNESCO declaration on bioethics and human rights: A canon for the ages? *Journal of Medicine and Philosophy* 34(3):195–203.

COMMENTARY 2.4.3: OPEN-LABEL EXTENSION STUDIES: ARE THEY REALLY RESEARCH?

MILDRED K. CHO

This consultation about the open-label extension phase of a drug trial raises at least two related questions. The first was posed by the requestor of the consultation: Should the sponsor of this clinical trial mandate that subgroups of subjects for whom the trial had so far shown no benefit discontinue use of the drug now that the study is in the open-label phase, or merely inform subjects and the participating physicians about the findings? Second, does the sponsor have an obligation to allow interested subjects to remain in the trial at no cost?

Central to this case is the assessment of risks and benefits of the intervention. However, the analysis is dependent on whether the primary purpose of the activity (the open-label extension phase of the study) is to create generalizable knowledge (i.e., research) or to provide clinical benefit according to the needs of individuals enrolled in the study (i.e., compassionate use). The usefulness of open-label extension studies for generating reliable and valid data has been challenged (Day and Williams 2007), even as they become more common, and their real purpose is somewhat ambiguous. Therefore, clarification of the intentions of the sponsor is important to the ethical analysis.

Several ethical concerns of open-label studies have been highlighted, primarily that the prospect of receiving interventions that would otherwise not be available or only be available at high cost to the subject is coercive (Micetich 1996), especially for subjects with serious and/or terminal illnesses. Indeed, 80% of subjects interviewed in a study ($n = 32$) conducted in a pain clinic reported that availability of study medications after hypothetical clinical trials would be an important factor in deciding whether to participate (Casarett et al. 2001). In addition, some have argued that subjects cannot give informed consent to participate in an open-label extension study unless they know to which arm of the main trial they were assigned (Wainwright 2002). Irrespective of the purpose of the activity, clinicians and subjects should be informed of the results and of any concerns the study has generated.

If the purpose of the activity is primarily research, federal regulations for protection of human subjects (45 CFR 46) require that risks be balanced by benefits. Data from the Cassarett study suggest that research subjects see potential benefit to themselves in the option to continue to take medications in an open-label extension phase of a study (Casarett et al. 2001) and that the data may "expand the range of normative judgments about open label studies" based on subject preferences. Nevertheless, if this primarily is considered a research activity, this particular trial should be discontinued for all patients because the benefits from generalizable knowledge would be very limited given this study design. In other words, researchers do not have an obligation to provide a drug as part of an open-label extension that is not effective. Ideally, this should have been made clear in the consent form.

If the purpose is primarily to provide clinical benefit to individuals, however, the sponsor should continue to provide access to the drug under the same conditions as in the main study (e.g., at no cost to subjects). Subjects' participation in the trial could be continued at the discretion of subjects and their physicians, assuming that they know in which arm of the main study they had participated. Thus, the research framework should not be used to guide the assessment of risks and benefits (Taylor and Wainwright 2005). However, the researchers could collect data to aid future study designs, such as whether individual subjects experience significant benefit other than the main study's surrogate endpoints (e.g., a six-minute walking distance), or whether physicians believe that there are clinically important benefits of the intervention, such as potentially providing a bridge to transplant.

References

Casarett, D., J. Karlawish, P. Sankar, K. B. Hirschman, and D. A. Asch. 2001. Open label extension studies and the ethical design of clinical trials. *IRB: Ethics & Human Research* 4:1–5.

Day, R. O., and K. M. Williams. 2007. Open-label extension studies: Do they provide meaningful information on the safety of new drugs? *Drug Safety* 30:93–105.

Micetich, K. C. 1996. The ethical problems of the open label extension study. *Cambridge Quarterly of Healthcare Ethics* 5:410–14.

Taylor, G. J., and P. Wainwright. 2005. Open label extension studies: Research or marketing? *British Medical Journal* 331:572–4.

Wainwright, P. 2002. Consent to open label extension studies: Some ethical issues. *Journal of Medical Ethics* 28:373–6.

CASE 2.5: SUPPORTING INVESTIGATORS IN CHALLENGING CASES: UNEASE IN THE FACE OF AN ETHICALLY APPROPRIATE ACTION

INTRODUCTION

As medicine and science advance, new ethical questions emerge. Over time, deliberation and analysis result in a somewhat settled approach to a problem. Often the settled approach is based on group consensus from investigator-initiated working groups, professional organizations, or national entities. However, the "settled approach" rarely remains static over time as new data emerge, social context changes, attitudes shift, and further scholarship emerges.

This "life cycle" has been played out on a wide range of topics in bioethics, such as disclosure of research results. When an investigator faces a seemingly novel ethical challenge in the conduct of research and seeks out the advice of a bioethics consultant, the investigator's problem may span this life cycle: ranging from truly novel to something that is new to the investigator, but for which a "settled approach" has already been defined by the research ethics community. For more settled questions, the consultant will have different resources available to address the problem, including analyses in the literature or consensus statements. However, for the investigator, the problem may still feel raw and palpable. In such a circumstance, how should the consultant address the "angst" that the investigator feels, even if the issue is reasonably settled?

The case below focuses on the distress experienced by an investigator who learns of a research result in a particular participant that he believes the participant would want disclosed, even though the study does not routinely disclose results. The first commentary by Toby Schonfeld and Cynthia M. A. Geppert from the Veterans Health Administration, Washington, DC, points out that the issue of requestor distress is common in clinical bioethics consultation and the consultant may need to spend time helping the investigator clarify the values at play that are resulting in the distress. They note that the overlapping roles of investigator and clinician can be one source of the distress. Shannon Blee, Claire Sibold, Margie Dixon, and Rebecca D. Pentz from the Winship Cancer Institute, Atlanta, GA, take an organizational ethics lens and query whether the institution has a general policy on results disclosure, which, if present, may reduce the angst. They also propose a particular policy for routine disclosure of aggregate data from studies, which could further preempt the distress. Ryan Spellecy and Alan Nyitray from the Medical College of Wisconsin, Milwaukee, WI, engage the question with nuance related to the particular result and its meaning to this participant and question whether, in fact, this result should be disclosed, even though they acknowledge that ultimately the plan for non-disclosure is reasonable. They appreciate that the angst is genuine and cannot be easily addressed other than to accept it as part of the investigator experience.

CASE SUMMARY

Anal cancer is caused by human papillomavirus, like almost all cervical cancers. Unlike cervical cancer, there is no uniformly accepted screening for anal cancer and screening methods are the subject of ongoing research. A common clinical approach is a high-resolution anoscopy (HRA)-directed biopsy to detect precancerous lesions; however, potentially complementary biomarkers are being tested in an ongoing clinical trial. The trial, open to men who have sex with men and transgender persons, collects cells from the anal canal and runs a methylation test to determine if methylation results are a promising biomarker for identifying persons at increased risk for anal cancer. Methylation scores are assessed for association with any precancerous lesions identified during the clinical evaluation (i.e., the HRA-directed biopsy). As the test is investigational, methylation results are not returned to participants.

Recently, the research laboratory performing the methylation analysis informed the principal investigator (PI) of a participant with a very high methylation score, urging the PI to disclose the result. Uncertain how to proceed, the PI requested a research ethics consultation. The consultant concluded that disclosure was not appropriate, given all participants will receive an HRA-directed biopsy and the meaning of methylation is uncertain. However, this seemingly straightforward consultation request, of whether to disclose the research results, became more complicated. The study participant was well known to the PI, and in fact, the PI has somewhat regular contact with the individual and believed that this person would want to know the results, even if the meaning of the test is uncertain. How do research ethics consultants support those who come to us for advice when the decision, even though reasonable and ethical, still carries angst?

COMMENTARY 2.5.1: RESEARCHERS EXPERIENCE MORAL DISTRESS TOO!

TOBY SCHONFELD AND CYNTHIA M. A. GEPPERT

Traditional approaches to human subjects protections in the United States focus on the ethical principles from the *Belmont Report*: respect for persons, beneficence, and justice. Since research regulations stem from, and are conceptually tied to, these principles, researchers and oversight bodies often default to compliance with federal regulation and institutional policy as a stand-in for a robust ethical analysis of a research project. This case presents one example of how this compliance orientation may fail to identify important ethical issues that can arise in the conduct of research. Here, the PI has lingering questions about the right action toward a specific participant despite understanding the process in the approved protocol not to disclose results of unknown scientific significance (Wilfond, Duenas, and Johnson 2021). Because the question is a form of moral uncertainty, we contend this case points to an important problem that has received insufficient attention: moral distress in research.

The PI in this case acknowledges a moral dilemma. He understands the uncertain implication of the findings and the danger of sharing information of unclear clinical import, and yet still feels as though he should inform the participant because the person "would want to know the results." This is a conflict in values: the value of respect for an individual, as compared with the value of protecting the integrity of the clinical trial. There is no value that supports providing erroneous or misleading information to participants or patients; such disclosure could cause considerable harm. Indeed, this is one of the reasons why informed consent and shared decision making rely on disclosure of information germane to the decision at hand (Childress and Childress 2020). Therefore, since the concern is not about straightforward truth-telling, something else must be going on here.

One possible explanation may apply if the PI is also the participant's healthcare provider. The ethical tension between the dual roles of researcher and healthcare provider is increasingly recognized (Morain, Joffe, and Largent 2019). In that case, the PI may have difficulty separating roles—and, importantly, correlative responsibilities—when acting as clinician and when acting as researcher. In the former role, the healthcare provider's obligation is to promote the patient's welfare. If the healthcare provider believes that the patient would want information consistent with their healthcare preferences, regardless of its potential import, the provider might feel they should disclose it out of respect for the patient's values. The researcher, however, does not have the participant's welfare as the central organizing principle. Instead, fidelity to the research protocol as a mechanism to answer an important scientific question is the focus. True, the PI must monitor and act on the participant's welfare during the course of the research in accordance with both the rules that govern and the values that ground human subjects research. Still, the end goal is *not* benefit to the individual participant. This difference in moral obligation is what may give rise to moral distress: standing by while the participant is not provided information that the investigator believes the individual would want to know.

While the concept of moral distress is well hewn in the clinical ethics literature, it is rarely applied in the context of research ethics (Resnik 2016). Traditional moral distress occurs when professionals cannot carry out what they believe to be ethically appropriate actions because of internal (e.g., fear of repercussions; self-doubt) or external (e.g., lack of administrative support or follow-up on concerns; hierarchies within healthcare systems) constraints. In this case, the PI is facing the external constraint of the requirement to follow the approved protocol. The root of his distress is that the protocol prohibits him from disclosing research results to the participant, despite his conviction that the person would want them: it is a conflict of values. The researcher does not appear to question the validity of the overall rule, as it results from the scientific process to which the researcher has voluntarily committed. Yet the researcher is also clearly conflicted about his obligations to the participant.

Feeling as though core values have been compromised even when there is an ethically justifiable resolution of a moral dilemma can still be morally distressing. "Being thrust into a moral dilemma can lead to feelings of compromise, loss of well-being, and so on, just as naturally as being faced with a morally right option that one is kept from taking" (Campbell, Ulrich, and Grady 2016). As the case states, the researcher understands that an ethical decision and action have been reached, and yet he still experiences angst. This happens because values often support competing actions, and even when properly adjudicated, moral agents can be left feeling as though they were not able to adequately discharge all of their responsibilities—and, sometimes, they can't. One action may preclude another, as is the case here. And that is distressing, especially when it involves human well-being.

Recognizing that researchers too encounter moral dilemmas that result in moral distress not only facilitates greater awareness of the problem but also suggests that solutions that have been found beneficial for healthcare providers may also be helpful to researchers. One strategy from the clinical literature on moral distress that has potential application to research is values clarification: a process that helps an individual identify their values as a means of facilitating decision making (Rushton 2006). This is an area where the research ethics consultant could have gone beyond merely indicating that not informing the participant was ethically justifiable. The consultant could have assisted the PI to identify the respective values of his role as a researcher and as a provider, as well as the values of the participant (to the extent these are known), and to analyze and reflect on how all of these values bear on the decision at hand. Adapting that process to this case would require more information about the participant's purported desire to know the information of uncertain clinical importance. Understanding the values that support that conclusion may provide a window into helping the researcher either meet those values in other ways or recognize that there is no value conflict after all (because, when he analyzes it, he realizes he does not have an obligation to provide uncertain and potentially misleading information).

Even more promising are the lessons learned in healthcare about how experiences of moral distress can be transformed into moral resilience. Resiliency strategies include (but are not limited to): (1) ensuring there are safe spaces in which researchers can reflect on the moral dimensions of their work, (2) incorporating moral distress identification and mitigation into research ethics training, and (3) promoting the moral agency of researchers. Morally resilient people also have developed self-confidence by confronting such situations so they can maintain their moral compass, no matter what happens in a protocol (Lachman 2016).

At the end of the day, the consultant must validate the researcher's feelings of distress and provide insight into both the causes and potential mitigation strategies for the researcher.

References

Campbell, S. M., C. M. Ulrich, and C. Grady. 2016. A broader understanding of moral distress. *The American Journal of Bioethics* 16(12):2–9.

Childress, J. F., and M. D. Childress. 2020. What does the evolution from informed consent to shared decision making teach us about authority in health care? *AMA Journal of Ethics* 22(5):E423–9.

Lachman, V. D. 2016. Moral resilience: Managing and preventing moral distress and moral residue. *Medsurg Nursing* 25(2):121–4.

Morain, S. R., S. Joffe, and E. A. Largent. 2019. Response to open peer commentaries: When is it ethical for physician-investigators to seek consent from their own patients? *The American Journal of Bioethics* 19(5):W3–4.

Resnik, D. B. 2016. Moral distress in scientific research. *The American Journal of Bioethics* 16(12):13–5.

Rushton, C. H. 2006. Defining and addressing moral distress: Tools for critical care nursing leaders. *AACN Advanced Critical Care* 17(2):161–8.

Wilfond, B. S., D. M. Duenas, and L.-M. Johnson. 2021. Supporting investigators in challenging cases: Unease in the face of an ethically appropriate action. *The American Journal of Bioethics* 21(4):98–9.

COMMENTARY 2.5.2: RELIEVING INVESTIGATOR ANGST AFTER AN APPROPRIATE BUT CONCERNING ETHICS CONSULTATION

SHANNON BLEE, HANNAH CLAIRE SIBOLD, MARGIE DIXON, AND REBECCA D. PENTZ

Even appropriate, ethically sound recommendations can generate angst. In this case, the PI is concerned about the ethics consultation recommendation to not inform the participant about the high methylation score, since the PI is convinced that the participant would want to know the results (Wilfond, Duenas, and Johnson 2021). We suggest three steps to relieve the PI's angst based on our own experience that angst can be relieved if we rethink the conclusion reached to make sure it is correct and then see if there is any positive action to take. First, we would carefully review the recommendation with the PI to see if and why it is ethically sound. Second, we would determine if this problem arose because of an organizational ethics issue that could be resolved with an institutional return of individual results policy. If the institution does not have such a policy, we suggest two acceptable approaches to establish one, both of which may address the PI's concerns at an institutional level, relieving the PI of his perceived responsibility to inform the participant of his results and helping to alleviate his personal angst.

The ethics consultant offers two reasons to justify no disclosure: As part of the trial, the participant will receive the commonly used approach of biopsying precancerous lesions, so he is not left without any information about his anal cancer risk. Second, since this is a research protocol to test if the methylation score is a biomarker for anal cancer, it is unknown whether a high score indicates cancer risk, making the results not medically actionable. After this review, it is likely that the PI still exhibits angst, since he is convinced that the participant wants all information, actionable or not. The PI is to be lauded for recognizing that the participant is an information monitor, since this promotes patient-centered, individualized care, even though it did result in his own angst (Roussi and Miller 2014).

Since reviewing the reasons for the ethics recommendation did not relieve the PI's angst, the next step could be to determine if there is an organizational ethics issue that could be solved and, by doing so, help the PI resolve his personal angst.

A major question is why this problem arose in the first place. Why was the PI called? Did the research lab think the results were actionable? If not, were the guidelines for returning individual results unclear? Or were there no guidelines?

If there is a return of individual results policy at this institution, education of the research team about this policy is needed. If there is no policy, we recommend that the institution develop one. There are three options. One option is to allow participants to opt in or out of receiving actionable findings, which would abide by the principle of respect for persons and patient autonomy (Long et al.

2019). Research indicates that the majority of participants want actionable results, especially if they are returned at no cost (Bollinger et al. 2014). In this case, the PI believes that his participant would want all the results returned, not just the actionable ones. However, while there are studies that suggest research participants want all results (Bijlsma et al. 2020), we do not recommend giving participants this option as it could lead to therapeutic misconception, participant harm, and participants' misunderstanding of the research results' significance (Long et al. 2019). Another concern that specifically applies to low-literate individuals is that low health literacy has been shown to be correlated with distress when receiving incidental findings (Phillips et al. 2015). Additionally, what the participants choose in the consent may not be indicative of their actual preferences due to misinterpretations of what returning results includes (Viberg et al. 2016). Returning all results could also slow down research, and studies have shown that if participants were aware that research length could be impacted if they were to receive all results, then they were satisfied with receiving only actionable ones (Bollinger et al. 2014). Finally, given that the participant is an information monitor, returning ambiguous results may heighten their anxiety and contribute to distress, since the monitor's goal is to find information that leads to certainty (Roussi and Miller 2014). Given this situation, we recommend that the institution adopt a second option: a policy of only returning medically actionable findings. If this policy had been in place, there would have been one of two ways to proceed: (1) If the study is so conclusive that the methylation score becomes actionable by the end of the study, the return of individual results policy that stipulates actionable findings will be returned would trigger disclosure of the result to the participants at the conclusion of the study. (2) However, more likely, more studies would need to be performed to establish whether methylation scores are true biomarkers. In this case, we propose a relatively underused approach—posting aggregate results after publication of the research study's findings.

Posting the aggregate results following publication treats the participants with respect and provides them with information, though admittedly delayed. The Children's Oncology Group (COG) has used this approach: At the completion and publication of a study's findings, aggregate results are published as a lay summary online on the COG website. The participants are informed at consent and at the participant's study completion that they can access this lay summary, and they can sign up on the COG portal to be informed when the lay summary is available. Furthermore, each lay summary is created in a multistep process by nurses and physicians with patient education experience and by a patient advocate to ensure understandability. Participants are advised to reach out to their home institution if they have any questions or concerns about the results (Fernandez et al. 2012). This approach ensures that the research itself will not be negatively impacted and that the results will be posted in an understandable manner so as to eliminate any health literacy challenges. Several caveats to the COG approach need to be mentioned: (1) Currently, COG does not post biomarker studies due to personnel constraints; and (2) since the publication process is a lengthy one, members of the research community may know whether or not a methylation score is a biomarker substantially before the lay summary is posted. This situation may trigger the PI's angst, since the PI will know the results before the lay summary is posted and may feel obligated to inform the participant as soon as possible. However, it is doubtful that the test would be standard of care and CLIA approved before publication of the research and completion of the lay summary.

Though not perfect, communicating aggregate results to all participants respects research participants and would allow the participant to know whether or not a high methylation score is a biomarker. If it is, he can determine his own risk by being retested in a CLIA lab, if the test is approved. In this way, the participant's desire for information is respected, though, admittedly, with what could be a significant delay.

In summary, we recommend that institutions adopt a return of individual results policy that recommends disclosure of actionable results to the participants in real time and return of the aggregate results after study publication. Implementing such a policy will help alleviate the organizational ethics issue present and provide a standardized process for returning results. Having this policy at the institutional level will decrease the PI's perceived responsibility to inform the participant of the results, helping to alleviate his personal angst. Hopefully, working with the PI to take action in addressing the concerns raised by this case will relieve some angst both for him now and for others in future studies.

References

Bijlsma, R., R. Wouters, H. Wessels, S. Sleijfer, L. Beerepoot, D. ten Bokkel Huinink, H. Cruijsen, J. Heijns, M. P. Lolkema, N. Steeghs, et al. 2020. Preferences to receive unsolicited findings of germline genome sequencing in a large population of patients with cancer. *ESMO Open* 5(2):e000619.

Bollinger, J. M., J. F. P. Bridges, A. Mohamed, and D. Kaufman. 2014. Public preferences for the return of research results in genetic research: A conjoint analysis. *Genetics in Medicine* 16(12):932–9.

Fernandez, C. V., K. Ruccione, R. J. Wells, J. B. Long, W. Pelletier, M. C. Hooke, R. D. Pentz, R. B. Noll, J. N. Baker, M. O'Leary, et al. 2012. Recommendations for the return of research results to study participants and guardians: A report from the Children's Oncology Group. *Journal of Clinical Oncology* 30 (36):4573–9.

Long, C. R., R. S. Purvis, E. Flood-Grady, K. S. Kimminau, R. L. Rhyne, M. R. Burge, M. K. Stewart, A. J. Jenkins, L. P. James, and P. A. McElfish. 2019. Health researchers' experiences, perceptions and barriers related to sharing study results with participants. *Health Research Policy and Systems* 17(1):25. doi:10.1186/s12961-019-0422-5.

Phillips, J. P., C. Cole, J. P. Gluck, J. M. Shoemaker, L. E. Petree, D. L. Helitzer, R. M. Schrader, and M. T. Holdsworth. 2015. Stakeholder opinions and ethical perspectives support complete disclosure of incidental findings in MRI research. *Ethics & Behavior* 25(4):332–50.

Roussi, P., and S. M. Miller. 2014. Monitoring style of coping with cancer related threats: A review of the literature. *Journal of Behavioral Medicine* 37(5):931–54.

Viberg, J., P. Segerdahl, S. Langenskiold, and M. G. Hansson. 2016. Freedom of choice about incidental findings can frustrate participants' true preferences. *Bioethics* 30(3):203–9.

Wilfond, B. S., D. M. Duenas, and L.-M. Johnson. 2021. Supporting investigators in challenging cases: Unease in the face of an ethically appropriate action. *The American Journal of Bioethics* 21(4):98–9.

COMMENTARY 2.5.3: ACKNOWLEDGING ANGST: RESEARCH ETHICS CONSULTATION IN DISCLOSING EXPERIMENTAL RESEARCH RESULTS OF UNCERTAIN BENEFIT

RYAN SPELLECY AND ALAN NYITRAY

In this case, it is noted that while DNA testing and methylation are being studied as biomarkers for high-grade squamous intraepithelial lesions (precancers) in the anal canal, their efficacy is not yet known (Wilfond, Duenas, and Johnson 2021). If these biomarkers are shown to be efficacious, a positive result may engage the next clinical step, which, in some medical practices, would be to look for the presence of cancerous and precancerous lesions as determined by a digital anal rectal exam and/or a HRA-directed biopsy. We begin our discussion by noting this because HRA-directed biopsy can carry significant morbidity, including pain, discomfort, and bleeding. Moreover, if precancerous lesions are found, there is currently no proven treatment for removing the lesions to prevent the occurrence of anal cancer. Thus, disclosing such a result is not simply informing the research participant and respecting his autonomy, and it must be balanced by the uncertain nature of the test and the very real harms that may follow.

In terms of respecting the autonomy of the research participant, it is noted that the PI knows the participant well and believes he would want to know the results. In fact, the PI believed that even if it were reinforced to the participant that the results are of unknown validity, he would still want to know. The disclosure of research results has been discussed extensively in the literature with strong arguments both for and against the practice (Burke, Evans, and Jarvik 2014; Dressler 2009; Fernandez, Skedgel, and Weijer 2004). Even if the results are of questionable significance to this individual's care, as there is no proven treatment for the removal of precancerous lesions to prevent cancer, there are other benefits such as life planning and other areas that are not strictly clinical. In addition, some private clinics and some public health entities recommend HRA screening among men who have sex with men (MSM), and there is growing awareness among this population of their high risk for anal cancer. Even though methylation testing has not been shown to be efficacious and is not recommended, it may seem inconsistent not to disclose test results given public health campaigns to increase screening among MSM, and more so as their awareness is rising.

First, we believe it is important to acknowledge the unease in this case. We contend that it is not a foregone conclusion that experimental test results should never be disclosed, particularly as we broaden considerations for disclosing results to benefits other than those that are clinically actionable. We also believe we should take seriously the values and preferences of research participants who give their time and literal bodies to further research. Respect for persons in this case requires that we proceed with caution and carefully consider the preferences of the participant. However, as the case states, the results of the methylation tests are not returned to participants, which would be covered in the informed consent process. That this individual enrolled in the study with that knowledge must also be considered in fulfilling the principle of respect for persons. With that in mind, we agree that it is ethically appropriate not to disclose the test results.

We are reminded of a quote from Fitz-James Stephen in *Liberty, Equality, Fraternity*, which, although it was discussing belief in God, is relevant to decision making amidst uncertainty and can be helpful in addressing the resulting angst.

> We stand on a mountain pass in the midst of whirling snow and blinding mist, through which we get glimpses now and then of paths which may be deceptive. If we stand still, we shall be frozen to death. If we take the wrong road, we shall be dashed to pieces. We do not certainly know whether there is any right one. What must we do? "Be strong and of a good courage." Act for the best, hope for the best, and take what comes.
>
> *(Stephen 1967, 158)*

We find this encouraging as it acknowledges the angst of the decision and can, in a sense, give permission to make a decision. The PI in this case has information, and he must decide what to do with it. It may also assuage the PI's angst to reiterate that, as part of the study, this participant is scheduled to receive HRA-directed biopsy and that results will be shared. It is important to relay to him that, through honest and careful deliberation, an ethically sound decision can be reached.

Thus, a thorough and robust discussion of these considerations; taking seriously the likely preferences of the participant; risks and benefits, including those that are not clinical; and acknowledging the difficulty of the decision and angst, without prematurely concluding that since the methylation test is experimental the result ought not be disclosed, are in our opinion how we ought to support the PI who requested this consultation.

References

Burke, W., B. J. Evans, and G. P. Jarvik. 2014. Return of results: Ethical and legal distinctions between research and clinical care. *American Journal of Medical Genetics Part C: Seminars in Medical Genetics* 166(1):105–11.

Dressler, L. G. 2009. Disclosure of research results from cancer genomic studies: State of the science. *Clinical Cancer Research* 15(13):4270–6.

Fernandez, C. V., C. Skedgel, and C. Weijer. 2004. Considerations and costs of disclosing study findings to research participants. *CMAJ: Canadian Medical Association Journal = journal de l'Association medicale canadienne* 170(9):1417–9.

Stephen, J. F. 1967. *Liberty, equality, fraternity*, Cambridge, UK: Cambridge University Press.

Wilfond, B. S., D. M. Duenas, and L.-M. Johnson. 2021. Supporting investigators in challenging cases: Unease in the face of an ethically appropriate action. *The American Journal of Bioethics* 21(4):98–9.

CASE 2.6: RECONTACT AND RECRUITMENT OF YOUNG ADULTS PREVIOUSLY ENROLLED IN NEONATAL HERPES SIMPLEX VIRUS RESEARCH

INTRODUCTION

Herpes simplex virus type 2 (HSV-2) infection is lifelong when it occurs, so that infants infected with HSV-2 will be infected with HSV-2 for life. HSV-2 is periodically shed from skin lesions in children who were perinatally infected, a condition that can episodically persist for years. The intensity of this shedding generally declines with time, although the rate of that decline is uncertain at both the individual and population levels. HSV-2 can be transmitted by asymptomatic shedding as well as by contact with genital lesions (a fact nicely reviewed by Mertz 2008). The case presented here along with three commentaries focuses on whether and how the investigators who enrolled the mothers of infants born with HSV should proceed in the recruitment of the infant cohort, who are now teens or adults, to participate in a novel research study to explore the long-term outcomes and complications of perinatal HSV infection.

Accompanying the case summary are commentaries by Ann J. Melvin, MD, MPH, Kathleen M. Mohan, ARNP, and Anna Wald, MD, MPH, of the University of Washington, along with Katie Porter, JD, MPH, and Benjamin S. Wilfond, MD, of Seattle Children's Research Institute, who posit that the value of the scientific knowledge to be gained must be balanced with the privacy rights of parents. Ross E. McKinney, Jr., MD, of Duke University School of Medicine, identifies and then prioritizes the rights and interests of key stakeholders involved in this case. Erin Talati Paquette, MD, JD, MBe, of Northwestern University and the Ann & Robert H. Lurie Children's Hospital of Chicago, and Lainie Ross, MD, PhD, of the University of Chicago, MacLean Center for Clinical Medical Ethics, argue that the key to the resolution of this case lies in what parents were told when they enrolled in the original study about whether they or their children would be contacted in the future.

CASE SUMMARY

Since 1980, approximately 140 newborns with documented herpes simplex virus (HSV) disease were treated with antiviral medications at a single U.S. children's hospital. For the majority of these early cases, the parents enrolled the newborn in the clinical research study because that was the only way to get access to HSV antiviral medications for many years. Researchers at the same site now want to study the long-term outcomes and complications of neonatal HSV infection. The 140 newborns who were previously in the HSV antiviral research study make up a known population of potential research subjects for this current study.

The initial plan was for the researchers to enroll newly identified infants, as well as to go back and interview older children and their families who were in the initial research study to learn about the child's current health and developmental status. The research also proposes to study whether these children who contracted HSV in the neonatal period are currently experiencing genital shedding of the virus, a question that has long been debated and for which any information would be valuable to treatment and prevention of the spread of the virus.

The IRB has made a distinction in approach based on current age of the potential research subject. For those who were diagnosed as infants who are currently under the age of 18 years, the IRB has approved a recruitment process by which researchers first contact the teen's parent or guardian (as documented in the initial neonatal study paperwork) and ask whether they would give permission for their teen to be enrolled in the current study.

For those who were diagnosed as infants who are currently 18 or older, the IRB has approved a recruitment process by which researchers contact the young adult's parent or guardian to ask whether they would forward study information to their child. If the parent or guardian is unwilling to do so, the researchers will request a telephone interview with the parent to collect limited information regarding the child's HSV history and functional status while under the parent's care and/or up to the age of 18. The IRB did not allow researchers to ask parents or guardians anything about the young adult's health after the child reached 18 years.

Using this recontact and recruitment strategy, the researchers have failed to enroll any of the children who were in the original neonatal HSV study into the current study. In cases where the researchers were able to talk to a parent or guardian, there has been a stated reluctance to pass information regarding the study on to the child, although the parents and guardians have been very interested to know how other children with a similar diagnosis have fared as they approach and enter adulthood. Researchers now question whether or not, for those former study subjects now over 18, it would be ethical to bypass the parent or guardian and instead contact the young adult directly to request participation in the follow-up study.

Is it appropriate to directly contact a young adult (over 18) who was enrolled in research as an infant? Does the answer change in a situation where divulging the initial research participation reveals the personal health status of the parent? Does the actual disease at issue, HSV, have bearing on the ethical questions?

REFERENCE

Mertz, G. J. 2008. Asymptomatic shedding of herpes simplex virus 1 and 2: Implications for prevention of transmission. *Journal of Infectious Diseases* 198(8):1098–100.

COMMENTARY 2.6.1: RESEARCH RECRUITMENT OF ADULT SURVIVORS OF NEONATAL INFECTIONS: IS THERE A ROLE FOR PARENTAL CONSENT?

ANN J. MELVIN, KATHLEEN M. MOHAN, ANNA WALD, KATHRYN PORTER, AND BENJAMIN S. WILFOND

Research on competent adult subjects does not require the consent of anyone beyond that of the adult subject. This case is complicated, however, because the targeted subjects were initially enrolled by their parents in a neonatal study and because the focus of the study, genital HSV, carries significant stigma in the community. In considering the ethical issue of directly approaching the young adults for participation in this research, there are three key themes that need to be evaluated and considered: (1) the importance of the research for anticipatory guidance about the long-term impact of neonatal HSV, (2) the concerns of parents in disclosing the diagnosis, and (3) the interests of affected teens and young adults and their future partners.

First, knowledge about the long-term effects of neonatal HSV infection is very limited. Follow-up for neonatal HSV has been limited to early childhood in the majority of studies (Kimberlin et al. 2011; Whitley et al. 1991). Apart from one small study involving children up to age 15 years (Malm et al. 1991), sparse data exist to inform families of the long-term clinical and psychosocial consequences of neonatal HSV infection. For example, while clinicians know that many children have periodic skin outbreaks of HSV that can continue for years (Kimberlin et al. 2011; Malm 1991), they do not know whether infection with HSV at birth will result in genital or oral recurrences or asymptomatic shedding of the virus later in life. Therefore, researchers do not know whether these individuals are at risk of passing the virus on to their sexual partners. This is particularly relevant to children who have survived neonatal herpes unscathed and thus would expect to have normal sexual activity during adulthood. The proposed research would address the questions that parents of children with neonatal HSV have about the long-term prognosis for their children and the risk of future genital shedding of HSV, for which there are no data on which to base an answer.

Second, the initial parental response to the proposed research demonstrates reluctance either to enroll their teen or now-adult children in this new research study or to pass the information about the study to them. Only the parents themselves can articulate their precise concerns, but it is possible to speculate about reasons for this reluctance. There is significant shame and stigma associated with HSV related to sexual behavior (Bickford, Barton, and Mandalia 2007; Newton and McCabe 2008), and a parent might be uncomfortable sharing this sensitive and personal information with his or her child. Telling a child about the neonatal HSV infection exposes the mother's HSV status, something that many parents would prefer not to share. This might stem from shame or even play into an issue of authority—it may be harder to maintain authority as a parent tries to instill values of safe sex or abstinence if the mother must also admit that she has a sexually transmitted infection (STI). Additionally, there may be parental guilt, knowing that the child acquired the infection from the mother. It could also be argued, however, that parental authority could be strengthened when speaking from an honest position of experience and lived consequences.

Finally, teens and young adults have a right to the health history contained in their medical record, which would contain documentation of a neonatal HSV infection. Thus, this information could be considered to be theirs already. They might want to know that they carry the virus, whether for their own health reasons or to protect their sexual partners. Their HSV infection might be detected later on during a requested STI screening, or even at the time of a woman's pregnancy, but could be wrongly attributed to the person's, or his or her partner's, sexual behavior.

The challenge is how to balance a young adult's direct interest in the information and the previously stated concerns of the parents, in the context of research that will benefit future parents and children in this community. One unique aspect of the research context is that the investigator's original relationship is with the parents. Two somewhat comparable research areas for examination that might provide some guidance into this situation are genetic diseases and human immunodeficiency virus (HIV), although these comparisons also highlight the unique aspects of this HSV research dilemma.

In genetics research, it is common practice to prioritize the interests of the person with whom researchers have a relationship. With hereditary genetic conditions, family members of an individual found to carry a specific genetic condition may benefit from knowing this information. However, because of concerns about respect and privacy, researchers typically do not inform a family member of his or her risk if the research subject is not willing to share the information (Shah et al. 2013). The researchers, however, may try to persuade the participant to share this information with family members who might be affected. In the current situation, there is a triadic relationship involving the child, the parent(s), and the researcher. Parents and researchers have an aligned obligation to consider the child's interests, but the actual interactive relationship is between the parents and the researchers, and this also must be acknowledged and respected.

In the HIV context, infected children are likely receiving lifelong treatment and the potential risk for transmission to future sexual partners is well established. There is a strong case for eventual disclosure to the adolescent who will need to manage the therapy for his or her HIV infection, even if some of the issues of parental discomfort are the same. In contrast, HSV infection may remain asymptomatic and never require treatment. Additionally, the risk of transmission to a sexual partner from an individual infected with HSV as a neonate is unknown. This is a large part of why a standard of routine disclosure for HSV has not emerged.

The examples of genetics and HIV suggest a challenging tension that may be mitigated by additional empirical data about the reasons for parental reluctance to disclose HSV information to their affected children. Further conversations with the parents of these young adults, possibly through focus groups or in one-on-one meetings, may be useful. Perhaps if parents understood the potential outcomes of the research, they would be more willing to encourage participation. Researchers could develop several research outcome scenarios and ask parents to share their opinions on participation after considering potential outcomes. Furthermore, in discussing concerns or potential harms, ideas may be developed to better support parents and reduce identified harms or risks.

Through interviews and discussion, parental concerns could be identified. Would parents consider allowing the researchers to follow up directly with the young adults? Would parents feel differently if they were given the opportunity to understand the importance of the research and were provided with counseling or tools to talk to their teen or adult children about the neonatal infection? While such data will not be fully dispositive to resolve the ethical tension, better understanding of the nature and intensity of parental concerns could allow researchers to develop materials that directly address those concerns and an ethically justified plan allowing for successful recruitment.

References

Bickford, J., S. E. Barton, and S. Mandalia. 2007. Chronic genital herpes and disclosure. The influence of stigma. *International Journal of STD & AIDS* 18: 589–92.

Kimberlin, D. W., R. J. Whitley, W. Wan, National Institute of Allergy and Infectious Diseases Collaborative Antiviral Study Group et al. 2011. Oral acyclovir suppression and neurodevelopment after neonatal herpes. *New England Journal of Medicine* 365:1284–92.

Malm, G., M. Forsgren, M. el Azazi, and A. Persson. 1991. A follow-up study of children with neonatal herpes simplex virus infections with particular regard to late nervous disturbances. *Acta Paediatrica Scandinavica* 80:226–34.

Newton, D. C., and M. P. McCabe. 2008. Sexually transmitted infections: Impact on individuals and their relationships. *Journal of Health Psychology* 13:864–9.

Shah, S. K., S. C. Hull, M. A. Spinner, et al. 2013. What does the duty to warn require? *American Journal of Bioethics* 13(10):62–3.

Whitley, R., A. Arvin, C. Prober, et al. 1991. Predictors of morbidity and mortality in neonates with herpes simplex virus infections. The National Institute of Allergy and Infectious Diseases Collaborative Antiviral Study Group. *New England Journal of Medicine* 324:450–4.

COMMENTARY 2.6.2: A KNOTTY PROBLEM OF INTERTWINED RIGHTS

ROSS E. McKINNEY

One of the most challenging problems for ethicists is a situation where there are multiple actors, each of whom has rights and fair expectations, and those rights do not squarely align. In this case, there are at least four main parties. To start with the encompassing set of actors, we should consider the rights of the parents, particularly the mother; the child, now a teen or adult; the investigators; and the future sexual partners of the child.

The first actor to consider is the parents. There is little question the mother of the child is HSV-2 infected, given the route of neonatal HSV-2 transmission. In most cases, the mother acquired HSV-2 as a sexually transmitted disease. This mode of transmission makes HSV-2 societally stigmatized, with the further result that parents may not want to discuss the mother's HSV status with their child. It's harder for parents to hold their child accountable for sexual behavior when there is clear evidence that when one or both parents were in the same position, they failed at least once to choose or effectively use barrier protection. In essence, in failing to protect themselves from a sexually transmitted infection, parents lose the moral high ground, and their sense of authority may erode as well.

My interpretation of the failure of parents to recruit their adult children for the study is that it's most likely they didn't want to have a difficult discussion with them about where the HSV-2 originated in the family. So the first set of rights has to do with the parents' privacy, even within a family.

The second actor is the adult child, who has the right to his or her own medical history and the right to make medical decisions based on it. If the adult children are, for example, shedding HSV-2 from their genital mucosa, they may opt to suppress the virus using acyclovir or a similar medication. The adult children can choose how to handle their sexuality with more knowledge of their HSV status, including the potential for abstinence. And while the risk is extremely low, a pregnant woman might want to know about her HSV-2 status to prevent transmission to her child.

The investigators don't intrinsically have a right to discuss the case with the adult children, given all of the privacy concerns. Instead, their most important role is to represent the interests of the class of people who had HSV as an infant and who might want to know their own status and potential contagiousness. I believe it has been a significant misconception to believe that the investigators are doing research primarily for their own good, whether it be for fame, grants, money, or curiosity. Instead, their most important role is to represent the broad needs of affected subjects, who would like to know more about their condition generally and, perhaps, about their own situation personally. It can be argued that the investigators are self-appointing themselves to be those representatives, and that by such self-appointment lack real authority. However, despite advances in community-engaged research, it is unlikely that anyone from a class of patients such as grown perinatal HSV-2 survivors could find a mechanism to self-represent in a situation like this one. Thus, investigators do play a key role, checked by IRB or ethics board review.

The final set of actors in this hierarchy of rights is the future sexual contacts of the infected adult children. While some might argue that the general caveat emptor that relates to sex with anyone applies, I would argue that the risk of HSV transmission can and should be minimized whenever possible. And, in this case, it is possible.

While the actors can be defined, the challenge is to sort the rights in some type of reasonable order. Among the actors, I believe the infected child intrinsically has the highest status in this case. First, the infected children, now teens and young adults, deserve to know their own condition, and to control their own sexuality and fertility. They should know whether they have the potential to infect another person, hopefully someone about whom they care. The question of shedding is an open one, scientifically, so the information is useful both to the infected individuals and to the class of people perinatally HSV infected—an increasing number with more effective perinatal treatment. Counterbalancing this right are a few factors: The probability of shedding is most likely low, HSV-2 is present in the community and might be acquired by other means, and the probability of a second generation of mother-to-child transmission also seems very low. In short, the self-knowledge is useful, but probably of marginal utility in a situation with basically low risk. The right to know, however, is substantive.

Prioritization of the infected adult child would seem to argue that the investigators should be able to contact the adult children directly. What are the costs if that approach is taken? Almost certainly, the biggest issue is how the now-adult children will view their parents. They now know that their mother was HSV-2 infected. They may also learn that there was important medical information withheld by their parents, who either didn't consider it important, or prioritized some aspect of their parental role and self-esteem (i.e., their own medical privacy) over the health rights of their child. We don't know why parents did not act to contact their children when asked, but some aspect of the privacy and respect equation seems most likely.

As a final note, there is another important counterbalance to the rights of the adult children and their sexual partners. Through the act of doing this research, particularly if contact is with the adult child, the investigators potentially have perturbed the current relationship between the parents and their child. The investigators have done this through what is essentially an intrusive step, contacting the adult child with whom they do not really have a relationship (the age of the research relationship was one where the investigators would be interacting with the parents). The failure of the parents to refer the investigators to their child is empirical evidence that the parents did not want to alter this aspect of the parent–child relationship. So I would judge that the new information to be gained is not a sufficient justification to intervene between parent and child, and I would work harder to communicate more effectively with the parents so that they understand the importance of this information for their child, while at the same time the parents have an opportunity for an honest conversation with their adult child, even if it is a difficult conversation to have.

COMMENTARY 2.6.3: CONSENT IS THE CORNERSTONE OF ETHICALLY VALID RESEARCH: ETHICAL ISSUES IN RECONTACTING SUBJECTS WHO ENROLLED IN RESEARCH AS A MINOR

ERIN TALATI PAQUETTE AND LAINIE FRIEDMAN ROSS

Informed consent is fundamental to the conduct of ethical research (U.S. Department of Health and Human Services, Office for Human Subjects Research, *Belmont Report* 1979; Nuremberg Code 1949). Consent requires disclosure regarding the methods, risks, benefits, and alternatives, and how long the subject will be expected to participate (U.S. Department of Health and Human Services 2009a). Parents or guardians provide permission for research involving minor subjects (<18 years of age). If subjects will be invited to participate in subsequent research based on their earlier participation, relevant considerations with respect to recontacting these individuals depend on what researchers told the parent as part of the consent process for the original research. We argue that attempts to directly contact individuals whose parents provided consent for their participation in an earlier study are not ethically permissible if the parents did not contemplate such contact when they initially consented to the child's participation.

In the current case, the investigators enrolled newborns in studies to evaluate neonatal HSV and disclosed as part of the original research study that there might be follow-up when the children were older. The original consent indicated that, prior to enrolling individuals for follow-up, the mother would be contacted and asked to forward information to her children age 18 years and older, and to provide permission for follow-up enrollment for her children 17 and younger. Mothers who agreed to enroll their child in the initial study did so with the understanding that they would be the point of contact for subsequent studies, and could decide then whether or not to forward information along to their children, who are now young adults. This recruitment strategy was approved by the IRB and presumably was included in the consent discussions with the parent or guardian.

The researchers are now finding universal unwillingness by the mothers to forward study information to their adult children. One must surmise that this unwillingness is due to the fact that it would disclose the mothers' own HSV status to their children. Under the approved research strategy, the mothers retain control over disclosure of their HSV status, which may have been relevant to their original agreement to enroll their child in the study. Even if it were not important at that time, their refusal to forward information to their adult children about the study indicates that it is important to these women now. They clearly are concerned about the potential for stigmatization related to HSV. As women might have had access to antiviral drugs only through experimental protocols, it is even more important that their original understanding of how personal information would be handled is not overlooked in permitting a different recruitment process that they could not have foreseen when they decided to participate.

While we contend that it is not ethically permissible for investigators to alter their recruitment process, even if it means that this research cannot be done, this case raises a number of important additional questions, including whether parents have an absolute right to privacy over their health information with regard to their children, whether adults have a corresponding right to know about research in which they participated as minors, and how to approach situations in which research cannot be conducted ethically under the current framework of human subjects protections.

The right to privacy over one's health information is well established (Annas 2002; Kulynych and Korn 2002; U.S. Department of Health and Human Services 2000). As their children's decision makers, parents have a right to access their child's health information, although this right is not absolute. For example, in most states, minors can seek care for some health conditions without their parents' knowledge or consent (Schlam and Wood 2000). In contrast, children do not have a right to access their parent's health information, although again, this right is not absolute. When a child becomes an adult, she has a right to access her own health information, which might contain information about her parents that was disclosed in a clinical encounter. In fact, the child's neonatal HSV diagnosis is most likely in her medical record. Similarly, one could argue that a child who was a subject in a research study ought to be able to learn about this participation as an adult if she so requests. In some situations, when a child's former research participation resulted in an exposure known to cause subsequent harm or risk, it may be necessary to affirmatively disclose that information even without parental consent. In this case, however, researchers seek to proactively disclose information about prior research participation without either a request by the former subject or a known harm that supports disclosure. Such a disclosure, particularly when it would reveal private information about another individual's health status, would be inconsistent with the fundamental principle of respect for persons that underlies research ethics (*Belmont Report*: U.S. Department of Health and Human Services, Office for Human Subjects Research 1979) and also would be noncompliant with privacy protections over personal health information (U.S. Department of Health and Human Services 2000).

We maintain that, even if it means that the investigators in this case cannot accomplish targeted enrollment and therefore must abandon their study without their proposed alternative recruitment strategy, it would be unethical for them to contact former subjects directly. If there were a compelling reason to motivate disclosure, such as a future threat to the health or safety of the former subjects, this situation might warrant disclosure of former research participation. However, we believe that such disclosures should only be permitted following a formal review of the proposed disclosure, possible consequences to others as a result of the disclosure, and the risks to individuals of nondisclosure. The formal review could be akin to a 407 review panel (Ross 2005). A 407 panel is requested by an IRB for research involving minors that would not otherwise be allowable but that "presents a reasonable opportunity to further the understanding, prevention, or alleviation of a serious problem affecting the health or welfare of children" (U.S. Department of Health and Human Services 2009b). We do not believe, however, that an exploratory study of the type described here would meet the 407 standard.

In the absence of a waiver that would permit disclosure without parental consent, investigators can consider alternatives. One option would be to design a new study that would enroll the mothers to understand their concerns and to see whether education about the importance of sharing their child's health history would change their minds. Alternatively, the researchers could consider offering an incentive to motivate the parents to engage their young adult children under the current recruitment strategy. Incentives in research can be ethically acceptable as long as they do not rise to the level of creating undue influence on decision making (VanderWalde and Kurzban 2011). An incentive that compensates a parent for the time and effort of engaging her child could be appropriate. An incentive that is excessive in order to overcome the parents' concerns about privacy or stigmatization would not be ethically acceptable.

References

Annas, G. J. 2002. Medical privacy and medical research—Judging the new federal regulations. *New England Journal of Medicine* 346(3):216–20.

Kulynych, J., and D. Korn. 2002. The effect of the new federal medical-privacy rule on research. *New England Journal of Medicine* 346(3):201–4.

Nuremberg Code. 1949. *Trials of war criminals before the Nuremberg military tribunals under control council law no 10*, Washington, DC: Government Printing Office.

Ross, L. F. 2005. Lessons to be learned from the 407 process. *Health Matrix* 15:401–21.

Schlam, L., and J. P. Wood. 2000. Informed consent to the medical treatment of minors: Law and practice. *Health Matrix* 10:141–74.

U.S. Department of Health and Human Services. 2000. Standards for privacy of individually identifiable health information. *Federal Register* 65:82462–829.

U.S. Department of Health and Human Services. 2009a. General requirements for informed consent. 45 CFR 46.116. C. Rule. Available at: http://www.hhs.gov/ohrp/humansubjects/guidance/45cfr46.html (accessed August 19, 2015).

U.S. Department of Health and Human Services. 2009b. Subpart D. additional protections for children involved as subjects in research. 45 CFR 46.407. Available at: http://www.hhs.gov/ohrp/humansubjects/guidance/45cfr46.html (accessed August 19, 2015).

U.S. Department of Health and Human Services, Office for Human Subjects Research. 1979. Belmont report. Ethical principles and guidelines for the protection of human subjects of research. Available at http://www.hhs.gov/ohrp/humansubjects/guidance/belmont.html

VanderWalde, A., and S. Kurzban. 2011. Paying human subjects in research: Where are we, how did we get here, and now what? *Journal of Law, Medicine & Ethics* 39(3):543–58.

CASE 2.7: GENOTYPE-DRIVEN RECRUITMENT IN POPULATION-BASED BIOMEDICAL RESEARCH

INTRODUCTION

Gene discovery research typically recruits research participants who have a particular phenotype. However, as population-based biospecimen repositories become more widespread, there is the opportunity to recruit participants on the basis of their genotype (ascertained as part of the research). The case described here is an example of this genotype-driven research about FMR1. FMR1, a gene on the X chromosome, contains long stretches of CGG repeats (mode = 30). The literature describes alleles with fewer than 40 repeats as "normal." People born with more than 200 repeats have fragile X syndrome (FXS), which involves some degree of intellectual disability, often accompanied by behaviors on the autism spectrum and other medical problems. Alleles with 55 to 200 repeats are "premutation" alleles; they can expand in length during reproduction, so female premutation carriers may give birth to children who have FXS (Birch et al. 2014; Grigsby et al. 2014; Maurin, Zongaro, and Bardoni 2014; Santoro, Bray, and Warren 2012; Wheeler et al. 2014).

Experts are not certain whether FMR1 premutation alleles cause medical problems in carriers. Some of the phenotypes associated with premutation alleles include fragile X–associated primary ovarian insufficiency (FXPOI), a dysfunction resulting in premature menopause; and fragile X–associated tremor/ataxia syndrome (FXTAS), a late-onset neurodegenerative disease. FXPOI and FXTAS reportedly affect ~20% and ~15%, respectively, of women with premutation alleles. Other symptoms that have been reported in clinical populations of premutation carriers include dizziness, migraines, anxiety, and depression. However, in certain environments (i.e., under conditions of low stress), premutation alleles have been reported to have positive health effects.

The case presented here and the three commentaries all address a study to explore the FMR1 phenotype among women known to carry the FMR1 premutation who had been recruited to join a population-based biospecimen registry. The commentaries explore whether it is appropriate to recruit these women without disclosing to them their FMR1 status, the balance of the potential harms that may accrue to the women, and how to navigate the informed consent process for participation in the study. Pilar Ossorio from the University of Wisconsin–Madison and Marsha Mailick of the Morgridge Institute for Research argue that nondisclosure of FMR1 status is key to the study design and propose two possible strategies for nondeceptive recruitment. Sam Doernberg and Sara Hull from the NIH argue that, based on the harms of nondisclosure, FMR1 premutation status ought to be disclosed during the consent process. Laura Beskow from Duke University School of Medicine also argues that FMR1 premutation status ought to be disclosed during the consent process and provides guidance for how the process ought to proceed.

CASE SUMMARY

Researchers propose to study phenotypes in women with FMR1 premutation alleles who did not know their FMR1 genotypes (mean age = 56 years). The study would also include control participants with normal-length alleles. Almost all previous studies of premutation phenotypes had been conducted in women who had children with FXS. Such women are not representative of the general population of women carrying premutations, as they may be experiencing parenting stress and because of ascertainment bias.

Each participant in the proposed study would complete a questionnaire and participate in an interview assessing neuromotor, neurocognitive, psychiatric, and health phenotypes. Any individual with symptoms would be given a referral for medical follow-up, regardless of genotype. The symptoms to be assessed have many etiologies, and symptoms in most women referred from the study likely would be caused by something other than an FMR1 genotype. Under this study design, all participants could potentially benefit.

Study participants would be recruited from a population-based research repository that contains individual genotype information linked to electronic health record (EHR) information. FMR1 allele status for individuals in the repository had been ascertained in a previous study. For the proposed study, repository personnel with access to genotype and contact information would compile a list of individuals eligible for recruitment. For both ethical and research design reasons, researchers involved in recruitment and data collection would not know any participant's FMR1 genotype.

Participants were recruited to the repository with consent materials clearly stating that no research results would be returned to them or placed in their medical records. They are reminded of this policy by statements in a newsletter sent to them two to four times per year, and by information on the repository's website. This "no return of results" policy was developed with input from a community advisory board. Repository participants to be recruited for the proposed FMR1 study all agreed to be contacted for future research, and they would undergo a study-specific consent process. Repository participants who are recruited would not be told about their personal mutation status.

This case raises ethical concerns regarding the disclosure of research results in the context of genotype-driven recruitment. Is it deceptive to recruit participants without disclosing the purpose of the study or why they were selected? Is it harmful to recruit participants without offering them information regarding their individual FMR1 genotype, either during recruitment or at the end of data collection? How can the researchers conduct an ethical consent process without disclosing FMR1 status?

REFERENCES

Birch, R. C., K. M. Cornish, D. R. Hocking, and J. N. Trollor. 2014. Understanding the neuropsychiatric phenotype of fragile X-associated tremor ataxia syndrome: A systematic review. *Neuropsychology Review* 24:491–513.

Grigsby, J., K. Cornish, D. Hocking, et al. 2014. The cognitive neuropsychological phenotype of carriers of the FMR1 premutation. *Journal of Neurodevelopmental Disorders* 6:28. doi:10.1186/1866-1955-6-28

Maurin, T., S. Zongaro, and B. Bardoni. 2014. Fragile X syndrome: From molecular pathology to therapy. *Neuroscience and Biobehavioral Reviews* 46:242–55.

Santoro, M. R., S. M. Bray, and S. T. Warren. 2012. Molecular mechanisms of fragile X syndrome: A twenty year perspective. *Annual Review of Pathology: Mechanisms of Disease* 7:219–45.

Wheeler, A. C., M. Raspa, A. Green, et al. 2014. Health and reproductive experiences of women with an FMR1 premutation with and without fragile X premutation ovarian insufficiency. *Frontiers in Genetics* 5:300. doi:10.3389/fgene.2014.00300.

COMMENTARY 2.7.1: GENOTYPE-DRIVEN RECRUITMENT WITHOUT DECEPTION

PILAR OSSORIO AND MARSHA MAILICK

Scholars have identified several ethical challenges for genotype-driven research (Beskow et al. 2010; Budin-Ljosne et al. 2013; McGuire and McGuire 2008; Michie et al. 2012). One group of commentators recommends that recruitment for genotype-driven studies usually should include an offer to disclose the individual genetic information on which recruitment is based, "because of the ethical importance of avoiding deception when explaining the purpose … and why prospective participants are eligible" (Beskow et al. 2012). Here, we argue that recruitment for the FMR1 study can be nondeceptive even though researchers will not offer to disclose individual genotype results.

We emphasize that double-blinding with respect to participants' FMR1 allele status is critical to this study's goal of addressing the role of FMR1 premutations in causing a variety of medical problems. There are good ethical reasons for double-blinded research designs—they help ensure that research produces high-quality, reproducible results and therefore manifest good stewardship of resources and respect for participants' contributions to research. However, the factors to which researchers are blinded usually are not material to recruitment.

Commentators may intuitively feel that failure to offer individual genotype results during recruitment for the FMR1 study would be deceptive because recruits will not know how their FMR1 allele status relates to their recruitment, but somebody affiliated with the study team will know this. Despite many people's intuitions, however, knowing information about a person without conveying it to her is not, by itself, deception.

Deception occurs when one person communicates to another with the intention of causing the recipient to believe something the speaker does not believe (Bok 1978; Lo 2013). One taxonomy of deception includes (1) lies; (2) truthful but misleading communication—communication made with the intention of creating false beliefs in another; and (3) misleading omissions—communication that strategically omits some information with the intention of permitting the recipient to continue with a false belief known to the speaker (Lo 2013). Under this taxonomy, failure to offer individual FMR1 results could constitute a misleading omission if done with the intent to perpetuate study recruits' false beliefs, which might relate to the study's purpose, the reason a woman was recruited, or the medical risks associated with FMR1 alleles.

This study's purpose is to develop evidence, in a population-based sample, regarding phenotypes caused by FMR1 premutations. One need not disclose individual genetic information to provide a comprehensible, non-misleading description of this purpose.

The more difficult question is whether researchers can nondeceptively explain why a particular individual is being recruited for the study. Might omitting information about individual FMR1 genotypes deceive women about the reason why they were invited to participate? In this case, blinding should prevent researchers who interact with participants from having beliefs about any individual's FMR1 alleles and, therefore, about whether any particular woman is being recruited as a premutation carrier or control. If researchers have no beliefs about the relevant matters, they cannot logically form an intention to create or perpetuate a false belief in the prospective participant.

Would omitting individual FMR1 information perpetuate false beliefs about risks associated with recruits' FMR1 alleles? The study design assumes that prospective participants will have no specific beliefs about their FMR1 alleles. This assumption is reasonable because no routine genetic screening assesses FMR1 alleles, and diagnostic assessments for the conditions to be studied, such as depression, do not include FMR1 testing. If pressed, most women probably assume their FMR1 alleles are medically unproblematic. Researchers conducting this FMR1 study might hypothesize that premutations may have medical or behavioral implications, but they are still in a state of uncertainty on this point. Researchers would not be omitting individual FMR1 information with the intention of perpetuating false beliefs. Therefore, they would not be engaged in deception.

In addition, we see no reason why a person's possibly false belief about the length of her FMR1 alleles would make her participation riskier or would inappropriately alter her willingness to participate. The study screening procedures are of low risk, and any risk associated with women's FMR1 alleles will not be increased by their choices to participate. The study could provide direct medical benefit for any participant via referral for an identified symptom, regardless of her FMR1 allele status. Given this potential benefit, a woman's willingness to participate in the research probably would not be affected by her beliefs, or lack thereof, about the length of her FMR1 alleles. The absence of individual FMR1 information will not cause women to inappropriately weight alternatives or otherwise change their participation decisions for the worse (Bok 1978).

One way that researchers can nondeceptively recruit women into the study is to convey the following points:

- This study aims to determine if any health or cognitive problems are associated with FMR1 pre-mutation alleles in a population-based sample of adult women.
- All research repository participants have already been genotyped to assess their FMR1 alleles.
- There is no plan to tell any participants their FMR1 status, as they agreed when they joined the repository.
- This study includes women with a range of FMR1 alleles. Some will have alleles with no previously reported health effects. Others will have alleles that might increase their risks for listed physical, neurological, or mental health problems, some of which can be serious.
- Researchers who work with participants will not know who has which alleles.

The bulleted information would be truthful, and it highlights important context: recruits' ongoing participation in the repository and their agreement not to receive individual genetic information from repository-based research. This information would decrease the likelihood of false beliefs among participants and the likelihood that participants would feel wronged by the omission of individual genetic information.

Alternatively, the recruitment and consent process could omit mention of the FMR1 gene and use more general language, such as "The purpose of this study is to determine how variation in a particular region of the genome affects neurological function, stress responses, and well-being." The rationale for this approach is that researchers and IRBs could worry that, if the name of the gene is disclosed, women recruited to this study might conduct internet searches and mistakenly assume they are at risk of developing FXS. Recruits and participants might also guess (rightly or wrongly) whether they are premutation carriers or controls. The researchers would not be in a position to verify or counter such guesses, which could lead women to make misguided reproductive or other life-course decisions.

Here, we have considered how recruitment for the FMR1 study can be conducted nondeceptively. We have not addressed the ethics of offering individual FMR1 information after the study's conclusions have been reached.

References

Beskow, L. M., S. M. Fullerton, E. E. Namey, D. K. Nelson, A. M. Davis, and B. S. Wilfond. 2012. Recommendations for ethical approaches to genotype-driven research recruitment. *Human Genetics* 131:1423–31.

Beskow, L. M., K. N. Linney, R. A. Radtke, E. L. Heinzen, and D. B. Godlstein. 2010. Ethical challenges in genotype-driven research recruitment. *Genome Research* 20:705–9.

Bok, S. 1978. *Lying: Moral choice in public and private life*, New York, NY: Random House.

Budin-Ljosne, I., K. J. Soye, A. M. Tasse, B. M. Knoppers, and J. R. Harris. 2013. Genotype-driven recruitment: A strategy whose time has come? *BMC Medical Genomics* 6:19. http://www.biomedcentral.com/1755-8794/1756/1719.

Lo, B. 2013. *Resolving ethical dilemmas: A guide for clinicians*, Philadelphia, PA: Lippincott Williams & Wilkins.

McGuire, S. E., and A. L. McGuire. 2008. Don't throw the baby out with the bathwater: Enabling a bottom-up approach in genomewide association studies. *Genome Research* 18:1683–85.

Michie, M., J. Cadigan, G. Henderson, and L. Beskow. 2012. Am I a control?: Genotype-driven research recruitment and self-understandings of study participants. *Genetics in Medicine* 14:983–89.

COMMENTARY 2.7.2: HARMS OF DECEPTION IN FMR1 PREMUTATION GENOTYPE-DRIVEN RECRUITMENT

SAM DOERNBERG AND SARA CHANDROS HULL

The research study in question proposes to recruit female participants with the FMR1 premutation from a biobank and evaluate their clinical symptoms and phenotypes, without disclosing the purpose of the study or participants' personal FMR1 status at any point during or after the study. The case asks two ethical questions about the nature of the study: whether the design as currently proposed is (1) harmful or (2) deceptive. We identify three ways that the research proposal is harmful, and we ultimately conclude that because of these harms, deception is not justified, and the research cannot be conducted ethically in the absence of disclosure.

The first harm of nondisclosure relates to knowledge of personally relevant health information. As currently proposed, women in this study who have medical conditions caused by the FMR1 premutation would not receive important information about their own health status. While concerns about the premutation are commonly focused on the potential for transmission of an expanded copy to offspring, 20% of women with the premutation have primary ovarian insufficiency (POI), which manifests as diminished fertility or infertility (Hantash et al. 2011). There is evidence that women who have experienced fertility problems such as POI wish to receive their personal FMR1 premutation status if offered testing and view premutation status as potentially explanatory as to the underlying cause of their fertility challenges (Pastore et al. 2014). This suggests that a portion of women in the study cohort have strong interests in understanding their own health conditions to mitigate anxieties and for purposes of clinical planning, and would be deprived of this if the researchers choose not to disclose.

The second harm of nondisclosure relates to missed opportunities for reproductive planning. We believe that many asymptomatic women in the study cohort would want to know their premutation status. While no surveys have been done on this precise question, there is clear evidence that asymptomatic women wish to know their full mutation status for two reasons: the possibility of termination, and planning for future fertility issues associated with FMR1 (Anido et al. 2005; Archibald et al. 2012). Both of these reasons are relevant to carriers of the premutation. There is a chance of having offspring with fragile X, because the premutation can expand during reproduction. Women with the premutation also have fertility challenges. It is therefore likely that asymptomatic women in the study cohort have reproductive interests in their premutation status, and not disclosing this valuable information would hinder or limit the reproductive choices these women have.

These first two harms relate to a failure to divulge useful information. However, even if participants have an interest in receiving this information, do researchers have a corresponding obligation to disclose? Answers to this question often focus on broad ethical duties to disclose results, such as a duty to rescue, but here we focus on three contextual factors that help determine when disclosure is warranted: benefit to participants, uniqueness of researcher access, and burden of disclosure (Gliwa and Berkman 2013). All three factors support an obligation to disclose genetic information in this particular study context. First, disclosing the premutation is likely to benefit participants by helping women with POI understand their condition and providing an opportunity for reproductive planning for all women in the study cohort. Second, the researchers likely have unique access to participants' carrier status, since the FMR1 premutation is not usually screened for during genetic testing. Finally, disclosure carries a low burden for the research team, since each participant's genetic status is already known. The researchers are therefore in a unique position to improve the welfare of participants at low cost to the research effort, indicating an obligation to disclose.

There are also potential concerns about harms of returning genetic information to participants. One concern is that unanticipated disclosure could provoke anxiety. However, this is unlikely to outweigh participants' strong interests in knowing the information, since women who learn they are

FMR1 carriers go through an adaptive process involving coping behaviors that lessen their level of upset (McConkie-Rosell et al. 2001). In addition, the study cohort, at 56 years old on average, is past typical childbearing age. Nevertheless, women show an interest in "the effects of their [FMR1] carrier status on their children and grandchildren" (Anido et al. 2005). This suggests that carrier status is welcomed even if it does not affect personal reproductive decisions, consonant with a broader conception of reproductive autonomy.

The third harm of the study results from unexplained referral to medical care. The researchers face a dilemma because the participants understood that they would not receive results, yet it seems apparent from the case description that the team expects to find clinically relevant information and considers it important to fulfill their ancillary care duties to maximize indirect benefits to participants. However, it will be difficult for the participants to be directed to medical care without revealing health-relevant genetic information. Referring participants to medical services without telling them the underlying reasons why is likely to provoke confusion and anxiety, especially in those who have experienced clinical symptoms. Even if there were clear scientific necessity not to disclose mutation status to participants at the outset of the study, for example due to a risk of biased symptom reporting (which is not an argument that has been presented by the researchers here), the information is not time sensitive and participants could be debriefed after their participation in the study is complete.

In order to evaluate these harms in context, we must note our view that this research is deceptive, given that the informed consent process withholds key information about the study such as its purpose and why participants were contacted to participate. The fact that research is deceptive does not necessarily mean it is unethical. Deception research can be justified when, for example, it is essential to answering an important scientific question. Such research has to comply with federal regulations that limit the kinds of deception research that can be conducted. Acceptable research must be of minimal risk, it cannot be practicably carried out without a waiver of informed consent, the waiver must not affect participants' rights and welfare, and participants should be debriefed after if appropriate (45 CFR §46.116.d: Department of Health and Human Services 2005). We believe that the study fails at least one of the required tests for research involving deception by neither disclosing health-relevant information nor even giving participants a choice about whether or not to receive this information. This omission negatively affects participants' welfare by depriving them of information they value for their personal health and reproductive interests—information that may be relevant to their choice about whether to participate in the research. Given the harms identified in this commentary, we do not believe the research can be conducted ethically in the absence of disclosure and informed consent. Details of the consent process are beyond the scope of this commentary, but researchers could consider a sequential consent process (e.g., Beskow et al. 2012) that entails sending a nonspecific letter to all potential participants, both controls and those with the premutation, explaining the topic and purpose of the study and providing an opt-in to the study and to receiving personal results. Alternatively, a modified process involving debriefing before referring participants to healthcare services could help to mitigate concerns about harms of nondisclosure.

References

Anido, A., L. M. Carlson, L. Taft, and S. L. Sherman. 2005. Women's attitudes toward testing for fragile X carrier status: A qualitative analysis. *Journal of Genetic Counseling* 14(4):295–306.

Archibald, A. D., C. L. Hickerton, A. M. Jaques, S. Wake, J. Cohen, and S. A. Metcalf. 2012. "It's about having the choice": Stakeholder perceptions of population-based genetic carrier screening for fragile X syndrome. *American Journal of Medical Genetics* 161A:48–58.

Beskow, L. M., L. Fullerton, E. E. Namey, D. K. Nelson, A. M. Davis, and B. S. Wilfond. 2012. Recommendations for ethical approaches to genotype-driven research recruitment. *Human Genetics* 131(9):1423–31.

Department of Health and Human Services. 2005. Protection of human subjects. 45 CFR 46.116d ("The Common Rule"). Available at: http://www.hhs.gov/ohrp/regulations-and-policy/regulations/45-cfr-46/index.html#46.116 (accessed November 16, 2016).

Gliwa, C., and B. E. Berkman. 2013. Do researchers have an obligation to actively look for incidental genetic findings? *American Journal of Bioethics* 13(2):32–42.

Hantash, J., D. M. Goos, and B. Crossley, et al. 2011. FMR1 premutation carrier frequency in patients undergoing routine population-based carrier screening: Insights into the prevalence of fragile X syndrome, fragile X-associated tremor/ataxia syndrome, and fragile X-associated primary ovarian insufficiency in the United States. *Genetics in Medicine* 13(1):39–45.

McConkie-Rosell, A., G. A. Spiridigliozzi, J. A. Sullivan, D. V. Dawson, and A. M. Lachiewicz. 2001. Longitudinal study of the carrier testing process for fragile X syndrome: Perceptions and coping. *American Journal of Medical Genetics* 98(1):37–45.

Pastore, L. M., M. Antero, K. Ventura, J. K. Penberthy, S. A. Thomas, and L. B. Karns. 2014. Attitudes towards potentially carrying the FMR1 premutation before vs after testing of non-carrier females with diminished ovarian reserve. *Journal of Genetic Counseling* 23:968–75.

COMMENTARY 2.7.3: GENOTYPE-DRIVEN RECRUITMENT AND THE DISCLOSURE OF INDIVIDUAL RESEARCH RESULTS

LAURA M. BESKOW

Research recruitment is typically considered less risky than research participation (Beskow et al. 2004). When contacted, individuals can choose to not respond, to express disinterest at the outset, or to learn more about the research and make a considered decision about taking part. Genotype-driven recruitment, however, entails both new promise and new concerns. The widespread adoption of such recruitment could significantly advance the pace of research on the functional significance of human genetic variation and progress toward the ultimate goal of benefiting human health (McGuire and McGuire 2008). At the same time, it is inextricably linked to the complex and much-debated issue of disclosing individual research results to participants. Specifically, genotype-driven recruitment raises the potential for harm if previously unknown and perhaps unwanted genetic information is disclosed as part of the solicitation to participate in research, prior to consent. There is a central tension between avoiding these harms and avoiding deception when explaining to prospective participants the purpose of the research and why they are eligible (Beskow et al. 2010).

These challenges have been the subject of empirical research (Beskow et al. 2012; Beskow, Namey, and Cadigan 2011) and of a multidisciplinary workshop convened to formulate recommendations (Beskow et al. 2012). This literature suggests there is unlikely to be a "one-size-fits-all" solution, but rather several ethically acceptable approaches to genotype-driven recruitment depending on context. In general, recruitment should proceed incrementally, with close attention to preserving prospective participants' right not to know genetic information about themselves. For many studies—including the FMR1 premutation study—the purpose of the research should be explained clearly and individuals should be offered an opportunity to make an informed decision to learn their results.

The FMR1 premutation recruitment process

According to the case presentation, participants in the original population-based repository were informed that they might be contacted in the future about additional research. This is a good first step. Although silence in the original consent form about the possibility of contact for research recruitment should not necessarily rule out such contact, it is recommended practice to let participants know about this prospect up front (Beskow et al. 2012).

Recruitment for the FMR1 premutation study should include a clear statement of the purpose of the study, and of basic eligibility criteria. This transparency is essential as an ethical matter, and also as a practical matter. In an interview study about a biobank consent form that included a basic statement about recontact for additional research, the most common assumption was that something must have been found in participants' blood:

> I can't imagine they would contact me unless they saw something in my blood that interested them and they needed more, needed to know more.
>
> I don't want anyone calling me out of the blue because that would make me feel like 'what did you find that makes you want to do the study so much?'

(Beskow and Dean 2008, 1445)

Indeed, in an actual study at Duke University (Beskow et al. 2010), researchers attempting genotype-driven recruitment sought ethics consultation precisely because, upon contact with prospective participants, they were often met with immediate concerns about "Did you find something wrong with me?"

Transparency about study purpose and general eligibility should not come at the cost of an individual's right not to know unwanted genetic information. Recruitment materials should be carefully crafted so that prospective participants can grasp the basic premise of the study, but not infer their individual FMR1 premutation status. One example of an ethical approach would be to:

- Remind recipients of their participation in the population-based repository.
- Include a brief, lay description of the FMR1 gene and why researchers want to learn more about it.
- State that people with or without the FMR1 premutation are being recruited, and that the recipient should not assume that contact means they have the variant.
- Provide instructions for how to opt out of further contact.

The FMR1 premutation study consent process

The consent form for genotype-driven studies like the one proposed should not disclose (or allow inference of) an individual's genetic status, but should clearly state whether or not results will be disclosed. If results will be disclosed, the risks and benefits should be plainly stated so that prospective participants can decide whether to proceed with enrollment. Unlike the original population-based repository, for which future research was likely unspecified, researchers conducting genotype-driven studies can anticipate and describe the kinds of findings they might uncover and devise detailed plans for minimizing risks and managing ethically appropriate disclosure, advice, and referral.

Disclosure of individual FMR1 premutation status

Although it may be possible to conduct some genotype-driven studies without offering to disclose individual results, this will not be the case for many such studies (Beskow et al. 2012). In general, debate surrounding the disclosure of research results concerns what ancillary responsibilities researchers have to participants, that is, whether they should offer individual results not because doing so is intrinsic to answering their research questions, but rather because of potential net benefits to participants outside the research context. In contrast, in genotype-driven recruitment, the question of whether to offer individual results is integral to the ethical conduct of the research itself. These are fundamentally different motivations, and thresholds established for the return of individual results in general should not be used for decision making about return of results in the context of genotype-driven studies (Beskow et al. 2012).

In the FMR1 premutation study, it seems unlikely that the development of the "no return of results" policy for the population-based repository included explicit consideration of genotype-driven research. It would be interesting to elicit the community advisory board's input on this emerging form of recruitment. Furthermore, the FMR1 premutation study is a separate study with a separate consent form, enabling development of a study-specific policy concerning disclosure of results. Unlike research results for which clinical validity, much less clinical utility, is unknown, the FMR1 gene was discovered 25 years ago and the premutation is a well-defined variation for which clinical testing is widely available (Wheeler et al. 2014).

Thus, the ethics of disclosing versus withholding individual results in the context of the FMR1 premutation study merits in-depth discussion among stakeholders. One issue for particular scrutiny is the claim that "all participants could potentially benefit" from the phenotypic testing and referral for medical follow-up. The symptoms to be assessed have many etiologies, and it seems possible (if not likely) that referral without disclosure of the FMR1 genotype could send participants on a diagnostic odyssey without the benefit of them or their physicians knowing their status relative to a known cause. The potential for provoking expensive and potentially risky testing and treatment based on an avoidable misdiagnosis must be thoroughly assessed.

In addition to these ethical considerations, researchers and IRBs should again anticipate practical hurdles. Although it may be important not to disclose individual results at the start of the study in order to gather unbiased information, it seems a near certainty that participants found to have symptoms and referred for medical follow-up will want to know, "Am I one of the people who have that gene?"

References

Beskow, L. M., J. R. Botkin, M. Daly, et al. 2004. Ethical issues in identifying and recruiting participants for familial genetic research. *American Journal of Medical Genetics A* 130A (4):424–31.

Beskow, L. M., and E. Dean. 2008. Informed consent for biorepositories: Assessing prospective participants' understanding and opinions. *Cancer Epidemiological Biomarkers and Prevention* 17(6):1440–51.

Beskow, L. M., S. M. Fullerton, E. E. Namey, D. K. Nelson, A. M. Davis, and B. S. Wilfond. 2012. Recommendations for ethical approaches to genotype-driven research recruitment. *Human Genetics* 131(9):1423–31.

Beskow, L. M., K. N. Linney, R. A. Radtke, E. L. Heinzen, and D. B. Goldstein. 2010. Ethical challenges in genotype-driven research recruitment. *Genome Research* 20(6):705–9.

Beskow, L. M., E. E. Namey, R. J. Cadigan, et al. 2011. Research participants' perspectives on genotype-driven research recruitment. *Journal of Empirical Research on Human Research Ethics* 6(4):3–20.

Beskow, L. M., E. E. Namey, P. R. Miller, D. K. Nelson, and A. Cooper. 2012. IRB chairs' perspectives on genotype-driven research recruitment. *IRB* 34(3):1–10.

McGuire, S. E., and A. L. McGuire. 2008. Don't throw the baby out with the bathwater: Enabling a bottom-up approach in genomewide association studies. *Genome Research* 18(11):1683–85.

Wheeler, A. C., D. B. Bailey Jr., E. Berry-Kravis, et al. 2014. Associated features in females with an FMR1 premutation. *Journal of Neurodevelopmental Disorders* 6 (1):30.

Section 3

Fair participant selection

HOLLY A. TAYLOR

The principle of fair participant selection requires that investigators recruit eligible research participants based on the scientific objectives of their research. The key components of fair participant selection are that selection of study populations should be driven by research objectives and the likelihood that the study will generate reliable and valid data; study samples should be selected to minimize risks to study participants and maximize social value and potential benefit to participants; and, when study participants are vulnerable, appropriate protections ought to be in place.

The five cases in this section are also categorized under the principles of favorable risk–benefit ratio and/or informed consent. In addition, almost all the cases are related to the topics of pediatrics/adolescents and legal and regulatory oversight. It is perhaps not surprising that cases with fair participant selection at their core are related to whether and how children should be included. It is also the case that, in the absence of regulatory guidance about the inclusion of adults without decision-making capacity in research, the criteria used to categorize pediatric research are often invoked. Four of the five cases address the social value of the research under consideration, three address equity, and one addresses trustworthiness.

CASE 3.1: IS IT ETHICAL TO ENROLL COGNITIVELY IMPAIRED ADULTS IN RESEARCH THAT IS MORE THAN MINIMAL RISK WITH NO PROSPECT OF BENEFIT? (2015)

Principles: Fair Participant Selection, Favorable Risk–Benefit Ratio, Informed Consent

Topics: Pediatrics, Legal and Regulatory Oversight, Disability and Neurodiversity

Values: Social Value, Equity

This key question in this case regards under what circumstances a cognitively impaired adult can be included in research. The Common Rule does not have specific regulations relating to adults with cognitive impairment. Investigators and institutional review boards (IRBs) are then left to justify and consider the inclusion of these individuals in research. Investigators are conducting a natural history study of a condition associated with cognitive impairment. The inclusion of children and adults with cognitive impairment is proposed. The IRB has concluded that the trial is more than a minor increase over minimal risk and has no prospect of direct benefit, and it is

---

DOI: 10.1201/9781003335306-4

therefore approvable under pediatric category 45 CFR 46.406, which requires both parents to provide permission for their child's enrollment. The IRB is left then to consider whether to include adults who are cognitively impaired. While the Common Rule is silent on the topic, IRBs need to be aware as to whether their state has any relevant statutes on whether a surrogate (i.e., legally authorized representative) can consent to enrollment for a cognitively impaired adult. The IRB should consider the research objective of the project, the social value of the project, the magnitude of risk, and whether to authorize the use of a surrogate.

The first commentary (Yarborough, this volume, p. 140) opens with a review of efforts to set a national standard for the inclusion of adults with cognitive impairment. The lack of a national standard and range of state statutes lead to local variation across the types of research approved and protections put in place. The commentary notes that both investigators and IRBs should adopt the clinical standard of "substituted judgment" as a baseline for the inclusion of cognitively impaired adults in research. Those with surrogates could be included with their surrogate's permission, and those without a surrogate (or with a surrogate without the knowledge of the potential participant's prior views on research participation) would be excluded. The commentary then advocates for an even more permissive standard that would allow surrogates to instead rely on "constructed judgment" in their decision making. Surrogates construct (rather than aim to accurately predict) the values and preferences of the potential participant based on their familiarity with the potential participant. The commentary notes that adopting this approach, as well as asking those capable of doing so to designate the preferred surrogate, would move us from merely protecting impaired adults to respecting them and their life narratives.

The second commentary (Derse and Spellecy, this volume, p. 142) advocates for a similar approach. They endorse the clinical standard as the appropriate starting point, and while not using the term "constructed judgment," they advocate for allowing surrogates familiar with the potential participant's life narrative to make decisions on the potential participant's behalf. Adapting the protections found in pediatric populations, they suggest limiting this option to studies that would expose the cognitively impaired adult to a minor increase over minimal risk.

The third commentary (Danis, Wendler, and Kim, this volume, p. 145) begins by noting the social and scientific value of conducting research among those with conditions and disorders who may lack capacity to address gaps in our knowledge about how to prevent and treat such disorders. With this as background, they conclude that such research ought to be pursued and the key question is about the upper limit of risk allowed. They consider a couple of situations. They first conclude that an impaired adult potential participant who has a durable power of attorney (DPA) and can provide assent can be enrolled in research with greater than ordinary risk and no potential for direct benefit. This is "parallel" to the criteria used to consider enrollment of children. Next, they consider what level of risk an impaired adult with no DPA and who does not have the capacity to designate a DPA can be exposed to. They look to empirical data and note that many adults affected by memory disorders, as well as the general public, endorse surrogate decisions made by family members about enrollment. They conclude that such an approach, with safeguards, is reasonable and that more data need to be gathered on where the upper limit of risk lies.

All three commentaries endorse an approach to expand the enrollment to include adults with cognitive impairment, thereby expanding the social value that may accrue as a result of their participation. It is assumed they are all referring to adults who once had capacity, not those who never did. In the absence of a national standard, they suggest adopting minor increase over minimal risk as a reasonable standard when there is potential for direct benefit. They also suggest that a knowledgeable surrogate be allowed to provide consent on behalf of the impaired adult.

CASE 3.2: SHOULD PATIENTS BE REQUIRED TO UNDERGO STANDARD CHEMOTHERAPY BEFORE BEING ELIGIBLE FOR NOVEL PHASE I IMMUNOTHERAPY CLINICAL TRIALS? (2017)

Principles: Fair Participant Selection, Favorable Risk–Benefit Ratio, Informed Consent

Topics: Pediatrics, Legal and Regulatory Oversight, Drugs and Devices, Phase I Trials

Values: Social Value

Unique among the cases considered in this book, the source of the consultation was a potential research participant. A potential research participant with a rare cancer was interested in enrolling in an early-phase trial for which he was not yet medically eligible as he had not yet exhausted all standard treatment options. In order to become eligible for an innovative immunotherapy trial, the potential participant agreed to undergo standard treatment known to have limited benefit (i.e., palliative care was a reasonable alternative) and enrolled in the study after he failed standard treatment. The participant, a family medicine physician, sought a consultation regarding his concerns about the scientific justification for the trial as well as the ethics of requiring patients to exhaust standard treatments. His question was whether it was fair to exclude him (or others similarly situated) from enrollment in an early-phase trial when the standard treatment options are poor.

The first commentary (Doussau and Hanmer, this volume, p. 149) posits that the patient's choice to opt for palliative care over standard, toxic treatment known to have limited benefit would have been respected as an informed decision. The question is whether this refusal of noncurative treatment (rather than undergoing the treatment) could be added to the list of eligibility criteria for an early-phase trial. The commentary goes on to conclude that relaxing the eligibility criteria in this way (in this particular scenario) would not expose the participant to unreasonable risk and that including participants naïve to standard treatment could allow for additional research questions to be explored. They add that pursuing such a design would require additional resources and a robust consent process.

The second commentary (Collier and Danis, this volume, p. 151) uses this case to discuss the rise of citizen science, in particular citizen engagement in the design and conduct of clinical research. They note recent U.S. federal agency interest in and support of patient engagement activities. The commentary also notes the value of having a research ethics consultation service that is open to patient requests (not all offer this opportunity). Benefits of access include: opportunity for the potential participant or participant to engage with experts, facilitation of communication with the study team, and support in decision making. Finally, they note the value of having participant perspectives when facing challenging situations in the conduct of research.

The third commentary (Wetmore, this volume, p. 153) advocates expanding eligibility to allow the patient to join the trial, and she suggests that parents should be able to make similar decisions for their children. The current model of testing new agents in adults (i.e., through Phase III testing) before they are tested in children leads to the development of effective treatment but leaves children behind in terms of early access. The commentary advocates that children with poor prognosis (no curative treatment) with a new or recurrent cancer should be considered eligible for trials currently open only for adult patients.

These three commentators take very distinct approaches to this case. The first posits whether refusal of noncurative treatment could be reasonably added as an eligibility criterion, expanding the role that the participant may have in decision making about enrollment. The second notes the instrumental value of having patients engaged in the design and conduct of research and that research ethics consultation services should be open to potential and actual research participants. The third bemoans the fact that excluding children from early-phase trials leaves them behind in terms of access to promising treatments.

CASE 3.3: INVOLVING PREGNANT WOMEN IN RESEARCH: WHAT SHOULD WE RECOMMEND WHEN THE REGULATIONS SEEM ETHICALLY PROBLEMATIC? (2018)

Principles: Fair Participant Selection, Favorable Risk–Benefit Ratio

Topics: Pediatrics, Legal and Regulatory Oversight, Pregnancy

Values: Social Value, Trustworthiness

This case has a unique twist as it involves conflicting recommendations from two different research ethics consultation teams. The specific question in this case is whether people who can become pregnant should be excluded from a trial testing a novel intervention to prevent recurrence of urinary stone disease (USD). USD is relatively common, and those who have had USD are at risk of recurrence. The intervention under investigation is usual care plus a water bottle that can monitor fluid intake. Participants are randomized to self-monitoring the water intake or receive a behavioral intervention and personalize fluid intake recommendations. People who are capable of becoming pregnant are considered vulnerable by the U.S. Common Rule and are included in research under specific criteria directed at minimizing harm to the fetus. In the case of USD, pregnant women are at no greater or lesser risk of developing the condition, but pregnant people have different fluid metabolism when compared to nonpregnant people, and if included would need to forgo some research procedures. The question brought to the consultation teams was: Even if people who are pregnant were excluded, if someone becomes pregnant while enrolled, should they be withdrawn or allowed to remain enrolled? One research ethics consultation service favored the former, and the other the latter.

The first commentary (Shah and Porter, this volume, p. 157) concludes that the two different consultation recommendations may have come out of two different approaches to assessing the risk–benefit ratio: one that assesses the ratio prior to randomization, and one that assesses the ratio after randomization (component analysis). According to the first approach, people who became pregnant while enrolled would remain enrolled given the prospect of direct benefit. On the second approach, people capable of becoming pregnant would be excluded as the standard arm does not hold out a prospect of direct benefit. Based on the Common Rule requirement, people capable of becoming pregnant should be excluded as the research question can be answered in nonpregnant people. The commentary concludes that the first approach is justified as it would result in more inclusive enrollment (i.e., people capable of becoming pregnant).

The second commentary (Sharp and Allyse, this volume, p. 159) opens with the observation that when more than one consultation is sought, there is always a possibility that they will conflict. Rather than conclude that one consultation must be right and the other wrong, they note that in this case there is a clear tiebreaker. While the ethical analysis may lead to two different perspectives, this case is about whether the study is in compliance with the Common Rule. While ethical consultations can contribute to a discussion of the key considerations, it is the IRB's role to decide whether the study as designed is compliant with the Common Rule. In this case, the commentary concludes that when the question is about regulation, the role of the research ethics consultation services is to refer the study team to the IRB and/or offer to facilitate their engagement with the IRB.

The third commentary (Sullivan, Braverman, and Wendler, this volume, p. 160) quickly asserts that the study as designed does not meet the criteria needed to include individuals capable of pregnancy. People at risk of pregnancy should be excluded, and people who become pregnant while enrolled should be withdrawn. However, the commentators find this approach troubling given the intervention is minimal risk and procedures could be adjusted for people capable of becoming pregnant, as has already been done to include children 12 and over at risk of recurrence. The exclusion of people capable of becoming pregnant while in compliance with the Common Rule does not facilitate knowledge gained that could benefit people capable of becoming pregnant as a class. But the commentators conclude that it would not be appropriate for research ethics consultants to push for alternative interpretation of the Common Rule. Failure to do so could erode the public's trust in the research enterprise that relies on consistent interpretation and application of the Common Rule.

All three commentators agree that there may be ethical justifications for the inclusion of people capable of becoming pregnant in research in this particular study and more generally, but there is disagreement regarding how broad or narrow the consultations should be in interpreting the regulations.

CASE 3.4: ENROLLING ADOLESCENTS WITH RARE DISEASE FOR EARLY PHASE CLINICAL TRIALS WHILE UNDER CARE OF CHILD PROTECTIVE SERVICES: BALANCING PROTECTION AND ACCESS. (2022)

Principles: Fair Participant Selection, Favorable Risk–Benefit Ratio

Topics: Adolescents and Young Adults, Legal and Regulatory Oversight, Phase I Trials

Values: Equity

This case considers the inclusion of an adolescent who is temporarily a ward of the state and touches on fair participant selection as well as balancing risk and benefit. An adolescent with a rare genetic disorder is medically eligible for a potentially curative hematopoietic stem cell transplant (HSCT). The study team sees the HSCT as her only treatment option and that she will likely die without the transplant. In addition to the risks of the procedure itself, she faces many months of inpatient and outpatient recovery. Complicating the situation, she was recently placed in the care of Child Protective Services (CPS) due to medical neglect. In the balance are whether it is feasible to enroll a ward of the state in research and whether this adolescent can bear the burdens of enrollment given her current social circumstances.

The first commentary (Turnbull and Benedetti, this volume, p. 164) emphasizes the psychological and emotional support the potential participant will need in order to make a considered decision about enrollment as well as the time she will need to spend as an inpatient post-transplant. They share evidence of the positive relationship between social support and better psychosocial outcomes as well as better quality of life. They assume that CPS is unlikely to be able to provide the level of social support the potential participant will need to promote success, adding that poor adherence to posttransplant care could both compromise the participant's health and the integrity of the trial. The commentators next consider, if the necessary social supports are put in place, whether enrollment under these circumstances is compliant with the Common Rule. While not required for a study offering potential benefit, they conclude that an advocate ought to be appointed to represent the interests of the potential participant independent of CPS to avoid potential harms of being included in a risky trial without adequate support or being excluded from the trial based on her current social situation. The commentary concludes that only if an advocate is appointed and adequate social supports are in place (acknowledging the delay in receipt of the HSCT) would it be appropriate to move forward with enrollment.

The second commentary (Greiner and Antommaria, this volume, p. 166) acknowledges the complexity of enrolling children who are temporary wards of the state but highlights the cost of excluding these children given the harms to an individual child as well as wards as a class. The authors review the type of procedures in place to place a child in temporary custody as well as noting that, while in CPS custody, a professional from CPS will be responsible for the overall health and well-being of the child. The child will be placed with an alternative caregiver responsible for the day-to-day needs of the child. The commentators note that, because the potential participant in this case is an adolescent, she should be involved in the decision-making process regarding enrollment and her assent sought. The authority to provide permission is retained by CPS but should be pursued in collaboration with the temporary caregiver (and, to the extent possible, the potential participant's mother). The authors conclude with five key recommendations that, if fulfilled, should support inclusion in the trial.

The third commentary (Forte and Anderson, this volume, p. 168) begins by noting that it is essential that any patient eligible for a transplant meet medical and psychosocial criteria; it would be unethical to exclude the potential participant in this case due to social circumstances beyond her control. They note, in this case, the appointment of a caregiver to support the potential participant through the procedure as well as post-transplant, adding that caregiving possibilities may be shared by multiple individuals. If a caregiver (or multiple caregivers as needed) is present, the authors conclude that inclusion is warranted. As with the second commentary, the authors emphasize the important role the potential participant as well has her biological family, caregiver(s), and the individual from state with the ultimate authority to provide permission for enrollment participate in the decision to enroll. They emphasize the importance of respecting the adolescent's dissent if necessary, as her lack of cooperation with the transplant and aftercare is essential.

The final commentary (Sacks and Rhodes, this volume, p. 171) begins by noting that the ethical question in this case is clear. If the potential participant is willing, she should be included in the trial given the dire consequences of the alternative. But they note several key considerations similar to the previous commentaries: assuring the financial and human resources needed to support the potential participant, and considering her decision-making capacity. These authors elaborate regarding the landscape of state legislation regarding surrogate consent (permission in this case) for enrollment in research as well as the fact that local IRBs may have policies regarding the inclusion of wards of the state in otherwise IRB-approvable research. As such, the authors encourage the study team faced with these circumstances to fully investigate the relevant state laws and local IRB policy. They conclude, as the other commentaries do, that there is no ethical barrier to the inclusion of this potential participant in this potentially lifesaving procedure.

All four commentaries conclude that if the child is medically eligible to enroll, the appropriate social support resources are available, and the adolescent agrees to enroll, there is no ethical justification for excluding a ward of the state from a study likely to result in direct medical benefit. To exclude her based on her social circumstances would not promote equity. Some of the commentators are pessimistic that the type and amount of social support the adolescent will need can be provided by the relevant state authority.

CASE 3.5: SELECTING CHILDREN FOR AN AUTISM SPECTRUM DISORDER STUDY: JUSTICE AND GEOGRAPHY (2016)

Principles: Fair Participant Selection, Favorable Risk–Benefit Ratio

Topics: Pediatrics, Drugs and Devices, Disability and Neurodiversity, Family Impact, Genetics

Values: Social Value, Equity

This case focuses on the enrollment of children with a genetic disorder that presents with symptoms of autism spectrum disorder (ASD). The goal of the early-phase placebo-controlled cross-over trial is to assess the safety and effectiveness of a previously approved drug to treat common ASD symptoms. This case, like Case 3.4, highlights the high stakes of treating children with no other treatment options as well as the challenge of enrolling participants in trials that require attention to the social circumstances of potential participants. A key eligibility criterion for the study is that potential participants have stable routines and behaviors prior to enrollment. As such, only families who live close by or have the means to move closer to the study site for the length of the study (up to one year) will be included in the study. The ethical question is whether these restrictions violate the principle of fair participant selection.

The first commentary (Chen, this volume, p. 175) posits that at least two questions need to be considered to determine whether families with lower means will be excluded from enrollment: What is the study team's motivation for exclusion, and how accessible is the selected study site to a diverse population of potential participants? For the first question, the commentator concludes that the study team is appropriately balancing the obligation to complete a conclusive trial with opening the trial to children for whom travel could disrupt their routines and behaviors and compromise the ability of the team to generate useful findings. On the second question, it may not be feasible to relocate the site for a variety of reasons. The commentator counsels that, if moving the site to a location better able to recruit a diverse population is feasible, doing so should be considered. The commentator concludes that the study team could explore methods to financially support family relocation and offer the trial at multiple sites, but neither would be ethically required in the case of an early-phase trial.

The second commentary (Stein and King, this volume, p. 177) highlights concerns in tension similar to those raised in the first: namely, that the potential benefit of the intervention is uncertain and the need to complete a conclusive trial. In addition, the second commentary introduces a concern about undue influence. The first issue is about whether the study team has unique expertise related to this rare syndrome; the second is about whether any of the potential participants are currently under the care of the study team. Families may find the offer of enrollment an option they can't refuse either because they want access to expertise or because they don't want to disappoint their clinical team. The commentators conclude that, while the participants who live closer or relocate may benefit from their participation, they will also take on the risks and burdens of enrollment in an early-phase trial.

The third commentary (Rhodes and Kolevzon, this volume, p. 179) highlights the importance of balancing the risks and benefits to the potential participants as well as the population of patients with the disorder. Using similar arguments as shared by the previous commentators, they note that failing to consider those who may benefit in the future could distract from the importance of completing a well-designed trial. The commentators conclude that it is especially important to consider those who may benefit in the future when dealing with a rare, chronic disease, adding that the resources allotted ought to be maximized and others stand to benefit whether the findings are positive or negative.

The commentators agree that excluding families without the means to relocate from enrolling in this trial does not violate the principle of justice. The study team is appropriately balancing the risks to the potential participants, the integrity of the trial, and the future benefits a well-designed trial will generate. Addressing the social inequities that limit enrollment is not the responsibility of the study team.

CASE 3.1: IS IT ETHICAL TO ENROLL COGNITIVELY IMPAIRED ADULTS IN RESEARCH THAT IS MORE THAN MINIMAL RISK WITH NO PROSPECT OF BENEFIT?

INTRODUCTION

An important theme in research ethics involves limiting the risks that subjects can be exposed to when they do not have the capacity to provide informed consent. When investigators propose research that is more than minimal risk in this context, there may be ways to respect subjects' preferences (substituted judgment) to participate in research. Ideally, this can allow investigators to distinguish between potential subjects for whom the research participation might or might not be acceptable. There is a range of views, however, about how to understand the concept of substituted judgment, how explicit the preference needs to be, the implications of varying degrees of cognitive impairment, and how substituted judgment is applied in clinical research.

These issues are illustrated by the case given here, which involves a study of adults with cognitive impairment who would undergo lumbar puncture (LP) and other procedures that are not needed for clinical care. Accompanying the case summary is a commentary by Mark Yarborough, PhD, of the University of California, Davis, who discusses the lack of consistency of regulatory approaches for who is allowed to participate and what research to allow with cognitively impaired adults. He suggests that we should embrace a broad view of substituted judgment, relying on life narratives, as may be done in healthcare decisions. Arthur Derse, MD, JD, and Ryan Spellecy, PhD, of the Medical College of Wisconsin, offer a similar analysis for a broad view of substituted judgment and propose applying to adults the approach to risk underlying the pediatric regulations, which limits risk to "no more than a minor increase in risk." They suggest that the risk of the LP falls below this threshold. Marion Danis, MD, David Wendler, PhD, and Scott Kim, MD, PhD, of the National Institutes of Health (NIH), note that the public generally is supportive of research, even with some risks, and the ideal approach would be to expand the concept of DPA for healthcare to include research participation to facilitate substituted judgments. While the commentators have different approaches, they each acknowledge that involvement in research, even if it involves more than minimal risk, can be acceptable in some contexts for cognitively impaired adults.

CASE SUMMARY

A researcher plans a natural history study of a condition associated with varying degrees of cognitive impairment. The study proposes to enroll children and adults who will undergo magnetic resonance imaging (MRI) spectroscopy of the brain and collection of cerebral spinal fluid by LP. Conscious sedation will be used for subjects who need it to complete either or both procedures. Given the LP and the possible use of conscious sedation, the IRB categorizes the study as a minor increase over minimal risk with no prospect of direct benefit.

U.S. regulations allow IRBs to approve the enrollment of minors in this category of research (45 CFR 46.406) provided both parents (if reasonably available) give their permission and minors who are capable provide assent. For adults, the regulations stipulate that investigators must obtain the subject's consent or permission from the subject's legally authorized representative (LAR) (45 CFR 46.102). An LAR is a person who is "authorized under applicable law to consent on behalf of a prospective subject to the subject's participation in the procedure(s) involved in the research." Which individuals are authorized to make research decisions depends on the law of the state or local jurisdiction where the research is conducted. A few jurisdictions have explicit laws on who qualifies as an LAR for research purposes. All others are silent on this issue, including the state in which the research described here will be conducted. For research in these jurisdictions, the Office for Human

Research Protections (OHRP) counsels IRBs to look to who is legally authorized to make clinical decisions regarding the interventions used in the study to determine who should be authorized to make research decisions.

If a potential subject is unable to consent and does not have a legal guardian or an agent with DPA, the investigators plan to evaluate whether the individual is able to assign DPA. The study proposes to exclude those who do not have a legal guardian or DPA. Individuals who have a legal guardian or DPA may be enrolled, provided that the representative (1) understands the research, (2) has sufficient reason to believe enrollment is consistent with the subject's preferences and values, and (3) grants permission. A final requirement is that the subject understands the study to the extent he or she is capable, and assents. The researchers plan to monitor enrolled subjects during the study and to withdraw those who subsequently dissent (i.e., express distress).

This case brings up several ethical questions: Should investigators be allowed to enroll adults who cannot consent in research that offers no prospect of direct benefit and poses more than minimal risk? If so, what additional protections should be included in such research? Should an agent with DPA for healthcare be permitted to make research decisions? If a potential subject cannot consent and does not have an agent with DPA, is it appropriate to evaluate the potential subject's capacity to assign DPA?

COMMENTARY 3.1.1: INCONSISTENT APPROACHES TO RESEARCH INVOLVING COGNITIVELY IMPAIRED ADULTS: WHY THE BROAD VIEW OF SUBSTITUTED JUDGMENT IS OUR BEST GUIDE

MARK YARBOROUGH

This case study highlights some of the most challenging ethical issues in biomedical research: When and how can we justifiably use cognitively impaired adults to benefit other people? Forty years after the issuance of federal regulation 45 CFR 46, practice in this area remains unsettled. The Common Rule lacks specificity; guidance from the OHRP defers the matter largely to the states; and most states fail to explicitly address the topic, despite many thoughtful reports (American College of Physicians 1989), including from two Presidential Commissions (National Bioethics Advisory Commission 1998; Presidential Commission for the Study of Bioethical Issues 2015), recommendations (National Institutes of Health, Office of Extramural Research 2009), and commentaries (Berg 1996; Glass and Speyer-Ofenberg 1996; Yarborough 2002).

As a result, IRB practices, and thus research opportunities, can be wildly discordant. For example, in jurisdictions lacking state statutes that authorize surrogates to make research decisions for incapacitated adults, an IRB may prohibit all such nontherapeutic research, reasoning that the absence of a law authorizing surrogate consent for research means that that state does not want this research to occur. In that same state, another IRB may decide the exact opposite, reasoning instead that if the state had wanted to prohibit such research, it would have done so explicitly.

Discordance does not end at the question of whether we can legally conduct nontherapeutic research with impaired adults. Among those IRBs that determine such research is legal, we find divergence on what research is permitted. Some may prohibit all nontherapeutic research. Others may permit nontherapeutic research but restrict all research to health conditions relevant to adults with impaired decision making, like the research addressed in this case study. It might also be within the discretion of an IRB to restrict surrogate consent to, for example, surrogates able to employ the substituted judgment standard of consent, similar again to this case study.

In light of this confusing landscape, the Presidential Commission for the Study of Bioethical Issues has called for clear legal standards regarding surrogate consent (Presidential Commission for the Study of Bioethical Issues 2015). In their absence, we can never have consistent answers to substantive questions such as who is qualified to give consent and whether consent should be restricted to research related to the health and well-being of cognitively impaired adults.

The most critical step toward greater consistency is applying the settled policy for clinical decision making to research as well: Require the substituted judgment legal standard of surrogate decision making for research with cognitively impaired adults. This is the approach reflected in this case study: The protocol instructs the surrogate decision maker who has DPA to consider the subject's "preferences and values."

Two major implications would flow from this. First, research candidates without suitable surrogates could not participate in any nontherapeutic research, because nobody would be qualified to make substituted judgments on their behalf. Second, surrogates would have to be given appropriate guidance on how they exercise their discretion in making decisions for research candidates, regardless of the level of risk and potential for therapeutic benefit.

The literature is significantly divided on this guidance point. One school of thought severely restricts surrogates' discretion. It argues that substituted judgments that do not come close to matching actual prior decisions or previously expressed sentiments are invalid (Beauchamp and Childress 1994; Berg 1996). The problem with this approach is that it assumes that there is a prior research candidate decision or considered view about research participation that surrogates can accurately approximate, an assumption likely borne out in reality much less frequently than we would care to admit (Yarborough 2005). Following this school of thought, then, we would have to exclude surrogates who lacked information about the research candidates that closely approximates prior participation views. This would drastically restrict research.

An alternative approach more in line with the protocol in this case study grants substantially more discretion to surrogates by stressing characteristic rather than accurate decisions. Just because there is no prior research decision that a surrogate can accurately match, it does not follow that surrogates cannot make respectful decisions for candidates. According to this approach, surrogates construct, rather than match, decisions by using not just their prior knowledge of the values and preferences of research candidates, like the protocol in question does, but also their familiarity with the life narratives of candidates. This "constructed judgment" implementation method of substituted judgments better assures a respectful denouement of research candidates' lives during their time of dependency on others (Yarborough 2005).

Concern for respect leads directly to the question posed in this case study about evaluating the capacity of research candidates to appoint an agent with DPA if they do not have one. If we truly want to treat research candidates with the full measure of respect they are due, then this should be done. If we assume that people's life narratives often contain sufficient information to responsibly guide surrogate decisions, then it behooves us to work with individuals to identify their most appropriate surrogates. Determining whether or not a research candidate has the capacity to identify such a person extends this added demonstration of respect.

This more expansive interpretation of respectful treatment diverges from the *Belmont Report*, which restricts respectful treatment of people with diminished capacity to protection from harm (U.S. Department of Health and Human Services, Office for Human Subjects Research 1979). Hence, IRBs and investigators might be reluctant to move in this direction. This could prove unfortunate; adults with impaired decision making deserve more from us than simple protection. They deserve recognition for the individual people they are and the lives they are continuing to lead. Making good-faith efforts to consider what role research participation should play in those lives affords them that recognition.

It is disheartening that, after decades of deliberation, we have yet to reach consensus that surrogate research decision making for cognitively impaired adults should more closely parallel clinical decision making. This would guarantee that IRBs would defer to the substituted judgment standard of informed consent. Further consensus about how that standard is best implemented could yield important benefits. Agreement around the constructed judgment or some similar implementation method would mean that surrogate familiarity with the life narratives of research candidates is the most salient ethical consideration in research, not the degree of risk or the nature of the health condition being studied. Requiring investigators to seek out the most qualified surrogates would maximize the chances that respectful research decisions are made. This, in turn, likely would result in surrogate decisions that would permit more and varied research with this population of research candidates. Such judgments would be implicit in research candidates' life narratives, reflected by the fact that so many are motivated throughout their lives by the welfare and needs of others and not just themselves. There is no reason that diminished decisional capacity must rob people of their ability to continue such a legacy.

References

American College of Physicians. 1989. Cognitively impaired subjects. *Annals of Internal Medicine* 111:843–48.

Beauchamp, T. L., and J. F. Childress. 1994. *Principles of biomedical ethics*, 4th ed. New York, NY: Oxford University Press.

Berg, J. W. 1996. Legal and ethical complexities of consent with cognitively impaired research subjects: Proposed guidelines. *Journal of Law, Medicine & Ethics* 24:18–35.

Glass, K. C., and M. Speyer-Ofenberg. 1996. Incompetent persons as research subjects and the ethics of minimal risk. *Cambridge Quarterly Healthcare Ethics* 5:362–72.

National Bioethics Advisory Commission. 1998. *Research involving persons with mental disorders that may affect decisionmaking capacity: Report and recommendations*, vol. 1. Rockville MD: NBAC. Available at: http://hdl.handle.net/1805/21

National Institutes of Health, Office of Extramural Research. 2009. Research involving individuals with questionable capacity to consent: Points to consider. Available at: http://grants1.nih.gov/grants/policy/questionablecapacity.htm

Presidential Commission for the Study of Bioethical Issues. 2015. *Gray Matters*, vol. 2: *Topics at the intersection of neuroscience, ethics, and society*. Washington, DC. Available at: http://bioethics.gov/node/4704

U.S. Department of Health and Human Services, Office for Human Subjects Research. 1979. Belmont report. Ethical principles and guidelines for the protection of human subjects of research. Available at http://www.hhs.gov/ohrp/humansubjects/guidance/belmont.html

Yarborough, M. 2002. Adults are not big children: Examining surrogate consent to research using adults with dementia. *Cambridge Quarterly of Healthcare Ethics* 11:160–68.

Yarborough, M. 2005. Deciding for others at the end of life: Storytelling and moral agency. *Journal of Clinical Ethics* 16:127–43.

COMMENTARY 3.1.2: ETHICAL AND REGULATORY CONSIDERATIONS REGARDING ENROLLMENT OF INCOMPETENT ADULTS IN MORE THAN MINIMAL RISK RESEARCH AS COMPARED WITH CHILDREN

ARTHUR R. DERSE AND RYAN SPELLECY

In this case, the investigator should be allowed to enroll incompetent adults into this study, with certain safeguards. If an incompetent adult has an agent or an LAR, that person should be able to evaluate the appropriateness of enrollment in research participation in studies with a minor increment over minimal risk (like this study with LP and conscious sedation). The agent should base the decision on the person's prior expressed autonomous values, including altruism. Such an agent could be appointed by the potential subject, if capable of doing so.

The investigator is already allowed to enroll children under the current regulations that allow parents to evaluate research risks and enroll their children into studies with a minor increment over minimal risk. The guiding ethical consideration—constrained parental autonomy to make these decisions—is justifiably different from the justification applied to adults.

Adults

Regulatory guidance for enrolling incompetent adults in greater than minimal risk research is thin, stating only that when some or all of the subjects are likely to be incompetent, unspecified "additional safeguards" should be included to protect their rights and welfare (45 CFR 46.111 (b): U.S. Department of Health and Human Services 2005). Investigators should be allowed to enroll incompetent adults, even if that research offers no prospect of direct benefit, if the research has only a minor increase over minimal risk and the LAR grants permission, as provided for in the regulations (45 CFR 46.102: U.S. Department of Health and Human Services 2005). The additional safeguards that should be included in this type of research are that (1) the adult, while decisional, expressed or exhibited values of altruism; (2) the individual was not known to be unwilling to participate in research; and (3) there is documentation of these requirements by the LAR.

In this case we advocate not only for a surrogate role, but also for limiting possible enrollment to cases with, at most, a minor increase over minimal risk. We propose relying on a substituted judgment that might be inferred from the subject's values and preferences over a lifetime, honoring the person's autonomy.

If the adult's preferences or values before becoming incompetent are known or can be reasonably inferred from behaviors and statements while the adult was competent, then the LAR can apply those values in deciding about enrollment. Many people value and exhibit altruism and participate in opportunities to benefit society, such as blood donation, that are not without risk. For instance, individuals who participate in so-called "fun runs" as fundraisers for disease research know that, on occasion, these voluntary opportunities can lead to serious injury or even death. Many others demonstrate their altruism through donations of money, knowing that there is a minor risk that at some point in the future they might greatly need money, but they are willing to take that risk. Participation in such activities provides some evidence of altruism, giving insight into the values of the person whose autonomy we seek to protect. Volunteering for an LP for research can be an expression of autonomous altruism, with one volunteer stating that donating small amounts of cerebral spinal fluid "felt like the most useful thing I'd ever done" (Hedreen 2015).

In this case, if, while the subject was decisional, there was evidence of altruism and no known opposition to participation in research, an LAR could decide to enroll the subject in research, as long as this was consistent with the subject's values. On the other hand, in the case of an adult who was known not to be altruistic, or was known to be unwilling to participate in research, or was never competent and could not express values of altruism or desire to participate in research, the LAR should not be allowed to authorize participation in greater than minimal risk research.

Children

Compared to adults who are not competent, the federal regulations allow children to be enrolled in research that does not have a prospect of direct benefit if the research is likely to yield generalizable knowledge about the subjects' disorder or condition and poses only a minor increment over minimal risk (45 CFR 46.406: U.S. Department of Health and Human Services 2005). Children typically do not have formulated preferences with respect to research, yet parents may enroll their children in greater than minimal risk research based on constrained parental autonomy (Ross 1998, 2006), in which parents may wish to inculcate altruism in their children. Thus, we allow one set of parents to enroll their child in research that other parents might not authorize because we allow parents wide latitude in rearing their children.

The fact that parents can make choices based on the values they wish to impart to their children does imply that, similarly in adults, there may be certain situations in which a slight increment over minimal risk is within the authority of those who are charged with acting in an individual's best interest. The rationale, however, is different. The parental ability to make a choice for a child without preferences is based on the value of altruism the parents wish to impart. But for the incompetent adults, the LAR should act upon evidence of altruism or similar values.

Representatives

When there is no LAR appointed for research purposes, an agent with DPA for healthcare should be considered appropriate to weigh clinical research decisions.

Certainly, if the person's values are known or can be reasonably inferred from behavior and statements, this knowledge and judgment are the same kind that agents of a DPA typically evaluate in the healthcare situation and should be able to do likewise in a research situation. Evaluations concerning risks and benefits in healthcare are judgments that agents must make. If the adult's values and preferences are unknown, this is more akin to the best interest standard in healthcare, in which only the best interests of the individual should be considered, and research involving a minor increment over minimal risk should not be permitted.

Appointment of an agent of a DPA

When an adult is not able to evaluate research risks, but might have the capacity to identify an individual to make an evaluation on his or her behalf, it would be appropriate to evaluate the potential subject's capacity to assign an agent of a DPA under these circumstances. The agent with DPA should be someone who knows the preferences of the individual well enough to be able to determine expressed or demonstrated values of altruism as well as expressed or demonstrated unwillingness to participate in research.

Conclusion

In this case, just as the investigator can be allowed to enroll children under the current regulatory guidelines that allow parents to evaluate research risks and enroll their children into studies with a minor increment over minimal risk, using the guiding ethical consideration of constrained parental autonomy, so also the investigator should be allowed to enroll incompetent adults into research without direct benefit that has a minor increment over minimal risk, based on the person's expressed autonomous values of altruism, with certain safeguards outlined in this commentary.

References

Hedreen, A. 2015, June 29. My spinal taps for Alzheimer's. *Wall Street Journal*, A11.

Ross, L. F. 1998. *Children, families, and health care decision making*, Oxford, UK: Oxford University Press.

Ross, L. F. 2006. *Children in medical research: Access versus protection*, Oxford, UK: Oxford University Press.

U.S. Department of Health and Human Services. 2005. U.S. Code of Federal Regulations. Title 45. Public welfare. Part 46. Protection of human subjects. Available at: http://www.hhs.gov/ohrp/humansubjects/guidance/45cfr46.html (accessed May 18, 2015).

COMMENTARY 3.1.3: ACCEPTABLE APPROACHES TO ENROLLING ADULTS WHO CANNOT CONSENT IN MORE THAN MINIMAL RISK RESEARCH

MARION DANIS, DAVID WENDLER, AND SCOTT Y. H. KIM

Research on diseases that cause cognitive impairment is of vital importance. It provides the opportunity to improve methods to prevent, treat, and possibly cure illnesses that cause significant morbidity to millions of people. When possible, investigators should conduct this research with individuals who are able to provide informed consent. And we should note that many individuals with mild cognitive impairment, when carefully evaluated, show evidence that they retain the ability to consent. To understand the nature of Alzheimer's disease (AD), autism, and diseases associated with cognitive impairment, however, investigators sometimes need to conduct nonbeneficial procedures that pose greater than minimal risk with individuals who cannot provide informed consent.

When assessing the ethical appropriateness of this research, the first question should be whether the research is of sufficient value. Individuals, whether they can consent or not, should be enrolled in research only when it is socially valuable—especially when the research poses greater than minimal risk and enrolls adults who cannot consent.

Most guidelines and commentators permit minimal-risk, nonbeneficial research with adults who cannot consent (Secretary's Advisory Committee on Human Research Protections 2009). The present question is, what level of additional risk is acceptable? Specifically, given the regulatory definition of minimal risk, the question is: Is it acceptable to enroll individuals who cannot consent in research that poses risks exceeding those considered appropriate as part of ordinary, daily life?

It seems appropriate to expose adults who cannot consent to risks greater than those permitted ordinarily if the research has the potential to gather important information that cannot be obtained with individuals who can consent and cannot be obtained in a way that poses lower risks. The key questions are, under what circumstances would such research be permissible, and what is the upper limit of such risk?

Consider first a situation in which an individual has designated someone, through assignment of DPA, to make research decisions for them and there is sufficient reason to believe that participation in the study is consistent with the individual's values. Suppose further that this person, although quite impaired, is able to understand some rudimentary information (e.g., that he is being enrolled in a study, even though he cannot explain the details) and to provide assent—as is the case with many people with dementia (Kim, Cox, and Caine 2002; Marson et al. 1995). It seems appropriate to permit such a person to enroll in research with greater than ordinary risk without prospect of benefit, if the person assigned the DPA agrees.

The act of designating someone else to make decisions provides that designee with special moral authority to make decisions on the individual's behalf (Kim and Appelbaum 2006). There is good evidence that many people with cognitive impairments retain the ability to appoint a surrogate (over 90% of persons with early Alzheimer's will likely be able to appoint a DPA for research). Even some individuals who have lost the capacity to consent can appoint a surrogate (Kim et al. 2011a). These data highlight the importance of encouraging persons in early stages of diagnosis to designate a DPA for research, and the importance of evaluating whether or not individuals with moderate impairments who lack a designee with DPA are able to appoint one.

Moving on, we face the question of individuals who do not have and are unable to assign a DPA for research. Is it acceptable to rely on next of kin or the designee with the DPA for healthcare decisions to make research decisions in studies with greater than minimal risk and no prospect of benefit? As very few people fill out advance research directives or appoint a DPA for research, this is an important question from a policy perspective. The fact that an individual did not assign a surrogate for research decisions does not imply that next-of-kin decision makers are inappropriate. For instance, court-appointed guardians often are permitted to make research decisions even though they were not appointed by the individual. It may be, for example, that most people would be willing to allow their family to make decisions for them in the event of their incapacity, much as family is expected to do for treatment decisions. What is the evidence for the public's view on this issue?

First, people generally are willing to participate in research that might be categorized as more than minimal risk research with no prospect of benefit based on family surrogate consent. Surveys of people at increased risk of Alzheimer's (Kim et al. 2005; Wendler et al. 2002), elderly people in clinics and senior centers (Karlawish et al. 2009), caregivers of patients with dementia (Kim, Uhlmann, and Appelbaum 2010), and the older general public (Kim et al. 2009) indicate that all these groups highly value AD research and many are willing to consider participation. In a survey of U.S. adults aged 51 years and older, 71% were willing to consider participation in studies involving LP without prospect of benefit based on the permission of a family surrogate decision maker (Kim et al. 2009). Furthermore, most people are willing to give their future surrogate decision makers some or complete leeway regarding research participation decisions (Karlawish et al. 2009; Kim et al. 2009; Kim, Kim, and Ryan 2013; Wendler et al. 2002).

Second, the public generally supports a societal policy of family surrogate consent for dementia research when necessary. For example, after a day-long democratic deliberation session consisting of interactive expert education and peer deliberation, 92% of individuals drawn from the general public said they would probably (41%) or definitely (51%) support de facto family surrogate permission for studies involving LPs without prospect of benefit, and 67% would support first-in-human gene transfer research (Kim et al. 2011b).

Of course, when relying on a surrogate who is not chosen by the potential research subject for research decisions, it is important to follow certain safeguards. As in this case, this means that surrogates are evaluated to determine whether they (1) have a good relationship with the potential research subject, (2) understand the study involves research, and (3) have sufficient reason to believe that enrollment in the study is consistent with the subject's preferences and values.

Finally, while we believe research that poses some level of risks greater than minimal can be acceptable, we think there should be an upper limit on the net risks to which individuals who cannot consent may be exposed. However, we do not think that this level of risk can be settled by philosophical analysis. Philosophical analysis can support the claim that it can be acceptable to expose individuals who cannot consent to some risks for the benefit of others. Such analysis, though, will not be able to identify the precise limit to risks. Hence, it will be important to gather data on what level of risks is regarded as appropriate by a majority of the public, and to couple these data with judicious safeguards.

References

Karlawish, J., J. Rubright, D. Casarett, M. Cary, T. Ten Have, and P. Sankar. 2009. Older adults' attitudes toward enrollment of non-competent subjects participating in Alzheimer's research. *American Journal of Psychiatry* 166(2):131–34.

Kim, S. Y. H., and P. S. Appelbaum. 2006. The capacity to appoint a proxy and the possibility of concurrent proxy directives. *Behavioral Sciences & the Law* 24(4):469–78.

Kim, S. Y. H., C. Cox, and E. D. Caine. 2002. Impaired decision-making ability and willingness to participate in research in persons with Alzheimer's disease. *American Journal of Psychiatry* 159:797–802.

Kim, S., J. Karlawish, H. Kim, I. Wall, A. Bozoki, and P. Appelbaum. 2011a. Preservation of the capacity to appoint a proxy decision maker: Implications for dementia research. *Archives of General Psychiatry* 68(2):214–20.

Kim, S. Y. H., H. M. Kim, D. S. Knopman, R. De Vries, L. Damschroder, and P. S. Appelbaum. 2011b. Effect of public deliberation on attitudes toward surrogate consent for dementia research. *Neurology* 77(24):2097–104.

Kim, S. Y. H., H. M. Kim, K. M. Langa, J. H. Karlawish, D. S. Knopman, and P. S. Appelbaum. 2009. Surrogate consent for dementia research: A national survey of older Americans. *Neurology* 72(2):149–55.

Kim, S. Y. H., H. M. Kim, C. McCallum, and P. N. Tariot. 2005. What do people at risk for Alzheimer's disease think about surrogate consent for research? *Neurology* 65:1395–1401.

Kim, S. Y. H., H. M. Kim, K. A. Ryan, et al. 2013. How important is "accuracy" of surrogate decision-making for research participation? *PLoS ONE* 8(1):e54790.

Kim, S. Y. H., R. A. Uhlmann, P. S. Appelbaum, et al. 2010. Deliberative assessment of surrogate consent in dementia research. *Alzheimer's and Dementia* 6(4):342–50.

Marson, D. C., K. K. Ingram, H. A. Cody, and L. E. Harrell. 1995. Assessing the competency of patients with Alzheimer's disease under different legal standards. A prototype instrument. *Archives of Neurology* 52(10):949–54.

Secretary's Advisory Committee on Human Research Protections. 2009. Recommendations from the Subcommittee for the Inclusion of Individuals with Impaired Decision Making in Research (SIIIDR). Approved 2009. Available at: http://www.hhs.gov/ohrp/sachrp/20090715letterattach.pdf

Wendler, D., R. A. Martinez, D. Fairclough, T. Sunderland, and E. Emanuel. 2002. Views of potential subjects toward proposed regulations for clinical research with adults unable to consent. *American Journal of Psychiatry* 159(4):585–91.

CASE 3.2: SHOULD PATIENTS BE REQUIRED TO UNDERGO STANDARD CHEMOTHERAPY BEFORE BEING ELIGIBLE FOR NOVEL PHASE I IMMUNOTHERAPY CLINICAL TRIALS?

INTRODUCTION

Many Phase I oncology trials include an eligibility criterion requiring potential participants to fail standard chemotherapy. The rationale for this approach is to ensure that patients do not forgo established clinical approaches. The case described here has the additional feature of the consultation being requested by a research participant who wanted to challenge the ethical rationale for such an eligibility criterion. He also questioned the scientific validity of the premise that failure of standard treatments should be required. This may be particularly relevant when standard treatments have limited impact on survival, and when the experimental approach represents a biologically distinct approach such as immunotherapy (agents aimed at stimulating the immune system to attack the cancer cells, via T-cell lymphocytes).

Adélaïde Doussau, of the NIH, and Clark B. Hanmer, a retired family practice physician from Laurinburg, NC, share their perspectives as the ethics consultant and the consultation requestor and focus on allowing patients who have not received standard NIH Institutes of Health discuss the emerging role of patients in contributing to the research agenda, in the context of citizen science, and also point to the value of facilitating patients to have access to research ethics consultation services. Cynthia Wetmore from the Aflac Cancer and Blood Disorders Center at Children's Healthcare of Atlanta and Emory University Department of Pediatrics suggests that the scientific rationale for alternative approaches to Phase I studies is so compelling that it should be extended to include children, even though children cannot provide informed consent themselves. What is most striking is that all three commentary groups do not primarily justify their analysis on the basis of direct patient welfare, but rather on the role of patients in advocating for the well-being of other patients through research.

CASE SUMMARY

The patient was diagnosed with an advanced cholangiocarcinoma, a rare cancer affecting bile ducts. Untreated, about half the patients with such cancer survive six months (Park et al. 2009). The standard gemcitabine–cisplatin chemotherapy provides limited benefit: It prolongs median survival by a few months (median survival of 12 months), has severe side effects (71% of patients experience at least one severe side effect [Grade > 3, i.e., requiring hospitalization or limiting patient's ability to care for him- or herself], most frequently decreased neutrophil counts [25%], infection [18%], abnormal liver function [17%], or fatigue [19%]), and complete responses are extremely rare (0.5% to 1%) (Valle et al. 2010). The patient is a family medicine physician. Upon diagnosis, he entertained the options of standard chemotherapy and palliative care. He was leaning toward palliative care, given the prognosis even with standard treatment, but then decided he would like to have the opportunity to enroll in a clinical trial as a way to contribute to medical progress and to help future cancer patients. He contacted research teams to seek enrollment in a clinical trial testing an innovative immunotherapy. Eligibility in these trials was restricted to patients who had failed standard chemotherapy. He agreed to receive standard chemotherapy in order to become eligible for the Phase I immunotherapy trial. He became eligible when he developed pulmonary metastases (four months after diagnosis) and was enrolled (six months after diagnosis).

As he reflected on his own experience, he became concerned about the eligibility criteria for such trials. First, as an ethical concern, he questioned whether patients should be required to exhaust all available therapies to be eligible for early-phase clinical trials, particularly when the impact of the chemotherapy on the prognosis is relatively modest (risk of toxicity and limited increase in life expectancy). In his words, "The probability of becoming too sick or dying before getting the chance to enroll is unacceptably high."

Second is a scientific question about study design, in the context of highly lethal cancers where it is unclear whether immunotherapy will be best delivered before or after chemotherapy. Indeed, with immunotherapies, white blood cells (T cells) are stimulated to recognize and kill cancer cells. The mechanism of action is thus very different from traditional chemotherapies that are acting by a direct toxic mechanism on cancer cells and are accompanied by various side effects, including immunosuppression. Therefore, destruction of tumor cells by chemotherapy may uncover fragments of the tumor for the immune system to target via immunotherapy, but the depletion of the immune system due to adverse events of chemotherapy might also prevent optimal immunotherapy efficacy.

The patient sought a research ethics consultation to further reflect on these concerns about eligibility and design and learn more about the ethical and scientific implications of relaxing this requirement for patients to fail standard treatment prior to allowing them to be eligible for Phase I oncology research.

REFERENCES

Park, J., M. H. Kim, K. P. Kim, D. H. Park, S. H. Moon, T. J. Song, J. Eum, S. S. Lee, D. W. Seo, and S. K. Lee. 2009. Natural history and prognostic factors of advanced cholangiocarcinoma without surgery, chemotherapy, or radiotherapy: A large-scale observational study. *Gut and Liver* 3(4):298–305.

Valle, J., H. Wasan, D. H. Palmer, et al. 2010. Cisplatin plus gemcitabine versus gemcitabine for biliary tract cancer. *New England Journal of Medicine* 362:1273–81.

COMMENTARY 3.2.1: A RATIONALE FOR RELAXING THE REQUIREMENT TO UNDERGO A NONCURATIVE CHEMOTHERAPY FOR ADVANCED CANCER IN A PHASE I IMMUNOTHERAPY TRIAL

ADÉLAÏDE DOUSSAU AND CLARK B. HANMER

This patient-physician with advanced cholangiocarcinoma challenges the long-lasting widespread idea that Phase I cancer clinical trials ought to be conducted in patients who have failed all available therapies. Of course, it is not desirable that investigators recommend an experimental drug when an approved drug could offer a meaningful clinical benefit relying on a higher level of scientific evidence. In the case of lethal disease for which the available treatments provide a limited benefit, however, there is some ambiguity about which previous treatments should be considered mandatory by explicit eligibility criteria.

We review the case of this patient by examining medical decision making in the clinical care setting first. We further consider whether relaxing the eligibility criteria in clinical research would impact the risk and benefit for participants, or the scientific and social value of the study.

Let us first consider how medical decision making would proceed for such a patient in the clinical setting, outside of the scope of any research. For this patient, there is no curative treatment. It is reasonable for a patient to decide to forgo a chemotherapy that is likely to neither cure him nor have a major impact on his survival, given that the treatment has a significant burden in terms of treatment delivery and toxicities. Respecting his decision to forgo the chemotherapy would be respecting his values and his autonomy, provided that his decision-making capacity has not been impaired. Given that the patient is a physician, he is likely to have a good understanding of the consequences of his decision. It would, however, be advisable to ensure that he has an accurate understanding of the evidence and current professional recommendations, so that the decision is made in a shared decision-making process with his treating oncologist. Once the patient has made the decision to refuse the standard, recommended, but noncurative treatment, he should be considered as having no available therapy for his condition. The eligibility criteria for early-phase trials in advanced cancer could be relaxed to include those who chose to forgo noncurative chemotherapy.

Two important concerns about this approach are that (1) it could compromise the safety of the study participant or (2) it could compromise the attainment of the scientific objectives of the study (Emanuel, Wendler, and Grady 2000). We now consider each of these concerns.

First, given that the primary objective in Phase I trials is to study safety, the benefit–risk should be evaluated primarily in regard with safety concerns. It is unlikely that receiving immunotherapy without having received the chemotherapy would increase the risk of toxicity of the immunotherapy for an individual participant, as compared to receiving the immunotherapy after the chemotherapy. The risk of toxicity of immunotherapy could be either similar or even lower. Importantly, the disease could progress quicker without chemotherapy than with chemotherapy. However, (1) progression is the expected course of the disease irrespective of undergoing chemotherapy or not; (2) earlier progression would be a consequence of the autonomous decision of the patient before entering the trial, not a consequence of the participation in the trial; and (3) in this case, the prognosis without chemotherapy is still compatible with sufficient time participation enabling collecting scientific data to evaluate the safety of the experimental compound, thus not compromising the validity. Thus, allowing inclusion of patients who refused chemotherapy would neither increase the risk to the patient of participating in the trial, nor impede the scientific validity of the safety evaluation.

Second, little is known at the stage of Phase I trials about the activity of the experimental compound. Thus, it is not advisable to consider potential activity as a likely benefit for participants (Kimmelman 2016). However, it is important to consider how the evaluation of activity could be impacted by relaxing eligibility criteria. Indeed, Phase I trials set the grounds for future Phase II trials and thus need to be informative enough that signals of activity can be detected. Currently, it is not known whether having received chemotherapy or not could have a positive or negative impact on the activity of the immunotherapy. Including both types of patients—those with prior chemotherapy and those without—could allow for exploring this question while not compromising the study of safety. Being able to explore those two strata for activity might, however, require a bigger sample size, in order to be able to analyze the two groups of patients separately. While this might have an impact on the cost of the trial, it could also increase the feasibility of the study, as the pool of eligible patients would be bigger (fewer patients die or become ineligible before being able to enter the trial). This is particularly relevant in a rare disease such as cholangiocarcinoma. Therefore, the feasibility of the study would not be compromised, and the higher cost could be justified by the additional scientific question being investigated. Further studies could even consider randomizing three strategies to explore formally the question of the best sequence of treatments: (1) chemotherapy, then immunotherapy if chemotherapy fails (current program); (2) immunotherapy, then chemotherapy (reversed sequence); and (3) chemotherapy plus immunotherapy combined.

Widening the eligibility criteria of Phase I trials to allow patients to forgo standard chemotherapy would nevertheless require ensuring that patients be systematically first offered standard chemotherapy, and that their decision be truly informed, and not guided by either unreasonable hope of clinical benefit from the experimental drug or external constraints such as costs. This might be done through a multidisciplinary discussion or a bioethics consultation. The protocol should also be very explicit about any restrictions about access to standard chemotherapy later on: If the disease progresses under immunotherapy, the patient should know whether his decision to forgo the chemotherapy is revocable. In this case, the bioethics consultation was requested by the patient himself; as a family physician, he had a good understanding of what stage IV incurable cancer means and what palliative care entails, knew how to interpret data from the medical literature, had his own appraisal of what four to six months of prolonged survival might mean in regard to the burden and toxicity of chemotherapy, and could be expected to be less susceptible to unrealistic optimism (Hanmer 2016). He was clear that his motivation for participation in a Phase I study was mainly altruistic (i.e., intended to generate knowledge for future patients with a similar condition) and that he did not have unrealistic expectations of being cured by the experimental drug. This is particularly important in the setting of immunotherapy research, where there are currently concerns about unrealistic hopes and expectations (Garde 2016).

Overall, this analysis indicates that investigators and IRBs could consider allowing participants with advanced cancer and limited life expectancy to forgo noncurative chemotherapy before entering Phase I trials as a reasonable option in some cancers, as long as it is clear and documented that the decision of the patient is well informed, that the risk for study participants is not increased, and that relaxing this eligibility criteria does not threaten the validity and feasibility of the study.

References

Emanuel, E. J., D. Wendler, and C. Grady. 2000. What makes clinical research ethical? *Journal of the American Medical Association* 283(20):2701–11.

Garde, D. 2016. Separating hope from hype in the latest cancer treatment 'revolution'. STAT. Available at: https://www.statnews.com/2016/09/27/cancer-immunotherapy-hope-hype (accessed December 1, 2016).

Hanmer, C. B. 2016. Dancing with my cancer demon: All the way to a NIH/NCI immunotherapy clinical trial, edited by S. Hicks. Available at: http://www.lulu.com/spotlight/mycancerdemon

Kimmelman, J. 2016. Is participation in cancer Phase I trials really therapeutic? *Journal of Clinical Oncology. JCO* 67:9902. Epub ahead of print.

COMMENTARY 3.2.2: PARTICIPATION OF CITIZEN SCIENTISTS IN CLINICAL RESEARCH AND ACCESS TO RESEARCH ETHICS CONSULTATIONS

ELAINE COLLIER AND MARION DANIS

This case teaches us two important lessons. The first pertains to the valuable input that patients, prospective and active research participants, and others can provide to the research enterprise. The second pertains to the value of allowing patients as well as prospective and active research participants to request research ethics consultations.

The citizen scientist's role in clinical research

A citizen scientist is an individual who voluntarily contributes his or her time, effort, and resources toward scientific research in collaboration with professional scientists or alone. These individuals don't necessarily have a formal science background (Scistarter 2016). In this understanding of citizen scientist, patients, families, and the public are increasingly playing multiple roles in clinical research. They have brought new perspectives to the research questions to be addressed, funding models, appropriate primary and secondary outcomes, study design, data collection methodology, analyses, and dissemination of results (Anderson and McCleary 2015). While the value of citizen scientist involvement in clinical research is recognized, some have raised concerns about possible conflicts of interest when those individuals have industry relationships or advocacy roles (Harris 2016). Ethicists are beginning to address the ethics of the multiple roles of citizen scientists, which have similarities and differences to those of traditional scientists (Rose 2013).

Rare disease research in particular has a long history of contributions by nonscientists working closely with researchers. For example, Matt Might applied his computer and social media skills to the task of finding other children with the new genetic defect identified in his child (Mnookin 2014). His identification of other families facilitated research on the disease and the search for treatments (Might and Wilsey 2014). Recently, the Patient Centered Outcomes Research Institute (PCORI) (2016) and the All of Us Research Program or precision medicine initiative (National Institutes of Health [NIH] 2016) are two large clinical research programs that have embraced the multiple roles of patients and the general public in clinical research. The U.S. Food and Drug Administration (FDA) has increased its patient engagement through multiple mechanisms and at all stages of research (FDA 2016). The Nuffield Council on Bioethics' (UK) "Statement of Aspiration: Improving Research by Involving Children and Young People" emphasizes the value of contributions by children in development of research questions, protocols, and the conduct of research (Nuffield Council on Bioethics 2016).

In addition to their perspective as potential participants, patients can provide a different view of the value or impact of the research. The individual who initiated the consultation in this case was interested in advancing the treatment of future patients rather than addressing issues about his personal participation. While not a researcher, he investigated the literature on the disease, its known treatments, the effectiveness of those treatments, and possible new mechanisms for impacting disease not utilized by current treatments. His analysis, knowledge, and thoughtful exploration of available research studies and their requirements and outcomes were ones that he felt would be useful for researchers of this disease to consider. His approach and analysis were also informed by his experience as a practicing physician.

Accessibility of research ethics consultation services to patients, research participants, and others

The ethics consultation service to which this individual brought his request served as a formal mechanism for facilitating a dialogue with the research team and stimulating a broader discussion about the design and conduct of research and the impact of the research on diseases like his. This brings us to the second point about allowing patients, research participants, and others to access research ethics consultation services. This individual was able to access the bioethics consultation service at the NIH Clinical Center since this service allows all individuals with a stake in the research enterprise to request consultations (Danis et al. 2012). Potential and active research participants and their families may consult the service for any number of reasons. For example, they may be in the process of making a decision about whether to enroll and want assistance in understanding the difference between clinical care and research and sorting out competing personal values and goals. They may be already enrolled and come to a point where they wish to reconsider their voluntary enrollment. They may have a conflict with the research team and wish for help with resolution.

The justification for allowing those outside the research team to request ethics consultations is multifold. As in the healthcare delivery setting where patients may access an ethics consultation service, allowing patients, families, potential research participants, and already-enrolled participants access to a research ethics consultation service levels the playing field and gives them a voice in shaping their involvement in the research endeavor. This justification is both a matter of respect for the role of patients and others in research and an opportunity for ethicists to facilitate the evolution of patients' and others' role in clinical research. The ethics consultant can hear views or concerns about the research process from a different perspective and help provide a conversational space for successfully resolving concerns. Issues may impact the participation of the individual or could address additional concerns of the individual about the research conduct. The consultation may facilitate the successful continuation and completion of enrollment in the research effort that might not have occurred otherwise. Alternatively, the consultation may clarify the possibility that nonparticipation or the termination of a participant's enrollment would be the best course of action when the patient's interests and the research aims are carefully weighed.

Giving individuals outside of the research team an ability to request a research ethics consultation requires some effort. It requires publicity to let patients, potential research participants, research participants, and their families know of the existence and availability of the service to them. It requires letting research staff, particularly research nurses and research coordinators, know that they can serve as a conduit for bringing patients', research participants', and families' concerns to the ethics consultation team. It also requires setting a tone indicating that a request for an ethics consultation is an opportunity for ethical deliberation and not a sign of moral failing. It requires acknowledging that some requests are best referred to other resources such as the IRB, the patient representative, or the office of research integrity.

This consultation request was a mechanism not only for an individual to provide input from his perspective to the research team but also for a citizen scientist to contribute to clinical research. This individual's remarkable willingness to contribute his insights to advance research for others in such a constructive way, not necessarily for his own benefit, underscores the significant contribution patients can make to clinical research. This case also highlights the opportunity and duty ethicists have to offer guidance on the ethical issues raised by participation of citizen scientists in the research process just as they have for traditional scientists.

References

Anderson, M., and K. K. McCleary. 2015. From passenger to copilots: Patients roles expand. *Science Translational Medicine* 7(291):291fs25.

Danis, M., E. Largent, C. Grady, et al. 2012. *Research ethics consultation: A casebook.* New York, NY: Oxford University Press.

Harris, R. 2016. Patients increasingly influence direction of medical research. National Public Radio, November 28. Available at: http://www.npr.org/sections/health-shots/2016/11/28/502904826/patients-increasingly-influence-the-direction-of-medical-research (accessed December 26, 2016).

Might, M., and M. Wilsey. 2014. The shifting model in clinical diagnostics: How next-generation sequencing and families are altering the way rare diseases are discovered, studied, and treated. *Genetics in Medicine* 16(10):736–37.

Mnookin, S. 2014. Fighting a one-of-a-kind disease. *New Yorker,* July 21. Available at: http://www.newyorker.com/magazine/2014/07/21/one-of-a-kind-2 (accessed December 26, 2016).

National Institutes of Health. 2016. All of Us research program. Available at: https://www.nih.gov/allofus-research-program/participation (accessed December 26, 2016).

Nuffield Council on Bioethics. 2016. Statement on improving research involving children and young people. Available at: http://nuffieldbioethics.org/news/2016/statement-of-aspiration-improving-research-by-involving-children (accessed December 26, 2016).

Patient Centered Outcomes Research Institute (PCORI). 2016. Get involved. Available at: http://www.pcori.org/get-involved (accessed December 26, 2016).

Rose, S. L. 2013. Patient advocacy organizations: Institutional conflicts of interest, trust, and trustworthiness. *The Journal of Law, Medicine & Ethics* 41(3):680–87.

Scistarter. 2016. Citizen science. Available at: http://scistarter.com/page/Citizen%20Science.html (accessed December 26, 2016).

U.S. Food & Drug Administration (FDA). 2016. Patient engagement. Available at: http://www.fda.gov/ForPatients/PatientEngagement/default.htm (accessed December 26, 2016).

COMMENTARY 3.2.3: FORGOING CONVENTIONAL THERAPY IN PHASE I ONCOLOGY RESEARCH: DON'T FORGET ABOUT THE CHILDREN

CYNTHIA WETMORE

The nine-year-old girl turned her head sideways to focus her dark eyes on mine and asked, "Will I be able to play hockey again?" What her pediatrician first thought was a viral infection, causing weakness of the left side of her face and eye muscles, was now unmistakably a brainstem tumor called diffuse intrinsic pontine glioma (DIPG). DIPG arises primarily in the first decade of life and robs the patient of the remaining decades. There is no cure for DIPG, and only radiation therapy has been found to provide palliative relief of the effects of this tumor, with fewer than 5% of patients surviving more than two years from diagnosis.

Phase I clinical trials are designed to describe the toxicities of an agent not previously used in humans and to estimate, using a cohort-based progressive increase in dose, the maximum tolerated dose and the recommended Phase II dose of an agent to be used for subsequent studies of efficacy. In a Phase I study, the likelihood of benefit for a given patient has been, historically, exceedingly low. However, a well-designed and -conducted Phase I clinical trial will, in the best scenario, result in an increase in the "generalizable knowledge" of a therapy or drug that can be used to improve the health of future patients. Unfortunately, most agents that enter the clinical trial pipeline are never licensed by the FDA, and the majority of data from the outcome of these "failed" trials are often never published or shared with the medical community (Hakala et al. 2015). Manuscripts reporting the early closure of a trial due to "futility" or lack of efficacy of the agent rarely garner attention from editors of high-impact journals, if those manuscripts are even drafted and submitted for publication at all (Rising, Bacchetti, and Bero 2008).

The requirement under reflection by this case—that novel drugs be tested in patients whose disease has progressed through first- and second-line therapy—may not be the most effective or predictive process to assess the safety or efficacy of new agents. In this immunotherapy trial, the antitumor activity of the medication may actually be undermined by the decrement in immune function that can result from prior courses of the "standard of care" cytotoxic therapy. It may be that naïve patients have the greatest potential to respond to an immune-modulatory agent as an initial course of therapy, when their immune system is the most robust.

Cytotoxic therapy induces mutations in the tumor so that a recurrent/progressive tumor may have acquired 10-fold greater mutational burden than the original tumor. It has been reported that fewer than 12% of the molecular events noted in the recurrent tumor were present at diagnosis (Morrissy et al. 2016). Therefore, the requirement to investigate the toxicity and potential efficacy of new therapies on patients with recurrent tumors may, in fact, be doing a disservice to the clinical trial process. We now know that a recurrent tumor undergoes significant genetic divergence through exposure to cytotoxic chemotherapy and radiation therapy.

That novel drugs be tested in patients whose disease has progressed through first- and second-line therapy is particularly relevant to pediatric oncology. Genomic sequencing of tumors arising in children—which carry an overall lower mutation rate than do tumors arising in adults—reported that recurrent tumors have an eightfold increase in the mutational burden as compared to the original tumor (Lee et al. 2012). As a pediatric oncologist, I strongly support the inclusion of children in early-phase clinical research studies. Pediatric tumors often have a distinct genetic signature that differs from a tumor of the same type arising in the adult population. For example, an aggressive brain tumor known as glioblastoma multiforme (GBM) typically has an activating mutation in the epidermal growth factor receptor that promotes tumor growth. While a GBM arising in a child may look the same histologically, it does not have the same constellation of mutations. In fact, many high-grade brain tumors that arise in children have a unique and distinct mutation of the histone complex, the "spool" around which the genetic material is packed within the cell nucleus (Wu et al. 2014). It is a disservice to our pediatric patients to deny them access to early-phase trials of novel agents until they have been demonstrated safe and efficacious in adult disease, as that may not be predictive of the same activity in children. Children and adults with poor-prognosis new or recurrent cancer should have equal access to early-phase trials.

Those (future) patients with the most potential to gain from a clinical trial are usually not the same cohort of patients who are undertaking the greatest burden of risk by exposure to an untested therapy in the early phase of evaluation. However, the possibility of benefit to the study participant and the potential differential in risk versus benefit of study participation are tipped when the participant's disease has no standard curative therapy. Given the lack of data to support the standard sequence of events—testing novel drugs in patients whose disease has progressed through first- and second-line therapy—there is an opportunity to gain knowledge through the study of this patient in a rapidly evolving field of medicine. In the current environment of a growing number of molecularly targeted agents and "personalized medicine," the selection of a patient cohort with a given molecular signature may enhance the chance of that patient's tumor responding to the therapy. However, genomic sequencing of patients' tumor tissue for the presence of a given mutation as an eligibility criterion for a trial using a targeted agent is not straightforward, as most tumors have significant molecular heterogeneity within the mass. Despite this fact, the move to use the molecular signature of the disease to guide therapy is gaining momentum, and that may require us to also reconsider the eligibility criteria and, perhaps, to eliminate the requirement for patients to have undergone prior therapeutic regimens.

The patient in the related case summary is well informed (a family medicine physician) and able to understand the potential risks and benefits of participating in a Phase I immunotherapy trial. Given the gravity of the diagnosis of cholangiocarcinoma or DIPG and the dearth of curative options, one can argue that the choice of a novel yet unproven therapy may offer some clinical benefit and that the patient has the right to consider that option. But the rationale for changing eligibility should not be that he is well informed and thus should be allowed to participate in such a trial. The social value and scientific rationale for innovative approaches to Phase I oncology eligibility are compelling enough that such approaches should be applied to children as well. While the parent or legal guardian must provide consent on behalf of the minor child, it is critically important that any revisiting of the eligibility criteria for early-phase clinical research include children.

References

Hakala, A., J. Kimmelman, B. Carlisle, G. Freeman, and D. Fergus-son. 2015. Accessibility of trial reports for drugs stalling in development: A systematic assessment of registered trials. *British Medical Journal* 350:h1116.

Lee, R. S., C. Stewart, S. L. Carter, et al. 2012. A remarkably simple genome underlies highly malignant pediatric rhabdoid cancers. *Journal of Clinical Investigation* 122(8):2983–8.

Morrissy, A. S., L. Garzia, D. J. H. Shih, et al. 2016. Divergent clonal selection dominates medulloblastoma at recurrence. *Nature* 529(7586):351–57.

Rising, K., P. Bacchetti, and L. Bero. 2008. Reporting bias in drug trials submitted to the Food and Drug Administration: Review of publication and presentation. *PLoS Medicine* 5(11):e217.

Wu, G., A. K. Diaz, B. S. Paugh, et al. 2014. The genomic landscape of diffuse intrinsic pontine glioma and pediatric non-brainstem high-grade glioma. *Nature Genetics* 46(5):444–50.

CASE 3.3: INVOLVING PREGNANT WOMEN IN RESEARCH: WHAT SHOULD WE RECOMMEND WHEN THE REGULATIONS SEEM ETHICALLY PROBLEMATIC?

INTRODUCTION

Investigators conducting a trial to determine whether an intervention to prevent the recurrence of urinary stone disease (USD) were considering whether to exclude pregnant women. Two ethics consultations were sought, one with a NIH-funded investigator and the other with the NIH program officer responsible for the study. The resulting consultation reports are in conflict. One consultation report recommends excluding pregnant women from enrollment but retaining women on the study if they became pregnant while enrolled; while the other report concludes that, under the U.S. Department of Health and Human Services (DHHS) regulations, pregnant women should be excluded from the study. Once the conflict was identified, the consultants met by phone to discuss their different conclusions.

Given the conflicting results from the two consultation services, is it possible that both of the recommendations are ethically acceptable? To what extent should ethicists factor regulatory constraints into their analysis, and how much weight should they place on what they see as the best way to interpret regulations that involve some ambiguity? When ethicists think the regulations lead to problematic conclusions in a particular case, what should they do?

Seema Shah and Kathryn Porter from the Treuman Katz Center for Pediatric Bioethics at Seattle Children's Research Institute and the Department of Pediatrics at the University of Washington School of Medicine explain that, regarding the exclusion of pregnant women from research, there is growing recognition that the human subject regulations are unduly restrictive. They conclude that it would therefore be ethically acceptable for the investigators to resolve the dilemma they face by relying on a commonplace—if somewhat problematic—reading of the human subject regulations to lead to an ethically better result for this particular study. Richard Sharp and Megan Allyse from the Biomedical Research Ethics Program at the Mayo Clinic argue that the interpretation of regulatory guidance is the responsibility of oversight bodies, such as the IRB, and conclude that a bioethics consultant ought to refrain from regulatory interpretation and focus instead on the provision of advice regarding the ethical conduct of research. Haley K. Sullivan, Derek W. Braverman, and David Wendler from the Department of Bioethics and the Clinical Center of the NIH also conclude that ethicists should not endorse alternate interpretations when human subject regulations are clear but lead to problematic outcomes. Their focus, however, is on the need for the American research enterprise to maintain a common set of standards and the public's trust.

CASE BACKGROUND

USD involves the development of hard deposits of minerals and salts in the kidney, which can be very painful and, in some cases, require surgical intervention. USD affects approximately one in 11 individuals in the United States in their lifetimes, and stones occur more frequently in men, obese individuals, and older people. Half of all individuals who have had a urinary stone have another within 10 years (American Urological Association 2014). Existing clinical guidelines recommend increased fluid intake as a way to prevent urinary stone recurrence. These guidelines are directed at otherwise healthy adults (Cheungpasitporn et al. 2016; Qaseem et al. 2014).

The Preventing Urinary Stones with Hydration (or "PUSH") trial is a large-scale, randomized, multisite controlled trial designed to provide evidence on the effects of controlled fluid intake and behavioral interventions on USD recurrence in adults and children over the age of 12 years. The primary outcome of the trial is stone recurrence, a composite measure of clinical events and growth or recurrence of stones on imaging.

All PUSH participants will receive usual care and a "smart" water bottle that monitors fluid consumption and connects to a smartphone app for automated data collection. Participants will be randomized to be responsible for self-monitoring their fluid intake under the guidelines or receive a theory-based behavioral intervention and a personalized fluid prescription. Adult participants will undergo low-dose computed tomography (CT) scans annually for 24 months, and ultrasound will be used for pediatric participants. Inclusion criteria include being 12 years or older, having had one or more symptomatic stone events in the past three years, and having low urine volume. Proposed exclusion criteria include pregnant women and women currently breastfeeding. Including pregnant women would require developing specialized inclusion criteria for them as well, because there are no data on urine output for pregnant women to identify who would need the intervention. Additionally, pregnant women could not receive CT scans because of the increased risk to the fetus, and would have to receive less sensitive ultrasounds to measure urinary stone growth. Investigators sought an ethics consultation about whether their plans to exclude pregnant women were ethically sound and whether women who become pregnant once enrolled should complete the study.

REFERENCES

American Urological Association. 2014. Medical management of kidney stones guidelines. Available at: http://www.auanet.org/guidelines/medical-management-of-kidney-stones-(2014) (accessed December 12, 2017).

Cheungpasitporn, W., S. Rossetti, K. Friend, S. B. Erickson, and J. Lieske. 2016. Treatment effect, adherence, and safety of high fluid intake for the prevention of incident and recurrent kidney stones: A systematic review and meta-analysis. *Journal of Nephrology* 29(2):211–19.

Qaseem, A., P. Dallas, M. A. Forciea, M. Starkey, and T. D. Denberg. 2014. Dietary and pharmacologic management to prevent recurrent nephrolithiasis in adults: A clinical practice guideline from the American College of Physicians. *Annals of Internal Medicine* 161(9):659–67.

COMMENTARY 3.3.1: CONFLICTS BETWEEN REGULATIONS AND ETHICAL PRINCIPLES: RESOLVING AMBIGUITY IN FAVOR OF THE ETHICALLY PREFERABLE OUTCOME

SEEMA K. SHAH AND KATHRYN PORTER

This case presents a dilemma for the ethics consultants surrounding how to integrate regulatory constraints into ethical analysis, particularly when the regulations are ambiguous. The consultants could either recommend excluding pregnant women from the study altogether based on a way of interpreting the regulations that is generally favored in the ethics literature (even though it leads to an ethically inferior result in this case), or they could recommend allowing women to stay on the study under what seems to be a common but problematic way to interpret the regulations.

The requestors in this case raised important scientific concerns about including pregnant women in the study prospectively. The eligibility criteria for the study were based on urine output, but pregnancy is associated with higher urine volume in general, and there are no guidelines to follow to tell what urine output level is normal in pregnancy. Even if pregnant women were prospectively excluded, however, it was not clear what to do about women who became pregnant after being deemed eligible for the study.

The federal regulations governing research with pregnant women hold that research could proceed if there is a prospect of direct benefit to the pregnant women or the fetus (and other conditions were met). If there is no prospect of direct benefit, however, the purpose of the research has to develop important biomedical knowledge that couldn't otherwise be obtained (Department of Health and Human Services 2017).

Both ethics consultation services agreed that the study offers a prospect of benefit that outweighs the risk to the participants who receive the intervention. However, the control arm did not offer a prospect of direct benefit compared to alternatives because it was the same as the standard of care, with some additional research procedures such as blood draws and urine samples, resulting in a low level of net risk to the participants in this arm. For trials with more than one arm, there are two potential commonly used approaches to analyze the risk–benefit ratio: (1) Assess the risk–benefit ratio of the trial as a whole, before randomization; or (2) component analysis, under which the risk–benefit ratio of each arm is assessed separately.

Under the first approach, if the prospect of benefit from being in the intervention arm outweighs the net risk associated with the other arms, then the research could be considered a prospect of direct benefit as a whole. This would permit allowing women in the PUSH trial who become pregnant to stay on the study. For women with USD, not only would participation in the study offer benefit to them if they were enrolled in the intervention arm, but it also could generate some data for pregnant women with this condition. It therefore seems ethically appropriate, and possibly even advisable, not to automatically take women off the study if they became pregnant. It is also worth noting that there is growing recognition that the regulations governing research with pregnant women are unduly restrictive. Clinical research tends to exclude pregnant women and women of childbearing potential largely based on concerns about protecting fetuses, thereby leading to a dearth of data on interventions for pregnant women and fetuses, which is an injustice with serious consequences (Lyerly, Little, and Faden 2008).

Nevertheless, some ethicists favor the second approach, component analysis, because it ensures that excessively risky control arms cannot be ethically justified by the potential benefits to subjects in the intervention arm (Weijer 2004). Consider, for instance, a trial of a neurological implant where the control arm involves a sham surgical procedure that requires drilling holes into participants' skulls to control for the placebo effect (Horng and Miller 2003). In such a case, it seems ethically problematic not to evaluate the risks of the arm with the sham procedure separately to make sure they are not excessive. Ethicists have argued that conducting individual component analysis of each arm of a trial separately is ethically preferable and avoids what they call "the fallacy of the package deal" (Weijer 2004).

This second approach, however, would likely preclude the enrollment of pregnant women because the control arm does not offer a prospect of direct benefit, and the regulations therefore require that the research produce important biomedical knowledge that could not otherwise be obtained—a high bar that is likely not met in this case. It is also worth noting that many IRBs appear to assess risks and benefits as a package. Finally, although the fact that a non-ideal practice is commonplace is not a good reason to justify its use in a particular case, this does raise the possibility that if the requestors simply submitted their protocol to an IRB without raising these ethical issues, pregnant women would be allowed to stay on the study. This, in turn, suggests that calling for an ethics consultation in this case could have led to a less well-justified outcome, which both undermines the goal of providing ethics consultation and serves as a potential deterrent to those seeking ethics consultation in the future.

Clearly, the ideal solution would be to reform the regulations governing research with pregnant women. However, regulatory change is slow in the best of circumstances (Bierer, Barnes, and Lynch 2017), and research with pregnant women is fraught in ways that may make reform especially difficult. We therefore conclude that it would be ethically acceptable for the investigators to resolve the dilemma they faced by relying on a commonplace—if somewhat problematic—reading of the regulations to lead to an ethically better result for this particular study.

References

Bierer, B. E., M. Barnes, and H. F. Lynch. 2017. Revised 'Common Rule' shapes protections for research participants. *Health Affairs* 36(5):784–8. doi:10.1377/hlthaff.2017.0307.

Department of Health and Human Services. 2017. Code of Federal Regulations: Protection of human subjects, subpart B—Additional protections for pregnant women, human fetuses and neonates involved in research. Available at: https://www.hhs.gov/ohrp/regulations-and-policy/regulations/45-cfr-46/index.html#subpartb (access November 24, 2017).

Horng, S., and F. G. Miller. 2003. Ethical framework for the use of sham procedures in clinical trials. *Critical Care Medicine* 31(3 Suppl):S126–30.

Lyerly, A. D., M. O. Little, and R. Faden. 2008. The second wave: Toward responsible inclusion of pregnant women in research. *International Journal of Feminist Approaches to Bioethics* 1(2):5–22.

Weijer, C. 2004. The ethical analysis of risk in intensive care unit research. *Critical Care* 8(2):85–86.

COMMENTARY 3.3.2: WHEN TO AVOID GIVING ADVICE ON THE ETHICAL CONDUCT OF RESEARCH

RICHARD R. SHARP AND MEGAN A. ALLYSE

Bioethicists involved in research ethics consultation will find the basic structure of this case familiar. Investigators often seek input about ethical aspects of their work from bioethics colleagues, both informally and through structured consultation services, and the ethical tensions motivating these requests are often tied closely to issues of concern to a variety of research oversight committees, including IRBs, human embryonic stem cell oversight groups, and conflict of interest committees. When more than one advisor is consulted, it is quite possible to receive conflicting advice from one or more of these actors. These conflicts often stem from the fact that each brings a slightly different perspective and authority to their engagement with research oversight. Thankfully, these conflicts can most often be resolved through additional dialogue.

What is especially interesting about the case here is that multiple ethicists were consulted about the same case and gave substantively different advice. In the case described, the recommendations offered by two consulting bioethicists are irreconcilable; if one of these bioethicists has given good advice, the other must be wrong.

We suggest that this view oversimplifies the complex relationships among ethics, regulation, law, and institutional priorities. There is reason to believe that both consultants may bring legitimate considerations of the situation to the discussion. However, we wish to suggest that in this case, the primary issue raised is not a question of ethics but of how to interpret an ambiguous element of human subjects research regulation. The federal regulations regarding the inclusion of vulnerable populations in research include pregnant women as a protected class. In theory, exceptional provisions and justification should be made if studies wish to enroll women who are currently pregnant. However, the intent of the regulation is to ensure protection for research in which the fetus may conceivably be at risk, not to suggest that pregnant women per se should not participate in research. Thus, the central question raised by this case is not an ethical one, but a regulatory one. Does the current study entail a situation in which the federal definition of a protected class should be employed?

While bioethicists can certainly add to discussions of regulatory scope by clarifying the underlying ethical intent of a regulation, or how other research teams have interpreted these rules in the past, the decision about how best to interpret federal regulations falls squarely on the relevant institutional IRB. IRBs, often with input from legal counsel or the OHRP, are charged with ensuring that individual researchers are in compliance with federal regulations and are well positioned to determine the most appropriate interpretation of these and other research rules.

Our view is that the consulting bioethicist, when asked to assist with a direct question of regulatory interpretation, should offer to facilitate conversation with the appropriate oversight committee. The bioethicist may be in a good position to clarify the sources of regulatory ambiguity, and to respond to questions that the IRB will likely want to clarify in settling upon an interpretation. It may also be appropriate to assist the research team in engaging the IRB in exploring the practical implications of different approaches to enrolling pregnant women in the study, such as how to manage situations where women become pregnant during the course of their participation in research. However, the responsibility for ensuring compliance, including the proper management of any adverse events that may occur, rests with the IRB.

Nevertheless, few, if any, research ethics consultations are completely separable from matters of regulation. There is a careful balance to be struck in supporting our colleagues and assuming authority that is not ours. Although consulting bioethicists may be poorly positioned to serve as regulatory arbiters, they often are well positioned to assist investigators in considering how a complex array of societal views intersect with the work a scientist is proposing. In many of the most complex consultations, the investigator may not be able to articulate what is driving a request for help. Something may not feel right about a particular intervention; she may be concerned that the study violates some unspoken ethical norm, she may wonder how her colleagues will view her work, and so forth. In these cases, bioethicists can play a critical role in clarifying these issues. Furthermore, bioethicists often become very familiar with the specific regulations that constrain research, and IRBs themselves may seek counsel from bioethicists, especially with regard to precedent in the interpretation of contentious or ethically charged regulations.

At the end of the day, however, the role of the bioethicist is not to ensure research compliance or to provide regulatory guidance. We serve our scientific colleagues best when we are clear about not only the limited scope of our institutional authority but also the specific expertise we can and should contribute to discussions regarding the ethical conduct of research.

COMMENTARY 3.3.3: WHEN RESEARCH REGULATIONS AND ETHICS CONFLICT

HALEY K. SULLIVAN, DEREK W. BRAVERMAN, AND DAVID WENDLER

Many research ethics consultations pertain to whether a study is approvable under existing regulations. Sometimes, studies are ethically appropriate yet still conflict with regulations. Using the PUSH trial as an example, we first examine how to interpret the regulations on research involving pregnant people and then discuss more broadly how ethicists should respond when an otherwise ethical study is inconsistent with the regulations.

The U.S. regulations on research involving pregnant women, human fetuses, and neonates are found in subpart B of 45 CFR 46 (the Common Rule). Section 46.204 of subpart B mandates that research involving pregnant women may be conducted only when "scientifically appropriate" prior studies have been completed (Department of Health and Human Services 2017a). We understand the requirement for "scientifically appropriate" prior studies to mean that prior studies must be done to the extent that they are ethical, are feasible, and might yield information relevant to assessing the intervention in pregnant people. Preclinical studies involving smartphone-mediated behavioral interventions are not feasible in pregnant animals (although it might be useful to know the impact of increased water consumption on pregnant animals with urinary stones). In contrast, prior clinical studies with nonpregnant women would certainly be ethical and feasible and might yield information useful for assessing the risks of trial in pregnant women. In addition, as evidenced by the proposal to exclude people who are pregnant at enrollment, the PUSH trial could achieve its scientific goals without enrolling pregnant people. It follows that enrolling people who are pregnant in the PUSH trial is inconsistent with existing U.S. regulations.

This conclusion raises a question regarding people who become pregnant after they have enrolled in the trial. May they continue to participate under existing U.S. regulations? In ordinary English, retaining in the trial women who become pregnant after they enroll would be a case of research "involving" pregnant women. If an investigator performs a research procedure on a woman who is eight months pregnant, that would constitute research involving a pregnant woman, even if the woman became pregnant after she had enrolled in the study. This suggests that the regulations also apply to women who become pregnant after they have enrolled in research.

Subpart B does not explicitly address whether this is the correct interpretation. However, the OHRP provides guidance on an analogous situation involving research with prisoners (laid out in subpart C of the Common Rule): If a participant becomes a prisoner after enrolling in a study, the prisoner regulations apply, and the researchers must satisfy the conditions for research with prisoners or disenroll the participant (Department of Health and Human Services 2017b). This reasoning seems even more salient in the case of pregnant people. The primary concern with enrolling prisoners is their ability to provide uncoerced consent, a concern that arises primarily at the time of initial enrollment. In contrast, the concern with involving pregnant people arises after they enroll and are exposed to the risks of research procedures. Therefore, consistency with existing guidance from the OHRP suggests that the regulations in subpart B apply to women who become pregnant following enrollment.

The conclusion that the involvement of pregnant women in the PUSH trial is not approvable under existing U.S. regulations is troubling. The study intervention— reminders to consume water—is clearly minimal risk. The CT scans used to monitor urinary stone growth pose some risks to the fetus but could be replaced with ultrasound scans, a modification already made for pediatric participants. This case thus illustrates a concern with the U.S. regulations. Although the regulations are intended to protect pregnant women and their fetuses, the requirements to first conduct preclinical studies on pregnant animals and clinical studies on nonpregnant people seem overly restrictive, particularly for low-risk research using familiar procedures, and may preclude ever obtaining useful data on pregnant people. Indeed, many have argued that the current regulations are overly strict and that the consequent lack of research with pregnant people undermines the health of both pregnant people and fetuses (Lyerly, Little, and Faden 2008). This concern raises the broader question of what ethicists should do when a valuable and ethically acceptable study seems inconsistent with the regulations.

Ethicists could work with researchers to redesign a study to conform to the regulations, but investigators pursuing ethical research may not always be able to modify their protocols to conform to existing regulations. For instance, the PUSH trial researchers may not be able to recruit enough pregnant people for appropriate subgroup analyses. Alternatively, ethicists might propose an interpretation of the regulations that leads to the ethically preferable outcome. In some cases, there might be sufficient ambiguity to support this approach. In other cases, the challenge is not one of ambiguity, but of regulations that seem clear but too restrictive. This, we believe, is the present case. Is there anything ethicists can do to encourage needed research with pregnant people in such cases?

In our view, ethicists should not endorse alternate interpretations when the regulations are clear but lead to problematic outcomes. For example, we do not think that ethicists should argue that research with women who become pregnant after they enroll in a study does not constitute research "involving" pregnant women. Even though the Common Rule is not perfect, the American research enterprise and the public's trust in it depend on the existence of a common set of standards that everyone agrees to abide by. Ambiguous regulations need to be interpreted and, at least in many cases, it makes sense to endorse the interpretation that leads to the ethically best outcome.

A system that empowers stakeholders to pursue whatever interpretation they regard as ethically preferable, independent of the actual wording of the regulations, may lead to better results in isolated cases; however, the ultimate result could be disastrous. Specifically, the end result could be every stakeholder pursuing his or her own understanding of what counts as ethical research, a result that in effect eliminates the regulations governing clinical research. To avoid this result, ethicists should not endorse alternative interpretations when the Common Rule provides clear, if unfortunate, guidance.

References

Department of Health and Human Services. 2017a. 45 CFR 46: Protection of human subjects. Available at: https://www.hhs.gov/ohrp/regulations-and-policy/regulations/45-cfr-46/index.html (accessed November 24, 2017).

Department of Health and Human Services. 2017b. Prisoner research FAQs. Available at: https://www.hhs.gov/ohrp/regulations-and-policy/guidance/faq/prisoner-research/index.html (accessed November 24, 2017).

Lyerly, A. D., M. O. Little, and R. Faden. 2008. The second wave: Toward responsible inclusion of pregnant women in research. *International Journal of Feminist Approaches to Bioethics* 1(2):5–22.

CASE 3.4: ENROLLING ADOLESCENTS WITH RARE DISEASE FOR EARLY-PHASE CLINICAL TRIALS WHILE UNDER THE CARE OF CHILD PROTECTIVE SERVICES: BALANCING PROTECTION AND ACCESS

INTRODUCTION

For many rare diseases, the availability of effective interventions is limited or nonexistent. In this context, clinical research evaluating emerging interventions may be the only potentially "therapeutic" option. In some cases, the interventions themselves can be risky. Hence, the benefit–risk balance can be especially precarious. Hematopoietic stem cell transplants (HSCTs) are a paradigmatic example of a clinical intervention that offers the potential for lifesaving benefits as well as life-ending risks. All six individuals reported in the first publication on HSCTs in 1957 died within months (Thomas et al. 1957). However, as experience and knowledge evolved over the last 60 years, HSCT has become a standard clinical intervention for many hematological conditions, and ongoing research continues to expand the range of conditions and patients for whom this may be effective, including metabolic disorders and immune deficiencies. In many cases, HSCTs are considered in children, and as such, parents typically plan a critical role in decision making for a high-risk but potentially high-reward intervention.

This can be even more important in the research context, especially if the lack of alternative clinical approaches further exaggerates the potential benefits and risks. In this case, HSCT is the only significantly disease-modifying option for an adolescent (Sam) with an inherited immune disorder at a referral hospital for whom CPS now has decision-making authority because of parental neglect based on the experience of a community hospital. The accompanying commentaries address the special challenges that arise when there are concerns about the parent's ability to make decisions and guide the adolescent.

The four commentaries each identify similar themes: the significance of the research–clinical distinction, the special importance of psychosocial support following the transplant, the role of the adolescent in the decision, and implications of the status as a ward of the state. However, the four commentaries distinctly draw our attention to different aspects of the case.

Two of the commentaries include authors who practice in oncology, and these two commentaries draw our attention to the psychosocial support needed for the HSCT to be successful. Jessica M. Turnbull and Daniel J. Benedetti from Vanderbilt University consider this concern as a presumptive reason to defer enrollment in research until it is clear that there is an effective plan to provide this support. In contrast, Kathy J. Forte and Emily E. Anderson at Loyola University Chicago presumptively assume that the care team has both the capacity to address these issues and an obligation to do this efficiently.

The next two commentaries draw similar conclusions to the second, but follow different pathways based on specific reflections on experiences with wards of the state. Henry Sacks and Rosamond Rhodes at the Icahn School of Medicine at Mount Sinai remind us about babies with HIV in the 1980s, many of whom were in state custody and for whom clinical trial participation was their only option. Finally, Mary Greiner and Armand Antommaria at Cincinnati Children's Hospital share their experiences with nuances of how the foster care system operates to both support the parents and the child and conclude that clinical need should be the focus of all involved in supporting this adolescent.

CASE SUMMARY

Sam is a 15-year-old with a rare genetic immune disorder who is transferred from a community hospital to an academic medical center. She has end-stage manifestations of her underlying genetic disease. The clinical team concludes that the only treatment option at this point in her disease progression is an HSCT. Her only access to an HSCT is enrollment in a clinical trial open only at this institution. The institution has performed 15 HSCTs in patients with the same diagnosis, and the early results are promising. Following the actual transplant, Sam will face an extended inpatient stay so the team can closely monitor her progress. The institution requires that any patient under 18 has a caregiver on site to help navigate and implement a program to continue the patient's education and social development. Sam has been living with her mother and an older sibling in a rural setting in another state that is over four hours away. On the day of her admission, the team is notified that CPS in Sam's home state is seeking emergency removal from her mother due to medical neglect reported by the community hospital. Sam will soon be a ward of the state. The state where the HSCT will be done requires review and approval by the state IRB. The team has sought a consultation to assure that they consider all relevant regulatory, practical, and ethical concerns of enrolling Sam in their trial, including whether the team should pursue enrollment and who should be involved in the decision making if Sam is approached to enroll.

REFERENCE

Thomas, E. D., H. L. Lochte Jr., W. C. Lu, and J. W. Ferrebee. 1957. Intravenous infusion of bone marrow in patients receiving radiation and chemotherapy. *The New England Journal of Medicine* 257(11):491–6.

COMMENTARY 3.4.1: FUZZY LOGIC: HOW THE PRACTICALITIES OF STATE INVOLVEMENT SHAPE THE MOST ETHICALLY SUPPORTABLE WAY FORWARD

JESSICA M. TURNBULL AND DANIEL J. BENEDETTI

The case presents a teenage girl, Sam, in the end stages of a rare disease with no proven therapeutic options, and an investigational HSCT has been offered through a clinical trial. CPS is taking custody due to medical neglect, and the clinical research team seeks guidance about whether and how to proceed. While the consultation has come from the research team, untangling the practical clinical dilemmas present is of the utmost importance to ascertain whether her involvement in the trial is ethically supportable.

Examining the dilemma using a strictly principle-based approach, it is appealing to argue that the best interests of the child would be achieved through study enrollment and receipt of the HSCT. In the judgment of her clinical team, it is the "only treatment option," and has promising early results—facts not changed when she is a ward of the state. In the face of certain death, the burdens (maleficence) of the HSCT would be outweighed by the benefits (beneficence) of ongoing life.

The most notable practical issues to scrutinize include: (1) whether a child removed from her family can be emotionally supported during an arduous hospital course; and (2) whether the multifaceted aspects of required psychosocial care can be mobilized quickly enough for her to benefit from HSCT.

HSCT is both physically and emotionally demanding for the transplant recipient, requiring prolonged hospitalization with acute toxicities, chronic risks from immunosuppression and graft-versus-host disease, and prolonged social isolation post-hospitalization. Psychosocial support during HSCT is critical (Packman et al. 2010), and a psychosocial assessment is part of the standard pre-HSCT workup in order to "address any potential psychosocial … concerns or barriers … that may negatively impact the success of the [HSCT]" (Bingen and Hoag 2016). Positive social support is associated with lower distress and improved ability to cope with the demands of HSCT (Bingen et al. 2012). It is likely that a child who has been medically neglected, then separated, from her parent would be experiencing distress and poor psychological functioning heading into her transplant hospitalization, both risk factors for lower health-related quality of life and negative psychosocial outcomes of HSCT (American

Academy of Pediatrics, Committee on Bioethics and Committee on Hospital Care 2000). In the state where the authors practice, it is unlikely that CPS could provide adequate social support for a child to receive a HSCT, and unrealistic that it could do so in an urgent timeframe.

If HSCT were standard of care for this disease, clinicians might weigh whether to accept suboptimal social circumstances in order to offer a proven, beneficial therapy to this patient. Because the proposed HSCT is research, the benefits are unproven, and CPS must provide a comprehensive and well-resourced plan for satisfactory psychosocial support. This is critical to optimize the patient's transplant outcome and for the integrity of the research study. Poor adherence to posttransplant care could impair HSCT outcomes such as graft or patient survival. If she were to suffer a poor outcome as the result of a lack of social support, the results of the trial would be undermined, possibly at the expense of future patients who might benefit from the therapy.

Another reason to optimize psychosocial resources is that if she has a poor outcome (e.g., one of many potential life-threatening complications of HSCT), she should face her declining health and the end of her life with as much support as possible. The worst possible outcome would be that she enroll in the study, have a bad outcome, and have little emotional support outside of a rotating cast of healthcare providers and CPS workers unfamiliar to her and unable to support the needs of a dying child (Clarke, Eiser, and Skinner 2008). We may hope for a smooth course, but the high morbidity and mortality of allogeneic HSCT obligate we plan for a greatly difficult one, including assuring that her family be able to visit her as she will likely be maximally comforted by them despite prior medical neglect.

If CPS can meet the required threshold of support, the research team must then determine whether trial participation remains justifiable after she becomes a ward of the state. This study falls under the Code of Federal Regulations, Part 46, subpart D, category 405 (U.S. Department of Health and Human Services 2021), as one with greater than minimal risk, with the possibility of direct benefit to the participant. A ward of the state enrolling in such a study typically does not need an independent advocate assigned to guard her interests (Varma and Wendler 2008). In the authors' state, parents retain medical decision-making rights when a child enters CPS custody; however, as the patient is being removed from her mother's care due to medical neglect, the state must scrutinize and independently adjudicate the decision regarding enrollment in such a high-risk, high-reward study. We believe that while HSCT has the possibility of direct benefit to the participant, the CPS-provided psychosocial care required to optimize success obligates us to identify an independent advocate to assure Sam's interests—as a vulnerable research participant due to her status as a minor and perhaps even more vulnerable given her family of origin's difficulties—are met. As the advocate cannot be a member of the patient's guardian organization (in this case, CPS) (U.S. Department of Health and Human Services 2021), a participant advocate can be assigned per institutional policy. Interdisciplinary team members such as social work and palliative care may be able to provide additional wrap-around support. Should an independent advocate not be named for the patient, she risks two potentially avoidable harms: either being enrolled in a study that only causes her harm without the social support to fully benefit from the HSCT; or being passed over for the chance at a potentially lifesaving intervention because her social situation is "too difficult" to manage in a research setting.

Given that there did not appear to be ethical concerns regarding trial participation prior to CPS's involvement, it seems most ethically supportable to attempt to mobilize the psychosocial resources necessary to support trial enrollment. The new dilemmas should delay admission to coordinate the patient's psychosocial support for transplant while she receives ongoing standard medical therapies for her condition. The clinical and research teams should balance delaying HSCT long enough to allow supportive relationships to be formed, while avoiding delay that reduces potential benefits of HSCT. The team should delineate specific clinical parameters—ones indicating irreversible progression of underlying disease—which would preclude the patient from receiving a HSCT. Should the requisite psychosocial support not be secured prior to reaching those clinical markers, she should not be enrolled or undergo HSCT. However, in the unlikely event that support is mobilized to the satisfaction of the IRB, the research team and CPS should proceed with enrollment, feeling good about their commitment to research integrity while trying their absolute best to help a child with nearly insurmountable odds stacked against her.

References

American Academy of Pediatrics, Committee on Bioethics and Committee on Hospital Care. 2000. Palliative care for children. *Pediatrics* 106(2 Pt 1):351–7.

Bingen, K., and J. A. Hoag. 2016. Pediatric Hematopoietic Stem Cell Transplantation: Psychosocial Assessment and Care. *Pediatric psychosocial oncology: Textbook for multidisciplinary care.* Edited by N. A. Annah, C. M. Anna, and W. Lori. Cham, Switzerland: Springer International Publishing, pp. 219–42.

Bingen, K., M. W. Kent, A. M. Rodday, S. J. Ratichek, M. J. Kupst, and S. K. Parsons. 2012. Children's coping with hematopoietic stem cell transplant stressors: Results from the journeys to recovery study. *Children's Health Care* 41(2):145–61.

Clarke, S. A., C. Eiser, and R. Skinner. 2008. Health-related quality of life in survivors of BMT for paediatric malignancy: A systematic review of the literature. *Bone Marrow Transplantation* 42(2):73–82.

Packman, W., S. Weber, J. Wallace, and N. Bugescu. 2010. Psychological effects of hematopoietic SCT on pediatric patients, siblings and parents: A review. *Bone Marrow Transplantation* 45(7):1134–46.

U.S. Department of Health and Human Services. Protection of human subjects. 45 CFR part 46, subpart D. Accessed October 16, 2021. https://www.hhs.gov/ohrp/regulations-and-policy/regulations/45-cfr-46/common-rule-subpart-d/index.html#46.405.

Varma, S., and D. Wendler. 2008. Research involving wards of the state: Protecting particularly vulnerable children. *The Journal of Pediatrics* 152(1):9–14.

COMMENTARY 3.4.2: ENROLLING FOSTER YOUTH IN CLINICAL TRIALS: AVOIDING THE HARM OF EXCLUSION

MARY V. GREINER AND ARMAND H. MATHENY ANTOMMARIA

In this case, an adolescent with a life-threatening immune disease experiences increased social complexity, child welfare involvement, and placement into foster care, which could disrupt a medical treatment plan offered through a clinical trial. Unfortunately, social and legal complexity is often an unjust barrier to healthcare for youth in foster care and can lead to fewer opportunities for medical treatment. Despite this complexity, however, an understanding of the process of foster care placement and the roles of adults in the life of a child in foster care can help identify ethically sound and legally authorized decision makers (Greiner et al. 2018).

There are approximately 430,000 children in foster care in the United States (Administration on Children, Youth and Families, Children's Bureau 2020). A child enters foster care when CPS investigates a reported concern for abuse and/or neglect and identifies a risk of serious, imminent harm for the child if the child stays in the home. The child welfare professional then must obtain a judge's (or magistrate's) approval, and the judge issues a court order to place the child in the temporary protective custody of child welfare. The judge will also appoint a guardian ad litem (GAL) or court-appointed special advocate (CASA) who is charged with advocating for the child's best interests until the case is closed and the child is reunited with the family of origin or placed in an alternate safe and permanent home. During the period of temporary custody, the child welfare professional is responsible for the safety and well-being of the child and must identify an out-of-home placement, such as a kinship home, a nonrelative foster home, a group home, or an independent living placement.

Placement in foster care does not sever the family of origin's rights. The family of origin often maintains limited parental rights, including some medical decision making, unless special circumstances exist or until parental rights are terminated. Termination of parental rights typically does not occur in less than two years to allow time for efforts toward successful reunification. A child in the temporary custody of child welfare still has an important connection, legally and otherwise, to the family of origin.

Once placed, the child now also has a new caregiver, either a kinship or foster parent or a staff member depending on placement type, who is charged with the child's day-to-day care. Importantly for healthcare, the new caregiver will be the one bringing the child to appointments, giving medications, and providing supervision of diet, exercise, and so on. The child and foster placement may have other supports in place, such as foster network agency workers, case managers, mentors, and others.

In this case, the clinical team has learned that Sam will soon be in the protective custody of child welfare and so will be soon gaining adults in the roles described above. It is not the clinical team's job to investigate the medical neglect concerns; their responsibility is to continue to provide the best healthcare possible. While foster placement creates a sense of complication and diffused responsibility, a collaborative and comprehensive decision-making process for the patient is possible. Sam's preferences and assent should be sought, she should be supported by individuals who know her preferences and can assess her interests, and informed consent should be provided by an individual or entity with legal authority (Greiner, Beal, and Antommaria 2020).

It is imperative to involve the youth in the decision making when possible. There is no reason to believe that youth in foster care have less capacity to assent than other youth. In this case, because the clinical trial has the prospect of direct benefit, Sam's assent is preferable but not required. Her preferences should nonetheless be strongly considered in evaluating what is in her best interest.

Who has the most knowledge of a child's preferences and is best situated to determine which choice is in the child's best interest is variable. For a child who has not been in custody long, such as Sam, or is close to reunification, it may be the parent of origin. If the child has been in custody for a longer period, reunification is not close, and the caseworker has been stable, it may be the caseworker. In some cases, it might be the GAL, the CASA, or even a long-term foster caregiver. Care should be taken to ensure that there is at least one participant in the decision who knows the child's history, likes, dislikes, fears, comforts, and future goals.

In most cases of children in protective custody, the child welfare system is the entity legally authorized to consent for medical care or participation in research. While the caseworker may have the most knowledge of the child's preferences, the director of the child welfare agency is likely to have the legal and institutional authority to consent. Because of the magnitude of the risks involved in a bone marrow transplant (BMT) and the uncertainty regarding the likelihood of success, the decision will also have to be made in concert with the family of origin. If the child welfare organization and the family of origin reach consensus, the organization may consent. If they do not, a judge may need to make the final decision.

In this case, the child welfare agency will need to consider the requirement for there to be a caregiver at the medical center to help navigate and implement a program to continue educational and social development in its placement decision. While fulfilling this requirement for a child in foster care may be more challenging, it is likely not insurmountable. One possibility is allowing the biological mother to be present at the bedside if deemed safe by child welfare. Alternatively, child welfare in Sam's home state could consider placing her in a foster home located in the same state as the hospital. The foster parent would be the bedside caregiver. This would require collaboration between the two state child welfare systems. A last and least desirable possibility would be identifying a child welfare or foster care network staff member to take on the role.

In this case, the research ethics consultant could make the following recommendations:

1. The team should pursue the opportunity to enroll the patient in this clinical trial with appropriate consent and assent.
2. The patient's assent should be sought.
3. The child welfare system, in collaboration with the patient's biological mother, should provide consent. The child welfare system and the mother together can meet criteria for both ethically assessing the patient's interests and legally providing informed consent.
4. The child welfare team should consider the trial's inclusion criteria—e.g., proximity to the hospital, medical background, and any other relevant details—in making a foster placement and putting supports into place.
5. Information, progress updates, and treatment decision plans should be shared between child welfare and the biological mother, with updates to the foster caregiver on the day-to-day needs of the child.

Through this process, Sam will have the opportunity to consider a potentially lifesaving clinical trial, just as a teen would who is not in foster care. This approach is essential to promoting equity for children in foster care and allowing the benefits of scientific process and discovery to impact this highly vulnerable population.

References

Administration on Children, Youth and Families, Children's Bureau. 2020. The AFCARS report. Preliminary FY 2019 estimates as of June 23, 2020. *U.S. Department of Health and Human Services, Administration for Children and Families.* https://www.acf.hhs.gov/sites/default/files/cb/afcarsreport26.pdf.

Greiner, M. V., S. J. Beal, A. Allen, V. Patel, J. Meinzen-Derr, and A. H. M. Antommaria. 2018. Who speaks for me? Addressing variability in informed consent practices for minimal risk research involving foster youth. *Journal of Health Disparities Research and Practice* 11(4):111–31.

Greiner, M. V., S. J. Beal, and A. H. M. Antommaria. 2020. Perspectives on informed consent practices for minimal-risk research involving foster youth. *Pediatrics* 145(4):e20192845.

COMMENTARY 3.4.3: NO JUSTIFICATION TO EXCLUDE A STATE WARD FROM PEDIATRIC TRANSPLANT RESEARCH

KATHY J. FORTE AND EMILY E. ANDERSON

With an overall estimated five-year survival rate of 67%, BMT is a potential cure for patients with primary immune regulatory diseases (Chan et al. 2020). Given that Sam is described as end stage and the early results from the trial are promising, it appears to be in her best interest to enroll in the clinical trial and proceed with the transplant, with a few considerations discussed below.

Ethical issues in using psychosocial evaluation in pediatric transplant research

Evaluation of a patient's suitability for transplant always includes a disease assessment as well as laboratory evaluation and organ assessment (Kanate, Perales, and Hamadani 2020). Many transplant centers also require a psychosocial assessment, which is more subjective than evaluation of the patient's physical ability to proceed. Pre-transplant psychosocial evaluation includes domains such as adherence to medical management, self-management, neurocognitive considerations, patient and parent adjustment, and family functioning (Lefkowitz et al. 2014). Considerations include the age and developmental level of the child and the child's previous experience with illness and treatment, including medication adherence.

For a child with a severe disease in need of a transplant and without other options, considerations for enrollment in a clinical trial should not differ from considerations for a non-research transplant. In practice, transplant centers are hesitant to deny a child a potentially lifesaving treatment based on psychosocial factors. It is a violation of the ethical principles of beneficence and justice to base a decision about enrollment on factors that the child cannot control (Sharma and Johnson 2019). Furthermore, there is a lack of empirical data to support that pre-transplant behavior predicts posttransplant behavior in children (Lefkowitz et al. 2014). In a pediatric research setting, the primary goal of psychosocial screening is to identify necessary supports, not for the sole purpose of excluding potential participants.

The need for a caregiver on site and at home

Sam is about to become a ward of the state, and enrollment requires a caregiver who will remain on site during an extended inpatient stay. However, this should not exclude her from participation in the research. Although her mother is not able to fill the caregiver role and Sam does not yet have a state-appointed guardian, identifying an appropriate person or persons should be feasible.

To be sure, caregivers play an even more integral role in transplant success post discharge, by helping patients adhere to medication schedules, attend clinic appointments, care for central lines, and maintain a clean environment. Infections are a major cause of morbidity and mortality in the first year post discharge after an allogeneic HSCT (Ifversen et al. 2021). Poor adherence to medications is associated with increased infections post HSCT (Pai et al. 2018). Although a majority of transplant centers (89%) in the National Marrow Donor Registry require a caregiver to be identified as a condition of transplant eligibility for both adult and pediatric patients (Preussler et al. 2019), there are solutions when a caregiver cannot be easily identified. For example, a patient can have multiple caregivers, or funds can be identified to hire caregivers and community volunteers. In this case, the child could be supported by a combination of other family members, volunteers, and/or guardians appointed by the state CPS. Pediatric centers reported contacting CPS to help provide care as a last resort (Preussler et al. 2019).

Protection of children who are wards of the state

For children who are wards of the state, there is concern that they will be exploited to carry an unfair share of the burden of research and that their individual interests will not be protected (Varma and Wendler 2008). However, in this case Sam is in desperate need of a transplant to survive, and while this type of therapy carries risk, the alternative of allowing her to die contradicts the goal of protection. The only ethically sound reasons to deny a child a lifesaving treatment would be if lack of parental support would necessarily jeopardize the success of the treatment itself and if the treatment is in short supply, meaning that another child would not receive the treatment if this child proceeds in the study (Foster et al. 2006). In this case, as alternative caregivers can be identified and stem cells are renewable, neither is true.

Determining who can give consent

State laws vary in terms of who can make medical decisions for children in protective custody. In some circumstances, unless the biologic parental rights have been terminated, the birth parents may retain the right to give consent for treatment or research. Any restrictions that will be placed on the mother's participation, both as a support during the hospital stay or in the future, should be clarified.

In many instances, medical decision making is shared between the biologic parents, foster parents, case workers, and clinicians (Seltzer, Henderson, and Boss 2016). In this case, while the biologic parent's consent may be sufficient for research participation, it is clear that this parent will not be able to participate in posttransplant care, whether inpatient or at home. It is not necessary that the same person who provides consent for research participation must also be the onsite caregiver. But whoever will provide onsite and home care should participate in conversations about the decision to enroll the child in the study, even if they are not the person (or persons) who ultimately can provide consent.

Since Sam is 15 years old, some might argue that she be evaluated to determine if she can provide consent for herself (Iltis 2013). In this case, we do not have information about her level of cognitive development, her prior abilities to take medications on her own, or her desire to proceed with the transplant. However, regardless of Sam's ability to legally provide consent for herself, she should be included in all discussions, and her dissent should be taken seriously as lack of cooperation could jeopardize her posttransplant recovery.

Conclusion

In this case, offering an experimental HSCT provides the best medical option for a cure of a life-threatening disease. While the lack of parental presence or support may pose some challenges to the requirements of the study and some risk for decreased compliance post discharge, these risks should not prevent the child from getting the best curative option. Psychosocial support can be provided during the hospital stay from various members of the healthcare team as well as volunteers, foster parents, and/or family members. Post discharge, the practical concerns of getting the patient to clinic visits, adhering to the medication regimen, and caring for the central line may all be addressed if Sam is properly placed with a foster family adept at caring for children with special medical needs. The healthcare team will need to work closely with the case worker, foster family, and possibly extended biologic family and friends to carefully coordinate a plan for supporting this child during her stay but more importantly post discharge.

References

Chan, A. Y., J. W. Leiding, X. Liu, B. R. Logan, L. M. Burroughs, E. J. Allenspach, S. Skoda-Smith, G. Uzel, L. D. Notarangelo, M. Slatter, et al. 2020. Hematopoietic cell transplantation in patients with Primary Immune Regulatory Disorders (PIRD): A Primary Immune Deficiency Treatment Consortium (PIDTC) Survey. *Frontiers in Immunology* 11:239.

Foster, L. W., L. J. McLellan, L. A. Rybicki, J. Dabney, E. Welsh, and B. J. Bolwell. 2006. Allogeneic BMT and patient eligibility based on psychosocial criteria: A survey of BMT professionals. *Bone Marrow Transplant* 37(2):223–8.

Ifversen, M., R. Meisel, P. Sedlacek, K. Kalwak, L. Sisinni, D. Hutt, T. Lehrnbecher, et al. 2021. Supportive care during pediatric hematopoietic stem cell transplantation: Prevention of infections. A report from workshops on supportive care of the Paediatric Diseases working Party (PDWP) of the European Society for Blood and Marrow Transplantation (EBMT). *Frontiers in Pediatrics* 9:705179.

Iltis, A. S. 2013. Parents, adolescents, and consent for research participation. *The Journal of Medicine and Philosophy* 38(3):332–46.

Kanate, A. S., M.-A. Perales, and M. Hamadani. 2020. Eligibility criteria for patients undergoing allogeneic hematopoietic cell transplantation. *Journal of the National Comprehensive Cancer Network* 18(5):635–43.

Lefkowitz, D. S., C. J. Fitzgerald, N. Zelikovsky, K. Barlow, and J. Wray. 2014. Best practices in the pediatric pretransplant psychosocial evaluation. *Pediatric Transplantation* 18(4):327–35.

Pai, A. L. H., J. Rausch, S. Drake, C. F. Morrison, J. L. Lee, A. Nelson, A. Tackett, S. Berger, L. Szulczewski, C. Mara, et al. 2018. Poor adherence is associated with more infections after pediatric hematopoietic stem cell transplant. *Biology of Blood and Marrow Transplantation* 24(2):381–5.

Preussler, J. M., L.-W. Mau, N. S. Majhail, M. Bevans, E. Clancy, C. Messner, L. Parran, K. A. Pederson, S. Stickney Ferguson, K. Walters, et al. 2019. Caregiver availability and patient access to hematopoietic cell transplantation: Social worker perspectives inform practice. *Supportive Care in Cancer* 27(11):4253–64.

Seltzer, R. R., C. M. Henderson, and R. D. Boss. 2016. Medical foster care: What happens when children with medical complexity cannot be cared for by their families? *Pediatric Research* 79(1–2):191–6.

Sharma, A., and L.-M. Johnson. 2019. Should poor social support be an exclusion criterion in bone marrow transplantation? *American Journal of Bioethics* 19(11):39–41.

Varma, S. D., and Wendler. 2008. Research involving wards of the state: Protecting particularly vulnerable children. *The Journal of Pediatrics* 152(1):9–14.

COMMENTARY 3.4.4: LIFESAVING EXPERIMENTAL TREATMENT FOR A TEENAGE WARD OF THE STATE

HENRY SACKS AND ROSAMOND RHODES

This case raises a number of complex ethical, legal, and practical issues, some of which cannot be resolved by a research ethics consultation. Sam is an adolescent who has end-stage manifestations of her rare underlying genetic disease. She is soon to become a ward of a state. A study of a potentially lifesaving treatment is available in another state. Although this teenager would meet the study enrollment criteria, questions remain about whether she should or could be included.

The ethical question seems relatively clear-cut: So long as Sam is willing or eager to participate in the trial, she should be enrolled because the early results of HSCT for this condition are promising while the alternative is dire. In reality, our ethics committee would ask for more details about Sam and her condition. For example, we would want to know how urgently the treatment is needed, what is the prognosis with and without treatment, does this young woman adequately understand and appreciate her situation, and is she likely to comply with the study requirements and sustain the confinement entailed. Nevertheless, this teenager has a fatal disease, for which there is no standard treatment. The experimental treatment may be beneficial. If the patient is on board and capable of withstanding the ordeal involved in study participation, given what we know about the situation, it seems ethically appropriate for the patient to be enrolled in the trial and receive the HSCT.

Because Sam may have inadequate family support, or perhaps no family support at all, the treating institution will have to muster their resources to provide additional support from their psychologists, child life program staff, social workers, chaplains, volunteers, and any additional services they can commandeer to help her make it through the treatment. Unfortunately, the legal issues may be even more difficult to navigate. Addressing them may require the assistance of lawyers, courts, state agencies, and possibly new legislation.

This situation is similar to what clinicians and researchers faced in the 1990s when children were living with HIV infection. In many cases, their parents had become incapable of caring for them, or they had died from HIV themselves. Thus, many HIV+ children were in foster care. At that time, a small number of drugs had been proven effective in adults with HIV, but they had not yet been approved for children. Those drugs were, therefore, only available through clinical trials. At that time, while most states had established procedures for obtaining consent to treat children who were wards of the state, they did not have procedures for obtaining consent to enroll those children in research. A survey in 1989 found that the majority of states had children with HIV in their custody, but their child welfare agencies did not have the authority to consent for research on behalf of the children in their care (Martin and Sacks 1990).

Another study that surveyed the legal landscape found considerable variability between states and within states in how IRBs handle surrogate consent to research (Gong et al. 2010). As of 2010, only three states—California, Kansas, and New Jersey—had legislation that addressed the issue of surrogate consent for research. Some IRBs were restrictive to the extent of either not accepting surrogate consent at all or accepting consent from only specific surrogates (e.g., healthcare proxy, guardian, power of attorney, spouse, or parents). Other IRBs were rather permissive about accepting surrogate consent. Furthermore, the study revealed that many IRBs (39%) would allow only minimal-risk studies, and a significant number (25%) would allow only studies involving minimal and minor increase over minimal risk. A study employing HSCT clearly involves risks exceeding those standards.

An additional barrier to enrolling this adolescent patient in the study is the Code of Federal Regulations Title 45 Part 46 (the Common Rule). It requires parental or guardian permission for a child to participate in research (Section 46.408 b). This requirement can create a barrier to adolescent participation in research whenever adolescents and parents have different opinions on research participation and whenever adolescents are reluctant to inform parents about their participation.

Taken together, the lacuna in state legislation, the variability in IRB practices with respect to both the authority to consent and the degree of risk that may be accepted, and the Common Rule requirement of parental consent for research leave this patient in a desperate medical situation with a regulatory morass to navigate. The teams involved need to investigate the legislation, policies, and procedures in the adolescent's home state as well as the state where the treatment is to be administered. They also have to explore the treating institution's IRB policies on consent for adolescents' participation in research and the degree of risk that would be acceptable in research involving a minor. They may also have to deal with the home state's court's willingness to accept recommendations from the research team and the IRB. An additional complication might be the status of the mother who was accused of medical neglect. Until that issue is adjudicated, the mother's consent may still be required. If the mother's rights are terminated, a court-appointed advocate (or two) to review the pros and cons of participation in the trial and an onsite guardian may be required by the pediatric medical center.

A separate issue in this case will be the decisional capacity of the patient. Is she able to ask questions and understand her situation? If so, at a minimum, her assent will be required for enrollment. Many adolescents are capable of understanding the risks and benefits of HSCT and their role in adherence to the posttransplant treatment regimen, but some are not. Some states have emancipated minor laws that allow some adolescents to make their own treatment decisions, but they may not cover research participation.

If these issues cannot be quickly resolved, there may be another possible path forward. Again, similar to the foster children with HIV, this situation lies at the juncture of research and clinical care. The *Belmont Report* made a sharp distinction between research and clinical care, which has since been challenged by some ethicists (Faden et al. 2013; Rhodes 2005). In some situations, such as this case, the neat distinction that isolates these two legitimate medical activities creates avoidable problems. There is no obvious reason for allowing surrogates broad authority for decisions regarding treatment while drastically limiting their authority for enrolling their wards in IRB-approved clinical research.

Both the HIV drug trial and this HSCT trial are for diseases that are uniformly fatal if untreated. The HIV studies with children and the proposed HSCT study involve no control group: They provide the treatment to all participants and offer a potential for direct benefit. For that reason, in some states where child welfare authorities lacked the authority to consent for research, the child welfare authorities themselves decided that the HIV drug trials should be considered clinical care over which they had authority. Because every child involved in the studies received the "treatment," the child welfare authorities considered their agencies authorized to provide consent on that basis. Most of the children who were enrolled in HIV trials back in the 1990s did well, and the drugs were ultimately approved for use in children. A similar approach of regarding study participation as "treatment" may be a possible solution in this complicated case.

References

Faden, R. R., N. E. Kass, S. N. Goodman, P. Pronovost, S. Tunis, and T. L. Beauchamp. 2013. An ethics framework for a learning health care system: A departure from traditional research ethics and clinical ethics. *The Hastings Center Report*: S16–S27.

Gong, M., L. Richardson, R. Rhodes, G. Winkel, and J. Silverstein. 2010. Surrogate consent for research involving adults with impaired decision-making: Survey of institutional review boards' practices. *Critical Care Medicine* 38(11):2146–54.

Martin, J., and H. S. Sacks. 1990. Do HIV infected children in foster care have access to clinical trials of new treatments? *AIDS & Public Policy Journal* 5(1):3–8.

Rhodes, R. 2005. Rethinking research ethics. *The American Journal of Bioethics* 5(1):7–28.

Wilfond, B. S., D. M. Duenas, and L.-M. Johnson. 2022. Enrolling adolescents with rare disease for early phase clinical trials while under the care of child protection services: Balancing protection and access. *The American Journal of Bioethics* 22(4):81–82.

CASE 3.5: SELECTING CHILDREN FOR AN AUTISM SPECTRUM DISORDER STUDY: JUSTICE AND GEOGRAPHY

INTRODUCTION

Clinical research conducted in contexts where clinical alternatives for effective interventions are not well established raises special challenges for investigators and affected populations. One traditional concern is that some desperately ill patients have limited treatment options and are at risk of conflating the option of enrollment in clinical research with access to beneficial therapy. But an alternative perspective is that constrained availability to early-phase clinical trials limits the opportunity for desperately ill patients to have access to promising new therapies. The case presented here along with three commentaries focus on whether an early-phase clinical trial to be conducted at a single site creates an unjust allocation of benefits and burdens if close proximity or relocation is required for enrollment.

The three commentaries take different paths to the conclusion that the requirement for geographic proximity (or relocation) is just. Stephanie C. Chen from the NIH supports the proposed approach for this Phase II trial by distinguishing between positive obligations for inclusion and negative obligations to not exclude participants. She suggests that for a Phase III trial, it would be more important to ensure that a wider range of participants are included by conducting a multisite trial or offering relocation reimbursements. Mark A. Stein and Bryan H. King of the University of Washington and Seattle Children's Hospital also point to the scientific rationale for the requirement and suggest that the affected community, as a whole, has a compelling interest in ensuring the study is able to effectively determine whether this intervention is potentially efficacious, even if only a limited population is eligible to enroll. Rosamond Rhodes and Alex Kolevzon from the Icahn School of Medicine at Mount Sinai offer a conceptual analysis of the requirement of justice for both individual participants and future patients. They highlight that justice considerations are particularly critical when a condition is chronic and rare, as occurs in this novel study.

CASE SUMMARY

An investigator has IRB approval and an investigational new drug (IND) application from the FDA for a Phase II study to evaluate the safety, tolerability, and impact of insulin-like growth factor 1 (IGF-1) on autism-specific impairments. IGF-1 has shown promising results in mouse and human neuronal models of Rett syndrome, suggesting that this pathway may be a target in diverse forms of autism spectrum disorder (ASD). The study aims to assess changes in socialization, language, and motor functioning in children with Phelan–McDermid syndrome (PMS; also known as *SHANK3* deficiency or 22q13 deletion syndrome).

The study involves a double-blind placebo-controlled crossover design in 18 children aged 5–12 years. IGF-1 and placebo are each administered for 12 weeks with a four-week washout period in between.

Worldwide, approximately 1,200 children with PMS have been identified to date. There currently are no therapies available to manage the severe cognitive and behavioral manifestations of this syndrome. IGF-1 is an FDA-approved, commercially available compound that promotes neuronal cell survival, synaptic maturation, and synaptic plasticity. Although this agent is commercially available, it can cost as much as $40,000 per year. Parents and caregivers within the ASD community are interested in potential therapies for this disorder, and they are keenly aware of research possibilities as they arise. This study in particular has attracted a lot of attention from families with an affected child diagnosed with PMS.

Because the primary outcome for this study is behavioral, eligibility criteria require that potential participants live in an environment in which the child's routines and behaviors are stable for three months prior to enrollment. Furthermore, any therapeutic interventions currently received by an eligible child must be stable for three months prior to enrollment. Finally, given the severe disability and the behavioral problems characteristic of this disorder, frequent long-distance travel to and from the study center may confound the collection of accurate data. It is, therefore, important for subjects to live close to the study center to minimize the burden of biweekly travel to appointments throughout the 32-week study. These limitations will restrict study participation to families who live within close proximity to the site and those with the economic means to relocate for the entire study period. There are not likely to be enough eligible children within the study site catchment area to meet the target enrollment.

The investigator requests a clinical research ethics consultation for guidance related to the plan for participant selection. The investigator is confident that he will be able to recruit 18 participants who will be able to comply with the study requirements. He is, however, concerned about the ethical acceptability of offering an investigational drug only to those who have the economic resources to move to the region for a year. The investigator has two primary questions: (1) Does this enrollment plan meet the requirement of justice in clinical research? (2) Is it fair to conduct a study using enrollment criteria that favor economically advantaged patients with Phelan–McDermid syndrome and exclude those with lesser means?

COMMENTARY 3.5.1: FAIR PARTICIPANT SELECTION: A NEGATIVE OBLIGATION NOT TO EXCLUDE

STEPHANIE C. CHEN

The trial in question is testing the safety and efficacy of insulin-like growth factor 1 (IGF-1) in patients with Phelan–McDermid syndrome (PMS). To participate, patients must remain in close proximity to the site for the entire duration of the study. They cannot travel a long distance to the research site, and those who do not live nearby will therefore need to relocate for 32 weeks. The investigators are concerned that the travel restriction would favor economically advantaged patients and exclude those with lesser means.

Fair participant selection is a tenet of ethical research (Emanuel, Wendler, and Grady 2000). Groups should not be excluded from the opportunity to participate without a good scientific reason or particular susceptibility to risk. The trial would indeed be unfair and unethical if the research team had imposed the travel restrictions primarily to exclude less wealthy individuals from participating, or chosen a site that is largely homogeneous and affluent over sites that are more accessible to a wider range of PMS patients and equally good in other respects. In this case, the fairness of the trial seems to depend mainly on two aspects, one being motivations behind the travel restrictions, the other site selection.

First, the travel restrictions are motivated by research considerations, not discriminatory attitudes. PMS patients tend to have severe disabilities and behavioral difficulties. To ensure accurate measurements of behavioral outcomes, including the primary outcome for the trial, they need to maintain stable routines and refrain from long-distance travel for the duration of the study. Therefore, requiring that patients and their families live near or stay in the vicinity of the research site seems necessary for collecting quality data and conducting quality research. Since the goal of research is to generate useful knowledge, the travel restrictions are not unfair.

In addition, the travel restrictions do not violate a general right, as access to research participation is not typically construed as such (American Medical Association 1998). One reason is that research involves investigational interventions that carry risks. Although there is no current treatment for PMS, the investigators are not denying children a proven and clinically indicated drug that they could not otherwise afford. The study is a Phase II clinical trial. There is no proof of efficacy of IGF-1 in this patient population. In fact, there may be risks associated with the intervention, given that part of the study is to determine the safety and tolerability of IGF-1 among children with PMS.

Given the nature of the research, the investigators are not ethically obligated to ensure that all PMS patients have the same opportunity and ability to participate in the trial regardless of their place of residence and financial means (American Medical Association 1998). To do so would require relocation reimbursements for all participants who do not live close to the site. Although the trial only requires 18 participants to reach its scientific goals, we know some will need to relocate. Paying for multiple participants to relocate for 32 weeks seems impractical and prohibitively expensive.

One possibility is to relax the travel restrictions, so that some patients who cannot afford to relocate but can afford to travel to required visits will be able to participate. Scientifically, the results may be less conclusive, or more children may need to participate, and incur research risks, to generate useful data. Ethically, being more inclusive ameliorates some of the investigators' concerns, but if the results will be inconclusive, some children will have incurred research risks without sufficient justification. The research team needs to assess the scientific and ethical trade-off between having more children, some traveling further than others, and having fewer children all in close proximity of the site to assess the viability and value of this approach.

The second element that is relevant to fair participant selection in this trial is the location of the study site. Specifically, is the study site accessible to a diverse range of patients without compromising the scientific goals of the study? If the principal investigator has an academic appointment at the site, it would be unreasonable to expect him to relocate to increase accessibility. Other legitimate reasons for selecting this particular site may include the local concentration of eligible and interested patients. Although there are not 18 participants at the current site, it may have access to the largest number of participants of all potential sites, thereby minimizing concerns associated with relocation. The investigators may also take into account whether participants at a certain site will likely adhere to research requirements. If a different site is accessible to more potential participants or participants who are more socioeconomically diverse, but fewer of them will likely complete the study or adhere to all research requirements, then the scientific goals of the study would be compromised. Indeed, it would be unethical to enroll anybody in a trial that is not expected to collect enough quality data to produce useful knowledge (Halpern, Karlawish, and Berlin 2002).

Even if the investigators do not violate fair participant selection, they might nonetheless consider other methods for increasing accessibility to patients who are more socioeconomically diverse (Pace, Miller, and Danis 2003). The trial may be conducted at multiple sites, through the Rare Disease Clinical Research Network, for example (Hampton 2006). Investigators might establish a program to provide resources and assistance to families who would not otherwise be able to relocate and participate. Both strategies will require considerable funding and effort to facilitate, but can increase the size and diversity of the sample. A more diverse sample may also improve the state of understanding on aspects of the disease that are less well understood, such as the role of environmental factors in the presence and severity of various features of the disease (Phelan 2008). For a Phase II trial, these advantages may not warrant increasing accessibility at significant costs. However, if investigators conducted a Phase III trial in the future, these scientific gains might be substantial. By then, there will be safety and some preliminary efficacy evidence for IGF-1, creating a more ethically compelling case to provide the expensive treatment for PMS to more affected children through a larger clinical trial. At that time, the research team will need to weigh the scientific and ethical gains against the costs and burdens of expanding the study.

References

American Medical Association. 1998. Subject selection for clinical trials. *IRB* 20(2–3):12–15.

Emanuel, E. J., D. Wendler, and C. Grady. 2000. What makes clinical research ethical? *Journal of the American Medical Association* 283(20):2701–11.

Halpern, S. D., J. H. T. Karlawish, and J. A. Berlin. 2002. The continuing unethical conduct of under-powered clinical trials. *Journal of the American Medical Association* 288(3):358–62.

Hampton, T. 2006. Rare disease research gets boost. *Journal of the American Medical Association* 295(24):2836–38.

Pace, C., F. G. Miller, and M. Danis. 2003. Enrolling the uninsured in clinical trials: An ethical perspective. *Critical Care Medicine* 31(3):S121–25.

Phelan, M. C. 2008. Deletion 22q13.3 syndrome. *Orphanet Journal of Rare Diseases* 3(14):7.

COMMENTARY 3.5.2: UNEQUAL INDIVIDUAL RISK AND POTENTIAL BENEFIT BALANCED BY BENEFITS TO THE POPULATION AT LARGE IN AUTISM CLINICAL TRIALS?

MARK A. STEIN AND BRYAN H. KING

The investigator seeks guidance related to a planned recruitment strategy of requiring participants to live within close proximity to the study site for the 32-week Phase II study examining the safety, tolerability, and impact of insulin-like growth factor 1 (IGF-1) on autism-specific impairments in 18 children with 22q13 deletion or Phelan–McDermid syndrome. Study subjects must either reside in the geographic area or have the economic ability to relocate, creating the potential for a biased sample of participants with regard to social and economic status.

22q13 Deletion syndrome is a rare disorder with a heterogeneous phenotype associated with intellectual disability, ASD, and hypotonia. Since there are no established pharmacologic treatments of core symptoms of ASD, and a specific reason to believe that IGF-1 may be helpful in 22q13 deletion syndrome, there is much interest in the study and motivation for families to participate.

An important ethical question is whether restricting study participation to those who live in the geographic area or can afford to relocate for the trial is justifiable. This question relates to the ethical principal of justice, which suggests that there should be a fair distribution of research burdens as well as research benefits. In recent years, and highlighted by issues related to the development and selective availability of HIV treatment, the discussion of fairness in research has shifted from fair distribution of risks and burdens to a fair distribution of research benefits, including study participation and access to study treatments (reviewed in Meltzer and Childress 2008).

Indeed, although not the specific focus of this ethics consultation request, access to treatment can be particularly salient where very rare disorders are concerned. Just as there are relatively few individuals in the world with known 22q13 deletions, there are very few clinician scientists who are experts. This raises two issues that should be considered and addressed during the consenting process and in carrying out the study. First, it is possible that access to the clinical expertise offered by the study team is available to the families only through enrollment in this study. In such a case, protections against possible undue influence must be considered. For example, families with access to such a clinical investigator may consider themselves so fortunate that they do not appreciate the risks and burdens of being in a particular study, and may consent to participate without a thorough understanding of what is involved. A second concern is that families already under the care of a member of the team may not wish to disappoint their clinician-investigator for fear of jeopardizing their clinical relationship and access to treatment. This possible undue influence may also impact the study design, and perhaps introduce bias and even inflate placebo effects due to high expectations and a desire to please the investigator to increase opportunities to connect.

It is also important to remember that relocation for study participation can be detrimental to children with ASD. While there may be a concern about fairness related to limiting study access only to those out-of-town families who can afford to do this, relocation may be harmful to some children, as children with ASD do poorly with change. Indeed, in his original description, Kanner first highlighted their "obsessive preoccupation with the preservation of sameness" (Kanner 1943). It is difficult to quantify the risk to the child participants of having to relocate from their homes for several months in order to participate in a study. There is the potential, at least in the short term, of adversely affecting children due to this instability related to study participation. Participants should be given adequate time to adjust and effects of relocating monitored to ensure the burden on children and families is not excessive.

In a Phase II trial such as this one, the potential for individual benefit is unknown, despite promising preclinical or pilot data. It is known, however, that the research participants, children with intellectual disability and ASD, will be exposed to additional burdens and risks associated with a clinical research study involving both placebo and IGF-1 treatment. Phase II trials typically involve careful monitoring, frequent procedures, and blood draws to ensure safety and measure efficacy. There are the known risks of treatment with IGF-1, such as metabolic changes, hyperlipidemia, and hepatotoxicity, as well as the unknown risks in a vulnerable population with characteristic moderate to severe cognitive impairments and medical comorbidities, especially neurologic and endocrine. As this is a crossover design and there are no established treatments, the risks of placebo are arguably reduced, but risks associated with treatment and withdrawal of active treatment are unknown with this population.

If IGF-1 treatment is effective for persons with 22q13 deletion syndrome, individual benefit will be limited initially to study participants and their families. However, the benefits from a well-designed randomized controlled trial (RCT) extend to the broader population of nonparticipants with 22q13 deletion syndrome who will not be exposed to the burdens and risks of clinical research. Indeed, determining the efficacy of this treatment in an RCT has the potential to benefit those with 22q13 deletion syndrome regardless of the findings. If effective, this will lead to more research and potentially increased availability to participate in studies or to receive an effective treatment. Once efficacy has been established, future Phase III studies can determine the generalizability through larger sample sizes with more representative enrollment that have the potential to directly benefit a larger number of individuals. On the other hand, if this study of IGF-1 treatment is negative, specifically because the study population was nonrepresentative in some way (e.g., limited to relatively higher functioning or less symptomatic individuals who can travel), and the intervention does not move on to additional trials, the broader population may be forever denied access to this therapy.

Families of children with ASD would also benefit from a well-designed and well-carried-out negative study. Indeed, over the past 50 years, the autism field has been marked by numerous false treatment leads that, despite claims of early success, have not demonstrated success when scientifically tested in an RCT. These include studies of fenfluramine (Ritvo et al. 1986), secretin (Coniglio et al. 2001), mecamylanine (Arnold, Aman, and Hollway 2012), hyperbaric oxygen therapy (Arnold et al. 2012), and omega-3 fatty acids (Mankad et al. 2015). Parents of children with 22q13 deletion syndrome and ASD who are desperate for a cure are at high risk of exploitation in terms of trying unvalidated and possibly unsafe treatments (Nye and Brice 2002; Rimland 1998).

In examining the ethics of this study, a primary consideration should be ensuring the scientific goals of the study are met. Although the researchers should certainly strive to recruit a diverse socioeconomic sample from their own geographic area, given the rarity of the disorder and the importance of the study question, a selection bias favoring those with the means to participate may be unavoidable. This may lead to unequal perceived benefit in terms of individual participation in the treatment study to those living near the investigators or possessing the resources and ability to relocate. This same group will be exposed to the research burdens and risks, suggesting proportionality for participants in terms of benefits and risks while also providing group benefits to the population of affected individuals and families who cannot participate in this initial study.

The fact that the investigator is asking for a consultation bodes well for an inclusive approach to participation. More importantly, this sensitivity will be critical to ensuring that the actual risks and burdens of study participation are not disproportionate to the unknown benefits, and that study subjects, whose parents may theoretically have moved across the world to enroll, are still afforded the right to assent to research as appropriate, and also to withdraw if they need to.

References

Arnold, L. E., M. G. Aman, J. Hollway, et al. 2012. Placebo-controlled pilot trial of mecamylamine for treatment of autism spectrum disorders. *Journal of Child and Adolescent Psychopharmacology* 22(3):198–205.

Coniglio, S. J., J. D. Lewis, C. Lang, et al. 2001. A randomized, double-blind, placebo-controlled trial of single-dose intravenous secretin as treatment for children with autism. *Journal of Pediatrics* 138(5):649–55.

Kanner, L. 1943. Autistic disturbances of affective contact. *Nervous Child* 2:217–50.

Mankad, D., A. Dupuis, S. Smile, et al. 2015. A randomized, placebo controlled trial of omega-3 fatty acids in the treatment of young children with autism. *Molecular Autism* 6:18.

Meltzer, L., and J. Childress. 2008. What Is Fair Participant Selection? *The Oxford textbook of clinical research ethics*. Edited by E. J. Emanuel, C. Grady, R. A. Crouch, et al. Oxford, UK: Oxford University Press, pp. 377–85.

Nye, C., and A. Brice. 2002. Combined vitamin B6-magnesium treatment in autism spectrum disorder. *Cochrane Database of Systematic Reviews* 4:CD003497.

Rimland, B. 1998. Critique of efficacy of vitamin B6 and magnesium in the treatment of autism. *Journal of Autism and Developmental Disorders* 28(6):580–81.

Ritvo, E. R., B. J. Freeman, A. Yuwiler, et al. 1986. Fenfluramine treatment of autism: UCLA collaborative study of 81 patients at nine medical centers. *Psychopharmacology Bulletin* 22(1):133–40.

COMMENTARY 3.5.3: JUSTICE IN SELECTING PARTICIPANTS FOR A STUDY IN PHELAN–McDERMID SYNDROME

ROSAMOND RHODES AND ALEX KOLEVZON

This case describes the first clinical trial in the United States in PMS. News of the trial generated significant attention from the community. Given the rare prevalence of PMS, few interested families live near the study site. The investigators want to limit the possibility of external stressors that might confound the results, such as long-distance travel. This raises the question of whether it is just to include only families able to reside close to the study site as an enrollment criterion. Relocating participants to the study site area is possible, but such flexibility is likely to reflect financial wherewithal and thereby exclude participants with limited financial resources who reside far from the study site. Could this exclusion be ethically justified?

To determine whether insulin-like growth factor 1 (IGF-1) is effective as a treatment for PMS, the study will rely on measurements of behavioral outcomes; all can be significantly affected by changes in the child's environment and routines. Although other study designs could be considered, decreasing the sample size to allow investigators to travel to families or reducing the number of assessments could compromise the scientific integrity and safety of the study. Assuring the safety and rigor of the study should be the standard for establishing inclusion and exclusion criteria.

Justice in research

This study design may appear to favor those who are rich over the poor, and may therefore seem unjust. But determining whether or not a practice is just requires a thorough and thoughtful analysis. Aristotle's formal principle of justice requires that people who are similarly situated receive similar treatment (Aristotle 1971). A superficial reading of the formal principle of justice implies that as long as the same inclusion and exclusion criteria are applied in the enrollment decisions for all children, the proposal would be just. By raising the question, however, the investigator suggests that simply applying the same criteria to all participants may not be sufficient attention to the subtle justice issues involved in this study. That insight is actually fully consistent with Aristotle's view that justice is complex and contextual.

Going beyond the formal principle of justice, contemporary philosopher T. M. Scanlon presents persuasive arguments to show that clarifying the requirements of justice is not a simple matter (Scanlon 1998). It requires us to consider the array of reasons that incline people to make different decisions in different circumstances. As Scanlon explains, justice requires that we base our judgments about what we owe to others on principles that others could not reasonably reject. Employing his formulation in considering whether it would be unreasonable to reject the investigators' proposed study design can inform us about whether their enrollment criteria meet the high bar of justice.

To determine whether or not this study design is not only scientifically sound but consistent with justice, we need to evaluate the harms and benefits involved and to whom they accrue. In clinical research, there are two populations to consider: (1) the study participants and (2) the population living with the disease. Typically, the ethical evaluation of research focuses on the participants' experiences during the trial. Achieving justice, however, requires a broad perspective that examines all of the effects on all of those who are likely to be affected by an action. This involves determining whether the risks of harm are reasonable under the circumstances and whether the distribution of burdens and benefits is fair and attends to legitimate claims.

(1) For participants enrolled in this trial, the obvious risk is the harm associated with receiving the drug and, for those who are required to relocate, also the risks of harms associated with being uprooted and transported away from familiar surroundings and relationships. The obvious potential benefit is the reduction of symptoms associated with the condition. (2) The population of people with PMS is harmed by not having good evidence available to guide physicians in the treatment of their devastating disease. The population of those with PMS clearly benefits from a well-designed, carefully executed trial. All PMS patients receive a definitive answer to questions about the study drug's efficacy or lack thereof, and that information benefits patients over the entire course of their lives. The study question will be answered sooner and with fewer participants when the design optimizes the quality of data collection. A definitive positive answer could facilitate FDA approval and ultimately mitigate their symptoms and diminish patients' disability. A definitive negative answer will prevent families from investing time and money in an ineffective treatment and avoid patients' needless exposure to possible drug-related side effects. Everyone in the population is entitled to be protected from the promulgation of ineffective treatments. In addition, having a definite answer will facilitate insurance coverage for an effective drug.

This analysis explains why the PMS population should be willing to endorse a study that would provide these significant benefits sooner rather than later. No reasonable person with the diagnosis, or a parent of a child with PMS, should refuse to endorse a study design that would provide a clear answer to the study question. Therefore, every patient and their parents should be willing to accept a study design that would achieve those ends. This is a study design that they could not reasonably reject.

Understanding the requirements of justice in clinical research allows us to go beyond the superficial concern over the apparent advantage for wealthy patients and appreciate why we should accept the investigator's enrollment plan as the route that is ethically required. This analysis also reveals two frequently overlooked, yet significant, factors that should be taken into consideration in determining whether a study design is just.

One is the fact that clinical research on chronic illness is different from clinical research on acute illness. People living with chronic illness always stand to benefit from the findings of a well-conducted efficient study because the findings will not only provide them with a theoretical possibility of a future benefit, but will certainly be relevant to them and that benefit will be lifelong. That difference deserves attention in the ethical review of studies related to chronic disease, and it should make an especially significant difference in the assessment of the risks and benefits for study participants. Specifically, this point suggests that IRBs need to take chronicity into account and appreciate how all study participants (those in the active arm and those in the placebo arm) will directly benefit from the findings.

The other factor is the rarity of the condition being studied. Although research on common diseases is relatively well funded and can draw on large pools of potential study participants, neither of these is the case with research on rare diseases. Both the financial resources to conduct studies and the availability of participants for studies are severely restricted in research on rare diseases. These limitations mean that people in the affected populations cannot afford to squander their limited opportunities to improve the state of knowledge. Thus, choosing a study design that can answer the study question within the existing constraints becomes a moral imperative because of the impact on the entire affected population.

Conclusion

When decisions about study design have an impact on the lives of others, weighing all of the study's repercussions is critical. Taking a broad, comprehensive, and contextual view of justice in biomedical research allows us to appreciate that equality is only one piece of a complex set of issues that should be considered in designing a study in accordance with the highest ethical standards. Because the design of this study actually reflects the interests of the affected populations, reasonable people should find it just and not reject it.

References

Aristotle. 1971. *The Nicomachean ethics of Aristotle.* Edited and translated by W. D. Ross. London, UK: Oxford University Press.

Scanlon, T. M. 1998. *What we owe to each other,* Cambridge, MA: Harvard University Press.

Section 4

Favorable risk–benefit ratio

LIZA-MARIE JOHNSON

In the design and review of clinical research, one must consider the basic ethical principles of beneficence and nonmaleficence. The balance of these two principles is applied in the assessment of the risk–benefit ratio of a proposed study. Risk is the possibility of experiencing harm from study participation and considers both (1) the magnitude of any potential harm as well as (2) the likelihood of the harm to occur. Harms exist on a spectrum—from transient to permanent and from minimal to serious, even including significant morbidity or mortality. Harms can include physical, psychological, social, or economic harms that occur because of study participation.

Benefits of research broadly include the potential of a study to generate generalizable knowledge impacting others beyond study participants. Some studies also confer the potential for direct benefit to participants, generally Phase III intervention-based research where the research intervention may ameliorate a condition or treat a disease. Participants may also incur indirect benefits (e.g., increased health screenings and feelings of altruism), although these are generally not included in an analysis of the risk–benefit ratio of a given study.

The five cases included in this section focus on study design and ask if risks to participants have been sufficiently minimized or if researchers have additional obligations to potential participants to further minimize risks or maximize benefits. The final two cases in this section involve risk–benefit assessments in pediatric research. There are additional protections within the Code of Federal Regulations (subpart D) for children regarding allowable risks.

CASE 4.1: OBLIGATIONS TO ACT ON PATIENT-REPORTED OUTCOMES IN ELECTRONIC HEALTH RECORDS (2016)

Principles: Favorable Risk–Benefit Ratio, Informed Consent

Topics: Privacy, Electronic Health Records, Clinician and Researcher Obligations

Values: Equity

Research involving patient-reported outcome (PRO) information to clinical electronic health record (EHR) data can blur the line between research commitments and clinical obligations, particularly when the reported information may be clinically actionable in nature. This case considers the risks associated with reviewing PRO data for clinical actionability and risks to privacy if such

---

DOI: 10.1201/9781003335306-5

data are placed in the EHR, and raises several questions. How should consent be obtained for such research, do clinicians have obligations to review PRO data entered by research staff, and should there be any privacy protections such as a firewall around the data?

The first commentary (Whicher and Evans, this volume, p. 188) argues against exceptionalism in PRO research and posits that the informed consent process be the same as for any other survey research study. They add that any future research on PRO data, after the data have been placed in the EHR, be subject to the same regulatory and ethical guidelines as any study that seeks to use EHR data.

The second commentary (Swirsky and Boyd, this volume, p. 191) also emphasizes the need for a quality informed consent process that outlines for participants what information will be placed into the EHR and elicits permission to notify a patient's care team when appropriate. Given the volume of data in the EHR, it is likely impractical to rely on clinicians to scan the EHR for potentially relevant PRO; therefore, there is a duty on study teams to report relevant results to clinical teams. Some PRO data may contain sensitive information where participants would prefer privacy from the clinical team. Some, but not all, EHRs may be able to segregate access to sensitive PRO data, but as this functionality is not universal, investigators working with PRO data have an obligation to consider aspects of data security and individual privacy when designing studies that link PRO data with the EHR.

The final commentary (Crites et al., this volume, p. 193) also believes there is an ethical obligation to respond to clinically actionable PRO information, although note that to whom this responsibility falls remains uncertain. Like Swirsky and Boyd, the commentators have concerns about protection of participant privacy and suggest the segregation and limited access of PRO data collected for research use. Given the obligation to act upon actionable findings, they suggest training members of the PRO team to review PRO data in a timely manner and to identify "triggers" for when data should be shared with a clinical team.

Patient-centered outcomes research and the integration of PROs comprise an increasingly key component of the effort to improve the quality of clinical care and ensure that research includes outcomes that are meaningful to participants. The linkage of PRO to EHR data raises several ethical questions around privacy risks to participants, obligations to intervene on PRO data, and the process around informed consent. All the commentaries in this case choose to emphasize at least one of these aspects in their analysis of the case.

CASE 4.2: A TRIAL TO TEST A NOVEL APPROACH TO DIABETES PREVENTION (2017)

Principles: Favorable Risk–Benefit Ratio, Informed Consent

Content: Drugs and Devices, Pragmatic Trials

Values: Social Value

In designing a randomized trial, the principle of clinical equipoise requires investigators to have uncertainty over whether a treatment will be beneficial, thus providing an ethical basis for randomization of participants to a novel versus standard treatment (or placebo) arm. In this case, investigators are evaluating whether the use of positive airway pressure (PAP) during sleep plus lifestyle coaching are superior to lifestyle coaching alone to prevent progression to type 2 diabetes in individuals who are found to be prediabetic with concomitant moderate to severe obstructive sleep apnea (OSA). Individuals will be recruited from a general community clinic and are not currently seeking OSA treatment. The recommendation for OSA is PAP at night, so a research ethics consultation asks if it is appropriate to randomize individuals found to have OSA to a study arm that does not include PAP.

The first commentary (McCormick, Wu, and Doussau, this volume, p. 196) examines the importance of the study aims given the burden of diabetes, noting that PAP is not always frontline therapy for OSA, with some affected individuals benefiting from lifestyle modification and weight loss. The commentators believe there is sufficient uncertainty around whether the intervention of lifestyle modification plus PAP is superior to lifestyle modification alone (control) in preventing conversion to diabetes, to conduct the trial as planned. Lifestyle modification alone may benefit individuals with OSA, so participants in the control arm may receive a benefit from participation. They go on to argue that a "clear and meaningful informed consent" process could inform potential participants about a reasonable alternative: deferral of the clinical trial to pursue access to PAP for their OSA. A final obligation, they argue, is to offer alternative referrals for participants with OSA who cannot be randomized due to intolerance of PAP.

Like the first commentary, the second commentary (Taylor and Punjabi, this volume, p. 198) agrees there is value in confirming (or disconfirming) the potential benefit of PAP plus lifestyle coaching in the prevention of diabetes, and that enrollment on the control arm does not expose individuals to undue risk. Their recommendations come with three conditions for the ethical implementation of the study: (1) Offer referral to a physician for clinical follow-up in lieu of trial participation, (2) adhere to voluntariness and continue to follow participants who enroll but later wish to cross over to the other intervention (i.e., discontinue or initiate PAP depending on the study arm), and (3) facilitate continued access to PAP at the end of the trial.

In contrast, the final commentary (Miller and Kim, this volume, p. 200) questions the clinical utility of the trial given that (1) PAP is already indicated for participants with OSA and (2) the plans for a run-in period testing tolerance of PAP is not generalizable to ordinary practice, where clinicians will regularly face patients unlikely to use PAP.

These cases show the differences in recommendations that can arise given the subjective nature of assessments around study value and risk–benefit analysis.

CASE 4.3: IS IT ETHICALLY APPROPRIATE TO REFUSE TO COMPENSATE PARTICIPANTS WHO ARE BELIEVED TO HAVE INTENTIONALLY CONCEALED MEDICAL CONDITIONS? (2018)

Principles: Favorable Risk–Benefit Ratio, Informed Consent

Topics: Payment

Values: Trustworthiness

This case examines compensation for research participants, but rather than focusing on the more common research ethics debates over how much to compensate participants, the potential role of compensation in an individual's decision to participate, and the risk of undue inducement, this case examines the ethical appropriateness of withholding compensation. In this case, individuals who use certain prescribed or recreational drugs or those with certain chronic medical conditions are excluded from enrollment. Participants receive $100 for a screening visit, and those who pass the screening can participate in the study itself. Unfortunately, the study team has discovered participants who have failed to disclose drug use (failed associated drug screen) or a chronic medical condition that would exclude them from study participation. The team now asks if it is appropriate to withhold the screening visit compensation from individuals who are believed to have intentionally concealed a chronic medical condition.

In the first commentary (Lynch, Gelinas, and Largent, this volume, p. 204), the commentators argue that it is acceptable to withhold payment to participants who intentionally deceive investigators as to their eligibility, but suggest that if payment is offered as part of the screening process, it is important for investigators to be clear about the conditions that must be met to receive it. The goal should be to design a screening process that minimizes any incentive to lie to investigators in order to receive payment.

The second commentary (Danis et al., this volume, p. 207) also outlines a framework for withholding payment, but notes that in some circumstances it may be difficult to distinguish outright deception from participant ignorance. For example, a potential participant may not yet know they have a certain medical condition, have learned about it under a different name or diagnosis, or simply forgot. Based on the challenges ascertaining intent, they conclude that while it is necessary to exclude from study participation, it is still necessary to pay participants for their time.

The final commentary (Rhodes and Danziger, this volume, p. 208) argues that while participants should not lie, researchers have an obligation to pay them for their time and effort, having undergone the screening visit. The commentary notes that denying compensation is ethically problematic because it is judgmental (requires investigators to judge participant actions) and punitive. They argue that there are obligations not to purposefully inflict harm and to being nonjudgmental in participant interactions.

All three commentaries highlight the real-world irregularities in human self-reporting, be it concealing information or simply forgetting information. They also observe the consequences of relying on self-report—be it the risk that the misinformation impacts study outcomes and/or that it increases the risks of study participation. Despite these shared observations, the commentaries ultimately reach different conclusions about the withholding of compensation to participants who deceive.

CASE 4.4: ETHICAL DRUG DEVELOPMENT FOR RARE CHILDHOOD DISEASES: WHEN THERE ARE LIMITED BUT PROMISING DATA IN ADULTS, HOW TO CHOOSE BETWEEN SAFETY OR EFFICACY STUDIES? (2020)

Principles: Favorable Risk–Benefit Ratio

Content: Drugs and Devices, Pediatrics, Phase I Trials

Values: Equity

This case is the first of two cases involving early-phase clinical trials involving pediatric participants. Early-phase trials commonly consist of two phases: the first phase ("Phase I trials") begins with safety, tolerability, and often dose finding, while the second phase ("Phase II trials) enrolls a small number of additional participants to look at efficacy. In this case, an investigator has designed a Phase I study to look at the safety of low-dose interleukin-2 (LD IL-2) in children with pediatric-onset systemic lupus erythematosus (pSLE). While high-dose IL-2 is a U.S. Food and Drug Administration (FDA)-approved treatment for some malignancies, a lower dose of IL-2 is not approved for any condition or disorder. The FDA has issued a clinical hold, stating the study design (safety and tolerability of escalating doses of LD IL-2) was more than a minor increase in risk with no clear prospect of direct benefit. The FDA proposes additional efficacy studies in adult patients and then a larger early-phase trial in pediatrics looking at efficacy, potentially offering participants a direct benefit. The investigator does not have funding to conduct a larger such trial and requests assistance in responding to the FDA.

The first commentator (Nelson, this volume, p. 214) outlines the regulatory landscape, which does not allow for approval of research interventions that exceed a minor increase in minimal risk without the prospect of direct benefit. He concludes that the repeated exposure to LD IL-2 over six weeks does not provide a sufficient prospect of direct benefit to participants. Citing information from adult studies, he agrees with the FDA position that the design of a pediatric efficacy trial is the most clinically, scientifically, and ethically appropriate way to proceed and would offer enrolled adolescents enough prospect of direct benefit to justify the risks of participation.

The second commentary (Porter, Stevens, and Wilfond, this volume, p. 216) reviews the standard approach to many pediatric trials: Data from adult-only trials provide the background evidence for potential benefit to participants in a pediatric trial. However, they note that this approach fails when the disorder under study exists only in children or presents with a difference in disease trajectory. The commentary argues that because the biology and trajectory of pediatric SLE are sufficiently different from those of adult SLE, it is not appropriate to follow the traditional adults-first approach. The commentators suggest it is better to start with a small safety study involving a minimal number of participants rather than a larger pediatric efficacy study based on the extrapolation of adult data. They note that the concept of a "minor" increase in risk is subjective, and, given what is already known about the drug, the risks of exposure may be modest enough to meet the criterion for minor and thus be approvable. Finally, focusing on the broader context of rare pediatric conditions for which few good clinical options exist, the commentary argues that risk assessments should consider parental perspectives on risk as trials are designed.

The final commentary (Matsler and Young, this volume, p. 218) is also critical of the FDA proposal to further study efficacy in adults and extrapolate the information to a pediatric efficacy study, noting that pediatric lupus is associated with higher morbidity and mortality. The commentators recommend the trial be referred out for approval through CFR 50.54, a pathway for pediatric clinical trials that include more than a minor increase over minimal risk without potential for direct benefit, but that present an opportunity to "understand, prevent, or alleviate a serious problem affecting the health or welfare of children" (FDA 2019).

This case is the first of two in this section looking at risk assessments in pediatrics and highlights the tension between innovative research in pediatrics and subjectivity around defining when an intervention is "more than a minor increase" in risk.

CASE 4.5: GREATER THAN MINIMAL RISK, NO DIRECT BENEFIT: BRIDGING DRUG TRIALS AND NOVEL THERAPY IN PEDIATRIC POPULATIONS (2020)

Principles: Favorable Risk–Benefit Ratio

Content: Drugs and Devices, Pediatrics, Phase I Trials

Values: Social Value

In this case, an investigator seeks to study the tolerability of plerixafor, a medication used for stem cell mobilization, in pediatric patients with sickle cell disease (SCD). While this medication is approved in adults, its use in pediatric patients with SCD would be "off-label," and as designed, the trial will not directly benefit participants. Like the previous case, evaluation of risk is the central question. Should the IRB consider the trial as only a minor increase in minimal risk approvable under 45 CFR 46.406, or should it be referred to the Department of Health and Human Services for potential approval under 45 CFR 46.407? Approval of research under 45 CFR 46.407 occurs after an IRB referral to federal agencies (i.e., the FDA or Office for Human Research Protections [OHRP]) for formal review by an expert panel with input from public stakeholders.

The first commentator (Unguru, this volume, p. 222) considers the side effects of plerixafor and considers that its use would be more than a minor increase in risk for pediatric participants, thus necessitating referral to a 407 panel to assess the ethical acceptability of the trial as currently designed.

The second commentary (Sharma and Johnson, this volume, p. 224) takes the opposite position. Citing data from the use of plerixafor in adults with SCD, the permissibility of some novel vaccine safety studies in pediatric populations (without potential for direct benefit), and the development of well-defined stopping rules, the commentary argues that the trial is approvable under 45 CFR 46.406 as only a minor increase in minimal risk.

The final commentators (Lee and Ginsberg, this volume, p. 227) focus on the "socially acceptable" standard, wherein a "minor increase over minimal risk" is the level of risk experienced by children who face greater, yet socially acceptable, risks. Given the increased morbidity and mortality faced by children with SCD, IRBs should evaluate whether the few adverse effects of plerixafor exceed a socially acceptable risk given that, as compared to healthy children, the lives of these children include greater risks.

In this case, the ambiguity around the term "minor increase over minimal risk" leads commentators to reach different conclusions around the level of risk in a proposed study for pediatric patients with serious illness.

CASE 4.1: OBLIGATIONS TO ACT ON PATIENT-REPORTED OUTCOMES IN ELECTRONIC HEALTH RECORDS

INTRODUCTION

As part of the effort to improve the quality of clinical care, investigators have been conducting research using novel methods of collecting and sharing data across patient populations and institutions. One example of this is linking biospecimen data with data from EHRs. More recently, an emphasis has been placed on collecting PROs directly from patients both for clinical use and to enhance the research utility of these population-based databases. Some institutions have opted to collect PROs through patient portals that are stored electronically in the participant's EHR.

The case presented here, along with three commentaries, focuses on how patients need to be informed when their PRO data will be used for research purposes and who has the responsibility to review PROs for clinically actionable data. Danielle Whicher and Emily Evans from Patient-Centered Outcomes Research Institute (PCORI) argue that the use of PRO data for research purposes should use the same approach for informed consent as other survey research and does not require any additional consent requirements than the use of EHR data for such purposes. Eric S. Swirsky and Andrew D. Boyd from the University of Illinois at Chicago suggest what information should be included in patient consent for use of the PRO data for research, the segregation of sensitive data, and the clinicians' duties to review PRO data and take clinical action when necessary. Joshua S. Crites from the Cleveland Clinic as well as his national collaborators on a PCORI-funded network propose a practice standard for how to identify clinically actionable information.

CASE SUMMARY

To collect PRO data through the individual's EHR, a typical process is as follows: (1) The researcher "orders" a survey, as if it were a lab test, prompting the patient-participant to complete the survey; (2) data are automatically populated in the EHR of the patient-participant; and (3) a researcher—but often not the individual's clinician—will review the data. This data collection method shows great promise for linking PRO data acquired as part of a research project to variations in clinical care that might be associated with patient outcomes.

The practice of collecting PRO data from research participation in an individual's EHR, however, raises several significant ethical questions. First, how should informed consent be obtained for research studies where PROs will be linked to participants' EHRs? Second, what are the responsibilities of clinicians—who may not be associated directly with the research project—to review PRO data that are collected and linked within the individual's EHR for clinically relevant and/or potentially actionable information? Third, are there responsibilities to "firewall" any sensitive information confidentially reported in EHR-linked PROs that does not have direct clinical relevance but that could be visible to the multitude of clinicians and other care providers who might be accessing an individual's EHR?

COMMENTARY 4.1.1: INFORMED CONSENT FOR PROs IN EHR RESEARCH: ARE ADDITIONAL REQUIREMENTS NECESSARY?

DANIELLE WHICHER AND EMILY EVANS

The use of electronic health records (EHRs) by providers and healthcare organizations has increased substantially over the past decade (Heisey-Grove and Patel 2015). By improving the collection, organization, and accessibility of patients' medical information, EHRs offer substantial advantages over paper-based medical records in terms of improving healthcare delivery and patient outcomes. In addition to these clinical benefits, EHR data can support rigorous clinical and health services research.

Research using EHRs faces a number of important challenges, however, including that EHRs generally lack data on patient-reported outcomes (PROs) (Snyder et al. 2013). Broadly defined by the FDA as "any report of the status of a patient's health condition that comes directly from the patient, without interpretation of the patient's response by a clinician or anyone else" (U.S. Department of Health and Human Services et al. 2009), PROs are intended to improve assessments of patients' health, the quality of clinical care, and the benefits and risks of interventions. That EHRs do not routinely collect PROs in a systematic manner limits their usefulness for research purposes, especially given the growing emphasis on ensuring that research includes outcomes that are meaningful to the individuals impacted by it (Snyder et al. 2013).

To overcome this limitation, efforts have been made to embed the collection and storage of PRO data into EHRs (see, e.g., Kozak, Mugavero, and Yo 2012). Although these efforts are designed to improve the usefulness of the evidence generated by research to patients and other end users, they raise questions regarding informed consent. In what follows, we argue that, with respect to informed consent, PRO collection and integration of the data into EHRs for research purposes should be treated the same as other survey research. Future uses of PRO data once it has been entered into the EHR should then be subject to the same requirements, with respect to informed consent, that apply to research using EHR data.

Informed consent for pro collection and use

Requirements for informed consent are based on the principal of autonomy, ensuring that individuals have the ability to choose what activities they are willing to participate in and what risks they are willing to assume. The question of whether and how informed consent should be obtained for survey research as well as for research that leverages EHR data has received substantial attention in the literature and regulatory context (see, e.g., Miller 2008; Whicher and Wu 2015).

A central question regarding the collection of PROs as part of a patient's EHR is whether the act of collecting a PRO for research purposes creates the need for different informed consent requirements compared to (1) other survey research and (2) research using EHR data. All PROs involve the administration of standardized survey questions to individuals, which can be used to inform patient care and/ or for research purposes.

For survey research, defined as research in which "a sample of participants is drawn … from a larger population … [and] is asked a series of questions related to a topic about which they should have some knowledge or attitude" (Gliner, Morgan, and Leech 2010), the risks of harms that individuals may be asked to assume depend on the nature of the questions asked and how that information will be used. If the questions themselves could result in psychological harm to individuals or if the use of the information obtained could result in psychological, legal, or social harms, it is important to disclose those risks, as well as the voluntary nature of participation, to potential survey respondents in advance (Whicher and Wu 2015). Importantly, such risks can exist in both clinical and research contexts.

Therefore, regardless of whether the PRO data will be used for research purposes, clinical purposes, or both, all PRO surveys should include a statement that describes how the data will be used; that the responses will be included in the individual's EHR; and, if applicable, any risks of harms associated with completing the survey or with how the information will be used. Within the contexts of both clinical care and research, it is also critical that patients be informed that they may refuse to answer any questions about their health or healthcare and about the privacy protections in place for clinical and patient-reported information. In situations where competent adults have received this information, completing the survey should imply consent for the specified uses of the survey responses as well as for inclusion of those responses in the EHR.

If a proposed research project plans to link PRO survey responses with clinical information in the individual's EHR, this should be disclosed in the statement included at the beginning of the survey. If, in addition to collecting data from surveys and linking the data to clinical information, studies also involve the manipulation of clinical care, more extensive consent processes may be required, depending on the nature of the interventions and risks of harms imposed on research participants.

Beyond the use of the PRO data for the intended purposes (clinical and/or research), requirements for future research using PRO data from EHRs should be the same as those for other research relying on data from EHRs. For research involving EHR data, the risks of harms to individuals generally depend on whether the research will use identifiable or deidentified data and, similar to survey research, whether disclosure of these data could result in harms to the individual, as well as whether the research involves intervening in a patient's medical care. Under current U.S. regulations, informed consent is not required for use of existing data that have been deidentified in accordance with the HIPAA Privacy Rule (45 CFR Parts 160, 164: U.S. Department of Health and Human Services 2007). Informed consent requirements may also be waived in situations where it is not practicable to obtain consent and where the risks of harm to individuals are minimal (45 CFR 46.116(d)(1): U.S. Department of Health, Education, and Welfare 2009).

Although the integration of PRO data in the EHR is relatively new, there is nothing inherently different about these data compared to other health information contained in an EHR. Therefore, requirements for research using previously collected PRO data in EHRs should be determined based on the risks of harms imposed on participants. A waiver for informed consent is reasonable when the study includes PRO data that has been sufficiently deidentified, since the risks of harms to individuals are expected to be minimal. If the study will rely on identifiable PRO data and could impose risks of harms on individual patients, informed consent should be obtained consistent with applicable regulations and requirements.

Conclusion

Given the benefits of PRO data for both clinical practice and clinical research, as well as the movement to create a learning healthcare system (Olsen et al. 2007), we expect that the collection of PROs as part of the clinical encounter will become increasingly routine and standardized. However, regardless of whether PRO collection becomes a more routine part of clinical practice, individuals should always be provided with information about the purpose of the PRO survey, the intended uses of the data (including storage in the EHR), and any risks associated with completing the PRO survey. Once PRO data have been entered into an individual's health record, informed consent requirements for the use of these data should be the same as those for research involving any other data contained in a patient's EHR.

References

FDA. 2019. https://www.accessdata.fda.gov/scripts/cdrh/cfdocs/cfcfr/CFRSearch.cfm?fr=50.54

Gliner, J. A., G. A. Morgan, and N. L. Leech. 2010. *Research methods in applied settings: An integrated approach to design and analysis*, pp. 338–39. Mahwah, NJ: Lawrence Erlbaum Associates.

Heisey-Grove, D., and V. Patel. 2015. Any, certified, and basic: Quantifying physician EHR adoption through 2014. ONC Data Brief 28. Available at: https://www.healthit.gov/sites/default/files/briefs/oncdatabrief28_certified_vs_basic.pdf (accessed October 30, 2015).

Kozak, M. S., M. J. Mugavero, and J. Yo, et al. 2012. Patient reported outcomes in routine care: Advancing data capture for HIV cohort research. *Clinical Infectious Diseases* 54(1):141–47.

Miller, F. G. 2008. Research on medical records without consent. *Journal of Law, Medicine and Ethics* 36(3):560–66.

Olsen, L. W., D. Aisner, J. M. McGinnis, and Roundtable on Evidence-Based Medicine. 2007. *The learning healthcare system: Workshop summary (IOM roundtable on evidence-based medicine)*, Washington, DC: National Academies Press.

Snyder, C. F., R. E. Jensen, J. B. Segal, and A. W. Wu. 2013. Patient-reported outcomes (PROs): Putting the patient perspective in patient-centered outcomes research. *Medical Care* 51(8 Suppl. 3):S73–79.

U.S. Department of Health and Human Services, Food and Drug Administration, Center for Drug Evaluation and Research, Center for Biologics Evaluation and Research, and Center for Devices and Radiological Health. 2009. Guidance for industry: Patient-reported outcome measures: Use in medical product development to support labeling claims. Available at: http://www.fda.gov/downloads/Drugs/GuidanceComplianceRegulatoryInformation/Guidances/UCM193282.pdf (accessed October 30, 2015).

U.S. Department of Health and Human Services. 2007. *Code of Federal Regulations*, Title 45, Parts 160 and 164.

U.S. Department of Health, Education, and Welfare. 2009. *Code of Federal Regulations*, Title 45, Part 46.116 (D) (1).

Whicher, D., and A. W. Wu. 2015. Ethics review of survey research: A mandatory requirement for publication? *The Patient* 8(6):477–82.

COMMENTARY 4.1.2: PATIENT-REPORTED OUTCOMES AT THE CROSSROADS OF CLINICAL RESEARCH AND INFORMATICS

ERIC S. SWIRSKY AND ANDREW D. BOYD

Patient-reported outcomes (PROs) provide a new dimension of patient narrative to clinical care. PROs are structured representations of the patient's voice that appeal to clinical values of autonomy, patient-centered care, and shared decision making, and as such they can serve to incorporate the patient perspective into research and clinical care. Using a study involving PROs as an example, this commentary addresses matters related to patient consent, clinicians' duties to review PRO data linked to their patients' electronic health records (EHRs) by independent investigators, and segregation of sensitive data. We conclude that, in the absence of guidance, an interdisciplinary approach is required to satisfy the ethical, clinical, and technical demands of protocols involving PROs and health information technology.

A recent study by Boyd, Brown, and Henrickson (2012) screening for depression, sleep disorders, and anxiety in patients being treated for pancreatic adenocarcinoma provides an example of a PRO in use. Patients enrolled in the study completed psychometric evaluations over time to assess changes in their depression, anxiety, or other conditions. These PROs were simultaneously entered into participants' EHRs through the in-house M-Strides system, given their likely therapeutic value. Once entered, the information was available through a tab within the EHR to all providers with access rights. Patients were notified during the consent process that they would be asked psychiatric questions, the results would be posted in their medical records, and their primary providers would be notified if additional follow-up was appropriate and necessary for care. Prior to the implementation of the study, patient providers were notified that their patients would be completing PROs as part of the study and they would be notified if the PRO data revealed significant signs of depression, such as suicidal ideation (Boyd et al. 2012).

The lessons learned from this study provide an example of issues attendant to use of PROs containing sensitive data in large academic medical centers. Many of the challenges faced by the sample may not be applicable in every case, but taking a generalized approach we can glean some insight. For example, protocols involving access to an EHR containing protected health information should include the patient's written consent or an appropriate waiver in keeping with HIPAA and best practices for protection of confidentiality and privacy in clinical research. Consent should include permission to notify the patient's care team when appropriate; providers have to know when information is being entered into the record and in some cases may have to be contacted directly.

Once the research team meets its duty to report, the burden shifts to the care team to review the PRO data inasmuch as it holds clinical utility. How information is handed off directly impacts a clinician's duty to review it. Many EHRs such as those implemented at large academic medical centers are low-density, high-volume information systems that too frequently suffer problems related to clinical usability and value of information. Even if a hospital has specialized PRO systems like M-Strides, providers outside the research protocol or clinical specialty may view it as one tab among others in the EHR for which they have received little training. Moreover, the EHR is large and complex with many points of access and deposits of information. Alerts regarding the deposit of potentially clinically actionable information are essential, and the flow of information must be coordinated and operationalized. With participant-patient safety on the line, it is too risky to rely upon clinicians to perpetually scan electronic patient records for potentially relevant information among myriad points of changing data. In addition, while an investigator may consider some PRO responses to be actionable information, a provider will need to exercise clinical judgment in deciding what PRO responses are significant. Some clinicians are not inclined to embrace PRO data in their practices. Of course, providers who fail to review these data also run the risk of liability if actionable information is revealed in the record. Whether and how the information is utilized by the provider will remain his or her responsibility. Efforts ought to be made to develop guidelines and/or best practices as the field matures. In the interim, researchers and clinicians will need to negotiate how to communicate and their individual and mutual responsibilities on a case-by-case basis.

Considering the possibility that a breach of confidentiality of PRO information may lead to patient harm, investigators using PROs ought to erect a firewall to protect sensitive information. For example, raw data can be segregated in some health information systems, while role-based access, patient aliases, independent databases, and audit trails can provide security. Segregation of data occurs regularly with high-risk clinical information in EHRs, such as information related to sexually transmitted diseases and alcohol and drug abuse, which require a higher degree of security to prevent unauthorized access. Other types of PROs, such as patient satisfaction surveys, may not be directly relevant to clinical care yet may contain sensitive information that a research participant would prefer to have kept from her provider. However, functionality and accessibility of features vary widely among information systems and providers. In the march toward interoperability, many health information systems, such as pathology, radiology, and custom systems such as M-Strides, have been designed to enter results directly into the EHR regardless of whether tests are performed for research or clinical care. Thus, researchers should engage system experts when designing their protocols, as some environments do not have functionality that will allow for the creation of customized pools of segregated PRO data.

Until best practices emerge for linkage of PRO data with EHRs, balancing patient confidentiality and clinical utility of PROs requires careful and systematic consideration (Snyder et al. 2013). Investigators in this area must consider their responsibilities regarding privacy and security of patient data and how to best engage with and share actionable information with clinical teams. IRBs must be prepared to meet the interdisciplinary demands of this line of inquiry so that they can properly assess protocols and assist researchers with clear guidance. Here at the intersection of research and health information technology, where matters of patient care, information governance, and technology converge, clinical informaticians can and should play an essential role in protocol preparation and IRB approval processes.

References

Boyd, A. D., D. Brown, C. Henrickson, et al. 2012. Screening for depression, sleep-related disturbances, and anxiety in patients with adenocarcinoma of the pancreas: A preliminary study. *Scientific World Journal* 2012:650707.

Snyder, C. F., R. E. Jensen, J. B. Segal, and A. W. Wu. 2013. Patient-reported outcomes (PROs): Putting the patient perspective in patient-centered outcomes research. *Medical Care* 51(8 Suppl. 3):S73–79.

COMMENTARY 4.1.3: PROs IN THE BALANCE: ETHICAL IMPLICATIONS OF COLLECTING PATIENT-REPORTED OUTCOME MEASURES IN THE ELECTRONIC HEALTH RECORD

JOSHUA S. CRITES, CYNTHIA CHUANG, ANNE DIMMOCK, WENKE HWANG, BOBBIE JOHANNES, ANURADHA PARANJAPE, AND ALBERT W. WU

As outlined in the case description already presented, efforts to collect PROs may improve the quality of healthcare delivery by identifying relationships between current standards of clinical practice and the positive and negative outcomes that patients experience. In this commentary, we argue that there is an ethical obligation to flag clinically actionable PRO information collected for research purposes, but to whom the responsibility falls and the extent of this obligation are uncertain. We claim that this uncertainty stems from a tension between risks of failing to act on clinically relevant information on the one hand, and research priorities such as maintaining participant privacy and a commitment to producing generalizable knowledge on the other. We then conclude with recommendations for future research directions.

In the context of PRO research, the primary obligation of investigators is to collect data that will improve delivery of patient care by analyzing patient-provided information about patients' health and experiences following a clinical encounter. The content of this information is likely to include reports of quality-of-life measures, pain scores, adherence to recommended medications, and ongoing symptoms (Calvert et al. 2013). In many instances, this will include information related to a clinical encounter but is within the scope of expected symptoms (e.g., "I had pain at the incision site"). Other reports may include information that is within the bounds of expected experiences but the extent of which was unanticipated and warrants clinical follow-up (e.g., severe pain and drainage at the incision site that made it impossible for the patient to make dinner for his family for the past several days). This information may have health implications and therefore be clinically actionable (Wolf et al. 2008).

Because much of the information contained in a completed PRO measure is inseparable from clinically relevant data, we follow Richardson and Belsky in recognizing that there is a high degree of "entrustment" between research participants and investigators when it comes to their obligations to address healthcare needs of participants (Richardson and Belsky 2004). As such, we accept that investigators have a strong duty to care when an actionable health need is identified in the process of research data collection (i.e., to provide or facilitate provision of ancillary care based on clinically relevant information discovered in a completed PRO measure). We also agree with Belsky and Richardson that researchers have no obligation to seek out healthcare needs beyond the scope of what investigators ask for in the PRO and what research participants permit in their informed consent. More specifically, "the permission [provided by participants] entrusts only specific aspects of their health to researchers [in the context of PRO research, data found in specific completed PRO measures], *not their health in general*" (Belsky and Richardson 2004, 1495, emphasis added). Searches for clinically relevant information not specifically contained in a completed PRO measure are not likely to reveal significantly more actionable incidents than what would emerge in the regular course of PRO data review and would unnecessarily conflate the goals of research with the goals of clinical care.

Instead of searching for all possible occurrences of actionable data present in but outside the scope of a specific PRO measure, we propose that PRO research team members be trained to identify "triggers" among the PRO data (e.g., a participant report of symptoms of severe depression on a standard depression rating scale). In practice, the process would involve an initial screen of whether the information is clinically relevant and, if so, who should be notified. Research team members should complete this process, given their familiarity with the context of the research and facility for interpreting PRO scores, and it should occur in a timely fashion. It also should be made clear in the EHR those situations in which PRO data are for research purposes only and thus should only be viewed by members of the research team unless directed otherwise—a "break seal only in the case of emergency" approach. It may, in fact, be possible to technically limit permissions for who can view PRO data in the EHR only to those associated with the research team or who have been authorized by the principal investigator (PI) to view PRO data that have been identified as clinically relevant. Although not failsafe, limiting access in this way could add a layer of privacy protection for participants. This approach is justified by the principle of beneficence—it maximizes benefits while neither compromising the ability to produce generalizable knowledge nor unjustifiably breaching participant expectations of privacy—and is supported by a duty to care created by the nature of PRO research.

The practical goal of the proposed approach is twofold. First, researchers ought to feel confident in their ethical responsibilities when engaging in the type of research outlined in the preceding case description. It should be made clear to investigators that research involving PROs linked to individual participants' EHRs creates a relatively novel research setting where the boundaries between research commitments and clinical commitments might be blurred. Second, concerns about clinically relevant information should not detract significantly from the scientific goals of the research. The intention of using PROs in this context—like most research—is not to provide clinical care but to generate knowledge that would improve the care of future patients. That said, all research involving human subjects must make every effort to minimize harm and maximize benefit, and information that falls within the scope of research aims should be assessed for its potential to affect the health and well-being of research participants.

More empirical research investigating participants' general expectations regarding both access to PRO data linked to their EHRs and disclosure of information researchers believe to be clinically relevant to third parties ought to be conducted. The results of this research would further refine our understanding of the ethics involved in PRO research and would facilitate a better understanding of whether PRO research participants find the approach proposed in this commentary commensurate with their expectations. In the meantime, we believe that the framework proposed in this commentary establishes an ethically supportable path forward that will allow investigators conducting this type of patient-centered research to continue to meet their divergent obligations.

References

Belsky, L., and H. S. Richardson, 19 Jun. 2004. Medical researchers' ancillary care responsibilities. *British Medical Journal* 328(7454):1494–96.

Calvert, M., J. Blazeby, D. G. Altman, D. A. Revicki, D. Moher, M. D. Brundage; CONSORT PRO Group. 2013. Reporting of patient-reported outcomes in randomized trials: The CONSORT PRO extension. *Journal of the American Medical Association* 309:814–22.

Richardson, H. S., and L. Belsky. 2004. The ancillary-care responsibilities of medical researchers: An ethical framework for thinking about the clinical care that researchers owe their subjects. *Hastings Center Report* 34(1):25–33.

Wolf, S. M., F. P. Lawrenz, C. A. Nelson, et al. 2008. Managing incidental findings in human subjects research. *Journal of Law, Medicine & Ethics* 36(2): 219–48.

CASE 4.2: A TRIAL TO TEST A NOVEL APPROACH TO DIABETES PREVENTION

INTRODUCTION

Randomization is generally considered ethically sound when there is uncertainty about whether the novel treatment to be tested against the standard treatment (or placebo when warranted) is of potential benefit to eligible participants. The study under consideration plans to randomize patients at risk of type 2 diabetes to positive airway pressure (PAP) therapy to prevent the progression from prediabetes to type 2 diabetes. PAP is often prescribed to those suffering from sleep apnea. Potentially eligible patients at risk of diabetes will be identified and recruited from a general clinic population, not from those patients actively seeking care for obstructive sleep apnea (OSA). The prevalence of diabetes worldwide has been growing at an alarming rate (International Diabetes Federation 2015). It is well established that individuals with diabetes are at an elevated risk to develop heart disease, stroke, and death due to other vascular causes (Sarwar et al. 2010). Although pharmacologic therapy and weight loss postpone disease onset, progression to diabetes still occurs in the vast majority of those with prediabetes.

There is a growing recognition that OSA may be an independent risk factor for diabetes (Wang et al. 2013). OSA is associated with intermittent hypoxemia (low concentration of oxygen in blood) and sleep fragmentation, which can impair insulin sensitivity and possibly impair insulin secretion. It is hypothesized that treatment of OSA can improve insulin sensitivity and glucose disposal, preventing the conversion of prediabetes to diabetes.

A research ethics consultation was sought in the development of a clinical trial to determine whether exposure to PAP therapy could prevent conversion from prediabetes to diabetes. Accompanying the case summary are three commentaries. Jennifer B. McCormick, from the Department of Humanities at Penn State College of Medicine; Joel T. Wu, from the Division of Health Policy and Management at the University of Minnesota School of Public Health and the Clinical Ethics Department at Children's Minnesota; and Adélaïde Doussau, from the Biomedical Ethics Unit at McGill University School of Medicine, consider the case and conclude that the study as designed is ethical if the consent process is meaningful, if participants are offered appropriate referrals if they choose to not enroll or choose to withdraw, and if the objective of the study is explanatory rather than pragmatic. Holly A. Taylor, from Johns Hopkins Bloomberg School of Public Health and Johns Hopkins Berman Institute of Bioethics, and Naresh M. Punjabi, from the Johns Hopkins School of Medicine, agree with McCormick and colleagues and highlight the limited number of eligible patients who seek and/or are adherent with PAP compared to the large number who may benefit and affordable posttrial access for those who want to continue on or have access to PAP. D. Gibbes Miller and Scott Y. H. Kim, from the Department of Bioethics at the National Institutes of Health, conclude that the trial as designed has inadequate social value and lacks the potential to produce clinically relevant findings to justify exposing potential participants to the level of risks and burden described.

CASE SUMMARY

The overall objective of the proposed multicenter randomized controlled trial (RCT) is to determine whether treatment of moderate to severe OSA with PAP therapy, in addition to an effective lifestyle coaching program, will decrease the number of people with prediabetes who convert to diabetes.

Eligible participants will be randomized to either PAP therapy with lifestyle coaching or lifestyle coaching alone based on the U.S. Diabetes Prevention Program (DPP) intervention (The Diabetes Prevention Program 1999). The DPP has been found to be effective in preventing prediabetes-to-diabetes conversion. Patients not currently seeking care for OSA will be recruited via EHRs and public advertising (Ackermann and Marrero 2007; Whittemore 2011). Patients who are screened and found to have prediabetes and moderate to severe OSA will be asked whether they want to join the trial.

Adherence to PAP therapy is perhaps the most cited challenge in clinical trials related to OSA. Instituting motivational enhancement therapy (MET) with the introduction of PAP improves adherence (Bakker et al. 2016). A related challenge of equal importance to PAP adherence is defining the amount (or dose) of PAP use needed to yield benefit. The proposed trial will (1) utilize a run-in period to identify people who are likely to use PAP therapy consistently, and (2) incorporate the principles of MET to optimize PAP adherence. The research question is not whether PAP is effective in treatment of OSA but whether exposure to PAP will reduce the likelihood that a prediabetes patient converts to diabetes. The key ethical issue is whether and/or under what circumstances participants recruited from the general community diagnosed with moderate to severe OSA during a screening for eligibility should be randomized to a study arm that does not include PAP.

REFERENCES

Ackermann, R. T., and D. G. Marrero. 2007. Adapting the diabetes prevention program lifestyle intervention for delivery in the community: The YMCA Model. *Diabetes Education* 33(1):69, 74–75, 78.

Bakker, J. P., R. Wang, J. Weng, et al. 2016. Motivational enhancement for increasing adherence to CPAP: A randomized controlled trial. *Chest* 150 (2):337–45.

International Diabetes Federation. 2015. *IDF diabetes atlas*, 7th ed. Brussels, Belgium: International Diabetes Federation.

Sarwar, N., P. Gao, S. R. K. Seshasai, et al. 2010. Diabetes mellitus, fasting blood glucose concentration, and risk of vascular disease: A collaborative meta-analysis of 102 prospective studies. *Lancet* 375 (9733):2215–22.

The Diabetes Prevention Program. 1999. Design and methods for a clinical trial in the prevention of type 2 diabetes. *Diabetes Care* 22(4):623–34.

Wang, X., Y. Bi, Q. Zhang, and F. Pan. 2013. Obstructive sleep apnoea and the risk of type 2 diabetes: A meta-analysis of prospective cohort studies. *Respirology* 18(1):140–46.

Whittemore, R. 2011. A systematic review of the translational research on the diabetes prevention program. *Translational Behavioral Medicine* 1(3):480–91.

COMMENTARY 4.2.1: IS IT ETHICALLY ACCEPTABLE TO SCREEN PATIENTS FOR OBSTRUCTIVE SLEEP APNEA AND NOT OFFER THEM POSITIVE AIRWAY PRESSURE THERAPY IN A CLINICAL TRIAL?

JENNIFER B. McCORMICK, JOEL T. WU, AND ADÉLAÏDE DOUSSAU

The study in question proposes to examine a preventative intervention for type 2 diabetes (T2D). When considering the ethical nature of a research study, we find it helpful to specify the potential social relevance or importance of the research study's goals (Emanuel, Wendler, and Grady 2000). T2D has numerous comorbidities, can lead to death, and incurs an approximately $254 billion cost on society ($176 billion in direct medical costs and $69 billion in reduced productivity) annually (American Diabetes Association 2013). Identifying mechanisms to limit the progression of prediabetes to T2D has the potential for significant impact by reducing harms and costs, both at the individual and at the societal levels.

Our next step is to evaluate the approach the investigators propose. First, we ask: What evidence supports the proposed intervention? Studies suggest that OSA increases the risk of being diagnosed with T2D due to the negative impact of sleep disruptions and oxygen desaturation that occur as a result of sleep apnea–related conditions (Collop 2007). PAP therapy is a known and effective intervention for OSA; however, the study question here is not about the resolution of OSA. Rather, the aim of this study is to describe how a standard intervention for prediabetes when combined with PAP affects progression to T2D.

This proposed study is a RCT involving individuals with prediabetes and moderate to severe OSA who are currently not seeking treatment for their OSA. The fundamental concern here would be what the benefit–risk ratio is for participants in both arms of the trial. If the ratio is significantly different, then is it ethically permissible to randomize these specific participants into a control arm that does not receive the PAP intervention, given the health status of eligible participants?

PAP is not always considered the first line of therapy for individuals with OSA; for those individuals who are overweight or obese, lifestyle change including losing weight and exercise is the recommended therapy. Both arms will receive lifestyle coaching that has been successfully demonstrated to benefit overweight, prediabetic individuals.

We suggest that the control arm (non-PAP) will potentially provide benefit to individuals with OSA, given that diet, exercise, and lifestyle change are collectively a recognized first-line intervention in the care for overweight and obese individuals with OSA. That is, control-arm participants are being offered appropriate care given their health status. As such, randomizing participants to the control arm would not expose them to any risk exceeding the risks they would encounter if not participating in the study.

If the hypothesis of the study is confirmed, we could consider the possibility that there is a higher risk for individuals to convert to T2D during the course of study in the control arm than in the experimental arm. One might then argue that could have been prevented had they been randomized to the experimental arm. However, this is not a valid argument: The effect of the intervention prior to the study was uncertain. This uncertainty, also known as clinical equipoise, is a necessary aspect of ethical clinical research. There must be a real uncertainty about the relative efficacy of the intervention prior to the trial for the trial to have scientific merit, and also for the trial to be ethically permissible. Since there is equipoise, we conclude randomization as the investigators describe is ethically justifiable (Freedman 1987). Finally, when the study is completed, any individual in the control arm will be free to seek treatment for his OSA. Furthermore, should the study findings suggest that PAP therapy helps prevent T2D, the study team should share this information with all participants and provide them with resources to learn more about PAP therapy and how to obtain it.

Clear and meaningful informed consent is important. As with any other study, investigators will need to be transparent about the study goal: to obtain data on whether exposure to PAP can reduce the likelihood that a prediabetes patient converts to T2D. It is also critical that participants are made aware of their current risk for conversion to T2D, and that they understand that participation in the study may not reduce their risk for T2D any more than the standard interventions available.

In addition, individuals should be informed of the alternatives to study participation. This would include that if they want to be sure to be able to access the PAP, they could seek access to it outside the study, but that if they do so they would be ineligible for the study. Thus, if some enrolled participants do not understand what participation entails and do not accept the likelihood of not receiving the PAP, there is a risk for participants randomized to the control group dropping out if they later decide to begin PAP therapy for their sleep apnea. This in turn could be a threat for the validity of the study.

Furthermore, those who are screened and not enrolled due to intolerance to PAP should also be provided with an adequate referral for OSA. Indeed, another aspect of the study that calls for some ethical consideration is that all screened participants will undergo a run-in with the PAP to confirm eligibility to be randomized. This can be justified due to the high proportion of individuals not tolerating PAP; not doing this run-in would lead to a high proportion of participants randomized to the experimental arm being unable to receive the intervention. However, there are two issues: one for screened participants and the other for the practical application of the findings. First, some participants will be diagnosed with OSA and not enrolled in the trial due to intolerance to PAP; thus, a proper care plan should be provided to them, given that they are identified as participants with high risk factors for cardiovascular complications. Implementing a lead-in before randomization can be a reasonable option in an explanatory trial where the objective is to isolate the effect of the intervention under optimal experimental conditions (Schwartz and Lellouch 2009). Second, should the investigators want to evaluate the benefit of the intervention in a pragmatic trial, it would be advisable not to conduct the lead-in, so that the impact of the intervention can be based on both efficacy and tolerance in a broader population. While we do conclude that the lead-in can be justified in this case, it has ethical implications both for screened participants and for the social value of the study (Emanuel, Wendler, and Grady 2000).

The key ethical question the investigators have is whether participants recruited from the general community who are diagnosed during a study screening with moderate to severe OSA can be randomized to the control study arm, and how to ensure the welfare of those screened who cannot be randomized due to PAP intolerance. We determined that the planned study design is ethical if a meaningful informed consent process is followed by the investigators, appropriate referrals are offered, and the objective of the study is explanatory rather than pragmatic. These will ensure protection and respect of the participants and optimal social value.

References

American Diabetes Association. 2013. Economic costs of diabetes in the U.S. in 2012. *Diabetes Care*. Available at: https://doi.org/10.2337/dc12-2625

Collop, N. A. 2007. The effect of obstructive sleep apnea on chronic medical disorders. *Cleveland Clinic Journal of Medicine* 74(1):72–8.

Emanuel, E. J., D. Wendler, and C. Grady. 2000. What makes clinical research ethical? *Journal of the American Medical Association* 283:2711.

Freedman, B. 1987. Equipoise and the ethics of clinical research. *New England Journal of Medicine* 317:141–5.

Schwartz, D., and J. Lellouch. 2009. Explanatory and pragmatic attitudes in therapeutical trials. *Journal of Clinical Epidemiology* 62(5):499–505.

COMMENTARY 4.2.2: CAN WE BREATHE EASY IF PAP THERAPY IS WITHHELD?

HOLLY A. TAYLOR AND NARESH M. PUNJABI

In answering the key question about this study, we considered two empirical issues as key to our assessment of whether it is ethically acceptable to withhold PAP therapy to those diagnosed with moderate to severe (M/S) OSA. The first regards what is known about diagnosis and treatment of M/S OSA. Being male, getting older, and weight gain are strong predictors of developing M/S OSA (Peppard et al. 2013). According to a recent systematic review, the prevalence of M/S OSA in the general population is between 9 and 38% (Senaratna et al. 2017). Of those with M/S OSA, only 20 to 30% seek treatment and are diagnosed (Kapur et al. 1999). Once an individual is diagnosed, the typical approach is to encourage and facilitate weight loss and/or prescribe PAP therapy (Qaseem et al. 2013). Whether an M/S OSA patient is prescribed PAP may vary depending on the type of healthcare provider who has made the diagnosis (e.g., sleep physician vs. primary care physician). Obviously, those who do not seek care are neither diagnosed nor treated (i.e., 70 to 80% of those with M/S OSA). According to a review of 20 years of data, of those who initiate PAP, 30 to 50% are able to be adherent (Rotenberg, Murariu, and Pang 2016).

Taken together, this evidence indicates that there are a large number of individuals in the population with undiagnosed and untreated M/S OSA. One conclusion from this analysis would be to advocate for efforts to raise awareness of the prevalence of M/S OSA and encourage individuals at risk to seek out diagnosis and care. While this would likely increase the number of patients encouraged to lose weight and/or prescribed PAP, it would leave more than half of the patients at risk of nonadherence and therefore at risk of developing additional health complications such as diabetes. A well-designed trial with an adequate sample size will confirm or disconfirm the benefit of PAP along with lifestyle coaching, leading to a more convincing call for clinical action or inaction and patient motivation for adherence.

A second empirical consideration prior to our ethical analysis is whether there is evidence that individuals diagnosed with M/S OSA are put at an unreasonable amount of risk if they do not initiate PAP and adhere to PAP as soon as they are diagnosed. According to a recent article assessing the value of PAP among patients with coronary or cerebrovascular disease randomized to PAP or sham PAP, PAP has no beneficial effect on cardiovascular risk factors (McEvoy et al. 2016). PAP did improve quality-of-life outcomes (McEvoy et al. 2016). These results do not indicate that withholding PAP has no physical risk but that the impact of postponing treatment is likely minimal, and/or the quality-of-life implications could be easily described to a potential subject who could then make an informed decision about enrollment. That is, are subjects willing to risk that exposure to lifestyle intervention alone will reduce their risk of sleep apnea?

All of the preceding leaves us to conclude that, with consent, voluntary withholding of PAP therapy from patients diagnosed with M/S OSA recruited from the general community who are otherwise not seeking medical attention would not expose individuals to undue risk. We conclude that, with the adoption of the three conditions that follow, this study could be conducted ethically.

Alternatives are offered to those identified as eligible for the trial

Once diagnosed with M/S OSA, eligible patients ought to be offered the option of enrolling in the trial or being referred to a physician for clinical follow-up. This assures the patients that they do not have to enroll in the trial to receive typical care. This requires that the study team identify in advance a resource for referral, including for those who do not currently have access to health insurance. For example, this may be referral to a resource at the institution that assists patients in accessing public benefits for which they are eligible or accessing a clinic that provides care for free or at a reduced rate.

Follow-up of those who enroll but decide they are no longer willing to continue with PAP or do not want to initiate PAP

Once enrolled, a patient ought to be reminded that their participation is voluntary. A participant who wants to withdraw ought to have access to the same route of referral as described above. If possible, the trial could follow those participants who cross over during the trial. Such an option could respect the fact that participants may change their mind, as well as facilitate further data collection relevant to the research question and track how often such a request occurs and how often in either direction. The latter may have implications for how clinical care is delivered after the trial is completed.

Adopting both of these approaches may have implications for the success of the trial. If too many individuals opt for PAP off trial, accrual may lag. If many more subjects once enrolled opt to seek PAP off trial, the comparability of the two arms of the study will be reduced. On the other hand, if potential subjects are well informed, they may favor the option of preventing the onset of diabetes by engaging in exercise and being well monitored while enrolled, compared to the relative discomfort of PAP. We would suggest that the study team track these outcomes carefully as the trial progresses and make adjustments as needed.

Access to PAP at the end of the trial

Any participant who would like to continue with PAP therapy ought to have the opportunity to do so. If participants have a primary care physician, the study ought to share relevant details with the physician, with the patients' permission, to facilitate a transfer of care. If a patient would like to continue but does not have a primary care physician, the study team should refer the patient to a resource to facilitate continued access, similar to those who chose clinical care rather than enrolling in the study.

References

Kapur, V., D. K. Blough, R. E. Sandblom, et al. 1999. The medical cost of undiagnosed sleep apnea. *Sleep* 22(6):749–55.

McEvoy, R. D., N. A. Antic, E. Heeley, et al. 2016. CPAP for prevention of cardiovascular events in obstructive sleep apnea. *New England Journal of Medicine* 375:919–31.

Peppard, P. E., T. Young, J. H. Barnet, M. Palta, E. W. Hagen, and K. M. Hla. 2013. Increased prevalence of sleep-disordered breathing in adults. *American Journal of Epidemiology* 177(9):1006–14.

Qaseem, A., J. E. Holty, D. K. Owens, P. Dallas, M. Starkey, and P. Shekelle. 2013. Clinical guidelines committee of the American College of Physicians. Management of obstructive sleep apnea in adults: A clinical practice guideline from the American College of Physicians. *Annals of Internal Medicine* 159(7):471–83.

Rotenberg, B. W., D. Murariu, and K. P. Pang. 2016. Trends in CPAP adherence over twenty years of data collection: A flattened curve. *Journal of Otolaryngology—Head and Neck Surgery* 45(1):43.

Senaratna, C. V., J. L. Perret, C. J. Lodge, et al. 2017. Prevalence of obstructive sleep apnea in the general population: A systematic review. *Sleep Medicine Reviews* 34:70–81. pii:S1087-0792(16)30064-8.

COMMENTARY 4.2.3: RISKS OF CLINICAL RESEARCH MUST BE REASONABLE AND NECESSARY

D. GIBBES MILLER AND SCOTT Y. H. KIM

A central ethical issue in evaluating a clinical trial is whether a study's scientific and clinical value justifies the risks and burdens imposed on research subjects. We are doubtful that this justification is present for the proposed RCT—at least as the study's rationale and design are described.

Value of the clinical trial

The proposed study asks whether treating prediabetic patients who have moderate to severe OSA with PAP therapy, along with lifestyle coaching, will decrease the risk of converting from prediabetes to diabetes. The trial provides an opportunity to establish proof-of-concept that OSA contributes to the development of diabetes, and a positive result might eventually reinforce the use of PAP therapy among prediabetic patients with OSA. However, the study's value is limited by two factors.

First, since the trial participants have both prediabetes and moderate to severe OSA, PAP is already an indicated treatment for all trial participants (Qaseem et al. 2013). Thus, even a positive result is not likely to alter clinical practice substantially because it will not expand the group of patients indicated to receive PAP therapy. Second, this trial uses a run-in period to identify participants who are most likely to adhere to PAP therapy, in order to boost observed PAP effects (if any). This limits the study's generalizability because in ordinary practice, clinicians will not face only those patients who are likely to use PAP.

We therefore wonder how much clinical value this study adds. At best, a positive trial result might reiterate the benefits of PAP therapy or assess a pathophysiological hypothesis about PAP therapy for prediabetics with OSA. However, it is not clear that the proposed design is appropriate, given these limited goals.

Risks of research participation

In this trial, clinical equipoise exists for prediabetes but not for OSA. In fact, when considering prediabetes alone, the risk–benefit ratio of participation seems favorable since all participants will receive lifestyle coaching (a standard intervention for prediabetes), and risks associated with PAP therapy are low (Qaseem et al. 2013).

When considering OSA, however, the risk–benefit ratio is more complicated. Because PAP therapy is an indicated treatment for all participants, it is important to consider the risks the control participants will take on by forgoing PAP therapy for the duration of the trial. For patients with moderate to severe OSA, forgoing PAP therapy means forgoing its potential benefits such as improvements in blood pressure, daytime sleepiness, memory, and daily functioning (Qaseem et al. 2013). There are also emerging data showing that PAP therapy may decrease one's risk of serious cardiac morbidity and mortality among those with OSA if they maintain high adherence to the therapy. Although observational studies have shown mixed results, some have shown significant reductions in mortality with PAP therapy (Qaseem et al. 2013). A recent international multicenter RCT did not find significant effects of PAP therapy on risk of cardiovascular events or mortality (McEvoy et al. 2016), but limitations of the trial (such as low PAP adherence rate in the intervention arm) may have decreased its ability to detect possible mortality differences (Mokhlesi and Ayas 2016). A large two-year RCT in Greece comparing standard PAP versus an intensive PAP (to increase adherence) showed—even compared to an active PAP arm—that higher adherence among the intensive-PAP group resulted in significantly fewer deaths and hospitalizations (Bouloukaki et al. 2014). Even if the data are not yet definitive, if the proposed RCT identifies persons with OSA who are willing to use PAP with a high likelihood of adherence, then asking them to forgo its use would mean asking them to risk higher rates of serious morbidity and mortality.

It is worth emphasizing that the risks faced by the trial participants are amplified by the use of a run-in period. The selected patients are those most likely to benefit from PAP therapy. Consequently, the selected participants (compared to a standard OSA population) are at greatest risk of forgoing significant clinical benefits if placed in the control arm.

Permissibility of forgoing effective treatment in clinical trials

Even if the control arm does face greater risk of negative events, does this risk exceed what should be allowed in a clinical trial like this one? The debate over the use of placebos in RCTs when effective treatments exist provides a framework for considering the permissible level of risk that study participants can be asked to take on. Considerable debate exists about the exact threshold of permissible risk in such situations, but there is agreement that the use of placebos (or otherwise untreated controls) is unethical if it would increase risk of mortality or serious, long-term morbidity (Emanuel and Miller 2001; Temple and Ellenberg 2000), while some also include the risk of severe discomfort or serious but reversible harm (Emanuel and Miller 2001).

Conclusions and recommendations

With the limited information provided in the case report (e.g., it is not clear how long the intervention period is), it is not possible to provide conclusive recommendations. We therefore highlight issues that the investigators and their IRBs should consider.

First, are the control-arm subjects being asked to forgo likely reduction in risk of serious morbidity and mortality? There is some evidence to suggest this to be the case. Independent expert input should determine this issue. If the answer is affirmative, then by any account, the study goes beyond the currently accepted level of permitted risk in RCTs. Furthermore, the no-PAP control arm cannot be justified by the reasoning that "they aren't getting the treatment outside the RCT anyway." Once these participants are identified and are allocated to the control arm, they are taking on risks attributable to research since the investigators are controlling the allocation of interventions. After all, the investigators do not know whether those patients would in fact have gone on to receive PAP outside the trial, even if, at the time the participants were identified, they were not receiving PAP.

Second, even if it is debatable whether the risks to subjects would involve increased morbidity and mortality, IRBs must determine whether the risks and burdens are justified by the benefits, and whether the risks are minimized in pursuing the scientific question. At least as currently described, the scientific and clinical value of the proposed RCT seems limited—even positive results will not likely change clinical decisions. Furthermore, the mandate to minimize research risks probably requires that other trial designs be considered to answer the scientific question, for example by "piggybacking" onto a larger PAP therapy trial or by using a different type of control arm (similar to Bouloukaki et al. 2014).

The proposed study could provide interesting insights into the relationship between PAP therapy and the development of diabetes. However, the trial's clinical value seems limited, especially when considering the potential risks that participants in the control arm would be taking on by forgoing PAP therapy. This concern is increased by the "enrichment" of the sample with those who are likely to use, and therefore benefit from, PAP therapy.

References

Bouloukaki, I., K. Giannadaki, C. Mermigkis, et al. 2014. Intensive versus standard follow-up to improve continuous positive airway pressure compliance. *European Respiratory Journal* 44(5):1262–74.

Emanuel, E. J., and F. G. Miller. 2001. The ethics of placebo-controlled trials—A middle ground. *New England Journal of Medicine* 345(12):915–19.

McEvoy, R. D., N. A. Antic, E. Heeley, et al. 2016. CPAP for prevention of cardiovascular events in obstructive sleep apnea. *New England Journal of Medicine* 375(10):919–31.

Mokhlesi, B., and N. T. Ayas. 2016. Cardiovascular events in obstructive sleep apnea—Can CPAP therapy SAVE lives? *New England Journal of Medicine* 375(10):994–96.

Qaseem, A., J. E. C. Holty, D. K. Owens, P. Dallas, M. Starkey, and P. Shekelle. 2013. Management of obstructive sleep apnea in adults: A clinical practice guideline from the American college of physicians. *Annals of Internal Medicine* 159(7):471–83.

Temple, R., and S. S. Ellenberg. 2000. Placebo-controlled trials and active-control trials in the evaluation of new treatments: Part 1: Ethical and scientific issues. *Annals of Internal Medicine* 133(6):455–63.

CASE 4.3: IS IT ETHICALLY APPROPRIATE TO REFUSE TO COMPENSATE PARTICIPANTS WHO ARE BELIEVED TO HAVE INTENTIONALLY CONCEALED MEDICAL CONDITIONS?

INTRODUCTION

Whether to compensate research participants, how much to compensate participants, and the role compensation may play in a participant's decision to enroll in research have been long debated in the research ethics literature. In some settings, investigators utilize a screening protocol in advance of enrolling a participant in a trial. The screening protocol is an opportunity to collect medical information and/or biological samples from the participant in order to determine their eligibility. The goal of the screening protocol is most often to screen out individuals for whom enrollment in the research protocol would involve exposure to unnecessary risk. In this case, the investigators sought a research ethics consultation as to whether it was ethically acceptable to withhold compensation when they suspect that potential participants agreed to the screening with the knowledge that a medical condition they have makes them ineligible for the research protocol.

Accompanying the case summary are three commentaries. Holly Fernandez Lynch, Luke Gelinas, and Emily A. Largent from the Department of Medical Ethics and Health Policy at the Perelman School of Medicine, University of Pennsylvania, argue that it is acceptable to withhold compensation when the consequences of deception are clear from the start. They conclude that such disclosure avoids burden and waste all around, and also serves to clarify that deceivers are failing to uphold their end of the mutual obligations of research participation. They add that, in the case of a medical condition diagnosed during the screening process, it may be hard to determine whether the participant knew of their status in advance. Marion Danis, Sam Doernberg, Matthew Memoli, and Joseph Millum from the Bioethics Department of the Clinical Center at the National Institutes of Health argue that, in the case of a participant who fails to disclose a medical condition, it may be hard to distinguish lying from ignorance, and they conclude that the participant ought to be excluded from participation but compensated for their time. Rosamond Rhodes and Michael Danziger from the Icahn School of Medicine at Mount Sinai agree with Lynch and colleagues with regard to the importance of disclosing the circumstances under which compensation will be withheld. They conclude that the participant ought to be compensated even when found to have knowingly withheld information relevant to his or her eligibility to the investigators, as the participant invested time and energy in the screening process.

CASE SUMMARY

A clinical investigator has been conducting virus challenge studies. Such studies involve the deliberate inoculation of a host with a virus, allowing for improved understanding of the infecting pathogen and testing of vaccine candidates. Volunteers in such studies need to be healthy individuals so they are at less risk of complications of infection. They need to be willing to reside in an inpatient unit for a period of time so that they can be observed carefully and so that they do not expose others who might be at greater risk from such infections, such as children and the elderly. The investigator and his team have a screening protocol through which they identify appropriate participants for the challenge studies. The screening protocol allows the research team to exclude individuals who use either prescribed or recreational drugs and individuals who have certain chronic medical conditions. There are two justifications for these exclusion criteria. The first concerns safety: For example, cocaine use can increase the risk of myocardial infarction, and inhaled drugs can increase susceptibility to respiratory infections. The second concern relates to confounding of study results: Drugs and chronic illnesses can cause clinical symptoms and laboratory abnormalities that would make adverse events difficult to interpret.

The screening consists of a single visit to the research center and involves a questionnaire, clinical evaluation, and diagnostic workup. Participants are compensated $100 at completion of the screening. Individuals who pass the screening protocol can participate in the challenge study itself.

Several years ago, the study team found that multiple participants who were using illicit drugs had participated in the screening protocol, presumably for the compensation. It was assumed that these participants had lied when asked about their drug use, as determined through drug tests that the study team runs on each screened individual. The study team submitted to the IRB a protocol amendment, which was approved, stating that participants in the screening protocol who lied about their drug use would not be compensated if the drug test later found them to be using drugs. Participants who were honest in acknowledging their drug use would still be compensated for the time required to attend the screening visit. The justification relates to trust: If the investigator knows that an individual has not disclosed relevant information during screening, the investigator might doubt the veracity of subsequent reporting of information by the study participant during participation in the challenge study. In turn, this may affect the health and safety of participants and others and the quality of the data collected.

Recently, the study team has identified several instances of participants apparently lying about exclusionary medical conditions, including asthma and HIV. In both cases, the study team found out about these medical conditions from medical records related to prior enrollment or attempted enrollment in other protocols at the research center.

The study team considered amending the protocol to deny compensation to participants in the screening protocol who were discovered to have not reported an exclusionary medical condition. An ethics consultation was requested to consider whether it is ethically appropriate for a research team to refuse to compensate participants who are believed to have intentionally concealed medical conditions.

COMMENTARY 4.3.1: MUTUAL OBLIGATIONS IN RESEARCH AND WITHHOLDING PAYMENT FROM DECEPTIVE PARTICIPANTS

HOLLY FERNANDEZ LYNCH, LUKE GELINAS, AND EMILY A. LARGENT

Paying research participants can be ethically charged, both when payment is offered and—as demonstrated in this case—when it is withheld. When individuals undergoing screening intentionally deceive investigators as to their eligibility, withholding payment to which they would otherwise be entitled is both ethically acceptable and practically important.

The problem of payment-induced deception

In addition to conceptual concerns related to the validity of informed consent, one worry about offering payment to research participants is that such offers will induce them to lie about eligibility criteria or other factors, such as experiencing adverse events. This sort of deception is problematic because it may place research participants at increased risk of harm and/or jeopardize the scientific integrity and social value of the study (Largent and Lynch 2017a). Thus, investigators are prudent to take steps to avoid payment-induced deception.

Although deception was evident to the investigators in this case, it is important to note that the frequency of payment-induced deception in research is unknown. In one study of 100 "experienced research participants" (all of whom had participated in at least two studies during the past year), three-quarters self-reported that they had, at some point in their life, concealed information from investigators to avoid exclusion, and one-third had engaged in some form of fabrication (Devine et al. 2013). This study did not assess the relationship between payment and deception, although there is anecdotal evidence of a link, particularly among "professional" Phase I participants (Walker, Cottingham, and

Fisher 2018). Another study assessing the reactions of pharmacy students to offers of payment for a hypothetical study showed that higher payments may influence behaviors around concealing information about restricted activities (Bentley and Thacker 2004).

Relevant principles

More evidence is needed, but common sense suggests that payment-induced deception can be a legitimate concern. How, then, should deception by research participants be addressed? Two principles can help resolve the apparent ethical dilemma: (1) consistency, or asking how similar deception would be handled outside the research setting; and (2) responsibility, or acknowledging the obligations of potential research participants.

AVOIDING PAYMENT EXCEPTIONALISM

Consider the following example: A hospital advertises a job for a Spanish-speaking interpreter. During the interview process, candidates sit for a proficiency exam and conduct a mock patient interview, for which they are paid $100 for their time. Imagine that a non-Spanish-speaking individual hoping to make an easy $100 applies, knowing that he does not meet the obvious criterion. Even if the applicant sits through the exam and interview, it seems reasonable to withhold payment when it becomes evident that he lied about his qualifications. He could have easily avoided wasting his time by being truthful, and he made no meaningful contribution to the hospital's search process. Now imagine a second applicant who applies in good faith, but whose Spanish is determined through screening not to be good enough. Paying this individual for completing the screening would be appropriate, as the purpose of the screening was served.

This seems to be a clear-cut case. Why, then, should we feel any differently about research? We (EL and HFL) have argued elsewhere that exceptionalism as to paying research participants is unjustified (Largent and Lynch 2017b). If we are comfortable paying people to take on risks, burdens, and uncertainty for the benefit of others outside of the research context, we should be comfortable doing so for research participants as well. The reverse is also true: If payment could be withheld outside research in the face of evident deception about obviously meaningful aspects of whatever it is that payment is being offered for, the same should be true in the research setting. There is nothing exceptional about research participants that suggests they need to be insulated from the consequences of violating basic social norms.

RECOGNIZING RESEARCH AS A MUTUAL ENDEAVOR

It is also important to recognize that participating in research is a mutual endeavor. Investigators commit to adequately protecting research participants, to enrolling them only in research that is socially valuable, and—sometimes—to paying them. But these commitments are not one-sided; investigators make these promises to research participants in exchange for the participants' agreement to contribute to the advancement of science. Thus, research participants should be expected to be truthful and not misleading during screening and to otherwise comply with the clearly stated terms of research participation—for example, to show up for study appointments, take medications as indicated, and report adverse events.

The question of whether individuals should be paid despite knowingly and purposefully lying to investigators about relevant information strongly implies that they lack obligations to the research enterprise for which they can be held to account. This is not only exceptional as compared to other endeavors that involve reciprocity, but also disrespectful and infantilizing of research participants. Respecting and protecting participants do not entail rewarding them for behaving badly. To the contrary, potential or enrolled participants should not be permitted to deceive without consequence, given the potentially serious consequences of such deception for them and for research. For research to succeed, participants need to be able to count on investigators, and vice versa.

Application to the case

With these tools in hand—avoidance of payment exceptionalism and recognition of research as a mutual endeavor—we can turn to solutions to the problem of payment-induced deception at the screening phase of study recruitment, as seen in this case.

One potential approach might be to simply avoid payment altogether to prevent the temptation of deception. Withholding payment from all individuals in order to prevent some from deceiving, however, risks inadequate recruitment and may fail to fairly compensate the real burdens incurred during extensive screening (Largent and Lynch 2017a). Thus, it is not an ideal solution, and certainly not the only one.

A more promising approach would be to design the screening process to minimize the possibility of lying. For example, whenever possible, it is best to rely on objective measures rather than self-reports regarding eligibility criteria. As an additional safeguard, to the extent that there are any criteria that seem to be most susceptible to deception (or most dangerous should deception occur) in a given study, it is ideal to assess them as early in the screening process as possible to quickly identify ineligible individuals, saving burdens and resources for all parties.

As a next step, when payment is being offered for screening, it is important to be clear about the conditions that must be met to receive it. Stating that there will be no payment if deliberate deception about eligibility criteria is detected alerts potential participants to the consequences of lying and is likely to dissuade at least some would-be deceivers. It is important to avoid the appearance of (or actually) behaving punitively toward potential participants, which is potentially damaging to the research enterprise and not permitted by research regulations. However, when the terms on which payment would be provided are clear and appropriate, withholding payment in the face of deception is not punitive because there is no entitlement to payment when those terms are not satisfied. Instead, it is simply refusal to pay for a service not provided, and can be explained as such.

Ultimately, there are three types of potential participants who may seek to proceed with screening once the consequences of deception are made clear: (1) individuals who are in fact eligible; (2) individuals who reasonably believe they may be eligible, but turn out not to be; and (3) individuals who know they are not eligible, but seek to deceive. Paying individuals in categories 1 and 2 is appropriate because they have not been deceptive and have fulfilled their obligations to the investigators. However, it is ethically appropriate to withhold payment from individuals in category 3, and doing so may be important to preserve the scientific integrity of research. These individuals have adequate information to know better than to proceed with a screening visit, and therefore could have avoided any burdens they ultimately undertake in screening simply by being truthful; a burden need not always be compensated with payment if the individual could have reasonably avoided it because he knows, or should know, that he does not satisfy conditions for receiving payment. Although the issue becomes somewhat more challenging if deception is not uncovered until after enrollment, the same principles apply, such that it may be appropriate to withhold payment from deceivers in that context as well. Again, because the participant can easily self-protect in these cases, it is not unfair to impose consequences for inappropriate enrollment.

Discretion is important in these cases, however. Payment should only be withheld for deception as to elements that are important to participant protection or study integrity, and it should go without saying that the point is certainly not to catch participants on "technicalities" to avoid having to pay them. Moreover, it will not always be possible for investigators to know with certainty that an individual has been deceptive. For example, if eligibility is conditioned on being HIV− negative and an individual says he is HIV− but then tests positive, this could be a case of mistake or ignorance about one's HIV status.

Under the circumstances, it is reasonable to give the potential participant the benefit of the doubt. For other types of eligibility criteria not subject to similar mistakes or ignorance, such as recent illicit drug use, deception may be identified with greater certainty, and payment can justifiably be withheld.

Conclusion

Although it is certainly true that some individuals will lie out of financial need rather than malice, this is a larger problem beyond the scope of the research enterprise to resolve. Making the consequences of deception clear from the start avoids burden and waste all around, and also serves to clarify that deceivers are failing to uphold their end of the mutual obligations of research participation. As a rule, when the terms of payment are clear, it is reasonable to withhold payment from deliberately deceptive individuals seeking to enroll or participating in research. Cheating should not pay.

References

Bentley, J. P., and P. G. Thacker. 2004. The influence of risk and monetary payment on the research participation decision making process. *Journal of Medical Ethics* 30(3):293–98.

Devine, E. G., M. E. Waters, M. Putnam, et al. 2013. Concealment and fabrication by experienced research subjects. *Clinical Trials* 10:935–48.

Largent, E. A., and H. F. Lynch. 2017a. Paying research participants: The outsized influence of 'undue influence.' *IRB: Ethics & Human Research* 39(4):1–9.

Largent, E. A., and H. F. Lynch. 2017b. Paying research participants: Regulatory uncertainty, conceptual confusion, and a path forward. *Yale Journal of Health Policy, Law, and Ethics* 17(1):61–141.

Walker, R. L., M. D. Cottingham, and J. A. Fisher. 2018. Serial participation and the ethics of phase 1 healthy volunteer research. *Journal of Medicine and Philosophy* 43(1):83–114.

COMMENTARY 4.3.2: BEST TO EXCLUDE BUT PAY

MARION DANIS, SAM DOERNBERG, MATTHEW MEMOLI, AND JOSEPH MILLUM

Surveys indicate that a substantial percentage of research participants provide inaccurate information to investigators. In a survey of 100 individuals who had previously enrolled in at least two studies in the prior year, Devine and colleagues found that many respondents reported concealing some health information from researchers to avoid exclusion from enrollment in a study (Devine et al. 2013). Health problems had been concealed by 32% of the sample, use of prescribed medications by 28%, and recreational drug use by 20%. One-fourth of participants reported exaggerating symptoms in order to qualify for a study, and 14% reported pretending to have a health condition in order to qualify (Devine et al. 2013). Thus, the problem brought to the consultants in this consultation request is a prevalent one.

The justification for excluding individuals who attempt to deceive the investigators from protocols is compelling. If included in the study, the participants may compromise the study findings, may be at greater risk of physical harm, and—in studies like the one under consideration—may put personal contacts at greater risk of harm. But the decision about enrollment in the vaccine challenge study is separate from the question of whether to reimburse individuals for their participation in screening.

One might think that it is outside the bounds of the relationship for investigators to be judging the actions of prospective research participants and withholding payment on this basis. By analogy, it is usually inappropriate for clinicians to judge their patients. Clinicians are expected to address the health needs of patients regardless of patient behavior, including lying and other forms of deception.

Moralistic judgments are typically irrelevant to the therapeutic interaction and therefore outside the bounds of the relationship.

However, when a patient does something that poses a direct threat to him- or herself or others, or repeatedly exceeds some boundaries of reasonable behavior, it is acceptable for the healthcare provider to judge and respond (Lippman and Davenport 2011). For example, when patients threaten clinical staff, it is justifiable for clinicians to discharge them from their practice; when patients fail to keep appointments without warning, clinicians have the prerogative to charge them for the missed appointment. In both cases, the grounds for imposing these consequences on the patient are that the patient's behavior runs the risk of imposing harms or other negative effects on others. If this analogy holds, it might be reasonable for the investigator not only to exclude participants who intentionally deceived the investigator during the screening process from the vaccine challenge study but also to impose financial consequences by withholding payment.

A more promising argument in favor of paying potential participants who intentionally deceive the investigator during the screening process is based on the epistemic situation of the investigator. It may be fairly straightforward to determine, through a carefully conducted drug-screening test, whether a person is giving a deceptive response to a question about substance use or abuse. But it may be difficult to know whether a person who denies having a chronic disease may have, in all honesty, not known yet of their diagnosis, forgotten the diagnosis, or learned about it under a different name. Thus, it can be difficult to distinguish lying from ignorance. To falsely accuse someone of lying disrespects that person—through the message that it conveys—and is liable to shatter their trust in the investigator and the research enterprise. Under these circumstances, the moral cost entailed in occasionally falsely accusing an individual may outweigh the benefits to be gained for the scientific project and for patient safety. It may be too difficult for investigators to know with certainty that an individual has deceived. Best to exclude but pay.

References

Devine, E. G., M. E. Waters, M. Putnam, et al. 2013. Concealment and fabrication by experienced research subjects. *Clinical Trials* 10:935–48.

Lippman, H., and J. Davenport. 2011. Patient dismissal: The right way to do it. *Journal of Family Practice* 60:135–40.

COMMENTARY 4.3.3: TO PAY OR NOT TO PAY? WITHHOLDING PAYMENT FROM RESEARCH PARTICIPANTS

ROSAMOND RHODES AND MICHAEL DANZIGER

In an ideal world, study participants would always be truthful, compliant with study protocols, and honest reporters of their study-related experiences. This is not, however, an ideal world, and the onus is on investigators to deal with irregularities in human reporting, including concealing information, as well as misremembering or forgetting.

From the researcher's perspective, the effects of intentional and unintentional misleading responses are the same. Misinformation may compromise the findings of their study. Investigators have to account for potential discrepancies in participants' statements in both study design and data analysis.

The investigators in this virus challenge study inquired about prescribed and recreational drug use and chronic medical conditions and expected potential participants to be honest in their responses. Poor health status related to either could put them at risk of complications or contracting infection. Additionally, drug use and chronic illnesses could confound the study results by exacerbating underlying conditions or with unexpected laboratory abnormalities. Whether a potential participant answered honestly may also predict the person's willingness to remain within the inpatient unit during the required time period both for observation and to prevent others from being exposed to the virus. Investigators also need to rely on participants, once enrolled, to report accurate information during the challenge study.

Although denying compensation to participants who had deliberately deceived them seemed appropriate to the investigators and IRB members, we argue that there is no functional difference as it relates to study outcome between the participants who lie and those who failed to remember the same type of information. In other words, the quality of data collected from either participant is equally compromised. This fact raises three questions about the legitimacy of denying compensation: (1) Should all participants be told that they will be paid for completing the screening survey when investigators intend to withhold payment from some of them? (2) Should investigators treat volunteers who mistakenly provide false information differently from those who deliberately try to mislead them? (3) Should volunteers who intentionally conceal information be denied compensation for participating in the screening procedure?

Should all participants be told that they will be paid for completing the screening survey when investigators intend to withhold payment from some of them?

Volunteers travel to the study site and participate in the screening survey only because of what investigators tell them prior to their arrival. In other words, they rely upon what investigators convey.

There is no way of knowing precisely which details were most salient for which volunteer, but, based on past research experience, it is fair to expect that some of those who presented themselves for the screening survey would not have done so without the promise of compensation. If investigators make an offer without intending to honor it, they violate a basic tenet of morality and thereby undermine the trust they need to rely on to complete their work. Particularly when in this case the volunteer has fulfilled her part of an agreement by coming in for the screening, it is a prima facie duty of the investigator to provide compensation. Thus, investigators who intend to deny compensation to some participants must refrain from making a promise that they do not intend to keep.

Should investigators treat volunteers who mistakenly provide false information differently from those who deliberately try to mislead them?

Informing volunteers in advance of a study that payment will be withheld from those who provide inaccurate information could have a positive effect by encouraging casual responders to be more attentive in reporting their history and more thoughtful about considering what information the screening questions are requesting. The threat of withholding payment could also discourage volunteers from concealing information about their medical history that may result in their being deemed ineligible for enrollment. Nevertheless, denying compensation to individuals who are found to have lied during participant screening is ethically problematic.

On the one hand, denying compensation requires a judgment by the investigator that some volunteers are unworthy of the compensation that others will receive. That is disconcerting because medicine and, by extension, biomedical research are committed to being nonjudgmental in patient and participant interactions.

On the other hand, withholding compensation is punitive. Volunteers are punished (in this case, by withholding promised payment for actions already performed) because their intentional deception is discovered by investigators. Punishment is always morally compromising because it involves deliberately inflicting harm on another, that is, doing something that is prima facie wrong. Purposefully inflicting harm on a person can sometimes be justified, but in this case the reasons are not persuasive.

Should volunteers who intentionally conceal information be denied compensation for participating in the screening procedure?

Participants who are found to have deceived investigators have already traveled to the study site and completed the screening survey. Thus, refusing them compensation after the fact serves no study aim. It also devalues the time of participants who invested effort in participation. Even those who lied altered the normal course of their day in order to participate. Therefore, they should be compensated.

The study design employs a two-tiered system of compensation. First, volunteers receive a small payment for completing the screening survey. Second, they receive a more robust amount for participation in the virus challenge study. Participants are given reason to expect that they will be compensated for the time and effort that they invest in undergoing the screening survey. They are led to expect that the second payment is, however, contingent upon satisfying the enrollment criteria and conforming to all of the study requirements. Because volunteers who submit to the screening protocol have given their time and effort, they should be compensated for what they have done.

Participation in activities at the behest of others warrants acknowledgment that the participant's time and efforts could be spent elsewhere. Take the example of jury duty. Jurors receive compensation irrespective of being chosen to serve on a jury. They are remunerated for their time, not for service performed. This practice acknowledges that an individual's time is valuable, even when the service is mandated and only nominally compensated.

In contrast to jury duty, participation in research studies is voluntary and contingent upon the willingness of volunteers to contribute. To maintain this system requires that the trust between researchers and study participants be preserved. Anything that is likely to erode that trust compromises future research by dissuading participation. Not paying research participants is likely to result in a reduction in the number of volunteers, while paying participants enables future human subjects research to be conducted. Even though research participants should not lie, their willingness to inconvenience themselves and participate in biomedical research should be rewarded.

CASE 4.4: ETHICAL DRUG DEVELOPMENT FOR RARE CHILDHOOD DISEASES: WHEN THERE ARE LIMITED BUT PROMISING DATA IN ADULTS, HOW TO CHOOSE BETWEEN SAFETY OR EFFICACY STUDIES?

INTRODUCTION

The pathway for conducting clinical research for FDA approval of drugs for rare pediatric diseases is complicated. The traditional pathway begins with Phase I (safety), followed by Phase II studies (efficacy), and then larger Phase III studies (effectiveness). Recently, more studies are designed to combine the Phase I and Phase II components into a single protocol under the umbrella term "early-phase research." For many diseases that affect children and adults, it is preferable to first obtain approval in adults. However, there are some conditions where this is not feasible, for example disorders presenting in childhood or conditions that are not of concern in adult populations. Additional pediatric considerations include the impact of the study agent on a participant's growth and development, the potential for differential pharmacokinetics based on age, and variable disease severity (and potential genotype) when a typically adult-onset condition presents in childhood.

This case is about an investigator-initiated Phase 1 study of the safety of low-dose interleukin-2 (LD IL-2) in adolescents with pediatric-onset systemic lupus erythematosus (SLE). High-dose IL-2 was approved in 1992 for cancer, but LD IL-2 has not been approved for any condition or disorder, although it has been used in adult patients with autoimmune disease. The investigator submitted the protocol with an investigational new drug (IND) application to the FDA, but the FDA issued a clinical hold. The FDA commented that a stand-alone safety study for pediatric patients with SLE was not allowable under the FDA regulations.

The FDA regulatory framework for human subjects research enrolling children is based on the level of risk. Most drug development studies are considered to be greater than minimal risk. In these cases, it is necessary for there to be the prospect of direct benefit to pediatric participants (FDA 2019a) or, if there is no prospect of direct benefit, there can only be a minor increase over minimal risk and the study must be likely to yield generalizable knowledge about the disorder (FDA 2019b).

The case raises questions about the definition of minimal risk, and how to balance potential risks in research in the context of rare serious pediatric diseases with limited effective treatment options. The case is further complicated because the IND is requested by an academic research team with limited philanthropic funding to expand the trial into a combined Phase I/II trial.

Three commentaries accompany this case report. In the commentary by Robert "Skip" Nelson at Johnson & Johnson, he reviews the ethical principles that guide pediatric clinical development programs, highlighting that the trial, as presently designed, does not hold a prospect of benefit yet exceeds the threshold of a minor increase over minimal risk. Dr. Nelson argues that the study should not be considered for approval under 21 CFR 50.54 (or HHS 45 CFR 46.407) and should be redesigned as an early-phase (Phase I/II) efficacy trial. In contrast, Kathryn Porter and Benjamin Wilfond of the Treuman Katz Center for Pediatric Bioethics and Anne Stevens of the University of Washington School of Medicine and Janssen Research and Development argue that the current model of pediatric trial design is not a good fit for rare pediatric-onset disorders and the concept of a "minor increase in risk" is subjective. The authors argue that the FDA determination to begin with a larger early-phase efficacy study may miss important pediatric safety signals and, in the case of rare pediatric disorders such as pediatric-onset SLE, that stakeholders such as patients, parents, and pediatric providers have the most insight and perspective into assessing trial-related risks. Given this, the authors suggest that the use of IL-2 in this setting would likely be considered a minor increase in risk by such stakeholders while arguing for a pediatric-centered approach that facilitates drug development for rarer disorders.

In the commentary by Jeff Matsler and Jamila Young of WellStar Health System, the authors argue that the 21 CFR 50.53 criteria of minor increase in minimal risk represent an undefined value and, given the importance of studying pediatric-onset conditions in pediatric populations, the investigators should request a hearing with potential approval through the 21 CFR 50.54 pathway.

CASE SUMMARY

Pediatric SLE is not as common as adult-onset SLE, and children with the disorder have worse outcomes than patients with adult-onset disease (Ardoin and Schanberg 2012; Hersh et al. 2009, 2010, 2011, 2018; Hui-Yuen et al. 2011; Mina and Brunner 2010, 2013; Son et al. 2014; Tucker et al. 2008; Webb et al. 2011). Interventions in children with SLE have the potential to prevent disease morbidities, such as end-stage organ damage, but the current pharmaceutical therapies used (i.e., corticosteroids, chemotherapy, and immunosuppressive biologics) are only partially effective and poorly tolerated by patients.

Although there are no data in children with SLE, LD IL-2 has been studied in children and adults with other autoimmune conditions and was well tolerated, suggesting it has the potential to be a safer intervention in pediatric patients with SLE (He et al. 2016; Humrich et al. 2015; Jyonouchi et al. 2017; Kennedy-Nasser et al. 2014; von Spee-Mayer et al. 2016).

As presently proposed, the study is a multisite dose-escalation study with three cohorts (four participants each, total 12 participants) for six weeks for individuals between 13 and 21 years of age whose onset was before the age of 18.

The FDA was concerned that the study, as proposed, was designed as a safety and tolerability study with no clear prospect of direct benefit to the children in the study. The recommendation from their review was that if LD IL-2 could be studied in consenting adults, then that would be the preferred method to study the drug. The FDA was also concerned about the efficacy data around LD IL-2 in adult patients with SLE because the trials were open-label, uncontrolled trials in foreign countries. The dose and duration of treatment in the available studies differ from those in the proposed study, and do not support the potential for direct benefit in pediatric patients. The FDA suggested additional efficacy studies in adults and then a larger efficacy study of longer duration in children that would offer a prospect of benefit.

The investigator requested an ethics consultation to consider how to respond to the FDA to ensure the research plan has adequate safety and is within the bounds of regulations. This case raises several important questions:

- Can a safety study for a drug ever be considered no more than a minor increase over minimal risk?
- The FDA recommendation for a larger efficacy study of longer duration would offer a prospect of benefit, but would it be justified by the risks of exposing a larger cohort for longer?
- Which approach is ethically more appropriate?

REFERENCES

Ardoin, S. P., and L. E. Schanberg. 2012. Lessons from SLE: Children are not little adults. *Nature Reviews Rheumatology* 8(8):444–445.

Food and Drug Administration (FDA). 2019a. 21 CFR Part 50.52. Clinical investigations involving greater than minimal risk but presenting the prospect of direct benefit to individual subjects. Revised 1 April 2019. https://www.accessdata.fda.gov/scripts/cdrh/cfdocs/cfcfr/CFRSearch.cfm?CFRPart=50&showFR=1&subpartNode=21:1.0.1.1.20.4 (accessed December 24, 2019)

Food and Drug Administration (FDA). 2019b. 21 CFR Part 50.53. Clinical investigations involving greater than minimal risk and no prospect of direct benefit to individual subjects, but likely to yield generalizable knowledge about the subjects' disorder or condition. Revised 1 April 2019. https://www.accessdata.fda.gov/scripts/cdrh/cfdocs/cfcfr/CFRSearch.cfm?CFRPart=50&showFR =1&subpartNode=21:1.0.1.1.20.4 (accessed December 24, 2019)

He, J., X. Zhang, Y. Wei, X. Sun, Y. Chen, J. Deng, Y. Jin, Y. Gan, X. Hu, R. Jia, et al. 2016. Low-dose interleukin-2 treatment selectively modulates CD4+ T cell subsets in patients with systemic lupus erythematosus. *Nature Medicine* 22(9): 991–993.

Hersh, A. O., E. von Scheven, J. Yazdany, P. Panopalis, L. Trupin, L. Julian, P. Katz, L. A. Criswell, and E. Yelin. 2009. Differences in long-term disease activity and treatment of adult patients with childhood- and adult-onset systemic lupus erythematosus. *Arthritis Care and Research* 61(1):13–20.

Hersh, A. O., L. Trupin, J. Yazdany, P. Panopalis, L. Julian, P. Katz, L. A. Criswell, and E. Yelin. 2010. Childhood-onset disease as a predictor of mortality in an adult cohort of patients with systemic lupus erythematosus. *Arthritis Care and Research* 62(8):1152–1159.

Hersh, A. O., S. M. Case, and M. B. Son. 2018. Predictors of disability in a childhood-onset systemic lupus erythematosus cohort: Results from the CARRA Legacy Registry. *Lupus* 27(3):494–500.

Hersh, A., E. von Scheven, and E. Yelin. 2011. Adult outcomes of childhood-onset rheumatic diseases. *Nature Reviews Rheumatology* 7(5):290–295.

Hui-Yuen, J. S., L. F. Imundo, C. Avitabile, P. J. Kahn, A. H. Eichenfield, and D. M. Levy. 2011. Early versus later onset childhood-onset systemic lupus erythematosus: Clinical features, treatment and outcome. *Lupus* 20(9):952–959.

Humrich, J. Y., C. von Spee-Mayer, E. Siegert, T. Alexander, F. Hiepe, A. Radbruch, R. Burmester, and G. Riemekasten. 2015. Rapid induction of clinical remission by low-dose interleukin-2 in a patient with refractory SLE. *Annals of the Rheumatic Diseases* 74(4):791–792.

Jyonouchi, S., B. Gwafila, L. A. Gwalani, M. Ahmad, C. Moertel, C. Holbert, J. Y. Kim, N. Kobrinsky, S. Roy-Ghanta, and J. S. Orange. 2017. Phase I trial of low-dose interleukin 2 therapy in patients with Wiskott-Aldrich syndrome. *Clinical Immunology* 179:47–53.

Kennedy-Nasser, A. A., S. Ku, P. Castillo-Caro, Y. Hazrat, M. F. Wu, H. Liu, J. Melenhorst, A. J. Barrett, S. Ito, A. Foster, et al. 2014. Ultra low-dose IL-2 for GVHD prophylaxis after allogeneic hematopoietic stem cell transplantation mediates expansion of regulatory T cells without diminishing antiviral and antileukemic activity. *Clinical Cancer Research* 20(8): 2215–2225.

Mina, R., and H. I. Brunner. 2010. Pediatric lupus – Are there differences in presentation, genetics, response to therapy, and damage accrual compared with adult lupus? *Rheumatic Disease Clinics of North America* 36(1):53–80.

Mina, R., and H. I. Brunner. 2013. Update on differences between childhood-onset and adult-onset systemic lupus erythematosus. *Arthritis Research and Therapy* 15(4):218–226.

Son, M. B., V. M. Johnson, A. O. Hersh, M. S. Lo, and K. H. Costenbader. 2014. Outcomes in hospitalized pediatric patients with systemic lupus erythematosus. *Pediatrics* 133(1):e106–e113.

Tucker, L. B., A. G. Uribe, M. Fernandez, L. M. Vila, G. McGwin, M. Apte, B. J. Fessler, H. M. Bastian, J. D. Reveille, and G. S. Alarcon. 2008. Adolescent onset of lupus results in more aggressive disease and worse outcomes: Results of a nested matched case-control study within LUMINA, a multiethnic US cohort (LUMINA LVII). *Lupus* 17(4):314–322.

von Spee-Mayer, C., E. Siegert, D. Abdirama, A. Rose, A. Klaus, T. Alexander, P. Enghard, B. Sawitzki, F. Hiepe, A. Radbruch, et al. 2016. Low-dose interleukin-2 selectively corrects regulatory T cell defects in patients with systemic lupus erythematosus. *Annals of the Rheumatic Diseases* 75(7):1407–1415.

Webb, R., J. A. Kelly, E. C. Somers, T. Hughes, K. M. Kaufman, E. Sanchez, S. K. Nath, G. Bruner, M. E. Alarcon-Riquelme, G. S. Gilkeson, et al. 2011. Early disease onset is predicted by a higher genetic risk for lupus and is associated with a more severe phenotype in lupus patients. *Annals of the Rheumatic Diseases* 70(1): 151–156.

COMMENTARY 4.4.1: THE USE OF PEDIATRIC EXTRAPOLATION TO AVOID UNNECESSARY PEDIATRIC CLINICAL TRIALS

ROBERT M. NELSON

The proposed clinical trial (Johnson, Duenas, and Wilfond 2020) of LD IL-2 for the treatment of adolescents with SLE should be evaluated from two perspectives: (1) the ethical principles that guide the design of a pediatric clinical development program, and (2) the necessity of the data for the further development of IL-2 as a treatment for pediatric SLE. Although an academic investigator with limited funding may be unable to conduct a full pediatric development program, the proposed clinical trial must be viewed from the overall perspective of such a program for the exposure of adolescents with SLE to the risks of IL-2 to be justified.

Three ethical principles guide the design of the pediatric clinical development program. First, children should not be enrolled in a clinical investigation unless it is necessary to achieve an important scientific and/or public health objective concerning the health and welfare of children. This ethical principle of scientific necessity is grounded on considerations of social justice and is reflected in the regulatory requirements for minimizing risk and selecting participants equitably (Roth-Cline et al. 2011; Roth-Cline and Nelson 2014). This principle is also the moral justification for the use of extrapolation of efficacy from a reference population (e.g., adults with SLE) to a target population (e.g., adolescents with SLE) when clinically and scientifically appropriate. Second, interventions that do not offer a sufficient prospect of direct clinical benefit to the enrolled children must present no more than low risk. Under U.S. regulations, there are two categories of low risk, that is, minimal risk and a minor increase over minimal risk. Since the adolescents to be enrolled in this proposed clinical trial have SLE, the relevant category would be a minor increase over minimal risk. In this case, the administration of IL-2 exceeds the threshold of minimal risk, and the adolescents have a condition. Third, interventions that present more than a minor increase over minimal risk must provide a sufficient prospect of direct benefit to justify that risk, and the balance of risk and potential benefit must be comparable to the available alternatives. This requirement reflects the ethical principle that children should not be placed at a disadvantage by being enrolled in a clinical trial, either through exposure to excessive risks or by failing to get necessary healthcare.

These three ethical principles are reflected in the FDA regulatory framework found in 21 CFR 50, subpart D, which formed the basis for the FDA placing the proposed clinical trial on clinical hold. Among other criteria, the FDA may place a proposed or ongoing clinical trial on hold if it finds that the participants are or would be exposed to an unreasonable and significant risk of illness or injury (FDA 2019). As a matter of policy, failure to be in compliance with the ethical requirements of 21 CFR 50, subpart D, is sufficient to establish that the enrolled children would be exposed to an unreasonable and significant risk. In effect, the FDA placed the study on clinical hold because the duration (i.e., six weeks) of exposure to IL-2 did not provide a sufficient prospect of direct benefit to justify the risks of IL-2 exposure. Although arguably a low exposure to IL-2 may present no more than a minor increase over minimal risk, a dose-escalation study involving repeated exposure to IL-2 (i.e., increasing the risk of medication-related adverse effects) clearly exceeds that threshold.

A more important question is whether the data that would be generated by this study are in fact necessary for the further development of IL-2 as a treatment for pediatric SLE. The administration of LD IL-2 over six months has been shown in adult patients to activate and expand regulatory T cells, a biomarker of immunological improvement, and ameliorate the clinical manifestations of SLE (He et al. 2016; Rosenzwajg et al. 2019; von Spee-Mayer et al. 2016). A Phase II, multicenter, randomized, double-blind, placebo-controlled trial to evaluate the efficacy, safety, and pharmacokinetics of IL-2 in adult patients with active moderate to severe systemic SLE has recently been completed (ClinicalTrials. gov 2019). The results have not yet been disseminated. Once the efficacy of IL-2 for the treatment of

SLE has been established in adults, it may be possible to establish the efficacy of IL-2 in adolescents with SLE using an extrapolation approach (Brunner et al. 2019; Gamalo-Siebers et al. 2019). For example, belimumab was recently approved by both the FDA and European Medicines Agency (EMA) for the treatment of pediatric SLE using two different extrapolation approaches, a Bayesian analysis with 55% weighting of the adult response (Division of Pulmonary Allergy and Rheumatology Products [CDER] 2019) and a matching of exposure and clinical response (Committee for Medicinal Products for Human Use [CHMP] 2019). The exact design of a clinical trial in adolescents with SLE that would be sufficient to establish the safety and efficacy of LD IL-2 when combined with adult efficacy data is beyond the scope of this commentary. In addition, the adolescent dosing regimen to be used in an efficacy trial would be the same as the adult dosing regimen, as has been demonstrated for other compounds (e.g., monoclonal antibodies) (Yang, Xu, and Yao 2019). Given the known safety profile of IL-2, it is highly unlikely that the relatively small cohort to be enrolled in the proposed study would provide any additional safety information to inform a future efficacy trial. In summary, it is unclear that the current proposed design would provide any additional data about dosing and safety to inform a subsequent pediatric SLE efficacy trial.

In conclusion, the most appropriate course of action from an ethical, clinical, and scientific perspective is to design a pediatric efficacy trial that would provide a sufficient IL-2 exposure to offer a prospect of direct benefit to the enrolled adolescents to justify the risk. To minimize the required pediatric sample size, the clinical trial should be designed to allow for the extrapolation of adult SLE efficacy data to support an assessment of pediatric efficacy using either a Bayesian framework, matching of exposure and/or response, or both. This recommended course of action will be challenging for the academic investigator. However, the existence of well-established investigator networks in pediatric rheumatology in both the United States and Europe may render this task less daunting (Brunner et al. 2019).

References

Brunner, H. I., A. Martini, D. J. Lovell, and N. Ruperto. 2019. Clinical trials in children and adolescents with systemic lupus erythematosus: Methodological aspects, regulatory landscape and future opportunities. *Annals of the Rheumatic Diseases* 78(2):162–170.

ClinicalTrials.gov. 2019. Identifier NCT02955615, ILT-101 in Patients with Active Moderate to Severe Systemic Lupus Erythematosus (SLE) (LUPIL-2). National Library of Medicine (US). https://clinical-trials.gov/ct2/show/NCT02955615 (accessed December 30, 2019)

Committee for Medicinal Products for Human Use (CHMP). 2019. Assessment report: Benlysta (Procedure No. EMEA/H/C/002015/II/0062). Amsterdam, The Netherlands: European Medicines Agency. https://www.ema.europa.eu/en/documents/variation-report/benlysta-h-c-2015-ii-0062-epar-assessment-report-variation_en.pdf. (accessed December 30, 2019)

Division of Pulmonary Allergy and Rheumatology Products (CDER). 2019. BLA 125370/s-064 and BLA 761043/s-007 Multi-disciplinary Review and Evaluation, Benlysta® (belimumab) for Intravenous Infusion in Children 5–17 Years of Age with SLE. Silver Spring, MD: Food and Drug Administration. https://www.fda.gov/media/127912/download (accessed December 30, 2019).

Food and Drug Administration (FDA). 2019. 21 CFR Part 312.42. Clinical holds and request for modification. Revised 1 April 2019. https://www.accessdata.fda.gov/scripts/cdrh/cfdocs/cfcfr/CFRSearch.cfm?fr=312.42 (accessed December 30, 2019)

Gamalo-Siebers, M., L. Hampson, K. Kordy, S. Weber, R. M. Nelson, and R. Portman. 2019. Incorporating innovative techniques toward extrapolation and efficient pediatric drug development. *Therapeutic Innovation and Regulatory Science* 53(5):567–578.

He, J., X. Zhang, Y. Wei, et al. 2016. Low-dose interleukin-2 treatment selectively modulates CD4(+) T cell subsets in patients with systemic lupus erythematosus. *Nature Medicine* 22(9):991–993.

Johnson, L., D. Duenas, and B. S. Wilfond. 2020. Ethical drug development for rare childhood diseases: When there are limited but promising data in adults, how to choose between safety or efficacy studies? *The American Journal of Bioethics* 20(4):102–103.

Rosenzwajg, M., R. Lorenzon, P. Cacoub, H. P. Pham, F. Pitoiset, K. E. Soufi, C. Rlbet, C. Bernard, S. Aractingi, B. Banneville, et al. 2019. Immunological and clinical effects of low-dose interleukin-2 across 11 autoimmune diseases in a single, open clinical trial. *Annals of the Rheumatic Diseases* 78(2):209–217

Roth-Cline, M., and R. Nelson. 2014. The ethical principle of scientific necessity in pediatric research. *The American Journal of Bioethics* 14(12):14–15.

Roth-Cline, M., J. Gerson, P. Bright, C. S. Lee, and R. M. Nelson. 2011. Ethical considerations in conducting pediatric research. *Handbook of Experimental Pharmacology* 205:219–244.

von Spee-Mayer, C., E. Siegert, D. Abdirama, A. Rose, A. Klaus, T. Alexander, P. Enghard, B. Sawitzki, F. Hiepe, and A. Radbruch, et al. 2016. Low-dose interleukin-2 selectively corrects regulatory T cell defects in patients with systemic lupus erythematosus. *Annals of the Rheumatic Diseases* 75(7):1407–1415.

Yang, N., M. C. Xu, and Z. Yao. 2019. Evaluation of weight thresholds for pediatric patients to use adult dosage of therapeutic monoclonal antibodies. *Journal of Clinical Pharmacology* 59(10):1309–1318.

COMMENTARY 4.4.2: FLEXIBILITY REQUIRED: BALANCING THE INTERESTS OF CHILDREN AND RISK IN DRUG DEVELOPMENT FOR RARE PEDIATRIC CONDITIONS

KATHRYN M. PORTER, ANNE STEVENS, AND BENJAMIN S. WILFOND

There exists a standard approach to developing drugs for adults. The process begins with animal studies focused on toxicity, followed by Phase I safety and dosage studies in humans, Phase II efficacy and side effect studies, and, finally, Phase III effectiveness studies, all before a drug can be approved for use (U.S. Food and Drug Administration [FDA] 2018). Historically, most drugs were only approved in adults and were used in children off-label. More recently, a series of laws, such as the Pediatric Research Equity Act and the Best Pharmaceuticals for Children Act, have encouraged researchers and drug manufacturers to study those drugs in children as well (U.S. Congress 2002, 2003). For common conditions that can affect both children and adults, such as asthma or hypertension, safety and efficacy studies are first completed in adults and pediatric drug research then begins with efficacy studies. The reason for this is that the FDA regulations require that research on children that is more than minimal risk have the prospect of direct benefit, and Phase I/II adult studies can provide evidence of this potential benefit. In general, this process works effectively because of the large number of potential participants, researchers, and drug manufacturers focused on common conditions.

However, there are some diseases that do not appear in the adult population at all, for example medical conditions that are exclusively within the realm of neonatology or pediatric conditions for which life expectancy does not reach adulthood. Drug research does exist in these contexts, taking a modified approach that begins with safety studies involving very small numbers of children and then progressing to efficacy studies. As an example, preclinical (animal) evidence suggested that, when started immediately after birth, erythropoietin could have a neuroprotective effect on the cognitive development of infants who are born prematurely. Human research began with a safety study of 30 infants receiving the drug intervention at varying doses, followed by an efficacy study (Juul et al. 2008).

Drug development for rare pediatric diseases frequently struggles to fit into the standard adult-first model. In these cases, there may be justifiable reasons to forgo this adult-first approach and develop a process, similar to that used for conditions that do not appear in adults, that protects children while simultaneously allowing for a more efficient process to study possible therapeutic drugs. However, this case (Johnson, Duenas, and Wilfond 2020) was reviewed by the FDA with the standard adult-first approach in mind.

The FDA indicated a preference that, rather than conduct a safety study in children, researchers further evaluate the drug in adults, and then, when there is more evidence of efficacy, conduct a Phase I/II safety–efficacy study in children. We argue, however, that there are compelling reasons to deviate from this adult-first approach for this drug development study for pediatric-onset lupus. First, for many rare diseases, as with SLE, affected children have limited clinical options. While some rare diseases do not affect adults at all, in others, such as SLE, the biologically driven adult experience differs significantly from the pediatric experience (i.e., growth, immune developmental stage, and genetic load), thereby potentially warranting different interventions and also diminishing the relevance of adult-focused research. Second, even if adult research is warranted and relevant, subjectivity exists in terms of the amount of efficacy evidence from adult studies considered adequate to move forward with pediatric clinical trials. For this particular case, there is evidence of efficacy for LD IL-2 in adults with SLE and other autoimmune conditions in single-arm studies and case reports (He et al. 2016; Humrich et al. 2015; Humrich et al. 2019; von Spee-Mayer et al. 2016), and yet the FDA did not find it to be sufficient, despite the fact that the adult experience differs from the pediatric experience and therefore may not be as relevant as might be desired. Third, the number of potential research participants is very small, and the number of researchers interested and qualified in leading relevant studies is also very limited. For many rare diseases in children, the research is less commonly initiated by large drug manufacturers with exhaustive resources and more frequently by clinician scientists who primarily care for children and work with limited financial research resources. An expectation for these pediatric clinician scientists to conduct adult efficacy studies, for what is essentially a different condition, is likely not practicable.

To be clear, it is necessary for the drug development process to avoid exposing children to unnecessary risk. However, interpretation of the FDA regulations is widely variable across IRBs (Shah et al. 2004). There is subjectivity in the interpretation of relevant terms such as "minimal risk" and "minor increase." In considering what risk falls within a minor increase over minimal risk, one should consider the perspectives of those with an intimate knowledge of the disease and its impact on daily life, such as physicians, patients, and families. This better assures that all risks associated with living with inadequately treated SLE are considered. This is not to say that parents should be making risk determinations, but these parties are all important stakeholders in considering the real-life impacts of the interpretation of regulatory terms.

Because of the subjective nature of what is meant by a *minor* increase over minimal risk, it is possible that some drugs, such as LD IL-2 where risk appears to be modest, could meet the threshold to permit an initial safety study. Additionally, because of the subjective nature of risk, there is great value in seeking out the views of the families of children living with these conditions. When few good clinical options exist, the priorities of families to find effective treatments should hold some weight. Parents may believe that it is in the long-term interest of their children, as well as other children with the condition, to allow the initiation of safety studies in children for drugs with a reasonable adult safety profile when there is at least moderate evidence of efficacy in adults, rather than delay research to develop treatment. One of the authors (AS) conducted a focus group of parents and patients with pediatric-onset SLE who shared that they supported this view.

Finally, as proposed in this case, a safety study in a small cohort of children exposes fewer children to risk than does beginning with a larger Phase II efficacy study, such as was proposed by the FDA. Because the biology of SLE in adults is different from that of children, more adult safety and efficacy data still may not decrease the possibility of unexpected safety signals in either a pediatric safety study or a pediatric efficacy study. Thus, beginning the pediatric research with safety in mind and subjecting a smaller number of children to potential risk have merit.

There are good systems in place for the protection of pediatric human participants in research, but real-life situations shed light on the potential limitations that come from strict interpretation of regulations without any flexibility. Sometimes, interpretation should include the intent of the rules and consider what is in the best interest of children struggling with a devastating disease. If the ultimate goal of drug development for rare pediatric conditions such as pediatric SLE is to help children quickly yet safely, stepping away from the standard adult-first approach and instead modeling a drug development approach on that used for conditions for which there is not a comparable adult counterpart could better facilitate the drug development process. This pediatric-only approach could be better for children and their families, as well as more feasible for the researchers dedicated to helping these children, while still ensuring adequate safety for the pediatric research participants.

References

He, J., X. Zhang, Y. Wei, et al. 2016. Low-dose interleukin-2 treatment selectively modulates CD4(+) T cell subsets in patients with systemic lupus erythematosus. *Nature Medicine* 22(9):991–993.

Humrich, J. Y., C. von Spee-Mayer, E. Siegert, et al. 2015. Rapid induction of clinical remission by low-dose interleukin-2 in a patient with refractory SLE. *Annals of the Rheumatic Diseases* 74(4):791–792.

Humrich, J. Y., C. von Spee-Mayer, E. Siegert, et al. 2019. Low-dose interleukin-2 therapy in refractory systemic lupus erythematosus: An investigator-initiated, single-centre phase 1 and 2a clinical trial. *The Lancet Rheumatology* 1(1):e44–e54.

Johnson, L. M., D. M. Duenas, and B. S. Wilfond. 2020. Ethical drug development for rare childhood diseases: When there are limited but promising data in adults, how to choose between safety or efficacy studies? *The American Journal of Bioethics* 20(4):102–103.

Juul, S. E., R. J. McPherson, L. A. Bauer, K. J. Ledbetter, C. A. Gleason, and D. E. Mayock. 2008. A phase I/II trial of high-dose erythropoietin in extremely low birth weight infants: Pharmacokinetics and safety. *Pediatrics* 122(2):383–391.

Shah, S., A. Whittle, B. Wilfond, G. Gensler, and D. Wendler. 2004. How do institutional review boards apply the federal risk and benefit standards for pediatric research. *The Journal of American Medical Association* 291(4):476–482.

U.S. Congress. 2002. Best Pharmaceuticals for Children Act. 107th Congress, S. 1789. Available at: https://www.congress.gov/107/plaws/publ109/PLAW-107publ109.pdf (accessed February 26, 2020).

U.S. Congress. 2003. Pediatric Research Equity Act of 2003. 108th Congress, S. 650 Available at: https://www.congress.gov/108/plaws/publ155/PLAW-108publ155.pdf (accessed February 26, 2020).

U.S. Food and Drug Administration (FDA). 2018. The drug development process: Step 3: Clinical research. https://www.fda.gov/patients/drug-development-process/step-3-clinical-research. (accessed December 31, 2019).

von Spee-Mayer, C., E. Siegert, D. Abdirama, et al. 2016. Low-dose interleukin-2 selectively corrects regulatory T cell defects in patients with systemic lupus erythematosus. *Annals of the Rheumatic Diseases* 75 (7): 1407–1415.

COMMENTARY 4.4.3: WHEN HIGHER RISK DOES NOT EQUAL GREATER HARM: DOING THE MOST GOOD IN A LIMITED PEDIATRIC STUDY POPULATION

JEFF MATSLER AND JAMILA M. YOUNG

In society's quest for scientific gains, particularly when conducting medical research, it is imperative our ethical standards are never sacrificed on the altar of knowledge. This is particularly true for research conducted with human participants—and exponentially so for individuals who lack the ability to consent for themselves, a category of individuals that includes, among others, children (FDA 2019a). This intentional ethical restraint in human subjects research makes it particularly complicated to think about conducting research for either diseases that only occur in youth or those, such as pediatric systemic lupus erythematosus (pSLE), that manifest and exhibit differently and with different mortality and morbidity rates than when onset occurs in adulthood (Weiss 2012). In these instances, it becomes necessary to determine which is the lesser harm: not learning about the potential treatments designed specifically to counter the progress of a disease and its unique progression in younger participants; or taking limited, controlled risk (even if greater than minimal) in an effort to benefit those who are currently suffering and potentially ease the suffering of those who may encounter the condition in the future. The FDA has very specific guidelines that restrict and/or allow research with children in studies that impose greater than minimal risk upon their participants; these are listed in the Common Rule, specifically in 21 CFR 50 subpart D (FDA 2019a).

This specific case is about an investigator-initiated Phase I study considering the safety of low-dose interleukin-2 (LD IL-2) in adolescents with pSLE. As noted in the case, LD IL-2 has never been approved for treatment in pSLE participants or for any other disease; however, high-dose IL-2 (HD IL-2) was approved in 1992 for cancer patients. Moreover, LD IL-2 has been successfully studied in adult participants with autoimmune disease. Upon submission to the FDA, a clinical hold was placed on this study with comments indicating a stand-alone safety study for pSLE participants is not permissible under current regulations. Their recommendation suggests the best route for research of LD IL-2 in pSLE involves conducting efficacy studies in adults with SLE and then a larger study of longer duration in children with pSLE. Concerns were threefold: (1) The study posed a greater than minimal risk to participants; (2) it provided no prospect of direct benefit; and (3) existing data in adults lack efficacy—or, at best, if situationally accurate are not applicable to this study.

It will be shown that following the FDA's current recommendation unnecessarily places a large adult test population (and, later, a larger sampling of pSLE participants) at risk with little or no benefit of learning anything about how the drug actually impacts pSLE symptoms, and defers any potential knowledge to be gained into an indeterminable future. Considering the limited resources of the academic institution proposing the study, it seems unlikely that these large, long-term studies would ever be conducted (certainly a greater harm than the potential harm in consideration). With these facts in mind, it seems that the trial, as proposed, would provide greater understanding of the disease and the drug's impact on specific aspects of the disease not observed in adult-onset populations. Even so, if the proposal is to advance beyond its current clinical hold, the FDA concerns must be addressed.

If one is resolved that the study as presently designed is the most ethical route for LD IL-2 research in pSLE participants, there are two potential pathways to progress for a study such as this that presents no immediate benefit to participants (both of which require consent by parents and assent by the minor). The first is to demonstrate that while the study may indeed pose a "greater than minimal risk" to its participants, that risk poses only a minor increase over what is considered minimal (FDA 2019b). The second option requires direct approval from the FDA's commissioner once it is determined that the investigation is grounded in ethical principles and "presents a reasonable opportunity to further the understanding, prevention, or alleviation of a serious problem affecting the health or welfare of children" (FDA 2019c). It must be noted that, as the FDA has not defined what constitutes a "minor increase over minimal risk," there is great dissention and disagreement over what this actually looks like in a research trial (Wendler 2013).

There is a great deal of evidence to support pursuing the commissioner's direct approval as outlined in 50.54.

1. pSLE manifests differently in children than it does in adults. Many of the symptoms that define the disease in pediatric-onset SLE—such as major organ system degradation, neuropsychiatric involvement, and psychological manifestation—are not defining factors for those diagnosed with adult-onset SLE. Furthermore, those who contract pSLE have significantly higher morbidity and mortality rates than those with SLE (Weiss 2012).

2. A second consideration is that all study participants are teenagers or young adults. It is long established that teenagers, while not autonomous adults, do in many instances possess the cognitive ability to understand and provide assent (Ackerman 1980).

3. Finally, it should be noted that most adolescents cite altruism as a reason for participation in medical research. Data confirm that minors involved in research they perceive to be altruistic often experience the individual benefit of psychological/psychiatric improvement. This is significant considering the potential neuropsychiatric aspects of pSLE (Pediatric Advisory Committee 2008).

In conclusion, as the path laid out in CFR 50.53 contains the potentially insurmountable hurdle of proving an undefined value ("minor increase over minimal risk") to an agency that has already rejected the institution's proposal on these grounds; and as it is shown that simply complying with the FDA's initial recommendation would put a greater number of individuals at risk in a study that would not successfully monitor the effects of LD IL-2 on pSLE symptoms (or conclude whether doses given to them—adults—would be safe for minors), it is evident that addressing the FDA concerns in an appeal to the commissioner as laid out in CFR 50.54 is not only the most ethical but also the most practical solution for those seeking approval of this submission.

References

Ackerman, T. F. 1980. Moral duties of parents and nonther-apeutic clinical research procedures involving children. *Bioethics Quarterly* 2(2):94–111.

Food and Drug Administration (FDA). 2019a. 21 CFR Part 50 Subpart D. Additional safeguards for children in clinical investigations. Revised 1 April 2019. Available at https://www.accessdata.fda.gov/scripts/cdrh/cfdocs/cfcfr/CFRSearch.cfm?CFRPart=50&showFR=1&subpartNode=21:1.0.1.1.20.4 (accessed December 24, 2019).

Food and Drug Administration (FDA). 2019b. 21 CFR Part 50.53. Clinical investigations involving greater than minimal risk and no prospect of direct benefit to individual subjects, but likely to yield generalizable knowledge about the subjects' disorder or condition. Revised 1 April 2019. Available at https://www.accessdata.fda.gov/scripts/cdrh/cfdocs/cfcfr/CFRSearch.cfm?CFRPart=50&showFR=1&subpartNode=21:1.0.1.1.20.4 (accessed December 24, 2019).

Food and Drug Administration (FDA). 2019c. 21 CFR Part 50.54. Clinical investigations not otherwise approvable that present an opportunity to understand, prevent, or alleviate a serious problem affecting the health or welfare of children. Revised 1 April 2019. Available at https://www.accessdata.fda.gov/scripts/cdrh/cfdocs/cfcfr/CFRSearch.cfm?CFRPart=50&showFR=1&subpartNode=21:1.0.1.1.20.4 (accessed December 24, 2019).

Pediatric Advisory Committee. 2008. Children's Oncology Group protocol ASCT0631: A phase III randomized trial of granulocyte colony stimulating factor (G-CSF) stimulated bone marrow vs. conventional bone marrow as a stem cell source in matched sibling donor transplantation. http://www.fda.gov/ohrms/dockets/ac/08/transcripts/2008-4406t-01.pdf

Weiss, J. E. 2012. Pediatric systemic lupus erythematosus: More than a positive antinuclear antibody. *Pediatrics in Review* 33(2):62–73.

Wendler, D. 2013. Do U.S. regulations allow more than minor increase over minimal risk pediatric research? Should they? *IRB* 35(6):1–8.

CASE 4.5: GREATER THAN MINIMAL RISK, NO DIRECT BENEFIT: BRIDGING DRUG TRIALS AND NOVEL THERAPY IN PEDIATRIC POPULATIONS

INTRODUCTION

Sickle cell disease (SCD) affects approximately 100,000 individuals in the United States and millions worldwide. Although mortality from SCD has improved for children, affected individuals continue to suffer from severe morbidity and premature mortality; therefore, novel therapies for SCD are needed.

Recently, due to advancement in gene therapy techniques, several curative approaches using genetic manipulation of hematopoietic stem cells (HSCs) have been developed. If successful, these may provide benefit to patients with SCD. The starting material for these gene therapy approaches is mobilized peripheral blood–derived HSCs that must be collected from the affected patient. Granulocyte colony-stimulating factor (G-CSF), the most common medication for mobilizing blood stem cells prior to collection in other settings (i.e., bone marrow transplant), is contraindicated in patients with SCD due to severe side effects, including death. To successfully mobilize stem cells in this patient population and allow for future gene therapy trials, another safer method of mobilization is necessary.

An alternative drug, plerixafor, is FDA approved for use in patients with non-Hodgkin's lymphoma and multiple myeloma to mobilize and collect peripheral blood–derived HSCs. Plerixafor appears to be an attractive alternative to G-CSF, especially in patients with SCD, since it does not cause activation of immune cells. Thus, theoretically, the side effect profile of plerixafor in patients with SCD is expected to be much better tolerated. Additionally, limited experience with the use of plerixafor in adults with SCD shows that it is associated with fewer adverse events. However, pediatric patients with SCD are a special population where this drug has never been used before.

An investigator would like to design a clinical trial to study the toxicity/safety and efficacy of plerixafor in children with SCD. The question is whether it is ethical to study a drug in a population that will not receive direct benefit from the study itself, but rather will set the foundation for future studies. The regulatory question is how such a study may be approvable under the regulatory definition of minor increase over minimal risk, which requires a values-based assessment.

Three commentaries accompany this case report. Yoram Unguru of the Herman and Walter Samuelson Children's Hospital at Sinai and Johns Hopkins University considers the specific risks of plerixafor to exceed the minor increase threshold and concludes that using a 407 panel to assess the ethical acceptability of this study is warranted. However, Akshay Sharma and Liza-Marie Johnson from St. Jude Children's Research Hospital argue that this risk could be considered below the threshold, pointing to the examples of safety studies for pediatric vaccine development, the data in adults for this drug, and efforts to minimize risks using well-defined stopping rules governed by an independent data and safety monitoring committee. Similarly, Susannah Lee and Jessica Ginsberg from Wellstar Health System agree that the risk in such a study would not be more than a minor increase, drawing on the concept that risks should be evaluated on whether the risk would be considered a "socially acceptable" risk, by acknowledging that it is considered socially acceptable to expose children to a low probability of serious harms in some non-research contexts (e.g., shoveling snow for an elderly neighbor).

CASE SUMMARY

The investigator hopes to enroll children with SCD for upcoming gene therapy trials using plerixafor, as they are likely to benefit the most from a curative gene therapy approach, before they develop any irreversible complications of SCD. But he would like to first evaluate the safety and toxicity of plerixafor in an independent study *prior* to the use of the agent in an early-phase gene therapy trial. The rationale for the preliminary study of plerixafor, given the uncertain risks of a gene therapy trial, is to elucidate the tolerability of plerixafor without potential confounders.

Although a small number of adults with SCD have received plerixafor without major side effects, plerixafor has yet to be studied in a large pediatric patient cohort with SCD. Such a drug trial of plerixafor would entail more than minimal risk but have no direct benefit to the participants. At the same time, it is foreseeable that such a study would yield valuable generalizable information that will help children with SCD in the future.

Plerixafor is currently marketed in the United States, the investigation is not intended to be reported to the FDA in support of a new indication, and there is no intent to use it to support any other significant change in the labeling or advertising for the drug.

SPECIFIC QUESTIONS

1. Should the IRB approve this clinical trial under 45 CFR 46.406 (greater than minimal risk and no prospect of direct benefit, but likely to yield generalizable knowledge about the condition), or should this be referred to the Department of Health and Human Services (HHS) for approval under 45 CFR 46.407 (does not meet the conditions of 45 CFR 46.404, 46.405, or 46.406, but the research presents a reasonable opportunity to further the understanding, prevention, or alleviation of a serious problem)?

2. Can this study be IND exempt, or should the investigator apply to the FDA for an IND for the use of this drug in children?

COMMENTARY 4.5.1: BALANCING RISK AND REWARD: GREATER RESEARCH OVERSIGHT IS APPROPRIATE FOR NOVEL THERAPIES FOR CHILDREN WITH LIFE-LIMITING ILLNESS

YORAM UNGURU

Sickle cell disease (SCD) is a lifelong disease associated with significant morbidity and mortality. The clinical hallmark of SCD is painful vaso-occlusive crises. In addition to painful crises, SCD has protean manifestations, affecting nearly every organ system. Recently, there has been heightened interest in developing novel therapies for patients with SCD, including gene therapy, with many clinical trials currently, or soon to be, underway (American Society of Hematology 2019).

Given the burden of disease and substantial toll on those affected by SCD, some patients and families may be willing to assume significant risk when considering potentially curative interventions. This has been illustrated in several studies of both adult patients with SCD as well as parents of children with SCD. In a study of 100 adults with SCD, van Besien et al. found that in exchange for a cure, 63% of patients were willing to accept a greater than 5% risk of short-term mortality and 12% of patients were willing to accept a short-term mortality risk higher than 40% (van Besien et al. 2001). Nearly 30 years ago, in a study of parents of children with SCD, Kodish et al. assessed parental willingness to proceed with curative bone marrow transplantation (BMT) and found that 37% of parents would proceed with BMT if there was a 15% or higher risk of short-term mortality, while 12% of parents were willing to proceed with BMT if there was a 50% or higher mortality risk (Kodish et al. 1991). Nearly 25 years later, in the era of more widespread knowledge of transplantation for SCD, Meier et al. conducted a follow-up to Kodish's study to determine parents' willingness to proceed with potentially curative hematopoietic stem cell transplantation (HSCT) and found that 72% of parents were willing to proceed with HSCT if there was a 5% or higher mortality risk, while 57% would proceed with BMT if there was a 10% risk of graft-versus-host disease (Meier, Dioguardi, and Kamani 2015). These data have very real implications for clinical trials investigating potentially curative therapies for SCD, in particular those including pediatric patients.

Research with children is necessary to gain greater understanding of pediatric disease processes and develop more effective treatments and potential cures. Yet, medical research entails risks. As a result of their limited decision-making capacity (i.e., the ability to make reasonable decisions), children are a vulnerable population. Children's vulnerability places them at heightened risk for research-related harms, necessitating added protections (U.S. Department of Health and Human Services 1983).

Federal regulations that oversee pediatric research are protectionist in nature and are based upon a risk–benefit analysis, to be determined by local IRBs. The notion of minimal risk is both the backbone and the reference point adopted by the regulations. Accordingly, when there is no prospect of direct benefit, IRBs widely accept research that represents only a minor increase over minimal risk. When a prospect of direct benefit exists, approval is often granted when the risks are justified by the potential benefits. The regulations thus can simultaneously protect pediatric research participants from excessive risk while permitting important research to occur (Miller and Weijer 2005).

Understandably, many parents look to clinical research as a way to achieve the goal of cure, in particular as viewed through the lens of genetic and stem cell therapies (Kodish 2003; Samson et al. 2009). Clinician-investigators and oversight bodies like IRBs must carefully balance protecting children involved in risky research with parental, personal, and investigators' hope for cures (Unguru 2015).

We are told that the investigator has proposed to evaluate the safety and toxicity of plerixafor in children with SCD, suggesting that this *independent* study of plerixafor is a Phase I trial. Given the study design, there is no meaningful chance of direct benefit for prospective enrollees. Although the gene therapy trial to include plerixafor holds the prospect of potential benefit to study participants, we must evaluate the independent plerixafor trial on its own merits, separately from the gene therapy trial. Although the relative risk is small, the toxicity profile of plerixafor nonetheless includes several potentially serious side effects, including hyperleukocytosis, splenomegaly and splenic rupture, and hypersensitivity reaction and anaphylaxis. Given the lack of direct benefit and the trial-related risks, which represent more than a minor increase over minimal, the study should be referred to HHS for approval under 46.407. Research under this heading fails to meet criteria of 46.404, 46.405, and 46.406, yet presents a reasonable opportunity to further the understanding, prevention, or alleviation of a serious problem. If the trial were to include an efficacy arm, e.g., assessing the ability to successfully collect adequate stem cells for subsequent gene therapy, given the prospect of direct benefit, ostensibly, the study could be considered approved under 46.405.

Is the use of plerixafor in children IND exempt? Current federal guidance explicitly requires that each of the following four criteria are met for IND exempt status: (1) The drug product is lawfully marketed in the United States; (2) the investigation is not intended to be reported to the FDA as a well-controlled study in support of a new indication, and there is no intent to use it to support any other significant change in the labeling of the drug; (3) in the case of a prescription drug, the investigation is not intended to support a significant change in the advertising for the drug; and (4) the investigation does not involve a route of administration, dose, patient population, or other factor that significantly increases the risk (or decreases the acceptability of the risk) associated with the use of the drug product (21 CFR 312.2(b)(1)(iii): FDA 2019).

As plerixafor has yet to be studied in a large pediatric patient cohort with SCD, its use in this patient group represents a new patient population with the potential for an altered risk profile; and therefore, as appreciated by the aforementioned FDA guidance, the investigator must apply for an IND.

Novel treatments like gene therapy hold great promise with the potential to affect positive change in human health. Patients and parents of children with life-limiting diseases, as well as clinician-investigators who care for these patients, often view such innovative technologies favorably. The promise of gene therapy must be tempered by the limited experience with this emerging technology and the potential risk to research participants, including risks that may extend beyond the individual participant. Clinical investigators and IRBs must balance the hope for reward with the risk of harm.

References

American Society of Hematology. 2019. American Society of Hematology to launch sickle cell disease clinical trials network. https://www.hematology.org/Newsroom/Press-Releases/2018/8952.aspx (accessed November 6).

FDA. 2019. Guidance for clinical investigators, sponsors, and IRBs. Investigational new drug applications (INDs) - determining whether human research studies can be conducted without an IND. https://www.fda.gov/media/79386/download (accessed November 7).

Kodish, E. 2003. Pediatric ethics and early-phase childhood cancer research: Conflicted goals and the prospect of benefit. *Accountability in Research* 10(1):17–25.

Kodish, E., J. Lantos, C. Stocking, P. A. Singer, M. Siegler, and F. L. Johnson. 1991. Bone marrow transplantation for sickle cell disease - A study of parents' decisions. *New England Journal of Medicine* 325(19):1349–1353.

Meier, E. R., J. V. Dioguardi, and N. Kamani. 2015. Current attitudes of parents and patients toward hematopoietic stem cell transplantation. *Pediatric Blood and Cancer* 62(7):1277–1284.

Miller, P. B., and C. Weijer. 2005. Evaluating Benefits and Harms in Research on Healthy Children. *Ethics and research with children: A case-based approach*. Edited by E. Kodish. New York: Oxford University Press, pp. 29–45.

Samson, A., E. Tomiak, and J. Dimillo, et al. 2009. The lived experience of hope among parents of a child with duchenne muscular dystrophy: Perceiving the human being beyond illness. *Chronic Illness* 5(2):103–114.

Unguru, Y. 2015. Ethical challenges in early-phase pediatric research for life-limiting illness. *Seminars in Pediatric Neurology* 22(3):177–186.

U.S. Department of Health and Human Services. 1983. 45CFR46. Subpart d. Additional protections for children involved as subjects in research. *Federal Registrar* 48: 9818.

van Besien, K., M. Koshy, and L. Anderson-Shaw, et al. 2001. Allogenic stem cell transplantation for sickle cell disease: A study of patients' decisions. *Bone Marrow Transplantation* 28(6):545–549.

COMMENTARY 4.5.2: BRINGING KNOWN DRUGS TO PEDIATRIC RESEARCH: SAFETY, EFFICACY, AND THE AMBIGUOUS MINOR INCREASE OVER MINIMAL RISK

AKSHAY SHARMA AND LIZA-MARIE JOHNSON

Sickle cell disease (SCD) is associated with significant morbidity and early mortality in affected individuals, and new treatments are urgently needed. Until recently hydroxyurea, an oral medication that increases the production of fetal-type hemoglobin in red blood cells (RBCs), was the only FDA-approved medication for use in patients with SCD. Hydroxyurea can ameliorate some of the symptoms of SCD but does not provide a cure. BMT with a human leukocyte antigen (HLA)-matched donor remains the only available curative therapy, but most individuals lack a suitable donor, limiting its use as a viable treatment for most affected individuals.

Now, advances in gene therapy allow researchers to manipulate the genes for hemoglobin production in the HSCs from individuals affected with SCD. The ability to harvest, genetically manipulate, and reinfuse these HSCs following a myeloablative conditioning regimen offers a potential cure to every person affected by SCD. If successful, every patient could be their "own donor" and not be dependent on the availability of an HLA-matched donor, who are not commonly available for all, to perform the transplantation. Unfortunately, harvesting HSCs from an individual affected with SCD to perform ex vivo gene therapy remains challenging.

The traditional medication for mobilizing HSCs, GCSF, causes life-threatening complications in individuals with SCD, limiting its use in this population (Abboud, Laver, and Blau 1998; Adler et al. 2001). Plerixafor is a relatively new medication that has emerged as a novel alternative for the mobilization of HSCs. While it has been used in patients with conditions other than SCD for several years, it was recently shown to be efficacious and safe in adults with SCD (Boulad et al. 2018; Esrick et al. 2018; Lagresle-Peyrou et al. 2018). Being able to use this drug successfully and safely in children with SCD will allow researchers to offer a curative therapy for SCD before the development of significant irreversible SCD-related comorbidities.

This case (Wilfond, Duenas, and Johnson 2020) raises the question of whether a study of the safety and efficacy of plerixafor, without the confounders of gene therapy adverse events, is approvable under 45 CFR 46.406. It is obvious that, as currently designed, such a trial exposes the participants to risk with no immediate prospect of direct benefit. We argue that such a study is approvable as a minor increase over minimal risk provided the investigators have a rigorous data and safety monitoring plan and well-designed stopping rules.

For children with SCD to eventually benefit from potentially curative gene therapy, it is first important to know whether plerixafor is even safe and efficient for mobilizing HSCs in children with SCD. While the results will not yield generalizable information about SCD itself, the study may provide valuable information about how SCD might eventually be cured using gene therapy. Harvesting HSCs safely and successfully is the first step toward development of gene therapy as a curative modality for SCD, and if this can be successfully accomplished, it would be a significant milestone toward advancing a potential cure for children with SCD. Thus, a successful clinical trial of plerixafor-based mobilization and collection of HSCs in children with SCD could alter the clinical management of SCD entirely and would indeed be valuable "generalizable" information about the disease.

Although it would be possible to administer plerixafor as a first step in a larger gene therapy trial that potentially offers the prospect of direct benefit to the pediatric participants, this trial design may not be ideal. Combining two novel therapies (plerixafor-based mobilization with gene therapy) and conducting such a clinical trial in children add levels of complexity and may confound the success (or failure) of the larger combined trial. Gene therapy for SCD is still in its infancy, and while early results are promising, combining the two experimental aims may make recruitment of pediatric patients to the trial much more challenging. Given the unknown risks of gene therapy in SCD, these first-in-human trials are likely to first occur in adult populations. Participation in a plerixafor mobilization trial is a relatively easier decision to make for a potential participant, as it does not require the commitment needed to enroll in a first-in-human clinical trial of an experimental gene therapy that carries lifelong consequences. Likewise, parents of children with SCD may feel more comfortable enrolling their children on a clinical trial exploring plerixafor mobilization before having to decide on the more challenging decision to enroll on a gene therapy clinical trial.

We realize that a more conservative view may suggest that our interpretation potentially overlaps with the 45 CFR 46.407 definition of "opportunity to further the understanding, prevention, or alleviation of a serious problem." It is also completely reasonable to suggest that, while successful mobilization and collection of HSCs comprise a first step, translation into successful gene therapy is not guaranteed. But since the two steps are dependent and sequential, it is justifiable that being able to safely harvest sufficient HSCs is just as important as the final gene therapy itself. At the same time, given the historical mistreatment of African Americans in clinical research and some persistent distrust of clinical research (Braunstein et al. 2008; Scharff et al. 2010; Sewell 2015), some would argue that a proposed new therapy should bear a higher burden of demonstrating potential benefit to the community at large and be vetted through a 407 panel.

We believe these criticisms can be addressed in the design and execution of the trial. First, early-phase trials without expectation of direct benefit exist in other settings; for example, early-phase vaccine trials designed to assess participants' immune response to antigen exposure rather than efficacy of the vaccine (such as infant trials involving novel RSV vaccines). The safety and efficacy data from other plerixafor trials indicate that it is well-tolerated and effective in mobilizing HSCs in other non-SCD pediatric populations as well as in adults with SCD (Boulad et al. 2018; Esrick et al. 2018; Lagresle-Peyrou et al. 2018). This information provides important background data to suggest that plerixafor itself, when used in limited doses to mobilize HSCs, is relatively safe, is well-tolerated, and provides only a minor increase in minimal risk. Enrollment of participants with an existing vascular access device (such as those who have an indwelling central venous catheter for chronic transfusion therapy) removes placement of a line for HSC collection as an additional research procedure subject to component analysis. Using a continuous reassessment method or other design that enrolls the minimum number of participants necessary to answer the question about efficacy and tolerability will be important, and stopping rules should be conservative. Investigators should involve parents of children with SCD to incorporate important patient-reported outcome data and to develop education and informed consent materials. To further optimize the protection of human participants, investigators may consider opening enrollment to older adolescents using a staged design for enrollment of younger participants. Investigators may strongly wish to bank the collected HSCs for future use, such as a future gene therapy or other transplantation trial where participants could later potentially directly benefit from the previous collection of their stem cells.

Thus, by incorporating trial design characteristics and a rigorous monitoring plan, one could potentially limit the adverse outcomes, and we believe that such a trial can be potentially approvable under 45 CFR 46.406; and, based on the criteria outlined in the case, we do not believe this requires a new IND application.

References

Abboud, M., J. Laver, and C. A. Blau. 1998. Granulocytosis causing sickle-cell crisis. *The Lancet* 351(9107):959.

Adler, B. K., D. E. Salzman, M. H. Carabasi, W. P. Vaughan, V. V. Reddy, and J. T. Prchal. 2001. Fatal sickle cell crisis after granulocyte colony-stimulating factor administration. *Blood* 97(10):3313–3314.

Boulad, F., T. Shore, K. van Besien, et al. 2018. Safety and efficacy of plerixafor dose escalation for the mobilization of CD34+ hematopoietic progenitor cells in patients with sickle cell disease: Interim results. *Haematologica* 103(9): 1577–1577.

Braunstein, J. B., N. S. Sherber, S. P. Schulman, E. L. Ding, and N. R. Powe. 2008. Race, medical researcher distrust, perceived harm, and willingness to participate in cardio-vascular prevention trials. *Medicine* 87(1):1–9.

Esrick, E. B., J. P. Manis, H. Daley, et al. 2018. Successful hematopoietic stem cell mobilization and apheresis collection using plerixafor alone in sickle cell patients. *Blood Advances* 2(19): 2505–2512.

Lagresle-Peyrou, C., F. Lefrère, E. Magrin, et al. 2018. Plerixafor enables safe, rapid, efficient mobilization of hematopoietic stem cells in sickle cell disease patients after exchange transfusion. *Haematologica* 103(5): 778–786.

Scharff, D. P., K. J. Mathews, P. Jackson, J. Hoffsuemmer, E. Martin, and D. Edwards. 2010. More than Tuskegee: Understanding mistrust about research participation. *Journal of Health Care for the Poor and Underserved* 21(3):879–897.

Sewell, A. A. 2015. Disaggregating ethnoracial disparities in physician trust. *Social Science Research* 54:1–20.

Wilfond, B. S., D. M. Duenas, and L. M. Johnson. 2020. Greater than minimal risk, no direct benefit: Bridging drug trials and novel therapy in pediatric populations. *The American Journal of Bioethics* 20(4):102–10.

COMMENTARY 4.5.3: BALANCING SCIENTIFIC PROGRESS WITH PEDIATRIC PROTECTIONS: NO DIRECT BENEFIT NOW, BUT POTENTIAL NOVEL THERAPY IN THE FUTURE

SUSANNAH W. LEE AND JESSICA C. GINSBERG

Pediatric research that provides no direct benefit to participants raises ethical questions regarding fundamental permissibility and acceptable risks. Because children with SCD continue to face severe morbidity and premature mortality, novel therapies for SCD are urgently needed. Early intervention for children with SCD is paramount to mitigating the disease's severity (Quinn 2013; Ware, McGann, and Quinn 2019). The proposed study seeks to evaluate the safety and efficacy of administering plerixafor, a drug used to mobilize stem cells, to children with SCD, thereby working toward curative approaches for these patients through gene therapy. Because children are a vulnerable population who cannot provide informed consent, certain protections must be in place. The central question, in this case, is what level of risk is inherent in this trial, which impacts what regulation is applicable for this study and whether it qualifies for an IND exemption.

Which regulation applies?

Because the proposed patient population consists of children with a condition but who will receive no direct benefit, the study must (1) pose not more than a "minor increase over minimal risk," and (2) produce generalizable knowledge about the subjects' condition, which is of vital importance to understanding the condition in order to receive IRB approval under 45 CFR 46.406 (U.S. Department of Health and Human Services 2018, 45 CFR 46.406). Assuming the associated study risks are determined to be socially acceptable and the outcome will produce vital information about pediatric SCD, we find it ethically supportable for the IRB to approve the investigation under 46.406.

Regarding the first issue, the federal regulations do not define what constitutes a "minor increase over minimal risk." Instead, 45 CFR 46.102(i) defines "minimal risks" as those where the likelihood and severity of harm anticipated in the investigation are not greater than those "ordinarily encountered in daily life or during the performance of routine physical or psychological examinations" (U.S. Department of Health and Human Services 2018, 45 CFR 46.102(i)). Consequently, the IRB must determine whether the risks associated with administering plerixafor to children with SCD fall within the nebulous boundaries of "minor increase over minimal risk." Because the law fails to elucidate this risk category, an ethical analysis is necessary to clarify the appropriate risk standard.

Much debate in pediatric ethics exists over how best to interpret minimal risk; perspectives range from highly restrictive to highly permissive. The "objective" standard is a popular proposal whereby "minimal risk" is based on the level of harms that "average, healthy, normal children" face in "their daily lives or … in routine examinations" (Wendler and Emanuel 2005, 575). This is a broad standard that, if interpreted conservatively, could have a chilling effect on pediatric research, and potentially exclude non-healthy children from studies (Field and Behrman 2004). The "socially acceptable" standard assumes that some children encounter greater risks in daily life than others, with some of these risks being socially acceptable and others not—e.g., farming and unsafe housing conditions, respectively. Per this standard, a "minor increase over minimal risk" constitutes the level of risk experienced in the lives of children who face greater, yet socially acceptable, risks (Wendler and Emanuel 2005, 577). The IRB should apply the socially acceptable standard to the risks associated with plerixafor injections since the case summary stipulates that the trial entails greater than minimal risk. Though imperfect, this standard appeals to a collective intuition that tries to balance allowing risks greater than those faced by most healthy children and protecting children from exposure to socially unacceptable risks.

In the present case (Johnson et al. 2020), more empirical information is needed to determine if the risks are socially acceptable. On its face, the administration of subcutaneous injections appears to pass the socially acceptable test. For example, children undergo subcutaneous injections as part of their routine MMR vaccination protocol. Not only is the administration of these subcutaneous vaccinations socially acceptable, but it is recommended by the Centers for Disease Control and Prevention (CDC) for young children to receive multiple doses through age six (Centers for Disease Control and Prevention 2019).

More problematic, however, are the unknown effects of plerixafor in patients with SCD. Though limited published data on the effects of plerixafor in adult SCD patients reveal a safe, rapid, and efficient mobilization of stem cells with few adverse effects, we still recommend that the IRB consult with experienced clinicians who have administered plerixafor to these patients and obtain their unpublished data (Lagresle-Peyrou et al. 2018). After collecting both published and unpublished data, the IRB should assess whether the risks of the procedure exceed the socially acceptable risks faced by children whose lives pose greater risks than those of average children. If, for example, the IRB finds very few adverse effects associated with administration of plerixafor to adult SCD patients, then these results further weigh in favor of a socially acceptable level of risk and thus permissibility of approval via 46.406.

The second element for 46.406 approval is whether an intervention is likely to yield "generalizable knowledge about the subjects' condition which is of vital importance for the understanding or amelioration of the subjects' condition" (U.S. Department of Health and Human Services 2018, 45 CFR 46.406). The case stipulates that this study is likely to yield this important information. Furthermore, because of a paucity of therapeutic options, and the potential for this medication to safely mobilize stem cells and provide curative therapy, this knowledge is of vital importance to ameliorating SCD in children.

Is an investigational new drug application necessary?

Generally, investigators who study new drugs must submit an IND application and receive approval from the FDA (Center for Drug Evaluation and Research 2015). However, clinical investigations of already FDA-approved drugs may be exempt from IND requirements if all criteria for an exemption per 21 CFR 312.2(b) are met, which are (1) the drug is lawfully marketed in the United States; (2) the investigator does not intend to report to the FDA for a new indication or significant change in labeling, or (3) advertising; (4) the investigation does not involve a route of administration, dose, patient population, or other factor that *significantly increases the associated risk*; (5) the investigation complies with informed consent requirements and the IRB process; and (6) the investigation does not promote the drug as safe or effective for the purposes for which it is under investigation (Food and Drug Administration 2019, 21 CFR 312.2(b)).

The case explicitly provides that the first three requirements are satisfied. Regarding the fourth requirement, the only factor implicated as a change from the current administration of the drug is the patient population. Because children are younger and less likely to have comorbidities or more severe forms of SCD compared to adults with SCD, this factor would likely represent a decrease in the risk associated with plerixafor and could not reasonably be thought to pose a significant increase in risk (Kanter and Kruse-Jarres 2013). Presumably, the investigation will comply with informed consent requirements and is stated to be reviewed by an IRB, thus satisfying the fifth criterion. Because the safety profile of plerixafor use in children is unknown, the investigator likely would not represent its use as safe and effective while the investigation is ongoing. If the assumptions in this analysis prove to be true, then the investigation would satisfy all the 21 CFR 312.2(b) criteria and thus qualify for an IND exemption.

Ultimately, the IRB is tasked with the challenge of balancing scientific progress with child protection. In this case, more data must be collected about the administration of plerixafor in SCD patients. If, after collecting more information, the IRB's intuitive judgment coupled with acquired data determine the risks of plerixafor are socially acceptable, then the IRB should approve the investigation under 45 CFR 46.406 and not require an IND application.

References

Center for Drug Evaluation and Research. 2015. IND application procedures: Exemptions from IND Requirements. U.S. Food and Drug Administration. https://www.fda.gov/drugs/investigational-new-drug-ind-application/ind-application-procedures-exemptions-ind-requirements (accessed December 19, 2019).

Centers for Disease Control and Prevention. 2019. Administering MMR vaccine" https://www.cdc.gov/vaccines/vpd/mmr/hcp/administering-mmr.html (accessed December 19, 2019).

Field, M. J., and R. E. Behrman, eds. 2004. *Ethical conduct of clinical research involving children.* Institute of Medicine (US) Committee on Clinical Research Involving Children, Washington (DC): National Academies Press. https://www.ncbi.nlm.nih.gov/books/NBK25542/. (accessed December 19, 2019).

Food and Drug Administration. 2019. 21 CFR §312. Investigational new drug application. Revised April 1. https://www.accessdata.fda.gov/scripts/cdrh/cfdocs/cfcfr/CFRSearch.cfm?fr=312.2 (accessed December 19, 2019).

Johnson, L. M., D. M. Duenas, and B. Wilfond. 2020. Greater than minimal risk, no direct benefit: Bridging drug trials and novel therapy in pediatric populations. *The American Journal of Bioethics* 20(4):102–103.

Kanter, J., and R. Kruse-Jarres. 2013. Management of sickle cell disease from childhood through adulthood. *Blood Reviews* 27(6):279–287.

Lagresle-Peyrou, C., F. Lefrère, E. Magrin, et al. 2018. Plerixafor enables safe, rapid, efficient mobilization of hematopoietic stem cells in sickle cell disease patients after exchange transfusion. *Haematologica* 103(5): 778–786.

Quinn, C. T. 2013. Sickle cell disease in childhood: From newborn screening through transition to adult medical care. *Pediatric Clinics of North America* 60(6):1363–1381.

U.S. Department of Health and Human Services. 2018. Final rule 45 CFR §46. Protection of human subjects. Revised July 19. https://www.hhs.gov/ohrp/regulations-and-policy/regulations/45-cfr-46/index.html (accessed December 19, 2019).

Ware, R. E., P. T. McGann, and C. T. Quinn. 2019. Hydroxyurea for children with sickle cell anemia: Prescribe it early and often. *Pediatric Blood and Cancer* 66(8):e27778.

Wendler, D., and E. J. Emanuel. 2005. What is a "minor" increase over minimal risk? *The Journal of Pediatrics* 147(5):575–578.

Section 5

Informed consent

LIZA-MARIE JOHNSON

The principle of "informed consent" arises from the historical misrepresentation of research and should have three key components: disclosure, comprehension, and voluntariness. Informed consent begins with a process of sharing relevant information for a proposed research study, including the purpose, associated risks and benefits (if any), and relevant alternatives. There is also an obligation on investigators to share information in a way that individuals can comprehend and ask questions, while also conveying to potential research participants the voluntariness of participation for those who decide to enroll. In the United States, federal regulations outline regulatory requirements of informed consent and include protections for vulnerable populations. This regulatory guidance also details criteria for when formal informed consent, or written documentation of it, can be waived. As outlined in the case examples in this chapter, research ethics questions arise in the actual operationalization of these requirements.

The eight cases included in this section focus on both the process and content of recruitment and informed consent developed by study teams prior to study approval and review by institutional review boards (IRBs). Process questions relate to the "how" of recruitment and consent. Content questions focus on the "what," i.e., the information that should be included in the informed consent form or discussed in conversation. Not surprisingly, many of these cases involve vulnerable subject populations such as pediatric participants (both neonates and adolescents), patients with psychological concerns (suicidal individuals), or individuals vulnerable due to a job role and the nature of research (i.e., active military members engaging in performance research).

CASE 5.1: THE ETHICS OF DISCLOSING TO RESEARCH SUBJECTS THE AVAILABILITY OF OFF-LABEL MARKETED DRUGS (2014)

Principles: Informed Consent, Respect for Participants

Topics: Drugs and Devices, Off-Label Drug Use and Availability

Values: Trustworthiness

U.S. regulations governing human subjects research require investigators to disclose to potential participants "appropriate alternative procedures or courses of treatment, if any, that

DOI: 10.1201/9781003335306-6

may be advantageous to the prospective subject" (CFR 46.116.a.4). This information is also included as a required element of the "key information section" under the revised Common Rule. Although this is a required element of consent, there may be subjectivity in what is defined as an "appropriate" alternative. In this case, the study team questioned whether the possibility of obtaining the same study drugs off-label via clinical prescription is an "appropriate alternative" to study participation and should thus be disclosed to potential participants. "Off-label" is the term used when a clinician prescribes a medication approved for one indication for a different, non-approved indication where the clinician believes the medication may still have a clinical benefit.

In the first commentary (Silber, this volume, p. 241), the commentator argues that investigators have a firm moral obligation to disclose the availability of the drugs off-label based on the ethical principles of (1) respect for persons and (2) veracity. The commentary argues that researchers have an obligation to disclose information that can influence decision making and allow potential participants to exercise autonomy. He notes that potential participants expect researchers to be honest, which is inconsistent with withholding information about off-label access to the study drugs. He believes that IRBs should insist this be disclosed under the category of "appropriate alternative" and states that investigators can place this information in context when explaining the rationale for the study.

The second commentary (Baskaran and Sade, this volume, p. 242) takes a more nuanced approach, arguing that the regulatory requirement to disclose appropriate alternatives may be dependent on the phase of the clinical trial. In early-phase trials (Phase I and Phase II studies), the determination of "appropriate" may depend on the persuasiveness of the evidence in suggesting effectiveness for the condition under study given the aims of early-phase trials. In Phase III trials, where the purpose of the trial is to confirm effectiveness and compare the intervention to commonly used treatments, the requirement for clinical equipoise in the trial rationale likely tips the weight of the evidence toward disclosure of off-label access as an "appropriate alternative." Finally, the commentary notes that outside of the regulatory requirements, it is ethically appropriate to disclose off-label availability whenever a clinician would judge there to be sufficient evidence for potential efficacy in clinical contexts.

The final commentary (Phillips and Wendler, this volume, p. 243) argues that disclosure must be evaluated on a case-by-case basis depending on varying contextual considerations. Like Silber, they argue for the role of IRBs in deciding when disclosure of off-label availability should be required; and like Baskaran and Sade, the commentators argue that the more favorable the safety and efficacy information, or if there is reason to believe the off-label use will be medically better than research participation, there is an obligation to disclose. On the contrary, if there is evidence that treatment outside of the research setting may be worse for patients or when off-label use may mislead individuals about a drug's effectiveness, the commentators argue these are contextual reasons not to disclose. Finally, the commentary considers that disclosures to facilitate understanding are appropriate when it is unlikely to overwhelm participants and potentially detract from the understanding of other key aspects of the trial.

All three commentaries endorse reasons to disclose the availability of off-label access to a study medication, whereas the latter two commentaries also elaborate on reasons why off-label access may not meet the regulatory criteria of "appropriate alternative." This case asks readers to consider the regulatory requirements of disclosure as well as when it may be ethically appropriate to disclose, regardless of whether the federal regulations require it.

CASE 5.2: A PRAGMATIC TRIAL OF SUICIDE RISK ASSESSMENT AND AMBULANCE TRANSPORT DECISION MAKING AMONG EMERGENCY MEDICAL SERVICES PROVIDERS: IMPLICATIONS FOR PATIENT CONSENT (2019)

Principles: Informed Consent, Risk–Benefit Ratio

Topics: Pragmatic Trials

Values: Trustworthiness

Pragmatic trials focus on the correlation between a treatment or intervention and outcomes as conducted in real-world health-systems practice. Each year, a large number of individuals present to emergency departments via emergency medical services (EMS) with a chief complaint of suicidal ideation, yet most are discharged home and do not receive specialty inpatient care. The pilot pragmatic clinical trial at the center of this case seeks to train EMS personnel to identify patients expressing suicidal thoughts and conduct a risk assessment to see who might be referred to a crisis lifeline for assistance in lieu of transport to the emergency department. The study team will use administrative-level data to assess the impact of this intervention and will not directly interact with patients. The question at hand for this case, and other pragmatic trial designs, is whether informed consent should be obtained from patients when the project seeks to study the implementation of the health-systems intervention. If so, how should it be done?

The first commentators (DeCou, Shah, and Porter, this volume, p. 248) note that the EMS providers and individuals expressing suicidality are *both* research participants, and thus conventional models of informed consent have low feasibility in this setting. The commentary outlines why standard regulatory exceptions to informed consent (waiver of consent, waiver of documentation of consent, and exceptions for emergency research) are impractical or not applicable and argue that novel models of consent are needed for research involving community-based care, particularly in an era where mobile integrated healthcare is expanding in many communities.

The second commentators (Goldstein and Weijer, this volume, p. 250) suggest that three tenets from the 15 recommendations in the Ottawa Statement on the Ethical Design and Conduct of Cluster Randomized Trials might be applied to this case. The three questions highlighted by the commentators include: how to conceive of the study intervention, who to consider as research participants, and finally if informed consent is required. Similar to the first commentators, this commentary highlights that study interventions apply to both EMS personnel (educational intervention to change their professional behavior) and patients (the risk assessment intervention is experimental at the patient level), and thus both groups are research participants. Given that both groups are research participants, the commentary suggests that at this stage in the trial design, consent should be obtained (from EMS personnel) or waived (in patients), and then propose a community notification mechanism during the future, larger pragmatic trial.

In the final commentary (Canavera and Parris, this volume, p. 253), the commentators define suicidality as a behavioral health emergency and argue for treating suicide research as emergency medicine research where informed consent can be waived. Although there are circumstances where a complete waiver is necessary (e.g., an unconscious or psychotic patient), there is most commonly a continuum of capacity and thus an "integrated consent model" is most appropriate. This model would mirror the approach used in daily clinical practice during behavioral crises, where a brief verbal discussion outlines the forthcoming intervention.

In this case, all commentators agree that patients expressing suicidality are research participants, whereas two of the commentaries also highlight EMS as being additional research participants. Despite their general agreement, nuances exist around the commentators' recommendations for informed consent.

CASE 5.3: THE OBLIGATIONS TO REPORT STATUTORY SEXUAL ABUSE DISCLOSED IN A RESEARCH STUDY (2014)

Principles: Informed Consent, Respect for Persons, Collaborative Partnership

Topics: Clinician and Researcher Obligations, Legal and Regulatory Oversight, Adolescents and Young Adults, Pregnancy, Privacy, Family Impact

Values: Trustworthiness, Social Value

This case highlights the value of anticipating circumstances in advance in order to disclose relevant information in the consent form. In this case, an adolescent pregnant person (age 15) was recruited to participate in a study measuring the effect of a co-parenting intervention on adolescents and their sexual partners. In reference to the need for parental permission for enrollment, a member of the study team asked the potential participant about the age of her partner. She reported that he was 18, and the team concluded that he could consent to his own participation if interested. The study team later learned that the partner was 24 years old. In the state where this study was taking place, given the age of the adolescent and her partner, statutory rape had occurred and potential sexual abuse was continuing. The question presented in the consultation was whether the study team had an obligation to report this crime.

The first commentary (Paquette and Ross, this volume, p. 258) reviews the likely legal landscape and concludes that at least one of the members of the study team would be legally considered a "mandatory reporter" of sexual abuse. They note that this reporter could be acting in a research rather than clinical role but that mandatory reporting laws do not make this distinction as the goal is to protect the well-being of the children involved. The authors review the current status of the Certificate of Confidentiality issued by the National Institutes of Health (NIH) and conclude that little guidance has been provided about what must be reported regardless of whether a Certificate of Confidentiality is in place. The commentary concludes that, in retrospect, the study team (and the IRB) should have anticipated this situation and made it clear in the consent form exactly what would have to be reported if disclosed and what would occur if the information is disclosed.

The second commentary (Hodgkinson et al., this volume, p. 261) covers similar territory as the first regarding mandatory reporting and the limits of Certificates of Confidentiality. They agree with the first commentary about the type of language that should have been included in the consent form and bring our attention to the potential harms of disclosure to law enforcement on the relationship between the adolescent and her partner and the likely disruption of social and financial stability. While adding that there is some social value to gathering information on this not-uncommon study, teams and IRBs should consider and minimize leaving the adolescents in this study worse off.

The third commentary (Finder and Korenman, this volume, p. 263) concludes, as the other two, that the statutory rape must be reported to the appropriate authorities. They then take a step back and consider how the study team should have considered the context and community in which their research was taking place. They advocate for community collaboration in the design and implementation of the study, most importantly to engage with community members and organizations to better understand the phenomenon under study. This would have allowed them to better consider what types of circumstances they may encounter and build trust with community partners. The latter is important regardless, as study teams may encounter challenges that would benefit from community input.

There is a clear consensus among the commentators that the sexual abuse discovered must be reported to the appropriate authorities. They each make recommendations to anticipate and prevent engagement with participants that could leave them worse off as a result of research participation.

CASE 5.4: CONJOINED CONSENT: INFORMED CONSENT WHEN DONOR AND RECIPIENT ARE BOTH RESEARCH PARTICIPANTS (2021)

Principles: Informed Consent

Topics: Drugs and Devices, Family Impact

Values:

This case considers a clinical trial that clearly involves multiple research participants, and an IRB has asked for assistance in understanding how potential participants should be approached and enrolled. In the study at hand, investigators are studying the investigational use of a medication among kidney donors to determine if it improves outcomes among recipients of the human leukocyte antigen (HLA)-matched kidney, thus enrolling donor and recipient as dyads. Given the preexisting relationship between the individual who has already agreed to donate a kidney in a clinical context and the recipient who will receive the organ, how should investigators approach the potential participants for enrollment in the ongoing clinical trial?

While the first commentary (Aaron, Ginsberg, and Lesandrini, this volume, p. 267) does not directly name therapeutic misconception, the commentators clearly articulate that in order for the donor to adequately assess the risks and benefits of the clinical trial, discussions of the research study should occur separately from and after all discussions related to the clinical decision to donate a kidney. They suggest that investigators check for adequate understanding concerning the research proposal and suggest the use of a donor advocate to help ensure the donor's decision is voluntary. Conversations about enrollment should occur separately from potential enrollment of the kidney recipient and should be timed such that the recipient does not have an opportunity to pressure the donor to enroll in the trial.

In the second commentary (Ghobrial, Akkina, and Anderson, this volume, p. 269), the commentators note how the interrelatedness of the donor and recipient may complicate decision making. Like the first commentary, they agree that researchers should first approach the donor and offer them the opportunity to enroll or refuse before ever approaching the kidney recipient. However, given the interrelatedness of the dyad, they argue that these separate consent discussions should be followed by a facilitated discussion around the independent decisions, unless there is a concern for harm, in order to promote shared decision making under a relational model of autonomy.

The final commentary (Kraft, this volume, p. 272) argues that due to the inherent interrelatedness between the donor and recipient, investigators should facilitate a joint decision-making process through a combined approach with both the donor and recipient present. This approach not only honors individual autonomy but also recognizes the role of relationships in decision making.

Although this case involves an HLA-matched kidney donor and recipient, other study contexts can involve the enrollment of dyads. Examples include other cases of organ donation, sibling or family research, some genomic studies, and donors and recipients in hematopoietic stem cell transplant. Ultimately, contextual features and other circumstances of family or dyad research may influence informed consent practices for participants when their participation is in some way relational.

CASE 5.5: NAVIGATING PARENTAL PERMISSION FOR NEONATAL RESEARCH (2015)

Principles: Informed Consent

Topics: Pediatrics

Values: Trustworthiness

In pediatric research, parents, as the legal guardians of their children, typically provide parental permission for research. This case, which involves a randomized, multicenter trial designed to test the efficacy of a drug on extremely premature infants, explored the other side of this interaction by asking who is appropriate to obtain parental permission for the research at a time when parents may be especially vulnerable due to the serious nature of extreme prematurity. As originally designed, study enrollment would not be completed by the attending physician but, rather, a study coordinator or investigator. During enrollment, circumstances arose where a child was enrolled at one site by an individual with the dual role of attending physician and study investigator, and another site requested permission to use a similar approach. As the regulations do not specify who can obtain permission for research, the case requestors ask if the role of the person obtaining consent might influence participant voluntariness or understanding and therefore who should be authorized to obtain parental permission for study participation.

The first commentators (Fiore and Cushman, this volume, p. 276) outline three ethical considerations when determining who should or should not obtain informed consent (parental permission) for trial participation. The first consideration is the obligation of study teams to minimize therapeutic misconception; and in cases when an attending physician obtains consent, an individual's ability to differentiate between research and treatment may be compromised given the role of the physician as medical advocate. A second requirement is to minimize factors that might cause an undue influence on potential participants, and the authors wonder if the physician in their role as investigator might unduly influence an individual's decision to participate in the trial. Finally, the commentary questions whether the dual role, as both physician and researcher, might create a conflict of commitment given the different ethical duties attached to each role, and recommends that clinicians should generally not enroll their patients in research trials. In circumstances when this is allowed by local IRBs, the commentators suggest that IRBs require a mitigation plan to address potential ethical concerns.

The second commentator (Eisenberg, this volume, p. 278) is also concerned about therapeutic misconception and undue influence, but also the timing of informed consent conversations.

She argues that unless enrollment issues necessitate postnatal enrollment, obtaining permission prenatally is the most ethical way to minimize therapeutic misconception and maximize parental understanding of key study information. Regardless of the timing of enrollment, the commentary argues that informed consent done by the attending physician is never appropriate.

The third commentators (Shah et al., this volume, p. 279) acknowledge the responsibility of investigators to (1) minimize therapeutic misconception and undue influence and (2) maximize understanding and voluntariness among potential study participants; however, they do not conclude that dual-role consent is necessarily problematic. The commentators note that an attending physician may be well positioned to explain the risks and benefits of the trial in the context of the neonate's ongoing medical concerns. Anyone, they argue, has the potential to unduly influence potential study participants, and they conclude with two strategies to mitigate this bias. One strategy is presenting three reasons why some might choose to participate and three reasons why others may not, to emphasize that both choices are reasonable. A second strategy would be to provide the opportunity to talk with another person about the study before deciding. The commentators conclude that it can be acceptable for a person who has a clinical role with a particular participant to be responsible for enrolling that participant.

All three commentaries in this case highlight two important threats to informed consent for clinical research: therapeutic misconception and undue influence. Regardless of whether it is a pediatric clinical trial where parents are providing permission for their child to participate or research where one is consenting for oneself, study teams have an ethical obligation to develop consent processes to ensure that individuals understand the purpose of the trial without conflating the research interventions with standard clinical care and to ensure that enrollment occurs voluntarily.

CASE 5.6: CLICK HERE TO COMPLETE THIS SURVEY: ONLINE RESEARCH, ADOLESCENTS, AND PARENTAL CONSENT (2020)

Principles: Informed Consent

Topics: Adolescents and Young Adults, Social Media

Values:

In the United States, pediatric research requires parental permission and child assent unless criteria for a waiver are met as outlined in 45 CFR 46.116 (U.S. DHHS 2018). In this case, an investigator would like to recruit adolescents who have undergone solid organ transplantation and ask them to complete an online minimal-risk survey about medication adherence. The investigator plans to advertise online through websites frequented by recent donors and their parents, and has asked for assistance on how to consent potential adolescent participants in the digital environment for minimal-risk research.

In the first commentary (Taylor and Mogul, this volume, p. 283), the commentators highlight the minimal-risk nature of the research with completion of the anonymous survey the only burden placed on adolescents, all of whom have already undergone a solid organ transplant and are thus familiar with medical care. While IRBs have the authority to waive parental permission, they conclude that many IRBs will be unwilling to do so and thus propose two alternatives: (1) recruitment through parents, whose forwarding of the survey link to the child would imply parental permission; or (2) through use of an honor system asking the adolescents to verify that parental permission has been obtained.

In the second commentary (Caruso Brown, this volume, p. 284), there is an emphasis on constrained adolescent autonomy: a concept that allows adolescents to make some of their own healthcare decisions and suggests that requiring parental permission is likely to hinder participation and potentially contribute to selection bias by enrolling only those adolescents willing to discuss the study with their parents in advance of completing the survey. She argues that while it may be technically possible to carry out the study without the waiver of parental permission, the potential for bias may compromise the ability of the study to produce meaningful results, which the author notes is in itself unethical.

The final commentary (Knapp, this volume, p. 286) takes the opposite approach of Caruso Brown, arguing that it is not impractical to carry out the survey without a waiver of parental permission, and like Taylor and Mogul, suggests alternative approaches for obtaining parental permission.

All three commentaries discuss circumstances when a waiver of parental permission may be warranted in pediatric research, but only one argues strongly for this approach in the case at hand. In thinking of online research for older children (teens > 13 years), it is important to consider involving the adolescent during the informed consent process. In designing or evaluating research with adolescents, it is important to determine if this group should consent independently (i.e., "click here"), provide assent in conjunction with formal parental permission, or participate via an honor system or other mechanism of verifying parental permission.

CASE 5.7: HOW SHOULD RESEARCH STAFF ADVERTISE ON SOCIAL MEDIA FOR RESEARCH OPPORTUNITIES? (2021)

Principles: Informed Consent, Fair Participant Selection

Topics: Social Media

Values: Equity

This case considers recruitment for research through online channels such as social media, and if this is chosen as a recruitment tool, *how* research staff should advertise research studies online through social media. Guidance exists for IRBs to review and approve any direct advertising to study participants as part of the evaluation of the recruitment and informed consent process, but what is ethically appropriate behavior when sharing approved content across sites, potentially across personal social media accounts?

The first commentator (Anderson, this volume, p. 290) argues that in the absence of clear regulatory guidance, the practice of recruitment through personal social media should be avoided unless there is sufficient reason to believe that such recruitment would promote diversity, equity, and inclusion. The commentary notes that many personal networks are nonrandom, potentially homogeneous groups: Recruitment through such networks may result in a sample population that is unrepresentative of the target population as a whole.

The second commentators (Spellecy and Nelson, this volume, p. 293) also acknowledge the potential for selection biases to include overselection of participants with similar demographics to the recruiting investigator, but they also note the potential for social media to democratize recruitment by potentially reaching a wider audience than through traditional methods. A more major concern of the commentators concerns professionalism and the potential for the recruitment post to be viewed as an endorsement of the research or conflated with other personal beliefs of the poster, potentially in a negative manner. Given the diversity of research opportunities, the commentary ultimately concludes that the appropriate approach for online recruitment is likely study-specific and will not be well serviced by rigid, across-the-board policies.

In this case, which asks how staff should advertise on social media, the two commentaries both raise concerns about selection bias and professionalism, but ultimately have differing opinions on the permissibility of recruitment through personal social media channels. This case and the associated commentaries highlight how the digital sharing of information on social media channels may blur the line between professional and personal roles. As recruitment moves online, it will be important for research ethicists and IRBs to evaluate the how and where of sharing research studies on social media sites. It may be that the scope of the activity (i.e., copying a link versus adding personal comments) and the nature of the research study are important factors as IRBs seek to determine the ethical permissibility of evaluating research when online advertising is part of the recruitment plan.

CASE 5.8: THE LIMITATIONS OF "BOILERPLATE" LANGUAGE IN INFORMED CONSENT: SINGLE-IRB REVIEW OF MULTISITE GENETIC RESEARCH IN MILITARY PERSONNEL (2019)

Principles: Informed Consent

Topics: Genetics, Legal and Regulatory Oversight

Values: Equity

Single-IRB (sIRB) review is a mechanism in the United States where a single IRB is responsible for the review and oversight of research conducted across multiple domestic clinical trial sites. The aim of sIRB review and oversight is to streamline the review process by reducing systemic inefficiencies and reducing administrative burden. In this case, the sIRB questioned the proposed "boilerplate" (i.e., standardized) language contained in the informed consent and wondered if it adequately captured information relevant for participants across sites. While this study involved differential risks across civilian and military sites, it is possible that boilerplate language may not apply to all participants based on a variety of factors. Examples include differential cultural or local contexts that would require different language, or the standardized language is required by an institution but not applicable to a particular study. This case considers the role of boilerplate language in informed consent forms and, in the context of sIRB review, which boilerplate language an IRB should apply.

The first commentator (Botkin, this volume, p. 296) highlights that boilerplate language is often equivalent to "legalese" and is frequently written in formats that do not prioritize reader comprehension and, in general, should be improved to enhance accessibility. Regarding which boilerplate template should be prioritized in the consent form, the author highlights that in the era of sIRB review, the regulations do not require identical consent forms to be used across sites; thus, nothing should change around site-specific language used by institutions: sIRBs should review and approve multiple versions of the consent form when relevant local laws or context require section-specific customization across sites.

The second commentary (Hull and Schiffenbauer, this volume, p. 298) acknowledges that while one goal of sIRB review is to minimize arbitrary variability in consent form language across sites, IRBs also have an obligation to ensure consent forms contain relevant site-specific contextual features and meet local policy requirements. Like Botkin, they argue that IRBs should accommodate requests to customize the consent form to recognize the substantive differences unique to military personnel offered enrollment in the study. Regarding the role of sIRBs in the oversight of multisite research, the commentators note the challenges that may arise as IRBs attempt to assess local context considerations. To address this challenge, they suggest research ethics consultation as a potential resource for IRBs struggling to interpret local context requirements.

The final commentary (Abraham, Hohmann, and Morash, this volume, p. 300) also highlights that boilerplate language is often institutionally mandated language related to privacy, confidentiality, and HIPAA that is typically fixed for consistent use across studies and hard to change. They quickly move on to highlight pragmatic solutions for the case at hand: Use of multiple IRBs (civilian and military) if a sIRB is not mandated or, in the case of a sIRB, asking the civilian and military sites to compromise on language applicable across states. Unlike the other commentaries, the authors offer multiple consent forms as a final option if there is no room to compromise across local stakeholders. They suggest that sIRBs, particularly for consortia groups, proactively develop consensus templates, negotiate boilerplate language for the group, and develop a standardized process for disagreements.

All three commentaries highlight some of the challenges associated with boilerplate language and sIRB review of research across sites with different local context considerations. Although approaches vary, all agree that consent language must contain information that is relevant to potential participants across all study sites and agree that despite sIRB review, multiple consent forms may be necessary to achieve this aim.

CASE 5.1: THE ETHICS OF DISCLOSING TO RESEARCH SUBJECTS THE AVAILABILITY OF OFF-LABEL MARKETED DRUGS

INTRODUCTION

This case explores what information investigators must disclose to potential subjects. Physicians are allowed to use their clinical judgment when treating patients. Among the options a physician has is to prescribe an intervention approved for one indication to treat a patient for a different indication—referred to as "off-label" use. The question in this case is whether an investigator must disclose the option of off-label use to a patient offered enrollment in a trial to determine whether the intervention previously approved for one indication is effective for a new indication.

Tomas Silber, MD, MASS, from the Children's National Medical Center, argues that an investigator is morally obligated to inform the patient that the intervention under investigation has been approved for another indication and could therefore be made available to them by prescription. Amrutha Baskaran, MD, MSCR, and Robert M. Sade, MD, from the University of California, San Diego, and the University of South Carolina, respectively, argue that whether the investigator is obligated to inform the patient about the option of off-label use may depend on the phase of the trial underway. John Phillips and David Wendler, PhD, from the Department of Bioethics at the NIH, discuss whether the investigator should disclose the option of off-label use, and argue that the decision rests on whether such a disclosure can increase the potential subject's understanding of the study under consideration and available treatment options.

CASE SUMMARY

Members of a group involved in testing novel applications for approved drugs want to know whether to disclose to potential research subjects the possibility of receiving the same drugs off-label. Specifically, once a drug has been approved for one indication, providers may prescribe it for other conditions. This practice, known as off-label use, allows providers to use their clinical judgment to decide when an approved drug may be beneficial for conditions other than the ones for which it has been approved. Should investigators testing approved drugs disclose this option in consent forms?

Several of the requestors' colleagues argued that because clinical trials are carried out only when there is some reason to believe that the drug may be beneficial for the condition in question, the option of receiving the drug by prescription in the clinical setting should be disclosed to potential subjects. The requestor was concerned that clinical trials frequently study agents for which the existing evidence does not support novel uses in the clinical setting; hence, it seems inappropriate in these cases to disclose the possibility of off-label use as an option.

The U.S. regulations governing human subjects research mandate that investigators disclose to potential subjects "appropriate alternative procedures or courses of treatment, if any, that might be advantageous to the subject" (CFR 46.116.a.4). However, the regulations do not specify or otherwise provide means for determining which courses of treatment qualify as appropriate alternatives.

This research ethics consultation raises two questions. When does the off-label availability of a study drug constitute an "appropriate alternative" that must be disclosed under federal regulations? When is it ethically appropriate for researchers to disclose off-label availability, regardless of whether the regulations require them to do so?

COMMENTARY 5.1.1: RESEARCHERS HAVE AN ETHICAL OBLIGATION TO DISCLOSE THE AVAILABILITY OF OFF-LABEL MARKETED DRUGS

TOMAS J. SILBER

At issue is whether a researcher testing novel applications for approved drugs has an obligation to disclose to prospective research subjects the possibility of receiving the drugs off-label. The answer is a firm *yes*.

Researchers have the ethical obligation to reveal to research subjects that a drug that has been approved for one indication may be prescribed off-label for other conditions. This obligation is based on the principle of respect for persons (National Commission for the Protection of Human Subjects of Biomedical and Behavioral Research 1979), which includes the appreciation of subjects' autonomy, which in practice requires researchers to provide information that can influence decision making. Clearly knowing alternatives to research study enrollment is essential to the exercise of autonomy. One could also add that subjects should expect researchers to be honest, which is incompatible with withholding information.

The ethics consultation requestor's concern is legitimate: that before the completion of clinical trials, there is not sufficient evidence to support the novel use of the study drug in the clinical setting. It does not follow, however, that therefore it seems inappropriate to disclose the possibility of off-label use as an option. The following information can be explained well under the rubric of "reasons for this study" during the informed consent process: (1) the lack of sufficient evidence and (2) the problems with off-label use.

The *Belmont Report* (National Commission for the Protection of Human Subjects of Biomedical and Behavioral Research 1979) informs the U.S. regulations governing human subjects research, which in turn clarify the ethical obligations of researchers (Department of Health and Human Services 2009). Figuring prominently is the federal mandate that investigators disclose to potential subjects "appropriate alternative procedures or courses of treatment, if any, that might be advantageous to the subject" (CFR 46.116.a.4). The federal regulations remain silent about, and do not specify or otherwise provide means for determining, which courses of treatment qualify as appropriate alternatives, but they clearly make this a matter for IRB consideration. Therefore, the IRB can and should insist that when a study drug is available off-label, this must be disclosed to research subjects.

Conclusion

The principle of respect for persons and the corollary of a right to information that can impact decision making indicate an ethical obligation for researchers to disclose off-label availability, regardless of whether the regulations require them to do so. An IRB imprimatur is highly desirable, and research ethics consultation should always be available to the IRB. In response to such consultation, I would not only propose that this is the right thing to do, but further argue that the disclosure of the availability of the study drug off-label falls within the category of an "appropriate alternative" that must be disclosed under federal regulations.

References

Department of Health and Human Services. 2009. Protection of human subjects. 45 CFR 46.
National Commission for the Protection of Human Subjects of Biomedical and Behavioral Research. 1979. Ethical principles and guidelines for the protection of human subjects of research. Available at: http://www.hhs.gov/ohrp/humansubjects/guidance/belmont.html.

COMMENTARY 5.1.2: THE RELEVANCE OF THE RESEARCH STUDY PHASE TO DISCLOSURE OF OFF-LABEL DRUG AVAILABILITY

AMRUTHA BASKARAN AND ROBERT M. SADE

Off-label use of drugs is widespread in medical practice, accounting for 21% of all prescribed drugs in the United States (Stafford 2012). U.S. Food and Drug Administration (FDA) regulations allow physicians to use an approved product for non-approved indications based on their best knowledge and judgment. For example, the vast majority of drugs used in pediatric practice are prescribed off-label, because few drugs have been tested sufficiently in children to receive FDA approval for pediatric use (Bush 2006).

In clinical practice, it is neither legally mandated nor ethically required to disclose to the patient that the use of a particular drug has not been approved by the FDA, that is, that it is being used off-label, although some have argued to the contrary (Wilkes and Johns 2008). In research, federal regulations require a clinical investigator to disclose, during the informed consent process, appropriate alternative procedures or courses of treatment for potential research subjects to consider as alternatives to participating in the study.

Whether an investigator is required by regulation or it is ethically appropriate to disclose an off-label alternative to a potential research subject may be related to the phase of the planned investigation. In a Phase I study, a new drug or treatment is used "in a small group of people for the first time to evaluate its safety, determine a safe dosage range, and identify side effects" (National Institutes of Health n.d.). In such cases, there must be reason to believe that the drug might be efficacious. But if there is not sufficient evidence of effectiveness for the condition being treated to persuade a physician that off-label use is indicated, off-label use of the drug is probably not an "appropriate alternative," and therefore should not be disclosed as such to a potential study subject.

In a Phase II study, "The drug or treatment is given to a larger group of people to see if it is effective and to further evaluate its safety" (National Institutes of Health n.d.). The same reasoning as that used for Phase I studies applies here: It might or might not be necessary to discuss off-label use of the drug as an appropriate alternative, depending on whether the evidence supports such use.

In a Phase III study, "The drug or treatment is given to large groups of people to confirm its effectiveness, monitor side effects, compare it to commonly used treatments, and collect information that will allow the drug or treatment to be used safely" (National Institutes of Health n.d.). Here, we argue, the reasoning shifts in favor of discussing off-label use of the drug because there is at least some evidence of effectiveness. Furthermore, study design is based on the existence of clinical equipoise, which requires that, at a minimum, there be sufficient emerging evidence to believe that the drug is likely to be efficacious for the condition under investigation or at least as effective as available standard treatments. In such a case, a clinician could decide based on best knowledge and judgment that use of the off-label drug qualifies as an "appropriate alternative" under federal regulations and the option should be disclosed to the potential research subject as an alternative to study participation.

We conclude that the off-label availability of a study drug might or might not constitute an "appropriate alternative" in Phase I and Phase II studies, depending on the persuasiveness of the evidence supporting its use for the target condition. By the time a drug is in a Phase III trial, however, the requirement for clinical equipoise has ensured that it has sufficient effectiveness for the drug to be considered a possible alternative, and thus it should be disclosed as such to a potential subject, as required by federal regulations. Finally, it is ethically appropriate for researchers to disclose off-label availability of an investigational drug, regardless of whether the regulations require them to do so, whenever there is sufficient evidence of potential efficacy for a physician to judge it useful in the relevant clinical circumstances.

References

Bush, A. 2006. Clinical trials research in pediatrics: Strategies for effective collaboration between investigator sites and the pharmaceutical industry. *Pediatric Drugs* 8(5):271–277.

National Institutes of Health. n.d. Clinical trial phases. U.S. National Library of Medicine. Available at: http://www.nlm.nih.gov/services/ctphases.html (accessed November 18, 2013).

Stafford, R. S. 2012. Off-label use of drugs and medical devices: A review of policy implications. *Clinical Pharmacology & Therapeutics*. Advance online publication 4 April.

Wilkes, M., and M. Johns. 2008. Informed consent and shared decision-making: A requirement to disclose to patients off-label prescriptions. *PLoS Medicine* 5(11):e223.

COMMENTARY 5.1.3: WHICH ALTERNATIVES SHOULD INVESTIGATORS DISCLOSE TO RESEARCH SUBJECTS?

JOHN PHILLIPS AND DAVID WENDLER

The decision whether to disclose to potential research subjects the possibility of obtaining a study agent on an off-label basis in the clinical setting involves two questions: (1) Under existing regulations, are investigators required to disclose this possibility? (2) Ethically, should investigators disclose this possibility?

We are aware of two cases in which the Office for Human Research Protections (OHRP n.d.) cited researchers for not disclosing the possibility of off-label use of the study agent. These determinations suggest that off-label use sometimes qualifies as an alternative that must be disclosed, and present the challenge of identifying the conditions under which this is the case. The present attempt to address this challenge is based on the assumption that, in cases of uncertainty, the regulations should be interpreted in ways that respect research subjects, and protect and promote their interests (National Commission for the Protection of Human Subjects of Biomedical and Behavioral Research 1979). Because respecting and protecting subjects are central to treating them ethically, this analysis also provides insight into when investigators ethically should disclose the possibility of off-label use as an alternative to research enrollment.

Why not?

The natural first response to whether investigators should disclose the possibility of off-label use is, "Why not?" Disclosure of this information requires essentially no additional resources, and may be of interest to some individuals (Menikoff 2003; Resnik et al. 2008). Yet the same is true for almost any piece of information. Hence, this line of reasoning suggests that investigators should disclose extensive information about essentially every aspect of the study in question.

This approach would involve significant costs, and likely would confuse potential subjects. If investigators disclosed every possible alternative that has a nonzero chance of being of interest to some subjects, the consent form would be virtually endless, and potential subjects likely would end up understanding important aspects of the study, such as the major risks, less well. This result highlights the difficulties that arise if one tries to determine in isolation whether a given piece of information should be disclosed and points to the need for a general analysis. Among all the pieces of information that have a nonzero chance of being of interest to some potential subjects, which should investigators disclose?

Medical interests

Investigators should be required to disclose a piece of information when there is good reason to believe that it is relevant to protecting or promoting subjects' medical interests. This standard suggests that investigators should be required to disclose an alternative when there is good reason to believe that it is medically better for potential subjects than enrolling in the research. For example, obtaining the study drug on an off-label basis may offer a more favorable risk–benefit ratio than enrolling in a study that provides the same drug but includes several invasive research biopsies.

In contrast, for the purposes of promoting individuals' medical interests, off-label use need not be disclosed when there is good reason to believe, given the nature of the condition and the study agent being tested, that enrolling in the trial offers a more favorable risk–benefit ratio than obtaining the study agent in the clinical setting. For example, when the study intervention is complex or novel, researchers who possess a high level of expertise may employ it more effectively than inexperienced clinicians. In these cases, off-label use in the clinical setting does not represent an appropriate alternative that must be disclosed to potential subjects. Protection and promotion of subjects' medical interests also do not provide a reason to disclose the possibility of off-label use in two further cases: when there is no evidence that off-label use is medically better than research enrollment, and when there is good reason to think that off-label use and research enrollment are medically equivalent.

Nonmedical interests

Reasonable persons have nonmedical values and preferences that can provide a reason to prefer some alternatives to research participation, even when there is no evidence to believe that they are medically better than research participation. For example, some may prefer to receive treatment locally, rather than travel to the study site.

When investigators are aware that a particular alternative is important to an individual or particular group, respect for persons suggests that they should disclose the alternative. At the same time, investigators and IRBs typically are not in a position to know which alternatives are relevant to certain individuals. Recognizing this limitation, the alternatives section of research consent forms should include a statement like: "You may want to ask the investigators or your physician about what options you have besides enrolling in the present study." Investigators also should ask potential subjects if they have any specific concerns that may be relevant to whether they enroll, and encourage them to ask questions.

Finally, disclosure of the possibility of off-label use may provide potential subjects with a better understanding of the study and their options. Whether this possibility provides a strong reason to disclose it depends on the circumstances.

1. Disclosure as a way of increasing potential subjects' understanding makes sense only when it is not likely to detract from their understanding of more important aspects of the study, such as the risks.
2. Whether disclosure makes sense depends on how much evidence exists regarding the safety of the test article, and whether there is good evidence regarding its efficacy for the condition in question (e.g., data from an early-phase trial conducted in advance of the current trial). The more favorable data that exist regarding safety and efficacy, the more reason there is to disclose off-label use as an alternative to research enrollment.
3. It is important to consider whether disclosure may lead even reasonable persons to assume that there must be data that the medication is effective for their condition. When that assumption is mistaken and cannot be corrected easily, investigators have a positive reason not to disclose the possibility of off-label use to potential subjects.

The relevance and strength of these considerations depend on the context. Recognizing that IRBs are charged with making determinations of what is included in the consent form and consent process based on the individual study, the best approach may be to allow IRBs to decide in these cases whether disclosure of off-label availability should be required and in what form.

Conclusion

This analysis suggests that, in all cases, investigators should ask potential subjects whether they have any questions or individual concerns that may be relevant to deciding whether it makes sense for them to enroll in the study. Whether, in addition, the off-label availability of study drugs must, should, or should not be disclosed varies from study to study.

When there is reason to believe that off-label use will be medically better than research participation, this alternative must be disclosed. Evidence that off-label use is important to some individuals provides reason to disclose it to them. At the same time, this consideration must be weighed against the extent to which treatment outside of a research setting will be medically worse for patients and the possibility that the disclosure of off-label availability may mislead even reasonable persons about the drug's effectiveness. Given that these determinations depend on the circumstances, the decision of whether investigators should be required to disclose the possibility of off-label use in these cases should be left up to the investigators and IRBs to decide on a case-by-case basis.

References

Menikoff, J. 2003. The hidden alternative: Getting investigational treatments off-study. *Lancet* 361(9351):63–67.

National Commission for the Protection of Human Subjects of Biomedical and Behavioral Research. 1979. Belmont report. Ethical principles and guidelines for the protection of human subjects of research. Available at: http://www.hhs.gov/ohrp/humansubjects/guidance/belmont.html (accessed October 17, 2013).

Office for Human Research Protections (OHRP). n.d. Informed consent guidelines. Available at: http://www.hhs.gov/ohrp/policy/consent/index.html (accessed October 17, 2013).

Resnik, D. B., S. Peddada, J. Altilio, N. Wang, and J. Menikoff. 2008. Oncology consent forms: Failure to disclose off-site treatment availability. *IRB* 30(6):7–11.

CASE 5.2: A PRAGMATIC TRIAL OF SUICIDE RISK ASSESSMENT AND AMBULANCE TRANSPORT DECISION MAKING AMONG EMERGENCY MEDICAL SERVICES PROVIDERS: IMPLICATIONS FOR PATIENT CONSENT

INTRODUCTION

Current approaches to caring for patients with suicidal ideation are neither well tailored to their needs nor efficient in the use of healthcare resources, including emergency medical services (EMS) response and transport. For instance, approximately one-third of patients who present to the hospital for psychiatric care, including those in suicidal crises, arrive by ambulance (Larkin et al. 2006). However, most patients who are seen at an emergency department (ED) with suicidality are discharged home, and do not receive specialty inpatient psychiatric care (Kroll et al. 2018). EDs typically have lengthy waits, and most do not have psychiatrists or psychologists to address the needs of patients with suicidal ideation. By contrast, suicide crisis lines can offer immediate and suicide-specific intervention from trained crisis line operators under the supervision of a licensed mental health practitioner. A study has been proposed with an objective to enhance the ability of EMS providers to assist patients with suicidal thoughts in accessing appropriate crisis intervention services. The study would involve training EMS providers to direct appropriate patients to these crisis services. The impact of the study would be assessed through administrative databases, and the research team would not directly engage with patients.

This study is typical of pragmatic studies that focus on changing health system practices to improve patient outcomes (Weinfurt et al. 2017). This study raises questions about whether patients should be notified or whether informed consent from patients should be obtained. The companion case in this issue regards issues that can arise during the implementation of a cluster trial when the study reveals potentially problematic practices within a health system (Johnson, Zabrowski, and Wilfond 2019).

The first commentary, by Chris DeCou of Harborview Medical Center and the University of Washington, Seema Shah of Lurie Children's Hospital and Northwestern University, and Kathryn Porter of Seattle Children's Hospital and Research Institute, outlines the regulatory options to address the question of consent and highlights the challenges with each approach. They also point out that these issues are likely to become more frequent in the context of care innovations using mobile technologies to provide mental health services. The other three commentators collectively conclude that traditional consent is not practical but that patients should be made aware of the study. They all agree that the regulatory solution would be grounded in considering this study to be minimal risk. However, each commentary looks at the question from a distinct vantage point to reach its conclusion. Cory Goldstein and Charles Weijer from Western University, whose scholarship focuses on the ethical complexities of research within the learning health system, propose specific steps to consider the ethical issues for any cluster randomized trial. They point out the implications for consent from their systematic approach. Kristin Canavera and Kendra Parris, from St. Jude Children's Research Hospital, look at this case in the context of clinical psychiatric care and contend that there is not a meaningful distinction between research and clinical care that requires a different approach to research consent. Neal Dickert from Emory University has recently developed a systematic framework to consent that relies on identified goals of informed consent to determine the ethical approach. He applies this framework to the case to conclude that while consent from patients is not necessary, efforts to engage patients are necessary.

CASE SUMMARY

The study will develop an intervention protocol for EMS providers to use to identify patients who express suicidal thoughts and facilitate obtaining immediate risk assessment, safety planning, and outpatient treatment referrals without requiring transport to the ED. Then a preliminary pragmatic trial will observe EMS providers who have been trained in the intervention protocol. The trial will assess barriers to, and facilitators of, implementing the protocol.

The study will identify two fire stations and recruit at least 10 EMS providers from each station. Providers who volunteer to participate will provide informed consent, including consent for evaluation of their adherence to the intervention protocol, and will provide self-report data related to the intervention. Providers will be trained to administer a brief evidence-based suicide risk screening tool that will include standardized clinical cutoffs to stratify patients' level of suicidality.

Patients who screen negative for suicidality will be provided crisis lifeline information, as no specific intervention is required. For patients who screen positive for suicidality, EMS providers will contact the local suicide crisis lifeline together with the patient, and the crisis lifeline will conduct a brief assessment to guide appropriate treatment decision making. If a patient is deemed to be at low to moderate risk and agrees to engage with crisis lifeline services, the crisis lifeline will complete brief suicide-specific interventions over the phone, and the patient will be released from EMS. Patients who are determined to be at moderate to high risk, and/or who are unable or unwilling to engage with crisis lifeline services, will be transported to the ED for additional evaluation and treatment, including possible referral to inpatient psychiatric care. Patients who have previously attempted suicide or engaged in other self-directed violence will also be transported to the ED for evaluation and treatment.

The investigators will not directly engage with EMS patients in the study. Instead, administrative data and patient services utilization will be collected across all city and county EMS services, and from local crisis lifeline services records, to characterize the treatment course and outcomes of usual care provision by EMS providers for suicidality. Additionally, EMS providers' self-reports will include their perceptions of implementation outcomes, including acceptability, appropriateness, and feasibility.

The study proposes to establish a technical advisory board to develop and evaluate the protocol for EMS providers to assess and refer suicidal patients. The committee will include representatives from EMS, fire, and police services; local hospital administration and EDs; the suicide crisis lifeline; mobile crisis and emergency shelter services; and a suicide attempt survivor who previously presented for care via EMS. The study will also utilize a data safety monitoring board, which will comprise three individuals independent of the study.

An ethics consultation was requested by the primary investigator and study team to discuss the issue of informed consent as they were developing the study. Should informed consent be obtained from patients for a project studying the implementation of a screening and referral tool that targets EMS providers and addresses the needs of patients with suicidal ideation in prehospital settings? If so, how should this be done?

REFERENCES

Johnson, L., J. Zabrowski, and B. Wilfond. 2019. A cluster randomized trial to screen for abusive head trauma in the pediatric intensive care unit - How to manage site-specific evidence of racial/ethnic disparity. *American Journal of Bioethics* 19(10):108–109.

Kroll, D. S., J. Karno, B. Mullen, S. B. Shah, D. J. Pallin, and D. F. Gitlin. 2018. Clinical severity alone does not determine disposition decisions for patients in the emergency department with suicide risk. *Psychosomatics* 59(4):388–393.

Larkin, G. L., C. A. Claassen, A. J. Pelletier, and C. A. Camargo. 2006. National study of ambulance transports to United States emergency departments: Importance of mental health problems. *Prehospital and Disaster Medicine* 21(2):82–90.

Weinfurt, K. P., A. F. Hernandez, G. D. Coronado., et al. 2017. Pragmatic clinical trials embedded in healthcare systems: Generalizable lessons from the NIH collaboratory. *BMC Medical Research Methodology* 17(1):144–147.

COMMENTARY 5.2.1: IMPROVING CARE FOR SUICIDAL PATIENTS WHILE PROTECTING HUMAN SUBJECTS: ADDRESSING ETHICAL CHALLENGES IN MENTAL HEALTH RESEARCH INVOLVING EMERGENCY MEDICAL SERVICES PROVIDERS

CHRISTOPHER R. DeCOU, SEEMA K. SHAH, AND KATHRYN M. PORTER

Limited research has been conducted on emergency medical services (EMS) providers' provision of psychiatric services and/or suicide-specific interventions outside of the hospital setting. This study seeks to fill this gap by proposing to test an intervention with potential benefit to patients who EMS engages within the community (Wilfond, Zabrowski, and Johnson 2019). Because these patients fall within the federal definition of human subjects (U.S. Department of Health and Human Services 2009, 45 CFR 46.102(f)), their informed consent is typically required for research.

However, it is unclear whether conventional models of informed consent are feasible in this instance, and perhaps in community-based suicide prevention research more generally. First, EMS providers participating in the delivery of this particular intervention are not members of the research team, and thus lack the requisite knowledge about the study that might be necessary to obtain consent from EMS patients. Not only are EMS providers not research staff, they are research participants themselves. If conventional informed consent were required for this study, some research participants would have to obtain consent from other research participants—which is far from standard and not necessarily a protection. Moreover, the time required for typical research informed consent procedures might be prohibitive; EMS visits are brief by design, so that EMS providers can be available for other emergencies that arise in the community.

There are existing regulatory exceptions to the traditional rules governing informed consent. These include waivers of informed consent (U.S. Department of Health and Human Services 2009, 45 CFR 46.116(d)), waivers of documentation of consent (U.S. Department of Health and Human Services 2009, 45 CFR 46.117(c)), and emergency medicine research regulations (Food and Drug Administration 2018, 21 CFR 50.24). Although sound arguments can be made for applying each of these regulatory exceptions to the proposed study, there are also unique challenges with each exception within the context of suicide prevention research in the community setting.

First, a waiver of informed consent requires that the research involve no more than minimal risk to the subjects. While a proposed risk mitigation plan may be able to reduce the risk considerably, risk involves both the probability and the magnitude of the harm. Research involving potentially suicidal patients may not have a high probability of harm, but the magnitude of potential harm is great. The primary concern is ensuring that patients are able to access the appropriate level of care, and that no patient in need of suicide-specific care is incorrectly diverted from ambulance transport to pursue necessary and urgent treatment at a medical facility. However, this severe adverse event is highly unlikely, given the low base rate of suicidal behavior, even among high-risk clinical populations (Owens, Horrocks, and House 2002). For example, in a recent study of suicide after presenting to a hospital for nonfatal self-harm, less than 1% of patients died by suicide in the year after discharge (Vuagnat et al. 2019). Moreover, one way to reduce the risk further is to employ a technical advisory board and a data safety monitoring board to closely monitor data and standard operating procedures throughout the trial. It is also important to consider the frequently experienced burdens and harms associated with the current standard of care approach of unnecessary ambulance transport and ED care. For example, ED treatment includes long waiting periods, limited access to mental health treatment, and substantial financial costs for individuals and their families (Harris et al. 2016).

The second option, a waiver of documentation of consent, would require either EMS providers (themselves study participants) to carry out the informed consent process, or the insertion of a study team member into the EMS system, potentially impacting the flow of service. Because there is no way to know in advance whether a particular call will involve a suicidal patient, this may add unnecessary burdens and inefficiencies to the system. Finally, the third option of an exception for emergency research creates challenges because community-based care for suicidality and other behavioral emergencies is often not focused on the resolution of an imminent life-threatening illness or injury, such as cardiac arrest or overdose. Therefore, regulations designed for research involving interventions that must be applied urgently do not seem applicable to this proposed health services intervention.

These challenges highlight significant ethical issues raised within the context of informed consent for EMS-focused suicide prevention studies, and addressing them is crucial to improving care for suicidal patients. For example, are EMS providers effective in making determinations about appropriate "treatments and the settings of care" (Lezzoni, Dorner, and Ajayi 2016, 1108)? In general, there is a dearth of evidence on alternatives to transportation for ED care for suicidal patients seen by EMS providers in the community. Carefully designed pragmatic clinical trials and other prospective research methods can address this gap, but these studies will require a rigorous and feasible approach to informed consent for the numerous settings and stakeholders involved.

Developing effective models of consent for research involving community-based care of suicidal patients is particularly important given the proliferation of mobile integrated healthcare (MIH) (Choi, Blumberg, and Williams 2016). MIH is an approach to out-of-hospital care that expands conventional EMS responses to include nursing, social work, and other health professions that may be more effective for certain types of nonurgent EMS calls. MIH responses can include referrals to primary care or mental health providers in the community, assistance in accessing housing or other public welfare benefits, and ongoing community-based follow-up by a member of the MIH team. MIH is particularly relevant to issues of mental health and persistent psychiatric illness that often require coordinated community-based responses and lack sufficient ED resources.

There are several aspects of MIH that could be considered in assessing the feasibility of implementing modified versions of informed consent. First, EMS encounters are typically brief, though this could vary greatly within the setting of MIH services and could include extended time on scene (MedStar Mobile Healthcare 2014). Other features of MIH could include provision of mental health services by nurses or social workers in the field (King County Public Health 2017), or structured follow-up contacts performed by MIH team members after the initial incident has resolved. It may be that modified informed consent could be more appropriate for such interactions, particularly given the additional time allowed for these types of patient contacts, or that opt-out or other deferred models of consent could be incorporated within follow-up contacts for MIH patients engaged in additional services.

In the case of both conventional EMS operations and emerging models of MIH, innovative models of informed consent and appropriate consideration of modifications and waivers of consent are needed. It may be necessary to reconsider how emergency medicine settings and situations are conceptualized within regulatory and ethical review for studies conducted in prehospital settings. This could include a more nuanced understanding of the time frames, personnel, and potential for follow-up, in addition to an improved understanding of immediate threats to life. EMS and MIH care includes a spectrum of exigency that is not well incorporated within conventional research ethics guidelines and regulations. Yet it is increasingly important that research ethics evolve to protect EMS patients by minimizing potential harms associated with research and allowing EMS patient populations to benefit from new approaches to EMS and MIH treatment that result from research conducted in the setting in which these patients receive care.

References

Choi, B. Y., C. Blumberg, and K. Williams. 2016. Mobile integrated health care and community paramedicine: An emerging emergency medical services concept. *Annals of Emergency Medicine* 67(3):361–366.

Food and Drug Administration. 2018. Final rule 21 CFR §50.24. Exception from informed consent requirements for emergency research. Revised 1 April 2018. https://www.accessdata.fda.gov/scripts/cdrh/cfdocs/cfcfr/cfrsearch.cfm?fr=50.24 (accessed June 28, 2019).

Harris, B., R. Beurmann, S. Fagien, and M. M. Shattell. 2016. Patients' experiences of psychiatric care in emergency departments: A secondary analysis. *International Emergency Nursing* 26:14–19.

King County Public Health. 2017. *Division of emergency medical service - annual report.* Seattle, WA.

Lezzoni, L. I., S. C. Dorner, and T. Ajayi. 2016. Community paramedicine — Addressing questions as programs expand. *New England Journal of Medicine* 374:1107–1109.

MedStar Mobile Healthcare. 2014. *Mobile integrated healthcare: Approach to implementation,* Burlington, MA: Jones & Bartlett Publishers.

Owens, D., J. Horrocks, and A. House. 2002. Fatal and non-fatal repetition of self-harm. Systematic review. *The British Journal of Psychiatry: The Journal of Mental Science* 181(3):193–199.

U.S. Department of Health and Human Services. 2009. Final rule 45 CFR §46. Protection of Human Subjects. Revised January 15. https://www.hhs.gov/ohrp/regulations-and-policy/regula-tions/45-cfr-46/index.html (accessed June 28, 2019).

Vuagnat, A., F. Jollant, M. Abbar, K. Hawton, and C. Quantin. 2019. Recurrence and mortality 1 year after hospital admission for non-fatal self-harm: A nationwide population-based study. *Epidemiology and Psychiatric Science,* advanced online publication.

Wilfond, B., J. Zabrowski, and L. Johnson. 2019. A pragmatic trial of suicide risk assessment and ambulance transport decision making among emergency medical services providers. *American Journal of Bioethics* 19(10):97–98.

COMMENTARY 5.2.2: A STEPWISE APPROACH TO ETHICALLY ASSESS PRAGMATIC CLUSTER RANDOMIZED TRIALS: IMPLICATIONS FOR INFORMED CONSENT FOR SUICIDE PREVENTION IMPLEMENTATION RESEARCH

CORY E. GOLDSTEIN AND CHARLES WEIJER

Is informed consent in this study required, and, if so, from whom and for what (Wilfond, Zabrowski, and Johnson 2019)? These are the first questions that come to mind for almost anyone—be they investigator, IRB member, or ethicist—working through the ethical issues in research involving humans. But pragmatic trials studying implementation interventions are complex, and accordingly require a stepwise approach to their ethical analysis.

The proposed study of suicide risk assessment and ambulance transport decision making among EMS providers is a pilot study that will inform a future pragmatic cluster randomized trial. Pragmatic trials seek to evaluate interventions in real-world settings to inform the decisions of patients, providers, and system managers. Cluster randomized designs are an increasingly popular choice for pragmatic trials (Ford and Norrie 2016). Cluster randomized trials are complex studies in which groups—as opposed to individuals—are allocated randomly to study interventions, while outcomes are measured on the individuals.

In the future pragmatic trial based on the findings from the pilot study, fire stations would be randomized either to adopt a novel EMS provider training program for suicide risk assessment and transportation, or to continue the usual practice of transporting all patients to EDs. The design could compare the two interventions in parallel, or it could assess the novel intervention with a stepped wedge design as it is rolled out across fire stations. Outcomes would be measured from self-reported EMS providers' data and from anonymized patient data collected from electronic health records.

While these implementation studies raise interesting questions about consent, pragmatic cluster randomized trials raise other important questions. The Ottawa Statement on the Ethical Design and Conduct of Cluster Randomized Trials provides 15 recommendations to aid investigators and research ethics committees (Weijer et al. 2012). Using the Ottawa Statement as guidance, we address three questions raised by the case. Each, as it turns out, has downstream implications for how to approach informed consent.

How should we conceive of the study interventions?

Study interventions in a cluster randomized trial can be delivered at a number of different levels, two of which are relevant in this case (Eldridge, Ashby, and Feder 2005). Professional-level interventions, such as education or training, are delivered to healthcare providers with consequences for their patients. Individual-level interventions, such as drugs or treatment strategies, are delivered to patients.

In the case, EMS providers will administer a brief evidence-based suicide risk tool to assess risk of suicidality. Those patients at low risk of suicidality will be directed to crisis lifeline services, while patients at high risk or who have previously attempted suicide or self-harm will be taken directly to an ED.

Interventions in implementation research are often complex and difficult to categorize. In this case, the intervention comprises professional-level and individual-level components. In brief, the EMS providers are targeted by the educational aspects of the intervention, and education seeks to change their professional behavior. EMS providers also deliver the intervention to patients, and the intervention itself is experimental at the level of the patient. How we conceive of the interventions has implications for the identification of research participants.

Who are the research participants?

National and international ethical guidelines require investigators and research ethics committees to clearly identify participants to ensure they are appropriately protected (CIHR et al. 2014; CIOMS 2016; DHHS 2018). According to the Ottawa Statement, "a research participant can be identified as an individual whose interests may be affected as a result of study interventions or data collection procedures" (Weijer et al. 2012). This includes all individuals who are the intended recipient of an experimental or control intervention, with whom an investigator interacts for research purposes, or about whom an investigator obtains identifiable private information.

Health providers in knowledge translation and health services trials are the oft-forgotten research participants. In the case, they receive an educational intervention; moreover, they are required to self-report data related to the intervention. Thus, EMS providers should be considered research participants.

But are the patients research participants? The Ottawa Statement states, "If the study intervention is designed to promote evidence-based practice by health professionals, and does not directly intervene in patient care, and if the investigators do not interact with patients or collect their identifiable private information, then those patients are not research participants" (Weijer et al. 2012). However, in this case, it is not yet known whether EMS provider triage and referral to suicide prevention lines are safe and effective for patients. As the intervention is experimental at the patient level, the patients should be considered research participants.

Is informed consent required?

There is a general presumption that the informed consent of research participants is necessary unless conditions for a waiver of consent obtain. As both EMS providers and patients are research participants, their informed consent is required unless a research ethics committee approves a waiver of consent. A research ethics committee may approve a waiver of consent when (1) the research is not feasible without a waiver of consent and (2) the study interventions and data collection procedures pose no more than minimal risk (Weijer et al. 2012).

In the case, the educational interventions would pose no more than minimal risk to the health providers. Since EMS providers are routinely trained as part of their employment, the risks posed by a novel evidence-based training program would be no more than the risks they commonly incur in other training programs. Thus, a waiver of consent hinges on the feasibility of obtaining it. Since only 10 volunteer EMS providers are sought in two fire stations, it is difficult to see how their informed consent could not feasibly be obtained. The future pragmatic cluster randomized trial might be a case in which EMS providers would not be able to meaningfully refuse the interventions, as the interventions would be delivered to the entire healthcare team as a unit.

Obtaining informed consent from patients is plainly not feasible. The question, then, is whether the study interventions and data collection procedures pose no more than minimal risk. Minimal risk, according to U.S. regulations, means that "the probability and magnitude of harm or discomfort anticipated in the research are not greater … than those ordinarily encountered in daily life" (U.S. Department of Health and Human Services 2018, 45 CFR 46). In the case, data are collected from administrative databases and from crisis lifeline services records. With sufficient confidentiality procedures, data collection would pose no more than minimal risk. Moreover, the incremental risk posed to patients who receive the study interventions—either a referral to a suicide prevention line or being directly transported to the ED—is no greater than that ordinarily encountered by this patient population. Thus, the informed consent from patients can be waived.

In the event that requirements for a waiver of informed consent are met for both patients and providers in the future pragmatic trial, there is a final question worth considering: Should we notify people of ongoing research? Notification may serve a number of purposes, including the preservation of trust with communities and participants. In this case, trust with the community may be promoted by a study website and media messaging about the study (e.g., radio broadcasts, newspapers, and social media). Furthermore, participant trust may be enhanced by letting patients know about their participation after the fact and informing them of the study results.

References

Canadian Institutes of Health Research (CIHR), Natural Sciences and Engineering Research Council of Canada (NSERC), and Social Sciences and Humanities Research Council of Canada (SSHRC). 2014. Tri-council policy statement: Ethical Conduct for Research Involving Humans. http://www.pre.ethics.gc.ca/eng/policy-politique/initiatives/tcps2-eptc2/default/ (accessed June 25, 2019).

Council for International Organizations of Medical Sciences (CIOMS). 2016. International Ethical Guidelines for Health-related Research Involving Humans. http://www.pre.ethics.gc.ca/eng/policy-politique/initiatives/tcps2-eptc2/default/ (accessed 25 June 2019).

Eldridge, S. M., D. Ashby, and G. S. Feder. 2005. Informed patient consent to participation in cluster randomized trials: An empirical exploration of trials in primary care. *Clinical Trials (London, England)* 2(2):91–98.

Ford, I., and J. Norrie. 2016. Pragmatic trials. *The New England Journal of Medicine* 375(5):454–463.

U.S. Department of Health and Human Services (DHHS). 2018. Electronic Code of Federal Regulations. 45 CFR 46. https://www.hhs.gov/ohrp/regulations-and-policy/regulations/revised-common-rule-regulatory-text/index.html (accessed June 25, 2019).

Weijer, C., J. M. Grimshaw, M. P. Eccles., et al. 2012. The Ottawa statement on the ethical design and conduct of cluster randomized trials. *PLOS Medicine* 9(11):e1001346.

Wilfond, B. S., J. Zabrowski, and L.-M. Johnson. 2019. A pragmatic trial of suicide risk assessment and ambulance transport decision making among emergency medical services providers. Implications for patient consent. *American Journal of Bioethics* 19(10):97–98.

COMMENTARY 5.2.3: INFORMED CONSENT IN A PRAGMATIC EMERGENCY SUICIDE TRIAL: REJECTING THE RESEARCH–PRACTICE DISTINCTION

KRISTIN CANAVERA AND KENDRA PARRIS

Managing suicidality is fraught with unique ethical issues, including limits to confidentiality, questions about decision-making capacity, and tensions related to beneficence overriding patient autonomy during behavioral health crises (Lakeman and Fitzgerald 2009). This case study raises ethical questions in suicide research using pragmatic trials. Does informed consent need to be obtained in an emergency suicide pragmatic trial (Wilfond, Zabrowski, and Johnson 2019)? Is obtaining informed consent feasible in a behavioral health emergency? Are waivers or alterations to informed consent ethically justifiable for a vulnerable population, or should added protections be implemented? We draw parallels to the impracticalities of obtaining informed consent in emergency medicine research. We also propose use of informed consent processes used in daily clinical practice during behavioral health crises, which account for patient safety as well as vulnerability.

By definition, suicidality is a behavioral health emergency. Suicide research involving EMS providers should be conceptualized as equivalent to emergency medicine research, in which informed consent can be waived. Historically, informed consent and protection of participants in emergency medicine research faced challenges due to the many ethical issues that emerged. The debate on how to ethically ensure protection of participants even led to a moratorium on emergency research for several years (Karlawish 2008). When considering suicide research, a similar pattern of reluctance from investigators and IRBs consequently leads to delays in research due to the ethical issues that emerge when involving a high-risk population (Lakeman and Fitzgerald 2009). As an example, approval of the Suicide Prevention Outreach Trial (SPOT), as part of the Health Care Systems Research Collaboratory, which aims to implement large-scale pragmatic clinical trials, was extended several months (10) longer than other trials due to disagreements regarding whether minimal-risk studies could be carried out in a high-risk population (Weinfurt et al. 2017).

The same challenges faced in emergency medicine apply to suicide research within a crisis context, including various practical barriers precluding obtainment of consent (Flory, Mushlin, and Goodman 2016). Time constraints, the need for immediate intervention, and significant emotional distress contribute to these impracticalities of having a meaningful consent conversation or locating legally authorized representatives for consent. Further complicating matters, patients experiencing suicidality can be considered vulnerable due to their potential for incapacity or underlying mental illness. Having a mental health disorder does not indicate automatic incapacity, and capacity is not a strict either/or concept when encountered within the context of suicidality. However, there is a reason to presume that some degree of incapacity may be evident in suicidality, due to depressive symptomology or even psychosis that may impair decision-making capacity (Fisher et al. 2002). In clinical practice, informed consent is not required during an emergency risk assessment or safety planning when managing suicidality. Minimizing risk of self-harm is prioritized over rights to persons and consent. Furthermore, within the context of pragmatic trials, the need for informed consent is not an absolute and some would argue is not necessary (Faden et al. 2013; Goldstein et al. 2018).

Given this possibility of vulnerability, though, should additional protections be implemented for obtaining informed consent? What approach is the most prudent in balancing this tension of respect for autonomy while simultaneously addressing increased safeguards for vulnerability? Traditional approaches appealing to prospective consent or delayed consent are troubled with logistical and practical concerns, as evidenced in emergency research. An alternative approach is proxy consent through a legally authorized representative, though this option too is laden with impracticalities in a behavioral health crisis. Obtaining delayed or proxy consent may also substantially minimize involvement and enrollment, thus inadvertently contributing to the underlying problems of justice and the need for additional research regarding suicidality (Fisher et al. 2002; Karlawish 2008). Although an emergent literature questions the consent waiver in pragmatic trials due to infringements of respect for persons (Flory, Mushlin, and Goodman 2016), we argue that waivers are ethically justifiable given the emergency nature of the situation, as well as the broader benefits for this population specifically and society as a whole (Faden et al. 2013).

To address this conundrum of implementing adequate safeguards, we advocate for efforts to fully respect persons to the extent possible. While we hold that the consent waiver is justifiable in this case study, we also advocate for consideration of a conceptual model that applies a continuum approach to capacity and vulnerability, akin to a "sliding scale" (Biros 2018). As Biros (2018) proposes, waivers for consent involve the most extreme cases, in which capacity is completely lacking (e.g., an unconscious patient or a psychotic patient). But participants' capacity and vulnerability often fall somewhere in between the extremes. In the current case study, patients may be likely to have some decisional capacity. In these cases, rather than a consent waiver, investigators should strive to implement modified or adapted consent, comparable to the standard of care currently in clinical practice during suicide risk assessments. For these participants, a brief discussion, assent, or an abbreviated verbal consent, or even refusal would suffice. As one moves along the continuum of cases involving more distressing experiences (e.g., severe pain or significant emotional distress), a meaningful conversation may not be feasible and a more judicious approach may instead be brief disclosure of the study and intervention. Regardless of approach, the obligation of disclosure should be maintained, with the exception of no disclosure in the most extreme cases (e.g., unconsciousness). In this continuum model, the consent process is comparable to everyday clinical practice in suicide risk assessment and safety planning. This approach is also similar to the "integrated consent model" (Kim and Miller 2014), in which the clinical practice of verbal consent is considered for pragmatic trials, with the purpose of being a "mirror" and reflection of everyday delivery of care. As others argue, the distinction between clinical and research practice in pragmatic trials is unnecessary (Faden et al. 2013; Goldstein et al. 2018).

Could it be harmful to obtain consent in the midst of a mental health crisis? Obtaining consent in this clinical emergency may carry the risk of being misconstrued by patients, at worst perceived as coercive. Imagine a patient expressing suicidal ideation as a cry for help. They are met with study procedures and detailed consent forms, and may imagine denial of services if they do not agree to participate. While respect for persons seems on the surface to be prominent in this case, ultimately harm and justice are the core ethical issues. Unquestionably, there is a need for more research to inform care for this underserved population who have traditionally been excluded from trials (Fisher et al. 2002). Exclusion in trials and delays in research due to ongoing ethics debates regarding consent, risk, and protections are subsequently harmful to the population; that is, strict research regulations inadvertently exacerbate the paradoxical problem of inequitable access to research that will inform care (Fisher et al. 2002; Goldstein et al. 2018; Welch et al. 2015). In this case, simplifying and minimizing research burdens related to consent would be the most prudent approach to maximize research participation. As we have proposed, applying the approach to consent used in daily clinical practice during behavioral health crises corresponds to the underlying features of pragmatic trials in which the clinical–research practice distinction is indistinguishable.

References

Biros, M. 2018. Capacity, vulnerability, and informed consent for research. *The Journal of Law, Medicine & Ethics* 46(1):72–78.

Faden, R. R., N. E. Kass, S. N. Goodman, P. Pronovost, S. Tunis, and T. L. Beauchamp. 2013. An ethics framework for a learning health care system: A departure from traditional research ethics and clinical ethics. *Hastings Cent Report* 43(s1):S16–S27.

Fisher, C. B., J. L. Pearson, S. Kim, and C. F. Reynolds. 2002. Ethical issues in including suicidal individuals in clinical research. *IRB: Ethics and Human Research* 24(5):9–14.

Flory, J. H., A. I. Mushlin, and Z. I. Goodman. 2016. Proposals to conduct randomized controlled trials without informed consent: A narrative review. *Journal of General Internal Medicine* 31(12):1511–1518.

Goldstein, C. E., C. J. C. Weijer, D. A. Brehaut, et al. 2018. Ethical issues in pragmatic randomized controlled trials: A review of the recent literature identifies gaps in ethical argumentation. *BMC Medical Ethics* 19(1):14.

Karlawish, J. T. 2008. Emergency Research. In *The Oxford textbook of clinical research ethics*. Edited by E. J. Emanuel, C.C. Grady, R. A. Crouch, et al. New York, NY: Oxford University Press.

Kim, S. Y., and F. G. Miller. 2014. Informed consent for pragmatic trials-the integrated consent model. *New England Journal of Medicine* 370(8):769–772.

Lakeman, R., and M. Fitzgerald. 2009. Ethical suicide research: A survey of researchers. *International Journal of Mental Health Nursing* 18(1):10–17.

Weinfurt, K. P., A. F. G. D. Hernandez, L. L. Coronado, et al. 2017. Pragmatic clinical trials embedded in healthcare systems: Generalizable lessons from the NIH collaboratory. *BMC Medical Research Methodologies* 17(1):144.

Welch, M. J., R. J. E. Lally, S. Miller, et al. 2015. The ethics and regulatory landscape of including vulnerable populations in pragmatic clinical trials. *Clinical Trials: Journal of the Society for Clinical Trials* 12(5):503–510.

Wilfond, B. S., J. Zabrowski, and L.-M. Johnson. 2019. A pragmatic trial of suicide risk assessment and ambulance transport decision making among emergency medical services providers. Implications for patient consent. *American Journal of Bioethics* 19(10):97–98.

COMMENTARY 5.2.4: A PRAGMATIC TRIAL FOR EMERGENCY MEDICAL SERVICES PROVIDERS' PREHOSPITAL RESPONSE TO SUICIDALITY: CONSENT IS NOT ESSENTIAL, BUT LIMITED PATIENT ENGAGEMENT MAY BE MEANINGFUL

NEAL W. DICKERT

This case focuses on the role of and need for informed consent in a pragmatic trial of prehospital triage for patients with suicidal ideation (Wilfond, Zabrowski, and Johnson 2016). As proposed, there is no plan to seek consent from individual patients, primarily because the intervention being tested—prehospital screening and use of a suicide crisis line—is being assigned at the provider level and because patient-level outcome data are not being collected. The critical questions are the extent to which consent has ethical value and the extent to which consent is practical.

The proposed study involves several departures from traditional trial design that drive questions about consent and must be addressed first from a scientific perspective. Most notably, treatment assignment is at the level of the provider, and this design is grounded in important scientific considerations.

Randomization at a patient level would presumably be problematic, because EMS providers would have difficulty changing their "approach" from patient to patient. Their experience with one arm seems likely to influence their approach to patients in the other arm. Assignment at the provider level may thus be ethically advantageous by minimizing contamination. Another notable feature is that the study involves no interactions with individual patients to gather data. As is common in pragmatic designs, outcomes will be assessed using administrative data and data from providers. There are practical advantages to this approach, and it does obviate one reason to solicit consent (data use). However, it is not clear that these data sources will provide reliable insights into how well the proposed intervention works or how implementable it is. The focus of this commentary is on consent, but these scientific considerations are essential to acknowledge. If a study cannot provide valuable data, questions about consent are moot. Assuming the science is sufficiently strong, questions about the extent to which consent is practical and valuable become important.

From the perspective of practicality, the argument against individual consent is reasonably strong. Introducing patient-level research consent on top of provider-level treatment assignment to a behavioral intervention runs a risk of introducing selection bias, could change the nature of the interaction being tested in a way that might not reflect real practice, and would increase the logistical complexity and resources necessary to run the trial. Importantly, it may be very difficult for EMS providers to determine whether patients who are suicidal are able to make an informed decision regarding research participation. These patients, as described, are at low to moderate risk for suicide, but assessments of suicide risk and decision-making capacity have different purposes. Though it would be critical for any institutional review board reviewing a study like this to hear from or include experts in psychiatry, it seems that there is a reasonable case for waiving formal written research informed consent from the perspective of practicality.

The tougher question is whether some form of consent process would be valuable. One key consideration is the level of risk to which patients will be exposed. On the one hand, the study intervention only involves a screening protocol and a telephone crisis line. There are no medications or invasive procedures, and interaction with crisis lifeline services is an accepted practice. The process that takes place in the intervention arm is essentially what would happen if an individual were to call a crisis line rather than EMS. However, the outcome the interventions are designed to prevent is a major one, suicide. There has been active debate about risk evaluation in the context of comparative trials in emergency settings, in part because the stakes are often high and in part because assessment of risk carries regulatory implications (Dickert et al. 2016; Wendler et al. 2017). If the study is considered to present more than minimal risks, waiver of consent is difficult to justify from a regulatory perspective unless the study is proposed under the exception from informed consent for research in emergency settings. It appears that this intervention (when fully developed) likely does not present more than minimal risk, but careful expert review is essential to make sure that this assessment is robust.

There are additional questions that must be addressed in assessing whether consent, or some form of engagement with patients, would serve important functions in this case. Several of these functions—authorization and promotion of welfare interests—are closely connected to the risk assessment discussed in the preceding. If the risks associated with the study are considered minimal, for example, it becomes less critical that they be substantively authorized or accepted by an individual participant. Other functions, however, also warrant consideration (Dickert et al. 2017). One important function of consent is simply to allow patients to control what happens to them. As described, patients can refuse to speak with the crisis line and can be taken to the ED instead. The function of control may thus be achieved to some extent without a formal, in-depth consent process. In order to enhance this function and the extent to which patients are treated consistently with their preferences, the EMS provider in the intervention group could simply tell patients, "We have typically taken patients in your position to the emergency department, but we are working with a crisis line now to learn whether we can help patients avoid having to come to the hospital. If you feel you need to go to the hospital at any point, let us know." Such simple disclosure that the crisis line is being implemented as a new approach may also enhance transparency and promote trust, two other functions that consent processes frequently serve. We have learned from work in other emergency settings that patients value being engaged in decisions about research, even in situations where their understanding is poor (Dickert et al. 2019; Gammelgaard et al. 2004). Simple engagement like this, which does not require any form of capacity assessment, may have value while avoiding problems introduced by more complex processes.

In summary, there are practical and scientific reasons to avoid in-depth formal research consent for the proposed study. There may, however, be value in simply informing patients that the crisis line approach is novel and that they have the option to refuse that form of treatment. Such targeted provision of limited information may be sensitive to the clinical context and may accomplish some functions of consent without compromising the science.

References

Dickert, N. W., J. Brown, C. B. Cairns., et al. 2016. Confronting ethical and regulatory challenges of emergency care research with conscious patients. *Annals of Emergency Medicine* 67(4):538–545. doi: 10.1016/j.annemergmed.2015.10.026.

Dickert, N. W., N. Eyal, S. F. Goldkind., et al. 2017. Re-framing consent for clinical research: A function-based approach. *The American Journal of Bioethics* 17(12):3–11. doi: 10.1080/15265161.2017.1388448.

Dickert, N. W., V. M. Scicluna, O. Adeoye., et al. 2019. Emergency consent: Patients' and surrogates' perspectives on consent for clinical trials in acute stroke and myocardial infarction. *Journal of the American Heart Association* 8(2): e010905.

Gammelgaard, A., P. Rossel, O. S. Mortensen, and DANAMI-2 Investigators. 2004. Patients' perceptions of informed consent in acute myocardial infarction research: A Danish study. *Social Science & Medicine (1982)* 58(11):2313–2324.

Wendler, D., N. W. Dickert, R. Silbergleit, S. Y. H. Kim, and J. Brown. 2017. Targeted consent for research on standard of care interventions in the emergency setting. *Critical Care Medicine* 45(1):e105–e110.

Wilfond, B. S., J. Zabrowski, and L.-M. Johnson. 2016. A pragmatic trial of suicide risk assessment and ambulance transport decision making among emergency medical services providers. Implications for patient consent. *American Journal of Bioethics* 19(10):97–98.

CASE 5.3: THE OBLIGATIONS TO REPORT STATUTORY SEXUAL ABUSE DISCLOSED IN A RESEARCH STUDY

INTRODUCTION

Conducting research studies with children requires that stringent federal and state regulations are met. In the case presented here, the biological father of a baby disclosed to a researcher that he was nine years older than the adolescent mother. The research was conducted in a state where statutory rape is defined as sexual contact between a minor and someone four or more years older. What obligations do the researchers have to meet, and what are the roles of the various oversight and regulatory bodies charged with ensuring that research is conducted responsibly and ethically?

Commentators Erin Talati Paquette, MD, JD, MBe, and Lainie Friedman Ross, MD, PhD, from Lurie Children's Hospital of Chicago and the University of Chicago, respectively, discuss the implications of Certificates of Confidentiality on the approach to disclosure. Stacy Hodgkinson, PhD, and colleagues from Children's National Health System consider the implications of this case for the approach to informed consent. Stuart Finder, PhD, from Cedars-Sinai Medical Center, and Stanley Korenman, MD, from the University of California, Los Angeles School of Medicine, discuss the role of the community context and the roles of researchers compared to clinicians.

CASE SUMMARY

A 15-year-old woman (here called "D") was referred to a study evaluating a co-parenting intervention for pregnant teens and their partners. A research assistant determined that she met the following eligibility criteria: age from 15 to 18 years, no previous children, 15 to 32 weeks gestation, and the baby's father interested in participating. The researchers asked D about the age of her partner to determine whether it would be necessary to obtain parental consent for his participation. She reported that he was 18 years old; therefore, his participation would not require parental consent. Because D was a minor, parental consent was required for her to participate in the study. The consent process required the participation of the pregnant teen, the girl's mother, and the father of the baby. On the day of the interview, the father did not show up. The girl was interviewed, but the father's interview had to be postponed. Two weeks later during his interview, he reported that he was 24 years old, not 18 (an age differential of nine years).

The study took place in a jurisdiction where child sexual abuse is defined as sexual contact between a minor below the age of 16 and a partner who is four or more years older. Therefore, this was classified as a case of statutory rape. This research had a Certificate of Confidentiality. How should the researchers proceed? Whom can they consult? Should they report? Is there anything they could have done to avoid this situation? What is the role of the IRB?

COMMENTARY 5.3.1: THE MORAL AND LEGAL NEED TO DISCLOSE DESPITE A CERTIFICATE OF CONFIDENTIALITY

ERIN TALATI PAQUETTE AND LAINIE FRIEDMAN ROSS

This case raises four central questions: (1) Is there a duty to disclose? (2) What protection does the Certificate of Confidentiality (COC) provide? (3) What, if anything, could have been done to avoid this situation? (4) What are the next steps? In answering these questions, we must consider the ethical and legal obligations of researchers and IRBs with research involving children.

Is there a duty to disclose?

Is there a legal duty to report this case of statutory rape? Generally, state laws regarding mandated reporters encompass four types of reporters: (1) broad mandates to general citizens aware of any child abuse or neglect; (2) mandates to narrower groups of individuals who in the course of their professional activities suspect child abuse or neglect; (3) mandates to those who come into contact with children through their employment; and (4) mandates to specifically identified types of reporters, which may or may not include psychosocial researchers (Liss 1994). The first three types of laws require that researchers who learn of potential child abuse report it to the proper authorities. Even for states with a narrower list of mandated reporters, it is likely that at least one member of a research team would be included. If any member of the research team is a mandated reporter, arguably the entire team should be held to this standard.

Irrespective of legal obligations to report, researchers have ethical obligations to preserve the well-being of children they enroll, even if it adversely affects their research. Known as either the "jeopardy principle" (Scott-Jones 1994; Society for Research in Child Development 2013) or the "scientist-citizen dilemma" (Fisher 1994; Veatch 1987), there is broad ethical consensus to prioritize the well-being of children over the production of generalizable knowledge. Some researchers object to this requirement, arguing that (1) generalizable knowledge is important; (2) reporting of uncertain abuse may disproportionately place scrutiny on low-income families who may be overrepresented in studies of risky behaviors; and (3) some team members lack adequate training to detect abuse, although their reports will be taken quite seriously (Fisher et al. 1996; Scott-Jones 1994). Like all mandatory reporters, researchers should be thoughtful regarding decisions to report. When abuse is uncertain, state laws mandating reports of abuse and neglect encourage good-faith reports. In this case, the team learned that a child enrolled in their study had experienced certain statutorily defined sexual abuse based on the age difference between the adolescent mother and the father, such that they are legally obligated to report this (Fisher 1994). Even if the adolescent denied abuse, the ethical obligation to report still exists because the obligation to protect a child does not depend on the child's ability to recognize the harm. Therefore, the researchers are obligated both ethically and legally to disclose the abuse they discovered.

What protection does the certificate of confidentiality provide?

An unanswered question is whether procuring a COC abdicates the legal responsibility of researchers to report. The Public Health Service Act (2012) protects the privacy of research subjects by "withholding from all persons not connected with the conduct of such research the names or other identifying characteristics of such individuals" (42 USC 241(d)). COCs, issued under the Public Health Service Act, restrict "compelled disclosure of identifying information about subjects enrolled in sensitive ... research" (Office for Human Research Protections 2003). COCs are obtained for a broad array of research (Coffey and Ross 2004; Earley and Strong 1995; Lutz et al. 2000), where researchers show that the risk of loss of confidentiality would be damaging to individual subjects (Carney et al. 2000). Some have argued that COCs exempt researchers from compelled disclosure of all confidential information learned in the course of research (Liss 1994).

There is ongoing confusion over whether COCs afford absolute protection against certain disclosures, including child abuse and neglect. Study investigators, research subjects, IRBs, and legal counsel differ in their knowledge level and familiarity with COCs (Beskow et al. 2012; Catania et al. 2007; Coffey and Ross 2004; Wolf et al. 2012). In part, differences arise because only one court has spoken directly to the issue of the certificate's validity, upholding the COC, and promoting a widespread belief of absolute protection of confidentiality under COCs (Beskow, Dame, and Costello 2008).

Guidance documents issued by the NIH and OHRP indicate limits on the certificate's scope. The NIH advises that "personally identifiable information protected by a certificate may be disclosed under the following circumstances, [including] voluntary disclosure … on such things as child abuse." The NIH asserts only that COCs issued for communicable diseases must provide assurance "that reporting requirements for communicable diseases will be met," remaining silent about child abuse (U.S. Department of Health and Human Services, NIH Office of Extramural Research n.d.). Some have interpreted this silence to mean that the investigator is released from other reporting requirements (Earley and Strong 1995). OHRP, on the other hand, clarifies that "Certificates of Confidentiality protect subjects from compelled disclosure of identifying information, but do not prevent … voluntarily disclosing certain information about research subjects, such as evidence of child abuse" (Office for Human Research Protections 2003).

What, if anything, could have been done to avoid this situation?

In planning studies where investigators can anticipate a possible need for these types of disclosures, federal regulations and NIH guidance on COCs insist that informed consent documents outline limits to confidentiality (U.S. Department of Health and Human Services, NIH Office of Extramural Research n.d.). Prior to requesting a COC, researchers must obtain IRB approval (Carney et al. 2000). IRBs can require revisions if appropriate risks and disclosure limits are not enumerated, including the risk of abuse and neglect. Then, when the certificate is obtained, limits on confidentiality have already been identified.

Data show that adolescent girls are more likely to get pregnant when they have older sexual partners (Lindberg et al. 1997). Five to 10% of all sexually active and pregnant adolescent girls have partners who are more than five years older (Darroch, Landry, and Oslak 1999; Lindberg et al. 1997). As such, (1) the consent forms should have incorporated the risk of identifying statutory rape, and (2) the study protocol should have included how to address such findings. This would have allowed the adolescent to decline participation. Investigators may object that placing such limits on confidentiality may bias and reduce enrollment. As discussed earlier, this scientist-citizen dilemma should always be resolved in the direction of protecting a child at risk (Fisher 1994).

Given that the risks were not anticipated, the researchers were correct to seek institutional legal advice and then to ask their IRB how to proceed. As mandated reporters, the COC does not legally prevent them from voluntary compliance with mandated reporter statutes. Morally, the investigators have an obligation to seek assistance for a minor who may be at ongoing risk for abuse. Investigators who discover possible abuse or neglect that is not as clearcut as in this case, however, may turn to their IRB or legal counsel to provide guidance prior to making a voluntary disclosure.

Next steps

The IRB should work with the investigator to amend the protocol and consent documents in case future situations necessitate disclosures. Those involved in consenting subjects must be trained to discuss the protections of confidentiality and the limits of confidentiality, including the reporting of child abuse and neglect. Investigators will also need to work with an NIH Certificate Coordinator to amend their certificate, as a change in the limits of confidentiality to consent forms likely would constitute a "significant" change, requiring an amended application for a certificate (U.S. Department of Health and Human Services, NIH Office of Extramural Research n.d.).

Moving forward, the most useful intervention to provide the broadest safety net for children would be for the NIH to publish definitive guidance on the expectation of researchers to meet mandatory reporting laws about child abuse and neglect—even when a COC is procured—to eliminate concerns about liability for voluntary disclosure of identifying information in these circumstances (Earley and Strong 1995). Still, most would agree that the certificate, which is meant to prevent compelled disclosures from investigators, does not prevent voluntary disclosures from researchers regarding abuse and neglect (Coffey and Ross 2004).

References

Beskow, L. M., D. K. Check, E. E. Namey, et al. 2012. Institutional review boards' use and understanding of certificates of confidentiality. *PLoS One* 7(9):1–9.

Beskow, L. M., L. Dame, and E. J. Costello. 2008. Certificates of confidentiality and the compelled disclosure of research data. *Science* 322(5904):1054–1055.

Carney, P. A., B. M. Geller, H. Moffett, et al. 2000. Current medicolegal and confidentiality issues in large, multicenter research programs. *American Journal of Epidemiology* 152:371–378.

Catania, J. A., L. E. Wolf, S. Wertleib, B. Lo, and J. Henne. 2007. Research participant's perceptions of the certificate of confidentiality's assurances and limitations. *Journal of Empirical Research on Human Research Ethics* 2:53–59.

Coffey, M. J., and L. F. Ross. 2004. Human subjects protections in genetic research. *Genet Test.* 8:209–213.

Darroch, J. E., D. J. Landry, and S. Oslak. 1999. Age differences between sexual partners in the United States. *Family Planning Perspectives* 31:160–167.

Earley, C. L., and L. C. Strong. 1995. Certificates of confidentiality: A valuable tool for protecting genetic data. *American Journal of Human Genetics* 57:727–731.

Fisher, C. B. 1994. Reporting and referring research participants: Ethical challenges for investigators studying children and youth. *Ethics & Behavior* 4:87–95.

Fisher, C. B., A. Higgins-D'Alessandro, J. M. Rau, T. L. Kuther, and S. Belanger. 1996. Referring and reporting research participants at risk: Views from urban adolescents. *Child Development* 67:2086–2100.

Lindberg, L. D., F. L. Sonenstein, L. Ku, and G. Martinez. 1997. Age differences between minors who give birth and their adult partners. *Family Planning Perspectives* 29:61–66.

Liss, M. 1994. Child abuse: Is there a mandate for researchers to report? *Ethics & Behavior* 4:133–146.

Lutz, K. F., K. Shelton, L. Robrecht, D. C. Hutton, and A. K. Beckett. 2000. Use of certificates of confidentiality in nursing research. *Journal of Nursing Scholarship* 32:185–188.

Office for Human Research Protections. 2003. Guidance on certificates of confidentiality. February 25. Available at: http://www.hhs.gov/ohrp/policy/certconf.html (accessed June 20, 2014).

Public Health Service Act. 2012. 42 USC §241 (d).

Scott-Jones, D. 1994. Ethical issues in reporting and referring in research with low-income minority children. *Ethics & Behavior* 4:97–108.

Society for Research in Child Development. 2013. Principle 9: Jeopardy. *Ethical Standards in Research.* Available at: http://www.srcd.org/about-us/ethical-standards-research (accessed September 22, 2013).

U.S. Department of Health and Human Services, National Institutes of Health Office of Extramural Research. n.d. Frequently asked questions: Certificates of confidentiality. Available at: http://grants1.nih.gov/grants/policy/coc/faqs.htm (accessed June 20, 2014).

Veatch, R. M. 1987. *The patient as partner,* Bloomington IN: Indiana University Press.

Wolf, L. E., L. A. Dame, M. J. Patel, B. A. Williams, J. A. Austin, and L. M. Beskow. 2012. Certificates of confidentiality: Legal counsels' experiences with and perspectives on legal demands for research data. *Journal of Empirical Research on Human Research Ethics* 7(4):1–9.

COMMENTARY 5.3.2: INFORMED CONSENT AND THE IMPLICATIONS FOR STATUTORY RAPE REPORTING IN RESEARCH WITH ADOLESCENTS

STACY HODGKINSON, AMY LEWIN, BORA CHANG, LEE BEERS, AND TOMAS J. SILBER

The case presented illustrates the ethical and scientific challenges that face researchers working with pregnant and parenting adolescents, when the obligation to uphold local statutory rape laws conflicts with the research needs and/or the needs of research subjects. To address this question, we need to expand it to include how such a situation can be prevented by addressing the issue of informed consent.

The traditional definition of statutory rape is unlawful sexual intercourse between an adult and a minor, based on the age discrepancy between the two parties. The age and the age difference vary according to the jurisdiction. There are differences in how statutory rape is defined across state statutes, but essentially, there is agreement that this is a crime with mandatory reporting. In some states, researchers are not mandated reporters of child abuse unless they are teachers, health professionals, or child care providers (Donovan 1998). In at least two dozen states, however, a mandated reporter is anyone who has suspicion of child abuse (Socolar, Runyan, and Amaya-Jackson 1995). Additionally, most IRBs apply state child abuse reporting laws to researchers (Steinberg et al. 1999). Even when a study has a certificate of confidentiality, this does not apply to reportable abuse and does not provide protection to the study participants from the researcher's obligations to report statutory rape. The researchers have to report statutory rape. Reporting, of course, means that confidentiality has been breached and the IRB needs to be informed.

In reviewing this case, it appears that pregnant research participants and their partners were not fully informed about the limits of confidentiality, and they were not specifically warned to take into account the illegality of their relationship and the potential consequences they would face when they revealed their age discrepancy.

Our recommendation for this type of research is that the protocol be amended so that at intake, and before asking the age of the subjects, it is made clear that if statutory rape information surfaces, the researchers will have to notify authorities and/or Child Protective Services. In addition, the consent and assent forms and processes need to be modified to contain this protocol information.

There are some special considerations to keep in mind here. Pregnant adolescents and their adult male partners have persistently been a difficult population to engage in research. The proposed warning at the time of intake potentially will create additional barriers to engaging a group that is sorely underrepresented in research. Informing prospective subjects of reporting requirements and limitations to confidentiality certainly may jeopardize the ability of researchers to establish trust and rapport, which in turn may affect the veracity and accuracy of the information subjects provide (Findholt and Robrecht 2002). This is a fact of life that researchers need to accept, as it is unlikely that these research subjects will ever be exempted from the reporting of statutory rape. Why, then, warn subjects? Because it is the decent thing to do. This is no minor matter: Statutory rape legislation advocates have often portrayed men who father children of adolescent women as predatory and irresponsible, but this might be an inaccurate description of many men who seek to be responsible fathers to their children (Donovan 1996). Concern has also been voiced that this legislation can interfere with access to care (Teare and English 2002).

Although reporting statutory rape is designed to protect adolescents from abusive and exploitive relationships, it also has the potential to harm them. The enforcement of statutory rape laws might threaten the financial and social support that adolescent mothers receive from the fathers of their children, and thus may potentially deepen the level of poverty often experienced by young mothers and their children. No less importantly, it can jeopardize the relationships between adolescent mothers and their partners. Researchers therefore cannot ignore the challenge of weighing the social benefits of statutory rape laws against the possibility of doing more harm. To complicate matters, only a small fraction of statutory rape cases are prosecuted and hence enforcement of these laws may be capricious, as many law enforcement and child protection agencies are not equipped to respond to these reports.

In conclusion, reporting is mandatory and this is something researchers need to address. Therefore, it is better to clearly inform subjects of the risk beforehand. This might result in the loss of potential participants, as adolescents might not enroll to avoid the disclosure of a statutory rape. This is a preferred outcome to unwittingly misleading and possibly harming them.

References

Donovan, P. 1996. Can statutory rape laws be effective in preventing adolescent pregnancy? *Family Planning Perspectives* 29:30–40.

Donovan, P. 1998. Caught between teens and the law: Family planning programs and statutory rape reporting. *Guttmacher Report on Public Policy* 1:5–7.

Findholt, N., and C. Robrecht. 2002. Legal and ethical considerations in research with sexually active adolescent: The requirements to report statutory rape. *Perspectives on Sexual and Reproductive Health* 34(5):259–264.

Socolar, R., D. Runyan, and L. Amaya-Jackson. 1995. Methodological and ethical issues related to studying child maltreatment. *Journal of Family Issues* 16:565–586.

Steinberg, A., R. Pynoos, A. Goenjian, H. Sossanabadi, and L. Sherr. 1999. Are researchers bound by child abuse reporting laws? *Child Abuse and Neglect* 23:771–777.

Teare, C., and A. English. 2002. Nursing practice and statutory rape. Effects of reporting and enforcement on access to care for adolescents. *Nursing Clinics of North America* 37:393–404.

COMMENTARY 5.3.3: COMMUNITY, CONTEXT, AND THE CONTRASTING ROLES OF CLINICIANS AND RESEARCHERS: CHALLENGES RAISED BY STATUTORY RAPE

STUART G. FINDER AND STANLEY KORENMAN

The scope and limits of responsibility in the context of human subjects research are more complex than many researchers (and subjects) typically think (Easter et al. 2006). Many factors contribute to such complexity, including that the functions of clinicians and researchers are often indistinguishable, even while their focus and aim are quite distinct (a point well established since at least the Declaration of Helsinki [World Medical Association 2013], reiterated in the *Belmont Report* [U.S. Department of Health and Human Services, Office for Human Subjects Research 1979], and ingredient to current federal regulations governing IRB function). In the most general sense, the care and well-being of an individual patient serve as a clinician's focus, whereas for a researcher, the generation of "good data" frames one's practices. Despite considerable effort to separate the functions and the people who carry out each function, confusion between the role of "clinician" and "researcher"—and between "patient" and "subject"—remains all too common, as do the obligations associated with each role. This is often true among clinical researchers; among those who review, approve, and oversee research (IRBs, data safety monitoring boards, etc.); and for study subjects (Liddle 1967).

We draw attention to this issue of role confusion and to the parallel fact of differences in role responsibility, because the issue of whether to report statutory rape in the context of a research study as presented here is susceptible to similar complexity and confusion. Several issues need further examination to clarify how to answer the question of the obligation to report.

First, we acknowledge that researchers' legal and ethical role obligations are distinct (even if intertwined). There certainly *appears* to be little legal uncertainty that the sexual contact here is child sexual abuse and must be reported because the age difference between the pregnant adolescent girl and the fetus's father is greater than four years. What is not clear is whether this legal obligation is absolute in all contexts and circumstances.

For instance, when developing this study, researchers might have (and we suggest *should* have) anticipated this possibility of the mother–father dyad satisfying the statutory rape criteria (Bunting and McAuley 2004). Accordingly, the researchers could have sought input from local courts, Child Protective Services, and other legal entities to learn possible options for responding when such situations arise. By doing so, they would have been prepared to satisfy the need for protecting adolescent mothers (the basis for the legal requirement to report) as well as the (assumed-to-be-justified) need for performing this research. For the same reasons, a similar responsibility for contacting these kinds of legal and social agents rests on the shoulders of the IRB charged with reviewing this research prior to approval.

This case illustrates how the seemingly simple and straightforward legal obligation to report demands deeper exploration. Obligations more traditionally identified as "ethical" too are multidimensional. For instance, the pledge of confidentiality is undergirded by a commitment to be worthy of the trust given, meaning the researchers and, by implication, the institution that reviewed (through its IRB) the research must demonstrate such trustworthiness. There is considerable experience with research on illegal behaviors, especially in addiction, in which confidentiality rules protect subjects (Fitzgerald and Hamilton 1997). Similar confidentiality rules ought to have been incorporated into this study.

While this case provides little contextual information, we surmise some features that highlight the challenges for understanding the breadth and depth of ethical obligation. Consider the aim of this study: to evaluate a co-parenting intervention for pregnant adolescents and their partners. Given the well-established evidence that adolescents from lower socioeconomic groups have higher rates of pregnancy (Penman-Aguilar et al. 2013) and that children born into lower socioeconomic contexts experience greater health issues (Bradley and Corwyn 2002), it is reasonable to conjecture that the targeted subjects were adolescents in lower socioeconomic contexts.

This draws attention to another dimension of the issue of responsibility. Researchers do not shoulder the weight of responsibility alone; IRBs can and *should* play a significant role. At a minimum, adequate review of the scope of risks and potential harms for a study drawing subjects from a community that differs from those who propose and review the research demands explicit and direct outreach to that community—ideally during the earliest phases of developing the research, and certainly as part of the review and evaluation of the research (Baker et al. 1999). Doing so provides opportunity to develop an appreciation of how risks and harms are understood within that community, as well as what kind of activities and relational dynamics are taken as norms, thereby allowing greater likelihood of respecting the community social custom regarding, for instance, reporting when the biological father remains with the family.

This latter point is not meant to collapse ethical evaluation into relativism. Rather, the point is to highlight the need to develop sensibilities for differences concerning how those whom we study understand not merely the fact of our studying them, but their own experiences in being studied. We are required to do this when pursuing international research and interventions in cultural contexts vastly different from our own, such as developing countries (Emanuel et al. 2004). The same should be done here at home. Indeed, community-based IRBs are beginning to be formed to ensure there is appropriate partnering between researchers and communities in creating community-based research proposals so that cultural sensitivities are more clearly represented (Shore et al. 2011).

The upshot of all of the preceding is that research will be better, and better accepted, not only when we avoid confusing responsibilities we have as clinicians with those we have as researchers, but when we more actively involve the communities from which we draw research subjects. We will be better prepared to answer questions such as whether, and to whom, we have an obligation to report potential sexual abuse disclosed in a research study. As for this case, although there is no indication that the researchers proactively sought input from their local court system and Child Protective Services (as they should have), nor does it seem that they engaged the community from which they hoped to enroll subjects (as they should have), they nonetheless still have the opportunity to do so.

Accordingly, upon learning of the age difference between D and her partner, the researchers' first steps should be to go to community organizations connected to D, her partner, and their families. The aim for doing so is to learn how D's community understands such couplings and the ways in which they help and protect young women such as D (as well as the children they bear). What the researchers do next will depend on what they come to learn. The crucial point is that acting responsibly in this context demands reaching out to, and learning from, D's community. This community—of which she, her partner, and their families are part—provides crucial contextual grounding for understanding what it actually means, practically as well as morally, to "protect" or "care" for D—as research subject, as patient, and as a human being.

References

Baker, E. A., S. Horman, R. Schonhoff, and M. Kreuter. 1999. Principles of practice for academic/ practice/community research partnerships. *American Journal of Preventive Medicine* 16(3 Suppl):86–93.

Bradley, R. H., and R. F. Corwyn. 2002. Socioeconomic status and child development. *Annual Review of Psychology* 53:371–399.

Bunting, L., and C. McAuley. 2004. Teenage pregnancy and parenthood: The role of fathers. *Child & Family Social Work* 9(3):295–303.

Easter, M. M., G. E. Henderson, A. M. Davis, L. R. Churchill, and N. M. King. 2006. The many meanings of care in clinical research. *Sociology of Health & Illness* 28(6):695–712.

Emanuel, E. J., D. Wendler, J. Killen, and C. Grady. 2004. What makes clinical research in developing countries ethical? The benchmarks of ethical research. *Journal of Infectious Diseases* 189(5):930–937.

Fitzgerald, J. L., and M. Hamilton. 1997. Confidentiality, disseminated regulation and ethico-legal liabilities in research with hidden populations of illicit drug users. *Addiction* 92(9):1099–1108.

Liddle, G. W. 1967. The mores of clinical investigators. *Journal of Clinical Investigation* 46(7):1028–1030.

Penman-Aguilar, A., M. Carter, M. C. Snead, and A. P. Kourtis. 2013. Socioeconomic disadvantage as a social determinant of teen childbearing in the U.S. *Public Health Reports* 128(suppl. 1):5–22.

Shore, N., R. Brazauskas, E. Drew, K. Wong, L. Moy, A. Baden, K. Cyr, J. Ulevicus, and S. D. Seifer. 2011. Understanding community-based processes for research ethics review: A national study. *American Journal of Public Health* 101(suppl. 1):S359–S564.

U.S. Department of Health and Human Services, Office for Human Subjects Research. 1979. *Belmont Report. Ethical Principles and Guidelines for the Protection of Human Subjects of Research.* Available at: www.hhs.org/ohrp/humansubjects/guidance/belmont.html

World Medical Association. 2013. *Declaration of Helsinki—Ethical Principles for Medical Research Involving Human Subjects.* Available at: www.wma.net/en/30publications/10policies/b3

CASE 5.4: CONJOINED CONSENT: INFORMED CONSENT WHEN DONOR AND RECIPIENT ARE BOTH RESEARCH PARTICIPANTS

INTRODUCTION

In clinical trials, informed consent is the process by which an investigator or study team member informs potential study participants of the purpose of the trial, the risks and benefits of participation, and the alternatives to participation. To appropriately honor individuals, this process is about more than "getting the consent" or complying with regulations for human subjects research. The role of the investigator is to communicate this key information to potential participants in a manner that meets the informational needs of potential participants and promotes informed decision making. High-quality informed consent conversations should ensure that participants have an adequate understanding of the key information about the trial such that they can make an informed decision about participating that is consistent with their beliefs and values. A final key component of this process is the voluntariness of participation and ensuring that a potential participant is not subjected to any undue influence when agreeing to enroll.

In this case, investigators wish to study the role of donor stem cells in preventing rejection following a solid organ (kidney) transplant. While the kidney transplant is a clinical intervention, both the donor and recipient are potential research participants in the investigational collection and transfer of stem cells from the kidney donor to the recipient. In this case, where the study design requires the mutual enrollment and voluntary consent of two separate, autonomous, but related individuals to execute the trial intervention, what is the optimal way to obtain informed consent from each participant while honoring the principles above? The commentaries explore the obligations of investigators to ensure the adequacy of informed consent when both the donor and recipient are research participants. In the commentary by Brooklyn Aaron, Jessica Ginsberg, and Jason Lesandrini of Wellstar Health System, the authors emphasize the importance of obtaining the research consent after clinical consent has been obtained and conducting research consent conversations with the potential donor separately from the recipient. They emphasize the importance of a research advocate to help assess donor voluntariness of participation and understanding of study purpose. In the commentary by Philip Ghobrial, Sanjeev Akkina, and Emily Anderson of Loyola University Chicago, the authors note the potential psychosocial harms surrounding both clinical transplantation and the potential research study, given the interrelatedness of the donor and recipient. The authors also argue for a stepwise process of first obtaining consent from the donor and then, if the donor has agreed, approaching the kidney recipient to participate in the interventional trial. Going further than the previous commentary, the authors argue that investigators have an obligation to bring the donor and recipient in for a joint discussion about the implications of their independent decisions, acting as facilitators in the sharing of each person's individual decision. In the final commentary by Stephanie Kraft of the Treuman Katz Center for Pediatric Bioethics, Seattle, Washington, the author examines the role that people's relationships with others play in their "individual" decision making and uses this to support her argument that investigators should not ignore the interrelatedness of the donor and recipient. In contrast to the first two commentaries, the author contends that investigators should facilitate a joint decision-making process by bringing together both the donor and recipient for informed consent conversations about participation in the research study.

CASE SUMMARY

An investigator would like to conduct a study to determine if a single infusion of stem cells from an HLA-matched kidney donor into the recipient can induce tolerance and ultimately preserve transplant function and prevent transplant rejection. The study will harvest stem cells from the donor to create an investigational cellular immunotherapy. Several weeks prior to kidney donation, the donor will undergo twice-daily injections of granulocyte colony-stimulating factor (G-CSF) for five or six days in order to stimulate the bone marrow to release large numbers of stem cells into the bloodstream. Then, peripheral blood stem cells will be collected over 1–2 days of apheresis by the placement of a central venous catheter if adequate peripheral venous access is not available. If an insufficient number of stem cells is released or an insufficient amount of investigational product is created, a donor may need to undergo a second apheresis procedure over another 1–2 days. The kidney recipient will then receive infusions of the investigational cellular immunotherapy 10 days after the kidney transplant.

While G-CSF is FDA-approved for other uses, it is considered investigational in this study. Therefore, informed consent will be obtained from the kidney donor and the recipient as they are both research participants receiving investigational interventions. A research ethics consultation is requested after an IRB member raises concerns about the informed consent process, particularly the presentation of the clinical trial and its associated risks and benefits to the kidney donor. Given the preexisting relationship between the donor, who has already agreed to donate a kidney, and the recipient, how should the clinical trial and relationship concerns be addressed with the potential research participants?

COMMENTARY 5.4.1: MOVING BEYOND STANDARD INFORMED CONSENT FOR INTERVENTIONAL ORGAN TRANSPLANT RESEARCH

BROOKLYN AARON, JESSICA C. GINSBERG, AND JASON LESANDRINI

Introduction

Achieving valid informed consent from a human research participant involves an ongoing process designed to protect the participant and ensure their rights, safety, and well-being are not compromised. This can become increasingly challenging in situations involving organ donors and recipients, where both the donor and the recipient are research participants. The proposed G-CSF study poses a unique set of questions surrounding informed consent as the donor has already consented to donating an organ, an action that provides no direct benefit to the donor and involves risk, and now would take on additional risk by agreeing to donate stem cells in the clinical trial (Johnson, Duenas, and Wilfond 2021). Similarly, the recipient, who has already agreed to receiving an organ—likely out of necessity— is now being asked to engage in a trial that deviates from standard practice while knowingly placing the donor at additional risk (Heffernan and Glazier 2017). In presenting interventional donor research to participants, the framework used to discuss risks and benefits of biological donation research applies (Shaw et al. 2010; Skillern, Cedars, and Huddleston 2013). Given the complex donor–recipient relationship, investigators should place additional emphasis on voluntariness, disclosure, and ensuring participant understanding, particularly of the donor, who, excluding altruism, does not directly benefit from participation. Similar frameworks for presenting risks and benefits in research, such as in deceased donor intervention research and clinical research in general, should apply with additional precautions surrounding the ethical concerns around voluntariness, disclosure, and understanding particularly as they pertain to the donor.

Moving beyond standard informed consent

FDA guidelines and ethically accepted practices for clinical trials involving human participants require investigators to obtain informed consent from all participants, which includes: disclosing relevant information about the research, undertaking steps to ensure the participant's understanding of that information, allowing time for the potential participant to ask questions and make a decision regarding participation, and ensuring that participation is voluntary (U.S. Food and Drug

Administration 2018). Careful consideration should be taken to ensure that both the donor and recipient are made aware of the benefits and risks associated with not only the G-CSF injections but also the transplantation and the potential effects on the long-term outcome of the transplantation. Regarding the voluntary nature of the research, it should be made clear to both the donor and the recipient that declining to participate in the trial will not affect the ability to move forward with the organ donation and transplant.

To ensure the living donor has optimal opportunities to weigh the risks and benefits of the clinical trial, the donation decision for the solid organ should be made prior to and independent from the discussion of research. Doing so ensures that the decision to participate in the clinical research trial is not influenced by the decision to donate. This is akin to organ donation in deceased donors after circulatory death (donation after circulatory death [DCD]), where the decision to remove life-sustaining treatment is decided prior to the initiation of a donation conversation and likewise the decision to donate is decided prior to the conversation about interventional donor research (Cooper, Harvey, and Gardiner 2020). In the case of a living donor, the donor may agree to assume certain risks if it means directly saving the life of a loved one but may be unwilling to or apprehensive about assuming additional risks for the purpose of clinical research. In this case, it appears this criterion has already been met as the donor had previously agreed to donate the organ.

Additionally, to protect the donor from undue influence, pressure, or coercion, the use of a donor advocate is recommended. Donor advocates are trained to recognize signs that a donor's decision may not be voluntary, and this expertise may extend into the donor's decision regarding clinical research. A donor advocate is particularly useful to offer additional precautions and donor protections when a prior relationship exists between the donor and recipient, and may serve as a buffer for potential pressure to participate in the clinical study because the donor has already agreed to donate a kidney. Furthermore, the consent process for the donor should be conducted independently and separately from the consent process for the recipient. If possible, the timing of these independent conversations should occur such that the recipient does not have an opportunity to pressure the donor to participate in the clinical trial, or vice versa.

Practical guidelines for further confidence in consent

Further confidence that adequate informed consent is being obtained from the donor can be gained by following established examples of "testing" the donor/potential research participant by asking the donor a series of both objective and subjective questions concerning the research proposal (Joffe et al. 2001; Skillern, Cedars, and Huddleston 2013). Objective questions a clinician might ask the donor to assess the donor's understanding of the research include:

What are the potential short-term risks of receiving G-CSF and apheresis?
What follow-up will be available and required for trial participants? How does follow-up for trial participants differ from follow-up for traditional organ donation and transplantation?
What is the purpose of this research?
Will participating in this research study compromise the success of the organ transplantation?

In the same way, subjective-based questioning of the donor further confirms the donor's understanding and voluntariness by bringing awareness to their reasoning and motivations for participating in the research and the subjective benefits and risks of participation that may not be as obvious as clinical benefits and risks. The answers to subjective questions can be used to assess donor reasoning, potential influences, and relationship concerns and test whether the donor's understanding aligns with the realities of the research. Specifically, the investigator should look to ensure the donor understands the distinction between the act of donating the kidney, which will provide direct benefit to the recipient, and the actions associated with participating in the clinical trial, which may not provide direct benefit to the recipient. Questions that address these subjective aspects include:

Why do you want to participate in this research?
What do you hope to gain by participating in this research?

Answers to these questions can help investigators reinforce concepts where potential participants lack full understanding and moderate expectations if a large degree of therapeutic misconception is identified.

Conclusion

If a decision to donate the organ has been made, both the recipient and donor should be presented with the research using a similar framework of informed consent as is used for deceased donor interventions and clinical research in general, taking special precaution to differentiate between the organ donation/transplantation and the research study. Once a donor advocate has met with a potential participant and assessed their understanding of the trial and identified potential areas of concern, further objective and subjective questioning of the donor should help investigators address any ethical concerns in the donor's understanding and clarify the voluntariness of participation.

References

Cooper, J., D. Harvey, and D. Gardiner. 2020. Examining consent for interventional research in potential deceased organ donors: A narrative review. *Anaesthesia* 75(9):1229–35.

Heffernan, K. G., and A. K. Glazier. 2017. Are transplant recipients human subjects when research is conducted on organ donors? *The Hastings Center Report* 47(5):10–14.

Joffe, S., E. F. Cook, P. D. Cleary, J. W. Clark, and J. C. Weeks. 2001. Quality of informed consent: A new measure of understanding among research subjects. *Journal of the National Cancer Institute* 93(2):139–47.

Johnson, L.-M., D. M. Duenas, and B. S. Wilfond. 2021. Conjoined consent: Informed consent when donor and recipient are both research participants. *The American Journal of Bioethics* 21(4):106–107.

Shaw, B. E., L. Ball, M. Beksac, M. Bengtsson, D. Confer, S. Diler, M. Fechter, H. Greinix, M. Koh, S. Lee, et al. 2010. Donor safety: The role of the WMDA in ensuring the safety of volunteer unrelated donors: Clinical and ethical considerations. *Bone Marrow Transplantation* 45(5):832–8.

Skillern, A., M. Cedars, and H. Huddleston. 2013. Egg donor informed consent tool (EDICT): Development and validation of a new informed consent tool for oocyte donors. *Fertility and Sterility* 99(6):1733–8.

U.S. Food and Drug Administration (FDA). 2018. Informed consent for clinical trials. https://www.fda.gov/patients/clinical-trials-what-patients-need-know/informed-consent-clinical-trials (accessed October 28, 2020).

COMMENTARY 5.4.2: RISKS TO RELATIONSHIPS IN KIDNEY TRANSPLANT RESEARCH WITH LIVING DONORS AND RECIPIENTS

PHILIP GHOBRIAL, SANJEEV AKKINA, AND EMILY E. ANDERSON

In order to consider how best to address relationship concerns with potential research participants arising in this study (Johnson, Duenas, and Wilfond 2021), we will first describe unique features of the research and the ethical concerns these raise. Then we will argue that because of these unique concerns, investigators have additional responsibilities to both organ donors and recipients in inviting them to participate. After outlining these obligations, we will suggest how investigators can fulfill them.

Unique features of this study and ethical concerns

Given the requirement for an HLA-matched donor, this study will primarily include donor and recipient pairs with preexisting relationships. In order to test the effectiveness of the proposed intervention, both parties—kidney donor and recipient—must agree to participate in the research. This challenges the traditional conceptualization of informed consent as an individual, autonomous decision.

Prior to being invited to participate in the research, both parties will have already been rigorously screened and will have agreed to the donation and transplant procedures with an understanding that there are differential risks and potential benefits for each of them. Participation in the research slightly alters these differential risks and potential benefits. Research participation presents a minor increase in risk to the kidney donor (Tigue et al. 2007), who does not stand to benefit directly from the donation or participation in the research. There is a possibility that the kidney recipient may experience additional benefits from research participation, but there is also uncertainty about any potential for increased harm. During the consent process, the additional risks of the experimental procedures must be carefully differentiated from the baseline risks of the donation and transplant, as there is potential for the donor and recipient to errantly view participating in the research as more likely to result in better outcomes.

While the proposed research does not significantly increase the potential for physical harm to the donor from the donation or to the recipient from the transplant, it is not only medical risks and benefits that should be considered. There is a vast literature on the potential psychological harms and benefits of living organ donation to both donors and recipients. Empirical research on the decision making of potential living organ donors reveals that some donors do feel pressure to donate (Gordon 2012). Inviting a donor to participate in research following a compelled or tentative decision to donate could exacerbate these feelings of pressure. Most donors report psychosocial benefits, with only a minority reporting psychosocial harms. Indirect benefits to organ donors include the satisfaction of altruistic tendencies and helping a loved one and increased self-esteem. Psychosocial risks include potential guilt or regret if the graft fails or the recipient experiences other complications (Clemens et al. 2006). Organ recipients may feel unworthy, indebted, or fearful of receiving a transplant from a living donor, and feel responsibility for inconvenience to the donor as well as for medical and financial risks (Hanson et al. 2015). It is possible that participation in an experimental protocol may alter the donor's and the recipient's perceptions as well as their experiences of these harms and benefits.

Given that the invitation to research presents an additional decision with new risks and benefits to consider for both parties, this invitation has the potential to negatively impact the relationship between donor and recipient. The donor and recipient may evaluate these additional risks and potential benefits of the research differently, and therefore come to divergent decisions about participation. This disagreement may strain the relationship, whether or not the pair actually participates in the research.

Investigator responsibilities

Federal regulations require that researchers minimize risks to research participants (U.S. Department of Health and Human Services 2018) and inform them of any reasonably expected risks and benefits (U.S. Department of Health and Human Services 2018). This includes social and psychological risks as well as risks of physical harm. Because the invitation to participate in research may impose specific additional risks on the relationship between the donor and recipient, the research team has certain limited obligations to take steps to mitigate those particular risks. Researchers can fulfill these obligations during the informed consent process with minimal burden.

First, researchers should approach the donor and offer them the opportunity to refuse research participation before ever approaching the recipient. This is consistent with standard practice in organ donation of supporting potential living donors to refuse or change their mind without informing the potential recipient of the reason for doing so (Olbrisch et al. 2001). Risks and potential benefits to both parties should be presented to the donor. Unique risks to the relationship of one party's refusal to participate should also be included in the discussion. Then, only if the donor does not refuse participation at this stage should the researchers approach the recipient to discuss the risks, benefits, and procedures individually with them. Risks and benefits to both parties as well as risks to the relationship should be outlined for the kidney recipient as well.

At this point, however, regardless of the recipient's initial decision, the informed consent process should deviate from usual research practice in that researchers (perhaps with support from the transplant coordination team) should facilitate a discussion between donor and recipient, unless there are clear reasons that suggest this would be harmful. While legally and ethically each party's final decision to participate in the research is to be made autonomously by signing the consent form, researchers should promote a shared decision using a relational model of autonomy (Walter and Ross 2014). To treat parties as completely independent participants ignores important ethically salient, contextual realities and risks further harm to the relationship—and potentially the donation and transplant.

The donor and recipient may evaluate the research differently, and the pair may ultimately not participate due to the refusal of one party. This may strain the relationship. However, promoting a transparent, shared decision to the extent possible demonstrates respect for the relationship and protects each party from enrolling in research without providing truly voluntary informed consent.

It might be argued that it is overly paternalistic for researchers to consider the risks of the proposed research to the relationship and attempt to facilitate a discussion between adults who are related. Some may even argue that it is even dangerous for researchers to get involved in a family matter. However, it is generally agreed that researchers have obligations to research participants that are different from obligations to patients (Miller and Wertheimer 2007), given the uncertainty, real potential for harm, and limited potential for direct benefit. Our recommendations balance considerations for protecting individual participants and promoting both individual and relational autonomy.

In order to inform specific modifications to the consent process in future similar studies, empirical research is needed that explores how organ donors and recipients perceive an invitation to participate in transplant intervention research. Research should also assess the extent to which participation in an experimental living transplant protocol alters donors' and recipients' perceptions of risks and benefits as well as their actual experience of psychosocial harms.

References

Clemens, K. K., H. Thiessen-Philbrook, C. R. Parikh, R. C. Yang, M. L. Karley, N. Boudville, G. V. Ramesh Prasad, and A. X. Garg. 2006. Psychosocial health of living kidney donors: A systematic review. *American Journal of Transplantation* 6(12):2965–77.

Gordon, E. J. 2012. Informed consent for living donation: A review of key empirical studies, ethical challenges and future research. *American Journal of Transplantation* 12(9):2273–80.

Hanson, C. S., S. J. Chadban, J. R. Chapman, J. C. Craig, G. Wong, A. F. Ralph, and A. Tong. 2015. The expectations and attitudes of patients with chronic kidney disease toward living kidney donor transplantation: A thematic synthesis of qualitative studies. *Transplantation* 99(3):540–54.

Johnson, L.-M., D. M. Duenas, and B. S. Wilfond. 2021. Conjoined consent: Informed consent when donor and recipient are both research participants. *The American Journal of Bioethics* 21(4):106–107.

Miller, F. G., and A. Wertheimer. 2007. Facing up to paternalism in research ethics. *The Hastings Center Report* 37(3):24–34.

Olbrisch, M. E., S. M. Benedict, D. L. Haller, and J. L. Levenson. 2001. Psychosocial assessment of living organ donors: Clinical and ethical considerations. *Progress in Transplantation* 11(1):40–49.

Tigue, C. C., J. M. McKoy, A. M. Evens, S. M. Trifilio, M. S. Tallman, and C. L. Bennett. 2007. Granulocyte-colony stimulating factor administration to healthy individuals and persons with chronic neutropenia or cancer: An overview of safety considerations from the research on adverse drug events and reports project. *Bone Marrow Transplantation* 40(3):185–92.

U.S. Department of Health and Human Services (U.S. DHHS). 2018. Electronic Code of Federal Regulations. 45 CFR 46. Accessed November 5, 2020. https://www.hhs.gov/ohrp/regulations-and-policy/regulations/revised-com-mon-rule-regulatory-text/index.html

Walter, J. K., and L. F. Ross. 2014. Relational autonomy: Moving beyond the limits of isolated individualism. *Pediatrics* 133(Supplement):S16–S23.

COMMENTARY 5.4.3: RESPECTING DONOR–RECIPIENT RELATIONSHIPS IN RESEARCH DECISION MAKING: WHEN A LIVING DONOR AND KIDNEY TRANSPLANT RECIPIENT ARE BOTH RESEARCH SUBJECTS

STEPHANIE A. KRAFT

Introduction

The standard paradigm of individual informed consent in research ethics focuses on an individualized conception of autonomy. Yet humans are relational beings whose decisions—including whether to participate in a research study—are shaped by the relationships they have with their families, friends, and countless others. In this case the living kidney donor and recipient have a unique and profound relationship, and each individual's participation in the study depends on the participation of the other (Johnson, Duenas, and Wilfond 2021). This relationship is relevant and should be central to the ethical analysis of the informed consent process. This commentary will examine how to conceptualize the informed consent process in a way that respects the relationship between these potential participants, focusing on the principle of respect for persons and the weighing of risks and benefits within this relational context.

Respect for persons—not just individual autonomy

The informed consent process for research is founded in the ethical principle of respect for persons and is intended to provide potential participants an opportunity to make an informed decision about research participation. In practice, consent processes typically focus on promoting individual autonomy, as emphasized in the *Belmont Report*'s directive that researchers must "give weight to autonomous persons' considered opinions and choices" (National Commission for the Protection of Human Subjects of Biomedical and Behavioral Research 1979). But what constitutes a "considered" choice? A narrow, individualized conception of autonomy might suggest that consideration of one's choices is a solitary activity. However, every potential participant is situated in a broader clinical and social context, and many incorporate these contextual and relational factors as part of a fully considered choice. Informed consent processes are typically designed with a focus on disclosure and understanding of individual risks and benefits, without explicitly recognizing that a person may be thinking about how their participation might affect the people they care about, their relationships with them, or countless other factors. Nor do consent processes typically provide space to explore how those outside factors may inform one's decision, which in some cases may involve discussing the possibility of participation with others. Researchers familiar with the conventional approach to informed consent may feel uncomfortable with the idea that a potential participant wants to make a choice in a way that does not neatly fit into the paradigm of individual decision making, but to respect a person's considered choice means recognizing the broad set of considerations that may be part of their process.

Respecting potential participants also requires recognizing their values. In addition to supporting autonomous decision making, the informed consent process can promote values-concordant choices (Dickert et al. 2017). Recent empirical work suggests that participants feel respected when the research team takes the time to understand what is important to each individual and provides them with the space to make the decision that is right for them (Kraft et al. 2020). To the extent that a potential participant values the involvement of another person in their decision, this preference holds significant ethical weight.

In this study, it is important to assess how best to promote respect for persons and consider if the standard approach to informed consent, with an emphasis on individual decision making, may be making it harder for potential participants to make a fully considered choice that reflects their values. The unique relationship between the donor and the recipient in this case is such that each may place a particularly high value on the perspective of the other—for instance, the donor may care deeply about the recipient's perspectives on how study participation may affect their health, and the recipient may hold great concern for the donor's perspectives in recognition of the sacrifice they have already committed to make for them. To ignore the reality of this relationship and place unjustified barriers preventing joint decision making would not only impede their ability to make a fully informed decision, but also may convey disrespect for the values and experiences that may hold great significance in their lives. While a joint decision-making process could raise the possibility of undue or otherwise outsized influence on one or the other's decision, a stepwise process could be used to first assess each individual's desired involvement of the other in the decision before bringing the question to the other for further—and, if desired, collaborative—discussion. Provided these safeguards are in place, a respectful consent process should work within, not against, the preexisting donor–recipient relationship.

Weighing the risks and benefits to both potential participants

Respecting people's values may also include recognizing and accepting how they think about the risks and benefits of research, even if they fall outside those traditionally encompassed in the informed consent process. Risks and benefits to the individual must be disclosed (U.S. Department of Health and Human Services 2018), but a potential participant may also find risks and benefits to others relevant to their decision making. Altruistic motivations to advance science and health on a societal level are often framed as potential benefits of trial participation, but direct potential benefits to specific other individuals may also be highly relevant for individual decision making. Furthermore, explicit discussion of potential impacts on others may show recognition of and appreciation for the participant's choice; prior empirical work has shown that people feel respected in research when the benefits to not just themselves, but also others, are emphasized during the consent process (Kraft et al. 2020).

In this case, there is a prospect of direct, and potentially significant, benefit to a specific beneficiary: the kidney recipient. The donor does not have a prospect of direct clinical benefit but is being asked to take on risks as part of the clinical trial. Whether the donor should weigh the potential benefit to the recipient in their decision to participate is an individual choice, but many—if not all—will, whether this is included in the consent process or not. Disclosing risks and benefits of the research without acknowledging this reality could send a message that the donor's reasons for making their choice are neither valid nor valued by the research team. Safeguards on this process should be in place to ensure that individual risks are not excessive and are minimized to the extent possible, and that the potential benefits to the recipient and to society are sufficient to justify the risks to the donor (Emanuel, Wendler, and Grady 2000). Provided this bar is met and that the individual risks are clearly disclosed to the donor, it is ethically justifiable to include the potential benefits to the recipient in the donor's informed consent process so they can be part of the risk–benefit calculus. Likewise, the recipient may wish to understand the risks to the donor as a part of their decision whether the potential benefits are sufficient to justify moving forward. As discussed above, in many cases this will necessitate discussion between both parties and a joint decision-making process.

Conclusion: Centering the role of relationships in research decision making

People's relationships play a critical role in all research decisions, but they are often hidden from view by our reliance on the paradigm of individual informed consent. In a context like that of live organ donation, it is especially important to account for and accommodate potential participants' relational values as part of their decision-making process. With appropriate safeguards in place to minimize the possibility that people feel undue pressure to make a choice, research teams should explicitly acknowledge the donor–recipient relationship during the informed consent process, clearly state the risks and benefits to both parties, and, if desired by the potential participants, allow and even encourage discussion and joint decision making. Centering this profound relationship in the decision-making process is ethically justifiable as a way of promoting respect for persons, and may optimize each person's ability to make a decision that is in concordance with their values.

References

Dickert, N. W., N. Eyal, S. F. Goldkind, C. Grady, S. Joffe, B. Lo, F. G. Miller, R. D. Pentz, R. Silbergleit, K. P. Weinfurt, et al. 2017. Reframing consent for clinical research: A function-based approach. *The American Journal of Bioethics* 17 (12):3–11.

Emanuel, E. J., D. Wendler, and C. Grady. 2000. What makes clinical research ethical? *JAMA* 283(20):2701–11.

Johnson, L.-M., D. M. Duenas, and B. S. Wilfond. 2021. Conjoined consent: Informed consent when donor and recipient are both research participants. *The American Journal of Bioethics* 21(4):106–107.

Kraft, S. A., E. Rothwell, S. K. Shah, D. M. Duenas, H. Lewis, K. Muessig, D. J. Opel, K. A. B. Goddard, and B. S. Wilfond. 2020. Demonstrating "respect for persons" in clinical research: Findings from qualitative interviews with diverse genomics research participants. *Journal of Medical Ethics*. Published Online First: 06 October 2020.

National Commission for the Protection of Human Subjects of Biomedical and Behavioral Research. 1979. *The Belmont Report: Ethical principles and guidelines for the protection of human subjects of research.*

U.S. Department of Health and Human Services (U.S. DHHS). 2018. Electronic Code of Federal Regulations. 45 CFR 46. Accessed November 5, 2020. https://www.hhs.gov/ohrp/regulations-and-policy/regulations/revised-com-mon-rule-regulatory-text/index.html

CASE 5.5: NAVIGATING PARENTAL PERMISSION FOR NEONATAL RESEARCH

INTRODUCTION

Ethical study recruitment is one of the most challenging aspects of medical research. Who is in the best position to recruit subjects? Are there people who should be excluded from the recruitment process? What are the advantages and disadvantages to individuals in the roles of clinician, researcher, and study coordinator being permitted or assigned to obtain consent? The case we present here, along with three accompanying commentaries, address these issues, made even more complex in the context of conducting interventional research with neonates.

Robin Fiore, PhD, and Reid Cushman, PhD, from the University of Miami Miller School of Medicine, focus on the importance of minimizing therapeutic misconception, undue influence, and conflict of commitment when enrolling vulnerable populations in research studies. Leah Eisenberg, MA, JD, at the University of Arkansas Medical School, reminds researchers that parents of neonates face many difficult decisions and that the timing (prenatally or postnatally) of presenting clinical research options matters. Anita Shah, MD, MPH, Kathryn Porter, JD, MPH, Sandra Juul, MD, PhD, and Benjamin Wilfond, MD, of the University of Washington and Seattle Children's Research Institute, address the trade-offs associated with parental permission being sought by attending physicians, researchers, or study coordinators.

CASE SUMMARY

A randomized, multicenter, placebo-controlled trial was established to test the efficacy of a drug on extremely premature infants. The drug at issue is already FDA-approved for a different purpose in children and adults. Parental permission was obtained either prenatally or postnatally, depending on the availability of the parent. Prenatally, the standard approach was for the obstetrician caring for a hospitalized high-risk expectant mother to ask whether she was interested in being referred to a study investigator or study coordinator to discuss the study. Postnatally, however, consent had to be obtained within the first 24 hours of the child's life. The study protocol required that the person obtaining permission postnatally could not be the attending physician of record.

It came to the attention of the principal investigator at one of the trial centers that an attending physician admitting the baby was also a study investigator and obtained permission from the family to enroll the baby and initiate study procedures. After this event was discussed by the data coordinating center, the attending physician contacted the institution's IRB, which confirmed that this was an acceptable practice. At another trial site, the study investigators anticipated being short-staffed for a few days and asked the coordinating center for permission to use a similar approach of allowing the attending to enroll study subjects, again with local IRB approval. The coordinating center decided to allow the local IRB to guide the approach to recruitment, but there remained uncertainty as to what was the ethically correct approach.

The regulations do not specify who can obtain parental permission. These two separate events motivated the investigators to request an ethics consultation to discuss the range of acceptable approaches for parental permission. To what extent might the role of the person obtaining parental permission (attending physician or trial investigator) influence the parent's voluntariness or understanding? Who should be authorized to obtain parental permission?

COMMENTARY 5.5.1: INFORMED CONSENT AND PARENTAL PERMISSION FOR RESEARCH: RULES, ROLES, AND RELATIONSHIPS

ROBIN N. FIORE AND REID CUSHMAN

This is a multicenter, placebo-controlled, clinical trial involving pregnant women at high risk and "extremely premature infants." The regulations do not specify who can obtain parental permission, but the protocol specifically disqualifies the attending physician of record. Nevertheless, two local IRBs, with the study coordinating center's concurrence, approved allowing attending physicians to obtain parental permission. As described in the case, without specific regulations, the situation is one of "uncertainty as to what was the ethically correct approach" (Taylor, 2015, 76). On the contrary, we argue that ethical analysis precedes regulation—as well as justifying it—and therefore can be relied upon to resolve the confusion.

The question posed is who should be authorized to obtain parental permission and, furthermore, whether and to what extent the role of the individual obtaining permission influences the parents' voluntariness or understanding, two essential criteria for ethically valid informed consent or permission. In considering the ethical criteria for determining who should or should not obtain informed consent or permission, we identify three guiding ethical considerations: therapeutic misconception, undue influence, and conflict of commitment.

Therapeutic misconception occurs when study subjects "inaccurately attribute therapeutic intent to research procedures" (Lidz and Appelbaum 2002). That is, they fail to appreciate important differences between research and treatment such that they cannot adequately judge the risks and benefits of participation and nonparticipation. This may occur if, as here, parents mistake the therapeutic value of a study because they are introduced to it by their physician, whom they understand to be their personal medical advocate. Better study designs seek to mitigate the potential for therapeutic misconception and avoid compromising the validity of consent/permission by having someone other than the attending physician enroll research subjects. This is the approach the coordinating center originally undertook, but was unable to sustain.

Both FDA regulations (FDA 2014a, 21 CFR 50.20) and the Common Rule (U.S. Department of Health and Human Services 2009b, 45 CFR 46.116) require that investigators minimize the possibility of undue influence. This usually refers to the appropriateness of incentives or rewards offered to subjects for participating in research. OHRP guidance, however, notes that "undue influence can be subtle" and specifically mentions the obligation to participate in research that patients might feel if their physician is also the investigator (OHRP 2011). The FDA advises that "influence is contextual and undue influence is likely to depend on an individual's situation" (FDA 2014b). In the case at hand, special care must be taken with respect to children and pregnant women: OHRP cautions that what "would ordinarily be acceptable in some populations may become undue influences for these vulnerable subject groups" (U.S. Department of Health and Human Services 2009a, 45 CFR 46.111(b)).

Conflicts of commitment can undermine efforts to minimize both undue influence and the exercise of patients' rights. A conflict of commitment might arise because of the different ethical duties attached to the roles of *physician* and *researcher*. Physicians are duty-bound to treat each patient for the patient's benefit, in accordance with that patient's values and preferences. Researchers are obligated to comply with a rigid protocol, which aims to yield results that are reproducible and generalizable. Study participation, then, might not serve a particular patient's best interest. Thus, a treating physician who is also a clinical researcher is a "dual agent" in that the physician's professional commitments—patient benefit and pursuit of knowledge—can be in conflict.

Furthermore, patients have the right to access medical care that is not conditioned upon participating in clinical trials. As the FDA acknowledges, however, "because of a potential conflict of interest and the nature of the physician-patient relationship, when the investigator is also the prospective subject's physician, the physician should be careful to ensure that the prospective subject understands that enrollment in the clinical investigation is voluntary and that a decision to forego enrollment will not adversely affect his/her medical care" (FDA 2014b). That is, an individual who is both the patient's physician and a researcher might inadvertently cause a patient to conclude that the patient has no choice but to enroll in a study to preserve access to a particular doctor or healthcare institution.

Despite a lack of regulations on the specific question posed to the IRB, there is more than sufficient guidance to lay out the underlying ethical concerns that a resolution must attend to. According to the FDA and OHRP, both researchers and IRBs have a responsibility to minimize undue influence, and both the FDA and OHRP warn against conflicts of commitment generated by attendings who obtain informed consent or parental permission. In the preceding discussion, it is clear that when attending physicians obtain research consent or permission, they are more ethically burdened than others who ask subjects for consent, by virtue of their important primary relationship with patients. That is, for attendings, all three of the identified ethical concerns are in play. Therefore, as a matter of ethics, attending physicians should not be the ones who obtain consent or permission, especially in the case of a vulnerable subject population. If local IRBs allow attendings to do so, the IRB must also require a plan to mitigate the ethical concerns.

Variation is inevitable when IRBs or research ethics consultation services reflect on research ethics questions, although deliberations likely will cluster along certain themes, and arguably will be driven largely by regulation. As this case illustrates, even when specific regulations are lacking or vague—which is not an uncommon occurrence—a sound ethical analysis can and should provide guidance and empower local IRBs and research administrations.

References

Food and Drug Administration. 2014a. Final rule 21 CFR part 50.20. Additional safeguards for children in clinical investigations of Food and Drug Administration-related products. *Federal Register* 78(38):12937. [Revised 1 April 2014.] Available at: http://www.accessdata.fda.gov/scripts/cdrh/cfdocs/cfcfr/CFRSearch.cfm?CFRPart=50&showFR=1&subpartNode=21:1.0.1.1.20.2 (accessed 12 October 2014).

Food and Drug Administration. 2014b. Draft guidance, July. Informed consent information sheet: Guidance for IRBs, clinical investigators, and sponsors. http://www.fda.gov/downloads/RegulatoryInformation/Guidances/UCM405006.pdf (accessed 12 October 2014).

Lidz, C. W., and P. S. Appelbaum. 2002. The therapeutic misconception: Problems and solutions. *Medical Care* 40(9 suppl):V55–V63.

Office for Human Research Protections (OHRP). 2011. Policy and guidance. Frequently asked questions: What does it mean to minimize the possibility of coercion or undue influence? U.S. Department of Health and Human Services. Available at: http://www.hhs.gov/ohrp/policy/faq/informed-consent/what-does-coercion-or-undue-influence-mean.html (accessed 20 October 2014).

Taylor, Holly A., Ellen Kuwana, and Benjamin S. Wilfond. Navigating parental permission for neonatal research. *The American Journal of Bioethics: AJOB* 15.4(2015):76.

U.S. Department of Health and Human Services. 2009a. Final rule 45 CFR Part 46.111(b). Criteria for IRB approval of research. Revised January 15. Available at: http://www.hhs.gov/ohrp/humansubjects/guidance/45cfr46.html#46.111 (accessed 7 January 2015).

U.S. Department of Health and Human Services. 2009b. Final rule 45 CFR Part 46.116. General requirements for informed consent. Revised January 15. Available at: http://www.hhs.gov/ohrp/humansubjects/guidance/45cfr46.html#46.116 (accessed 7 January 2015).

COMMENTARY 5.5.2: RESEARCH INVOLVING PREMATURE INFANTS: TIMING IS EVERYTHING

LEAH R. EISENBERG

Under what circumstances is it ethical to ask and allow parents to give permission for research on their newborn premature infant? Generally, parents can agree to enrollment in IRB-approved clinical research as long as the infant is eligible for inclusion and the parents are willing and able to give permission. A high-quality permission process demands that the parents be provided with information about their child's condition, why the infant is invited to join the study, the investigational procedures, and the risks, benefits, and alternatives to participation. Such data must be presented clearly and using language that the parents can understand. They must be given time to ask questions and to consider how they wish to proceed. Permission that is provided absent any one of these conditions, or that is the result of undue influence, is inadequate.

It is therefore important to evaluate whether the role of the person obtaining permission influences the parent's voluntariness or understanding. Research has shown that, in general, parents have a difficult time understanding details about the information presented on pediatric research consent forms (Flory and Emanuel 2004). Such difficulties are magnified when the child in question is a neonate in the first day of life, as the parents are still adjusting to having a child, learning about their child's condition, and recovering from the birth itself (Ballard et al. 2004). In some instances, the infant may not be located in the same hospital where the birth occurred; the parents may have had to travel, and could be far from their support system. They will almost certainly be contending with a setting and medical team that are unfamiliar, yet they will still be striving to make decisions that they feel are best for their child. Thus, perhaps what is most important for this decision is whether the study is presented to the parents prenatally or postnatally. It is my contention that getting an expectant mother's agreement to enroll her child in the clinical trial described here prior to giving birth is ethically acceptable, while postnatal permission obtained by the attending physician is not.

In this case study, the protocol for enrollment required that someone other than the attending physician of record discuss potential enrollment with the parents. However, the principal investigator has learned that in at least one instance the attending was the study physician, and that another trial site was given IRB approval to allow an attending to enroll infants when the hospital is short-staffed. Prenatally, enrollment discussions could be handled by the study coordinator, once the mother's obstetrician asked the mother whether she was interested in learning about the study. An advantage of speaking to the mother before the birth is that she and the study coordinator can talk during a relatively calm time, and the pregnant woman can be given some time to make her decision. As it is likely that the study coordinator would not be someone the expectant mother had dealt with before, it could be easier for the pregnant woman to appreciate the difference between her clinical care and the research study. She would see that she was not meeting with a physician, and that the interaction was different from what occurs at a typical prenatal appointment. There would be no examination, just a discussion about the study. The research team should always emphasize the experimental and voluntary nature of the trial when speaking with parents; the prenatal study setting would reinforce the separation between research and clinical care.

Postnatal permission will necessarily take place in a higher-stress environment. Parents will probably need extra time to take in all the information that is being presented to them then, but in reality they will receive less, because study enrollment must occur in the first 24 hours of life. If the study information is presented by a physician, it will be easy for parents to believe that they are being told to do something for the infant's benefit (de Vries 2011). At that point in their infant's life, they are meeting many new care providers, so they may not be able to identify their baby's attending, or to differentiate the role of attending from that of study physician, particularly if one person is fulfilling both roles.

Even if they are able to do so, they may falsely believe that study enrollment is an important piece of the infant's clinical care (this is known as the therapeutic misconception). This all reinforces why postnatal enrollment by an attending, complicated as it is by exhaustion, time, worry, and faith in the physician, is the setting where there is the most risk for undue influence. That risk of permission, given without a clear understanding of the trial, outweighs potential benefits in this case, as data can still be obtained using infants for which prenatal permission was obtained.

Does this mean all postnatal permission is unethical? No. It is important to recognize that improvements in care for premature infants cannot be made without, at some point, trying them on premature infants. Prohibiting all postnatal study enrollment would greatly slow the pace of research, either because parents won't give permission prenatally because they do not expect a premature infant, or because they were not invited to participate at that time. Infants born before 28 weeks of gestation often face a long and complicated medical course that can impact them during their whole lives.

Research on neonates is therefore a necessity, and, as such, permission for such research will sometimes need to be obtained after birth. The question of whether it is ethical to allow postnatal parental permission must be considered on a study-by-study basis. However, study enrollment by a neonatal patient's attending physician is never appropriate. The risk of the therapeutic misconception impacting the parents' ability to give permission in a critical situation is too high. Furthermore, parents might give permission simply because they do not want to jeopardize their relationship with their child's physician. It is also important to note that the methodology of the trial presented here makes postnatal permission especially problematic, because infants must be enrolled so soon after birth, when stress and chaos are often at their highest. Studies for which enrollment can come later not only allow parents time to adjust to life with a premature infant, but also present an opportunity for a study coordinator to visit with them in order to answer their questions and explain research participation.

For all the reasons discussed here, the most ethical way to proceed with this trial is to seek prenatal permission. If enrollment numbers lag, postnatal enrollment can be considered, but a firm plan will need to be in place for getting a study staff member to speak to the family about participation, and for clearly highlighting the investigative nature of the trial before such enrollment can begin. Physicians involved in the infant's clinical care, particularly the infant's attending, should never be involved in trial enrollment. While improving care for premature infants is a goal everyone can agree upon, such improvements cannot come at the expense of ethical research conduct.

References

Ballard, H. O., L. A. Shook, N. S. Desai, and K. J. S. Anand. 2004. Research and the validity of informed consent obtained in the perinatal period. *Journal of Perinatology* 24(7):409–415.

de Vries, M. C. 2011. Ethical issues at the interface of clinical care and research practice in pediatric oncology: A narrative review of parents' and physicians' experiences. *BMC Medical Ethics* 12:18.

Flory, J., and E. Emanuel. 2004. Interventions to improve research participants' understanding in informed consent for research. A systematic review. *Journal of the American Medical Association* 292(13):1593–1601.

COMMENTARY 5.5.3: PRECLUDING CONSENT BY CLINICIANS WHO ARE BOTH THE ATTENDING AND THE INVESTIGATOR: AN OUTDATED SHIBBOLETH?

ANITA SHAH, KATHRYN PORTER, SANDRA JUUL, AND BENJAMIN S. WILFOND

The question raised by this case about who should obtain parental permission can be clarified by considering four general requirements for informed consent: (1) Individuals must have the capacity to give consent, (2) the information must be disclosed, (3) the information must be understood, and (4) the decision must be voluntary (Faden and Beauchamp 1986). This case highlights challenges related to two of these concepts: understanding and voluntariness. Specifically, does a parent's ability to comprehend and give voluntary permission differ depending on whether such permission is obtained by the attending physician, a researcher, or a study coordinator?

This research protocol utilized a standard approach of having a researcher not involved in the infant's care obtain permission. The rationale for this approach is that parents can more readily distinguish trial participation from regular clinical care when approached about participation by a researcher who is not directly responsible for their infant's clinical care. Additionally, the researcher has a thorough understanding of the study and therefore may be better suited to convey accurate information about the research. Furthermore, there is the potential concern that the attending physician in charge of the infant's clinical care might exert undue influence on a parent's decision, perhaps stemming from the possibility of the parents' belief that the attending physician would suggest participation only if it was clearly in the best interest of their child. These are speculative concerns for which there are limited empirical data.

However, there is an alternative perspective, also speculative, that it is preferable for the attending physician responsible for the infant's clinical care and not involved in the research to obtain permission. First is the concern that a researcher has so much personal investment in a trial that he or she will be overly enthusiastic, overstate the benefits, and thereby unduly influence a parent to grant permission for the child to participate. An attending physician will be better suited to present the trial, including its risks and benefits, in the context of the child's ongoing medical issues. The attending physician also might be better positioned to be aware of multiple clinical trials underway in the intensive care unit for which the infant may be eligible, and perhaps be more balanced in presenting all of these options to the parents.

An even more complicated scenario arises when the researcher is also the attending physician. In those cases, attempts to keep the roles separate can lead to additional logistical complexities. Of course, it is possible that either the attending physician or the researcher role can complicate understanding and voluntariness, but it is not clear that these concerns should preclude those in either role from obtaining parental permission. For both ethical and pragmatic reasons, however, study coordinators often are viewed as the happy medium, as they stand at a distance from clinical care while also presumably having the ability to be more balanced about presenting the research in which they are engaged (Davis et al. 2002).

IRBs have a range of practices and may specify or exclude individuals in these roles from obtaining the parental permission. For example, one IRB might determine that study coordinators cannot obtain parental permission because they might not have as deep an understanding of the trial (or of the clinical condition), while another IRB might prohibit the researcher or the attending physician from obtaining permission. In this case, it is clear that the IRBs for the different sites came to differing conclusions. In large part, this is because the Common Rule does not specify who can obtain parental permission (U.S. Department of Health and Human Services 2009, 45 CFR 46, Subpart D). Rather, each IRB sifts through the considerations addressed above regarding the advantages and disadvantages of individuals in different roles obtaining parental permission. Therefore, a range of possible solutions are ethically acceptable.

Two points require further consideration. First, what exactly is meant by "obtaining parental permission"? If a particular IRB determines the researcher must be the one to "obtain permission," this probably means, in its most simplified form, that the researcher must be the person sitting with the parent when the parent signs the permission form. However, signing the permission form is but the final step in the consent process as a whole. Numerous people in various roles might have conversations with the parents about the study during the time the parents are making their decision. If a problem exists with individuals in a certain role pressuring parents, designating an individual of a different role to "obtain permission" by simply obtaining a signature will not solve the underlying problem because the pressure may already have been exerted. Conversely, if a parent is giving permission with true understanding and voluntariness, then the specific role of the person handing the parents the pen should not make a difference.

Second, just as normative arguments can be made for every side of this issue, parents who find themselves in this situation also have varying opinions. While the literature fails to provide clarity on parental preferences for these different options (Hoberman et al. 2013; Singhal et al. 2002; Tait, Voepel-Lewis, and Malviya 2003), anecdotes from the clinical and research experiences of the authors reveal a wide range of preferences. Some parents are more comfortable talking with their attending physician regardless of that person's role in research, while others prefer to talk with a researcher who is not involved in their child's clinical care.

Study recruitment for neonatal research requires a very delicate balance. Facilitating trial enrollment is itself an important ethical goal, and exploring approaches that improve recruitment are desirable. Nevertheless, the primary goal in recruitment should be to promote the parents' understanding and their ability to give voluntary permission. What is of critical importance is that the attending physician, researcher, or study coordinator establishes a trusting relationship with the infant's family. This requires that whoever is charged with obtaining permission should be explicitly aware of his or her own potential to unduly influence the parent. Two simple strategies include (1) offering three reasons some parents choose to participate and three reasons some do not, and (2) offering parents the opportunity to talk with another person about the study before making a decision. With further empirical research, additional strategies to promote ethical recruitment can be developed.

References

Davis, A. M., S. C. Hull, C. Grady, B. S. Wilfond, and G. E. Henderson. 2002. The invisible hand in clinical research: The study coordinator's critical role in human subjects protection. *Journal of Law, Medicine & Ethics* 30(3):411–419. Available at: http://dx.doi.org/10.1111/j.1748-720X.2002.tb00410.x

Faden, R. R., and T. L. Beauchamp. 1986. *A history and theory of informed consent*, New York, NY: Oxford University Press.

Hoberman, A., N. Shaikh, S. Bhatnagar, et al. 2013. Factors that influence parental decisions to participate in clinical research: Consenters vs. Nonconsenters. *JAMA Pediatrics* 167(6):561–566.

Singhal, N., K. Oberle, E. Burgess, and J. Huber-Okrainec. 2002. Parents' perceptions of research with newborns. *Journal of Perinatology* 22(1):57–63.

Tait, A. R., T. Voepel-Lewis, and S. Malviya. 2003. Participation of children in clinical research: Factors that influence a parent's decision to consent. *Anesthesiology* 99(4):819–825.

U.S. Department of Health and Human Services. 2009. Final rule 45 CFR 46, Subpart D. Additional protections for children involved as subjects in research. Revised January 15. Available at: http://www.hhs.gov/ohrp/humansubjects/guidance/45cfr46.html (accessed 5 January 2015).

CASE 5.6: CLICK HERE TO COMPLETE THIS SURVEY: ONLINE RESEARCH, ADOLESCENTS, AND PARENTAL CONSENT

INTRODUCTION

Today we are living in a progressively digital society, where our communications are increasingly moving online through either traditional internet/email, video communications, or apps downloaded on mobile devices such as tablets and smartphones. Adolescents are no exception to the use of online digital technologies—in fact, a 2018 Pew Center Report found that 95 percent of adolescents reported owning or having access to a smartphone, and nearly half (45 percent) endorsed the statement "they are online almost constantly" with nearly all of the remainder (44 percent) sharing they were going online "several times a day," with YouTube and Snapchat as the most frequently used social media sites (Anderson and Jiang 2018). Their experience is likely identical to those of our own, where at least once daily we interface with content that asks us to "click here" for an ad, contest, survey, quiz, game, or other hyperlink. Occasionally, for some sites, we must click an additional box stating that we are of legal age (i.e., 18 or 21, depending on the content of the website), but these sites generally don't require actual verification that the user is of the stated age. All things considered, then, most adolescents engaging with the digital world can easily and regularly encounter a variety of content with the simple click of a finger and minimal parental supervision.

In this digital environment, what are the responsibilities of researchers who wish to enroll adolescent participants in an online survey that most IRBs would consider minimal risk under 45 CFR 46.404? Approval requires assent of the child and permission of the parent or guardian, as outlined under 45 CFR 46.408, unless the criteria for a waiver of consent are met as defined in 45 CFR 46.116 (U.S. DHHS 2018). In this situation, the waiver criteria applicable for an online survey would include an evaluation that: The research involves no more than minimal risk, the research could not practicably be carried out without a waiver or alteration to the consent process, it will not adversely affect the participant's rights and welfare, and, in the case of children, parental (guardian) permission is not a reasonable requirement to protect the pediatric participant.

Three commentaries accompany this case report. In the first commentary, Holly Taylor of the NIH and Doug Mogul of the Johns Hopkins School of Medicine argue that the spirit of the federal regulations can be met through a waiver of formal written consent: either by recruiting through the parents, whose forwarding of the survey to the adolescent implies parental permission, or by recruiting through the adolescent and using an honor system verifying that parental permission was obtained prior to survey completion. Amy Caruso Brown of the State University of New York (SUNY)-Upstate argues for a full waiver of parental consent and promoting adolescent autonomy; she notes that requiring parental permission is burdensome to adolescents and may introduce a selection bias of who ultimately enrolls, potentially limiting the generalizability of the research findings. Meanwhile, Esther Knapp of the University of Louisville argues that it is not impractical to carry out the survey without obtaining a waiver and suggests potential options for obtaining parental permission for online survey-based research.

CASE SUMMARY

Young adults who undergo solid organ transplantation are at risk of nonadherence with their anti-rejection medications, increasing their risk of rejection and graft failure after transplant (Dobbels et al. 2005). Based on a 2005 meta-analysis (Dobbels et al. 2005), which found that up to one-third of adolescent patients were nonadherent, an investigator wants to develop and test a digital tool to support adherence among teens and young adults. As a first step, the investigator would like to survey teenage and young adult transplant recipients to identify the barriers and facilitators of adherence. The investigator would like to enroll teenagers ages 13 and above in addition to those ages 18–30. The survey does not include any sensitive questions and will have no direct benefit for respondents but may benefit future young transplant recipients. The investigator would like to post the survey online and advertise the availability of the survey on websites frequented by recent organ recipients and their parents. A consultation is requested around how to consent participants for this survey study.

SPECIFIC QUESTIONS

Is parental consent necessary to engage the potential pediatric participants? If so, what is needed for the researchers to develop an online parental permission process, and how should it be implemented? What is the role of adolescent participants in online survey research—should they be allowed to consent independently, verify parental permission first, or assent in conjunction with formal verification of parental consent?

COMMENTARY 5.6.1: DIGITAL NEGOTIATIONS: NAVIGATING PARENTAL PERMISSION AND ADOLESCENT ASSENT FOR ONLINE SURVEY PARTICIPATION

HOLLY A. TAYLOR AND DOUGLAS B. MOGUL

Current federal regulations require that prior to conducting research with children, parental permission must be obtained (U.S. Department of Health and Human Services [U.S. DHHS] 2018, 45 CFR 46 Section B). In this study, adolescents (ages 13–18) who have received solid organ transplants in the past will be asked to complete an anonymous survey about their experience with treatment adherence (Johnson, Duenas, and Wilfond 2020). As described, children will be exposed to no more than minimal risk, if any risk at all (U.S. DHHS 2018, 45 CFR 46.404). The time it takes to complete the survey will be the only burden placed on the adolescents. One could argue that adolescents who have received solid organs are likely more familiar with medical care and more likely than the average child to appreciate the purpose of the study and have the capacity to make an informed decision about enrollment. As indicated in the regulations, IRBs have the authority to conclude that parental permission is not required to protect the adolescents eligible to join the study (U.S. DHHS 2018, 45 CFR 46.408(c)). We think IRBs ought to consider this option but will assume for the rest of the analysis that the average IRB may be unwilling to do so.

Here, we consider how best to obtain parental permission and adolescent assent. As noted in the case, the investigator is aware that parents of adolescents who have received a solid organ transplant, and their children, frequent particular websites in search of information and community. The proposal is to utilize these sites for recruitment. There are two ways to attract attention to the survey—through the parent or the adolescent. In the case of the parent, we believe it would be reasonable to notify them about the survey and ask them to recruit their adolescent to participate. They would be introduced to the survey purpose and content and be directed to ask their adolescent to consider participating. Prior to entering the survey, there would be the opportunity for the parent to indicate that they have provided permission for the adolescent to participate. Once the adolescent opens the survey, the same information about the study that was shared with the parent is displayed for the adolescent to review.

In the case of recruiting an adolescent directly, prior to the parent being made aware of the survey, we believe it would be reasonable to notify adolescents about the survey and ask them to seek permission from one of their parents prior to completing the survey. Adolescents would be asked to delay completion until they can direct their parent's attention to information about the survey. Parents would be oriented to the purpose and content of the survey. Prior to entering the survey itself, adolescents would be asked to check a box to confirm that they sought and received their parent's permission to continue. They would then be asked to affirm their assent to participation.

Either of these approaches meets the spirit of the regulations (respects both parent and child) but relies on the trustworthiness of parents and adolescents who are recruited to participate. The most likely violation of this approach would be that adolescents would fail to seek their parent's permission, but tick the box that they have and complete the survey. Given the close to zero risk of harm to the adolescent if they complete the survey, we believe it is reasonable to accept that some number of adolescents will do so. One could argue that accepting this possibility is disrespectful to parental authority. While it may be disrespectful, it is a harm that parents will not likely suffer from, as the adolescents who fail to seek their permission are unlikely to disclose their completion of the survey to their parents. It is possible that the parents of the adolescents may also become aware of the survey and share the opportunity with their adolescents. Under these circumstances, the worst case is that adolescents complete the survey a second time to cover up their choice not to seek their parent's permission. While this could undermine the validity and reliability of the survey results, the study team can review their dataset for duplicates and consider removing one set.

While we set aside the option of making a case to the IRB that parental permission could be waived in this setting, our proposal does in fact belie our bias in that direction. That is, the social value of the information to be gathered is such that accepting a process that relies on the integrity of the relevant parties and accepts some level of adolescent consent is a reasonable trade-off. For those IRBs willing to utilize their authority to waive parental permission, we think doing so in this case is justifiable. The focus of the IRB in this case ought to be the potential risks to the adolescent (none), the potential benefits to future adolescents similarly situated, and the relative maturity of the adolescents (likely). These adolescents are no doubt familiar with the medical environment and in many cases played a role in medical decision making in collaboration with their parents and healthcare providers. These same adolescents would likely have the maturity to accept or refuse the option of completing an anonymous survey about their experience. The only risk, as noted above, is that some parents may be offended that the investigators left them out of the process. The slim chance of this outcome is not reason enough to complicate the study with the approaches described above.

References

Anderson, M, and Jiang J. 2018. Teens, social media, and technology 2018. Pew Research Center, Available at: https://www.pewresearch.org/internet/2018/05/31/teenssocial-media-technology-2018/ (accessed August 20, 2020).

Dobbels F, Van Damme-Lombaert R, Vanhaecke J, and De Geest S. 2005 Gorwing pains: Non-adherence with the immunosuppressive regimen in adolescent transplant recipients. *Pediatric Transplantation* 9(3):381–390. doi: 10.1111/j.1399-3046.2005.00356.x. [PubMed: 15910397]

Johnson, L. M., D. M. Duenas, and B. S. Wilfond. 2020. Click here to complete this survey: Online research, adolescents, and parental consent. *The American Journal of Bioethics* 20(10):82–83.

U.S. Department of Health and Human Services (U.S. DHHS). 2018. Electronic code of federal regulations. 45 CFR 46 Section B. https://www.hhs.gov/ohrp/regulations-and-policy/regulations/revised-common-rule-regulatory-text/index.html (accessed March 23, 2020).

COMMENTARY 5.6.2: CONSTRAINED ADOLESCENT AUTONOMY FOR HEALTHCARE SHOULD INCLUDE PARTICIPATION IN SURVEY RESEARCH

AMY E. CARUSO BROWN

In situations like the one presented here (Johnson, Duenas, and Wilfond. 2020), adolescent participants should be allowed to consent independently, without parental permission being required or even solicited.

The proposed study involves psychosocial research with minimal risks. Even the risk to privacy should be minimal for a one-time, online survey, as it is not necessary to collect identifying information. Furthermore, both the potential benefits (namely, enhanced well-being or self-efficacy due to feeling that one has contributed meaningfully to future patients) and potential burdens (the time spent completing the survey and any negative emotions that might arise from reflecting on one's health or nonadherence) are fully borne by the adolescents themselves.

This form of research participation parallels clinical situations in which adolescents are generally granted constrained autonomy over healthcare decisions (e.g., Weiss et al. 2018). The exception that allows adolescents to independently seek outpatient mental health treatment is particularly analogous because the most salient benefits and burdens of the proposed study are psychological (Boldt 2012). Altruism can be a meaningful benefit of research participation, and contribute to a sense of agency for a sick teen who otherwise has few positive choices, perhaps even enhancing adherence, but only the participant can truly evaluate the extent of that benefit. Parents may underappreciate the positive psychosocial impact that participation in this type of research can have on their child, just as they may misconstrue the extent to which participating in the study might cause distress (Flicker and Guta 2008).

Current research supports the idea that adolescents have the capacity to provide independent consent to this type of research (Bruzzese and Fisher 2003; Michaud et al. 2015; Steinberg 2013). At least one study has suggested that the addition of simple multiple-choice questions to verify understanding of a study might be helpful in mitigating the risk of an adolescent participating in an online study without fully reading the consent document (Friedman et al. 2016). Although it is not at all clear that the tendency to sign documents without carefully reading them is unique to teens, the study investigators might consider adopting a similar approach, which would also allow them to assure that participants are aware of resources available to them to mitigate any psychological distress related to the survey or identified by the survey.

Parents may also have differential concerns regarding the potential loss of privacy from survey participation. Although this risk can be minimized by avoiding the collection of identifying information, study investigators may want to offer participants the option to be contacted in the future in order to receive results of the current study or be invited to participate in subsequent studies of the digital tool. This choice, too, should reside with the participant, not the parent, given the nature of the risk. The study, by design, will be advertised online, attracting the attention of teens who are already using the internet and who are, very likely, active on social media, a space in which most teens make their own decisions with regard to the disclosure of personal information.

As with the comparable exceptions that permit adolescents to consent to their own healthcare, there are also pragmatic reasons to advocate for this approach to consent (Flicker and Guta 2008). Chiefly, requiring parental permission is likely to significantly hinder participation and contribute to selection bias. For some adolescents, the extra step of discussing the study with a parent may mean that they never return to complete the survey; and one can imagine that for teens from families already experiencing the psychological, social, and economic challenges that contribute to nonadherence, this barrier may have a greater impact on some populations than others. For example, a study of school-based survey research noted that, when researchers accepted parental non-response "implied parental consent," they recruited more teen boys, African Americans, students with poor grades, and students who smoked (Unger et al. 2004). Similarly, a requirement for parental permission might skew this study's sample toward teens who are more adherent to treatment, as teens who are less adherent may be more hesitant to raise the subject of the study with their families. In addition, unlike most pediatric research, there is no pragmatic reason to involve the participants' parents at all, as neither their time nor resources are needed to support the adolescents' participation.

Ultimately, these practical reasons are important regulatory considerations, allowing for a waiver of parental permission on the grounds that the study cannot be "practically carried out" without a waiver (U.S. DHHS 2018, 45 CFR 46.116(d)). Though it may seem technically possible to conduct such a study without a waiver of parental permission, the risk of bias, as noted above, is potentially so significant as to invalidate the results. In a general sense, the risks of research, no matter how minor, are only ever justifiable by the prospect of benefit to participants or others. Information from those teens at the great risk of nonadherence will be of greatest value to the design of tools aimed at teens with low adherence, and requiring parental permission adds a potential barrier to reaching those participants. To require parental permission when it is ethically unnecessary, thereby compromising the likelihood that the study will produce meaningful results, is itself unethical.

References

Boldt, R. C. 2012. Adolescent decision making: Legal issues with respect to treatment for substance misuse and mental illness. *Journal of Health Care Law and Policy* 15(1):75. https://digitalcommons.law.umaryland.edu/jhclp/vol15/iss1/5

Bruzzese, J. M., and C. B. Fisher. 2003. Assessing and enhancing the research consent capacity of children and youth. *Applied Developmental Science* 7(1):13–26.

Flicker, S., and A. Guta. 2008. Ethical approaches to adolescent participation in sexual health research. *The Journal of Adolescent Health* 42(1):3–10.

Friedman, M. S., C. J. Chiu, C. Croft, T. E. Guadamuz, R. Stall, and M. P. Marshal. 2016. Ethics of online assent: Comparing strategies to ensure informed assent among youth. *Journal of Empirical Research on Human Research Ethics* 11(1):15–20.doi: 10.1177/1556264615624809.

Johnson, L. M., D. M. Duenas, and B. S. Wilfond. 2020. Click here to complete this survey: Online research, adolescents, and parental consent. *The American Journal of Bioethics* 20(10):82–83.

Michaud, P. P. A., R. W. Blum, I. Benaroyo, J. Zermatten, and V. Baltag. 2015. Assessing an Adolescent's capacity for autonomous decision-making in clinical care. *The Journal of Adolescent Health* 57(4):361–366.

Steinberg, L. 2013. Does recent research on adolescent brain development inform the mature minor doctrine? *The Journal of Medicine and Philosophy* 38(3):256–267.

Unger, J. B., P. Gallaher, P. H. Palmer, L. Baezconde- Garbanati, D. R. Trinidad, S. Cen, and C. A. Johnson. 2004. No news is bad news: Characteristics of adolescents who provide neither parental consent nor refusal for participation in school-based survey research. *Evaluation Review* 28(1):52–63.

U.S. Department of Health and Human Services (US DHHS). 2018. Electronic Code of Federal Regulations. 45 CFR 46. https://www.hhs.gov/ohrp/regulations-and-policy/regulations/revised-common-rule-regulatory-text/index.html (accessed March 23, 2020).

Weiss, C., E. C. Kwon, R. A. Shapiro, P. J. Vinett, M. Knodel, D. Lieberman, and K. Bodde. 2018. *Teenagers, health care, and the law: A guide to minors' rights in New York State*, New York, NY: New York Civil Liberties Union.

COMMENTARY 5.6.3: RESPECTING PARENTAL PERMISSION AND MAINTAINING FLEXIBILITY IN ONLINE RESEARCH INVOLVING ADOLESCENT PARTICIPANTS

ESTHER ELISE KNAPP

Online survey research offers many appealing advantages over more traditional methods of collecting research data: It is cheaper, it can make data collection and processing easier, it offers the opportunity to recruit broadly across populations, and it may improve inclusion of participants from diverse geographic and socioeconomic backgrounds (especially if mobile platforms are supported). This approach may be particularly useful for research with adolescents, as adolescent participants may feel more comfortable participating in an online survey rather than a face-to-face interview, especially when the research involves sensitive topics.

However, online research with minors also raises novel challenges, including potential barriers to obtaining parental permission online. These issues include verifying the roles of the different parties involved: For example, if the project described in this case (Johnson, Duenas, and Wilfond 2020) were to advertise on public websites, how would the investigators confirm that potential participants are indeed solid organ transplant recipients between the ages of 13 and 30? How would this impact the validity of the study's findings? Similarly, how do research personnel identify appropriate guardians of pediatric participants? How would the investigators know that the person signing a digital consent form is really the legal guardian, or even an adult?

Conversely, how would potential participants (and their parents) know that the project described in this case is a legitimate, IRB-approved study? If recruitment is conducted via internet advertising, as opposed to a physical encounter within an academic medical institution, how do pediatric transplant patients know that the information being collected is going to be protected and not misused? It may also be more difficult to obtain true informed consent: In-person research encounters provide more opportunity for potential participants and their parents to ask questions, and for the study team to verify that the participants understand the risks and benefits of the study.

Despite these challenges, it is still possible to conduct online research with pediatric participants responsibly, and obtain appropriate consent. Perhaps the simplest way to administer an online survey to adolescents would be to obtain only the assent of the participant, without requiring parental permission. There is indeed precedent for allowing adolescents to agree to participation in research without requiring parental permission (Levine 1995). However, regulations on pediatric research participation are intended to protect children, and with good reason. In order to justify circumventing parental permission, the investigators would need a compelling reason to do so. Thus, in order to conduct research on children without formal parental permission, the burden is on the investigators to demonstrate that it would not be practicable to perform the study another way. In this scenario, that might not be the case.

Research at institutions that receive federal funding are subject to specific guidelines regarding informed consent: Section 46.116 (Subpart A) of the Common Rule stipulates that the informed consent requirement can be waived if certain conditions are met, including: The proposed research involves no more than minimal risk to participants, and the research could not practicably be carried out without the requested waiver or alteration (U.S. DHHS 2018).

There are certainly plausible situations in which a waiver or alteration of informed consent would be necessary in order to carry out a pediatric study: for example, a study focused on homeless teens who have run away from home, or pregnant teenagers, or a survey of transgender adolescents. Physical separation from parents or guardians may mean that they are not available to provide permission for research participation. Stigma or fear of punishment may also prevent adolescents from being truthful with their parents about topics like their adherence to medical treatments or gender identity. In such cases, it may be important to conduct research with adolescents without a requirement for parental permission.

For the research ethics consultant in this case, before addressing the question of parental permission, the first question should probably be, "Is an anonymous, online survey really the best way to achieve your scientific aims?" While online surveys are often attractive because they can be conducted relatively inexpensively and with very little local research infrastructure, they are not always the best choice. In this case in particular, adolescent solid organ transplant patients are a relatively small population who can be identified and reached through the relatively small number of pediatric transplant centers who provide care for this population. It might be possible to work with these pediatric transplant centers to receive direct contact information for eligible participants, distribute recruitment materials, or even administer the surveys in clinic. All of these alternatives would take more legwork than an anonymous online survey, such as obtaining central IRB reliance agreements, but these approaches might also produce better scientific answers. After all, anonymous online surveys pose numerous scientific challenges such as "spam" responses and difficulties measuring the response rate. In addition to the scientific benefits, these alternatives could create opportunities to obtain higher-quality assent and parental permission than an exclusively online survey could offer. In fact, the growing comfort with and availability of videoconferencing and telehealth tools as a result of the COVID-19 pandemic mean that it might even be practical for the investigator in this case to conduct the assent and parental permission process via video. This is not to say that there is no role for using online surveys to conduct valuable, scientifically rigorous research. Sometimes the approaches suggested above will not be feasible, due to issues such as cost and logistics. Simply, it is important to consider the scientific goals of the study, and how they are best achieved, when attempting to find a solution to a research ethics challenge.

If, after consideration, the investigator decides that an online survey with passive recruitment is still the best scientific approach, then the research ethicist will need to address the question of how best to obtain consent. Since it is important for studies like this one to enroll as diverse a group of transplant recipients as possible, and try to minimize potential barriers to participation, then it is also important to weight the accessibility of different assent and parental permission options for a wide array of families. The researchers should seek to respect the primacy of parental authority to the extent possible, while at the same time accounting for the reality that not all families are the same. Some families will have limited access to the internet or internet-enabled devices, and others will involve a parent or guardian who is not physically present with the child. In general, however, it should still be possible in most circumstances for the investigators to obtain adolescent assent and parental permission online. For example, digital signatures can be obtained from both adolescent participants and their parents (Brothers, Clayton, and Goldenberg 2020). These signatures can be collected at separate times, and the parent can be sent a link via email (or even text) to complete the signature easily. These approaches could be utilized while still permitting exceptions where parental permission would need to be waived: for example, if the adolescent does not live with the parent or legal guardian, or if the parent is serving overseas in the military. Overall, the goal is to make a good faith effort to honor the parent's role in giving permission for research participation, but avoid making onerous requirements that discourage enrollment.

In summary, there are situations in which certain research studies can only be properly conducted by waiving the requirement for parental permission; these situations may increasingly include studies designed to collect data from adolescents online. In these cases, the adolescent's assent alone could be considered sufficient. However, the investigators should consider alternative approaches that might improve the scientific merit and facilitate more traditional assent and parental permission. If the research cannot reasonably be conducted any other way than a public online survey, the investigator should be expected to justify that conclusion. In this case, the ethics consultant bears a responsibility to provide guidance on how to protect pediatric research participants. Even for online surveys open to the public, parental permission can still typically be obtained prior to collecting data from adolescent participants, although flexibility for how this is obtained is key, since any single strategy for obtaining parental permission could create an undue burden for some families.

References

Brothers, K. B., E. W. Clayton, and A. J. Goldenberg. 2020. Online pediatric research: Addressing consent, assent, and parental permission. *The Journal of Law, Medicine & Ethics: A Journal of the American Society of Law, Medicine & Ethics* 48(1_suppl):129–137. doi: 10.1177/1073110520917038.

Johnson, L. M., D. M. Duenas, and B. S. Wilfond. 2020. Click here to complete this survey: Online research, adolescents, and parental consent. *The American Journal of Bioethics* 20(10):82–83.

Levine, R. J. 1995. Adolescents as research subjects without permission of their parents or guardians: Ethical considerations. *The Journal of Adolescent Health* 17(5):287–297. doi: 10.1016/1054-139x(95)00175-r.

U.S. Department of Health and Human Services (US DHHS). 2018. Electronic code of federal regulations. 45 CFR 46. https://www.hhs.gov/ohrp/regulations-and-policy/regulations/revised-common-rule-regulatory-text/index.html (accessed March 23, 2020).

CASE 5.7: WHEN PROFESSIONAL MEETS PERSONAL: HOW SHOULD RESEARCH STAFF ADVERTISE ON SOCIAL MEDIA FOR RESEARCH OPPORTUNITIES?

INTRODUCTION

As part of the regulatory review process, both the FDA (U.S. Food and Drug Administration 1998) and OHRP (U.S. Department of Health and Human Services 2013) have issued guidance stating that IRBs should review and approve direct advertising to study participants. Research opportunities advertised online, and specifically through social media, would be included in this requirement. The FDA considers recruitment via direct advertising for study participants to be the start of the informed consent and subject selection process. Advertisements should be included in the IRB review to assure that they are not unduly influential and do not promise any expectation of cure beyond what is described in the consent materials and the protocol. This is especially critical when a study may involve participants who are likely to be vulnerable to undue influence. The previously published directives from federal agencies predate the widespread use of social media platforms as a method of health communication and participant recruitment and are largely silent on the potential blurring of personal and professional boundaries when study staff members advertise through their personal social media platforms. For example, should there be any concern if a team member simply shares an IRB-approved advertisement from an institutional account to their personal Twitter or Facebook news feeds? What if they attach a comment to the retweet or share?

Certainly, individual IRBs can't review and control the comments of every post reshared online; given questions like these, what then is the recommended course of action for investigators considering sharing advertisements for their own studies on their personal social media accounts? In the commentary by Emily Anderson of Loyola University Chicago, she acknowledges the importance of social media platforms as a recruitment tool, but outlines the ethical concerns, practical challenges, and biases that can arise with recruitment through personal channels. Given these concerns, she argues that investigators wishing to recruit via social media should focus on alternative methods of recruitment that ensure equitable subject selection agnostic of individual study staff's personal networks. In a subsequent commentary, Ryan Spellecy and Lindsay D. Nelson of the Medical College of Wisconsin are also concerned about the introduction of selection bias and concerns of professionalism when personal networks are used for recruitment. Ultimately, they focus not on *whether* studies should use social media for recruitment, but on *how* to recruit in an ethically appropriate manner, concluding that study-specific management plans are more likely to address the concerns than are rigid one-size-fits-all policies.

As evidenced by the issues raised in the case itself and subsequently by the commentary authors, it is clear that there are multiple layers to consider when formulating an answer to the seemingly simple question, "How should research staff advertise on social media for research opportunities?" The ease of sharing information broadly on social media platforms can blur the lines between professional and personal roles; this can be particularly complicated when individuals seek to maintain a "professional" presence on one or more platforms (e.g., Twitter) where they regularly communicate and share health-related communications. Further reconsideration of the issue is warranted, as additional guidance may bring consistency to the practice and benefit researchers, IRBs, and sponsors seeking to advertise clinical trials via social media platforms. Fortunately, as research ethicists we are not alone in trying to define appropriate boundaries for communication across social media networks.

CASE SUMMARY

As COVID-19 has increased challenges and barriers to conducting non-COVID-19 research, specifically lower recruitment rates, a research ethics consultation (REC) request is placed about the appropriateness of investigators and study personnel advertising research opportunities via their personal social media accounts. At the institution, investigators are permitted to post information about studies on official university, government, and sponsor websites. This also includes the social media accounts of those entities (i.e., their Facebook, Instagram, and Twitter accounts). Through these institutionally managed channels, participants are often invited to join dedicated social media groups to learn more. Since this is a form of direct advertising, IRB approval is also required for investigators or study personnel to properly post novel study information directly to their own social media feeds. However, if an individual were to simply share a link to an approved posting that already exists (e.g., on a university, government, or sponsor website), the information would already be IRB-approved.

But study personnel using their personal social media accounts for these professional purposes—even when just linking to an already-existing study advertisement—raises questions of subject selection and consent, as well as introducing risks for the individual doing the posting. Some of the REC questions about these issues, as well as the risks incurred, included: What are the differences between personal and professional interactions, especially with respect to the content of the information shared about the study with potential participants, when a study member is interacting with individuals they may be "friends" with online or who follow their accounts? How is selection affected or even biased by the population who has access to the research, when recruitment is posted on personal social media accounts? Are there social risks to study personnel if friends or followers who wish to participate are not eligible for participation in the study? Do friends of study personnel feel undue influence to participate when study advertisements are posted on personal social media accounts?

REFERENCES

U.S. Department of Health and Human Services. 2013. Attachment B: Considerations and recommendations concerning internet research and human subjects research regulations, with revisions. Accessed July 6, 2021. https://www.hhs.gov/ohrp/sachrp-committee/recommendations/2013-may-20-letter-attachment-b/index.html

U.S. Food and Drug Administration. 1998. Recruiting study subjects: guidance for institutional review boards and clinical investigators. Accessed July 6, 2021. https://www.fda.gov/regulatory-information/search-fda-guidance-documents/recruiting-study-subjects

COMMENTARY 5.7.1: SHARING RESEARCH OPPORTUNITIES ON PERSONAL SOCIAL MEDIA ACCOUNTS AND FAIR SUBJECT SELECTION

EMILY E. ANDERSON

Given that many clinical research studies struggle to meet their recruitment goals (Desai 2020), researchers are eager to identify and employ strategies that will maximize reach to eligible and interested participants. There is also a critical need to increase enrollment of racial and ethnic minorities and other underrepresented groups in research (Strauss, White, and Bierer 2021). Limited evidence suggests that social media advertisements may be effective at recruiting hard-to-reach populations to clinical research when compared with traditional recruitment methods such as print, radio, television, and email (Topolovec-Vranic and Natarajan 2016; Whitaker, Stevelink, and Fear 2017). Social media is an important research recruitment tool subject to the same regulatory and ethical norms as other types of advertisements, simply in a new context (Harvard Catalyst Regulatory Foundations Ethics & Law Program 2017).

Efforts to recruit participants to clinical research studies must adhere to ethical standards for privacy, voluntariness, and fair selection of subjects. Research regulations do not say much about research recruitment and say nothing about use of social media. Therefore, it is reasonable that different IRBs may respond differently to a request to allow investigators and study personnel to advertise research opportunities via their personal social media accounts (Johnson, Duenas, and Wilfond 2021). Here I will argue that in the absence of clear regulatory prohibition, the practice should be avoided unless there is sufficient reason to believe that doing so will promote diversity, equity, and inclusion.

Practical concerns

Addressing the broad use of social media platforms to recruit study participants, the Harvard Catalyst published this guidance:

> There should not be a presumption against recruitment using social media. So long as recruitment advances are undertaken transparently and with due respect for the privacy rights and interests of social media users, they will typically satisfy relevant ethical requirements.

(2017, 13)

In a companion article, Gelinas et al. (2017) suggested that in analyzing use of social media for research recruitment, when possible, a familiar "off-line variant or equivalent" be identified, along with the ethical considerations relevant to this equivalent.

Distributing flyers by leaving them out at a party attended by many friends and acquaintances or mailing flyers out to all the people in one's address book might be offline equivalents to a researcher or staff member sharing an announcement about a research opportunity on a personal social media account. In both examples, threats to privacy and voluntariness are minimal; as with posting the information on a social media account, the invitation can easily be ignored given the absence of direct personal interaction. However, both examples seem quite obviously outside the bounds of usual recruitment practices. From a practical standpoint, investigators have likely not included such strategies in their recruitment plans as they are resource intensive and unlikely to translate to increased enrollment. The effort involved in physically producing recruitment flyers and the relatively small size of our real-world networks are significant compared with the ease of sharing on social media, where large numbers of friends and followers can be reached in a matter of seconds.

Privacy concerns

To be sure, there are unique privacy risks of recruitment via social media; if a friend or follower clicks on a recruitment ad, this may inadvertently disclose personal health information to third-party companies tracking online behavior for commercial purposes. But sharing research opportunities does not significantly increase such risks of disclosure for online friends and followers as these risks are ever present, and actual recruitment materials and processes should inform potential participants about these risks when appropriate (Bender et al. 2017).

Diversity, equity, and inclusion

These aforementioned nontraditional strategies for recruitment raise concerns about fair subject selection. The recruitment plan for any research study should carefully consider strategies that will reach sufficient numbers of potentially eligible individuals and ensure that members of particular groups are not over- or underrepresented. Given the nonrandom makeup of personal social networks, sharing a research opportunity on personal social media accounts (or at a birthday party, or with friends and family members at their home addresses) may violate the ethical requirement for fair and equitable procedures. If an individual researcher or staff member has large and homogeneous social networks, the study may end up with a sample that is quite unrepresentative in terms of sex, gender, race/ethnicity, sexuality, education, socioeconomic status, insurance and employment status, geographic location, and other characteristics. Therefore, this practice should be generally avoided unless there is some reason to anticipate that such sharing would promote diversity, equity, and inclusion. However, individuals' private networks should not be assessed as a means of determining this.

If the study includes a screening process that accounts for diversity and inclusion in some way—for example, by aiming to enroll equal numbers of men and women, or of people from different ethnic minority groups—*and* the study aims to enroll large numbers of participants, then such "non-systematic advertising" through personal social media accounts may be ethically neutral. But it is unlikely that such a screening process would be in place for randomized clinical trials of medicines or medical devices. Similarly, posting on personal social media accounts may be ethically neutral if a behavioral/ social science study aims to recruit a convenience sample.

Undue pressure on researchers and study personnel

Lastly, it is worth considering the potential impact on investigator behaviors if recruitment via personal social networks becomes the norm. For example, some researchers might be tempted or study personnel might feel obligated to increase their numbers of friends and followers, or join and become active on new social media platforms, to reach additional participants. For this reason, researchers and study personnel sharing research opportunities from their personal social network accounts should generally be discouraged.

Ultimately, personal social media accounts are likely not a useful strategy in meeting the important ethical goal of increasing diversity among those reached with an opportunity to participate in research. Researchers and sponsors concerned about recruiting sufficient numbers of research participants should focus instead on using advertising channels designed to promote fair subject selection and, most importantly, should budget accordingly. For clinical studies that want to appropriately use social media for recruitment, funds should be allocated for targeted advertisements, respectful engagement with specific online groups that involve members likely to meet eligibility criteria, and development of project or institutional social media accounts that are independent of researchers' or other study personnel's existing social networks.

References

Bender, J., A. Cyr, L. Arbuckle, and L. Ferris. 2017. Ethics and privacy implications of using the internet and social media to recruit participants for health research: A privacy-by-design framework for online recruitment. *Journal of Medical Internet Research* 19(4):e104.

Desai, M. 2020. Recruitment and retention of participants in clinical studies: Critical issues and challenges. *Perspectives in Clinical Research* 11(2):51–3.

Gelinas, L., R. Pierce, S. Winkler, I. G. Cohen, H. F. Lynch, and B. E. Bierer. 2017. Using social media as a research recruitment tool: Ethical issues and recommendations. *The American Journal of Bioethics* 17(3):3–14.

Harvard Catalyst Regulatory Foundations, Ethics, & Law Program. 2017. The use of social media in recruitment to research: A guide for investigators and IRBs. https://catalyst.harvard.edu/pdf/ regulatory/Social_Media_Guidance.pdf.

Johnson, L.-M., D. M. Duenas, and B. S. Wilfond. 2021. When professional meets personal: How should research staff advertise on social media for research opportunities? *The American Journal of Bioethics* 21(10):38–39.

Strauss, D. H., S. A. White, and B. E. Bierer. 2021. Justice, diversity, and research ethics review. *Science* 371(6535):1209–11.

Topolovec-Vranic, J., and K. Natarajan. 2016. The use of social media in recruitment for medical research studies: A scoping review. *Journal of Medical Internet Research* 18(11):e286.

Whitaker, C., S. Stevelink, and N. Fear. 2017. The use of Facebook in recruiting participants for health research purposes: A systematic review. *Journal of Medical Internet Research* 19(8):e290.

COMMENTARY 5.7.2: HOW SHOULD INVESTIGATORS ADVERTISE ON SOCIAL MEDIA FOR RESEARCH OPPORTUNITIES?

RYAN SPELLECY AND LINDSAY D. NELSON

How research studies should use social media to recruit research participants (Johnson, Duenas, and Wilfond 2021) is a timely question. Importantly, the question is how, not if, studies should use social media. Social media have become integral to many people's daily lives, and participant recruitment has adapted to that fact. Below, we offer some considerations for how IRBs, investigators, ethicists, and institutions might think through social media and other internet-based study recruitment. While coercion or undue influence may be relevant to using personal social media accounts for study recruitment, we wish to draw attention to two other issues raised by this case.

The first issue is the potential for personal social media advertising to increase selection bias, of interest to both IRBs (when considering whether subject selection is equitable) and investigators (due to effects on the generalizability of findings). Similar to other approaches that leverage one's personal contacts, advertising through personal social media accounts may lead to overselection of participants from similar demographics as the recruiting investigator. Workforces at academic institutions lack diversity (Davis and Fry 2019), so this method of recruitment could propagate ongoing limitations in the diversity of research participants. Yet, leveraging social media for study advertising may reach a wider audience than traditional recruitment strategies. Social media recruitment can facilitate selection of diverse groups through design features that users routinely encounter (e.g., posts that are displayed to individuals beyond the poster's immediate contact list), and features are available that can further facilitate the reach of social media advertisements (e.g., use of the advertising tools embedded into platforms such as Facebook; see King, O'Rourke, and DeLongis 2014). It has even been suggested that social media advertising "democratizes" recruitment by allowing potential participants to be contacted directly, without requiring the approval of, employers or professional organizations (King, O'Rourke, and DeLongis 2014). Thus, it is perhaps not surprising that internet-recruited samples appear at least as diverse as other samples (Gosling et al. 2004). To what degree personally advertising a study from one's social media page affects sampling bias is an empirical question with, likely, different answers based on study-specific factors and the individual nature of the research team member's social media platform. However, it appears misguided to assume that such recruitment would lead to more sampling bias than many other common recruitment approaches.

The second issue, which we might broadly term "professionalism," is more concerning. Posting recruitment materials on one's personal social media account implies endorsement for the research. In turn, viewers of an advertisement may conflate the poster's online identity with the institution sponsoring the research, a problem if the individual's personal posts conflict with the institution's values or policies. Consider, for example, recent media reports of individuals fired by their employers after sharing false information on their social media accounts regarding the COVID-19 pandemic. If such individuals were research staff and shared recruitment materials for a study sponsored by their institution, immediately after posting conspiracy theories about the COVID-19 vaccine, a connection between those two posts could be made by viewers of those posts. This might have a number of unintended consequences, such as diminishing or altering the reputation of the institution or research study in the eyes of the public.

However, such a concern is not one that an IRB would or perhaps even could consider. The risks delineated in 45 CFR 46.111 are typically understood to be risks to research participants, not the institution at which the research takes place. To be clear, this specific concern is not primarily an issue regarding IRB review of recruitment materials, but rather of risks to the institution that may arise in this kind of recruitment. Consequently, considering such risks and whether or not study teams should use their personal social media accounts for recruitment purposes requires collaboration between ethicists, study teams, and other stakeholders. Of course, the IRB is not the only tool for facilitating ethical research and protecting research participants. Looking more broadly, a Human Research Protection Program (HRPP) can consider the issue of professionalism in a collaborative manner.

Ross et al. provide useful guidance for similar circumstances in which an IRB cannot provide oversight (Ross 2010; Ross et al. 2010). In their model, a Human Subject Protections Program, now commonly referred to as an HRPP, collaboratively considers risks not only to individual research participants, but to groups as well. A similar collaboration between ethicists, study teams, the IRB, and other stakeholders could provide useful guidance in this case. Ultimately, the most equitable, effective, and appropriate approach to using social media, including personal social media accounts, to advertise for research is somewhat study-specific, and rigid policies are unlikely to facilitate ethical, robust research across diverse topics and populations.

References

Davis, L., and R. Fry. 2019. College faculty have become more racially and ethnically diverse, but remain far less so than students. *Pew Research Center*, July 21, 2019. https://www.pewresearch.org/fact-tank/2019/07/31/us-college-fac-ulty-student-diversity/.

Gosling, S. D., S. Vazire, S. Srivastava, and O. P. John. 2004. Should we trust web-based studies? A comparative analysis of six preconceptions about Internet questionnaires. *The American Psychologist* 59(2):93–104.

Johnson, L.-M., D. M. Duenas, and B. S. Wilfond. 2021. When professional meets personal: How should research staff advertise on social media for research opportunities? *The American Journal of Bioethics* 21(10):38–39.

King, D. B., N. O'Rourke, and A. DeLongis. 2014. Social media recruitment and online data collection: A beginner's guide and best practices for accessing low-prevalence and hard-to-reach populations. *Psychologie Canadienne [Canadian Psychology]* 55(4):240–49.

Ross, L. F. 2010. 360 Degrees of human subjects protections in community-engaged research. *Science Translational Medicine* 2(45):45cm23.

Ross, L. F., A. Loup, R. M. Nelson, J. R. Botkin, R. Kost, G. R. Smith, and S. Gehlert. 2010. Human subjects protections in community-engaged research: A research ethics framework. *Journal of Empirical Research on Human Research Ethics* 5(1):5–17.

CASE 5.8: THE LIMITATIONS OF "BOILERPLATE" LANGUAGE IN INFORMED CONSENT: A SINGLE-IRB REVIEW OF MULTISITE GENETIC RESEARCH IN MILITARY PERSONNEL

INTRODUCTION

Informed consent forms have commonly included standardized language, often referred to as "boilerplate" language, that has been vetted by institutional officials. The implicit goal is to ensure that all participants have adequate explanations of critical information. However, sometimes this language is included even if it does not clearly make sense in the context of a specific study, because it is more expedient for the investigator and the IRB to include it. More recently, single-IRB review of multisite trials has been an additional mechanism that is intended to improve efficiency and consistency for investigators and IRBs while ensuring the quality of the content and presentation of information.

The case presented here illustrates the challenge related to how a single IRB considers different boilerplate language from different institutions. This case is quite nuanced and is related to language about privacy and discrimination related to research about genetic risks for myositis in participants who are active-duty military personnel. However, the underlying concern in this case challenges the conceptualization of both the role of informed consent and role of institutions. Thus, this case is salient for anyone thinking about the role and expectations of consent forms for participants.

Three commentaries accompany the case. Jeff Botkin from the University of Utah acknowledges that boilerplate language serves institutional functions, but claims that it is still necessary for IRBs to ensure this information is written in such a way that can actually help participants make decisions. He concludes that single IRBs or standard IRBs have the same obligation to ensure that information is understandable and accurate for participant groups. Sara Hull and Adam Shiffenbauer, from the National Human Genome Research Institute, National Institute for Environmental Health Sciences, and NIH Clinical Center, agree with Botkin but discuss the specific complexities related to how implications of genetic research may be different for different populations, to support the importance of the single IRB working with the other relying IRBs collaboratively to ensure that the information is accurate. Melissa E. Abraham, Elizabeth Hohmann, and Megan Morash, from Massachusetts General Hospital, Partners HealthCare, and Harvard Medical School, also agree, but they further explore pragmatic approaches that institutions can take to be responsive to the concerns raised by this case that also acknowledge the institutional challenges of that responsiveness.

CASE SUMMARY

Investigators are planning an observational study to characterize the environmental and genetic risks for the development of myositis. The study required a single study visit that involved completing a medical history and physical exam, questionnaires about environmental exposure, and a blood draw to test for evidence of environmental exposures; conducting targeted DNA and RNA analyses; and examining epigenetic changes. The study does not plan to disclose preliminary research results to participants but may notify them in the future if "meaningful information is developed from this study that may be important for [their] health." This multisite study plans to enroll active-duty and former military personnel at both civilian medical facilities and military medical facilities. An IRB at one of the civilian sites agreed to serve as the single IRB of record for the study.

This civilian IRB had a concern regarding the proposed standardized ("boilerplate") language in the consent form for the military facility enrollment sites. The language describing privacy protections related to genetic research was substantively different from the language included in the consent form for the civilian enrollment sites. The military consent form discussed information regarding the Genetic Information Nondiscrimination Act (GINA) and other genetic discrimination coverage, including an executive order and other military policies that may protect participants from genetic discrimination. The IRB concern was that these statements were vague and did not answer important questions regarding protections that would be relevant to active military participants' decision to participate in the research. The IRB was concerned about the overemphasis on GINA, which they assumed would not apply to active-duty military personnel, and felt there was not enough detail concerning the protections in place that apply to active-duty military personnel. Given that myositis is a condition that potentially affects the performance of specific military duties and might impact future job placement of the active-duty participants, the IRB was concerned about discrimination in military personnel and felt the boilerplate language inadequately captured this risk.

Although the IRB was aware of substantive differences between the legal rights of military personnel who participate in research and the rights of members of the general public, it was uncertain about how best to describe protections that do and do not apply to military personnel in this study. The IRB requested a bioethics consultation to help determine the standardized consent language for participants at military study sites. The IRB also requested advice regarding its standing to stipulate substantive changes to institutional boilerplate language on another institution's consent form, particularly for an institution operating under different privacy regulations. What is the role of boilerplate language in consent forms? Is it intended to be critical information for participants to understand, or is it information that should be anticipated will be ignored but for which the role is to ensure that legally accurate information is disclosed? In the context of single IRBs, which IRB boilerplate should be used, and should the primary IRB simply accept another institution's approach or expect the other IRB to alter or replace its boilerplate language?

COMMENTARY 5.8.1: THE BANE OF "BOILERPLATE" LANGUAGE IN RESEARCH CONSENT FORMS: ENSURING CONSENT FORMS PROMOTE AUTONOMOUS AUTHORIZATION

JEFFREY R. BOTKIN

"Boilerplate" language in consent forms is commonly understood to mean text that does not vary from one study to the next and is routinely inserted into an institution's consent forms. This contrasts with variable sections of the consent document such as the background, procedures, risks and benefits, and so on that must be individualized for each study. Standardized language is often used for sections that describe institutional approaches or policies regarding content like HIPAA (Health Insurance Portability and Accountability Act) protections or contact information for participant questions or concerns. While this need not be the case, boilerplate sections referencing institutional policies or other legal protections are often written by, or in consultation with, institutional attorneys who are trained to use carefully defined and thorough language. Accordingly, these sections can often be characterized as "legalese," meaning they are not written with reader comprehension as a priority.

In their classic volume on informed consent, Faden and Beauchamp distinguished between two forms of consent called Sense[1] and Sense[2] (Faden, Beauchamp, and King 1986). Sense[1] is characterized as autonomous authorization that flows from intent, understanding, and freedom from controlling influences. Sense[2] refers to legally authorized consent that flows from a signed consent form, protecting the investigator and the healthcare institution from allegations of battery or malpractice. These two forms of consent can be in tension. Legally valid consent (Sense[2]) can be obtained through the signing of a form even when the participant has little or no understanding of the research being proposed (Sense[1]).

This case presents challenges at several levels (Wilfond, Zabrowski, and Johnson 2019). First, there is the question about whether boilerplate language is appropriate in general. Second, there is a question about whether the information in the consent form, the boilerplate language specifically, is accurate for some of the participants. Lastly, there is the question of how a single IRB should deal with standardized text in consent forms when the IRB is overseeing research at multiple institutions where a single set of standardized language does not meet the needs of different participant groups.

Participation in research is supererogatory, and we largely rely on the altruism of individuals to place themselves at risk and inconvenience to help answer important questions. For this reason, consent forms in research are far more extensive and detailed than consent forms for clinical care. This is the concept, at least. In practice, consent forms are commonly written at a reading level that exceeds average abilities, and efforts to enhance comprehension are rarely used, such as illustrations or a teach-back approach (Krishnamurti and Argo 2016). Many participants do not understand basic elements of the research protocol and may have fundamental misconceptions about the purpose of the study (Appelbaum and Lidz 2008). Furthermore, to date, efforts to improve comprehension through simplification and other measures have shown only limited impacts (Schenker et al. 2011). It appears that the information in the form is not critical to decisions about enrollment for many individuals. More important to many is trust: trust in the professional(s) and trust in the healthcare institution (de Melo-Martin and Ho 2008).

Given the limited efficacy of consent forms in promoting autonomous authorization, one might conclude that particularly arcane language, as in much boilerplate language, becomes irrelevant. Who cares whether there is complex standardized text when the whole form is often beyond comprehension and largely irrelevant for its ethical purpose? I take the opposite view. Autonomous authorization is too important to surrender without a much more vigorous effort. Consent forms can be improved through multiple measures, at least to the extent that the important concepts are available to the average reader who might choose to pursue them. More importantly, perhaps, improvements in the consent process with the use of personal time and measures like teach-back can assist potential participants in walking through the important points prior to a decision. Making information available in an accessible form is a sign of respect, even if many people choose to decide based on other elements, like trust and hope.

Of course, investigators, IRBs, and institutions have legitimate interests in conveying the information contained in boilerplate text, and potential participants have interests in knowing this information, or at least in having a reference document, should questions arise later. The problem lies in the poorly accessible nature of the text. If clinical research were the focus of a significant amount of litigation, quasi-legal language in a consent form might have some justification. However, it is not clear that such language is necessary to reduce the risk of litigation. Standardized language can be written in a form that is respectful of potential participants and designed to foster understanding and autonomous authorization. IRBs and their institutions need to make a commitment to expressing the information in standardized text in an accessible form. There is certainly nothing in the regulations requiring standardized text or "legalese," and, indeed, the forthcoming changes to the Common Rule require attention to the readability of the consent form (Protection of human subjects: Requirements for informed consent 2017).

The second challenge raised by the case regards the accuracy of the standardized language for military personnel. The specific question is whether the text describing certain protections from genetic discrimination in the context of a genetic research study accurately describes the risks and protections for individuals in the military. Not enough specific information about the consent language is provided to assess this claim, but suffice it to say that concerns about different protections for military personnel are legitimate (Baruch and Hudson 2008). Prior to the era of single IRBs, this type of problem was less of a concern because a local institutional IRB would craft language relevant to its context. The form and process would be customized to state or tribal law, institutional policies, and the mix of participant languages, among other variables. In the era of single IRBs, nothing should change. The single IRB has the responsibility and the authority to review and approve more than one consent form for research sites with different local contexts.

The challenge of "local context" was an important part of the debate over whether the single-IRB requirements would become NIH policy or part of the revised Common Rule (U.S. Department of

Health and Human Services 2011). Requirements for a single IRB are now in place, and research institutions, both those serving as the single IRB and those deferring this responsibility, are involved in often extended negotiations about which institution is responsible for what elements of oversight and assurance. But at a minimum, research conducted at a local institution must be in compliance with local or relevant law and the consent form must be customized accordingly. In the context of the case, the single IRB should approve a consent form to be used by military personnel and a separate consent form to be used by members of the general public. Whether these separate forms are used at separate institutions or both are used at some or all recruitment institutions is not critical, although the protocol must outline how potential participants who are military personnel would be identified. In this way, information relevant to the potential individual participant will be accurate and consistent with a goal of autonomous authorization. In general, neither the use of standardized language nor the use of single IRBs should undermine the need to present each potential research participant with the information he or she should reasonably need to decide relevant to his or her own participation.

References

Appelbaum, P. S., and C. W. Lidz. 2008. Twenty-five years of therapeutic misconception. *The Hastings Center Report* 38(2):5–6, author reply 6-7.

Baruch, S., and K. Hudson. 2008. Civilian and military genetics: Nondiscrimination policy in a post-GINA world. *American Journal Human Genetics* 83(4):435–444.

de Melo-Martin, I., and A. Ho. 2008. Beyond informed consent: The therapeutic misconception and trust. *Journal of Medical Ethics* 34(3):202–205.

Faden, R. R., T. L. Beauchamp, and N. M. P. King. 1986. *A history and theory of informed consent*, Oxford: Oxford University Press.

Krishnamurti, T., and N. Argo. 2016. A patient-centered approach to informed consent: Results from a survey and randomized trial. *Medical Decision Making* 36(6):726–740.

Protection of human subjects: Requirements for informed consent. 2017. Code of Federal Regulations, Title 45 CFR 46.116(a)(5)(i), Federal Register 82(12):7265–7267. New York, NY: Oxford University Press.

Schenker, Y., A. Fernandez, R. Sudore, and D. Schillinger. 2011. Interventions to improve patient comprehension in informed consent for medical and surgical procedures: A systematic review. *Medical Decision Making* 31(1):151–173.

U.S. Department of Health and Human Services. 2011. Protections., Secretary's Advisory Committee on Human Research. October 13, 2011 SACHRP Letter to the HHS Secretary: SACHRP ANPRM Comments-Final. Available at: https://www.hhs.gov/ohrp/sachrp-committee/recommendations/2011-octo-ber-13-letter-final/index.html (accessed on Nov 2018).

Wilfond, B. S., J. Zabrowski, and L. M. Johnson. 2019. The limitations of "boilerplate" language in informed consent: Single IRB review of multisite genetic research in military personnel. *American Journal of Bioethics* 19(4):81–82.

COMMENTARY 5.8.2: SINGLE IRBs ARE RESPONSIBLE TO ENSURE CONSENT LANGUAGE EFFECTIVELY CONVEYS THE LOCAL CONTEXT

SARA CHANDROS HULL AND ADAM I. SCHIFFENBAUER

This case illustrates a challenge that will become more common as the use of single IRBs for the review of multisite research increases: specifically, how best to handle local context considerations when a single IRB is required to oversee research being conducted in unfamiliar settings (Wilfond, Zabrowski, and Johnson 2019). A recent survey confirms that IRB officials consider "reviewing the local research context" to be a significant challenge associated with new single-IRB review requirements (Resnik, Smith, and Shi 2018). In the case presented here, a single IRB that is more familiar with the context of civilian research settings and study populations has assumed responsibility for reviewing research that is enrolling both active-duty and former military personnel at a military medical facility for a study of genetic risk and myositis. Although the single IRB of record is aware of regulatory differences in the privacy protections that are available to military personnel and civilians who enroll in genetic research, this single IRB is faced with the difficulty of interpreting those protections and determining how best to describe them in the military site consent forms.

A potential goal of review by a single IRB is to minimize arbitrary variability in consent form language across multiple sites that are carrying out identical research procedures (Koyfman et al. 2013). However, this goal needs to be balanced with the single IRB's obligation to ensure that relevant contextual features of each institution under its purview, including unique aspects of the study population and local culture as well as different regulatory and policy requirements, are adequately considered. Although it would be operationally unwieldy for each relying institution in a large multisite study to submit a completely unique consent form, a single-IRB best practice that has been proposed is to permit limited customization of otherwise consistent consent form language to reflect local policies. Such customization could include a relying institution's standardized descriptions of applicable privacy laws and requirements (e.g., HIPAA), distinct signature block requirements, and institutionally developed "boilerplate" for compensation for research-related injury and other legal requirements, for example (Splinter et al. 2018). This practice was not designed to allow enrollment sites to tailor consent forms based on subjective language preferences, but rather to accommodate language that is indicated by local policy requirements. In the current case, it is clear that the risks of genetic research with an active-duty military population in a military medical center setting would require some customization of consent language to describe accurately the risk of employment discrimination and relevant legal protections in that setting.

Indeed, privacy protections related to all genetic research are complex and context dependent. Because myositis is an example of a condition that could potentially affect military duties and future job placements, an IRB of record would need to understand how a study of genetic factors associated with the development of this condition could pose additional risks to participants enrolled at a military medical institution. While GINA provides some protection against health insurance and employment discrimination for civilians, and discrimination based on genetic data has been relatively rare in civilian contexts (Green, Lautenbach, and McGuire 2015), GINA does not apply to military personnel, for whom a different set of protections governs how genetic information is managed (De Castro et al. 2016). Accordingly, one would expect the consent language describing privacy protections related to genetic research at a military enrollment site to be substantively different than the consent language for civilian enrollment sites, and it is generally appropriate for a single IRB to accommodate a military research institution's request to customize the consent forms being used in these distinct settings to reflect those substantive differences.

Yet it is also reasonable for the single IRB to question the applicability of the GINA-specific consent language that was proposed by the military site and to require that the language be presented in a clearer, more understandable manner. Although the single IRB in this case was not situated in the military setting, it appears that this IRB appreciated that the information that active-duty military personnel would need to weigh the risks and make an informed decision about voluntary enrollment in a genetic research protocol was different from the information that civilians—and perhaps retired military personnel as well—would need to make that decision. Even when a single IRB of record has a practice of allowing customization of the consent forms that are being used at different enrollment sites, that single IRB still needs to consider the consent form as a holistic document to ensure that it presents the required elements of informed consent clearly and appropriately for the populations being included in the research. Although it could be appropriate for a single IRB to accept precise "boilerplate" language that succinctly describes legal protections that apply in the military research setting, we believe it is well within the purview of the single IRB to explore whether the language could indeed be changed to ensure that enrolled participants have the relevant information that they need. Depending on the degree of pushback, a single IRB might need to work closely with the local (military) IRB to develop language that both adheres to what is required in the military context and ensures that potential nonmilitary research participants have been provided the relevant information to allow them to be adequately informed of the risks and potential benefits of the research.

Finally, this case underscores a potential role for research ethics consultation as a resource for single IRBs who are facing the challenge of interpreting local context requirements. Although using the single IRB is intended to reduce the overall burden of IRB review of multisite studies, it will present additional responsibilities to the IRBs that are selected to oversee research at diverse enrollment sites. Understanding unfamiliar local context requirements is challenging and may require access to specialized expertise. Ethics consultants can help facilitate conversations between the relevant institutional representatives to augment an IRB's understanding of how local context considerations apply to the research participants in a multisite protocol and how best to reflect those considerations in associated consent form language.

References

De Castro, M., L. G. Biesecker, C. Turner, et al. 2016. Genomic medicine in the military. *Nature Partner Journals: Genomic Medicine* 13(1):1–3.

Green, R. C., D. Lautenbach, and A. L. McGuire. 2015. GINA, genetic discrimination, and genomic medicine. *The New England Journal of Medicine* 372(5):397–399.

Koyfman, S. A., P. Agre, R. Carlisle, et al. 2013. Consent form heterogeneity in cancer trials: The cooperative group and institutional review board gap. *Journal of the National Cancer Institute* 105(13):947–953.

Resnik, D. B., E. M. Smith, and M. Shi. 2018. How U.S. Research Institutions are responding to the single institutional review board mandate. *Accountability in Research* 25(6):340–349.

Splinter, K., S. C. Hull, I. A. Holm, T. L. McDonough, A. L. Wise, and R. B. Ramoni, and Members of the Undiagnosed Diseases Network. 2018. Implementing the single institutional review board model: Lessons from the undiagnosed diseases network. *Clinical and Translational Science* 11(1):28–31.

Wilfond, B. S., J. Zabrowski, and L. M. Johnson. 2019. The limitations of "boilerplate" language in informed consent: Single IRB review of multisite genetic research in military personnel. *American Journal of Bioethics* 19(4):81–82.

COMMENTARY 5.8.3: SOLVING THE SINGLE-IRB/BOILERPLATE BIND: ESTABLISHING INSTITUTIONAL GUIDELINES

MELISSA E. ABRAHAM, ELIZABETH HOHMANN, AND MEGAN MORASH

There are ongoing efforts to improve efficiency and clarity in the ethical review process. IRBs often use standardized ("boilerplate") language for consent forms to accomplish goals of maintaining consistency, ensuring full legal accountability and compliance, and conveying accurate and complete information at a readable level to potential participants. The language is typically "fixed" and is meant to be used by researchers without the provision of authority to make any changes to the wording.

A potentially complementary mandate for efficiency is to use a single IRB for multi-institutional studies. This single IRB is charged with ensuring that the ethical and regulatory requirements for informed consent are brought to all sites and all participants under the purview of the study. The IRB would ensure that the foreseeable risks and benefits related to participation in the study are described as accurately as possible for all participants. A single IRB would in theory alleviate problems for both researchers and IRBs related to delays, trivial wordsmithing, and wasted resources associated with multiple-IRB reviews.

However, in the current case, the intersection of the two efficiency goals (streamlining with boiler-plate consent form language and centralizing IRB review) can create a bind (Wilfond, Zabrowski, and Johnson 2019).

Here, military personnel are enrolled at both civilian and military sites, and the civilian site is serving as the single IRB. This IRB concluded that the "boilerplate" language the military site uses in its consent form may not allow for accurate information about risks related to potentially sensitive genetic information.

Among the advantages of boilerplate language are improved consistency across studies at an institution, clarity, and completeness. In the current case, the standardized language in question is in a realm typically standardized by IRBs: consent form language related to privacy, confidentiality, and HIPAA. This language is typically fixed, and has often been fully and painstakingly negotiated and vetted by multiple parties (e.g., privacy officer, general counsel, genetic researcher stakeholders, the IRB, research management, medical records management, and others). The investment in time and critical examination with such a team is not insignificant. Any changes would likely require going back to the multiple stakeholders. The process serves to ensure that every study conducted at the institution is in compliance with regulations and that the participants have accurate and pertinent information related to the privacy and confidentiality of information gathered in the study. There are great benefits to boilerplate language to participants, researchers, and IRBs for studies conducted at a single institution, and the careful vetting leads to significant streamlining in the majority of circumstances.

However, the use of boilerplate wording becomes more complicated when one IRB reviews the boilerplate language of another IRB. A primary focus of concern about single IRBs has been around the loss of the benefits of local review, where the IRB is familiar with the participants, investigators, and institution (Check et al. 2013), and relatedly, about the willingness of IRBs to defer to other IRBs for review (Flynn et al. 2013). However, implementation of the single-IRB review can cause delays associated with the review of consent form language, which can negate the efficiency advantages of single-IRB review.

When an IRB is reviewing a study conducted by individuals at a single site, the research may be conducted off-site, or may not collect information relevant to certain parts of the boilerplate language. In some cases, the boilerplate language provides contradictory or false information. For example, if the language discusses use of medical records, but a study involves learning tasks in a school, the child's medical records will never be accessed or examined, but the consent form boilerplate language suggests this could occur. In some cases, though anecdotal, IRBs may tell researchers to say "just ignore this part, it doesn't apply to this study, it is just part of the form our institution uses." In other cases, the IRB doesn't suggest this, but it is still done. Both researcher and IRB/institutional reviewer are in a bind if there seems to be no room for flexibility, and this certainly sacrifices good research practice for the sake of efficiency.

The problem is compounded in single-IRB review. The conflict seems unresolvable if the boilerplate language cannot be changed, and the alternative, to rework or negotiate the language, could cause significant delays and end with an impasse.

Considerations for the case in the current environment

In general, IRBs may wish to generally decline to be IRB of record when asked to review an institutional setting that is starkly different from their own (e.g., civilian vs. military), citing lack of expertise. Despite the advantages of single-IRB review, in some cases local review may be preferable (Klitzman 2011). We suggest that a civilian IRB, for example, may not have the knowledge or perspective to review for a military institution.

In general, when there are a small number of institutions such as in this study and a single IRB is not mandated, it may be most expeditious to review at two IRBs that can approve their own language at their site. This of course does not address the ethical concerns raised by the civilian IRB review, but from a pragmatic standpoint, it would not be that IRB's responsibility to make sure the language in the consent form was acceptable.

If a single IRB is mandated, a potential solution is for the civilian IRB to write a report to the military IRB about its concerns and have a response or discussion to see whether they can come to an expeditious compromise.

If there is no room to compromise according to the local stakeholders, and an impasse is reached, one might consider the use of multiple consent forms for the same study. However, this is not recommended for substantive ethical and privacy differences, and is perhaps only acceptable when there is a highly specific reason (e.g., remuneration is by cash vs. check because of institutional policies).

Procedural solutions to anticipate the single-IRB/boilerplate bind

In the new era of centralized IRB review, IRBs serving as a single IRB will be in a bind at each turn unless a solution can be found to head the problem off at the pass. Institutions should develop a standard process for disagreements, such as a "rapid response team," rather than requiring months of back and forth across many stakeholders. The team could also establish prospective guidelines, if an institution can anticipate where problems will arise and, for those cases, what flexibility they will agree on to allow studies to move forward. Guidelines could help the IRB determine whether it is qualified to take on a single-IRB role by developing questions it should ask before agreeing.

In addition, consortium groups that have reliance agreements with each other for central review could develop consensus templates, agree that each institution will accept the other's boilerplate verbatim, or negotiate boilerplate from the outset. These documents might include boilerplate consent language that many sites have agreed upon, which could be used for most studies. Boilerplate language might be more successful if areas that are nonnegotiable are identified, while areas of flexibility could be identified as well. This might be successful for consortiums of academic medical centers, for example.

Although there is evidence that centralizing IRB review creates more consistency and efficiency (e.g., Neuman et al. 2018), it is unclear whether the use of single IRBs will increase efficiency, due to problems such as the boilerplate bind.

References

Check, D. K., K. P. Weinfurt, C. B. Dombeck, J. M. Kramer, and K. E. Flynn. 2013. Use of Central institutional review boards for multicenter clinical trials in the United States: A review of the literature. *Clinical Trials: Journal of the Society for Clinical Trials* 10(4):560–567.

Flynn, K. E., D. L. Hahn, J. M. Kramer, D. K. Check, C. B. Dombeck, S. Bang, J. Perlmutter, F. A. Khin-Maung-Gyi, and K. P. Weinfurt. 2013. Using Central IRBs for multicenter clinical trials in the United States. *PLoS One* 8(1):e54999.

Klitzman, R. 2011. How local IRBs view Central IRBs in the US. *BMC Medical Ethics* 12: 13.

Neuman, M. D., L. J. Gaskins, T. Ziolek, and REGAIN investigators. 2018. Time to institutional review board approval with local versus Central review in a multicenter pragmatic trial. *Clinical Trials* 15(1):107–111.

Wilfond, B. S., J. Zabrowski, and L. M. Johnson. 2019. The limitations of "boilerplate" language in informed consent: Single IRB review of multisite genetic research in military personnel. *American Journal of Bioethics* 19(4):81–82.

Appendix A

Cases organized by principles

Fair participant selection

Favorable risk–benefit ratio

Informed consent

Appendix B

Cases organized by topics

Study type

Research features

Legal and regulatory oversight

Appendix C

Cases organized by values

Equity

Trustworthiness

Index